DATE DUE

How Music Grew

HOW MUSIC GREW

FROM PREHISTORIC TIMES TO THE
PRESENT DAY

BY

MARION BAUER & ETHEL PEYSER

WITH AN INTRODUCTION BY
WILLIAM J. HENDERSON

With 53 Illustrations
COMPLETELY REVISED EDITION

G. P. PUTNAM'S SONS
NEW YORK :: LONDON

"It takes three to make music: one to create, one to perform, one to appreciate. And who can tell which is the most important?"

ROBERT HAVEN SCHAUFFLER, from
The Creative Listener (a revision) in
The Musical Amateur.

THE AUTHORS' GREETINGS

Dear Young Readers from Nine to Ninety:

Dear Young Readers from Nine to Ninety:

In writing this book we have not tried to write a history but rather have attempted to follow a lane parallel to the road along which music has marched down to us through the ages.

For this reason you will find what may seem upon first glance peculiar omissions, but which to us were prayerfully and carefully relinquished, lest the book become an encyclopedia and lest our kind publisher look upon us ungraciously and our readers despair.

Among the omissions which may be regarded as serious is a chapter on the singers, those who have delighted and thrilled the public through the years, but the nature of this book, in the minds of its authors, precludes details of the executive side of music, adhering as closely as possible to the actual creators.

In our experience every history of music, and we have read scores of them, leaves out many things, so our "lane" touches things in passing, only, owing to mechanical as well as willful reasons.

On the other hand we have enlarged greatly on many topics. This we have done when we have considered a subject particularly picturesque in order to attract and stimulate the novice reading about music, perhaps, for the first time!

Lastly we have tried to explain as simply as possible, without becoming infantile, the varying steps in Music's growth. Therefore, the book has assumed larger proportions than if we had been able to use scientific terms and cut the Gordian knot of explanation with one swiftly aimed blow, rather than three or four.

So, with the sincere hope that our book will help you to love music better, because you will have seen its struggle with politics, religion and its critics, we leave you to read it—from cover to cover—we hope!

HOW MUSIC GREW

Many things have happened in the world since 1925 when we wrote this book. We do not have to follow the tragedies of every political change. Had we been compelled to have done this our book would be too cumbersome for comfort. We do think it necessary, however, in order to make the book authentic and up to date, to make basic revisions. So we have recorded with sorrow the passing of the musicians who have died since 1925, as well as the happier facts about the coming of new music makers and the flowering of those too young to have distinguished themselves when this book first appeared. We have, we hope, made it clear (1) that music has traveled along interesting roads in the past fifteen years; (2) that music does not stand still, and (3) that it cannot escape the influences, good or bad, of the life from which it springs, because it is a living, palpitating, sensitive art. Moreover, since this book has been published, there has been much profound and careful research into the origins and ancient forms of music. In this edition we have tried to tell you of some of the important discoveries, especially those of interest to laymen and young students. And again we leave our book to the kindly consideration of you who love and need music and want to know it better.

MARION BAUER AND ETHEL PEYSER.

New York City, 1939.

ACKNOWLEDGMENTS

OUR book has had friends other than its authors. It has, in fact, had makers as well as authors, so it cannot go out into the world without proclaiming its "thank-yous." First it would thank Flora Bernstein, its indefatigable and patient typist, editor and general adviser, who worked night and day for many moons; second, it must thank Dorothy Lawton of the Music Library of the City of New York for her graceful but poignant criticism, and third it must thank Grace Bliss Stewart, who did some research and anything needed.

How Music Grew
and the
AUTHORS.

INTRODUCTION

NO one questions the need of histories of music. Few, however, define the need. It seems to be generally agreed that people ought to know something about the history of the principal arts. Who designed St. Peter's, who painted the *Descent from the Cross* who wrote *The Faerie Queen* and who composed the *Ninth Symphony.* These are things one ought to know. The reasons why one ought to know them are seldom made clear. But just at this time, when the word "appreciation" is so active in the world's conversation, there should be little difficulty in separating from the mass of unformed comment at least one reason for acquaintance with the history of music.

No one can "appreciate" an art work without knowing its period, the state of the art in that period, the ideals and purposes of composers, the capacity of their public and the particular gifts and aims of the writer of the work under consideration. It is extremely difficult for any person to begin the study of "appreciation" after he is old enough to have acquired a stock of prejudices and burdened his mind with a heavy load of misconceptions. It is better to absorb good art, music or other, in the early years and to grow up with it than to try at 18 or 20 to put away childish things and understand Bach's "St. Matthew Passion."

Miss Bauer and Miss Peyser have written a history of music for young people. It is not for the kindergarten class and yet it is not out of the reach of mere children. It is not for the seniors in a university and yet they might profit by examining it. The authors have surveyed the entire field. They have touched ancient music and the music of nations not usually considered in some more pretentious histories. They have apparently tried to give a bird's-eye view of the art as practiced by all the civilized and some of the uncivilized races of the earth. With this in mind they have shown how the supreme art forms and the greatest art works developed among the western European peoples, who, it is interesting to note, produced also the metaphysical and philosophical bases of the world's scientific thought, the mightiest inventions, and with all regard for Buddhistic poetry and speculation, the highest achievements in literature.

It seems to me that they have made a history of music singularly well adapted to young minds. They do not treat their readers as if they were infants—which might offend them—nor as college professors, which would certainly bore them. The book will undoubtedly have a large audience, for teachers of young music students, of whom there are legions, will surely exclaim: "This is just what we have needed."

W. J. HENDERSON.

CONTENTS

BABYHOOD OF MUSIC

CHILDHOOD OF MUSIC

Contents

Contents

ILLUSTRATIONS

xvii

Illustrations

xix

How Music Grew

How Music Grew

Babyhood of Music

CHAPTER I

Music is Born—How, When and Where

THERE was once a time when children did not have to go to school, for there were no schools; they did not have to take music lessons because there was no music; there was not even a language by which people could talk to each other, and there were no books and no pencils. There were no churches then, no homes nor cities, no railroads, no roads in fact, and the oldest and wisest man knew less than a little child of today.

Step by step men fought their way to find means of speaking to each other, to make roads to travel on, houses to live in, fire to cook with, clothes to wear, and ways to amuse themselves.

During this time, over one hundred thousand years ago, called "prehistoric" because it was before events were recorded, men had to struggle with things that no longer bother us.

Picture to yourselves this era when people lived out-of-doors, in mounds and caves surrounded by wild beasts which

3

though dangerous, were not much more so than their human neighbors. Remember, too, that these people did not know that light followed darkness as the day the night; summer followed winter as the seasons come and go; that trees lost their leaves only to bear new ones in the spring, and that lightning and thunder were natural happenings; and so on through the long list of things that we think today perfectly simple, and not in the least frightening.

Because they did not understand these natural things, they thought that trees, sun, rain, animals, birds, fire, birth, death, marriage, the hunt, caves and everything else had good and bad gods in them. In order to please these gods they made prayers to them quite different from our prayers, as they danced, sang and acted the things they wanted to have happen. When a savage wanted sun or wind or rain, he called his tribe together and danced a sun dance, or a wind dance, or a rain dance. When he wanted food, he did not pray for it, but he acted out the hunt in a bear dance. As the centuries went by they continued to use these dances as prayers, and later they became what we call religious rites and festivals. So here you see actually the beginning of what we know as Easter festivals, Christmas with its Christmas tree and mistletoe, spring festivals and May-pole dances with the Queen of the May, Hallowe'en and many other holiday celebrations.

This is how music, dancing, poetry, painting and drama were born. They were the means by which primitive men talked to their gods. This they did, to be sure, very simply, by hand-clapping and foot-stamping, by swaying their bodies to and fro, by shouting, shrieking, grunting, crying and sobbing, and as soon as they knew enough, used language, and repeated the same word over and over again. These movements and sounds were the two roots from which music grew.

If you can call these queer grunts and yells singing, the

men of those far-off days must have sung even before they had a language, in fact, it must have been difficult to know whether they were singing or talking. In these cries of joy, sorrow, pain, rage, fear, or revenge, we find another very important reason for the growth of music. These exclamations, however barbaric and rough, were man's first attempt at expressing his feelings.

We still look upon music as one of the most satisfying ways to show our emotions, and the whole story of music from prehistoric times to the present day is a record of human feelings expressed in rhythm and melody.

Gradually these early men learned to make not only musical instruments, but also the knife for hunting and utensils for cooking. The first step towards a musical instrument was doubtless the striking together of two pieces of wood or stone in repeated beats. The next step was the stretching of the skin of an animal over a hollowed-out stone or tree trunk forming the first drum. Another simple and very useful instrument was made of a gourd (the dried hollow rind of a melon-like fruit) filled with pebbles and shaken like a baby's rattle.

As early in the story of mankind as this, the love of decoration and need of beauty were so natural that they decorated their bodies, the walls of their caves, and their everyday tools with designs in carving, and in colors made from earth and plants. You can see some of these utensils and knives, even bits of wall pictures, in many of the museums in collections made by men who dig up old cities and sections of the countries where prehistoric peoples lived. These men are called archaeologists, and devote their lives to this work so that we may know what happened before history began.

A few years ago tools of flint, utensils made of bone, and skeletons of huge animals, that no longer exist, were found in a sulphur spring in Oklahoma; pottery and tools of stone, wood, and shell were dug up in Arizona; carvings, spear heads, arrow points, polished stone hatchets and articles of stone and ivory in Georgia, Pennsylvania and the Potomac Valley. This shows that this continent also had been inhabited by prehistoric people.

Even as we see prehistoric man using the things of nature for his tools, such as elephant tusks, flint, and wood; and as we see him making paint from earth and plants, we also see him getting music from nature. It would have been impossible for these early men and children to have lived out-of-doors and not to have listened to the songs of the birds, the sound of wind through the trees, the waves against the rocks, the trickling water of brooks, the beat of the rain, the crashing of thunder and the cries and roars of animals. All of these sounds of nature they imitated in their songs and also the motions and play of animals in their dances.

In Kamchatka, the peninsula across the Behring Strait from Alaska, there still live natives who sing songs named for and mimicking the cries of their wild ducks.

The natives of Australia, which is the home of the amusing-looking kangaroo, have a dance in which they imitate the peculiar leaps and motions of this animal. When you recall its funny long hind legs and short forelegs, you can imagine how entertaining it would be to imitate its motions. The natives also try to make the same sounds with their voices, as the kangaroo. The women accompany these dances by singing a simple tune of four tones over and over, knocking two pieces of wood together to keep time. If ever you go to the Australian bush (woods or forests) you will see this kangaroo dance. This is different, isn't it, from sitting in a concert hall and listening to some great musician who has spent his life in hard work and study so that he may play or sing for you?

We can learn much about the beginnings of music from tribes of men who, although living today, are very near the birthday of the world, so far as their knowledge and habits are concerned.

Primitive men love play; they love to jump, to yell, to fling their arms and legs about, and to make up stories which they act out, as children do who "make believe."

This love of mankind for make believe, and his desire to be amused, along with his natural instinct to express what he feels, are the roots from which music has grown. But, of course, in prehistoric times, men did not know that they were making an art, for they were only uttering in sound and movement their wants, their needs, in fact, only expressing their daily life and their belief in God.

CHAPTER II

The Savage Makes His Music

FORTUNATELY for our story there live groups of people today still in the early stages of civilization who show us the manners and customs of primitive man, because they are primitive men themselves.

We are going to learn how music grew from the American Indian and the African. We are using these two as examples for two reasons: because they are close enough to us to have influenced our own American music, and because all savage music has similar traits. The American Indian and the African show us the steps from the primitive state of music to the beginning of music as an art. In other words, these people are a bridge between prehistoric music and that of the civilized world.

In Chapter I about prehistoric man, we spoke of the two roots of music—movement and sound. Hereafter when we speak of rhythm it will mean movement either in tones or in gestures. Rhythm expressed in tones makes music; rhythm expressed in gestures makes the dance. The reason we like dance music and marches is that we feel the rhythm, the thing that makes us want to mark the beat of the music with our feet, or hands, or with head bobbings. This love of the beat is strong in the savage, and upon this he builds his music.

Our American Jazz is the result of our desire for strong rhythms and shows that we, for all our culture, have something in us of the savage's feeling for movement.

AMERICAN INDIANS

We have a name for everything, but the American Indian has a name and a song for everything. He has a song for his moccasins, for his head-gear, for his teepee, the fire in it, the forest around him, the lakes and rivers in which he fishes and paddles, for his canoe, for the fish he catches, for his gods, his friends, his family, his enemies, the animal he hunts, the maiden he woos, the stars, the sun, and the moon, in fact for everything imaginable. The following little story will explain the Indians' idea of the use of their songs:

An American visitor who was making a collection of Indian songs, asked an old Ojibway song-leader to sing a hunting song. The old Indian looked at him in surprise and left him. A little later the son-in-law of the Indian appeared and with apologies told the American that "the old gentleman" could not sing a hunting song because it was not the hunting season.

The next time the old Indian came, the American asked him for a love song, but he politely refused, saying that it was not dignified for a man of his age to sing love songs. However, the old warrior suddenly decided that as he was making a call, it was quite proper for him to sing Visiting Songs, which he did, to his host's delight.

This old man had been taught to sing when he was a very little boy, as the Indian boy learns the history of his tribe through the songs. He is carefully trained by the old men and women so that no song of the tribe or family should be forgotten. These songs are handed down from one family to another, and no one knows how many hundreds of years old they may be. So, you see, these songs become history and the young Indians learn their history this way, not as we do, from text books.

"What new songs did you learn?" is the question that

one Indian will ask of another who has been away on a
visit, and like the announcer at the radio broadcasting
station, the Indian answers:

"My friends, I will now sing you a song of—" and he
fully describes the song. Then he sings it. After he fin-
ishes, he says, "My friends, I have sung you the song
of—" and repeats the name of the song!

So great a part of an Indian's life is music, that he has
no word meaning poetry in his language. Poetry to the
Indian is always song. In fact an Indian puts new words
to an old tune and thinks he has invented a new song.

What Is Indian Music?

When the Indian sings, he starts on the highest tone he
can reach and gradually drops to the lowest, so that many
of his songs cover almost two octaves. He does not know
that almost always he sings in a scale of five tones. For
reasons hard to explain, most primitive races have used
this same scale. It is like our five black keys on the piano,
starting with F sharp. This is called the pentatonic scale,
(penta, Greek word for five, tonic meaning tones). This
scale is a most amazing traveler, for we meet it in our
musical journeys in China, Japan, Arabia, Scotland,
Africa, Ireland, ancient Peru and Mexico, Greece and many
other places. The reason we find these five tones popular
must be because they are natural for the human throat.
At any rate we know that it is difficult for the Indian to
sing our scale. He does not seem to want the two notes
that we use between the two groups of black keys which
make our familiar major scale.

It is very difficult to put down an Indian song in our
musical writing, because, the Indians sing in a natural
scale that has not been changed by centuries of musical
learning. They sing in a rhythm that seems complicated

Fig. 1

Drums and Sticks.

Fig. 2.

Sioux Drum.

Fig. 3.

A Pipe and Rattles from Alaska.

Fig. 4.

Bone Flutes.

(Courtesy of the Metropolitan Museum of Art, New York.)

Some Instruments of the American Indian.

From the Egyptian Collection in the Louvre, Paris.

Hieroglyphics on an Egyptian Tablet.

(Telling a story of a Prince.)

From a panel in a Museum (delle Terme) in Rome.

Greek Girl Playing a Double Flute (auloi).

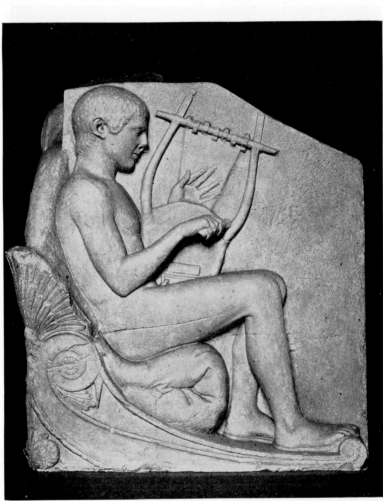

Greek Boy Playing the Lyre.

to our ears in spite of all our musical knowledge, and this, too, is difficult to write down. Another thing which makes it hard to set down and to imitate Indian music, is that they beat the drum in different time from the song which they sing. They seldom strike the drum and sing a tone at the same time. In fact, the drum and the voice seem to race with each other. At the beginning of a song, for example, the drum beat is slower than the voice. Gradually the drum catches up with the voice and for a few measures they run along together. The drum gains and wins the race, because it is played faster than the voice sings. The curious part of it is, that this is not an accident, but every time they sing the same song, the race is run the same way. We are trained to count the beats and sing beat for beat, measure for measure with the drum. Try to beat on a drum and sing, and see how hard it is not to keep time with it.

The Indian slides from tone to tone; he scoops with his voice, somewhat like the jazz trombone player.

INDIAN INSTRUMENTS

The Indian's orchestra is made up of the rattle and the drum. The white man cannot understand the Indian's love of his drum. However, when he lives among them he also learns to love it. When Indians travel, they carry with them a drum which is hidden from the eyes of the strange white man. When night comes, they have song contests accompanied by the drum which is taken out of its hiding place.

These contests, which are very real to the Indians, are somewhat similar to the tournaments held in Germany in the Middle Ages.

The drummer, who is also the singer, is called the leading voice and is so important that he ranks next to the chief.

His rank is high, because through knowing the songs he is the historian of his tribe.

The drum is made of a wooden frame across which is stretched the skin of an animal, usually a deer. Sometimes it is only a few inches across, and sometimes it is two feet in diameter. When it has two surfaces of skins, they are separated four to six inches from each other. It is held in the left hand by a leather strap attached to the drum frame, and beaten with a short stick. (Figure 1.)

The Sioux Indian sets his drum on the ground; it is about the size of a wash tub and has only one surface. Two or more players pound this drum at the same time and the noise is often deafening. The Ojibway drum always has two surfaces and is usually decorated with gay designs in color. (Sioux drum, Figure 2.)

The drum makes a good weather bureau! The Indian often forecasts the weather by the way his drum answers to his pounding. If the sound is dull, he knows there is rain in the air, if it is clear and sharp and the skin is tight, he can have out-door dances without fear of a wetting. You could almost become a weather prophet yourself by watching the strings of your tennis racket, which act very much like the drum skin.

Another instrument beloved of all Indians is the rattle. There are many different sizes and shapes of rattles made of gourds, horns of animals and tiny drums filled with pebbles and shot. Some of them are carved out of wood in the shape of birds and animal heads. (Figure 3.)

The Indians also have the flute, and although there is no special music for it, it is of great importance in their lives. No two flutes are made to play exactly the same tones, that is, they are not drawn to scale. They are like home-whittled whistles made of wood in which holes are burned. (Figure 4.)

The flute is never used in the festivals or in the dance

but it is the lover's instrument. A young man who is too bashful to ask his sweetheart to marry him, hides among the bushes near her teepee, close to the spring where she goes every morning for water. When he sees her, he plays a little tune that he makes up just for her. Being a well brought up little Indian maid, she pretends not to notice it, but very soon tries to find out who played to her. If she likes him, she gives him a sign and he comes out of his hiding place, but if she does not wish to marry him, she lets him go on playing every morning until he gets tired and discouraged and returns no more to the loved spring near her teepee in the early morning.

And this is the reason the Indian love songs so often refer to sunrise, spring and fountains, and why we use the melancholy flute when we write Indan love songs.

Because of the ceaseless beating of the drum, the constant repetition of their scale of five tones, and the rambling effect of the music like unpunctuated sentences, we find the Indian music very monotonous. But they return the compliment and find our music monotonous, probably, because it is too well punctuated. Mr. Frederick Burton in his book on Primitive American Music, tells of having given to two Indian friends tickets for a recital in Carnegie Hall, in New York City, where they heard songs by Schubert and Schumann. When he asked them how they enjoyed the music they politely said, "It is undoubtedly very fine, it was a beautiful hall and the man had a great voice, but it seemed to us as though he sang the song over, over and over again, only sometimes he made it long and sometimes short."

INDIAN SOCIETIES

The Indian is a great club man; every Indian belongs to some society. The society which he joins is decided by what he dreams. If he dreams of a bear, he joins the Bear Society; if he dreams of a Buffalo, he joins the Buffalo Society. Other names of clubs are: Thunder-bird, Elks and Wolves.

Dreams play a great part in the Indian's life. If he dreams of a small round stone, a sacred thing to him, he is supposed to have the power to cure sickness, to foretell future events, to tell where objects are which cannot be seen.

Every one of the societies or clubs has its own special songs. The Indians also have songs of games, dances, songs of war and of the hunt, songs celebrating the deeds of chiefs, conquering warriors, war-path and council songs.

In the first chapter we spoke of primitive man imitating animals and here we find that the Indians, in their societies named for animals, imitate the acts of the clubs' namesakes.

They have a dance called the grass dance, in which they decorate their belts with long tufts of grass, a reminder of the days when they wore scalps on their belts after they had been on the "war-path." In this dance they imitate the motions of the eagle and other birds. Even the feathers used in their head-dress is a part of their custom of imitating animals and birds. Some of these head-dresses are like the comb, and the Indian who wears this will imitate the cries of the bird to which the comb belongs. His actions always correspond with his costume.

The Indians have lullabies and children's game-songs,— the moccasin game, in which they search for sticks hidden in a moccasin. Then too, there is the Rain Dance of the Junis and the Snake Dance of the Hopis, in which they carry rattlesnakes, sometimes holding them between the teeth.

Dance often means a ceremony lasting several days. The Indians are worshippers of the Sun, and have a festival. which lasts several days, called the Sun Dance. This

festival took place particularly among the Indians of the
plains: the Cheyennes, the Chippewas and others. The
last Sun Dance took place in 1882. In this the Indian
offered to the "Great Spirit" what was strongest in his
nature and training,—the ability to stand pain. Self
inflicted pain was a part of the ceremony and seemed
noble to the Indian, but to the white man it was barbarous and heathenish and he put a stop to it.

The Medicine Man

Have you ever heard of the medicine man? He is doctor,
lawyer, priest, philosopher, botanist, and musician all in
one. The society of "Grand Medicine" is the religion of
the Chippewas. It teaches that one must be good to live
long. The chief aims of the society are to bring good
health and long life to its followers, and music is as important in the healing as medicine.

Every member of the society carries a bag of herbs, the
use of which he has learned, and if called upon to heal the
sick, he works the cure by singing the right song before giving the medicine. The medicine is not usually swallowed in
proper fashion as a child takes a dose, but it is carried by
the sick person, or is placed among his belongings, or a
little wooden figure is carved roughly by the Medicine
Man and must be carried around with the herbs to heal
the patient. But the song, and it must be the right song
for the occasion, counts as much as the medicine. Wouldn't
you like to be an Indian?

Often the Medicine Man is called upon for a love-charm,
for which there is a song. There are also songs of cursing
which are supposed to work an evil charm when used with
a certain kind of cursing herbs.

Both men and women may become members of the
Great Medicine Society, and they must go through eight

degrees or stages in which they are taught the use of the
medicines and the songs. Each member of the society
has his own set of songs, some of which he has composed
himself and others he has had to buy for large sums of
money or goods. No man is allowed to sing another man's
song unless he has bought the right to it. With the sale of
a song goes the herb to be used with that particular song.
The ceremony is very elaborate. It lasts for several days,
and sounds very much like a story book.

The Chippewa Indians have had a written picture lan-
guage by means of which they read the different songs.
These pictures were usually drawn on white birch-bark.
Here are a few samples:

INDIAN SONG
PICTURE

In form like a bird
it appears.

INDIAN Song
PICTURE

On my arm
behold my
pan of food.

INDIAN SONG
PICTURE

Wavy lines in-
dicate "the song."
Straight lines
indicate "strength."

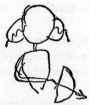

INDIAN SONG PICTURE

I have shot straight.

INDIAN SONG PICTURE

The sound of flowing
water comes toward my
home.

When we tell you about American music we will speak again of the Indian and how we have used in our own music what he has given us.

THE NEGRO AND HIS MUSIC

The place of the negro in the world of music has been the cause of many questions:

Is his music that of a primitive man?

Is it American?

Is it American Folk Music?

As we tell you the story of music we shall have to speak of the negro music from all these different sides. But, for you to understand why there is a question about it, we must tell you where the negro came from and what he brought from his primitive home.

When the English first came to Virginia and founded Jamestown in 1607 they started to grow tobacco on great plantations, and for this they needed cheap labor. They tried to use Indians, but as the work killed so many of them, they had negroes sent over from Africa to do it. A year before the Pilgrims landed at Plymouth Rock in 1620, negroes were already being sold as slaves in Virginia. Until 1808 these negroes were brought over from Africa; they were not all of one tribe, nor were they of one race. There were Malays from Madagascar, Movis from northern Africa, red skins and yellow skins as well as black.

These people were primitive and they all used song and dance in their religion, their work and their games. They brought from Africa a great love for music and ears that heard and remembered more than many a trained musician. A well-known writer has said that wherever the African negro has gone, he has left traces in the music of that country. The Spanish Habanera, which we have danced by the name of Tango came from Africa; even the name is African, "tangara," and was a vulgar dance unfit for civilized people. The rhythm of the African dance and of our tango is the same.

Like other savages, the African negro loved rhythm better than melody. His songs were monotonous and were made up of a few tones and short repeated phrases. They used the scale of five tones (called pentatonic), the same as the Indian's.

The African negro was a master at drumming. The Indian drumming was regular like the clock or pulse, but the negro played most difficult and complicated rhythms, almost impossible for a trained musician, to imitate. He had drums of all sizes and kinds.

These savages sang groups of tones which we call chords, which were not used by any of the ancient civilized people. By means of different rhythms they had hundreds of ways of combining the three tones of a chord as C–E–G. It is curious that these primitive people should have used methods more like our own than many of the races that had reached a much higher degree of civilization.

The Africans had an original telegraph system in which they did not use the Morse code, but sent their messages by means of drums that were heard many miles away. They had a special drum language which the natives understood; and the American Indians flashed *their* messages over long distances by means of the reflection of the sun on metal.

It is only a little more than a hundred years ago since we stopped bringing these primitive people into America and making slaves of them. Their children have become thoroughly Americanized now, from having lived alongside of the white people all this time and some have forgotten their African forefathers. But in the same way that the children of Italian, German, French or Russian parents remember the songs of their forefathers and often show traces of these songs in the music they make, so the negro without knowing it has kept some of the primitive traits of African music.

Later, we will tell you how this grew into two kinds of music, the beautiful religious song called the Negro Spiritual, and the dance which has grown into our popular ragtime and jazz.

If we were to study in detail the music of many savage tribes of different periods from prehistoric day to the uncivilized people living today, we should find certain points in common. They all have festival songs, songs for religious ceremonials, for games, work songs, war songs, hunting songs and love songs. In fact it is a beautiful habit for primitive people to put into song everything they do and everything they wish to remember. With them music has not been a frill or a luxury, but a daily need and a natural means for expressing themselves.

Another thing alike among these early peoples, is that all of them had drums and rattles of some kind and a roughly made instrument that resembles our pipes. But they had no stringed instruments and for their beginnings you will have to journey on with us in this,—your book.

After giving this book to the public, we came in direct contact with some remarkable songs of the Nootka (Canadian) Indians and of the Eskimos. Juliette Gaultier de la Verendry, a French Canadian, sang them in the original dialect. They were given to her by D. Jenness, an anthropologist who lived among the Eskimos for several years, studying their traits and at the same time he took the opportunity of writing down their songs. They are truly savage music and have the characteristics of which we have spoken in the use of intervals, drums, and in the type of songs, such as weather and healing incantations (medicine songs), work songs, and dances.

African music.

CHAPTER III

The Ancient Nations Made Their Music—Egyptian, Assyrian, and Hebrew

THREE thousand years before Jesus was born, a corner of south-western Asia and north-eastern Africa was the home of people who had reached a very high degree of civilization. They were the first to pass the stage of primitive man, and to make for themselves beautiful buildings, beautiful cities, monuments, decorations and music. Among these ancient, civilized people were the Egyptians, the Assyrians and the Hebrews. We will talk first about the Egyptians because they had the greatest influence not only on the Assyrian and Hebrew music, but also on the Greeks who went to Egypt. So, in European music we can trace the Egyptian influence through the Greeks.

The Egyptians were very fond of building and they decorated what they built with pictures in vivid colorings called hieroglyphics (heiro—sacred, glyphics—writings). As they had neither newspapers nor radio sets, they carved or painted the records of their daily lives, their festivals, battles, entertainments, and even marketing journeys on the walls and on the columns of the temples, on the obelisks, and in the tombs, some of which were the pyramids.

The climate saved these records from destruction, and the archæologists re-discovered them for us in the tombs full of Egyptian treasure and the temples and lost cities, buried for thousands of years.

The Egyptians built to inspire feelings of awe, mystery and grandeur. You probably remember pictures of obelisks, temples, pyramids, tombs and sphinxes, alongside of which a man looks but a few inches high.

They were very young as the world goes, and built huge structures because they were still filled with wonder at the immensity and power of the things they saw in Nature,— the Nile; the great desert which seemed vaster to them because they had only slow-moving camels, elephants and horses to take them about; they saw very long rainy seasons and the Nile overflowing its banks yearly, long dry seasons and the terrible wind and sand storms; the great heat of the sun, and the glory of their huge flowers, such as the lotus.

Just as primitive people did, they personified Nature in the gods. They had Osiris—god of Light, Health and Agriculture; Isis—goddess of the Arts and Agriculture; Horus (hawk-headed), the Sun god; Phtah, first divine King of Memphis, and many others. Again like primitive people, they had music for their gods, for their temple services, for their state ceremonies, festivals, martial celebrations and amusements.

Primitive music, we saw, had no laws to bind it, but was guided by the savage's natural feeling and he could make up anything he wished. In Egypt, because of state law which prevented it from changing, music was held down to the same system for three thousand years. New music was forbidden, and much of the old was considered sacred and so closely connected with religious ceremonies that it was allowed to be used only in the temples.

The priests lived in these magnificent temples and were the philosophers, artists and musicians, very like the medicine men of the Indians, but much more advanced in learning.

Like the American Indians, too, the profession of music

was handed down from father to son, and only the children of singers, whether they had good voices or not, could sing in the temples.

On the monuments we see these singers followed by players of instruments. The singers were of the highest caste, or Priest caste; the players were usually of the lower classes, or the Slave caste, although as pictured on the tombs of Rameses, one of Egypt's greatest rulers and builders, we see the priests dressed in splendid robes and playing large harps.

The temples of Egypt were so huge that the music had to be on a large scale. They thought nothing of an orchestra of six hundred players of harps, lyres, lutes, flutes and sistrums (bell rattles), whereas we today advertise in large type the fact of one hundred men in one orchestra! We see no trumpets in the picture writings of the Egyptian orchestra, for these were only used in war, and we find them only in their pictures of war and triumphal marches; nor do we see large drums, because the Egyptians clapped their hands to mark rhythm. However, the military instruments in the hands of players pictured on the monuments, show that they used trumpets and tambourines in the army.

From the names we find in the tombs—"Singers of the King" and "Singers of the Master of the World," we know that the Kings had musicians of high rank in their courts. The paintings on the walls and columns of the ruins of the temple Karnak, show funeral services with kneeling singers, playing harps of seven strings and other instruments.

Ptolemy Soter II, another famous Egyptian ruler, gave a fête in which were heard a chorus of twelve hundred voices, accompanied by three hundred Greek *kitharas* and many flutes.

It seems like a fairy tale that we can bring back the

manners and customs of three thousand years ago through
studying the writings in stone called hieroglyphics, and by
examining the things used every day, that were found in
the excavations. For a long time the hieroglyphics were
unsolved riddles until the discovery in 1799 A.D. of the
Rosetta stone, on which was an inscription in hieroglyphics
with its Greek translation. Although ancient Greek is
called a dead language, it still has enough life in it to bring
back the history and records of antiquity. Through this
knowledge of Greek, the Egyptian inscriptions speak to us
and tell us marvelous stories of ancient Egypt.

In one of the tombs at Thebes, was a harp with strings
of catgut, which when plucked, still gave out sounds
although the harp had probably not been played upon in
three thousand years!

Going once more to our ancient stone library—or collections of monuments in our museums or in Egypt—we
see many pictures of dancers. The Egyptians danced in
religious ceremonies as well as in private entertainments.
They loved lively dances, and the men did all sorts of
acrobatic steps and even toe-dancing like our Pavlowa,
while the women did the slow, languorous dances.

Egyptian music was greatest as far back as 3000 B.C.!
After that it grew poorer until 525 B.C. when Egypt was
conquered by Persia.

THE EGYPTIAN SCALE

The Egyptians must have used a musical scale of whole
steps and half steps, covering several octaves, not unlike
ours. Think of the piano keyboard with its black and its
white keys and you will get an idea of the Egyptian scale.
We learned this through the discovery of a flute that played
a scale of half steps from *a* below middle *c* to *d* above the
staff with only a few tones missing.

ASSYRIAN MUSIC

In the British Museum in London and in the Louvre in Paris, you can see ancient records which archaeologists unearthed from three mounds near the River Tigris in Asiatic Turkey. These mounds were the remains of the Assyrian cities of Nimroud (Babylon), Khorsabad, and probably the famous Nineveh, and date from 3000 to 1300 B.C.

Did Assyria influence Egypt or was it the other way around? The Egyptians excelled in making mechanical things such as instruments, utensils, tools, and in building temples and pyramids; while the Assyrians were sculptors, workers in metals and enamel, and knew the secret of dyeing and weaving stuffs, and of making beautiful pottery. But whose music was the better, the Egyptians or the Assyrians, is impossible to say. We do know, however, that the Assyrians, as well as the Egyptians and Hebrews, had perfected music far beyond the standard reached by many nations of our own time.

The Assyrians had the same families of instruments that we have,—the percussion (or drums), wind, and strings; and they used different combinations of instruments in concerts, either in instrumental performances or for accompanying vocal music. Everything that we know about them shows that the Assyrians were greater noise-makers than the Egyptians, for they not only had drums and trumpets, but they also marked rhythm by stamping their feet instead of clapping their hands.

The instruments pictured on the monuments, probably existed many centuries before the building of these monuments, which would make them very old indeed. In fact, almost all of them are still in use in the Orient today and are played in the same way. The monuments also prove that some of the special ceremonies in which music was used are still in existence.

Both the Assyrians and the Egyptians had flutes, and double flutes which were actually two flutes connected by one mouthpiece and looked like the letter v. The Assyrians also had harps that varied in size from some that could be carried in the hand, to some that stood seven feet high and had as many as twenty-two strings. The dulcimer, an instrument something like a zither, was very popular and was made so that it could be played standing upright or lying flat. They also had drums, castanets, cymbals, tambours or tambourines, and lyres, all of which could be easily carried.

The Assyrians being a warlike nation made their instruments so that they could be strapped to their bodies. So it seems that people in 3000 B.C. were practical.

The Assyrians were so fond of music that when their war-prisoners were musicians they were not put to death.

HEBREW MUSIC

We get our knowledge of the Hebrew music not from stone monuments and wall pictures, but from Biblical writings and other ancient Hebrew records. In the Second Commandment, God forbids the Hebrews to make images:

"Thou shalt not make unto thyself any graven image, nor the likeness of anything that is in heaven above, or in the earth beneath, or in the waters under the earth." (Exodus XXI: 4.) With so strict a commandment, you can understand why there are no pictures of singers and of instruments, and that we have to go to the greatest literary gift to the world,—the Old Testament, to find out about their music.

The first musician mentioned in the Bible is Jubal. It says in Genesis IV: 21, "he was the father of all such as handle the harp and pipe (or organ)." From an old Spanish book found in the early 18th century in a Mexican monastery, comes the story that Jubal was listening to Tubal-Cain's forge, and noticed the difference in pitch of the sounds made by the strokes on the anvil. Some tones were high, some low, and some were medium. He compared this to the human voice, and tried to imitate the sounds, high, low and medium, of the forge. Thus he became the first singer of the Hebrews. Jubal invented a flute and a little three-cornered harp called the *kinnor*. These small instruments were most convenient to carry about, for at this time the Hebrews were shepherd tribes wandering from place to place. Their music was simple as is the music of all primitive peoples.

We know from the Biblical story that the Children of Israel were sold into captivity and remained many centuries in Egypt; that Moses was found in the bulrushes by Pharoah's daughter, and was educated as an Egyptian boy and "was learned in all the wisdom of the Egyptians." Therefore, he must have learned music from the priests. It is natural then, that the Hebrews must have borrowed the music and instruments of their adopted country in the making of their own.

After Moses had been commanded by the Lord to lead the children of Israel out of the land of captivity, and after the Red Sea had divided to allow them to pass through, we read the great song of triumph sung by Moses:

"Then sang Moses and the Children of Israel: 'I will sing unto Jehovah, for he hath triumphed gloriously, the horse and his rider hath he thrown into the sea, Jehovah is my strength and my song and he is become my salvation.'" etc.—(Exodus XV: 1–2).

And "Miriam, the prophetess, the sister of Aaron, took a timbrel in her hand, and all the women went out after her with timbrels and with dances." (The timbrel is a small tambourine-like instrument.)

This story, like others in the Old Testament, is full of

the accounts of musical instruments, singing and dancing, and shows us that the ancient Hebrews used music and the dance for nearly every event. If you read carefully you will get the musical history of this poetic people.

While the Children of Israel were in the wilderness, Moses received from Jehovah the command: (Numbers X.)

"Make thee two trumpets of silver; of a whole piece shalt thou make them; that thou mayest use them for the calling of the assembly, and for the journeyings of the camp."

Then follow directions as to the meaning of the blowing of the trumpets. One trumpet alone called the princes; two trumpets called the entire tribe together; an "alarm" gave the signal for the camps to go forward, and so on. So, you see the ancient Hebrews used trumpets much as we today use the army bugle. The trumpets mentioned as one of the earliest of all instruments called the people to religious ceremonies too; it announced festivals, the declaration of a war, the crowning of a king, proclaimed the jubilee year, and gave warning of the anger of God.

One instrument has come down to our times and is still used in the Hebrew temple services. This is called the *shofar* and is usually a ram's horn on which two tones may be blown. Probably, as the ram was one of the animals of sacrifice, they used its horn as a sacred instrument. This shofar is 5,000 years old, at least. It is sounded in all the synagogues of the world on the Jewish New Year and on the Day of Atonement in memory of the wanderings of the Children of Israel.

When the twelve tribes, after their wanderings in the wilderness, had settled down in Palestine, they gave music a most important place in their daily life. Samuel, the last and most respected of the judges, built a school of prophecy and music. Here it was that young David hid himself to escape the persecutions of Saul. You remember that David is called the Great Musician and he gave us many of the Psalms, the most beautiful religious verse in the world. How much it would mean to us if we knew the music David sang to these songs! In spite of the fact that the music in which they were originally sung has been lost, the Psalms have been an inspiration to all composers of religious music throughout the ages. David learned so much at Samuel's school that he created a most beautiful musical service for the temple, which is the basis of the one used today in Jewish synagogues (temples).

The number that were instructed in the songs of the Lord was two hundred, four score and eight (288). There were in all four thousand, including assistants, students, players of instruments and the two hundred and eighty-eight professional singers.

All of these people did not perform at one time; for the ordinary services they used twelve male singers, twelve players on instruments,—nine harps, and two players of the psaltery and one of cymbals. Women were not allowed to sing in the temples but they were a part of the court and sang at funerals and at public festivities and banquets.

The great Jewish historian, Josephus, tells us that Solomon had two hundred thousand singers, forty thousand harpists, forty thousand sistrum players and two hundred thousand trumpeters. This is hard to believe, but as everything belonged to the kings in bygone days, probably this was only Solomon's musical directory.

The psaltery was an instrument something like our zither, with thirteen strings on a flat wooden sounding board, rectangular in shape. The sistrum was a metal rattle which made a very sweet sound.

It isn't easy to describe the instruments used thousands of years ago, for the names have become changed through the ages, and we find the same type of instruments called by different names in different countries and periods. For example, the psaltery is much the same instrument as the *dulcimer*, the Arab's *kanoun* and the Persian *santir*. We find the same psaltery in Chaucer's "Miller's Tale" as *sautrie*. By the addition of a keyboard this Biblical instrument became the *spinet*, which you will meet again in the 15th and 16th centuries. In the 13th century, in Italy, we find a kind of psaltery hung around the neck and called "Istroménto di porco" because it looked like the head of a pig.

Not all the songs of the Bible are religious. The Song of Solomon, a most beautiful poem of marriage, gives us a vivid picture of luxury and magnificence, as well as showing us that music was used for other than religious ceremonies.

After the death of Solomon, the music in the temple lost its splendor and again the Children of Israel were made captive. When one hundred years later Nebuchadnezzar (586 B.C.) the King of Babylon, destroyed their temple, the song of the Hebrews became sad and mournful, as you can read in the Book of Lamentations and in this beautiful song of grief, the 137th Psalm:

SORROWS OF THE EXILES IN BABYLON

By the rivers of Babylon
There we sat down, yea, we wept,
When we remembered Zion.

Upon the willows in the midst thereof
We hanged up our harps.

For there they that led us captive required of us songs,
And our tormentors required of us mirth, saying:
"Sing for us one of the songs of Zion."

How shall we sing Jehovah's song
In a foreign land?

If I forget thee, Oh Jerusalem,
Let my right hand forget her skill.

Let my tongue cleave to the roof of my mouth
If I remember thee not;
If I prefer not Jerusalem,
Above my chief joy.

During the next few centuries the Hebrews became scattered over the world, carrying with them their reverence for God, their love of poetry and song, and their religious customs. These qualities have persisted throughout the centuries, and some of the greatest musicians in the world have been of Hebrew origin.

Although most of the old music has passed away, there is still enough of its spirit left in their temple services to give some idea of the ancient Hebrew music.

CHAPTER IV

The Greeks Lived Their Music—The Romans Used Greek Patterns

THE Greeks "dwelt with beauty" and believed it to be a part of being good, and they strove to make everything beautiful. Beauty to the Greeks was a religion. Had this not been so, we would not have the Venus de Milo, the Parthenon in Athens, the Hermes, the Winged Victory (Niké of Samothrace) and all the other Greek masterpieces which no modern sculptor or builder has surpassed.

It is interesting to see a nation 400 years before the time of Christ and even earlier, making glorious art works in stone, and writing the greatest plays the world has ever had, being more grown up than modern nations, and yet as far as we know an infant in the art of music. We have only the slightest idea of how their music sounded as they had no accurate way of writing it, and had only very primitive instruments. Although when compared to their other arts their music was not great, still it was very important to them and they used it constantly with poetry, dancing, and in the drama.

The word music was first used by the Greeks and has been carried into nearly every language; we find *musique* in French, *Musik* in German, *musica* in Italian, and so on.

Music, according to the Greeks, was an art which combined not only the playing of instruments, singing and dancing, but also all the arts, particularly poetry and drama,

31

and sciences including mathematics. It took its name from the Muses, who were supposed to govern all the beautiful accord and harmony of the world.

The nine Muses were daughters of Jupiter, and each presided over some particular department of literature, art and science.

Clio: Muse of History and Epic Poetry. She is shown in statues and pictures holding a half open scroll.

Thalia: Muse of Joy and Comedy (drama) with a comic mask in one hand and a crooked staff in the other.

Erato: Muse of Lyric Poetry, inspired those who wrote of love. She plays on a nine-stringed lyre.

Euterpe: Muse of Lyric Song, patroness of music especially of flute players. She holds two flutes (*auloi*).

Polyhymnia: Muse of Sacred Song. She holds her forefinger to her lips or carries a scroll.

Calliope: Muse of Eloquence and Epic Poetry, holds a roll of parchment, or a trumpet.

Terpsichore: Muse of the Dance, presiding over choral, dance and song. She appears dancing with a seven-stringed lyre.

Urania: Muse of Astronomy, holds the globe and traces mathematical figures with a wand.

Melpomene: Muse of Tragedy (drama), leans on a club and holds a tragic mask.

MYTHS AND LEGENDS

The myths and legends of the ancient Greeks read like fairy tales, but to the Greeks they were what our Bible stories are to us. In their rich mythology we find many stories about the beginnings of music.

To Pan, the god of woods and fields, of flocks and shepherds, is given the credit of inventing the shepherd's pipe, or Pan's Pipes. He lived in grottoes, wandered on the mountains and in the valleys, and amused himself hunting, leading the dances of the nymphs, and playing on his pipes.

PAN'S PIPES

A beautiful nymph named Syrinx was loved by Pan, but every time that he tried to tell her of his love, she became frightened and ran away, for Pan was a funny looking lover with goat's legs, a man's body, and long pointed ears. One day he chased her through the woods to the bank of a river; she called out in fright, and was suddenly changed by her friends the Water Nymphs, into a clump of tall reeds. When he reached out to embrace her, instead of Syrinx, he had the clump of reeds in his arms! As he sighed in disappointment, his breath passing through the reeds, produced a sad wail. Pan, hearing in it a plaintive song, broke off the reeds in unequal lengths, bound them together, and made the first musical instrument, which he called a syrinx in memory of his lost sweetheart. These pipes comforted Pan, and he played many tender melodies, and often without being seen, was known to be near by his lovely music.

Pan, although adored, was feared. At one time, Brennus, a warrior, with a company of Gauls (a tribe from ancient France), attacked the Temple of Delphi (in Greece), and was about to destroy it, when suddenly they turned and fled in fear although no one pursued them. Their terror was supposed to have been of Pan's making, and to this day we use the word "panic" (Pan-ic) for all sudden overpowering fright.

APOLLO

Pan is supposed to have taught music to Apollo, the god of Music and of the Sun. You have seen statues of him with a lyre in his hands. As Pan's pupil he learned to play the syrinx so beautifully that he won a prize in a contest with Marsyas, a mortal who played the flute invented (ac-

cording to the Greek legend), by Pallas Athene. This
goddess was sometimes known as Musica or Musician.
When Cupid saw her play the flute he laughed at her because she made such queer faces. This angered her, and
she flung her flute away. It fell down from Mt. Olympus
to the earth, and Marsyas picked it up and became such a
skilfull player that he challenged the god Apollo to a contest for flute championship of the world! The day came
and Apollo won the prize, but put Marsyas to death for
daring to challenge him—a god. Apollo afterwards was
very sorry and broke all the strings of his lyre and placed it
with his flutes in a haunt of Dionysus (god of Wine), to
whom he consecrated these instruments.

These stories are not only a part of the ancient Greek
religion but they have become, on account of their beauty,
a rich source of plot and story for the works of musicians,
artists and writers from the days of antiquity to our own
time.

ORPHEUS

One of the favorite Greek stories has been that of Orpheus,
who went down to Hades to bring his dead wife whom he
adored, back to earth, and about whom Peri, Gluck, and
others wrote operas. He was son of Apollo and of Calliope,
the Muse of Epic Poetry, and became such a fine performer
on all instruments, that he charmed all things animate and
inanimate. He tamed wild birds and beasts, and even the
trees and rocks followed him as he played, the winds and
the waves obeyed him, and he soothed and made the
Dragon, who guarded the Golden Fleece, gentle and harm-
less.

On the cruise of the *Argo* in search of the Golden Fleece,
Orpheus not only succeeded in launching the boat when the
strength of the heroes had failed in the task, but when they

were passing the islands of the Sirens, he sang so loudly and so sweetly that the Sirens' songs could not be heard and the crew were saved.

Music in Their Daily Life

When a people have legends about music you may know that they love it. Such was the case with the Greeks. They did not call their schools high schools and colleges but Music schools, and everything that we call learning they included under the name of music. Every morning the little Greek boy was sent to the Music school where he was taught the things that were considered necessary for a citizen to know. Here he learned gymnastics, poetry, and music. At home too, music was quite as important as in school, and we know that they had folk songs which had to do with the deeds of ordinary life, such as farming and wine-making and grape-picking, and the effect and beauty of the seasons of the year. (See Chap. IX.) They can well be divided into songs of joy and songs of sorrow, and seem to have existed even before Homer the Blind Bard. If you ever have tried to dance or do your daily dozen without music, you will understand at once how much help music always has been to people as they worked.

Harvest Songs

All harvest songs in Greece had the name of Lytiersis. Lytiersis was the son of King Midas, known as the richest king in the world. Lytiersis was a king himself but also a mighty reaper, and according to Countess Martinengo-Cesaresco who has written a book called *Essays in the Study of Folk-Songs* it was his "habit to indulge in trials of strength with his companions and with strangers who were passing by. He tied the vanquished up in sheaves and beat them.

One day he defied an unknown stranger, who proved too strong for him and by whom he was slain." The first harvest song was composed to console King Midas for the death of his son. We can make a fable from this story which means that Nature and Man are always struggling against each other.

The harvest festivals founded in Greece led to others in Brittany, France, North Germany and England. So does the deed of one race affect other races.

THE LITURGIES

Among the taxes, or five special liturgies, that the Greeks had to pay, was the obligation for certain rich citizens to supply the Greek tragedies with the chorus. Every Greek play had its chorus and every chorus had to have its structures; a choregic monument to celebrate it; one or more flute players, costumes, crowns, decorations, teachers for the chorus and everything else to make it succeed. This cost, which would equal many thousands of dollars, was undertaken as a duty quite as easily as our men of wealth pay their income taxes. You can see a greatly enlarged copy of a choregic monument, the Soldiers' and Sailors' monument at 89th Street and Riverside Drive, in New York City, and also one at the Metropolitan Museum.

In old Greece the musicians were also poets. Homer, Hesiod, Pindar, Æschylus, Sophocles, Sappho, Euripides, Plato. not only wrote their dramas but knew what music should be played with them. In fact no play was complete without its chorus and its music and its flute-player. You have heard of the Greek chorus. Don't for a moment think it was like our chorus. It consisted of a group of masked actors (all actors in those days wore masks), who appeared between the acts and intoned (chanted) the meaning of the play and subsequent events. In fact the chorus took the

place of a libretto,—"words and music of the opera," for
it explained to the audience what it should expect. It spoke
and sang some of the most important lines of the play and
danced in appropriate rhythms. So it brought together
word, action and music, and was a remote ancestor of
opera, oratorio and ballet.

FESTIVALS

Besides the occupational songs and those for the drama
festivals, the Greeks had the great game festivals where
in some, not only competitions in sports took place but also
flute playing and singing. The oldest of these festivals was
the Olympic games, first held in 776 B.C. and every four
years thereafter. These games played so important a part
in the lives of the Greeks that their calendar was divided
into Olympiads instead of years. While music was evident
in the Olympic games, music and poetry were never among
the competitions.

The Pythian games were chiefly musical and poetic contests and were started in Delphi, 586 B.C., where they were
held every nine years in honor of the Delphian Apollo whose
shrine was at Delphi. The Isthmian and Nemean games
were also based on poetic and musical contests. Warriors,
statesmen, philosophers, artists and writers went to these
games and took part in them. Maybe some time we will
realize the power of music as did the Greeks nearly one
thousand years before the birth of Jesus.

THE GREEK SCALES

While, as we said before, we know very little about the
melodies of the Greeks, we do know something about their
scales, upon which the church music of the Middle Ages
was based, as are our own major and minor scales. In

fact the most important contribution Greece made to our music was the scale. They had a very complicated system and no one is quite sure how it worked.

We have the two modes or kinds of scales, major and minor, which we use in different keys, but the Greeks had at least seven different modes used in many different ways. They used one mode for martial or military music, another for funeral ceremonies, another for their temple music, and curiously enough, our own C major scale they used for their popular music, for drinking songs, and light festivities.

The Greek scales were based on *tetrachords*, from the Greek words tetra-four, chord-string that is, a group of four strings. If you play on the piano B C D E and C D E F and D E F G you will find the three tetrachords that formed the *primary modes* of the Greeks:—Dorian, Phrygian and Lydian.

You know in Greek architecture that the Doric column came from Doria, a province of Greece, and the Ionic column from Ionia, etc. The different provinces also contributed to the development of lyric poetry, and the various species of scales were likewise named after them: Dorian mode, Ionian, Æolian, Phrygian, Lydian, etc.

The Greek tetrachord was formed on the interval of a fourth, for example from E to A—these were called *standing tones*, because the intervals between the two standing tones or permanent tones could be changed but the first and the fourth always remained the same—

Dorian, E͡ F G A: Phrygian, E F͡♯ G A: Lydian, E F♯ G͡♯ A
$\frac{1}{2}$ step $\frac{1}{2}$ step $\frac{1}{2}$ step

By putting two tetrachords together all the other Greek scales were formed. These fell into two classes, and according to Cecil Forsyth in his *History of Music* these classes were called the *join* and the *break*. When the second tetrachord began on the fourth tone of the first tetrachord, Mr. Forsyth calls it the *joining* method, thus.

$$\overparen{EFGA}\cdots\overparen{AB^{\flat}CD}$$

When the second tetrachord began on the tone above the fourth tone of the first tetrachord, he calls it the *breaking* method, thus:

$$\overparen{EFGA}\ \overparen{BCDE}$$

By using the *join* and the *break* with each of the three modes, Dorian, Phrygian and Lydian, you can see to what a great variety of scales and names this would lead. The Greeks spoke of their scales from the top note down, instead of from the lowest note up, as we do.

The first *kithara* was supposed to have been an instrument of four strings that could be tuned in any of these different ways, with the half-step either between the first and second strings, or between the second and third, or between the third and fourth. Two instruments tuned differently formed the complete scale, but it did not take long to add strings to their lyres and kitharas so that they could play an entire scale on one instrument.

The little Greek boy was taught in school to tune the scale according to the fourth string of his lyre, which was the *home-tone* or what we should call *tonic*. Our tonic falls on the first degree of the scale, but in the *primary modes* of the Greeks, the tonic fell on the fourth degree, and was called the *final*. When the final was on pitch all the other strings had to be tuned to it.

These tetrachords are supposed to have been perfected by Terpander, in the six hundreds before Christ. His melodies were called *nomes* and were supposed to have had a fine moral effect on the Spartan youth in giving him spirit and courage. The Greeks thought that all music and that every one of their modes had a special effect on conduct and character.

After the Messenian war, Sparta was in such a state of upheaval that the Delphian oracle was consulted. The answer was:

" When Terpander's Cithar shall sound
Contention in Sparta shall cease."

So the Spartans called upon Terpander to help them, and through the power of his song all was peace again.

Terpander collected Asiatic, Egyptian, Æolian and Bœotian melodies all of which are unfortunately lost; he invented a new notation and enlarged the kithara from four strings to seven. Arion, Alcæus and the great poetess Sappho were his pupils, and Sappho is often shown in statues with a six stringed kithara.

Most of these poet-singers were called "lyric poets" because they sang to the accompaniment of the lyre.

PYTHAGORAS

The Greeks were the first to write down their music, or to make a musical notation whereby the singers and players knew what tones to use. Their system was their alphabet with certain alterations. They had names describing each tone not unlike our use of the word *tonic* for the first degree of the scale, and *dominant* for the fifth and so on.

Of course they did not have the *staff* and *treble* and *bass* *clefs* as we have, but they were groping for some way of recording music in those far away days.

Pythagoras as far back as 584–504 B.C., not only influenced the music in the classical Greek period (400 B.C), but down to and throughout the Middle Ages to the Renaissance (1500s). To this day music is based on his mathematical discovery. He worked out a theory of numbers based on the idea that all nature was governed by the law of numbers and modern scientists have proven that he was correct in many of his ideas. In fact our orchestras and pianos are tuned in accordance with his theories.

He invented an instrument called the monochord which consisted of a hollow wooden box with one string and movable fret. He discovered that when he divided the string exactly in half by means of the fret, the tone produced was an octave higher than the tone given out by striking the entire string; one-third of the string produced the interval of a fifth above the octave; one-fourth the length of the string produced a fourth above the fifth. The truth of Pythagoras' theory has been proved by experiments in physics carrying the tone relationships beyond the fourth division. The relation of the fifth of the string to the fourth is a large or major third; of sixth to fifth is a small or minor third; of seventh to sixth is a slightly smaller third; of eighth to seventh, a large second. The eighth tone is three octaves above the sound of the entire string:

An amusing experiment can be made by pressing silently any one of the tones marked 2, 3, 4, 5, 6, or 8, and striking the fundamental tone sharply, the key you are pressing silently will sound so that you can distinctly hear its pitch.

The Greeks seem to have had no harmony (that is, combining of two or more tones in chords) outside of the natural result of men's voices and women's singing together. But they had groups of singers answering each other in what is called *antiphony* (*anti*-against, *phony*-sound). Even our

American Indians have their song leader and chorus answering each other.

Greek rhythm followed the rhythm of the spoken word and was considered a part of their poetic system.

GREEK INSTRUMENTS

We have already spoken of the *syrinx*, Pan's Pipes, the instrument of Pan, the satyrs and of the shepherds; the *monochord*, Pythagoras' invention; the *lyre* and *kithara;* and the flute or *aulos*.

The lyre, of the family of stringed instruments, was the Greek national instrument. It was the first to be used in their musical competitions, and helped in the forming of the Greek modes. These were of two types, the lyre and the kithara. The first lyres which came down from the age of myths and fables were originally made of the shell of a tortoise and had four strings (the tetrachord) and later seven and even more strings. This form of the lyre was called *chelys*, or the tortoise, and was used for accompanying drinking songs and popular love songs.

The *kithara* was also called lyre, but was not made of the body of the tortoise, and it became the Greek concert instrument, and was only used by professionals, while the *chelys* was used in the home. It came originally from Asia Minor and Egypt. It had four strings at first but these were gradually added to, until there were fifteen and eighteen strings. It was sometimes small and sometimes large, and was held to the body by means of a sling and was played with a plectrum or pick.

The Greek flute or *aulos* was a wood-wind instrument more like our oboe than our flute. It was usually played in pairs, that is, one person played two flutes or *auloi* of different sizes at one time, and they were V shaped. There was a group of *auloi* differing in range like the human voice

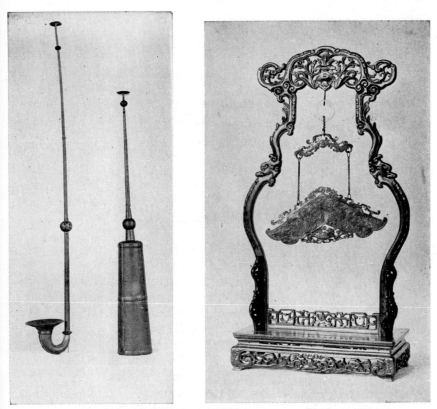

Fig. 5.

Fig. 6.

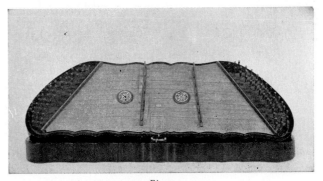

Fig. 7.

Courtesy of the Metropolitan Museum of Art.

Chinese Instruments.

Fig. 5.—Trumpets.
Fig. 6—Te'ch'ing—sonorous stone.
Fig. 7—Yang-Ch'in or Dulcimer.

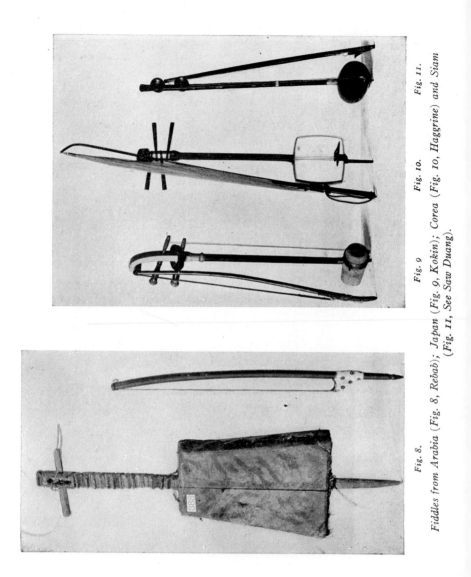

Fig. 8.   *Fig. 9*   *Fig. 10.*   *Fig. 11.*

Fiddles from Arabia (*Fig. 8, Rebab*); Japan (*Fig. 9, Kokin*); Corea (*Fig. 10, Haggrine*) and Siam
(*Fig. 11, See Saw Duang*).

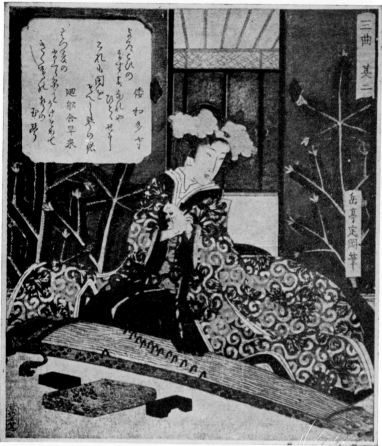

After a print by Gakutei—about 1840.

The Koto-Player.

After print by Kuniyasu—about 1830.

The Wandering Samisen-Player.

differs, and covering three octaves from the bass *aulos* to the soprano.

The *aulos* was first a single wooden pipe with three or four finger holes which later were increased to fifteen or sixteen so that the three modes Dorian, Phrygian and Lydian, could be played on one pair of *auloi*. About six centuries before the Christian era, the double flute became the instrument of the Delphian and Pythian musical competitions.

In the chorus too, we read that for each drama there was a special *aulos* soloist who always played the double flute.

There were other type instruments such as the war trumpets, trumpets used in the temple services, and harps (*magadis*) that were brought from Egypt, but the real instruments of the Greeks pictured in their sculpture and on their vases and urns, and spoken of in their literature, are the lyres and auloi.

Roman Music

The Romans, law givers, world conquerors and road builders, gave little new to music, for they did not show a great talent for art. They were influenced by Greek ideals and Greek methods. They were warlike by nature, and from defenders of their state they became conquerors. As they grew nationally stronger and more secure, they learned music, oratory, architecture and sculpture from Greek teachers. Many Romans well known in history were singers and gifted players on the Greek kithara, lyre, and flute (aulos).

The Romans seemed to have cared more about the performing of music than for the composing of it, and "offered prizes to those who had the greatest dexterity, could blow the loudest or play the fastest." (*Familiar Talks on History of Music.*—Gantvoort.)

As they come to America today the musicians of other lands flocked to Rome, especially those who played or sang, because they were received with honor and were richly paid.

The Romans, among them Boethius (6th century B.C.), wrote treatises on the Greek modes, were very much interested in the theory of music, and built their scales like the Greeks. To each of the seven tones within an octave they gave the name of a planet, and to every fourth tone which was the beginning of a new tetrachord, the name of a day of the week which is named for the planet.

B	C	D	E	F	G	A
Saturn	Jupiter	Mars	Sun	Venus	Mercury	Moon
Saturday			Sunday			Monday

B	C	D	E	F	G	A
Saturn	Jupiter	Mars	Sun	Venus	Mercury	Moon
		Tuesday			Wednesday	

B	C	D	E	F	G	A
Saturn	Jupiter	Mars	Sun	Venus	Mercury	Moon
	Thursday			Friday		

The days of the week in French show much more clearly than in English the names of the planets, in the case of Tuesday—mardi, (Mars); Wednesday—mercredi (Mercury); Thursday—jeudi, (Jupiter); Friday—vendredi. (Venus).

The Greeks brought their instrument, the *kithara*, to Rome, and with it a style of song called a *kitharoedic chant*, which was usually a hymn sung to some god or goddess. The words, until three hundred years after the birth of Jesus, were in the Greek language; the Latin kitharoedic songs like those of the poets Horace and Catullus were sung at banquets and private parties, Cicero too, was musical.

Edward MacDowell in *Critical and Historical Essays,* says that instrumental music was no longer used merely to accompany voices and had become quite independent. The flute (aulos) players performed better than the lyre and kithara players and were liked better. They played "dressed in long feminine, saffron (yellow)-colored robes, with veiled faces, and straps around their cheeks to support the muscles of the mouth." They played with an astonishing amount of technical skill. "Even women became flute players, although this was considered disgraceful." The prices paid to these flute players were higher than the amounts received by our opera singers.

The Roman theatre, unlike the Greek, was not a place to honor their gods. Greek plays, both tragedy and comedy, were replaced with pantomime, usually accompanied by orchestra and singing. The orchestra was made up of "cymbals, gongs, castanets, foot castanets, rattles, flutes, bagpipes, gigantic lyres, and a kind of shell or crockery cymbals, which were clashed together."

The Roman *tibia* or bagpipe is still popular today with the peasants of Italy. Although the bagpipe is first mentioned in Rome, there are some Persian terra cotta figures made before the Roman era, showing players of the bagpipes. It is always said that Nero played the fiddle while Rome burned and even our motion pictures show him playing the violin to the accompaniment of flames. How could he have played on a violin when it had not as yet been invented? If he played any instrument while Rome burned, it was probably the tibia.

CHAPTER V

The Orientals Make Their Music—Chinese, Japanese, Siamese, Burmese, and Javanese

TO hear two Chinamen exchanging greetings on a street corner, you would think they were singing or rather chanting, not because their tones are particularly pleasant for they are high and nasal and hard, but because they are talking in their own peculiar way. The Chinese have what is called an inflected language in which they use many tones. For example the syllable "hi" in one tone will mean one thing and it will mean something else entirely in each different inflection. Here again is a case where it is hard to say where speech ends and song begins. Another amusing thing about the Chinese is the way, according to our ideas, they seem to twist every thing around, so that what we call high tones they call low tones; they wear white for mourning and we wear black; their guests of honor sit at the left of the host and ours sit at the right; they consider taking off the hat very bad manners and of course we consider it bad manners for a man to keep it on in the house or when talking to a lady.

They never used their music as a way of expressing beauty as other nations have done, but treated it as we would a problem in arithmetic or a cross-word puzzle, and they loved to write articles on the subject that would seem long and dull to us. However, as far back as 2255 B.C. Ta Shao

composed a piece of music which Confucius, 1600 years
later, said, "enchanted him to such an extent that he did
not know the taste of food for months."

SCALES

Their scale was the pentatonic and they had the queerest
names for their degrees or steps.

F the first degree was called Emperor
G " 2d " " " Prime Minister
A " 3d " " " Loyal Subjects
C " 4th " " " Affairs of State
D " 5th " " " Mirror of the World

This shows that music must have been limited to a very
few subjects.

When the scale of five steps was changed into a scale of
seven steps about 600 B.C., every one thought that the end
of music had come. However these two new notes B and
E which formed half steps in the scale were given very interesting names: Leader and Mediator. We, today, call B
the leading tone, and E the mediant, so in this case, the
Chinese were not quite so topsy-turvy as usual. But in
true Chinese fashion they thought that a mythical bird
Fung-Woang and his mate had invented the steps and the
half steps. The whole steps to them stood for perfect
and independent things such as heaven, sun and man; the
half steps stood for dependent things such as earth, moon
and woman.

They had 84 scales! Think of that and be happy! For
we have only two modes, major and minor, and twelve
different sounding scales in each.

We get very little pleasure out of Chinese melodies for
they seem to wander about aimlessly and do not end comfortably, nor do they seem to begin anywhere! The best
melodies are found among the oldest sacred music and

among the songs of the sailors and mountaineers. The sacred hymns and the songs of the people have come down unchanged from earliest times. The music of their theatres we like least of all as it is sing-song, shrill and nerve racking.

Here is an example of an ancient hymn in the pentatonic scale:

CHINESE SACRIFICIAL HYMN TO THE IMPERIAL ANCESTORS

INSTRUMENTS

How the Chinese like noise! Their orchestras are seventy-five percent noise makers: drums of all kinds and sizes, bells, stones beaten with mallets, cymbals, wooden clappers, a row of tuned stones and copper plates strung up to be hammered, and wooden tubs beaten sometimes from the inside and sometimes from the outside. They also have wind instruments of clay and flutes of bamboo and metal. The *cheng*, their most pleasing wind instrument, is made of a hollow gourd with bamboo tubes of different lengths inserted. Their most popular stringed instruments are the *kin*, a primitive guitar, and the *cha*, a sort of large zither with twenty-five strings. These instruments date back to barbaric times.

One of the most curious that we have come across is the *king* which is supposed to have been invented by *Quei*, a mythical youth like the Greek Orpheus. It is a rack hung with two rows of sixteen different sized stones, which are struck with a wooden mallet. This instrument goes back to 2300 B.C. It seemed so important to the Chinese that they have a special kind of *king* called the *nio-king* upon which only the Emperor could play. Another little instrument almost as queer as the *king*, made of slats of wood tied together and shaped like a fan, used to beat time, was called the *tchoung-tou*. It was held in one hand and struck against the palm of the other much as one would play with a fan.

In making their instruments, the Chinese used eight different sounds in nature which they found musical—the sound of skin (drums), stone (*king* and *nio-king*), metal (flutes, bells, gongs, cymbals and trumpets), clay (instrument like an occarina moulded into fantastic animal shapes), wood (drums and boxes), bamboo (flutes and parts of the *cheng*), silk (strings on the *che* and *king* and other stringed instruments), gourds (sound boards which held the tubes of the *cheng*, one of the ancestors of the modern organ).

As early as the 5th century B.C., one of the first books on music in the world was written by a friend of Confucius, the great teacher and philosopher. We know about the ancient Chinese music, not from hieroglyphics and parchments, but from the music they use today, which is the same as that of barbaric times. The law against new things prevailed there as it did in Egypt, and where the government controls art, there can be little progress.

However we might have known much more about music had not Emperor She Huang-Ti "the book destroyer" ordered all musical instruments and books to be destroyed (246 B.C.) except those about medicine, agriculture and magic. For generations after, the people heard little music but the noise of tumbling bells and dancers' drums.

Their popular music has always been very poor with no particular form or system.

JAPANESE MUSIC

From the many Japanese prints, and cups and bowls decorated with fascinating pictures of the dainty little men and women playing the *samisen* and *koto*, we feel as if we had met these far away people before.

The *koto* and the *samisen* have remained unchanged for hundreds of years. It is said that the *koto* was first made of several hunting bows placed side by side and that later they were joined together as one long sounding board across which the strings were drawn. In the prints we see the long zither-like instruments lying flat on the floor and the dainty little players in fancy kimonos beside them.

Perhaps in the same print a companion will be seen playing a *samisen*, a long necked instrument whose strings are plucked with a pick or plectrum, such as we use for the mandolin. Whether these prints are a hundred years old or the work of an artist today, makes little difference, for we find the instrument unchanged and the little player in the same lovely kimono. These instruments have been in use in Japan for hundreds of years.

The music and instruments of the Japanese are very like those of the Chinese, not only because they are of like race, but because the Japanese are great imitators and have borrowed from China not only music but art. The Japanese love music for itself, not as the Chinese love it as subject for debate, but they have not written any better music than their neighbors on the mainland.

If you have listened to the music of *Madame Butterfly*, an opera by Giacomo Puccini, you will have heard a number of Japanese melodies, some of which are real. The composers of Europe and America love to imitate the oriental music because it gives them a chance to make effects quite different from those possible in our own music. Besides, the oriental people seem very picturesque to us and stir our imagination. Henry Eichheim of Boston has written Chinese and Japanese Impressions in which he has used many of the native instruments,—bells, rattles and drums.

The Japanese have great love of beauty which shows itself in their festivals, held in the spring when the cherry trees blossom and azaleas bloom. Then, too, their Geisha dances are full of grace and have the most winning names, such as, Leaf of Gold and the Butterfly dance. At the time of the festivals bands of musicians and dancers rove from place to place in gay costumes and add greatly to the fun. The Geisha girls are trained to sing and dance to the accompaniment of the *koto* and *samisen* to amuse the people.

The Japanese and Chinese are Buddhists, or worshippers of the prophet Buddha. In their temples they chant the whole service on one note accompanied by the sound of cymbals and the tolling of a deep rich gong. We know these gongs for we have often been called to dinner by them in America.

About 200 years ago a musician named Yatsubashi, the father of Japanese national music, invented a way of writing down music for the *koto*. Each string has a number and this number is set down and is read from top to bottom instead of from left to right on the staff, as we read music.

Since Commodore Perry of the United States Navy, in 1853, opened up Japan to western trade and influences, Japan has become the greatest imitator among the nations. She has borrowed western music, western ways of dressing, and western methods of warfare and industry. Starting with adapting Chinese music to her uses, she now enjoys symphony concerts, western singers and players. Even her own musicians compose in the western system and play and sing western music. Whether occidental music will banish oriental music in Japan, is beyond anyone but a prophet to foretell.

SIAMESE, BURMESE AND JAVANESE

The yellow races seem to like the same kind of music and use almost the same instruments. Nevertheless each nation has its own special instruments. For example, the Burmese have a drum organ made of twenty-one drums of different sizes, hung inside of a great hoop; they also have a gong organ in which fifteen or more gongs of different sizes and tones are strung inside a hoop. The player sits or stands inside the hoop and plays the surrounding gongs. Sometimes it looks very funny to see a procession in which this instrument is carried by two men while a third walks along inside a hoop, striking the gongs not only at the side and in front of him but also behind him. (Figure 14.)

This instrument is a very important part of the Javanese orchestra called the *gamelan* in Java. Their particular musical possession is the *anklong*, a set of bamboo tubes sounded by striking them. We have heard some Javanese songs sung by Eva Gauthier and we found great beauty in them. Many of these songs are centuries old.

In these countries the people are very fond of making musical instruments which look like animals and the things they see around them, as for instance, the Burmese *soung*, a thirteen stringed harp, with a boat shaped body and a prettily curved neck. Think, too, of playing as they do in Burma and Siam on a harp or zither shaped like a crocodile! (Figures 12 and 13.)

The Siamese use more wind instruments than the people of other Oriental lands. When Edward MacDowell, our famous composer, heard the Siamese Royal Orchestra in London, he decided that each musician made up his part as he went along, the only rule being to keep up with each other and to finish together. The fact that they thought they were doing a really lovely thing made the concert seem very comical. But the Orientals can return the compliment. A few years ago the Chinese government sent some students to study in Berlin but after a month's time they asked to be called home because, "It would be folly," they said, "to remain in a barbarous country where even the most elementary principles of music had not been grasped." (From *Critical and Historical Essays* of Edward MacDowell.)

INCAS AND AZTECS

Before leaving the Orientals, we want to cross the bridge with you between the Orient (East) and the Occident (West). Sometimes we find the same customs and ways of doing things in places very far apart. Sometimes this likeness will appear in a religious ceremony, a dance or song, a piece of pottery, or in a musical instrument. To find these similarities makes one believe that at sometime in the world's history, these people so far away from each other, must have been closely related. Such a likeness can be traced in the music of the ancient Chinese and the Aztecs of Mexico, and the Incas of Peru, some of which has been sung to us by Marguerite d'Alvarez, from Peru. The Peruvians played pipes and had music in the same rhythm as the sacred chants of the Chinese. The Mexicans had all kinds of drums, rattles, stones, gongs, bells and cymbals which resemble the Chinese instruments. On the other hand we read in Prescott's *Conquest of Peru* of a Sun Festival which recalls the Sun Dance of our own American Indian. The Inca or the ruler of Peru, his court and the entire population of the city met at dawn in June and with the first rays of the sun, thousands of wind instruments broke forth into "a majestic song of adoration" accompanied by thousands of shouting voices.

From the kind of instruments that the Aztecs in Mexico used, we know that their music was more barbaric than that of the Peruvians. A curious combination of love for music and barbarism is shown in the custom they had of appointing each year a youth to act as the God of music, whose name *Tezcatlipoca*, he was given. He was presented with a beautiful bride and for the one year he lived like a prince in the greatest luxury. He learned to play the flute and whenever the people heard it, they fell down and worshipped him! But this wonderful life was not all it seemed, for at the end of the year the beautiful youth was offered as a living sacrifice to the blood-thirsty God of Music whom he was impersonating.

CHAPTER VI

The Arab Spreads Culture—The Gods Give Music to the Hindus

ARABIA is the southwestern peninsula of Asia and is bounded by the Red Sea, Persian Gulf and the Arabian Sea. It was well situated to come in contact with the ancient nations of the world.

This story of Arabia and its music will include all those peoples to whom the Arabs gave of their learning. Saracen, Mussulman, Mohammedan and Islamite are different names for the same people, but they are all Arabs, even though they are not Arabians living in Arabia.

Arab music fills in the gaps between the ancient civilizations, the beginnings of early Christian music and the time of the Minnesingers and the Troubadours.

During the years called the Dark Ages (c. 476 to c. 1400), Europe was in a semi-barbarous state and there was little learning outside of the monasteries. All the culture and advances made by the Greeks and Romans seemed in danger of perishing in the raids and attacks of barbarous tribes, and wars among the early European peoples. But the Arabs, on whom we look today as almost barbarians, were the highly cultured race of that far-off time.

They were great mathematicians and from them we have Algebra and our Arabic numerals 1, 2, 3, 4, etc. From them we have the arabesques, or the intricate geometric

designs in carvings and traceries, seen on buildings in the
countries where the Arabs built, lived, roamed or studied.

Long before the Christian era there were very wonderful
Arabian universities in Bagdad and Damascus, so famous
that they attracted many Greek and Hebrew scholars to
learn from the Arabian philosophers and wise men.

Mohammed, their greatest prophet, who was born in
570 A.D., wrote their holy book called the *Koran*. While
he lived the Arabs were at the height of their power.

Because they had studied the learning of the past, and
had invaded and conquered parts of Europe, the Arabs
brought to Europe their arts and sciences and the learning
of the ancient nations. Through their conquests they also
carried their ways of living into the countries of the barbarians. For example, in 711, they drove the Goths out
from Spain and set up their own caliphs (rulers) in that
country, so that at this time they had two capitals—the
original Bagdad and one at Cordova. From these Arabs,
who came from Mauretania in Africa to Spain, descended
the people we call Moors. It is for this reason that we have
traces of Arab music and the Moorish architecture or Arab-
like buildings of which the Alhambra is best known, in
Spain. In Cordova, grew up a center of learning, far
greater than any in the surrounding countries. At the
university was a library of over 600,000 manuscripts not
yet in book form, for printing had not been invented.
Here, too, great chemists studied and discovered alcohol,
sulphuric and nitric acids. The clock also was invented by
the Arabs, and the game of chess was first thought out when
the Chinese were already playing Mah Jong! They were
responsible, too, for trigonometry as well as algebra, and
they knew how to make cotton goods, and were famous for
the Damascus steel out of which the swords of the heroes
for many generations were forged. Even today Damascus
steel is looked upon as excellent.

As they were worshippers of Mohammed, they were not permitted to make portraits of human beings in stone or on parchments for they believed that they would be deprived of their souls at the day of judgment should they reproduce the human form. So they put their artistic efforts into color and design.

Not satisfied with their conquest of the Goths, they decided to enter France, but were kept out by Emperor Charlemagne who thought differently, and stopped them. It was due to this conflict that the great epic *La Chanson de Roland* (The Song of Roland) was written.

Then came the Crusades, the expeditions which went on for many years to wrest the shrine of the Saviour from the hand of the Mussulman. These wars continued so long, that nearly every European group of people came in contact with the Arab, and in so doing, learned much from him.

The Arab was a courageous, loyal person, proud and ready to die for his own ideas; he was courtly, yet careful in all business dealings and many of his traits were passed on to his descendants. Very rapidly the rough warrior of the desert was transformed into a luxury-loving, cultured man.

The Arabians seemed to be great musical blotters; because they blotted up or absorbed music wherever they went and made it theirs! But they were unlike blotters for loving it; they made a science of it and passed it on to other nations and thence to us.

So much of the Persian music was absorbed by the Arab that it would be difficult to separate their systems here. The Arabs took the very loosely-put-together music of Persia and made it over into better form. Even before the Mohammedan conquests (700–800 A.D.), Arab music was well planned, and as they spread later to North Africa, Egypt, Morocco, Greece, Italy, and Spain, they left some traces of their own music and took something of the music of the natives. Furthermore, they adopted many of the instruments that they found and they became the ancestors of some of our own.

The ancient Arabs did not write down their music, but handed it on from musician to musician, gaining and losing very little from the many hands through which it passed. They have none of what we call harmony or accompaniment, as in their orchestras all the instruments except the drums play the same tune; the drums mark the time and often play very complicated rhythms. This makes their music sound confused to us, but by hearing it often you learn in what an orderly way it is done, and you will see why many people like it.

The caliphs (rulers) had court musicians and probably more music was played and more scientific treatises on music were written by these people than by any other mediæval or ancient race.

THE ARAB SCALES

There has been much argument about Arab music as to whether the scale was divided into seventeen steps or eight, as is our scale. Some people think they hear it as seventeen tones divided into one-third steps, but Baron d'Erlanger, a great authority on ancient Arab music, said that there are two distinct musical systems still in use. One comes from their ancient home in Asia, and the other from the Pharaohs of Egypt. And the fact that these two systems have been mixed in using them leads to the question of what the real scale is. Baron d'Erlanger found, as the result of his experiments, that if we could lower, ever so slightly, the third and seventh tones of our scale, we would have the old Pharaoh scale in its simplest form. The other scales can be played on stringed instruments on which there are no fixed tones as there are on a keyboard instrument like a piano, and can therefore play the intervals that do not exist on the piano.

It is impossible to say how many scales or modes the Arabs use, because each change of the tiniest part of a step creates a new mode, and there are many combinations possible. Some say that there are thirty-four modes; another says that there are twenty-four, one for each hour of the day. There are also modes for the four elements— fire, water, earth, and air; for the twelve signs of the zodiac, and for the seven planets.

Each mode has a name, called after all sorts of things like cities or tribes or ornaments, in fact, anything familiar to the people.

The weird effects made by the *Gloss* or musical ornaments like the trill, grace notes and slidings give the music a dreamy fascinating character, the charm of which is increased by its frequent changes from double to triple time, or from triple to double.

INSTRUMENTS

It is through the instruments that we can trace the Arab influence in our own music. When we come to the story of the Troubadours, you will find them using the lute, the principal instrument of the Middle Ages. This was called *el oud*, which gradually became *lute*, because the Europeans heard the words that way.

So, here you can see, how art travels through the chances and changes of wars, wanderings, conquests and political shiftings of power among the different nations.

Most of the Arab instruments are of Persian, Egyptian and Greek origin, but as we said above, the Arab became so mixed with other peoples of the world, that in wandering about, what is really theirs in music or instruments, or what was borrowed from others, is difficult to tell. But we can tell you that the popular music of the Arab, as you hear it to-day, in bazaars and cafés of Northern Africa and in parts of Asia where Arabs are still to be found, has remained practically unchanged throughout the centuries. Even the instruments are the same.

El oud still remains the popular instrument and shares its popularity with the *kanoun*, which is probably of Persian origin. This *kanoun* is like a zither, and is specially tuned for every scale. It is said that the Arab spends three-quarters of his life tuning his instruments.

Baron Rodolphe d'Erlanger, an Englishman who lived in Tunis, spent many years studying the ancient Arabian music in order to preserve it, for it is dying out through the arrival of modern European civilization accompanied by phonographs, jazz and radios.

Their viols are of real interest because it is claimed that they are the ancestors of the great violin family. These ancestors are of different styles and are called the *rebab* and *kemangeh*, sometimes played with the bow and sometimes without. They have *kissars* and *lyres* and various forms of zithers, besides the *kanoun*. The Arabs' fondness for strings is proof that they were indeed sensitive and fine, while most of their neighbors liked the drums and brasses much more, showing a lower grade of civilization. By this we do not mean that the Arabs were not fond of their drums, because the drum was one of the chief features of their music. Indeed they had many kinds—the *atambal* which looks like two kettle-drums hitched together; the *derbouka* which is really a vase with a skin stretched over the base; the *taar* like our tambourine; the *bendaair*, an open faced shallow drum, with snares (cords) stretched across inside the head somewhat like our own snare drum; and the *dof*, a squarish drum played with the hands and knuckles like the *taar*, but with the snares. The Hebrews had an instrument like this called the *tof* or *toph* and the

Persians also had the *dof* or *duff.* So, here again, you see
how one nation affects the other. (Figure 8.)

Then they had flutes called the *ijaouak* and *gosba* with
three or more holes, which they used for sad tunes.

Every visitor to a Mohammedan country is introduced to
Arab religious music at day-break, noon and sun-down, by
the muezzin (priest) who calls the faithful of Mohammed to
prayer, from an opening in the tower of a mosque. This

Mohammedan Call to Prayer

From "The Art Of Music"

call has been handed down to the Mohammedans from a
time even before the coming of Mohammed (6th century
A.D.).

The Gods Give Music to the Hindus

There had been so much conquest and battling in India,
that although we know much about Hindu music it is very
difficult to tell what really belonged to the Hindus and what
was brought to them.

The native legends tell us that the gods gave music to
the people and all through the music there are signs to show
their power and influence. The literature of India can be
traced back many centuries and through it we see what an
important place song held. There were minstrels in the
ancient courts whose duty it was to chant songs in praise

of their royal masters. In their religious ceremonies, too, music held a high place. One of their holy books says: "Indra (their chief god) rejects the offering made without music." The Hindu people are divided into many classes, which they call castes, and in ancient times the singers were members of the priest caste. The Hindus love music and have always used it for all festivities, in the drama, and in the temples.

The singing of poems from ancient time has always been popular and dancing too, and here, as among the Japanese, have grown up trained dancers called the Bayaderes or Nautch girls. (Chapter V).

Music is still used in India to appease and please the gods and to plead for rain or sunshine.

Travelers to India relate that they have heard the beating of drums, accompanied by solo voice or by a chorus, continued for several days at a time. When there has been a drought, and rain is needed, this long drawn out music is used as a means to ask the god to bring rain.

In the Temple of the Sacred Tooth in Ceylon (India) on each night of the full moon, the sacred books are chanted by relays of yellow-robed priests, following each other every two hours from dark to dawn. They chant in deep resounding voices without a pause. The Buddhist priests have repeated these sacred texts on every night of the full moon for twenty-eight centuries!

In India they have made a deep study of color and sound and things we know very little about, and to which we attach very little importance. Through their study of the laws of sound and color, the Hindus feel sure that they are related. Edward Maryon in "Marcotone" says: "Chemistry and Mathematics prove that the Natural Scales of Light and Sound in Principle are one, and therefore the Primary Colors of the Solar Spectrum, and the Primary Tones of the Musical Scale have the same *ratio* of speed

vibrations. Therefore both *Tone* and *Color* can be scaled
so that a given number of Lightspeeds (Colors), will equal
a given number of Soundwaves (Tones)."

When Edward Maryon was in India he visited one of the
temples and in watching the prayer wheels, noticed that a
certain wheel moving at a certain speed produced a certain
sound and a certain color, while another wheel moving at
a different speed produced a different tone and a different
color. It interested him so much that he learned from a
Hindu priest about the relation of light and sound. This led
to very interesting experiments and results which he has
used in teaching music. The color red is supposed to
correspond with the musical sound middle C, orange with
D, yellow with E, green with F, blue with G, indigo with A,
and violet with B. And recently in America we have been
interested in seeing a color organ, the "Clavilux" invented
by Thomas Wilfred which plays tones of colors instead of
tones of sound.

This is a direct twentieth century result of the so-called
"magic" of primitive times. From this you can see how
the magic of ancient days is explained by modern science.

HINDU RAGS

The Hindu songs presided over by special gods were called
rags, but of course, the name has no relationship whatever
to our *rag-time*.

It seems that religious feeling has dominated everything
in the Orient; for this reason every idea connected with
music has a corresponding idea in Hindu mythology. The
rags were all named after the gods who brought music down
from heaven to comfort man. The character of each god or
goddess was supposed to be reflected in the *rag*, and it was
not the result of scientific study as were, for instance, the
scales of the Chinese. Our knowledge of the *rag* has come

down to us from what Sanskrit writers on Indian music have
said, and what is practised today by the modern Hindu.
No doubt Arabia and Persia once had a music system very
much like this one of the Hindus.

Rags, ragas, or *raginis* were neither airs nor modes in our
sense of the words, but something like the modes of the
Arab songs, they were melodic forms, or themes, on which
musicians either improvised or composed new songs, by
using them in rhythms of endless variety.

There were many many *rags,* and they were under the
guidance of the gods of the rainy season, the cold season, the
mild, the hot, etc., and could only be sung during their
special seasons. It was thought that these songs sung at
the wrong time would bring down calamity. Again, as
with the American Indian (Chapter II), we find tribes who
are most careful to sing certain music at certain times.

It is told that a Hindu nobleman, long ago, tried to sing
a night song in the daytime and darkness covered all things
within the sound of his voice!

As important as was the song from the earliest time, instrumental music held almost an equal place.

Orchestra

The Hindu orchestra is sometimes large and sometimes
small. Hindu dances are lively and vigorous, and seldom
slow and romantic. Nevertheless there are many kinds of
songs, some spirited and some not, such as: songs in honor of
Krishna (one of their principal gods), official odes, war
hymns, love songs, evening songs, wedding songs, cradle
and patriotic songs. In some, the Arab seems to have
influenced the Hindu music, because they have the lively
rhythm and the variety of the Arab music, yet it is difficult
to know which one influenced the other. The Arab music
has the variety and luxurious soft beauty in popular dances

equal to anything our modern musicians or poets have composed.

The playing of instruments, accompanying songs with Sanskrit texts, was supposed to give energy, develop heroism, make a peaceful heart, and drive away harm and impurity.

The members of the different castes or sects had and still have meetings held sometimes in private houses and sometimes in the temples, when they sang religious hymns. Among the higher classes, they went to the expense of having good musicians and of giving artistic performances, but among the common people, their idea was that the greater the noise the more they showed their devotion, so they sang, beat drums and blew whistles without any regard for time or melody, and you can imagine the effect was pandemonium.

NOTATION

It is impossible to write the Hindu music in European notation, because instead of dividing the scale into semitones or half-steps, they use quarter tones.

Margaret Glyn, in her book, *Evolution of Musical Form*, writes:

"In the East notation is in an elementary condition, the staff being unknown. The Hindus, Chinese, and Abyssinians have ancient note-signs, consisting of a kind of letter to which some indication of time is added, but in this respect the Chinese system is wanting, having practically no time-notation. Probably note-signs existed in Persia and Arabia, but these do not appear to have survived. The modern Arabic notation is but three hundred years old, and is said to have been invented by one Demetrius de Cantemir who adapted the letters of the Turkish alphabet for the purpose. This has eighteen tones to the octave (we have twelve), and is used in Turkey and other countries of the near East."

The Hindus seem to like both triple (3 beats) and duple (2 or 4 beats) rhythm. The scheme changes according to the poetry of the song, and the pitch and the length of tones are shown by Sanskrit characters and special signs or words.

INSTRUMENTS

The Hindus have spent much time in studying music and the instruments of which they have many kinds. There are the strings, there are skins sounded by beating, instruments struck together in pairs, and those that are blown. They like the strings best. The characteristic instrument is the *vina*, usually of wood or bamboo strengthened by one to three gourds as sounding boards, and having five or seven wire strings played something like the zither, but sometimes with a bow. (Figure 16.) There are many varieties of the *sitar*, an instrument like a lute, and many viols of which the *sarinda sarunja* is typical and is played with a bow. (Figure 7.)

Among the percussion instruments are tambourines, castanets and cymbals; they had wind instruments such as flutes (seldom transverse or blown in from the side, and often played by blowing on them through the nostrils), trumpets, horns, bag-pipes and oboes. Certain instruments were used only by the priests, others by beggars, and others by dancing girls. Imagine how weird a story could be told in music if a modern symphony orchestra played a piece of music telling of life among the Hindus. Maybe some of the readers of this book will get an idea for a Hindu tone poem, who knows?

Childhood of Music

CHAPTER VII

What Church Music Imported from Greece

DURING the centuries when the Eastern nations were powerful the European continent was inhabited by primitive men, who had gradually formed tribes. They had rude songs, dances, and crude instruments. They used their music in religious ceremonies, to celebrate war victories and successful hunting expeditions, to sing to their sweethearts, and to accompany their work in the fields and homes, much as the American Indian did. Many manners and customs of the Anglo-Saxon (English), Teutonic (German), Norse (Danish, Swedish and Norwegian), Celtic (Irish) and Gallic (French) races may be traced back to these barbaric days, and even the beginning of national schools of music may be found.

Although a thousand years passed between the Greek musical era and the "Golden Age" of Christian Church music, much that happened in that time is hidden in darkness. The nations and tribes were fighting for existence and were developing into the nations which we know today.

Islam or the Mohammedan religion, and not Christianity, was the great influence.

Julius Cæsar (100–44 B.C.), the great Roman General, conquered Gallia (France), then invaded the land of the

Teutons (Germany) and even reached England. In parts of northern Europe, one still sees the remains of great roadways, aqueducts or water works, and bridges, that the Romans built during their invasions.

In the Cluny Museum in Paris is a great hall built as a bath by the Romans. In Bath, England, the city was named for the ancient Roman baths still existing, and you can see the pipe lines which carried the water.

Dark Ages

The world at that time was not a happy place in which to live. There was constant warfare between the once powerful Roman Empire and these barbaric tribes. The poorest people were oppressed and many were slaves, bought and sold by the rich land owners and army leaders.

Into such a world was the child, Jesus, born—a world with little love for humanity, little unselfishness, little sympathy for the down-trodden and unhappy, few kind words for the poor or the sick, little justice and less mercy. No wonder that His teachings brought new life and gave hope to the people!

A few centuries after the time of Jesus, the world went through a period called the Dark Ages, ushered in by the fall of the Roman Empire, 476 A.D. Rome, city of glorious victories and advanced culture, became the prey of barbaric tribes—Huns, Goths, Visigoths, Vandals, Franks, Saxons, and Slavs,—until it seemed that civilization would be wiped out and people would become primitive again.

Music was saved during the early centuries by a small band of faithful followers of Jesus Christ, who founded a church in His name. That their music should have been made up of existing tunes and words is very natural. Jesus, himself, brought up in the religion of the Hebrews, often sang the Psalms of David. The beautiful traditional music of the Jewish synagogues found its way into the services of the early Christian Church, because many of the believers were Hebrews. Soon the Hebrew Bible texts were translated into Latin—the everyday language of the Romans, and as most of these early Christians lived in Rome, they followed the rules of music the Romans learned from the Greeks. So, our Church music was influenced both by the Hebrews and Greeks.

For about three hundred years the early Christians had to hold their services in secret, as they were punished even by death when caught, for not worshipping Jupiter and the Roman gods. They were not rich and influential, but just humble folk to whom the teachings of Jesus came as a joyous comfort. They had no beautiful palaces where they could hold services, and at the same time hide from the Roman centurions, so they worshipped in dark and secret places and could not have much music as it would have attracted the attention of their enemies. The early Christians shunned music, too, because it had been used for the wild dances and festivals of their pagan oppressors. As they were poor and uneducated, they had had little training and lacked money to buy instruments, so all in all music had a hard time to keep alive.

From what we can gather, they chanted their Psalms much as did the Hebrews and had responses which sounded like soft and monotonous droning.

As time went on emperors like Constantine, began to take away the death penalty from those believing in Christ and gradually as the Romans saw the beauty of His teachings they became Christians in increasing numbers. Many of these Romans came from the upper classes, and as Greek was the language of culture they had had a thorough Greek education and owned many instruments, so they brought their Greek musical inheritance to the growing band.

Thus, the chants composed in Rome for the *kithara* were the direct ancestors of our Christian hymns. These early hymns were also a bridge between the single melody line of the Orient and Greece and Rome, and the many melody lines, called polyphonic music, of Europe.

In 325 A.D., Emperor Constantine made Christianity the national religion of Rome. He also founded the Christian Church in Byzantium, later called Constantinople, and all through the Dark Ages, in many parts of Europe, the cathedrals and church schools were the only gleam of learning in a time of darkness and struggle.

After the Roman Empire reached its greatest height, in the 2nd century, it gradually grew weaker and during the 4th and 5th centuries, the Goths, Vandals and Huns drove the government from Rome to Constantinople. In the 7th century Mohammedanism rose and swept over Syria, Egypt and North Africa, and reached Spain in the 8th century.

ANSWERING MUSIC

A legend says that St. Ignatius (49–107 A.D.) one of the early Christian fathers, had a vision in which he heard the Heavenly choirs praising the Holy Trinity, in alternating chants, and he was so impressed by it, that he introduced into the Church the idea of two choirs of singers answering each other.

In singing the Psalms of David, the Hebrews used this idea of antiphonal music. (Anti—against, phonal—sounding: antiphonal—sounding against each other.) We see it too in the Greek choruses, in the Roman kitharoedic chants (chants accompanied by the *kithara*), and now in the early Christian hymns. From this antiphonal music to the later polyphony (poly—many, phony—sounds: many voices or parts) is a natural step. Here again is an instance of the influence of one nation on another.

The Patron Saint of Music

Among the martyrs to the cause of the Christian faith, was St. Cecilia, a member of a noble Roman family, who was put to death for becoming a Christian about 177 A.D. She is probably buried in the Roman catacombs (underground burial chambers), is the patron saint of music, and is mistakenly credited with having invented the organ.

Greek Modes as Models

St. Ambrose (340?-397), Bishop of Milan, is supposed to have worked out a firm foundation for church music and to have composed some of the first Christian hymns. There were four so-called authentic *Ecclesiastical* or *Church* Modes known as Ambrosian Modes. These were scales modeled on the old Greek modes and called by Greek names. The names became mixed through the fact that the Greeks' words "high" and "low" for the stringing of their lyres were used in just the opposite fashion from our meaning of the terms. So the Dorian mode of Ambrose's time (from D to D on the white keys of the piano) was the Greek Phrygian; and the Ambrosian Phrygian (E to E) was the Greek Dorian; F to F was the Lydian mode; G to G, the Mixolydian.

St. Ambrose felt it his duty to make over the church music because popular street songs had crept in with the Hebrew Psalms and Greek and Roman chants! It was much the same effect as if you entered a church and heard the organ and choir performing "Yes, We Have No Bananas." About this time, schools were formed to train singers in these new hymns and church services, and a way to write down the music composed by St. Ambrose and his followers was needed. The Greek letters had been used in Rome, but in the 7th Century a new system called *neumes* appeared; this word comes from the Greek and means "nod" or "sign." Neumes did not show the exact sounds to be sung as did later methods of notation. There were eight signs with Latin names indicating groups of one, two, or three notes to be sung.

While the system of neumes-notation, which looks like our present day shorthand, was helpful, it had a serious shortcoming. It indicated whether the melody rose or fell, but just how much was a question not definitely shown. An unfamiliar chant could not be sung until the notation had been worked out. It took a long time for a choir singer to learn to sing all the music for the services.

When the singers sang solos, they ornamented the songs as they pleased! This made variety but it must also have caused confusion! The people may have learned this ornamental singing from *The Gloss* of the Arab.

GREGORIAN CHANT

The next step was the Gregorian chant which even today is sung in the Roman Catholic Churches. During the time of St. Gregory, who was Pope from 590 to 604, four scales, called *plagal*, were added to the authentic Ambrosian scales. These were based on the old Greek and Ambrosian modes, but St. Gregory did not invent them. To each authentic scale, a plagal scale starting four tones below it was added, and to the name of the authentic mode was added the prefix *hypo*. Each authentic mode and its *hypo* are related. Here is a table of these related modes, and their names:

AUTHENTIC SCALES OR MODES (St. Ambrose's Scales)	PLAGAL SCALES OR MODES (St. Gregory's Scales)
I. Dorian: d ef g a bc d	II. Hypo-Dorian: a bc d ef g a
III. Phrygian: ef g a bc d e	IV. Hypo-Phrygian: bc d ef g a b
V. Lydian: f g a bc d ef	VI. Hypo-Lydian: c d ef g a bc
VII. Mixolydian: g a bc d ef g	VIII. Hypo-Mixolydian: d ef g a bc d

We have marked the half-steps bc and ef, and in every mode they fall on different degrees of the scale. This shifting of the half-steps indicates the change of mode.

In order to try to give you some idea of how the modes affect music, we have written the familiar national hymn *America* in each mode (see page 74). Play them, and you will see how one differs from the other.

Katherine Ruth Heyman has used a similar idea in her little book *The Relation of Ultramodern to Archaic Music* in explaining Greek Modes.

It took many years to establish this music and it was not until the time of Charlemagne (742–814) that it became a real system called Plain Chant or Plain-song (from the Latin, *cantus planus*).

Pope Gregory encouraged the *Schola Cantorum*, school of singing, at Rome, and with trained singers he tried to establish for all Christian churches, a way to sing systematically and well. They studied nine years, and everything had to be memorized, for only the leader had a song book. Books were written by hand and were hard to get. The teacher had a monochord, the instrument invented by Pythagoras, to give the pitch, for all the singing was done without accompaniment. The singing must have improved

AMERICA

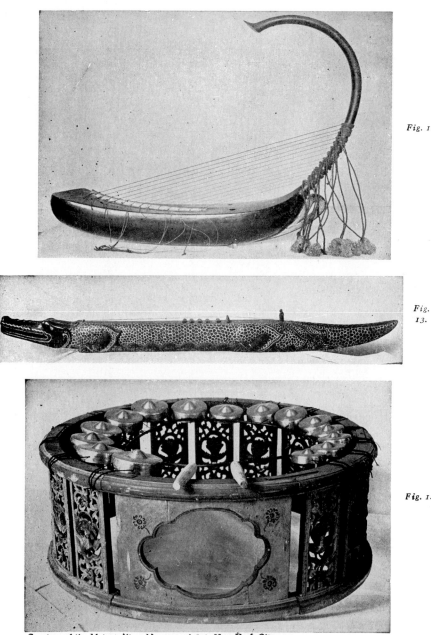

Fig. 12

Fig. 13.

Fig. 14.

Courtesy of the Metropolitan Museum of Art, New York City.

Instruments of Burmah and Siam.

Fig. 12.—Soung—boat-shaped harp.
Fig. 13.—Megyoung—crocodile harp.
Fig. 14.—Kyll Weing—gong organ.

A Burmese Musicale.

Fig. 15.

Fig. 16.

Courtesy of the Metropolitan Museum of Art, New York City.

Hindu Instruments.

Fig. 15.—Tabla—drum.
Fig. 16.—Kinnari—Vina, a stringed instrument.

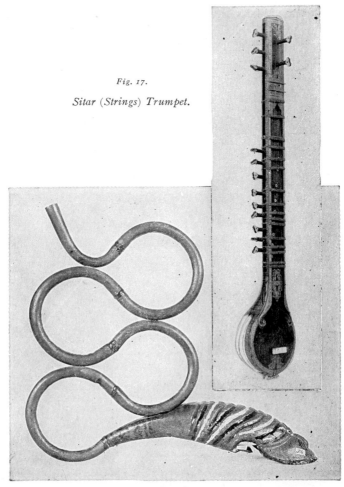

Fig. 17.

Sitar (Strings) Trumpet.

Fig. 18.

Hindu Instruments.

greatly after Gregory became Pope, for before his reform, music had become a stunt with no solemnity, and people in the churches waved handkerchiefs if the stunt pleased them!

A Long Journey

At any rate the Gregorian chant flourished and was so loved that Benedict Biscop, and other monks interested in music, came from far-off England to learn the chant invented by St. Gregory. A long journey! In 675 Biscop sent to Rome for singers and built monasteries very close to a pagan temple, where the Anglo-Saxons still worshipped the Roman Sun-god, Apollo, also god of music. These he filled with beautiful relics, paintings and stained glass windows, Bibles and service books illuminated in gold and color, which he brought from Rome.

Bringing things from Rome may sound easy to you, but fancy the travel and inconvenience when there were no steamships, no railroads, no aeroplanes, but only Roman roads, which however marvelous, were long and wearisome by foot or by horse, or mule and rude wagons. This shows how much the people of Britain desired music and beauty in their church services.

Venerable Bede

About this time, there lived a man in England so loved and respected that he was called the Venerable Bede. Although music had no such variety, melody and richness as today, just see what the Venerable Bede says about it: "Music is the most worthy, courteous, pleasant, joyous and lovely of all knowledge; it makes a man gentlemanly in his demeanor, pleasant, courteous, joyous, lovely, for it acts upon his feelings. Music encourages us to bear the heaviest afflictions, administers consolation in every difficulty, refreshes the broken spirit, removes headache and cures crossness and melancholy."

Isn't it remarkable for a man to have said this so long ago, when scientists, today, have just *begun* to think that music may have a power of healing ills of the mind and of the body! Truly—"there is nothing new under the sun!"

So Bede used the plain chant of Gregory and through his influence, spread this dignified music throughout England, and wherever a monastery was founded, a music school was started.

The Venerable Bede writes that Ethelbert of Kent, King of Britain, was a worshipper of Odin and Thor, Norse gods, but he married a French Princess who was a Christian. One day, writes the Venerable Bede, forty monks led in solemn procession by St. Augustine, passed before the king singing a chant. After hearing this marvelous hymn, he became a Christian and gave permission to the English to become worshippers of Christ instead of Norse and Druid gods. This hymn which converted Ethelbert in 597 A.D. was sung thirteen hundred years later (1897) in the same place, Canterbury, by another group of Benedictine monks!

At first the songs were sung unaccompanied, but as in the time of David, later the Church allowed instruments. The lyre and the harp were used first but the cymbals and the dulcimer, somewhat like our zither, were considered too noisy.

The Venerable Bede called music made by instruments *artificial* music, and that of the human voice, *natural* music. Whether at that time the viol, the drum, the organ or the psaltery (an instrument like the dulcimer) were used in the Church, is not known positively.

After Bede's death, Alcuin, a monk and musician, continued his work. He was appointed by Charlemagne, Emperor of France, to teach music in the schools of Germany and France to spread the use of the Gregorian chant.

A Curious Music System

About 900 an important thing happened, by which the reading and learning of music was much simplified. A red line was drawn straight across the page and this line represented "F" the tone on the fourth line of the bass staff. The *neumes* written on this red line were "F" and the others above or below, were of higher or lower pitch. This worked so well, that they placed a yellow line above the red line and this they called "C." These two lines were the beginnings of our five-line staff, but much happened between the two-line days and the five.

At this time people did not sing in parts, known as they are to us—soprano, alto, tenor, bass, but everybody sang the same tune, that is, sang in unison, and when men and women or men and boys sang together, the men's voices sounded an octave lower than the women's and the boy's. Some voices have naturally a high range and others low, and no doubt in these plain chant melodies the singers who could not reach all the tones comfortably, dropped uncon‑ sciously to a lower pitch, and in that way, made a second part. Soon the composers made this melody in the medium range of the voice a part of their pieces instead of trusting the singers to make it up as they went along. The principal tune sung or carried by most of the singers was given the name *tenor* (from the Latin *teneo*, to hold or carry). We use the same word to indicate the man's voice of high range.

Organum and Discant

Theorists in the tenth century first wrote about music with a second part a fifth above or a fourth below the tenor or "subject." (The Latin for the subject is *cantus firmus—* fixed song.) The fifth and fourth were probably used be‑ cause they were perfect intervals, and all others except the octave, were imperfect. There were often four parts including the *cantus firmus*, for two parts were doubled. This succession of fourths and fifths sounds crude now (just try the example), but people of the Middle Ages must have liked it, for it lasted several centuries and was one of the earliest attempts at combining melodies. This music was called *organum* or *diaphony* (*dia*—two, *phonai*—sound: two sounds). As early as 1100, singers tried out new effects with the added parts and introduced a few imperfect intervals, thirds and sixths, and sang occasionally in contrary motion to the subject,—this, also a form of *organum*, was called *discant*, the Latin word for *diaphony*. At first it may have sounded discordant and it was usually improvised. Soon it came to mean any part outside of the *cantus firmus* or subject. (See musical illustrations.)

Organum (IXth and Xth Centuries)

Diaphony

Discant (XIIth Century)

Example of Organum, Diaphony, Discant

There was also a three-voiced diaphony in which the bass, a fifth below the *cantus firmus*, was sung an octave higher than it was written. As it was a false bass, it was called *faux bourdon*. A second voice lay half way between the other two. This was the beginning of chords such as we use.

Hucbald (840–930), a French monk, left valuable information about music in his day. He was so learned that he was credited with books and inventions not his. He experimented with a system of writing music on a staff of six lines, in which only the spaces were used. Each space was marked with T or S, meaning that the singer was to sing a whole tone or a semitone (half-step). Instead of notes or neumes, the words of the text appeared in the spaces.

This system was clumsy and other experiments were attempted. In the monastery of St. Gall, Switzerland, a complicated system of letters, mixed in with the neumes, was used. In the 11th century Hermannus Contractus of Reichenau increased the number of letters and tried to indicate the exact interval to be sung.

Guido d'Arezzo and His Additions to Music

The next great name in music history is Guido d'Arezzo, a Benedictine monk (995–1050), famous for his valuable additions to music.

He invented the four-line staff, using both lines and spaces and giving a definite place on the staff to each sound:

> Yellow line C————————
> Black line. . . . .
> Red line   F————————
> Black line . . . .

In the Middle Ages, the men did most of the singing so the music was written in a range to suit their voices. C is middle C, and F the bass clef.

All church music was written by hand by the monks who made wonderful parchment copies. They grew careless about the yellow and red lines, so Guido placed the letters C and F at the beginning of the lines. The neumes had now developed into a notation of one, two or three square notes in groups, as in the Hymn on page 81.

Sometimes there were three lines to a staff, sometimes four, five, and even eleven! The use of clefs showing which line was C or F, made reading of music much easier. At the end of the 16th century the question of the number of lines to the staff was definitely decided, then they used four lines for the plain chant and five for all secular music. By calling the fifth line of the eleven, middle C, two staffs of five lines resulted—the grand staff of today.

Here is a table to show you how clefs grew:

CLEFS	13TH CENTURY	15TH CENTURY	17TH CENTURY	19TH CENTURY
C CLEF	C	C	⊟	𝕭
F CLEF	𝄢	⌐C	⌐𝄢	𝄢
G CLEF	ℭ	𝄞	𝄞	𝄞

(from Vincent d'Indy's "Cours de Composition Musicale")

Hucbald built his scales in groups of four tones like the Greek tetrachords but Guido extended this tetrachord to a hexachord or six-toned scale, and by overlapping the hexachords, he built a series of scales to which he gave the name, *gamut*, because it started on the G which is the first note of our grand staff (lowest line, bass clef) and the Greek word for G is "Gamma."

```
        F G ab͡b c d  ⎫
          ½ step      ⎪
     C D E͡F G a        ⎬  This was repeated starting
       ½ step          ⎪    an octave higher.
   G A B͡C D E         ⎪
     ½ step           ⎭
```

(Read from lowest line up.)

In the lowest hexachord, the B is natural, in the second hexachord there is no B and in the third hexachord, the B is flattened. Our sign (♭) for flat comes from the fact that this B was called a round B and the sign (♮) for natural was called a square B. The sharp (♯) came from the natural and both meant at first raising the tone a half-step.

Guido once heard the monks in the monastery of Arezzo singing a hymn in honor of St. John the Baptist. He noticed that each line of the Latin poem began on ascending notes of the scale,—the first line on C, the second on D, and so on up to the sixth on A. It gave him the idea to call each degree of the hexachord by the first syllable of the line of the Latin hymn, thus:

> *Ut*queant laxis,
> *Re*sonare fibris,
> *Mi*ra gestorum,
> *Fam*uli tuorum,
> *Sol*ve polluti,
> *Lab*ia reatum,

HYMN TO ST. JOHN THE BAPTIST

UT que-ant la-xis RE-so ne-re fi-bris, MI ra ges-to-rum FA-mu-li

to o rum, SOL ve pol-lu ti LA bi i re a-tum, Sancte Jo-an-nes

Here is a translation:

> Grant that the unworthy lips of Thy servant
> May be gifted with due harmony,
> Let the tones of my voice
> Sing the praises of Thy wonders.

We still call our scale degrees *ut* (frequently changed to *do*), *re, mi, fa, sol, la*. The French today use these syllables instead of the letters of the alphabet, and Guido is known as the man who originated this solmization (the word taken from the syllables *sol* and *mi*).

Where did the syllable *si*, the seventh degree of the scale, come from? This hymn was written to St. John and in Latin his name is *Sancte Ioannes*, the initials of which form the syllable *si* which came into use long after Guido's time.

This system was very difficult for the singers to learn as it was quite new to them, so Guido used his hand as a guide to the singers. Each joint represented a different syllable and tone, and a new scale began on every fourth tone. Look at the Guidonian hand on next page.

Guido was so great a teacher and musician that he was given credit for inventing much that already existed. He gathered all the knowledge he could find into a book, that was sent to the monasteries and music schools. He put in much that never before had been written down, explained many things that had never been clear, and added much that was new and useful.

Sometimes his name was written Gui or Guion. When he lived people had no last names but were called by the name of their native towns; as Guido was born in Arezzo, a town of Tuscany, he was called Guido d'Arezzo; Leonardo da Vinci, the great painter, was born in the village of Vinci; and the great Italian composer Pierluigi da Palestrina came from Palestrina.

Guido's work was considered revolutionary and not in

accord with the old ways which the church fathers reverenced. Because of plots against him, he was cast into

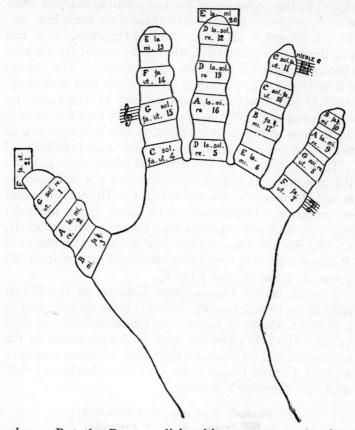

prison. But the Pope, realizing his greatness and value,
saved him. The inventors of new ideas always suffer!

MENSURAL MUSIC OR TIMED MUSIC

Before Guido invented it, there had been no system of
counting time.

If you are studying music, you know all about time signatures and what metre a piece is in, from the $\frac{3}{4}$, $\frac{6}{8}$, $\frac{2}{8}$, $\frac{2}{4}$, $\frac{4}{4}$ or sign C at the beginning of the composition, but you probably do not know how or when these signs came into use. In the Gregorian plain song and in Organum, there was practically no variety of rhythm and no need for showing time or marking off the music into measures. The accents fell quite naturally according to the words that were sung, much as you would recite poetry. But as music grew up and became more difficult, it was necessary for a chorus singing in three or four different parts, to sing in time as well as in tune, in order, at least, to start and finish together!

The first metre that was used was triple (three beats to the measure). It was called perfect and was indicated by a perfect circle, O, the symbol of the Holy Trinity and of perfection. Duple metre (two beats to the measure) was imperfect and was indicated by an incomplete circle, **C**. Our sign for common time (four beats to the measure), **C** comes from this incomplete circle. $\frac{2}{8}$ was written ⊙; $\frac{3}{4}$ was O; $\frac{6}{8}$ was ℂ; and $\frac{4}{4}$ was **C**.

A monk named Franco, from Cologne, on the Rhine, early in the twelfth century, invented these time signatures, and notes which in themselves indicated different time values. Hucbald's neumes were no longer suited to the new music, and besides time signatures it became necessary to have a music language showing very clearly and defi‧ nitely the composer's rhythm.

FRANCO'S NOTATION   OUR NOTATION

Franco's Notation		Our Notation	
▬	(maxima) =	𝆸	(whole note)
▇	(longa) =	𝅗𝅥	(half note)
■	(brevis) =	𝅘𝅥	(quarter note)
◆	(semi-brevis) =	𝅘𝅥𝅮	(eighth note)

Franco used four kinds of notes. Here they are translated into the time values of today.

Organs

In the 10th century, organs came into use in the churches, but they were ungainly and crude, sounding only a few tones, and were probably only used to keep the singers on pitch. The organ had been invented long before this, and had been used in Greece and Egypt. It was built on the principle of Pan's Pipes and was very simple. There were many portable organs, called portatives, small enough to be carried about.

One organ (not a portative!) at Winchester, England, had four hundred pipes and twenty-six pairs of bellows. It took seventy men to pump air into it and two men to play it by pounding on a key with their fists or elbows. The tone was so loud that it could be heard all over the town. Fancy that!

During these centuries, music was growing slowly but surely. Out of *organum* and *discant* and *faux bourdon*, arose a style called counterpoint, in which three, four or more melodies were sung at the same time. The writing of *counterpoint*, or horizontal music, is like a basket weave for the different melodies weave in and out like pieces of willow or raffia forming the basket. Later will come the *chorale*, written in chords or vertical music like a colonnade or series of columns. Keep this picture in mind. (St. Nicholas Tune, Chapter XI.) The word *point* means *note* so *counterpoint* means *note against note*. The word was first applied in the 13th century to very crude and discordant part-writing. But, little by little the monks learned how to combine melodies beautifully and harmoniously and we still use many of their rules.

Gradually great schools of church music flourished in France, Germany, Spain, England, Italy and the Netherlands in the 14th, 15th and 16th centuries.

Bit by bit this vast musical structure was built.   It did
not grow quickly; each new idea took centuries to become
a part of music, and as often the idea was not good, it took
a long time to replace it.

CHAPTER VIII

Troubadours and Minnesingers Brought Music to Kings and People

EXCEPT for the first few chapters in this book, we have told you of music made by men who wanted to improve it. You have seen how the fathers of the Church first reformed music, and gave it a short-hand called neumes; before that, the music laws of the Egyptians, the scales and modes of the Arab, the Greek scales which the churchmen used in the Ambrosian and the Gregorian modes. Then came the two-lined staff, and the beginnings of mensural or measured music by which they kept time. Then you saw how two melodies were fitted together and how they grew into four parts. All this we might call "on purpose" music. At the same time, in all the world, in every country, there was Song . . . and never have the world and the common people (called so because they are neither of the nobility nor of the church) been without folk song which has come from the folks of the world, the farmers, the weavers, and the laborers.

The best of these songs have what the great composers try to put into their music—a feeling of fresh free melody, design, balance, and climax, but more of this in the chapter on Folk Song.

This chapter is to be about Troubadours, Trouvères, and Minnesingers, who have left over two thousand songs. In most of these, they made up both words and music, but sometimes they used new words made up for folk tunes that everyone knew, or for melodies from the plain-chants which they had heard in church; sometimes they used the same melody for several different poems, and often they set the same words to several melodies.   Many of these troubadour songs and *minnelieder* became the people's own folk songs.

But now you must hear of the folk who lived hundreds of years before these poet singers.   Unknowingly, out of the heart and soul and soil of their native lands, they made songs and sang poetry and played sometimes other peoples' song, scattering their own wherever they went.

From these traveling singers and players, in all countries, came the professional musicians who were minstrels, bards, troubadours, etc., according to when, where and how they lived.

The Why of the Minstrel

The people sang and played not only because they wanted to, or because they loved it, but because they were the newspaper and the radio of their time, singing the news and doings of the day.   These minstrels who traveled from place to place "broadcast" the events.   No music was written down and no words were fastened by writing to any special piece.   The singer would learn a tune and when he sang a long story (an epic) he would repeat the tune many times so it was necessary to find a pleasing melody, or singers would not have been very welcome in the courts and market places.   These musical news columns entertained the people who had few amusements.   The wandering minstrels with their harps or *crwth* (Welsh harps), or whatever instrument they might have used in their particular country, were welcomed with open arms and hearts.

This sounds as if these singers and players traveled, and indeed they did!   They sprang up from all parts of Europe and had different names in different places.   There were bards from Britain and Ireland, skalds from the Norse lands, minstrels from "Merrie England," troubadours from the south of France, trouvères from the north of France, jongleurs from both north and south who danced and juggled for the joy of all who saw them, and minnesingers and meistersingers in Germany.

Druids and Bards

Centuries before this, Homer the great Greek poet was called the Blind Bard and he chanted his poems, the *Iliad* and the *Odyssey*, to the accompaniment of the lyre, the favorite instrument of the Greeks.   But when we speak of bards in this chapter we mean the poets and musicians of ancient Britain, when that island was inhabited and ruled by the Druids, 1000 B.C.   We do not know when the bards first began to make music or when they were first called bards, but it is certain that for many centuries before the Christian era, these rude, barbarous people of the countries we know as Wales, England, Ireland and Scotland, had many songs, dances and musical instruments.

Look at a map of France, and see how much like a teapot it is shaped.   The western part, the spout, is Brittany! As its name shows, this part of France was inhabited by the same race of people as were in Britain, they spoke the same language, had the same religion and made the same music. These people were Celts and their priests were called Druids. Much we said about primitive people is true of these early Britons.   They expressed their feelings, and tried to protect themselves from Nature and human foes by means of religious rites and ceremonies in which music and dancing played the leading part.

They had no churches, but held religious services in the open under the oak trees.   They piled boulders on top of each other to form altars, or built large circular enclosures of huge flat rocks, inside of which they gathered for worship, or to assist at some ceremonial in which sacrifices of animals and occasionally of human beings were made. These human sacrifices occurred once a year at the Spring Festival which was celebrated in much the same fashion as in Greece. These masses of stone are found not only in the British Isles, the most famous of which is Stonehenge (which was recently bought by an American), but there are also many of these so-called *cromlechs* and *menhirs* in Brittany.

It is curious how often men and women do the same things at times and places so completely separated that they could not have been influenced by each other, but did what was natural for them. It seems that between the state of being primitive or savage and of being cultured, mankind must pass through certain states of mind and certain bodily actions common to all men. In tracing the growth of any habits and actions of people,—in government, religion, amusements, art, music, manners and customs, and language, we find the same customs constantly repeated among different races. If you remember this point, you will be interested to watch, in this book, the difference between these experiences common to all mankind and those which later on, were caused by the influence that one race had on another through meeting, through conquest and through neighborly contact.

The bards belonged to the priesthood and were Druids. They sang in verse the brave deeds of their countrymen, praises of the gods and heroes, and legends of war and adventure, accompanying themselves on primitive harps, or on an instrument something like the violin without a neck, called a *crwth*. They wore long robes and when they were acting as priests, these were covered with white surplices somewhat like the gowns of our own clergy. From a bit of information handed down by the bards, we learn that in Ireland, the graduate bard wore six colors in his robes, said to be the origin of the plaid of the Scotch Highlanders; the king wore seven colors; lords and ladies, five; governors of fortresses, four; officers and gentlemen, three; soldiers, two, and the people were allowed to wear only one. Even their dress seemed important and marked the rank!

There were three kinds of bards: priestly bards who took part in the religious rituals and were also the historians, domestic bards who made music in honor of their masters, and heraldic bards whose duties were to arouse patriotism through songs in praise of their national heroes. They had to pass examinations to become bards, and the lower ranks were tested for knowledge and ability before being promoted to the higher ranks. Recently there has been a revival in Wales of the *Eisteddfod*, or song contests of the Druids.

"Minstrelsy," or singing to the *crwth* or harp, lived on long after Druidism had been replaced by the Christian faith. Did you ever wonder where the custom came from of mistletoe at Christmas time? Or of dancing around a Maypole? Or building bonfires for May-day and St. John's eve? Celebrating All-Hallowe'en with pumpkins and black cats? And of having Christmas trees? Well, these customs are all relics of Druidism of 2000 or more years ago.

SKALDS

In the land of the fierce Vikings or Norsemen, who inhabited Scandinavia, Iceland and Finland before and during the Middle Ages, there were bards called Skalds or Sagamen. They recited and sang stories telling of their Norse gods, goddesses and heroes, Woden, Thor, Odin, Freya, Brynnhild, and of the abode of the gods, Walhalla. These ballads formed the national epics called *sagas* and *eddas*, from which Richard Wagner drew the story for his immortal music dramas, the Nibelungenlied.

Odin, who was considered a Norse god, probably was a Saxon prince who lived in the 3rd century, A.D. He revived the Norse mythology and rites with the aid of minstrels, seers, and priests. His teachings lasted until the reign of Charlemagne, a devout Christian, who put an end to pagan rites.

In the 5th century came the Saxons, Hengist and Horsa, descendants of Odin, and much of Britain fell under their rule; with them, came the skalds whose duty it was to celebrate the deeds of their lords. They appeared at the great state banquets, and also on the battle fields, encouraging the warriors with their songs of heroism, and comforting the wounded soldiers.

When the Danes, the Angles and the Jutes came to Britain in this same century, the country was called England or Angle-land. Harpers and gleemen followed in the footsteps of the Scandinavian skalds. These musician-singers went as honored guests from court to court, and received valuable presents. A popular gleeman was given the title of poet-laureate, and crowned with a laurel wreath.

The songs were taught orally and learned by heart, as there was no notation at this early date (500 A.D.). They accompanied themselves on small harps which could be carried easily. The harp was handed around the banquet table so that each guest in turn might sing a song as his share of the entertainment. Singing and composing poetry were a necessary part of a gentleman's education.

The "Venerable" Bede (Chapter VII) wrote that "Cædmon the poet (600 A.D.) never could compose any trivial or vain songs, but only such as belonged to a serious and sacred vein of thought . . . he was not practised in the art of verse. So, oft, in an entertainment, where for the sake of merriment it had been agreed that each in turn should sing and harp, as the dreaded instrument was seen approaching, he arose in shame from the supper table and went home to his house." However, we learn that Cædmon who was a serving man, had a vision in which an angel asked him to "sing the beginning of creatures," and when the vision had passed, he remembered the heavenly song, and thus Cædmon ceased to be shy, became the first great poet of England and was permitted to be a monk.

As the gleemen and harpers were not fighting men, they had many privileges not granted to the warriors. They passed, unchallenged, through the fighting camps, and we have any number of stories of kings and warriors disguising themselves as harpers in order to get information about their enemies. A secret service system of the Middle Ages!

In 878, Alfred the Great had been robbed of power and authority by the Danes, so disguised as a gleeman and armed only with a harp, he went into the Danish encampment. The royal minstrel was received cordially, and while the Danish king was listening to the songs, the harper (Alfred) was getting the information he needed, and soon made a surprise attack with his troops and was victorious. This is spying with musical accompaniment!

The Battle of Hastings (1066) caused great changes not only in learning, customs, language, music, other arts and politics, but in life itself. The French who, under William of Normandy conquered Britain, were leaders in composing poetry and song, and they brought over to Britain all their talents. Now romance began and with it the art of glorifying in song and verse, deeds of valor and the charms of lovely ladies. And here the troubadours and trouvères make their entrance into our story.

France had had songs of deeds and action called *Chansons de Geste*, which were tales of the brave Charlemagne, celebrating his victory over the invading Moors from Spain. One of the greatest of these was the *Chanson de Roland*. Other songs or ballads on religious, historical, chivalric, or political subjects took the place of our modern newspapers and were powerful at the courts and among the people in the towns. When a man in court circles did anything that some one objected to, one of the minstrel-poets was hired to make up a song about it, which was sung everywhere until the news was well circulated, and the person punished, often undeservedly. However it made the men of those days think twice before doing things against the rights of others, for they were really afraid of these songs that were spread among their friends and enemies.

In the Battle of Hastings, Taillefer, a famous soldier-minstrel, led the attack of the Normans, singing songs of Roland and of Charlemagne. He struck the first blow in the fight, and was the first one killed, but he went to his death singing. Tales of our own soldiers in the great war tell us the same about the need and love of music.

Chanson de Roland

The *Chanson de Roland* is the national epic poem of France, and dates back to this Norman period. It celebrates the death at Roncevals, of Roland, Count of the "Marsh" of Bretagne, in Charlemagne's expedition against Spain in 778. The work is divided into three parts. The first tells of the fight between the French (Christians) and the Saracens (Spanish Arabs), of the valor of Oliver and of Roland, of the latter's death, of Charlemagne's miraculous victory over the Saracens. The second part is a poem not based on fact, in which Charlemagne fights Baligant, the chief of all the pagans of the Orient; the western chief is victorious over the pagan chief, who is utterly defeated and killed. This poem pictures the victory of Christianity over Paganism. In the third part, the revenge is carried further, by Charlemagne's taking the Saracen city Saragosse, and bringing back with him to France another of the leaders, Ganelon, who was tried and condemned to death.

This is the leading French work of the Middle Ages, as it sums up the greatest idealism, and brings to us that which they considered most vital—the call of patriotism, of honor and of duty.

Great Cathedrals and Feudal Castles

About this time began the building of the great Gothic churches in France, England, and Germany. Rome had fallen, paganism had gone, and the spirit of Christianity was taking great hold of the people's hearts. As a result of this feeling to praise God suitably the great churches which we copy even today were built.

If "architecture is frozen music," you can understand why music and architecture developed at the same time.

This was also the age of Feudalism, when the noblemen lived in castles with moats and drawbridges, and owned vast tracts of land and whole villages. People were retainers, vassals and serfs, with no freedom and no property rights except what the lords gave them. They even had to give their masters much of the produce of the lands which they cultivated. Of course, these feudal lords besides having to be fed and guarded had to be entertained, and had to know what was going on in the outside world. So, the minstrels and bards were cordially welcomed, and wandered from castle to castle, receiving presents of money or clothes, jewelry, horses, and sometimes even houses.

What Troubadours Learned Through Crusades

Every year during the early centuries of the Christian era, hundreds of pilgrims journeyed to the Holy Land undergoing much hardship on the way. They thought through this pilgrimage to be forgiven for their sins, and win the approval of the Church, then far more powerful than the

kings. Toward the end of the 11th century, Mohammedans
had seized Palestine, and prevented the Christian pilgrims
from doing penance or worshipping at the Holy Sepulchre.
This led to a series of expeditions against the Mohammedans in Palestine in which all the Christian countries of
Europe united. These expeditions were called the Crusades (1095-1271), and they have been celebrated in story
and song ever since. The Crusades gave the rough un-
cultured men of the Western world the chance to hear the
poetry and the songs of the Arabs (Chapter VI), who at
that time were the more advanced in culture and arts.
Although the Oriental music with its complicated rhythms
must have been hard to learn, the Crusaders brought back
much of real value and beauty,—a new way of singing, new
subjects for poems, and two new instruments, a kind of guitar
and *el oud*, in Europe called lute. The lute had a strong
influence on popular music, for it was the most commonly
used instrument for centuries.

ROMANCE LANGUAGES

Latin had been the language of France because the
Romans lived there so long, but later it became mixed with
the rough dialect and speech of the Franks and other
Gothic barbarous tribes and was much changed. From
this mixture came rustic Latin, or *Romanse rustique*, and
modern French, Spanish, Italian and Portuguese are still
called Romance languages. A new poetry was born in
Provence, the south of France, and in Normandy in the
north, written in this *Romanse rustique*, and the oldest
French songs were called *lais*, lay or ballad. The great
ruler Charlemagne collected these *lais* of barbarian period
and the trouvères and troubadours had wonderful old
songs of heroism to choose from.
In Provence they said "oc" for "yes" and in Nor-

mandy, "oui." So, the language of the south of France
was called "langue d'oc" and of the north "langue d'oui."

Troubadours, Trouvères, Jongleurs

The troubadours, whose very name brings to mind a
charming picture of romance, chivalry and adventure,
were the poet-composers of Provence a land of sunshine
where men were brave and courteous, and women beautiful
and gracious. The words *troubadour* and *trouvères*, come
from *trobar, trouver*, meaning to find or to invent, for these
troubadours and trouvères were the inventors or composers of poems which they set to music.

They wrote their songs on the four-lined staff in square
notes, without written accompaniment. The accompaniments played on the lute, the guitar, the vielle, or sometimes the harp, were probably made up by the *jongleur*,
(*joglar, jouglar*, in English,—juggler) who sang the songs,
had trained bears, danced and played tricks. Then as
now there were composers and performers. The troubadours and trouvères were as a rule, nobles and even
royalty. Five kings belonged to their number, the greatest
were Richard the Lion-hearted, William Count of Poi-
tiers, Alfonso, Thibaut de Champagne, and King of Navarre.

The troubadour seldom sang his own songs, as this was
the jongleur's duty. There were many more jongleurs
than troubadours, and they belonged to a much lower
grade of society. The jongleurs traveled from place to
place, from castle to castle, with their instruments slung
across their backs, and their songs in a little bag at their
side. They were heartily welcomed wherever they went,
but if they found the doors of the castles closed to them,
they soon gathered a crowd in the public squares, where
they performed to the joy of the townspeople.

Can you imagine the pleasure these strolling entertainers gave to the people who did not have motors, movies, radios, gramophones and theatres for their amusement? How happy the custodian of the castle must have been when he looked across the moat and lowered the drawbridge for the welcome minstrels!

The jongleurs grew so numerous, and their music became so poor that they were nuisances, little better than outlaws and beggars. How easily a good thing can be overdone!

In the 14th century they banded together in perhaps the first musical union on record. They appointed leaders, called kings of the minstrels or jugglers. At first they were hired by nobles and troubadours as entertainers with the rank of servants. Even the monasteries received them with joy during the early days; later they were denounced by the Church, and forbidden to enter the monasteries, for they had sung of evil things instead of lovely things and had acted unseemly. During Lent, they were forbidden to appear in public, so they wisely used that time to go to schools of minstrelsy, where they learned new songs, and tried their skill at composing. In these schools they were also taught to play their instruments. Sometimes we hear of women minstrels, who sang, played the flute, danced, and performed tricks to the endless delight of the audience. (See lining of the cover of this book.)

The jongleurs, at their best, seem to have "gotten in" everywhere,—at the courts of kings, in all the tournaments, festivals, pilgrimages, and weddings. A wedding wasn't complete without them! At the knightly tournaments and jousts, the minstrel was a most necessary person, for, did he not take the place of newspapers, and give accounts to a waiting world of the results of the exciting tournaments?

Massenet, the French composer, wrote a lovely opera

called *The Juggler of Notre Dame,* from one of the old miracle tales of a young juggler sheltered by the monks of Notre Dame. Everyone brought rich gifts to place at the feet of the Virgin Mary, but being a pauper, he had nothing but his songs, dances and tricks, which he offered the Virgin by going through them as best he could in front of the shrine. So shocked were the monks by his seeming lack of respect, that they wanted to drive him out! At this moment the miracle took place. The image of the Virgin came to life and stretched forth her arms protectingly to the young juggler, showing that she accepted his offering given in all sincerity and simplicity.

As all the countries of Europe took part in the Crusades, the troubadours' songs were heard by others than the French, and their music spread rapidly. Richard, the Lion-hearted, King of England, was a famous Crusader and a troubadour of skill. He invited jongleurs over from France, one of whom, Blondel de Nesle, became his devoted companion during the Crusade of 1193, and saved Richard's life. Richard was taken captive by Leopold, Duke of Austria, and was cast into a dungeon. The English did not know where to look for their monarch, but Blondel undertook the search, going from place to place, singing songs which he and the king had written together. One day as he sang, from the tower of a castle came a voice which he recognized as Richard's, singing the same song! And soon the royal troubadour was released.

THE TROUBADOURS

This new art of poetry and song was called "The gay science of chivalry and love-service." Indeed many of the poems about knightly adventure were addressed to some fair lady, real or imaginary, known or unknown. Curious as it may seem, the names of most of these songs came from the Arabian, because the Europeans met them during the crusades and during the Arabs' conquests and roam-ings in Europe.

The names tell you what the songs were about. *Chanson* and *canzo* both mean song, and we see these names to-day on our concert programs. There were story telling songs called the *chansons de toile*, songs of linen, which told of the lovely damsels at work weaving, of their beauty, and of their thoughts, for the women of castle and cottage alike wove the cloth out of which the clothes were made. Then, they had dramatic songs and dancing songs called *estampies* (from which comes our word stamping); the *reverdies*, or spring songs, to celebrate the Spring festivals; the *pastorelles* in which the heroine was always a charming shepherdess; the *sera* or *serenade*, an evening song; the *nocturne*, a night song, and love songs were often sung under the beloved ladies' windows! The *alba* was a morning song. The *sirvantes*, or songs of service, sung in praise of princes or nobles, or telling of public happenings were im-portant. These were often accompanied by drums, bells, pipes and trumpets.

We have debating societies in our schools and colleges, and questions of the day are discussed in the newspapers, but in the troubadours' day, debates were made into songs, sung by two people, and were called *tensons*. Many curi-ous and rather foolish questions were made the subjects of these songs.

Sometimes these popular songs found their way into the Church, and were made into fine church music, and some-times a bit of melody from the Church went through the hands of a troubadour poet and was turned into a *rounde*, *ballata*, *sera*, or *pastorella*.

This poetry and song of Provence lasted until the middle of the 14th century, for in the twelve hundreds the revolts against the abuses of the Church rose to such seriousness that massacres took place, towns were destroyed and many nobles and troubadours lost their lives.

TROUVÈRES

Shortly after the troubadours began to compose, in the north of France came the trouvères who profited much from the music and poetry of their southern brothers.

However, the trouvères did not have the warm, lovely dialect of the southern troubadours. As they were closer to the Church, their songs were more religious, had less variety of subjects, and the melodies were like Church music.

Although the troubadours did much to shape the rhyming stanzas in poetry, the trouvères helped in the gradual forming of the later French and Flemish schools of music, as you will see.

The jongleurs played on an instrument called the *vielle* which was great-grandfather to our violin. The short pieces played before the songs and accompanied by dances, were the first pieces of instrumental music in the Middle Ages. The combination of song, instrument and dance was called *balerie* or *ballada* from which comes our dance *ballet*. There was also a piece called *round*, *rota*, or *ronde*, composed so that different voices and the instrument came in at different points, each singing or playing the same tune, but arranged so that the parts sounded well together. Perhaps you know *Frère Jacques* or *Scotland's Burning* or *Three Blind Mice*. These are rounds or canons.

One of the most beautiful rounds in existence is an English song which dates from about 1240, the period of all this "gay science," and it is looked upon as a masterpiece. It is supposed to have been written by John Fornsete, a monk. It was notated in the old square neumes on a six line staff. The name of this "Six Men's Song" or round for six voices, is *Sumer is icumen in*. It seems to have been far ahead of its time as an art work.

One of the best known trouvères, Adam de la Hale, wrote *Le Jeu de Robin et Marion*, said to be the first comic opera. It was performed at the court of Naples in 1285.

The trouvères collected tales of Normandy, Brittany, and of Charlemagne's reign, and so preserved valuable musical and literary material.

So these troubadours and trouvères made the age of Chivalry romantic and beautiful to us who came long after them, in spite of much unpleasantness, prejudice, war, massacre and hardship.

Minnesingers

Along the river Rhine in Germany near that part of France where the trouvères sang, lived the Minnesingers. They sang love songs,—*minne* was the old German word for love. Like the troubadours the minnesingers were of the nobility, but they rarely hired jongleurs or anybody to perform their songs; they sang them themselves, playing their own accompaniments on lutes or viels (viols).

Many songs expressed adoration of the Virgin, and others praised deeds of chivalry. Differing from other minstrels, they made songs about Nature and Religion full of feeling, fancy and humor, but the minnesongs were not so light-hearted or fanciful as those of their French neighbors. They had marked rhythm, beauty of form and simplicity, and were more dramatic, telling the exploits of the Norse heroes in many a glorious story.

Their story was far more important to them than the music which for a long time was like the stern plain song of the Church. "We should be glad they were what they were, for they seem to have paved the way for the great

Protestant music of the 16th century," says Waldo Selden Pratt in his *History of Music*.

You can get an excellent idea of the minnesong in Wolfram von Eschenbach's *Oh Thou Sublime Sweet Evening Star*, which Wagner wrote in the spirit of the ancient minnesingers in the opera *Tannhäuser*. Tannhäuser was a real minnesinger, taking part in a real song contest, held by the Landgraf (Count) of Thuringia, 1206–7, who offered his daughter Elizabeth's hand to the winner, whatever his rank. We find Elizabeth also in Wagner's *Tannhäuser*, so when you hear it you will know that it is history as well as beautiful music! How remarkable that, in the days of feudalism, when the nobles practically owned the so-called common people, talent for music and verse stood even above rank! After all there is no nobility like that of talent. Even in the 13th century this was understood, and to either commoner or peer winning the song tournament, the lady of rank was given in marriage.

Wolfram von Eschenbach, the minnesinger, visited the courts and sang in many tournaments. Giving Wagner a character for the opera *Tannhäuser* was not all he did as Eschenbach wrote a poem from which Wagner drew the story for his *Parsifal*.

Walther von der Vogelweide, one of the most famous minnesingers, was so fond of birds, that when dying he asked for food and drink to be placed on his tomb every day for the birds. There are four holes carved in the tombstone; and pilgrims today, when they visit this singer's grave, still scatter crumbs for them,who probably in their bird histories record that Walther loved song even as they!

Prince Conrad, Konradin he was called, son of the last Swabian King, was the last famous minnesinger. Everyone battled for other people's countries and lands then, and so Conrad, heir to the crown, joined a Sicilian rebellion against France, and was killed by a troubadour, the Duke of Anjou.

MASTERSINGERS

After poor Conrad's time, the art of minnesinging declined, but as people must have music, a new activity sprang up among the people or "folk" instead of among the gentry and knights. The folk who took part in this were called the Meistersingers or mastersingers and their story is very thrilling and picturesque.

This was the day of the Robber Baron, when Germany was broken up into little kingdoms and principalities. Any rich and powerful noble could start a war to steal away the rights of another ruler, and become ruler himself. This was no pleasant state of affairs for the people, for they were in constant terror of death, of the destruction of their crops, or new taxes. Life became so perilous that people left the farms and went to the cities for protection. The feudal system began to fail, for the people would no longer be slaves, and gradually took up trades and formed themselves into guilds. The warring nobles had neglected music for conquest, so these workers and artisans, hungry for it, formed music guilds as well as trade guilds, drew up rules for making music and poetry, and held prize competitions. In these music guilds there were six grades of membership: first, member; second, scholar or apprentice; then, friends of the school; singer, poet, and finally mastersinger or *Meistersinger*. You can get a real picture of their day in the greatest comic opera ever written, Wagner's *Die Meistersinger*, and you can make the acquaintance of Hans Sachs, the most famous Meistersinger (1494–1576).

Heinrich von Meissen, known as *Frauenlob* (Praise of Women), is said to have founded the Meistersinger movement over a hundred years before Hans Sachs' time.

Till Eulenspiegel, whose merry pranks have been delightfully told in music by Richard Strauss, a composer who is still living, was said to have been a Mastersinger.

The origin of the name "Meistersinger" is disputed. One historian tells us that it was given to every minnesinger who was not a noble,—in other words, a burgher-minstrel. The other historian claims that the title *Meister* or master was given to any one who excelled in any act or trade, and afterwards came to mean all the guild members.

From the 14th century to the 16th, hardly a town in Germany was without music guilds and Mastersingers. Although they lost power then, the last guilds did not disappear until 1830, and the last member died in 1876. They must have passed the long winter evenings pleasantly for they met, and read or sang poems of the minnesingers or new ones composed by the members themselves. These guilds must have been great fun, for they had badges and initiation ceremonies and the kind of celebrations one loves in a club.

They had complicated, strict rules called *Tablatur* which today seem quite curious, so much has music matured and thrown off the chains which once bound it! Wagner states many of the rules in his opera.

When the guilds grew too large to be held in the different homes, the churches became the meeting places for practise and for the contests.

The highest praise we can give the Mastersingers is that they carried the love of music and song into every German home and made it a pastime of domestic life. Their influence spread not only through Germany, but throughout all lands. The composers who followed were glad to have their songs from which to draw inspiration for the popular religious songs at the time of the Protestant Reformation. Even though they did not make up any very great words or music, they spread a love for it and made people feel that the following of music as a career was worthy and dignified.

It is interesting to know before we close this chapter, that the English, well into the 16th century, after the

passing of the troubadours, trouvères, minnesingers and
mastersingers, still celebrated the exploits of the day in
ballads called the Percy Reliques.

VIELLE OR HURDY-GURDY

If you had lived in the Middle Ages you would have seen
the strolling players traveling around with a queer looking instrument known by many different names,—*vielle,
organistrum, Bauernleier* (peasant lyre), *Bettlerleier* (beggar's
lyre) or *hurdy-gurdy*. This was a country instrument, not
often seen in cities, and was shaped like the body of a lute
without a long neck. It had wire strings, sometimes gut,
and a set of keys; the sound was made by turning a little
crank at the bottom. The *vielle* or *hurdy-gurdy* is a cross
between the bowed and the keyed instruments. In the
12th century it was called the *organistrum*, a large instrument which took two men to play. It flourished in the
18th century throughout Europe.

And so, now on to folk songs, although we would like to
linger in this romantic period of wandering minstrels.

After a painting by Garofalo, National Gallery at Rome.

Saint Cecilia—Patron Saint of Music.

(Holding a portative organ.)

"The Music Making Boys," by Frans Hals, from the Kassel Gallery, Germany.

Boys with a Lute.

After a painting by Teniers, in the gallery at Munich.

A Peasant Wedding.

A Lady at the Clavier (Clavichord).

CHAPTER IX

The People Dance and Sing

FOLK MUSIC

ALL THE WORLD HAS DANCED AND SUNG

WE have watched the human race grow out of its state of primitive yells and grunts, or babyhood, telling its stories and expressing its feelings in crude music. We have seen it sing and dance its way through the ages during which its men were semi-barbarians, like the Franks, Gauls, Goths, Huns, Saxons, Celts, and Angles into the period when these same tribes became the French, German, Belgian and English nations.

Music was not a thing of learning as it is today, it was merely a way of talking, of enjoying life, and of passing on to others deeds and doings of the time. Early people said in poetry and song what was in their hearts. They knew nothing of musical rules and regulations and passed their songs along from father to son through the long years when the world was young, and their best songs have in them the seed of musical art! A modern Greek folk singer said: "As I don't know how to read, I have made this story into a song, so as not to forget it."

This music of the people, by the people and for the people is Folk Music and we shall see how these simple, tuneful bits have influenced the world of music because, as H. E. Krehbiel said "they are the heartbeats of the . . .

folk and in them are preserved feelings, beliefs and habits of vast antiquity." Don't you believe that studying history through folk tunes would be fascinating? People to-day have found out much about the different races and tribal events through them.

It is impossible to find out who wrote the five thousand folk songs of England and the more than five thousand of Russia and of Ireland and all the others, for it was not until the 19th century that folk songs and dances became subjects for serious study. The fact is, a true folk song doesn't want to find its composer for it loses its rank as a folk song if its maker should turn up! But this is not quite fair, for surely we should accept as folk songs those which have sprung up among the people, or have become a part of their lives through expressing their thoughts and feelings, even though the composer's name has not been lost. We divide folk songs into two classes,—Class A, the composerless songs, and Class B, those tagged with a name.

Isn't it exciting to think that folk songs and dances of the ancient Greeks, the Aztecs of Peru, the Chinese, the Irish and Russian peasants and our American negroes have things in common? It seems as if they might have had a world congress in primitive times and agreed on certain kinds of songs, for every nation has

1. Songs of childhood, games, and cradle songs.
2. Songs for religious ceremonies, festivals, holidays, and Chrismas Carols.
3. Love songs and songs for marriage fêtes, and weddings.
4. War songs, patriotic songs and army songs.
5. Songs of work and labor and trades.
6. Drinking songs, comical, political and satirical.
7. Songs for dancing, rounds, etc.
8. Funeral songs and songs for mourning.
9. Narratives, ballads and legends.

So it comes to pass, that many a time when nations, due to wars and wanderings and vast passings of time, have forgotten their origins, the singing of a song will bring back the fact of some far distant relationship.

One day a party of Bretons, in 1758 (long after the Welsh and Bretons had forgotten they were of the same race), were marching to give battle to some Welsh troops that had descended upon the French coast. As the Welsh soldiers marched forward, the Bretons were amazed to hear their enemies singing one of their own national songs! They were so surprised and so overcome with sympathy that the Bretons joined in and sang with the Welsh. Both commanders, speaking the same language, gave the order "Fire!" But neither side would or could fire. Instead, the soldiers dropped their weapons, broke ranks and in wild enthusiasm greeted each other as long lost friends. The song they sang is probably seven hundred years old or older.

(1) Songs of Childhood, Games and Cradle Songs

From the day of the obelisk to the day of the radio, every baby that has ever been born has been put to sleep to the soothing sound of the mother's song. The Greek mother sang to her baby,

Come, Sleep! come, Sleep! Take him away.
Come, Sleep, and make him slumber.
Carry him to the vineyard of the Aga,
To the Garden of the Aga,
The Aga will give him grapes; his wife, roses; his servant, pancakes.

Many early lullabies were sung in honor of the infant Jesus, which really gives them a very blessèd beginning. It is related by a Sicilian poet "When the Madunazza (mother) was mending St. Joseph's clothes, the Bambineddu (Bambino—the Infant Jesus) cried in his cradle, because no one was attending to Him. So the Archangel Raphael came and rocked Him and said these sweet little words to Him, 'Lullaby, Jesus, Son of Mary.'"

The Indians, too, sang lullabies, for you know the squaw is a gentle soul and takes beautiful care of her papoose. The Chippewas think of sleep as a big insect and they have named him Weeng. Weeng comes down from the top of a tree where he is busy making a buzzing noise with his wings and puts you to sleep by sending many little fairies to you who beat your head with tiny clubs!

We all know our own *Bye, Baby Bunting, Father's Gone a Hunting*, etc., and *Rockabye Baby on the Tree Top*.

The Germans, whose children songs and lullabies are so lovely, have the familiar *Schlaf, Kindlein, Schlaf!* It is a sweet name the Italians give their lullaby, the *ninnenanne!* And the mothers in Lyons, France, call sleep *souin-souin* and have a charming little song:

> Le Poupon voudrait bien do(r)mir;
> Le souin-souin ne peu pas venir.
> Souin-souin, vené, vené, vené;
> Souin-souin, vené, vené, vené!

> The infant wants to go to sleep;
> Sleep does not wish to come.
> Sleep come, come, come;
> Sleep come, come, come!

GAMES

We all have sung *The Farmer in the Dell, London Bridge is Falling Down, Ring Around the Rosy* and many other game-songs. We have told you of the Indian moccasin game, and we know that in all the other nations the children have had their game-songs.

(2) Songs for Religious Ceremonies, Holidays, and Christmas Carols, etc., May Songs and Spring Festivals

Spring is so full of the beginnings of life, and people can see the flowers begin to bloom and take on color and glory. Even as you and I, they have never been able to see them without rejoicing and every one's rejoicing sooner or later is a cause for music. In many countries this renewal of life is celebrated by rites and ceremonies that have been the source of much folk-lore and music.

The Greeks, as early as the 6th Century B.C., celebrated the coming of the spring with a religious festival named after the god Dionysus. Many songs and dances accompanied these festivals. On the evening before the festival, which lasted five days, there was an impressive procession by torch-light in which an image of the god Dionysus was carried to the theatre where the festival was held, accompanied by many handsome youths and a very splendid bull which was sacrificed.

In the excavations of Crete this ancient hymn has been found,—a spring song and a young man-song in one:

Ho! Kouros (young man), most Great, I give thee hail, Lord of all that is wet and gleaming; thou art come at the head of thy Daemones. To Dickte for the year, Oh, march and rejoice in the dance and song.

In Germany, it was thought that on Walpurgis-nacht (May night) witches rode on the tails of magpies and danced away the winter snows on the Brocken, one of the highest peaks of the Hartz Mountains. In Germany too, it was the custom for children to set May-flies (Maikäfer) free and to sing this song:

Maikäferchen fliege,
Dein Vater ist in Kriege
Dein Mutter ist in Pommerland
Pommerland ist abgebrannt
Maikäferchen fliege.

or

May-fly, fly away,
Your father is at war,
Your mother is in Pommerland.
Pommerland is all burned up!
May-fly, fly away.

Don't you think it is like our rhyme?

Lady-bug, lady-bug,
Fly away home.
Your house is on fire
Your children will burn.

And here is the French:

Avril, tu t'en vas!   Au firmament bleu,
Car Mai vient la-bas   Ton nid est en feu,
Pour balayer ta figure   Les Turcs avec leur épée
De pluie, aussi de froidure. Viennent tuer ta couvée.
Hanneton, vole!   Hanneton, vole!
Hanneton, vole!   Hanneton, vole!

or:

April, away!   Afar in the sky,
For here cometh May   With flames leaping high,
With sunshine again   The Turks with swords rude
To banish the rain.   Have slaughtered your brood.
May-beetle, fly!   May-beetle, fly!
May-beetle, fly!   May-beetle, fly!

The first comic opera, a *pastourale* six hundred years old, *Le Jeu de Robin et Marion* by Adam de la Hale, is full of May songs.

The King and Queen of the May and May Pole dancers and the English Jack-in-the-Green, the Thuringian Little Leaf Man and the Russian tree dressed up are only a few of the many examples of the rites of spring. And we have seen how the Druids and the Aztecs celebrated spring.

One of the most modern composers, Igor Stravinsky, has written a ballet called *Le Sacre du Printemps* (Rites of Spring) in which he has used the ancient Russian pagan rites of celebrating the spring. The music is wild and the rhythms primitive.

RELIGIOUS CEREMONIES

From legends, we know that songs and dances of the Polish people accompanied their religious ceremonies before Christianity. When they exchanged their pagan gods for the teachings of the early Christian fathers, many of these songs were lost, but some of them were handed down merely by changing the pagan name to the Christian. These songs have been traced by the fact that many of them are based on the old pentatonic scale. The Slavs, the Lithuanians and the Germanic races have kept this scale in Eastern and Middle Europe, and the Greeks, the ancient Italians and the Celts brought it into Western and Southern Europe. These scales are supposed to have come from Indo-China, for it must not be forgotten that the Polish along with all Slavs migrated from Asia, the cradle of the human race.

Two festivals,—St. John's Eve and Christmas, came down from the pagan era in Poland and the manner of celebration has changed little throughout the centuries.

CHRISTMAS CAROLS

The Polish Christmas Carol was also handed down from the days before Christ. The word "carol" comes from the old French *carole* which was a dance, and gave its name to the song by which it was accompanied.   In the pagan time there were summer carols, winter carols, Easter carols and carols that celebrated a religious winter festival.   As the winter festival occurred about the same time of the year as the Nativity or birthday of the Saviour, it was celebrated in the Christian Church as Christmas.   In England, the old Yule-tide of the Druids has influenced the present celebration of Christmas with its fun, festivities and Christmas trees!

Throughout Germany, Christmas Carols were sung early every Christmas morning, and many of the old hymns have thus been preserved.

The Christmas Carol in France is called *Noël* and the old English word was *Nowell*.

(3) Love Songs

It is safe to say that there are more love songs than any other kind of folk music, and among them is some of the most beautiful music in the world.   You will find charming folk love songs of every nationality on earth.

Different countries have different marriage customs which give an intimate picture of the life in different periods, of countries and tribes far apart.   Again we can trace forgotten relationships in like customs of bygone days.   Singing and dancing are very important in all marriage celebrations, and some wedding music is of great age.

In Russia, for example, the marriage customs and wedding music are very beautiful and impressive.   At the same time no folk dancing is wilder or gayer than that celebrating a peasant marriage.

Before going to a wedding ceremony, the Polish bride sings one particular song built on the pentatonic scale, that has probably been sung for more than two thousand years!

There are other wedding ceremony songs that can be traced back almost as far.

In Brittany, during the 11th and 12th centuries, the priest demanded a "nuptial song" from the newly-weds on the Sunday following the wedding, as a wedding tax!

In another place the feudal lord demanded that every new bride should dance and sing before him and in return he decorated her with a bonnet of flowers.

You haven't forgotten the Indian and his love music played on the flute, have you?

(4) Patriotic Songs

In the recent World War, we had examples of how folk songs were made. There were popular songs like *Over There* (George Cohan), *The Long, Long Trail* (by Zo Elliot), *Tipperary*, *Madelon*, that were sung by millions. They were songs of the people, by the people and for the people, and no one cared who wrote them.

Most of the national hymns and patriotic songs were born in a time of storm and stress. Words inspired by some special happening were written on the spur of the moment, and often set to some familiar tune. *America* was first sung to the tune of *God Save the King* on July 4, 1832. The words of *Star Spangled Banner* were written by Francis Scott Key during the War of 1812 as he watched the bombardment of Fort McHenry in Chesapeake Bay, and was set to an English drinking song, *Anacreon in Heaven*. *Yankee Doodle*, a song first sung to make fun of the young colonists, became the patriotic hymn of the Revolution! Where the tune came from is a mystery, but it shows a family likeness to a little Dutch nursery song, a German street song, an old English country dance, a folk tune from the Pyrenees and one from Hungary! But we love our old *Yankee Doodle* anyhow! *Hail Columbia* was adapted to a tune, *The President's March*, which had accompanied Washington when he was inaugurated, in New York, as our first president.

England's *God Save the King* was composed, words and music, by Henry Carey, and it was used first in 1743 during the Jacobite uprising. It has since served America, Germany, Denmark and Switzerland. *Auld Lang Syne* of Scotland was written by "Bobby" Burns and set to an old Scotch tune. *St. Patrick's Day* was originally a jig, and *The Wearing of the Green* was a street ballad of the Irish rebellion of 1798 mourning the fact that the Irish were forbidden to wear their national emblem, the shamrock. The Welsh song *Men of Harlech*, a stirring tune, dates from 1468.

The French have several thrilling national songs. If you heard *Malbrouk s'en va-t-en guerre* (Malbrouk to war is going) you would say, "Why! that's *For He's a Jolly Good Fellow.*" So it is, and it has had a long and chequered career. It is supposed to have been brought into Europe by one of the Crusaders, and was lost for five centuries; it cropped up again in 1781 when Marie Antoinette sang it to put the little Dauphin (the French prince) to sleep. Paris picked up the tune and it was heard in every café and on every street corner. Napoleon who had no ear for music hummed it. It crossed the English channel. Even the Arabs sing a popular song like it which they call *Mabrooka.* Beethoven used the air in a Battle Symphony (1813).

The stirring hymn of France, is the *Marseillaise* written by Rouget de l'Isle (1792) on the eve of the Revolution. It became the marching song of the French Army and was sung during the attack on the Tuileries (Paris), the king's palace. It has always been the Republican song of France.

In almost every book you read about the French Revolution, *La Carmagnole* and *Ça Ira* are mentioned. They accompanied thousands of victims to the guillotine. *Ça Ira* (It will go on!), was a popular song played by Marie An-

toinette on her *clavecin*. Little did she know that the same
tune would be shouted by the infuriated mobs as she was
driven through the streets of Paris in the tumbril to the
guillotine!

The Italians show their natural love for opera by the fact
that their national hymn is adopted from Bellini's opera
Somnambula.

The *Rakoczy March* of which you will hear later in the
chapter is the Hungarian national hymn.

We could write an entire book on this subject, but this is
only to give you a suggestion of how these songs grew and
where they came from.

(5) Songs of Work and Labor and Trades

We have shown you the American Indians singing their
songs as they fish and pound the corn; the boatmen rowing
to the rhythm of their songs; and we have tried to show you
that everybody loved songs as much when they worked as
when they danced. Haven't you, too, hummed or sung
while working? People who accompany dish cloths and
dusters with songs work better!

American negroes have used song to ease their work in
the hot sunny fields. They not only sang, but men were
hired to sing and act as song leaders in the slave days, to
set the pace for workers, for more work was done when the
slaves moved to the rhythm of music. In modern fac-
tories today, music is used to relieve the drudgery.

In Southern States the stevedores sing as they unload and
load ships. And haven't you often heard a rhythmic sound
uttered by men hauling ropes on ships or buildings?

The world over, sailors have their songs and dances,
farmers their reaping and planting songs, spinners and
weavers their songs, boatmen songs like those on the Nile
and the Volga boat song.

While few Greek folk songs have come down to our time, we know that they had songs for reaping the harvest, for grinding the barley, for threshing the wheat, for pressing the grapes, for spinning wool, and for weaving. They also had the songs of the shoemaker, the dyer, of the bath-master, the water-carrier, of the shepherd, etc.

There are innumerable spinning songs of all nationalities, and shepherds' songs,—you probably know the French *Il etait une Bergère.*

In Africa, we hear that the workers when cleaning rice were led by singers, who clapped their hands and stamped their feet to accompany the song. One man reports that he heard the negro women singing a national song in chorus, while pounding wheat always in time with the music.

Charles Peabody tells of a leader in a band of slaves in America who was besought by his companions not to sing a certain song because it made them work too hard!

The difference between the negro songs and the labor songs of other peoples and places is, that the negroes had no special labor songs but sang their religious songs, which they adapted to all purposes and occasions, while the true labor song was composed to fit the occasion.

In old England we hear of the "Labor-lilts" which were all work songs of spinners, milk-maids and shepherds. And we must not neglect the old night-watchman whom we meet in Wagner's *Die Meistersinger.* Neither can we let go by unnoticed the "town-crier" who told the news, good and bad. The street calls and cries of the Middle Ages were labor songs, later, in England and in France made into real compositions.

We, in America, have the old Cowboy songs, the Mining songs of California, and the Lumberjack songs of Maine. These are not exactly labor songs but are first cousins to them.

The stage coach *postillons* with their fascinating horn calls are really music of trades or occupations, too. Isn't it too bad that the inartistic jangle of the tram-car and the "honk-honk" of the automobile tear our ears instead of the tuneful hunting horns and postillon horns which are still occasionally heard in European forests!

The world's workers sing to make work slip along easily, so you see song is a great lubricant.

(6) Drinking Songs

In the great dining halls of the Middle Ages, when hunting parties gathered, and guests were received from near and far, or at Christmas time, when in old Britain the Wassail-bowl flowed freely, drinking songs were an important part of the banquet. At the elaborate feasts in Rome, drinking songs were popular. In fact, all over the world there are thousands of this kind of folk song.

The name Wassail dates back to the day when Vortigern, King of the Britons, visited Hengist, the Saxon. Rowena, Hengist's daughter greeted him with, "Was hail hla, ond cyning!" which means in plain English, "Be of health, Lord King!" to which the king replied, "Drink heil" (Drink health).

The Word Vaudeville

In the second half of the 15th century, two men named Basselin and Jean de Houx wrote many drinking songs. As they lived in the little valleys (in French called *vaux*) near Vire in Normandy, drinking songs came to be called *vaux-de-vire*. At the same time, songs that were sung in the streets, in fact, any folk songs with gay melodies and light words, were called *voix-de-ville*, (or voices of the city). So, in some way, these two terms became mixed, and the familiar word, *vaudeville* is the result!

(7) DANCING SONGS

In the folk dance, man shows the feelings and dispositions of his race. From this dance of the people, all music gradually took a measured form, a rhythmic shape that is lacking in the song of primitive people. In primitive times, all dances were sung, particularly was this the case with the Slav race. As instruments were perfected, they took the place of primitive drums and singing as accompaniment to the dance.

The plain chant, and in fact all music of the church, lacked the element we call metre or measure. It followed a rhythm needed by the words, but this was much more like talking than like singing. Even the ornamented chant of the soloists in the churches had no regularity of time or of phrase.

Rhythm as we know it, was developed in two ways,— through the singing of verses and through dancing. We must not forget that early peoples were much like children, and took pleasure in jingles, and in moving their feet and bodies in repeated motions which became dances.

It is most fascinating to see that the people who have the saddest songs, have the gayest and wildest dances. Maybe it is because the sadder the nation the more need it has for some gay way of forgetting its woes. The Russians, the Poles, the Norwegians and the people of all north countries where the songs are minor and tragic, have the wildest dances. The clothes, too, of the folk in these countries are decked in colored embroideries, and the decorations of the houses giddy and jolly. When the Russians get together they forget their sorrows in wild and almost frenzied dances, and directly after they will sing songs of deepest gloom.

POLISH DANCES

The Poles have several folk dances that are easily recognized by their rhythm and style. The great Polish composer Chopin used these folk dances in some of the loveliest piano music ever written. For more than six centuries
they have been used by Polish composers, yet there are people who say that folk song has no influence on musical art.

The Polonaise, in ¾ time, a stately dance of the aris-
tocracy and nobles rather than of the people, began as a
folk dance, and is supposed to have come from the Christ-

mas Carol. The rhythm of the Polonaise ♫♩♫♩♫♩ ,
is easily recognized and followed. In the early times, these
polonaises had no composer's tag, but were often named
for some Polish hero, and thus show the date in which they
were born.

One Polish writer dates the "courtly" polonaise from
1573. The year following the election of Henry III of
Anjou, a great reception took place at Cracow, in which all
the ladies of high rank marched in procession past the
throne to the sound of a stately dance. This was the beginning of the dignified polonaise, in which old and young
took part, marching all through the great drawing-rooms
and gardens.

The Mazurka, another very popular Polish dance, is also
in ¾ time, but faster than the polonaise, and slower than
the waltz. It is performed by a few couples at a time, two
to eight but rarely more. The accent of the measure falls
on the third beat, which distinguishes it from a waltz.

Other well known Polish dances are the *Krakowiak* in 2/4
time, the *Kujawiak* in ¾ time, the *Obertass* in ¾ time, the
dance of the mountaineers, called the *Kolomyjka* in 2/4 time,
and the *Kosah* in 2/4 time. All these dances are fast, and all
of them come directly from folk songs.

Spanish Dance-Songs

It is very hard to tell which of the Spanish folk pieces are dances and which at first were songs, because the favorite songs of Spain are nearly all sung as accompaniments to dancing. Spain had almost as rich troubadour music as France, because the influence of the troubadours and of the jongleurs was very strong, Provence being Spain's neighbor. In Catalonia the Provençal language has been used since the 9th century, and the folk music differs from that of other parts of Spain.

The songs of Spain divide themselves into four groups. The Basque, the music of Biscay and Navarre, unlike any music of which we have told you, is irregular in rhythm, melody, and scale, and the *jota* is one of its characteristic dances. Galicia and Castile have gay, bright, strong marked dance rhythms as may be seen from their characteristic *boleros* and *seguidillas*. Andalusian music and that of Southern Spain is perhaps the most beautiful of all, for here we find the influence of the Oriental music to a marked degree, in the use of the scale, in florid ornament, and in the richness of the rhythm; the dances *fandangos*, *rondeñas* and *malagueñas* are thought to be finer than the songs. The guitar is the king of instruments in Andalusia and how Spanish it is! The fourth group of songs is from Catalonia of French influence and less Spanish than the others.

The Ballad and the Ballet

In the English language we have the word *ballad*, which means a long poem in which a story is told. We also use the French word *ballet*, for a dance on the stage. These two words come from the same root, and show that at one time ballads and dance tunes were practically the same thing.

The English dance-song, the "round" or the same dance in France called the *ronde*, was a popular dance for many centuries, some of which are most amusing and curious. One dance-tune from the 12th century has Latin words; there is also a well known tune, Sellenger's Round, from the collection called the *Fitzwilliam Virginal Book.* Another famous ballad (dance) was *Trenchmore*, a good sample of English folk dance at the end of the 16th century:

TRENCHMORE

Wil-ly, pry-thee go to bed. For thou wilt have a drow-sy head; To-morrow we must be hunt-ing, And be-times be stir-ring. With a hey trol-ly lol-ly lo-ly-ly lo-ly-ly lo-ly-ly lo-ly-ly lo-ly-ly Hey, ho,— tro-lo-ly lo-ly-ly lo!

An English writer (how childlike was his fun!) in 1621 says of *Trenchmore*, "Who can withstand it? be we young or old, though our teeth shake in our heads like virginal jacks (see page 310), or stand parallel asunder like the arches of a bridge, there is no remedy; we must dance Trenchmore over tables, chairs, and stools!"

THE MORRIS DANCE

The English Morris Dance is a sort of pageant accompanied by dancing. It may have come from the *Morisco*, a Moorish dance popular in Spain and France, or perhaps from the Matassins, also called Buffoons, who did a dance in armor, which may have come from the Arabs. This dance of the Buffoons, popular in France during the 16th and 17th centuries, was performed by four men with swords, and bells attached to their costumes, used also

in the Morris Dance. It may have come into England at
the end of the 14th century, but in the 15th it was flourish-
ing. First it was given as a part of the May festival and
the characters who took part in it were a Lady of the May,
a Fool, a Piper, and two or more dancers. The dance then
became a part of the *Robin Hood* pageant, and the dancers
were called after the characters of the Robin Hood ballad:
Robin Hood, Friar Tuck, Little John, and Maid Marian.
Later, a hobby-horse, a dragon, four marshals, and other
characters were added. The Puritans stopped the Morris
Dance as they thought it too frivolous, and it was never
so popular again.

The Cushion Dance

In the *Story of Minstrelsy* is quoted a description of the
Cushion Dance from *The Dancing Master* (1686):
"This dance is begun by a single person (either a man or
woman), who, taking a cushion in hand, dances about the
room, and at the end of the tune stops and sings, 'This
dance it will no further go.' The musician answers, 'I
pray you, good sir, why say you so?' Man: 'Because
Joan Sanderson will not come too.' Musician: 'She must
come too, and she shall come too, and she must come
whether she will or no.' Then he lays down the cushion
before the woman, on which she kneels, and he kisses her,
singing, 'Welcome, Joan Sanderson, welcome, welcome.'
Then she rises, takes up the cushion, and both dance, singing, 'Prinkum-prankum is a fine dance!'" Why not try it?

Thomas Morley (1597) wrote of a kind of dance-part-
song called *villanelle* or *ballete*. "These and all other kinds
of light musick, saving the madrigal, are by a general name
called *aires*. There be also another kind of ballets commonly called *Fa-la's*. . . ."

When printing was invented these ballads (or ballets)

appeared in such quantities, that they became a nuisance. Any subject or event was made into a ballad. They were usually printed on single sheets so that an instrument like the viol could play the air, and were carried around in baskets and sold for a trifle. Ballad-singing in the streets took the place of the older minstrels, but the newer fashion never reached the dignity of the bards. These ballads were used as dances.

Both Henry VIII and Queen Mary issued edicts forbidding the printing of books, ballads, and rhymes, probably because many were political ballads uncomplimentary to them. In Elizabeth's reign the edict was removed, and many of these dance-songs are found in the plays of Shakespeare and are sung today in concerts as examples of English folk music.

Many of the better ones have been preserved for us in the *Fitzwilliam Virginal Book*, which is often wrongly called *Queen Elizabeth's Virginal Book*, and in Playford's *English Dancing Master* in which there are ninety-five songs used for dancing; they are also to be heard in the *Beggar's Opera* which contains sixty-nine airs, among which may be mentioned *Sally in our Alley*, *Bonny Dundee*, *Green Sleeves*, *Lilliburlero*, *Over the Hills and Far Away*, etc. John Gay gathered these folk songs and dances into *The Beggar's Opera* in 1727, and it was orchestrated by J. C. Pepusch. In 1920 it was revived with great success in London and New York.

Tiersot (an authority on French folk music) has shown that Adam de la Hale probably wrote the play of *Le Jeu de Robin et Marion* and then strung together a number of popular tunes, many of far older date, to suit his words. So this pastoral-comedy may be the oldest collection of French folk-tunes in existence.

In France, when a dance-air became popular, the rhymers made up words to fit the music; this was called *parodying* it. Our use of the word "parody" means to make fun of something, but at that time, the word meant to adapt words to a melody. One of the early French writers translated the Psalms for use in the Church, and these very Psalms which were dedicated to François I, the King, were "parodied," so that the people sang them to their favorite dance-tunes,— *courantes*, *sarabandes* and *bourrées*. This happened at a time when church music was being popularized, and one hears queer tales of the use of popular songs in the masses and motets of the 14th and 15th centuries. It sounds sacrilegious to us, doesn't it?

In spite of all the mixing-up of tunes and words, the folk dances of France, Italy, Spain, Germany, etc., besides being music of the people were the parents of a most important kind of composition. Just to keep you from being too curious, the name of this important musical form is the Suite.

(8) Funeral Songs and Songs for Mourning

All people from the savage state to the most civilized have had their funeral songs and songs for mourning which have been characteristic of the day and age to which they belonged and revealed many tribal and racial beliefs, superstitions and customs.

(9) Narratives, Ballads and Legends

We shall not tarry long on this subject for it has been covered in the chapter on Troubadours and Minnesingers.

All primitive races used this means of teaching and preserving their tribal history, legends, etc., of telling the news of the day and of praising their over-lords. Many hundreds of volumes of ballads of all countries are to be found and are most useful as well as entertaining in the story of mankind.

Among the most famous narratives known to us are: the *Sagas* and *Eddas* and *Runes* of the Northlands; the *Kalevala* of Finland; the *Percy Reliques* of Britain; the *Odyssey* and *Iliad* of ancient Greece; the *Song of Roland* of France, *Beowulf* of the Anglo-Saxons, and others, many of which have been translated and simplified for young readers.

CHAPTER X

National Portraits in Folk Music

THERE is one particularly lovely thing about folk songs and dances and that is the natural labels which they bear, marking them as belonging to France, Spain, Germany, Russia and so on. As with people, they all have similarities and yet no two are the same in looks or in actions. It would not take you long to know whether you were hearing a Spanish folk dance, an Irish Jig, a Russian Hopak, a Norwegian Halling or an American Foxtrot, because each has its own kind of rhythm and melody.

Some nations have gay, bright folk music, and others have sad, mournful music. In northern countries where living is hard on account of the long, dark, cold winters, and the people are forced to spend much time in-doors and away from neighbors, where money and food are scarce, they are likely to be sad and lonely. In the centuries gone by they made up songs that pictured their lives and their surroundings. On the other hand, in countries where the sun shines most of the time, where people live out of doors, are happy, and have many friends and much fun, the music is gayer and usually lighter. This is why the music of Finland, Sweden, Norway and northern Russia is so much in minor keys, and seems grey, and why the music of Italy, Spain, France and other southern countries is in major

keys and seems rosier in color and happier in mood. Other
reasons, too, for sad folk music is oppression, harsh rulers
and harsh laws. So the Finns and Russians, the American
negroes and the Hebrew tribes sang sad songs.

Russian Folk Music

Again you see history in the songs, particularly in the
Russian folk music, which shows us in musical portraits, the
tragedy of their lives under cruel czars and serfdom. They
sang in ancient scales which make the music all the more
mournful to our ears.

The rhythms in these songs are different from those of
romance languages or those derived from Latin, for the
Russians have a language of Slavic birth. The Russians
have some Oriental blood from the Tartars who invaded
Russia and who were descended from Tartar, a Mogul or
Mongol from Asia. When you hear Russian songs that
sound Oriental, you will agree with Rimsky-Korsakov, the
Russian composer, that the Russian, deep down below the
skin is an Oriental even though he has been living in Europe
for many centuries.

In Russia, from the Baltic Sea on the north to the Cau-
casus Mountains on the south, from the sunny slopes of the
Ural Mountains on the west, to the bleak desert wastes of
Kirghiz on the east, these mixed races have a common tie in
their love for folk story and folk music.

Marvelous tales have been handed down by word of
mouth about the river gods and the woodsprites, about the
animals who talked like men, and the ugly old witch, Baba-
Yaga, whose name alone was enough to quiet the naughtiest
child! Through these folk tales you can follow the Russians from the time they were primitive men and pagans
through all their battles and the invasions of barbarous
tribes, to the time when they became Christians and had

to struggle against the Tartars, the Turks and the Poles. All these happenings were put into songs and are the epic, or tale-telling folk music of the Russians.

But one of the most interesting things, we think, in all the growing of music into maturity, is that Russia never had anything but folk music until the 19th century! Music always belonged to the people, and there were no musical scholars making it the possession of the educated classes only.

Tchaikowsky, Rimsky-Korsakov and other Russians took the folk song from its humble surroundings and used it in their compositions, for they realized its beauty and its richness.

The Russians have instruments brought down from very early times, which are found today in no other country. Perhaps you may have heard a Russian *balalaika* orchestra. The *balalaika* is a stringed instrument, with a triangular body and long neck, having three or sometimes four strings, which are plucked and sound something like a guitar. It dates back to the end of the 13th century. They also have an instrument like a mandolin, with three strings, that dates from the 13th century also. It came from Asia at the time of the Mongolian invasion.

Another instrument, a descendant of the Greek *psalterion* and known to have been in Russia since the 9th century, is the *gusslee*. It is something like a zither, and is composed of a hollow box, strung with any number from seven to thirteen up to twenty-four strings. It is held on the lap, and the strings are plucked with the fingers.

There is also a sort of lute or *bandoura* with many strings, dating from the 16th century, played principally by the blind who belong to groups of minstrels. There is also a wooden clarinet, on which one scale can be played. Its special purpose was for use at funerals, and its name, which comes from a word meaning tomb, is *jaleika*.

Finnish Epics

The Finns, who have been dominated frequently in the past by Sweden or Russia, have retained their own characteristic songs. From the *Kalevala*, their narrative poem or epic which ranks with the *Iliad*, *Beowulf* and the *Eddas*, and the *Kanteletar* have come many folk tunes. Both are based on "runos." The Finnish heroes were music makers rather than warriors. The Finns also sing of their beautiful lakes and forests; and they have sleighing songs, spiritual songs and dance songs. The typical rhythm is in five beats. The ancient runos are still accompanied in some districts on the *kantele*, a plucked string instrument probably two thousand years old. The epics and songs have been a rich source of inspiration for Finnish composers.

Poland's Music

The Polish people have loved music as the Russians love it, and although Poland has been reconquered, divided and redivided among the surrounding kingdoms of Europe, it will always keep its own music. So we have another set of Slav songs but with certain rhythmical differences, not found in the music of other nations. (Chapter IX.)

There is an Oriental strain in this music, too, and it must be very ancient indeed, for Oriental tribes have not lived in this country for ages.

In addition to an instrument like the Russian *gusslee*, and a violin like the Arabian *rebab*, the Polish have a clarinet made of wood, called by its old name of *chalumeau*, the lute, and an instrument called the *kobza*, belonging to the bagpipe family. This is of great age, but is still in use among the mountaineers of Carpathia, and is made of goat skin with three pipe attachments. The *kobza* can replace an entire orchestra!

GYPSIES

Gypsies! The name fires our imagination and brings up
pictures of dark-skinned, black-eyed people with glossy
black hair, dressed in gay colored shawls, with bright ker-
chiefs wound around their heads. We think of them as
being on "one grand picnic," living out of doors, cooking
their meals over bonfires in the open, sleeping in their covered wagons or tents, or under the stars, always gay, care-
free and dirty! Then, think of the Gypsy music,—the
dances, the songs, and the wonderful violin playing! So
wild, so weird, so out-of-doors is it, that we are thrilled by
the very thought of it.

Where did these folk come from? Who are they?
What are they? They have spread over most of Europe,
and are found in Hungary, Bohemia, Roumania, Italy,
Spain, Germany, Russia, England, Turkey, and even America. They are a race and they have a language of their own.
Theirs is a mixture of the ancient *Prakrit* or Indian, with
the different languages with which they have come in contact in the course of many centuries. Men who make a
study of the history of languages say, that in their idioms,
they show traces of roving for many centuries in Asiatic
countries, before reaching Europe in or before the 15th century. They are often called "Bohemians" because Bohemia
(Czecho-Slovakia) seems to have been their main European
camping-ground. It is generally agreed that they came
from India and that they are Asiatic, but they got their
name *Gypsy*, a contraction of the word Egyptian, because people at first thought that they came from Egypt.

The Gypsies have an extraordinary gift for music. They
do not study it as an art, as we do, and cannot even read
musical notes, but they imitate and memorize, and reach
a high degree of skill in playing, particularly the violin.
They have such great power of imitation, that they rapidly

learn to play the instruments, and accustom themselves to the folk music they find wherever they wander. However, they always keep something of their own sadness and wildness. In Spain, they accompany themselves on the guitar, and mark the rhythm with castanets, as do the Spaniards themselves, borrowing the Spanish folk songs which they sing in their own way. In Russia, England, Turkey and everywhere they do the same with the folk music of those countries.

The special traits, then, of the music of the Gypsies, are found rather in the way they play, interpret and express the music of others, than as composers of their own music. Yet they use strongly marked rhythms, florid ornamentation, and scales that are Oriental, which show us from where they came. Here is one of their most used scales:

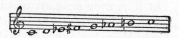

There are many kinds of scales among the Gypsies,—a mixture of the Oriental scale with the pentatonic, and with the European major and minor.

The Hungarian Gypsy has made more music than any other branch of the Gypsy people. In fact, when we hear music that makes us exclaim, "Oh, that is real Gypsy music!" it is almost always Hungarian. At least one quarter of the inhabitants of Hungary, a name which comes from the barbarian tribe of Huns, are Magyars, descendants of Tartars and Mongolians of Asia, who settled in the land of the Huns in the 9th century. In the national music of Hungary, we find it hard to tell just what is Magyar, and what is Gypsy, because the two have intermingled for so long.

The important thing is that this Magyar-Gypsy folk music has been the inspiration of hundreds of trained composers, like Haydn (see the Gypsy Rondo from his piano trio, also arranged for piano alone), Franz Liszt who wrote many famous Hungarian Rhapsodies, Hector Berlioz who made the Hungarian Rakoczy March famous, Johannes Brahms who used many folk songs in his compositions and wrote a set of Hungarian Dances. Even Bach, perhaps the greatest of all composers, seems to have been influenced by the Gypsy music as played on the Hungarian *cembalo*.

No Hungarian Gypsy orchestra is complete without a cembalo, which looks something like an old-fashioned square piano with the top off. This is strung with metal strings covering a range of four octaves, and is played with two small limber hammers. The cembalo players perform with great rapidity and agility; they are able to play scales, arpeggios, trills, and the tricks of Gypsy music with great skill and ease. It is not known just when this instrument came into use, but it is a descendant of the *dulcimer* and *psaltery*, instruments we hear of in the Bible, and in Arabia and Persia, probably brought into Europe during the Crusades.

The *czardas* (pronounced chardas) is an old Hungarian dance in which are all the national characteristics of this folk music, well marked in syncopated rhythms (rhythms out of focus, page 144, Chapter X), strong accents, many ornaments. The Gypsies dance the czardas every time they get a chance, for they love it. It has two contrasting parts, one is called *lassan* which is very slow and sad, and the other called *friska* which is very fast and fiery.

Panna Czinka, a Gypsy Queen, who lived in the 18th century was the daughter of the chief of a band of Gypsies and she inherited his title when she was very young. She married a 'cellist of her tribe and went all through Hungary, Poland and Roumania playing on a wonderful Amati violin, in a very wonderful way. She brought the *Rakoczy March* to the people, although it is not known whether or not she composed it. She always wore men's clothes of most picturesque type and when she died she requested to have her beloved violin buried with her! Long after her death she was still an inspiration to young Gypsy fiddlers, who all longed to play as beautifully as Panna Czinka.

BOHEMIAN FOLK SONG

Bohemia is rich in folk dances, most of which are named for places where they originated or the occasions for which they were used, or from songs by which they are accompanied.

The Bohemians have a bagpipe called the *Dudelsack* and the player is called a *Dudelsackpfeiffer!*

SPANISH AND PORTUGUESE FOLK MUSIC

To the outsider, there is a national color, rhythm, and charm in Spanish music that is unmistakable. We recognize it immediately as Spanish, but the Spaniard will be able to tell you the province from which it came, for there is as much difference between a Castilian song and a Basque, as we find between the speech of a Virginian and a Vermontian! (Chapter IX.)

Portugal, although Spain's next door neighbor, has quite a different music; it is peaceful, tranquil and thoughtful, but doesn't thrill you as does the Spanish music. The Portuguese are calmer and less excitable than the Spaniards, so here again you see the character and qualities of people coming out in the music or what we like to call the musical portrait of a nation. There are no exaggerated rhythms but instead a steady melancholy flow of melody.

FRENCH FOLK MUSIC

The portrait of France that we get from her folk music is much like the one we find in songs of her troubadours and trouvères. In southern France, the folk songs are gay and filled with poetic sentiment and religious feeling; from Burgundy come some of her loveliest Noëls (Christmas songs) and also the drinking songs. From Normandy, come songs of ordinary every-day doings; their mill songs, when sung out in the open on a summer night by the peasants are very beautiful and often show strong religious feeling. Brittany whose inhabitants were originally Celts have a music not unlike the Welsh, Scotch and Irish. Long ago, the famous French writer and musician of the 18th century, Jean Jacques Rousseau, said of it, "The airs are not snappy, they have, I know not what of an antique and sweet mood which touches the heart. They are simple, naïve and often sad—at any rate they are pleasing."

German Folk Music

The *Volkslieder* or folk songs of the Germans are the back-bone of the great classical and romantic periods of the 18th and 19th centuries which made Bach, Mozart, Schubert and Schumann, Wagner and Brahms the music masters of the world.

As early as the 14th century collections of these songs had been made, the subjects of which were mostly historical. By the 16th century music had grown so much that every sentiment of the human heart and every occupation of life had its own song: students, soldiers, pedlars, apprentices all had their songs. These are folk songs of Class A, because their composers forgot to leave their names and no musical archæologist has been able to dig them up. (Page 108. Chapter IX.)

These songs became melodies independent of the accompaniment. They also put the major scale on a firm basis which took the place of the church modes. Their spirit and power were felt in every branch of music, and they supplied melodies for the chorales or hymns, for the lute players and organists in the 15th, 16th and 17th centuries.

Every town had its own band called the *Stadt Pfeifferei* (town pipers). The peasant boys played the fiddle, and the shepherds the *schalmey*, (a kind of oboe). Every festivity was accompanied by song and dance.

Irish Folk Songs

No people in the world have more fancy and imagination, a keener sense of humor, are more fun-loving and more superstitious than the Irish. All these qualities come out in their vast treasure of folk music, which is considered the most beautiful and the most varied of all the music that has come from peasant folk. The subjects cover practically every phase of life from the castle to the cot, and songs of every heading we have included in the last chapter. There are reels, jigs, marches, spinning-tunes, nurse-tunes, planxties (Irish or Welsh melodies for the harp in the nature of a lament), plough-songs and whistles. The Irish folk songs are rich historically as well as beautiful musically.

The form of the Irish folk music is perfect, and is a model of what simple song form has been for several centuries. In fact, all large forms have been built on just such principles of balance and contrast as are found in an Irish folk song called *The Flight of the Earls*.

Scotch and Welsh Tunes

The Scotch and Welsh also have a very rich store of folk song and ballads. Along with the Irish they are children of the early Celts and have brought down to us the music of early times. In all this music we find the pentatonic scale, and a rhythm of this character ♪♫ ♪♫ a dotted note followed by a note of shorter value, which gives a real lilt to Irish, Welsh and Scotch music. We told you about the Welsh bards and their queer violin without a neck, called a *crwth*, and their little harp that was handed around their banquet tables from guest to guest.

The Gaelic music, or that of the Scotch Highlands, dates back to prehistoric times. You have seen a Scotch Highlander in his plaid and kilties playing on his bagpipe, and it has a special kind of scale (two pentatonic scales put together) like this:

G A B   D E   G
  A B C#   E F#   A

and a drone bass (one tone that does not change and is played all through the piece) which makes it hard to get the same effect on the piano. Scotch bagpipes are heard in districts where the milk-maids and serving folk get together in the "ingle," and still "lilt" in the good old-fashioned way.

The thing that makes us know Scotch music from any other is a queer little trick of the rhythm called the *snap* in which a note of short value is followed by a dotted note of longer value, instead of the other way around which is more commonly found. Thus: 🎵 but the two ways are always combined, thus: 🎵 and so on. If you want to make up a real Scotch tune yourself, just play this rhythm up and down the black keys of the piano from F# to the next F#!

Many of the lovely poems of Robert Burns have been set to old Scotch airs. He saved many of the old songs, for he gathered the remains of unpublished old ballads and songs, and snatches of popular melodies, and with genius gave life to the fragments he found. In his own words,

"I have collected, begged, borrowed and stolen all the songs I could meet with."

Canadian Folk Songs

Canada has the folk songs of the *habitant* which are French in character. They are very beautiful and full of romance and many of them can be traced back to France. Many, however, were born in Canada and reveal the hearts of people who lived in the great lonely spaces of a new country.

English Folk Songs

Most of the English folk songs are very practical accounts of the doings of the people. The English seemed more interested in human beings than in Nature, like the Scotch and Irish, or in romantic love songs like the Latin races in Spain, France and Italy. The English had to be practical for they were always leaders and at the head of things, while the Scots and Irish were further away from the center and rush of life and so went to Nature for their subjects.

There are about five thousand English folk songs which sing of the English milk-maid and her work, the carpenter, the hunter and his hounds, and hunting calls. They have the Morris Dance tunes, the May-day songs, the sailor's chanties, they even sing of criminals famous in history and always very definitely tell the full name and whereabouts of a character in a song. They also have songs of poachers (those who hunt on land forbidden them), of murderers and hangmen as well as shepherds and sailors. But England's finest songs are the Christmas carols which sing of the birth of Jesus. So, if they sang little of Nature they did sing of man and God and have given us much that is beautiful and worth while.

OLD ENGLISH CAROL

FROM THE TIME OF HENRY IV, OR EARLIER

Lullay! lullay! lytel child, myn owyn dere fode,
How xalt thou sufferin be nayled on the rode.
So blyssid be the tyme!

Lullay! lullay! lytel child, myn owyn dere smerte,
How xalt thou sufferin the sharp spere to Thi herte?
So blyssid be the tyme!

Lullay! lullay! lytel child, I synge all for Thi sake,
Many on is the scharpe schour to This body is schape.
So blyssid be the tyme!

Lullay! lullay! lytel child, fayre happis the befalle,
How xalt thou sufferin to drynke ezyl and galle?
So blyssid be the tyme!

Lullay! lullay! lytel child, I synge al beforn,
How xalt thou sufferin the scharp garlong of thorn?
So blyssid be the tyme!

Lullay! lullay! lytel child, gwy wepy Thou so sore,
Thou art bothin God and man, gwat woldyst Thou be more?
So blyssid be the tyme!

(From the Sloane MSS. Quoted from *The Study of Folk Songs*, by
Countess Martinengo-Cesaresco).

AMERICAN FOLK MUSIC

We come now to a question that has been the subject of
many arguments and debates. Many claim that we have
no folk music in the United States, and others claim that
we have. It would take a whole volume to present both
sides and we must reduce it to a sugar-coated capsule.

Although we know that Stephen Foster wrote *Old Folks
at Home, The Old Kentucky Home, Uncle Ned, Massa's in
the Cold, Cold Ground,* and *Old Black Joe,* they express so

perfectly the mood and spirit of the people that they are true folk songs. Harold Vincent Milligan in his book on Stephen Foster says: "Every folk-song is first born in the heart and brain of some one person, whose spirit is so finely attuned to the voice of that inward struggle which is the history of the soul of man, that when he seeks for his own self-expression he at the same time gives a voice to that vast 'mute multitude who die and give no sign.'"

And again speaking of Stephen Foster, Mr. Milligan says: "Although purists may question their right to the title 'folk songs' his melodies are truly the songs of the American people."

The folk music of which we have told you has been the music portraits of different peoples such as the Russian, the Polish, the French, the German, the English, the Irish and so on. If there has been a mixture of peoples or tribes as in England where there were Britons, Danes, Angles, Saxons and Normans, it happened so long ago that they have become molded into one race. We are all Americans but we are not of one race, and we are still in the process of being molded into one type.

We unite people of all nations under one flag and one government, but we have been sung to sleep and amused as children by the folk songs of the European nations to which our parents and grandparents belonged! And so we have heard from childhood *Sur le Pont d'Avignon, Schlaf Kindlein Schlaf, Wurmland, The Volga Boat Song, Sally in our Alley*, or *The Wearing of the Green*, none of which is American.

In spite of all these obstacles to the growth of a folk music in America, we have several sources from which they have come.

As our earliest settlers in Virginia and New England were English, they brought with them many of their folk songs and some of these have remained unchanged in the districts where people of other nations have not penetrated. *The Lonesome Tunes* of the Kentucky mountains, also of Tennessee, the Carolinas and Vermont are examples of this kind of English folk song in America.

In Louisiana which was settled by the French, we find a type of folk song that is very charming. It is a combination of old French folk song with negro spiritual, and is brought to us by the Creoles.

In California there is a strong Spanish flavor in some of the old ballads that date from the time of the Spanish Missions. There are also mining songs of the "days of '49," including *Oh Susannah*, by Stephen Foster, and we defy you to get rid of the tune if once it "gets you!"

Then there are cow-boy songs of the Plains, *The Texas Rangers*, *The Ship that Never Returned*, *The Cow-boy's Lament* and *Bury me not on the Lone Prairie;* the Lumberjack songs of Maine; the well known air of the *Arkansas Traveller*, which was a funny little sketch for theatre of a conversation between the Arkansas traveller and a squatter which is interrupted by snatches of a tune; and in addition a whole book full of songs sung in the backwoods settlements, hunting cabins and lumber camps in northern Pennsylvania.

So if you seek, you can find a large number of folk songs without going to the Indian or the Negro.

The Civil War brought out a number of new national songs among them *Glory Hallelujah* and *Dixie*. *Dixie* was written in 1859 as a song and "walk-around" by the famous minstrel Dan Emmett, and became a war song by accident. It had dash and a care-free spirit, and the rollicking way it pictured plantation life attracted the soldiers of the South when they were in the cold winter camps in the North. Its rhythm is so irresistible that it makes your hands and feet go in spite of yourself. Besides these two the soldiers of the Civil War marched to *Rally Round the Flag, Boys,*

Tramp, Tramp, Tramp, the Boys are Marching, Home, Sweet Home, Lily Dale, The Girl I Left Behind Me, Hail Columbia and *The Star Spangled Banner.*

We have told you so much about the Indian and his song that it is unnecessary now to dwell at length on his music. Of course some American composers have used Indian folk legend and music, but after all it remains the musical portrait of the Red Man and has not become the heart language of the white man.

We have, however, a real folk-expression that has had a great deal of influence on our popular music and will probably help to create a serious music to which we can attach the label "Made in America," and that is the music of the American Negro.

In Chapter II we showed you what the Negro had brought from his native Africa, and also that he had been influenced by his contact with the white race. His music is not the result of conscious art and of study but is a natural outburst in which he expresses his joys and sorrows, his tragedies and racial oppression. Also we find rhythms, melody and form that have grown as a wild flower grows, and are different from any we have met heretofore.

Mr. Krehbiel in his book *Afro-American Folksongs* says of the Negro slave songs: "They contain idioms which were transplanted hither from Africa, but as song they are the product of American institutions; of the social, political and geographical environment within which their creators were placed in America, of the influences to which they were subjected in America, of the joys, sorrows and experiences which fell to their lot in America."

The Negro has cultivated, like all races, songs and dances. As we said of the Russian, his song is sad and full of tragedy, but the dance is gay, wild and primitive. From the dance of the Negro we borrowed the rhythm formerly called ragtime, which is now jazz. The principle of the Negro rhythm

is syncopation, that is, the accent is shifted to the unac-
cented part of a measure or of a beat, like this,— ♩ ♩ ♩,
♪ ♩ ♪, ♫♫. All sorts of combinations are possible in
this rhythm, and it is this variety that is fascinating in a
good jazz tune.

The banjo is the instrument of the southern plantation
Negro, and when a crowd gathers for a "sing" or a dance,
the hands and feet take the place of drums and keep
time to the syncopated tune and is called, "patting
Juba."

A curious dance was the "shout" which flourished in
slave days. It took place on Sunday or on prayer meeting
nights and was accompanied by hymn singing and shouting
that sounded from a distance like a melancholy wail.
After the meeting the benches were pushed back, old and
young, men and women, stood in the middle of the floor
and when the "sperichel" (or spiritual) was started they
shuffled around in a ring. Sometimes the dancers sang
the "sperichel" or they sang only the chorus, and for a
distance of half a mile from the praise house the endless
thud, thud of the feet was heard.

In the beautiful Spiritual, the song of the Negro, we see
also the syncopated rhythm. The religious song is practically the only song he has, and he sings it at work, at
play, at prayer, when he is sick and his friends sing it after
he is dead. To our ears the words are crude and homely,
but always reveal a fervent religious nature as well as a
childlike faith.

No doubt you have heard *Nobody Knows the Trouble I
See*, *Deep River*, *Swing Low Sweet Chariot*, *Go Down Moses*,
Weeping Mary and many others.

Such a wealth of feeling and beauty could not fail to
leave its mark in the land where it was born.

Just how it will bear fruit we cannot say, but it is making

its appeal more and more, not only to the American, but to the foreign composers as well, and they believe that this music,—the syncopated rhythm that the American is at last developing in his own way—in spite of its humble origin, is the one new thing that America has given to the growth of music, and they envy us that wealth of rhythm that seems to be born in the American.

Music Becomes a Youth

CHAPTER XI

Makers of Motets and Madrigals—Rise of Schools
15th and 16th Centuries

WHILE most of the music before 1600 was vocal, instrumental music had begun much earlier to plant seeds which later blossomed as a great art. In the 13th century the minstrels and town pipers supplied music played on vielle, hurdy-gurdy, and trumpet, trombone and cornet. In the 14th, Paris had professional instrumentalists who formed a regular musicians union! German cities had their *Stadt-pfeifereien* (associations of town wind instrument players). In the 15th century, a blind organist, Conrad Paumann, in Nuremberg, wrote the oldest treatise on instrumental composition. It contains many arrangements for organ or clavier of sacred songs, dances, and also several preludes.

"Like children who break their toys to see how they work, they learned to break up the musical phrases into little bits which they repeated, which they moved from one part to another; in this way the dividing of themes (tunes) came, which led them to the use of imitation and of canon; these early and innocent gardeners finally learned how to make the trees of the enchanted garden of music bear fruit. Still timid, they kept the custom for three centuries of making all their pieces from parts of plain-song or of a popular song, instead of inventing subjects for themselves;

thus, what is prized today above everything else—the making of original melodies—was secondary in the minds of the musicians, so busy were they trying to organize their art, so earnestly were they trying to learn the use of their tools." (Translated from the French from *Palestrina*, by Michel Brenet).

By spending their time this way, they added much to the science of music, for these vocal works were full of interesting discoveries which composers used later, as we shall see, in fugues, canons, suites and many other forms.

The most popular forms of composition during these two centuries (the 15th and the 16th) were the motet for Church and the madrigal for outside the Church.

WHAT A MOTET IS

The *motet* gets its name from the French word *mot* meaning word, or the Latin word for motion. It dates back to the 13th century, and was called *motetus*. The first motets were used in the Church in the 13th and 14th centuries. Although crude to our ears, they are interesting historically. The composers of the different schools of this period wrote many motets. At first, any part of the Mass but the Credo, could be in motet form. Later, motets were not part of the Mass itself, but of the church ritual, varying with the day or season.

This motet, or part song, used as its central theme a tune already familiar to its hearers; this tune, the *cantus firmus*, was frequently a bit from a Gregorian chant or from a mass, but sometimes it was a snatch from a dance song or a folk song, or it may have been a troubadour love song with anything but the right kind of words for the Church. The text for one part was often from the Bible and for other parts very coarse words from popular tunes. Imagine singing them at the same time! Still more amazing, the words of the sacred song were sung in Latin and the popular song was sung in whatever language it happened to be written! Can you think of anything more ridiculous! The masses came to be known by the names from which the tune was taken and nearly every composer including the great Palestrina wrote masses on a popular tune of the day, *L'homme armé* (The Man in Armor). Yet they were all quite different, so varied had become the science of writing counterpoint.

Josquin des Près (1450–1521) the Flemish composer wrote a motet, *Victimae Paschali*, which is written around an old Gregorian plain-chant, interwoven with two popular *rondelli* (in French *roundel* from which come our terms *roundelay* and *rondo*) and a *Stabat Mater* of his. The *cantus firmus*, or subject of this motet is another secular or popular air.

The popular composers returned the compliment and took themes or tunes from church music and put secular words to them. History repeats itself, for someone stole a measure from Handel's *Messiah* and used it in *Yes, We Have No Bananas*, and, unfortunately, popular writers "swing" the beautiful music of Chopin, Schubert, Debussy, and others.

Yet this music—the child we are watching grow up—because of mixing up sacred and profane music soon had to be reformed.

The northern part of France seems to have been the birthplace of the motet; a little later it found its way into Italy where some of the finest music of the period was written, and the Italian influence reached into Spain in the middle of the 15th century; at the end of the century the Venetian school had spread its work into Germany. In the 17th century the name *motet* was given to a kind of composition between a cantata and an oratorio, but it had nothing to do with the famous motet of the 15th and 16th centuries which we are discussing.

To show you how clever the men were in these days, one composer wrote a motet in thirty-six parts!

In the Library of the Sistine Chapel in Rome are volumes containing the motets of the 14th century, copied, of course, by hand in notes large enough to be seen and read by the whole choir! These books are beautifully decorated in gold and lovely colors, or illuminated, and are of great value.

MADRIGALS OR POPULAR MOTETS

All music of this period not composed for the Church had the general name of Madrigal, but a real madrigal was a vocal composition for from three to six parts written on a secular subject, which often gave to the work a grace and lightness not in the motet. The vocal madrigals were to the music lovers of that day what chamber music is today, for instruments were hardly used without singing. Later, the lute played the chief melody with the voice, and it was only a step to have other instruments play the other parts of the madrigal. The instruments played a section of the composition alone while waiting for a solo singer to appear. He sang a part of the madrigal that was later called the *air* and the instrumental part was called the *ritournelle*, which literally meant that in this section of the work, the singer returned from "off-stage" where he had awaited his turn. By the end of the 16th century it had become the custom for motets as well as madrigals to have a solo *air* or aria, and an instrumental *ritournelle*, and this was the beginning of chamber-music,—a very great oak which grew from a very little acorn.

In the first printed music-books are many of the madrigals of the early period. We will tell you of the composers of this period separately, but remember that they all wrote practically the same kind of music,—masses, motets, and madrigals, but all with the subject borrowed from something they knew and with many parts for the voices. Often, too, the same tunes were used for Church and outside the Church. For this reason much music was published without the words, so that the singers could use sacred or profane words as they wished.

Strange as it may seem, it was the folk songs and ballads and not the *learned* church music, that had originality and came freely and sincerely from the hearts of the people.

Songs in Dance Form

Because the contrapuntal writings were serious (can you imagine dancing to a canon?) a new kind influenced by folk music grew up among these people who were naturally gay and jolly and wished to be entertained. Songs for three and four parts appeared, more popular in style and simpler in form than the church motet. These were the descendants of the music of the troubadours, and were in dance form, such as the French *chanson*, the *villanelle*, the Italian *canzona*, *canzonetta* or little canzona, *frottola*, *strambotto* and the German *lied*. Many of these songs in dance form later inspired composers to write music for instruments alone, so that people danced to music without singing. These dance songs were called *branles*, *pavanes*, *gaillardes*, *courantes*, *forlanes*, *rigaudons sarabandes*, *gigues*, *gavottes* and many other names.

The Lute

The favorite instrument of the 15th and 16th centuries was the lute. It fought for first place with the vielle, the viol, the harp, the psalterion and the portative organ, but won the fight and took its place beside the most famous singers of the day, sometimes for accompanying and again reaching the dignity of soloist, as we told you above. In the 15th century it took the form, which we see most often represented in pictures and in museums, with its six strings, graceful round body, and long neck bent back as you can see in plate opposite page 127 already described. As time went on this lute was made larger and strings were added until at the beginning of the 17th century, it was replaced by an instrument called the arch-lute or theorbo, which had twenty-four strings, a double neck, and two sets of tuning pins.

The spinets or virginals, the great-aunts of our piano-fortes first came into vogue in the 15th and 16th centuries.

TABLATURE

There was a notation called Tablature used in the 16th and 17th centuries to write down the music for lute and other stringed instruments such as the viol, cittern, theorbo. You will find, in pictures of Tablature, lines which look like our staff, but they do not form a staff, but simply represent the *strings* of the instrument. These lines vary according to the number of strings, from four for the cittern to six for the lute. The notation showed, not the position and fingering as we write music, but the position and fingering of frets and strings. Instead of *neumes* or notes you will find the alphabet up to the letter *j*, figures and queer dots and lines and slurs, but each sign had its own meaning and was important to the lutenist.

RISE OF SCHOOLS

As music outgrows childhood, Schools of Music are started. But these are not like the schools for educational purposes but are rather music groups or centers. Suppose you were a composer and lived in New York and knew a dozen or so musicians who were writing the same kind of music as you; the music, if good enough to be known and played, would be called the New York School, or it might be called the 20th century School! Or, if you were important enough to be imitated, it would be called the Smith School, if that happened to be your name, just as those who imitated Wagner were said to be of the Wagner School, and so it goes. Not a school to go to, but a school to belong to!

"What makes these schools start?" we can hear you ask. Many things. Sometimes people are oppressed by their rulers and in trying to forget their troubles, they naturally want to express themselves in the art they know, and in this way groups get together and a school grows. Sometimes the Church is the cause of schools of music, literature, and art, and we shall see in this chapter how the Church influenced the schools of music of this time and made it one of the most important periods in this story. Sometimes, too, the climate has caused the development of different styles as we told you in the chapter on folk music. It often happens too, that a great man or a great school in one country affects other countries.

FRANCO-FLEMISH SCHOOL

The first real group of composers to be called a "School" lived in the part of Europe that today covers the north of France, Belgium and the Netherlands. The composers who were born from 1400 to about 1530, in the so-called Low Countries belonged to this school. Some writers claim that there were three schools, and that the Franco-Flemish or Burgundian is a bridge between the Paris school of the 13th century and the Netherlands school of the 16th. But it would be difficult to say when one school began and another ended, as they all wrote much the same kind of music. The older composers were the teachers of the younger, and many of these masters of the north of Europe went to Italy, Spain, France, and to Germany, and spread the knowledge of the "new art" of counterpoint and vocal poly-melody (many melodies) and filled positions of importance in the churches. They were considered such splendid teachers, that many of the young students of other nationalities went to what is now Holland and Belgium to be taught.

Zeelandia, a Hollander, an important master in this new school, tried to get rid of the awkward intervals, fourths and fifths, which were used in organum (see Chapter VII), and was the first composer to give the subject or *cantus firmus* to the soprano voice instead of the tenor. Doesn't it seem strange that it took so long to let the soprano have the main tune?

But the most important composer of his period (1400–1474) was Guillaume Dufay, from Flanders, who was a chorister in the Papal choir (choir of the Pope) in Rome. He made the rules and imitation for the canon (a grown up round) and he was the first composer to use the folk song *L'homme armé* (The Man in Armor) in a mass.

The next important name is Jan Okeghem (1430–1495), a Hollander, who improved the science of counterpoint and of fugue writing. We have already mentioned his canon for thirty-six voices (page 149), and he wrote some puzzle canons, for use in secret guilds. No one could solve these without the key and they were much harder than the world's best cross-word puzzles. He tried to make music express the beauty he felt, and not merely be mathematical problems in tone, as was much of the music of his day. He was the teacher of several famous musicians among whom were Obrecht (who became the teacher of Erasmus, the learned Dutch religious reformer), Tinctoris, Josquin des Près, Loyset Compère, and Agricola who spent most of his life in Spain and Portugal. In fact, Okeghem taught so many,

that the art of counterpoint was taken into all countries by
his pupils, so he can be called the founder of all music schools
from his own day to the present.   He was chaplain at the
French court and, during forty years there, served three
Kings of France.

Tinctoris, a Belgian (1446–1511), founded the first public
school of music in Italy at Naples, and wrote a dictionary
of musical terms.

But the "Prince" of musicians of the 15th century, was
Josquin des Près, or de Près (1455–1525).   He was a pupil
of Okeghem, and although born in Flanders, spent much of
his life away from his home; he was a member of the Papal
choir in Rome and afterwards lived at the court of Louis
XII in France.   He also wrote a mass on the theme of
L'homme armé, and many other masses, motets, and madrigals.   Luther said of him,—"Josquin des Près is a master of
the notes.   They do as he wills.   Other composers must do
as the notes will.   His compositions are joyous, gentle and
lovely; not forced, not constrained, nor slavishly tied to the
rules, but free as the song of a finch."

Josquin des Près had many pupils, and among them were
many who became famous.   Clement Janequin, or Jannequin, is one of the best known from his music, and least
known from the facts of his life.   Most of his works are of a
secular nature and are original and amusing, and so perfect
that some people thought him as good as his popular teacher.
He was one of the first serious composers to imitate the
sounds of Nature in music!

One of his famous madrigals is the *Chant des Oiseaux*
(Song of the Birds) in which he tries to represent the sounds
of birds of all kinds.   In the middle of the piece is heard the
hoot of an owl; the birds get together and chase away the
poor hated owl, calling him a traitor, then all is quiet again.
Another of his pieces is named *The Cackle of Women!*   Another famous one still frequently sung is the *Battle of*

Marignan (1515), a lively piece in varied rhythm, which was one of the most popular army songs of the 16th century. The words and music imitate, first the tools of war, then the noise of the cannons and the crackling of the guns, the joy of victory for the French, and the retreat of the Swiss.

Another eminent pupil of Josquin des Près was Nicolas Gombert, of Bruges. Like Jannequin, he was a Nature lover, and many of his madrigals imitate its sounds. Secular music was now popular, and his works show that a composer was allowed to give expression to his feelings and ideas, for the prejudices of the earlier church music had disappeared.

Jean Mouton, a native of Metz, was in the chapel of Louis XII and of François I, King of France. His style was like his master's and some of his works were supposed to have been composed by Josquin.

WILLAERT FOUNDS THE VENETIAN SCHOOL

Willaert was a pupil of both Josquin and Mouton. He was chapel master at St. Mark's in Venice, and was so famous as a teacher that he attracted many good musicians, and became the founder of the famous Venetian school of composers. He wrote many madrigals, some of them on verses of Petrarch, the Italian poet. This work was accomplished after he was sixty years old!

Willaert was the first organist to use two and sometimes three choirs, each singing in four parts. Sometimes they sang in combination and sometimes answered each other antiphonally. According to Clarence G. Hamilton in his book *Outlines of Music History*, the idea of these choirs was probably suggested to Willaert because there were in St. Mark's two very fine organs. In this you see the influence instruments have on the growth of musical compositions.

Willaert made use too, of the idea that the different parts could be sounded together to form chords, instead of individual melodies as was the case in poly-melody (polyphony or in the contrapuntal style). This was a new idea, for up to this time the musicians had been writing horizontal music, the melodic line looking something like this:

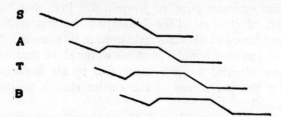

Willaert's idea, which probably came from folk-song and from some of the hymns that Luther created, was colonnade-like (see Chapter VII) or perpendicular music, which we might illustrate like this:

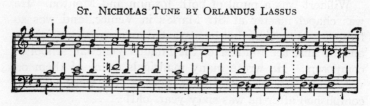

St. Nicholas Tune by Orlandus Lassus

in which each note is part of a chord, with the melody at the top. This is how Harmony, or the science of chords, came into use as we know it now.

Among Willaert's pupils were Cyprian de Rore of Antwerp, who succeeded his master at St. Mark's, and most of his works were madrigals which gained him much fame in Italy. He was one of the first to use the chromatic scale (scale in semi-tones like black and white keys on the piano).

An Italian, Zarlino, pupil of Willaert, must be mentioned here, not as a writer of music but as the author of three most important books on harmony and theory. These books seem to have been very much needed for they were reprinted many times. Another Italian pupil of Willaert was Andrea Gabrieli, like his master, also an organist at St. Mark's.

The greatest contribution from this Venetian school was its important use of instrumental music as an independent art, thus giving music a great push forward.

A composer whose motets and madrigals we still hear frequently is Jacob Arcadelt, a Netherlander, who spent most of his life in Italy, and shared with Willaert the glory of being one of the founders of the Venetian school. He was a singer at the court of Florence, singing master to the choir boys at St. Peter's in Rome, and then he became a member of the Papal choir.

The life of Claude Goudimel seems, from the little we know, to have been dramatic. He is supposed to have been in Rome and to have taught Palestrina, greatest composer of the age. Many now claim that he never was in Rome and was not the teacher of Palestrina! Even his birthplace is disputed. What is certain, however, is that he met his death in the massacre of the Huguenots (Protestants) at Lyons in 1572. He wrote many settings of Calvinist Psalms by Clement Marot which work led to his being a victim of the massacre.

Sweelinck Founds 17th Century Organ School

One of the last of the Netherland school was Jan Sweelinck (1562–1621), the greatest organist of his time. He had so many pupils from every country in Europe, that he became the founder of a very famous school of organists. Among them were Scheidt, Reinken of whom the story is

told that Bach as a boy walked miles to hear him play,
and Buxtehude, a Dane, one of the greatest, and an older
contemporary of Bach. Sweelinck perfected the Organ Fugue
which Bach later made more beautiful than any other composer. Sweelinck's talent and work were so deeply appreciated in his home, Amsterdam, that the merchants of that
city gave him a generous income for his old age. A splendid
thing to have done!

The Great Lassus

The greatest composer of this Netherland school was
Orlandus Lassus, or Orlando di Lasso, or Roland de Lattre,
take your choice! He was born in Mons, Belgium, some
time between 1520 and 1532. When he was a child he had
such a beautiful voice that he was kidnapped three times
from the school where he lived with the other choristers.
The third time he stayed with the Governor of Sicily,
Ferdinand Gonzague, and went from Sicily to Milan, then
to Naples and then to Rome where he became director of
the choir of one of the most celebrated churches. After
this he went to England and to France and finally returned
to Antwerp. In 1557 he was invited to the court of the
Duke of Bavaria in Munich to direct the chamber music.
There he married a lady of the court and had two daughters
and four sons, who were musicians. Later he was made
master of the chapel, and the men who lived at that time
said he was an inspiring choir director, a great composer,
and was deeply reverenced and loved. The Duke was a
splendid helper and patron of music, and encouraged him
to make their choir of ninety men one of the finest in the
world. Their lives were made so pleasant that a book,
published in 1568, says, "had the Heavenly Choir been
suddenly dismissed, it would straightway have made for
the court of Munich, there to find peace and retirement!"

Lassus used wind and brass instruments to accompany the voices which were kept quite separate from the strings. At a banquet, the wind instruments were heard during the early courses, then the strings directed by someone else, then, during the dessert, Lassus would direct the singing of the choir. So "chamber music" appears at this point in the growth of music.

At the Duke's suggestion, Lassus wrote music for seven *Penitential Psalms* which were sung to the unhappy King, Charles IX, after the massacre of the Huguenots on St. Bartholomew's eve.

He wrote secular music as well as sacred and showed a keen sense of humor in several of his secular pieces.

Soon after 1574, he wrote a set of twenty-four pieces for two parts: twelve have words and are vocal duets, and the other twelve are without words, to be played on instruments. The two groups are exactly alike in form which shows that many of the motets and madrigals for voices were often played on instruments alone.

The Hymn to St. John from which Guido d'Arezzo took the names of the scale-degrees, was made into a beautiful composition by Lassus; the tenor sings a *cantus firmus* of the tones of the scales, around which are woven many parts in counterpoint.

One festival day there was a violent storm in Munich, and orders were given that the usual procession from the Church through the town should not take place, but should be held inside the Church. As the head of the procession reached the porch of the Church, and the choir started a motet by Lassus, the sun suddenly came out and the procession went on as usual through the town. This was looked upon as a miracle, and whenever fine weather was wanted very much, this motet was chosen! This story does not tell whether the miracle always worked!

In Lassus' later church music, he simplified the complicated contrapuntal style, perhaps because he lived in the country where Luther had introduced the chorale. (Page 166.) Even though Lassus wrote masses and motets for the Catholic Church, he must have heard these new hymns, and was unknowingly influenced by them.

A complete edition of all his works would fill almost sixty volumes. This huge task was so taxing that his over-tired brain finally gave out and during the last five years of his life he did no more composing. He died in 1594.

Orlandus Lassus was the last and one of the greatest of this Netherland, or Franco-Flemish school, that for two hundred years had led the world of music. Music had changed from a cocoon, gradually developing into a radiant butterfly, or, in our book, we should say that music had left childhood and was becoming a stalwart lad.

RONSARD—FRENCH POET

The famous French poet, Pierre de Ronsard, who was born over four hundred years ago (1525), supplied more composers with words for their madrigals than any other poet of his age. He said that without music poetry was almost without grace, and that music without the melody of verse was lifeless. Today poetry and music have become so independent of each other, that many poets object to having verse made a servant of music, and many musicians think that music without words, that is, instrumental music, is the highest type of musical art.

In 1552, Ronsard asked four leading composers to set some of his sonnets to music. Jannequin, Pierre Certon, Claude Goudimel and Muret each composed music for the same ten sonnets. This experiment was so successful, that Ronsard published all the songs in his first volume of poetry. About the time that Shakespeare was born, in England, but long before he had said,

The man that hath no music in his soul
Is fit for treason, stratagem and spoils,

Ronsard wrote in a preface to a collection of songs: "How could one get along with a man who innately hated music? He who does not honor music, is not worthy to see the soft light of the sun."

Others who used Ronsard poems as texts for songs and madrigals were Philip de Monte (or Mons), G. Costeley, organist to Charles IX, de la Grotte, organist to Henri III, and Orlandus Lassus.

The Catholic Mass

For more than a thousand years famous composers have written music for the Roman Catholic liturgy, or public worship, known as the Mass. The officiating minister has dismissed the congregation with the words: "*Ite, missa est*" (Depart! The assembly is dismissed). From this came the word *missa*, Latin for Mass. The High Mass is typical of the various kinds. It is sung and chanted by the officiating priest and the choir. During the early centuries, masses were composed in plainsong, organum, and discant. The first epoch of the "polyphonic Mass" was ushered in by Guillaume de Machaut's mass in four parts (1364) for the coronation of Charles V. The ninth and last epoch includes masses by Palestrina, Haydn, Mozart, Beethoven, Weber, Schubert, Rossini, Gounod, etc.

The changeable parts of the service are according to the feast or season. The Mass, with unchanging Latin texts, is made up of the *Kyrie*, a humble cry for mercy; the *Gloria*, a song of triumphant jubilation; the *Credo*, a profession of faith; the *Sanctus*, a hymn of triumphant adoration, and the *Benedictus*, a greeting of the faithful to the Redeemer, and the *Agnus Dei*, a devotional and gentle plea.

CHAPTER XII

Music Gets a Reprimand—Reformation and Rebirth of Learning—How the Reforms Came to Be

HERE is a little reminder of how music grew:

A scale came into use in Greece about 700 B.C.

It was separated into modes by the Greeks about 400 B.C.

It was adopted by the Romans and by the early Christians and was used until the 10th century A.D. with little change.

450 years before the Christian era was the Golden Age of Pericles in Greece.

450 years after the Christian era was the beginning of the Dark Ages.

Harmony was first attempted about 900 A.D.

Between 900 A.D. and 1400, music made headway slowly.

Music has travelled along two roads,—the Church road and the People's road; they often crossed each other and became very much mixed up. You remember how popular songs had found their way into church music at the time of St. Gregory, and how the people took melodies from the masses, put profane words to them, and sang them in the taverns, at the street corners, in the tournaments and at work.

Early in the 15th century folk songs had again invaded the Church to the point that masses were known by the names of the folk songs from which they were taken. This led to a very important reform, as a result of which Palestrina, the greatest composer of the "Golden Age of Catholic Church Music," wrote his beautiful masses and motets, and Luther, the founder of the Protestant faith, made up hymns that are still sung and loved throughout Christendom.

Many things happened between 1400 and 1600, the period called the Renaissance, or rebirth of the ancient Greek and Roman learning. At this time the people in Italy (later in Spain, France, England and Germany), awakened to study after the Dark Ages of war and conquest. Now the people tried to bring back the literature, drama, music, and sculpture of the Greeks and Romans. Read this list of men whose genius developed through the new learning: Hans Memling, the Flemish painter; Albrecht Dürer, the German painter and wood and copper engraver; Hans Holbein, the German painter; Leonardo da Vinci, Italian artist, engineer and scientist, probably the most gifted man of all time; Michelangelo, the Italian sculptor and poet; Raphael, Correggio and Titian, Italian painters; Cervantes, the Spanish dramatist, author of *Don Quixote;* Edmund Spenser of England, who wrote *The Faery Queen;* Copernicus, the astronomer and Christopher Columbus.

INVENTION OF PRINTING

But the greatest event of this time was Gutenberg's invention of printing (1455) which has spread learning over the face of the earth. Soon people were able to get books cheaper than the hand written scrolls. Until this great moment the monks had been writing by hand all books and music scores. Only the great and wealthy owned them, and very few could read or write, for what would be the sense of learning to read if one had nothing to read? So the invention of printing awakened the desire to know how to read books and to learn poetry, which sharpened people's minds and enlightened them. 12,000 volumes were printed from 1463 to 1471 where perhaps a hundred had been written before.

The first press (wooden type) was set up by Charles VII (1459) in the Sorbonne in Paris, one of the greatest institutions of learning in the world which still attracts students from all countries. The first music was printed (1501) by Ottaviano dei Petrucci in Venice. It was a complete volume of part-music by contemporary Franco-Netherlandish composers. Music was benefited by being printed clearly and many changes were made to make it easier to read. Up to this time it was worse than cross-word puzzles! It seemed to be the object of the composers before the Renaissance to make music look just as difficult as it possibly could, and there are many examples of enigmatical canons which were used in the spirit of games and could be solved only by those having the key to the puzzles.

But now the printers who were learned men in those days, simplified the notation, and did away with many useless signs. People began to read it more easily, and music became more popular. After Ottaviano died, Antonio Gardane and his sons founded a publishing house in Venice, which was most useful to composers. Then Paris and Antwerp began to have fine printers, and in 1542 Ballard was made sole printer of music to the King and nearly all the music through Louis XIV's time (1638–1715) was printed by his descendants. Late in the 17th century the measures were separated by bars as they are today, and when metal was used for type instead of wood, the old square note became oval like ours.

At the beginning of the Renaissance Church music was again mixed with the most vulgar words from popular songs. "The bowsprit got mixed with the rudder sometimes"— as in *The Hunting of the Snark*.

At this time the people were beginning to think and read for themselves, and to question whether the Church had the right to dictate to and control them as it had been doing. They thought, too, that many of the church officers were not good enough, and by degrees the people protesting, broke away from the Roman Church and formed others. Through this protest the Protestant church won its name; this is known as the Reformation. With the new church came the need for new services, new music and new ways of singing.

MARTIN LUTHER, THE REFORMER

"Truth to Nature" was the *slogan* of the Renaissance.

In 1453, the Mohammedans captured Constantinople, and the Christian Church which had been there since the end of the 4th century, was driven out. Many of the learned Christians fled to Central Europe and brought with them a knowledge of Greek literature and art which they taught to the people.

Christopher Columbus, in his search for a passage to India, found a new continent, and in the same way these seekers for "Truth to Nature," although they may not have found exactly what they were looking for, certainly opened gates that swept men and women towards knowledge, appreciation, refinement and culture.

The outstanding person in the Reformation of the Church was Martin Luther (1483–1546) who interests us specially for what he did for the growth of music. Luther was a priest of the Catholic Church, but he was also a German; he believed in a national life free from Church government, and in singing hymns in the language of the people instead of in Latin, in order that the words could be understood. He spoke and wrote openly against certain actions of the Church and for this he was put out of the Church of Rome. But, very soon, he had enough followers to start a church of his own, and one of the first things he did was to make a new music for it. Up to this time the only music in Germany had been some hymns translated from the Latin into the "vernacular," the language of the people, the songs of the Minnesingers and Meistersingers, and a rich crop of folksongs that had appeared in the 14th century. There were also a few composers who had learned to write counterpoint in the Netherlands, Heinrich Isaak, Ludwig Senfl and Heinrich Fink, and they, too, influenced the music of the Reformation.

Luther, a musician himself, knew the love that his countrymen had for their hymns translated into German and for the folksongs, and realized that singing in which the congregation took part would be a power in the church. He had to gather material for new hymns simple enough for the people to sing, and besides he needed new music to replace the Mass. The result of his work is the *chorale,* the foundation of the great German school of music of the 18th and 19th centuries. He was helped in the work of creating these hymns by Johann Walther and Conrad Rupf. The first hymnal (1524) was selected from some of the finest Catholic hymns, Gregorian and Ambrosian melodies, dignified folk-melodies, and some original chorales by Luther himself.

He played the tunes of his chorales on a flute, and Walther wrote them down. He wrote to a friend, "I wish after the example of the Prophets and ancient Fathers of the Church, to make German Psalms for the people, and that is to say, sacred hymns, so that the word of God may dwell among the people by means of song also." The strength and beauty of these hymns can be seen in *Ein' Feste Burg ist unser Gott* (A Mighty Fortress is Our God).

The hymns were harmonized in four parts. They were usually sung in unison (all singing the same thing) with the accompaniment of the organ or a group of instruments. This great change, or revolt, broke the backbone of polyphonic music, freed the spirit of the people, and first brought into use modern scales (major and minor, as we know them). Curiously enough, this Reformed Church Music also brought about the "Golden Age of Catholic Music" with Palestrina as its leading composer.

PALESTRINA—PRINCE OF MUSIC

Martin Luther had hoped to reform the Church but instead founded a new one (another example of Columbus seeking a passage to India). But this action of Luther's was a challenge to the Mother-Church, and steps were taken to reform many customs and practices in the Church itself. As we have pointed out many times, popular tunes with vulgar words had crept into the Church services. These works composed for the Church were used to show the skill of the composer rather than to express the love of God. Questions dealing with the reforms for purifying the services of the Church were taken up by the Council of Trent, a gathering of the learned Church men and the Catholic kings. The council lasted for twenty years (1542 or 3–1562). The best minds of the era convened. At the end of its long session, the council decided that all music in the "impure mode" (in popular style), should be banished from the Church. They decided, and we cannot see why they waited so long, that the Mass with popular airs and words not approved by the Church fathers should be prohibited. Palestrina had both the genius and the understanding to meet the requirements, and his compositions for the Church are the highest achievement of the 16th century.

You will read in many histories of music that Palestrina was asked to write three masses to be sung before a group of Cardinals, in order to find out whether or not any composer could write music fit for the Church. These three masses were considered so fine, that he was claimed as the one who saved Church music. This would have been a great honor, but it did not happen, and was only a legend to show Palestrina's greatness. No doubt Palestrina wrote more carefully and beautifully on account of the decision of the Council of Trent, and was so great a composer that all vocal polyphonic music of the 16th century is said to be in the "Palestrinian" style.

Now this Palestrina was Giovanni Pierluigi, born in a humble home at Palestrina, a suburb of Rome. In English his name would be John Pierluigi of Palestrina. The year of his birth was about 1525 or 1526. He probably was a choir boy and was trained in music in one of the churches of Rome. You may hear that the Chapel master of Santa Maria Maggiore heard him singing on the road and picked him out for his music school, but this may be only one of many legends told of him. Even the name of his teacher is uncertain, some say that it was Goudimel, others that it was Gaudio or Claudio Mell, and still others that it was Cimello. However, his teacher's name seems to have had the letters "mel" in it, and all the rest is guess work. Before he was twenty, he played the organ in a church at Palestrina, sang in the daily service, taught singing and music, and shortly after was married.

In 1551 he became chapel master in the Capella Giulia (Julia Chapel) in the Vatican. His first published volume of five masses (1554) he dedicated to the Pope, Julius III. There had been many volumes of sacred music dedicated to the popes, but they had always been the work of musicians of the northern school, Hollanders or Belgians. This volume of Palestrina's was the first by an Italian composer to be written for a pope. As a reward, the Pope made him one of the twenty-four singers of his private chapel, but not having a good voice, and not being a priest, the next Pope dismissed him. But in 1571 he was again made chapel master in the Vatican.

It was the custom in those days for musicians to dedicate works not only to popes, but to rich and powerful nobles, monarchs, or other church officials. These attentions were often rewarded with gifts of money, positions at court or in the chapels. This "patronage," as it was called, made it possible for composers to do their best work. This was not only the case in music, but in poetry, painting and sculpture. Palestrina was kept busy dedicating his music to popes, for he lived during the reigns of at least twelve.

After the Council of Trent, one of his masses was recommended as a model, so it is said, of what church music should be. He was again granted the pay of singer in the Pontifical Choir, as he had been years before, but this time, due to his well-known skill, he did not lose his post when other popes succeeded in office. Many of his masses in manuscript are now in the Vatican library.

In 1575, fifteen hundred singers from Palestrina,—priests, laymen, boys and women, marched into Rome singing Giovanni Pierluigi's music, with the great composer leading them. This shows, that he was appreciated.

He was asked to revise some of the old church music and while he tried, he so hated to change the work of other composers whom he respected, that he never finished the task. It was like asking Stravinsky to put up-to-date harmonies into Beethoven.

A list of his compositions published by Breitkopf and Haertel include 93 Masses, 179 Motets, and 45 Hymns for the year, 68 Offertories, 3 books of Lamentations, 3 books of Litanies, 2 books of Magnificats, 4 books of Madrigals. A big list, isn't it? But his activities covered a long period, and he composed to the time of his death (1594).

He had very few pupils whose names have come down to us.

Palestrina never had great wealth, and some biographers make him seem poverty-stricken and suffering. At any rate, he was granted his heart's desire, to compose as much as he wanted to, and even if he was poor, he had the joy of success and the glory of being recognized as the greatest composer of his time in Italy. His works have outlived many other schools of composition, and today are looked upon as models of beauty and of masterly workmanship.

Palestrina was honored by burial in St. Peter's, and on his tombstone are the words "Princeps Musicæ" (Prince of Music).

You must not think that Palestrina was the only famous Italian composer of the 16th century, for Constanza Festa who died before Palestrina did his important work is called the first Italian master of the polyphonic school. There were also Animuccia, Andrea Gabrieli, and Andrea's nephew Giovanni Gabrieli. Giovanni was a Venetian, and the Venetians loved rich coloring in everything, even in their music. Gabrieli tried to get it by using cornets, trombones and violins with the organ, which at that time could not make a *crescendo*, that is, its volume could not be increased, but as these instruments could all be played soft or loud with *crescendo* effects, he created a color or quality that never had been before.

Chevalier Christoph Willibald von Gluck.
Father of Modern Opera.

From a statue by Barrias, in the Luxembourg Gallery, Paris.

The Boy Mozart.

After a "Portrait of a Young Man" (Mozart?) by Prud'hon, in the Louvre, Paris.

Wolfgang Amadeus Mozart.

From the head by Gourwitch.

Ludwig van Beethoven.

CHAPTER XIII

Birth of Oratorio and Opera—Monteverde and Heart Music

BIRTH OF ORATORIO AND OPERA

A FRIEND of Palestrina, Saint Filippo Neri, was the founder of Oratorio. In 1558, Father Neri started daily religious meetings to which all sorts of people came. These were held in a side room of the Church called the Oratory (chapel for private prayer), and in addition to his talks,—hymns, litanies and motets were sung, and scenes from the Bible were performed somewhat like opera. The name "Oratorio" was soon used, not only in Rome, but throughout all of Europe, wherever there were sacred dramas with music. Palestrina arranged and wrote some of the music for Father Neri.

BIBLE STORIES ACTED

The acted stories of the Bible can be traced back into the Middle Ages, and probably descended from the Greek and Roman theatre, for many early Christians were Greeks and Romans and had a natural love for drama. The Church understood this and saw in it a way to teach the history of the Scriptures. You know yourselves how much better you remember historical events when you have seen them in moving pictures! This natural love of play-acting in mankind goes back to primitive man who acted out his prayers in his religious rites. These theatrical performances were called "moralities," "mysteries," or "miracle-plays," and a very beautiful example is *Everyman*, which was revived in England and America a few years ago.

In the 8th century, Charlemagne's time, people gathered in the public markets, and the merchants entertained them by shows in which were singing and dancing. The priests forbade these performances because they were coarse and vulgar, but realizing how successful and how much loved they were, they themselves turned actors, built stages in many of the churches, turned the Bible stories into little plays, and added music. Sometimes when there were not enough priests to take part, dolls or puppets were used as in *Punch and Judy* shows. Isn't it interesting to think that operas and plays began in the Church?

One of the most famous of the church plays was the *Feast of Asses* in the 11th century.

The people did not have means of entertaining themselves as we have, and the Church was the place to which every one went for amusement as well as religion. In the 14th century some plays given in England were: *Fall of Lucifer, Creation, Deluge, Abraham, Salutation and Nativity, Three Kings, Last Supper, Resurrection*. The clergy hired minstrels during this period to supply the music.

In the 15th century there were also elaborate pageants.

The clergy soon saw that the people wanted to take part in the plays, so societies were formed in Paris, Rome, and in England for the people. In England, like in Germany in the 16th century, the guilds (trade-unions) performed plays that were based on religious subjects, although more or less comic. The trade-guild of water-drawers, who delivered water from door to door, liked to give the *Deluge!* The story goes: Mrs. Noah objected to going aboard the ark with her husband and children, because she did not want to leave her friends, "the gossips"; she even tells Noah to get himself another wife, but her son, Shem, forces her into the ark, and when she finally enters, she slaps Noah's face!

The subjects were not always comical, some were beautiful and inspiring, like the *Passion Play* still given in Oberammergau, Germany, every ten years.

MASQUES

During Henry VII's reign (1485–1509), which began the Tudor period, the moralities and religious pageantry were at their best, and the Masques began. Nobles, who appeared at balls in gorgeous costumes with masked faces, danced, had a jolly time, and usually surprised the guests with an elaborate entertainment in pantomime with much music and dancing. This became more and more important until it combined poetry, instrumental and vocal music, scenery, dancing, machinery, splendid costumes, and decorations in the Masque.

The greatest masques were written in the reigns of the Stuarts (17th century), by Ben Jonson, Beaumont and Fletcher, and John Milton. *Comus* and Shakespeare's *Tempest* were set to music in this form. While the Italians were experimenting with *Dramma per Musica* (drama with music), England was finding a new musical entertainment in the masque, and opera was its direct descendant.

The custom of masking for the ball came from Italy, and before that, the actors in the Greek drama (400 B.C.) wore masks, and that is why the mask is used in art to represent the theatre.

ITALIAN OPERA'S BEGINNINGS

In Italy during the second half of the 16th century, a group of people tried to combine music and drama to fit the new ideas of art. The Renaissance had influenced poetry, sculpture, painting, architecture, and now it was music's turn to profit by the return to Greek ideals. The Florentines and the Venetians felt that the madrigal was not the best form to express the feelings and emotions of the subjects of their plays. In the Middle Ages, the subjects were always Biblical, but now, as a result of the new learning they were chosen from Greek mythology and history. From the first operas at the close of the 16th century, to those of Gluck in the 18th, the names of Greek gods and heroes are used as the titles of operas: *Orpheus*, *Euridice*, *Daphne*, *Apollo* and *Bacchus*. These first operas were a combination of early *ballets*, and a sort of play called a *pastorale*.

Torquato Tasso, the Italian poet of the 16th century, wrote several *pastorales*, and was interested in music with drama. Like Ronsard in France, Tasso wrote beautiful poems for madrigals, which were set to music by the composers. He was a friend of Palestrina and of Don Gesualdo, Prince of Venosa, a famous patron of art, particularly of music. In the Prince's palace at Naples, a group of men met to spread and improve the taste for music. They also wished to create music that would fit the stage-plays better than the polyphonic or poly-melodic style imported from the Northern countries. They wanted melody and they wanted it sung by one voice alone, as were their popular songs, accompanied by the lute, called *frottoli*, *villanelles*, etc. Tasso, no doubt, talked over his ideas with composers from Florence who had formed a club, and who were directly responsible for the first opera in Italy, *Daphne* by Jacobo Peri.

The Camerata

This Florentine club was called the "Camerata"; it met at the home of Count Bardi, himself a poet, and among its members were Vincenzo Galilei, an amateur musician and father of the famous astronomer; Emilio del Cavalieri, a composer and inventor of *ballets;* Laura Guidiccioni, a woman poet; Giulio Caccini, a singer and composer; Ottavio Rinuccini and Strozzi, poets; and Peri, a composer and singer. They must have had wild times at their club meetings, for the musicians who were not amateurs did not want the popular song with lute accompaniment to replace polyphonic music, which was the "high-brow" art of that time. But the poets and singers and less cultured musicians won the day. Pretending to return to Greek music drama of which they knew less than nothing, they made a series of experiments which led to the invention of the artsong, or homophonic style (one voice, or melody, instead of polyphonic—many voices), which seemed to satisfy the Italian's natural love for melody.

Galilei set a scene from Dante's *Inferno*, for solo and *viola da gamba*, an instrument of the violoncello type. Following this, Peri invented the "speaking style" of singing now called *recitative*. This was a very important step in the making of opera and oratorio, for it did away with spoken words, and instead, the conversation was sung, or intoned, to satisfy the poets who wanted the meaning of their words made very clear. It was accompanied by simple chords on the lute, and later, the harpsichord.

Here were all the parts needed for a real opera,—the solo song, or aria; the recitative, or story-telling part; the chorus or ensemble, which was the old madrigal used in a new way; and the accompanying instruments which grew into the orchestra. Peri was the first to put all these parts together in an opera for which Rinuccini wrote a real play based on the Greek story of Daphne. Caccini and his daughter Francesca sang it, and no doubt made many suggestions as to how it should be done. Its first private performance (1597) was an important event for the closing of an important century. The audience thought that it was listening to a revival of Greek music-drama, but we know that it was another case of Columbus's passage to India! Although the Greek drama was not like this, after 2000 years it helped to create modern music.

Its success led to an invitation in 1600 for Peri and Rinuccini to write an opera, *Euridice*, for the marriage festivities of Henry IV of France and Marie de' Medici. Several noblemen, probably members of the "Camerata," took part in the first performance; one played the harpsichord, and three others played on the chitarrone (a large guitar), a viol da gamba, and a theorbo (double lute). The orchestra was completed by three flutes. This orchestral score was notated in a sort of musical shorthand called figured bass which shows the chords to be used as accompaniment to a melody by means of a bass note with a figure above it. Peri and his colleagues seem to have been the first to use this, but it was adopted by all composers into the 18th century, including Bach and Handel. It was called *basso continuo* or figured bass or thorough-bass.

Caccini also wrote an opera which he called *Euridice*, but it was in the style of a pastoral ballet with songs, dances, and recitatives. This work was probably the result of his having helped Peri in working out his ideas at the meetings of the "Camerata." This same year, 1600, which finished the 16th century, saw the presentation of Emilio del Cavalieri's mystery play, or oratorio, *La Rappresentazióne di 'Anima e di Córpo* (Representation of the spirit and body), for which Laura Guidiccioni wrote the text. This oratorio, with very elaborate decorations, was sung and danced in the oratory of a church. It must have been very like the operas except that it was based on a religious idea, and was performed in a church, while the opera by Peri was performed at the Pitti Palace and was from Greek mythology. The orchestra was composed of a

double lyre, a harpsichord, a double guitar, and a theorbo
or double lute.

BAIF'S CLUB IN FRANCE

While the Italians were trying to find the old Greek and
Latin methods of combining drama and music, there was a
movement in France to write poetry in classical verse.
Following Ronsard's example, Baif influenced the composers to write music that should express the feeling of
poetry, and also imitate its rhythm. They also tried writing madrigals arranged for a single voice with accompanying instrument, or group of instruments. While the Italians invented the recitative, the French developed a rich
fluent rhythmic song form, *musique mesurée à l'antique*, or,
music in the ancient metre.

Baif formed a club or an Academy of poets and musicians
much like Bardi's "Camerata" in Florence. They worked
hard to perfect mensural or measured music, and opened
the way for the use of measures and bars, which in the 16th
century were unknown. We are so accustomed to music
divided into measures by means of bars, that it is hard to
realize what a great step forward was made by Baif's
Academy. They were struggling to get rid of the plain-
chant which lacked rhythm as we know it, and which for
centuries had used "perfect" or "imperfect" time.

Two prominent composers of this group were Jacques
Mauduit (1557–1627) also a famous lute player, and Claude
Le Jeune (1530–1600), who worked with Baif to bring
"measured" music into favor, composer of many *chansons*
and of a Psalm-book used by all the Calvinist churches
(Calvin was a church reformer in Switzerland) in Europe
except in Switzerland! It went through more editions than
any other musical work since the invention of printing.
Le Jeune was a Huguenot, and on St. Bartholomew's eve

(1588), he tried to escape from the Catholic soldiers carrying with him many unpublished manuscripts. They would have been burned, had it not been for his Catholic friend and fellow-composer, Mauduit, who rescued the books, and saved his life. The title appears for the first time in history on one of his pieces, "Composer of Music for the King." (*Compositeur de la musique de la chambre du roy.*)

During the second half of the 16th century, in spite of serious political and religious troubles, the most popular form of entertainment at the French court was the very gorgeous ballet. No expense was considered too great, and no decoration too splendid for these ballets in which nobles and even the kings and their families appeared "in person." They were like the English Masques, and were the parents of the *French opera.* Baif, Mauduit and Le Jeune, together composed (1581) *Le Ballet comique de la Reine* (Queen's Comedy-Ballet) which was produced at the Palace of the Louvre in Paris.

Beaulieu and Salmon are often named as the composers of this ballet because in those days, one composer wrote the parts for voices, and another for instruments, so probably the musicians worked with the poets and dramatists to produce it. The characters in this musical drama were Circe and other Greek gods and demi-gods.

With Marie de' Medici and Cardinal Mazarin from Italy, Italian opera came into France. But this did not happen until the 17th century.

Monteverde and Heart Music

Wouldn't you be proud if you could compose a whole book of music at the age of sixteen? Monteverde did and besides he made music grow by composing things that had never been done before.

Claudio Monteverde (1567–1643) was born in Cremona,

a town made famous by the great makers of violins. Monteverde was one of the first great innovators in music, and he brought new ideas and vast changes into music as an art. His teacher, Marc Antonio Ingegneri, Chapel Master at the Cathedral, taught young Monteverde all the tricks of counterpoint and of the great polyphonic masters, and also gave him lessons on the organ and the viol. He must have been a very talented pupil, for he could play any instrument, and at the age of sixteen, published his first book of madrigals,—*Canzonette a tre voci* (Little Songs in Three Voices). The last song in this book has these charming words: "Now, dear Songs, go in peace singing joyously, always thanking those who listen to you and kissing their hands, without speaking." Evidently, little Italian boys were brought up to say nice things!

Even in this first book of madrigals and the four books that followed, Monteverde tried experiments in harmony and wrote music that sounded harsh to 16th century ears. He was trying to create a style that would combine the best points of the old school of polyphony (many voices) with the new school of monody (one melody), and this is why he is called the originator of the modern style of composition, which is, melody and accompaniment. Since his time there have been many originators of new styles in music, and when first heard they have usually been received with harsh words by the many and liked by the few. Monteverde was severely criticized in a book that appeared in Venice, in 1600, on the short-comings of modern music, (and they are still writing "on the short-comings of modern music" today!). The book was written by the monk, Artusi, who liked the old-fashioned music and believed that Monteverde's work was against all natural musical laws. But if we search we will find that music grows through experiments that are made by the composers, who "go against natural laws," then after the natural laws are broken, comes a learned theorist who shows that no law was broken at all, and so we go on stretching the boundaries of "natural law," and music goes on changing all the time. This is what we mean by the growth of music.

In 1590, Monteverde became viol player and singer to Vincenzo di Gonzaga, Duke of Mantua, a patron of arts and letters. At one time he took the poet Tasso from an insane asylum; he was patron of Galileo, the astronomer, who was considered to be a heretic because he said that the earth revolved around the sun, contrary to the teachings of the Bible; he also invited the great Flemish painter Rubens, to visit his court; and probably influenced Monteverde to write operas. The Duke engaged many musicians at his court, who formed a little orchestra to play dance music, solos, or parts in the madrigals. These were no longer sung alone, but were accompanied by instruments, or sometimes played by the instruments without voices, (see how music grows up!) because in Italy, the composers had not yet begun to write special music for instruments as they had in France.

The composer went with the Duke on many travels, even into battle, and in the evenings between military encounters, they sang madrigals and played on instruments!

The next trip with the Duke was pleasanter, for it gave Monteverde the chance to visit Flanders, where he heard the beautiful "new music" of Claude Le Jeune, Mauduit, and others. It impressed him so deeply that he began to write heart-music instead of head-music. He was one of the most successful in breaking down old rules and traditions and was enough of a genius to replace them with new things that were to point the way for all the opera writers and most of the composers that came after him.

Monteverde must have heard the music composed by the members of the "Camerata," but he was too much of a musician to brush aside all polyphonic writing and to value

words above music. However, their work opened the way
for his. Up to 1607, he had written everything in the form
of vocal madrigals, but his last book seems to have been
composed for string instruments instead of being madrigals
for voices. These sounded as though composed for viols
and lutes and not for voices, and were dramatic and full of
deep feeling as if written for an opera! No wonder they
sounded strange to the audience—even as Stravinsky,
Schoenberg and Milhaud have to most people today.

Until Monteverde was forty years old he had never written an opera, the greatest work of his life! He probably
would not have done so then had it not been at the command of his patron, Vincenzo di Gonzaga. His first and
second operas, *Orfeo* and *Arianna*, followed each other
quickly and were epoch making. Without the work of the
"Camerata," they might never have been written, but they
were much better than the best work of the "Camerata"
(Peri, Caccini, and Cavalieri). Monteverde was wise
enough to adopt their melodramatic form which he improved by his use of the devices of the Italian madrigalists
and organ composers, and the *airs de cour* (songs of the
court) and the ballets of the French composers.

Also, following the French ideas, Monteverde used a
large orchestra of forty pieces, including two clavichords;
two little organs called *organi di legno*, which sounded like
flutes; a regal, also a kind of small organ; a bass viol; a *viol
da gamba;* two very tiny violins called *pochettes*, because
they could be carried in the pockets of the French dancing-
masters; ten *viole da bracchia* or tenor viols; ordinary violins, two *chitarroni* or large lutes, and the usual trumpets,
cornets, flutes and oboes. In this Monteverde was a
pioneer for he had no other works to guide him, and had to
find out for himself the effects of combining different instruments. Today many of his musical effects sound crude
to us, but he had no symphony concerts, at which to hear

an orchestra, for such a thing did not exist. Neither were orchestral scores written out, but only indicated, and when instruments were used, their parts were made up at the moment and played, according to the "figured bass."

During the 16th century, the musicians had learned that trombones and cornets made a wonderful effect in scenes of the underworld (Hades, Inferno, Hell), of which there were many. They discovered, too, that trumpets and drums made battle scenes and war songs real; that flutes, oboes and bassoons gave a pastoral, or shepherd-like effect; that viols were for scenes of love and of sadness; and that to represent Heaven, they needed harps, lutes and regals. Monteverde brought them all together, and studied how to simplify the orchestra to give it a better balance in tone and variety. It must have been a wonderful time to live in this "young manhood" day of music.

The opera *Arianna* was written a year after *Orfeo*, to celebrate the wedding of the Duke's son. It must have been a sad task for Monteverde, as he had just lost his wife to whom he was very devoted. Ottavio Rinuccini, poet of the "Camerata" was his librettist (the writer of the words), and a famous Italian architect, Vianini, built an immense theatre in the castle for the first performance in 1608. Six thousand people assembled, the largest audience that had ever heard an opera! Nothing remains of the opera today, but the text, or words, some published accounts of the performances, and a very touching and beautiful *Lamentation* in which Arianna expresses her grief at being left by Theseus. This one piece is enough to show Monteverde's genius, also how freely he expressed human feelings in music. Not a house in Italy with either a clavichord or a theorbo was without a copy of the *Lamentation!*

About this time, Monteverde wrote a prologue for a comedy composed by five other musicians of the court, all well-known composers of their day, Rossi, Gastoldi, Gagliano, Giulio Monteverde, and Birt.

In 1613, a year after the death of the Duke, Vincenzo di Gonzaga, Monteverde was made Chapel-master of St. Mark's in Venice, which had long been famous for its fine music, where Adrian Willaert, Cyprian de Rore and Zarlino had been Chapel masters in the time of the "Golden Age of Polyphony." Monteverde had much to live up to! But, after his hard work at the court of Mantua, he found his position very agreeable, and he gave his time now to composing music for the Church, madrigals, intermezzos, and a new form of music called "cantata." His church music can be divided into works written in the old polyphonic style of Palestrina, and those written in the modern style of his day. So, when he did not write in the older church style, it was not because he did not know counterpoint, but because he wanted to make music express feelings through harmony and not through polyphony. He was able to do this as no one else had! His church music is not published for the parts have been so scattered, that a bass will be found in one collection and an instrumental part in another, and perhaps a soprano in still a third. So it would be very much like a jig-saw puzzle to find them all and put them together.

The Gonzaga family tried to persuade him to return to their court, but he refused, although he often wrote special operas for them or short dramatic spectacles which were called intermezzos. Of these, sad to say, almost nothing remains.

The recitative style invented by the "Camerata" had by this time taken such a firm hold upon the people, that it spread even to the music of the Church and to the madrigals. All the Italian composers began to write *recitative* for solo voices and accompaniment which they called *canzoni* (songs), *canzonetti* (little songs), *arie* (melodies).

Monteverde was one of the first to turn the madrigal into a *cantata da camera* which means the recitation to music of a short drama or story in verse, by one person, accompanied by one instrument. But, as things improve or die out, very soon another voice and several instruments were added. This composition is a musical milestone of the 17th century as the madrigal had been of the 15th and 16th. The cantata for more than one voice forms a little chamber music opera without any acting. Some of the best known cantata writers were Ferrari, Carissimi, Rossi, Gasparini, Marcello, and Alessandro Scarlatti. At the age of seventy, Monteverde took up this new style of composition with all the enthusiasm and freshness of a young composer! He was not the inventor of the *cantata da camera*, as is so often claimed for him, as no one man was its inventor. It was the result of the constant search of the composers of that day, who followed along the same path, and worked together to perfect a new form.

New Feelings Expressed

One of Monteverde's most important works in this style is the *Combat of Tancredi and Clorinda* (*Combattimento di Tancredi e di Clorinda*) a poem by Tasso, which is noteworthy for several new things. In the preface of the published edition, Monteverde says, that he had long tried to invent a style *concitato*, or agitated, that he had been struck by the fact that musicians had never tried to express anger or the fury of battle, but had expressed only tenderness and sweetness, sadness or gayety. (Perhaps he did not know Jannequin's *Battle of Marignan*.) So he wrote battle music.

The second innovation was the tremolo, which, however familiar to us today, he used for the first time to express agitation, anger and fear, and the musicians were so surprised to find something that they had never seen before, that they refused to play it! This was neither the first nor the last time that musicians balked at something new.

The third innovation was, that he wrote independent parts for the orchestra, and for the first time the instruments did not "copy" the voice, but had notes all to themselves, to play.

In 1630 there was a terrible epidemic in Venice, the "Black Plague" which lasted a year and took off one-third of her population! In gratitude for having been spared, Monteverde became a priest in the Church. This did not seem to interfere with his composing secular works, for after this, he wrote several operas.

Venice was the home of the first public opera house in the world! It was opened (1637) in the San Cassiano theatre by Benedetto Ferrari and Francesco Manelli, and for this in these last years of his life, Monteverde wrote some of his most important operas. Monteverde's operas of this time were a combination of the Roman *opera-cantate*, then in style, and his first operas, *Orfeo* and *Arianna*, written thirty-five years before. He had great enough genius to fit his work to the conditions that he found in the opera house, so that when they had to reduce expenses, Monteverde cut down the size of his orchestra to just a clavichord, a few theorbos, a bass viol and a few violins and viols, and wrote works without choruses!

The last work he composed at the age of 74 is one of his best! Is it not wonderful to think that he had not lost inspiration and enthusiasm after a long life of hard work? The Italian name for his last opera is *Incoronazione di Poppea*, or the "Coronation of Poppea." It is a story of the court of Nero, and Monteverde has sketched his characters in vivid music, and has made them seem true to life. Henry Prunieres, who has made an earnest study of this composer says in his book, *Monteverde*, "Monteverde saw Imperial Rome with eyes of genius and knew how to make it live again for us. No book, no historical account could picture Nero and Poppea as vigorously as this opera." It is the greatest opera of the 17th century, and actually created the school of Italian grand opera. With it, mythological characters gave way to the historical in opera, which enlarged the field of drama with music.

So Monteverde, the great innovator, died in Venice in 1643 and was given by the citizens of Venice a funeral worthy of his greatness.

He dug new paths for the composers who came after, and throughout his life he followed his ideal, which was to translate into the language of music, human feelings and ideas.

CHAPTER XIV

Musicke in Merrie England

YOU will recall how far away England was in the 16th century from Rome, the Pope, and the other nations. Not that it has been pushed any nearer now, but the radio, the aeroplane and the steamship have made it seem closer. In the 16th century it took a long time to reach the people of the continent, and for this reason England seemed to many, to have little musical influence, but in reality it had much for it was forced to develop what it found at home.

About 1420, John Dunstable wrote beautiful motets, canzonas and other secular music in the contrapuntal style of his period. He is supposed to have held a post in the Chapel Royal, founded during the reign of Henry IV, and to have taken part in the musical services held to celebrate Henry's victories in France.

Then came the War of the Roses between the Houses of York and Lancaster, and musical composition in England was checked for the sake of war-making. Yet, the Chapel Royal was maintained and the universities gave degrees to students of music. Judging from the number of singing guilds and cathedral choirs, and from the amount of singing and organ playing, music, even in spite of war, seemed to have its innings.

In the 16th century England made such strides forward that she holds a high place in the growth of music. Eng-

land loved the keyboard instruments such as the virginal,
and in this century, developed her own way of making a
successful combination of polyphony and harmony with the
new music for the Protestant Church service.

BLUFF PRINCE HAL

Right here came the Reformation of the English Church
under Henry VIII of the six wives. In 1535 he wanted
to divorce his first wife, Catherine of Aragon, to marry
Anne Boleyn, her lady in waiting, which the Pope would
not permit him to do, as the Roman Catholic Church pro-
hibits divorce. So, like Germany and Switzerland, England
cut herself off from the Pope and founded the English or
Anglican Church with the King as its head. You can
imagine the excitement this caused, can't you? People
lost their heads in very truth, for what they thought right
and religious, some of the rulers called sacrilegious and
heretical.

Breaking away from the Church of Rome, gave English
music a great push forward, for, the Mass (the musical setting of the main part of the service), the motet (the particular lines of the particular day) and the plain song
(which ministers intoned), were discontinued, and for these
were substituted, after Henry VIII's reign, the Church
"Services" founded on the Elizabethan Prayer book. On
this book, still in use, the new music was written and included such compositions as would fit this Liturgy (prayers)
the Litany, Creed, Psalms, Canticles (line verses), and the
Communion, the Plain Song, Versicles and Responses.
Then, too, came hymn tunes and anthems. Among the
composers of these in the Elizabethan reign were John
Shepherd, John Marbeck, Robert Whyte, Richard Farrant,
William Byrd and John Bull.

But let us go back to Bluff Prince Hal (Henry VIII),

who was good to music.   Not only did he love it, but he
played and composed himself.   One of his pieces is called
The King's Balade, or *Passetyme with Goode Companie* and
the pastimes of this monarch were many.   Read this list,
set down by one who knew him: "He spent his time in
shooting, singing, dancing, wrestling, casting of the bar,
playing at the recorders (a reed instrument), flute, virginals
(the English spinet) in setting songs and making ballads."
So with eating and sleeping and attending to affairs of state
and to his many wives as they came along, he must have
had plenty to do!   How many kings and governors today
write music as a "passetyme"?

In 1526 he had a band of players, says Edmundstoune
Duncan in his *Story of Minstrelsy*, "composed of fifteen
trumpets, three lutes, three rebecks, one harp, two viols, ten
sackbuts, a fife, and four drumslades"; a few years later a
trumpet, a lute, three minstrels, and a player of the virginals
were added.   (A rebeck is an early form of violin; a sackbut
is a reed instrument with a sliding piece such as we have today in the trombone; the drumslade is an old word for
drum.)

Anne Boleyn, second of King Henry's many wives, loved
music and dancing, and she too tried her hand at composing,
to which fact her *O death, rocke me on slepe* is proof.   It is
said that "she doated on the compositions of Josquin and
Mouton," and that she made collections of them for herself and her companions.

Up to this time there was no English Bible and only Latin
and Greek versions were used.   The Church did not consider it proper for the common people to read the Scriptures.   The Priests wanted to read and interpret it to them
instead.   You remember, too, one of the reasons that the
Reformation took place in Germany was because Luther
wanted to let the people think for themselves, read their
Bible, and choose their own ways of worshipping and inter-

preting it.   The same feeling crept into England, and William Tyndale made the first English Translation of the New Testament (1538).   Soon the Psalms were translated and set to music to any air from a jig to a French dance tune!   The gayer the air the more popular the Psalm!

CHAINED LIBRARIES

Because the Protestants did not want anything left that had been part of the old religion in England, a rather dreadful thing happened.   The monasteries were either destroyed or their libraries and organizations were discontinued.   On account of this, many fine manuscripts of music and poetry were lost, for as you know, the monks copied out, with much effort, the literature of their day, and these painstaking glorious bits of hand work were kept in the monasteries.

There are today four chained libraries in England, two of which are at Hereford, the old city that holds yearly musical festivals of the "Three Choirs."   The books are on the old chains and may be taken down and read on the desk below the shelves, as they were hundreds of years ago! Here they are, in the cloisters, a great collection of treasures beyond price, just as the medieval scholars read them in days when books were the costliest of luxuries, three hundred volumes dating back to the 12th century.   The earliest manuscript is the *Anglo Saxon Gospels* which was written about 800 A.D.   One of the greatest treasures is a Breviary (prayer book) with music (1280)—the plain-song notation as clear and as easy to read as modern print.

As something had to take the place of monasteries, the universities became the centers for study and the cultivation of music.   As far back as 866, King Alfred founded the first chair of music at Oxford.   Do you remember that this was the time of the bards and minstrels?   We do not seem very old in America, when we think of a college with a chair of music eleven hundred years ago!

Before the printers were expelled from England, Wynken de Worde, printed the first song book (1530) which contained pieces by men important at the time: Cornyshe, Pygot, Gwinneth, Robert Jones, Dr. Cooper, and Fayrfax.

MUSIC FOR THE NEW CHURCH

As the kingdom changed its king at the death of each monarch, the country swayed from Catholicism to Protestantism and back again, and many a poet and musician lost his head or was burnt at the stake because he wrote for the Protestant Church.   In the case of Marbeck who had made music for the *Book of Common Prayer*, he just escaped death for the crime of writing a *Bible* concordance (an index)!

Before Wynken de Worde's song book came out, William Caxton the great printer, published a book called *Polychronicon* by Higden.   In this, was an account of Pythagoras and his discovery of tone relations (Chapter IV); this proves the great interest in England for the science, as well as the art, of music.

In Frederick J. Crowest's book, *The Story of the Art of Music*, he tells very simply the state of music in England at this time:

"When the adventurous Henry VIII plunged into and consummated (completed) the reformation scheme, it was at the expense of considerable inconvenience to muscians obliged, perforce, to change their musical manners as well as their faith.   In double quick time the old ecclesiastical (church) music had to be cast aside, and new church music substituted. . . .   This meant pangs and hardships to the musicians, possibly not too industrious, accustomed to the old state of things.   Simplicity, too, was the order, a change that must have made musicians shudder when they, like others before them, from the time of Okeghem, had regarded the Mass as the natural and orthodox (correct) vehicle for the display of the contrapuntal miracles they wrought."

Now the Mass became the "Service," and the motet was turned into the "Anthem," which we still use in our churches. Most of the famous composers of the 16th and 17th centuries in England wrote for the new Anglican or Protestant Church, and made the new music lovely indeed. Many of them were organists or singers in the Chapel Royal, so they had been well prepared for their work.

To make this new music different from the old, the writers were ordered to fit every syllable with a chord (in the harmonic style). In the old counterpoint, of course, the words were somewhat blurred. These experiments with chords did much to free music for all time.

One of the earliest of the church composers is Thomas Tallis (about 1520-1585), a "Gentleman of the Chapel Royal" and father of English cathedral music. Through his long career, Tallis followed the different religions of the rulers from Henry VIII to Elizabeth, writing Catholic music or Protestant as was needed. You see he liked his head, so he changed his music with each new monarch. He, like some of the composers of the Netherlands school, wrote a motet for forty voices.

He shared with his pupil, William Byrd, the post of organist of the Chapel Royal, and together they opened a shop "to print and sell music, also to rule, print and sell music paper for twenty-one years" under a patent granted by Queen Elizabeth to them only. How successful the two composers were in the publishing business is not stated, but at least they could publish as many of their own works as they cared to! After Tallis' death, in 1585, for a while Byrd ran the shop alone, and published a collection of *Psalms, Sonets, and Songs of Sadness and Pietie.* In this

was written "Eight reasons briefly set down by the Author
(Byrd) to persuade every one to learn to sing" to which
he added:

> Since singing is so goode a thing
> I wish all men would learne to sing.

FAMOUS OLD MUSIC COLLECTIONS

England was the land of famous music collections in the
16th and 17th centuries. The first of these by Byrd was a
book of Italian Madrigals with English words, *Musica
Transalpina* (Music from across the Alps). The entire
title was (Don't laugh!): " *Musica Transalpina;* Madrigals
translated of foure, five, and sixe parts, chosen out of
diuers excellent Authors, with the first and second part of
La Virginella, made by Maister Byrd vpon two Stanz's
of Ariosto and brought to speak English with the rest. Published by N. Yonge, in fauer of such as take pleasure in
Musick of voices. Imprinted at London by Thomas Easy,
the assigne of William Byrd, 1588. *Cum Privilegio Regise
Maiestatis* (With permission of her Royal Majesty)." A
long title and one that would not make a book a "best-
seller" today! Do notice how they mixed u's and v's and
put in e's where you least expect them!

There were fifty-seven madrigals in the long titled collection including the two by "Maister Byrd"; the others
were by the Italian and Netherland madrigal writers, such
as Palestrina, Orlandus Lassus and Ferrabosco, a composer of masques and madrigals, who lived for years in
England.

Byrd's compositions in this work mark the beginning of
the great English school of madrigals, which were so lovely
that this period (from about 1588 to 1620 or a few years
later) was called the "Golden Age."

THE GOLDEN AGE OF MADRIGALS

Now the madrigal becomes the great English contribution to music. It was a part-song in free contrapuntal style and included the real Madrigal, the Ballet, and the Ayre. For the first time, secular music came to be held in great honor, and prepared the way for arias, dramatic solos and original melodies. After Byrd came other madrigal writers: Thomas Morley, John Dowland, George Kirby, John Wilbye, Thomas Campion, Thomas Weelkes, Thomas Ravenscroft, Orlando Gibbons, and others.

During this time part-song was being written in Germany. It was the companion of the chorale, as the madrigal was the secular partner of the motet. The chorale was harmonized in four parts, had a continuous melody and the same air was used for all stanzas. Although the Italian madrigal was used as a model, the German *Lied* shows itself in this type of part-song.

In Italy, the *villanella* or *villota*, is a part-song. In France it was the *chanson*, in England it was the madrigal or the *glee*.

"THE TRIUMPHS OF ORIANA"

Monarchs, besides ruling the country, inspired poets and composers from earliest times, and Queen Elizabeth was no exception. *The Triumphs of Oriana* is a collection of madrigals by many English composers in praise of Queen Elizabeth, made by Thomas Morley. Because William Byrd does not appear in it, it looks as if this collection had been published to show Byrd that the English could write good madrigals, too. Anyhow, it definitely proves that the English madrigals are as charming as the French, Italian or Flemish. There is a copy of the original edition in the British Museum.

Maister Byrd Gives Advice

In 1611, an important work of Byrd's appeared called *Psalms, Songs and Sonets: some solemne, others joyfull, framed to the life of the words: Fit for Voyces or Viols.* In the dedication, the composer gives this good advice: "Onely this I desire; that you will be but as carefull to heare them well expressed, as I have beene both in the composing and correcting of them. Otherwise the best Song that euer was made will seeme harsh and vnpleasant. . . . Besides a song that is well and artificially made cannot be well perceived nor vnderstood at the first hearing, but the oftner you shall heare it, the better cause of liking it you will discouer; and commonly the Song is best esteemed with which our eares are best acquainted."

Over the door of the music hall in Oxford University, is a canon (or round) for three voices, said to have been written by William Byrd. Some day, if you have not already seen it, you will have the thrilling experience of visiting the venerable college, and you may remember to look for this canon.

Ladies of the Realm Play Virginals

As today we consider no home complete without a piano (or pianoforte which is its real name), so in the 16th and 17th centuries we would have found a little key board instrument so small that it could easily be swallowed whole by one of our grand pianos, and you would never know where it had disappeared! It was known by several names,— spinet, clavecin, and virginal or virginals. Another instrument belonging to the same family and period is the harpsichord, which is more like our grand piano in shape. But later we will tell you more of the pianoforte's family tree, and of its tiny but important grand-parent.

It was quite the proper thing for all the ladies of the

realm to play the virginals, and the Queens, Mary, Eliza‑ beth, and Mary, Queen of Scots, were excellent performers.

The very first music printed for the virginals in Eng‑ land was called *Parthenia* (from the Greek word Parthenos, meaning unmarried woman or virgin). The printed title also tells us that it was "composed by three famous mas‑ ters, William Byrd, Dr. John Bull and Orlando Gibbons Gentilmen of his Majesties most illustrious Chappell." There are twenty-one pieces from the old dances which formed the Suites, of which you will soon hear,—Preludiums, Pavanes, Galiardes, a Fantasia, and one *The Queene's Command.* It was published in 1611, on staves of six lines, instead of five, as we use, and it was the first musical work engraved on copper plates.

MORE FAMOUS COLLECTIONS

Another most valuable collection was for many years called *Queen Elizabeth's Virginal Book*, but is now the *Fitzwilliam Virginal Book*, and the original manuscript is in the Fitzwilliam museum at Cambridge. It was sup‑ posed to have been "Good Queen Bess'" book, but it was not, as some of its compositions were composed after her death. It is not known who copied 220 pages of music, but it may have been a wealthy Roman Catholic, Francis Tregian, who spent twenty-four years in prison on account of his religious faith. This name, abbreviated or in initials, is found in several places in the manuscript. An edition in our notation has been made by J. A. Fuller Maitland and W. Barclay Squire. Many of the old songs of English min‑ strelsy are found among the numbers, and they were ar‑ ranged for the instrument by the famous composers of that day. There are also original compositions as well as "ayres" and variations. Among the composers we find Dr. John Bull, Thomas Morley, William Byrd, Orlando

Gibbons, Giles Farnaby, Richard Farnaby, Thomas Tallis, Jan Sweelinck, the Dutch organist, and many others. Here are some of the quaint titles: *St. Thomas' Wake, King's Hunt, The Carman's Whistle, The Hunt's Up, Sellenger's Round, Fortune My Foe, Pawles Warfe, Go from My Window, Bonny Sweet Robin,* besides many Pavanes, Galiardes, Fantasias, and Preludiums.

There is also a collection of Byrd's virginal music called *My Lady Nevell's Booke.* Lady Nevell may have been a pupil of Byrd. There are two collections of this same kind at Buckingham Palace, the home of the King of England,— *Will Forster's Virginal Book* and *Benjamin Cosyn's Virginal Book.* In the index of the latter, we read: "A table of these Lessons following made and sett forth by Ben Cos." In all, he copied more than 90 compositions!

Later came John Playford, music publisher, whose first musical publication, *The English Dancing-Master* (1650), contains almost a hundred old folk tunes. *Select Musical Ayres* appeared three years later, and is a typical 17th century song collection of first-class poems by Jonson, Dryden and others set to music by well-known composers. His book on the theory of music, used for almost a century, contained "lessons" for the viol, the cithern and flageolet. His *Dancing Master*, a collection of airs for violin for country dances, has brought to us many popular ballad tunes and dance airs of the period.

In these collections we often find the names *Fancies, Fantazia,* or *Fantasies,* a type of composition that grew out of the madrigal and led to the sonata. It was the name given to the first compositions for instruments alone like the *ricercari* of the Italians, which were original compositions and not written on a given subject (called in England "ground"), or on a folk song. The *Fancies* were sometimes written for the virginal, and sometimes for groups of instruments such as a "chest of viols" or even five cornets(!).

THE CHEST OF VIOLS

"Chest of Viols" may sound queer to you, but it isn't! It was the custom in England at that time for people to have collections of instruments in or out of chests. So, when callers came they could play the viols, instead, probably of bridge! You can read about these interesting old days in Samuel Pepys' *Diary*. He played the lute, the viol, the theorbo, the flageolet, the recorder (a kind of flute) and the virginal, and he was the proud owner of a chest of viols. He always carried his little flageolet with him in his pocket, and he says that while he was waiting in a tavern for a dish of poached eggs, he played his flageolet, also that he remained in the garden late playing the flageolet in the moonlight. (Poetic Pepys!)

Thomas Morley, Byrd's pupil, who was made a partner in the publishing house after Tallis's death, wrote his madrigals for virginal, and a collection called *First Book of Consort Lessons for Six Instruments, Lute, Pandora, Cittern* (an old English form of guitar), *Bass Viol, Flute, and Treble Viol*, and much sacred music. He also wrote a *Plaine and Easie Introduction to Practical Musick*, a book of great value and interest to musicians for the last three centuries, for it is a mirror of his time and of his fellow composers.

He tells of a gentleman, who, after dinner, was asked by his hostess to sing from the music she gave him. It was the custom in England to bring out the music books after dinner and for the guests to play and sing, as we wind up our graphophones and switch on the radio. The gentleman stammeringly declared that he could not sing at sight and "everyone began to wonder; yea, some whispered to others, demanding how he was brought up." He was so ashamed of his ignorance that he immediately took music lessons to remedy his woeful lack of culture. This proves that musical education was not looked upon as a luxury but a necessity in the 17th century.

Truly, it was a musical era, this time of Morley and Byrd! Fancy playing, while waiting for the barber, the viol, flute, lute, cittern, or virginal left for that purpose. Yet what would our dentist do today if he had to listen to a saxophone and jazz chorus from his waiting room? In those days, too, there was always a bass viol left in a drawing-room for the guest, to pass the time, waiting for the host to appear. Think of all the practising you could do waiting for the busy dentist or eternally late hostess!

The children of people who were poor, were taught music to make them fit to be "servants, apprentices or husband-men." Laneham, a groom who had been brought up in the royal stable, was advanced to the post of guarding the door of the council chamber and this is how he described his qualifications for the job: "Sometimes I foot it with dancing; now with my gittern, and else my cittern, then at the virginals (ye know nothing comes amiss to me); then carol I up a song withal; that by-and-by they come flocking about me like bees to honey; and ever they cry, 'Another, good Laneham, another!'" (From *The Story of Minstrelsy* by Edmundstoune Duncan.)

SHAKESPEARE AND MUSIC

This was the day in which Shakespeare lived, and from his plays we get a very good idea of the popular music of his time, for he used bits of folk songs and old ballads. *It was a Lover and his Lass* from *As You Like It* was set to music by Thomas Morley, and is one of the few songs written to Shakespeare's words in his own day that has come down to us. In *Twelfth Night* there is *O Mistress Mine, Hold thy Peace, Peg-a-Ramsey, O, London is a Fine Town, Three Merry Men be We,* and the Clown's song:

Hey! Robin, jolly Robin,
Tell me how thy lady does, etc.

In the *Winter's Tale, As You Like It, The Tempest, Merchant of Venice, Hamlet, Othello* are folk songs that are very well known and loved. Two songs from *The Tempest, Where the Bee Sucks* and *Full Fathoms Five*, were set to music by a composer, Robert Johnson, who lived at the same time as Shakespeare, but was not as famous as Morley, who also lived then. *O, Willow, Willow*, sung by Desdemona in *Othello* is one of the most beautiful and saddest folk songs we know.

One Shakespeare song has been made famous by the beautiful music which the great German song writer, Schubert, wrote to it. It is from *Two Gentlemen of Verona* and is called *Who is Sylvia?*"

Many of the English composers of the 17th and 18th centuries such as Henry Purcell and Dr. Arne made music for the Shakespeare songs because they were so lovely and so well written that they almost sang themselves; this we call lyric verse.

Thomas Weelkes (1575?–1623) whose madrigals were included in *The Triumphs of Oriana*, also wrote many *Fancies for Strings* which were the ancestors of the string quartets, the highest type of music.

CRYES OF LONDON

Several composers of this period, Thomas Weelkes, Orlando Gibbons (1583–1625) and Richard Deering (1580?–1630) wrote pieces using the old "Cryes of London" as their themes. Each trade had its own song, and the street pedlars used these tunes just as the fruit vendors, old-clothes men, and flower vendors cry their wares in our streets today. There is this difference, however; the street cries of today are mere noise, while the old "Cryes of London" were interesting and usually beautiful songs. *Cherry Ripe* is one of them, and Campion used it in 1617 in his famous old song, *There is a Garden in Her Face*. Some of the composers made rounds and catches based on the "Cryes," and Weelkes in his *Humorous Fancy* used the songs of the chimney-sweep, the bellows-mender, and the vendors of fruit, fish and vegetables. In telling about this "fancy," Frederick Bridge, a British composer and professor of music in Gresham College, says: "The Fancy at one point leaves its regular course, and for a few bars a delightful dance tune is introduced, to the words, whatever they mean, 'Twincledowne Tavye.' It is as if the vendors of fish, fruit and vegetables met in the street and had a bit of a frolic together." Bridge also says that he thinks all lovers of Shakespeare will be glad to make the acquaintance of the music of the "Cryes of London" which saluted the poet's ears in his daily walk.

Orlando Gibbons called his composition on the "cryes," a *Burlesque Madrigal*, and beside the cries, he has used in one of the inner parts for viol, an old plain-song melody, a form used very often by the Italian madrigalists of the 16th century. Richard Deering's *Humorous Fancy, The Cryes of London*, is the most elaborate of the three we have mentioned, having among many other tradesmen's songs, those of the rat-catcher (this makes us think of Browning's *Pied Piper of Hamelin*), the tooth-drawer, and the vendor of garlic.

SOME FAMOUS COMPOSERS

Orlando Gibbons was one of the composers of *Parthenia*. But he is famous as a composer of sacred music, in fact, he is looked upon as the greatest composer of the English contrapuntal school. His anthems are still sung in the English Cathedrals, and one of them made for James I, now known as the *Abbey Amen*, was sung, in part, at the coronations of Edward VII, George V, and George VI.

Gibbons, Byrd and Bull were very fine organists. Gibbons was organist of Westminster Abbey, and we are told by a writer of his own day that "the organ was touched by the best finger of that age, Mr. Orlando Gibbons."

Dr. John Bull (1563–1628) was brought up, as were many of the young English musicians, as one of the "Children of the Chapel Royal Choir." Later he became organist and player to King James I. Bull left England, entered the service of a Belgian archduke, was organist at the Antwerp Cathedral, and when he died in 1628, he was buried there. In the University of Oxford, where Bull took his degree as Doctor of Music, is his portrait around which is written:

> The Bull by force in field doth rayne
> But Bull by skill good-will doth gaine.

John Milton, father of the great poet, was an important composer of this period. It is well known that his famous son was very fond of music, was a good musician himself, and had many friends among these composers and musicians.

The music for Milton's famous Masque, *Comus*, was written by Henry Lawes (1595–1662) and was first produced in 1635. Lawes studied with an English composer named John Cooper who lived for so many years in Italy, that his name was translated into Giovanni Coperario. He turned the thoughts of his pupil to composing music for the stage, instead of church music. It looks as if Milton had been a pupil of Lawes, and had written *Comus* specially for him.

Lawes played a very amusing joke upon the concertgoers. At that time, as now, many thought that the music of other countries, and songs in foreign languages were bet-

Johann Sebastian Bach.

George Frederick Handel.

Franz Josef Haydn.

Carl Maria von Weber.

Three Classic Composers and an Early Romantic Composer.

The Piano and Its Grand-parents.
Courtesy of Morris Steinert & Sons, Company

ched by Kriehuber.

After the Painting by Bendemann.

Franz Schubert.

Robert Schumann.

After the Painting by F. V. Delacroix.

Felix Mendelssohn-Bartholdy.

Frédéric Chopin.

Poet Music Writers.

(Romantic School.)

Richard Wagner, the Wizard.

ter than their own. While Lawes himself knew the Italian music very well, he was eager to compose music that should be truly English. In the preface to his *Book of Ayres* he confessed: "This present generation is so sated with what's native, that nothing takes their ears but what's sung in a language which (commonly) they understand as little as they do the music. And to make them a little sensible of this ridiculous humor, I took a Table or Index of old Italian Songs and this *Index (which read together made a strange medley of nonsense) I set to a varyed Ayre, and gave out that it came from Italy, whereby it has passed for a rare Italian song.*" (Quoted from Bridge's *Twelve Good Musicians.*)

Lawes helped to compose a work that is looked upon as the first English opera, *The Siege of Rhodes*. This was played during the time of Oliver Cromwell and the Commonwealth, and in this piece for the first time in England, women appeared upon the stage.

A year after the Commonwealth was overthrown, Henry Lawes died and was buried in Westminster Abbey, but the spot where his body lies is not known.

From 1641 to 1660, music must have had a hard time for this was the period of the Commonwealth, when the country was going through all the horrors of civil war, and Cromwell's soldiers destroyed many things of great artistic value, that could never be replaced. Among them were the works of art found in the wonderful old English cathedrals, including organs and musical manuscripts. At Westminster Abbey, the Roundheads (the name given to Oliver Cromwell's soldiers) "brake down the organs for pots of ale."

Matthew Locke (1630?-1677) is looked upon as the "Father of English Opera." He wrote the music for *Psyche* and *The Tempest* (1673). Another Shakespeare play to which Locke wrote the music was *Macbeth*.

Captain Cooke's Choir Boys

Immediately after the Restoration, the Chapel Royal Choir was reorganized. For centuries it had been the great school of music for the sons of both rich and poor, and had produced nearly all the English musicians. Captain Henry Cooke, the first chapel master of the new choir, seems to have picked out unusually gifted children, some of whom wrote anthems while they were still in the Choir, and afterwards became very famous composers, among them John Blow, Pelham Humphrey and the great Henry Purcell. The Captain evidently knew how to train his boys!

Pelham Humphrey, having attracted the attention of the King, was sent to Paris to study with the famous opera composer, Lully. The effect of this study was felt in English music, as Humphrey was Purcell's master at the Chapel Royal, after the death of the good Captain Cooke, and he introduced his new ideas to his talented little choir boys and musical friends. Samuel Pepys says that the visit to Paris made a snob of "little" Pelham Humphrey: "He is an absolute *Monsieur*, full of form and confidence and vanity, and disparages everything and everybody's skill but his own. But to hear how he laughs at all the King's Musick here, . . . that they cannot keep time nor tune nor understand anything."

Dr. John Blow (1648–1708) composed Anthems while still a choir boy, and at twenty-one was organist of Westminster Abbey. In 1674 he was Master of the Children of the Chapel Royal, and became its organist as well, without giving up his post at Westminster. During part of the time Purcell was at Wesminster, and Blow was Almoner and Master of the choristers in St. Paul's Cathedral. Think of filling three of the greatest positions in musical London at the same time! He wrote an Anthem, *I was Glad*, for the opening of St. Paul's Cathedral in 1697.

He wrote many church compositions, masques, and pieces for harpsichord.

Purcell called him "one of the greatest masters in the world." Like Monteverde, he tried out new effects in harmony and made new combinations which have since been called "crude," but were signs of a musical daring and understanding that belong only to very gifted musicians.

He died in 1708 and is buried in Westminster Abbey.

MAISTER PURCELL

The last of the great 17th century English composers, and the greatest of them all, is Henry Purcell (1658–1695). His father was a well-known musician, and the uncle, who brought him up, was also a musician, so the young boy heard much music in his own home, and no doubt knew many composers.

Sir Frederick Bridge in *Twelve Good Musicians* tells us that the Purcell family came from Tipperary in Ireland and that Henry's father and uncle were Gentlemen in the Chapel Royal in London. Henry began his music studies at the age of six, for he, too, was one of "Captain Cooke's boys," and when he was twelve years old, "Maister Purcell" wrote a composition in honor of "His Majestie's Birthday."

The young Purcell, sometimes called the "English Mozart," gained much from Pelham Humphrey who told him of Lully in France. After Humphrey's early death (he was only twenty-seven), Purcell studied with Dr. Blow, and the two musicians were devoted comrades. Their tombs lie close together near the old entrance of the organ loft, where they must have spent many hours of their lives.

Matthew Locke was also a friend of Purcell's, and probably did much to interest the young composer in the drama.

for in spite of his early church training, Purcell's greatest offering to English music was his opera writing. While Purcell's are not operas in our sense of the word, they are the nearest thing to them that England had, before the Italians came with theirs in the 18th century. He wrote music to masques and plays, several of which were even called operas, yet only one really was an opera. Purcell's music "was so far in advance of anything of the sort known in any part of Europe in his day, in point of dramatic and musical freedom and scenic quality, that one can only regret his early death's preventing his taking to opera-writing on a larger scale." (W. F. Apthorp.) Among the things he put to music were the plays of Dryden and of Beaumont and Fletcher.

Purcell was one of the first English composers to use Italian musical terms, like *adagio*, *presto*, *largo*, etc. He was also one of the first composers to write compositions of three or four movements for two violins, 'cello and basso continuo, a part written for harpsichord or sometimes organ as an accompaniment to the other instruments. The name of this style of composition also came from the Italian, and was called *Sonata*. The first sonatas were composed by Italians. The word Sonata comes from an Italian word *suonare* which means to sound, and was first given to works for instruments. Another form of composition is the Cantata, from *cantare* which means to sing. It is a vocal composition with accompaniment of instruments, a direct descendant of the motet and madrigal, and of the early oratorios.

The Toccata, too, comes from the Italian *toccare*, meaning to touch, and was originally a work for instruments with key-boards. The Italian language gave us our musical names and terms, because Italian music was the model of what good music should be, and England, France and Germany copied Italian ways of composing. Everyone uses the Italian terms for musical expressions so that all nationalities can understand them.

When Purcell was only 17 years old, he composed an opera to be played by young ladies in a boarding school. This was *Dido and Æneas*, and it is so good that few writers on musical subjects believe that it was written in his youth.

In every branch of composition in which Purcell wrote, he excelled. His church music is the finest of his day, his chamber music and his operas are looked upon as works of genius. In fact, he is still considered the most gifted of all English composers.

He was only 37 when he died, and was a very great loss to the growth of English music.

Music Comes of Age

CHAPTER XV

Dance Tunes Grow Up—Suites—Violin Makers of Cremona

IN our range of musical mountains, we see just ahead of us one of the mightiest giants of them all, Johann Sebastian Bach, dwarfing everything around it and we must resist the temptation of skipping all the smaller mountains, for there is no musical aeroplane by means of which we can fly across and land safely on Mt. Bach. This grand old mountain, Bach, is such a tremendous landmark in the growth of music, that when we reach it we realize that everything that we have passed has been a journey of preparation. Bach is not the only peak, for there are Mozart, Haydn, Beethoven, Chopin, Schumann, Brahms, Wagner and others who stand out against the musical horizon.

Before coming to Bach, however, we must bridge over the time when music was still in its youth in the 16th and 17th centuries, to when it became full grown and mature in the 18th. Music has now come of age: it has perfected scales, notation, and developed form and instruments; it is ready to go into the world and take its place with painting, sculpture, poetry, drama and architecture as a full grown art!

Nothing through which music has passed has been lost, but it has been built like the great Egyptian Pyramids by adding one huge block on top of another. It has gone from the noise of primitive man with his drum, to the attempts of the savage to sing and to make crude instruments, to the music of the ancient nations in their religious ceremonies and entertainments, to the Arab singer who handed his art to the western world through the troubadours, to the people of all times and nations who danced and sang for the joy of it. It passed from the Greek drama and music schools where definite scales and modes were formed, to the early Christian Church which kept it alive during the Dark Ages and gradually invented ways to write it, and later to the "Golden Age" of the Catholic Church. It had seen the rise of schools and the perfection of the polyphonic system give way to the recitative and the aria, which in turn brought about opera, oratorio, and instrumental music. It has seen counterpoint give way to harmony, and yet the growth of music is not complete and never will be, but constantly new forms will blossom out of the old.

The 15th and 16th centuries were vocal. In the 17th, predominantly instrumental music was developed, and the way was opened for so-called modern music, that is, for Bach's compositions and all that followed.

BIRTH OF CHAMBER MUSIC

Gabrieli in the 16th century in Venice, sometimes wrote madrigals for instruments instead of for voices, and he added instruments to accompany the motets and masses (page 157); this led to composing works for groups of instruments instead of playing madrigals that had been composed for voices. The English often wrote on their compositions, "fit for voices and for viols." After they once started playing the part songs on viols, the composers soon found out that they could write more interesting and more difficult things for instruments than they could for voices, this led to the writing of very florid music for instruments alone. This florid part-writing, not unlike the Gloss of the Arabs, and the improvisations of the soloists in the early Catholic Church, soon became so overloaded with trills, fancy turns and runs that it had to be reformed again.

In the 17th century, the lute, the popular instrument of the court and the home for so many years, even centuries, suddenly found its rival in the little keyboard instrument called the *spinet* and *virginal* in England, and the *clavecin* in France. In Italy and France, as in England, there were famous performers and composers for these instruments, and many volumes of charming music were written for it.

DANCE TUNES GROW UP INTO SUITES

One of the first requirements of art works of all kinds is contrast. The line and the curve are found in primitive art, light must have shadow, one wing of a building must have another to balance it, and a slow serious piece of music is usually followed by a gay one for contrast. The Arabs understood this law of contrast, for in their ancient songs we find the seed of a form that has been most important in the growth of music. They made little suites by putting two, three, four or more songs together; each song had its mode, and one would be slow and sad, and the next fast and gay. The principal music of the 17th century was the Suite, a group of pieces which had grown out of the old folk dances. (Chapter IX.) The 17th century composers, like the Arabs, feeling the need of contrast, strung several of these dances together to form the Suite. So Suites were written for clavecins and harpsichords, for violins alone and for organs, for groups of stringed instruments and other chamber music combinations. Some of these dances were in duple time, some in triple; some were slow and some were fast; some were stately and some gay. The different pieces forming a suite, had to be written in the same key. These suites were known by different names in different countries, such as *partitas, exercises, lessons, sonate da camera, ordres.* In England the name *suite* was given to this form, then the Germans adopted it, and later the great Bach wrote suites which he also called *partitas.* In Italy, the suite was called *sonata da camera* (chamber sonata). The Italians also had a *sonata da chiesa* (church sonata) out of which has grown the very important sonata, symphony and chamber music quartet, trio, quintet, etc.

Here are some of the dance forms used in the suite:

Allemande (duple time or measure: moderately slow), Sarabande (triple time: slow, stately), Loure (duple time: slow), Gavotte (duple time: moderately fast), Musette (duple time: moderately fast), Bourrée (duple time: a little faster than the Gavotte), Minuet (triple time: moderately fast), Passepied (triple time: a fast minuet), Rigaudon (duple time: slower than the Bourrée), Tambourin (duple time: fast), Pavan (duple time: rather slow), Courante, Corrente (triple time: fast), Chaconne (triple time: moderately fast), Passacaglia (like Chaconne, but more stately) and Gigue (sometimes duple and sometimes triple time: very fast: almost always the last movement of a suite).

The Italians of the 17th century wrote suites, and Italy still held the place as leading the world in musical composition, just as it had in the 15th and 16th. We find the names of Frescobaldi, Michelangelo Rossi, Legrenzi, Bononcini, Giovanni Battista Vitali, Alessandro Scarlatti and his son Domenico, and going over into the seventeen-hundreds, Niccolo Porpora, Padre Martini, Paradies, and Baldassare Galuppi, whom we know through Robert

Browning's poem, *A Toccata of Galuppi's*. Most of these names you will find on the concert programs of today.

"Serious" Scarlatti and Opera Writers

Alessandro Scarlatti (1659–1725) is one of the most important Italian composers of the 17th century, and although he did not have great success during his lifetime, his compositions have outlived those of other writers, whose works were popular during his day. He was called "serious Scarlatti," and it was probably the very seriousness with which he looked upon his work that made him write without seeking public approval. Besides composing pieces for the spinet and harpsichord, and symphonies, sonatas, suites and concertos for different instruments, he wrote 125 operas, and over 500 cantatas, oratorios and church music. He was one of several Italians who continued the work of the first opera writers. Francesco Cavalli (1599–1676), Giacomo Carissimi (1603–1674), Luigi Rossi, Marc-Antonio Cesti (1628–1669), Francesco Provenzale (1610–1704), Stradella (1645–1682), Caldara (1670–1736), Lotti (1667–1740), Marcello (1686–1739), Leo (1694–1746), and others carried the ideas of Scarlatti into the 18th century. Many of these carried Italian opera into England, Germany and France, where it became the model for *their* opera.

Stradella is quite as famous for his romantic love story, as he is for the operas he left. This made an interesting libretto in the 19th century, for a German opera writer, Flotow, who was also the composer of the well-known opera *Martha*.

"La Serva Padrona" Points the Way

Giovanni Battista Pergolesi (1710–1736), who died when he was only twenty-six years old, was looked upon as a genius, and in his early youth had written two works that were models for many that followed, a *Stabat Mater* and a comic opera, *La Serva Padrona*, which is played often in America under the title of *The Mistress Maid*. When this little opera was performed in Paris (1752) it caused a very famous musical quarrel known as the "war of the buffoons." (Page 230.)

Jomelli (1714–1774), the composer of fifty-five operas, was a Neapolitan but he lived in Germany for so many years, that he had more influence on early German opera than on the Italian.

All the opera of this period, particularly the Italian, was very loosely put together and was not opera as we have it today. Later Gluck brought it to the point where it came of age.

Metastasio—Maker of Opera Librettos

These writers of the 18th century used the librettos of a poet and dramatist, Metastasio (1698–1782), who had a strong influence in the development of opera not only in his native Italy, but in other countries. He supplied texts for 1200 operatic scores! He understood music so well, that he was a great help to the composers who listened with attention to his advice. His life covered practically all of the 18th century.

A Celebrated Singing Teacher and Composer

When you read of Haydn, you will see that he played accompaniments and acted as valet to the eminent singing teacher Niccolo Porpora (1686–1767). This famous Italian had many pupils in the opera houses all over Europe, and was considered the greatest singing teacher in the world. One of his pupils in Dresden was the young princess Marie

Antoinette before she became Queen of France. Porpora was a fine composer, and wrote many operas, cantatas, masses, oratorios, and sonatas of which form he was one of the inventors. Among his pupils were Haydn, Marcello, Tartini, Leo, Galuppi, Padre Martini, Jomelli, Pergolesi, Caffarelli and Farinelli. This list shows that he trained composers as well as singers.

The Violin Makers of Cremona

Important changes, such as instrumental music coming into fashion, do not happen without good reasons. We are so accustomed to the violin, that we forget that there was a time when it did not exist, but until about three centuries ago, there was none. We are always eager to have new pianos, for the old ones wear out, but with violins the older they are, the better! But they must be masterpieces to begin with. All the famous violinists of the day like Kreisler, Elman, Heifetz, etc., have marvelous old violins that cost fortunes, and most of them were made by the violin makers of Cremona, a little town in northern Italy, the birthplace of Monteverde.

The troubadours played the accompaniments to their songs on stringed instruments called *violes* or *vielles*, which were the grandparents of the violins. In the 15th century bowed instruments were made similar in range to the human voice; these were called *treble* or *discant viol, tenor viol, bass viol* and the *double-bass*, and in England these went into the "chest of viols" (Page 198). Many improvements were made in the shape, size and tone of the instruments and by the middle of the 17th century the Italian makers were ready to create violins, perfect of their kind, which have never been surpassed. The secret of the tone of these instruments is said to be in the varnish which the Cremona makers used, the recipe of which has been lost. Recently a violin maker in Paris claimed to have discovered it in an old Italian book, and he has spent years in trying to reproduce it. The old Italian varnish and the mellowing of the wood with time are two reasons why age makes the old violins better.

For several centuries, practically all the lutes and the viols that supplied Europe were made by colonies of instrument makers who lived in Lombardy (North Italy) and the Tyrol (South Austria). Two towns in Lombardy became especially famous for their violins, Brescia in which Gaspara di Salo and Maggini lived, and Cremona, the home of the Amati, Stradivarius and Guarnerius families. In *The Orchestra and Its Instruments*, Esther Singleton says: "It is thrilling to realize that in this little town, in three workshops side by side, on the Piazza San Domenico, all the great violins of the world were made and in friendly competition by the three families." This covered the period from 1560 to 1760. These men worked together with just one object in life,—to turn out of their shops the most perfect instruments that could possibly be made! With what care they selected the wood! How they worked to make the tone of each instrument as beautiful as possible! Now you will know when you hear of an Amati violin, or a Stradivarius, a Guanerius or a Maggini, that they are worth their weight in gold and are among the rarest art treasures of the world. These were not the only violin makers in Lombardy, for there were long lists of them, and there were also many in the Tyrol. One of the most famous of these was Stainer who lived at Innsbruck. "It is said that this old maker used to walk through the wooded slopes of the Tyrolean mountains with a hammer in his hand and that he would knock the trunks of the trees and listen to the vibrations. When he found a tree that suited him, he had it cut down to use in making his instruments." (Esther Singleton.)

These instrument makers made not only violins, but also lutes, mandolins, guitars, violas, violoncellos, and double-basses. The Italians were the first to develop the last two. The 'cello, as we call the violoncello for short, was the child of an instrument named the *viola da gamba* (translated leg-viola because it was held against the leg), which for many years was the most popular of all bowed instruments. We do not find many examples of the instruments even in museums for they were made over into 'cellos when the latter came into fashion. There is one *viola da gamba* in the Metropolitan Museum of Art, however, which was imported from France by the Sisterhood of the General Hospital in Montreal before the conquest of Canada, and was used in the convent choir many years before there were any organs and pianos in the New World. The first 'cello to attract attention was made in 1691 by a famous wood carver and presented to the Duke of Modena. A member of the Amati family in the 16th century was the first to turn the *viola da gamba* into a violoncello. The 'cello and the double-bass were made more successfully by Bergonzi than by the Cremona makers, although Maggini, Amati and Galiano made very fine ones.

The viola is a descendant of the *viola d'amore*. These and the later violas, used in the string quartets, orchestras, and as solo instruments, were made by a Tyrolese named Gaspard Duiffaprugcar in the 16th century. His instruments are marvelous works of art. In the back of one is a riddle in Latin: can you guess the answer? "I was living in the forest; the cruel axe killed me. Living, I was mute; dead, I sing sweetly." When madrigals and motets were first played on stringed instruments, the principal melody was given to the tenor viol, the ancestor of the viola, even today called the alto or the tenor, but after the violin came into general use, the viola was treated like a step-child, for it is too large for a violin and too small for a

violoncello.   We have Mozart to thank for discovering that
the viola had something beautiful and important to say as a
solo instrument especially in passages where he needed a
tender, sad or melancholy voice.   You will read later that
Beethoven, too, loved the poor neglected viola.   He,
Berlioz and Wagner used the instrument to great advantage.

In 1572 Pope Pius V sent Charles IX, King of France, a
present of thirty-eight bowed instruments made by the
first Amati.   During the French Revolution, the mob
broke into the palace at Versailles, and all but two violins
and a 'cello were destroyed!   What a loss to art such destruction was!

Showing Off the New Instruments

With this development of exquisite instruments, came the
desire to use them and to write new compositions to show
them off.   These instruments gave unlimited possibilities
for technic and tone, and created the school of Italian
violinists and composers of the 17th and 18th centuries.   If
polyphonic music had still been in the lead, the development of solo instruments would have been impossible, but
in trying to find new forms, the first opera inventors had
broken the backbone of polyphony, and had replaced it
with monody, or single line melody.   Then, too, folk dances
had taken the public fancy and had been made into suites,
which could be played on solo bowed instruments with
accompaniments, on spinets and organs, or on groups of
instruments.   The *sonata da camera* was really a suite of
dances and was the first form used by these new composers
for violin.   About the middle of the 17th century, instrumental performances without any vocal music came to be a
part of the services of the Catholic Church for the priests
were quick to see in the violin playing, a refining influence.
Here the *sonata da camera* or " room sonata " was turned

into the more serious *sonata da chiesa* or "church sonata" gradually losing its dance character, and thus became the seed of the sonata form of Haydn, Mozart and Beethoven.

Giovanni Vitali (1644–1692) is the first great master of the violin sonata; after him, Giuseppe Torelli (1650?–1708) added a new and important kind of violin composition,— the Concerto. He called his compositions, *Concerti da Camera* and *Concerti Grossi*, which names and form were used by Vivaldi, Corelli, Handel and Bach. This *Concerto Grosso* was a *sonata da chiesa* accompanied not by a single instrument as was the habit with the *sonata da chiesa* and the *sonata da camera*, but by a group of bowed instruments to which a lute, organ and, later, a harpsichord were added.

At this time, all musicians were, as a matter of course, violinists, just as today all great composers can play the piano. One of the greatest of these composer-violinists was Arcangelo Corelli (1653–1713), whose works are often played by violinists of our own time, and have served as models for composers. He was one of the first to try to write music that should show off the beauty and possibilities of the violin.

The "Golden Age" of the Italian violin composers dated from 1720 to 1750, and was the time of Locatelli, Pugnani, Nardini, Veracini, Tartini and Vivaldi who added oboes and horns to the orchestral accompaniment of the *Concerti Grossi*. Corelli and Vivaldi were the models used by the German school of violinists who appeared about this time. Tartini was the musical authority of his century, and no violinist felt sure of his place as an artist until he had been heard and approved by Tartini. He was the composer of the famous piece called *The Devil's Trill*. Although Vivaldi was not looked upon with great esteem in his own time, he was used as a model by Johann Sebastian Bach.

Padre Martini, recognized by all Europe as the greatest authority on musical subjects, lived in Bologna where he was visited by such musicians as Grétry, Gluck, Mozart and one of the sons of Bach. Padre, or Father, Martini was a Franciscan monk, a fine composer, a learned historian, a master of counterpoint, and the owner of a musical library of 17,000 volumes! He helped everyone who sought him, and was loved by the entire musical world.

Once a year a great music festival was held in Bologna by the Philharmonic Society and new works by the Bolognese composers were performed. One hundred musicians took part in the orchestra and the choruses, and each composer conducted his own work. It was an honor to be present at this annual festival, and Italian and foreign musicians came from all over Europe to attend it. Young composers sometimes became famous over night here, for the critics were all invited and serious decisions were made as to the value of new music. Dr. Burney, a famous English musical historian of the 18th century, tells of meeting Leopold Mozart and his young son, Wolfgang Amadeus, at one of these festivals. Through the kind scheming of Padre Martini were they admitted!

Rome, in the 18th century was still the great music center, and guided the religious music of the world. It had wonderful collections of old music which attracted students from all over; it had seven or eight very famous theatres, where *opera seria* and *opera buffa* were given. (Today we call them grand opera and comic opera.) The Roman public was very difficult to please and because of the severity of their judgments, opera writers suffered every time their new works had first performances. Just think how you would feel if you had composed an opera, and by accident had put in a melody that sounded something like one that Mozart, Wagner, Puccini or Verdi had composed, if the whole house should break into shouts of "Bravo, Mozart!" or "Bravo, Wagner!" or "Bravo, Puccini!!" etc. This is what used to happen in Rome, but no doubt it was a good thing because it stopped a habit the composers had in those days, of helping themselves to each other's melodies.

DOMENICO SCARLATTI

But here we must pause for a moment to tell you of the life and work of Alessandro Scarlatti's son, Domenico, who was born in Naples in 1685, the same year as Bach and Handel. When you recall how many operas the father wrote, it seems queer that his son did not follow in his footsteps. The truth is that he did write operas for the private theatre of the Queen of Poland in Rome, and also sacred music while he was chapel master of St. Peter's, but he became immortal as a composer of harpsichord music. In the influence he had in the growing up of piano music, he can be compared to Chopin and Liszt, and is a founder of piano music style, an honor, which he shares with the French Couperin and Rameau, his contemporaries. The difference is that the two Frenchmen have a delicacy and grace that recall their period of wigs and satins and laces, while Scarlatti's works have strength, vigor and daring that take them out of any special period and place them beside the great piano compositions of all time.

Scarlatti's sonatas are sonatas in the Italian sense of a *scund-piece;* they are not, like the suites, in several movements, but each is in one movement, which forecasts the modern sonata form with its two main contrasting themes and development.

The "serious Scarlatti" understood his son's talent, for he sent him at the age of 20 to Florence to a member of the powerful de Medici family with this letter: "This son of mine is an eagle whose wings are grown; he ought not to stay idle in the nest, and I ought not to hinder his flight."

Three years later Handel and Scarlatti met in Rome in an organ and harpsichord competition, and while Handel won as organist, even Scarlatti declaring that he did not know that such playing existed, no decision was made as to which was the better harpsichord player. This contest seems to have caused no hard feelings for the two young men of the same age became devoted friends.

Scarlatti had a trick of crossing his hands in his compositions. Who does not remember with joy his first piece in which he had to cross his hands? But sad to relate as he grew old, he became so fat that he could no longer cross hands with comfort, so in the last compositions the crossing of hands is noticeably absent!

It is hard to know where an inspiration is next coming from, but wouldn't you be surprised were you a composer, if your pet cat presented you with a perfectly good theme? This happened to Domenico Scarlatti! His cat walked across the key-board, and the composer used his musical foot prints as the subject of a very fine fugue! Maybe Zez Confrey's *Kitten on the Keys* is a descendant of this pussy's piece.

The Scarlattis were the last of the great Italian instrumental composers. For two centuries Italy had been the generous dispenser of culture, and like an unselfish mother had sent her children out into the world to carry knowledge and works to all the nations of Europe. The sun of Italy's greatness was setting just as it began to rise in Germany.

CHAPTER XVI

Opera in France—Lully and Rameau—Clavecin and Harpsichord Composers

WE left French Opera in 1600 when Henry IV married Marie de' Medici. Ballets which resembled the English masques had been performed when Baif and his friends had produced *Le Ballet Comique de la Reine*, but no real opera had yet been written in France. In 1645, Cardinal Mazarin, the powerful Italian prime minister of France, invited a company of Italian singers to give a performance of Peri's *Euridice* in Paris. The French did not like the opera, as they said it sounded too much like plain song and airs from the cloister, and yet it led to Abbé Perrin's writing a work in 1658 which he called the *Pastoral*, and for which a composer named Cambert wrote the music. The *Pastoral* was a very great success, and was repeated by order of Louis XIV, King of France. Ten years later, Louis gave Perrin and Cambert permission "to establish throughout the kingdom academies of opera, or representations with music in the French language after the manner of those in Italy." Their next work, *Pomone*, was the first opera performed publicly in an opera house, built purposely in Paris for them. The opera was so enthusiastically received, that it ran nightly for eight months, and the crowds were so great, that the police had to be called out. This combination of poet and composer came to an end with *Pomone*, and a new man acquired the right to give opera in the new opera house. This man was Jean Baptiste Lully or in Italian, Giovanni Battista Lulli (1632–1687).

LULLY THE KING'S FAVORITE

You may hear that the first famous opera writer of France had been a pastry cook or kitchen boy, but no matter how humble his start in life, he rose to the highest social position ever reached up to that time by a composer in France. He became a great favorite of Louis XIV, he was covered with titles and honors, he was on friendly terms with all the nobility of the court, he was musical dictator of the opera and in fact of all the musical happenings of the court. The greatest literary geniuses of the period, such as Molière, Racine, La Fontaine, Quinault, Corneille and Boileau, worked with him when he wanted new librettos for his operas. He paid dearly for all his privileges, because his fellow composers were jealous of his genius and his opportunities, and they lost no chance to blacken his character.

Lully was born in Florence, Italy, in 1632, but we can tell you little or nothing of his parentage or of his childhood. A monk taught him a little about music and how to play the guitar. When he was about twelve years old, he was picked up by the Duke de Guise who saw him with a group of traveling comedians, and was so attracted by his vivacity, his singing and talent for mimicry, that he took him back to Paris, where he placed him in the household of his cousin, Mlle. de Montpensier. In her memoirs, Mademoiselle said that she had been studying Italian and had asked her cousin to bring back from Tuscany where he lived, a little Italian *garçon de la Chambre* a sort of personal errand boy. However, his guitar playing and musical gifts soon lifted him out of a servant's position and he became one of the musicians of the great lady's household, playing at concerts, balls and in the ballets. He learned to play the violin, and soon began to compose popular dances. He remained a member of Mademoiselle's household until he was nineteen when he asked permission to leave her service, as she had moved to the country, and he liked the gay life of Paris better.

He had no difficulty in attaching himself to the King's court, first as actor and dancer in the ballets, and soon as "composer of instrumental music." Louis XIV was only fourteen years old, and was evidently highly entertained by the capers of the young Italian who was willing to play any rôle, dance any kind of a dance, or play the violin "divinely" for his young monarch's amusement. The King remained Lully's faithful friend always. Louis loved music, and played the lute, the guitar, the harpsichord, and sang very well. Feeling that he needed to know more, Lully studied counterpoint, composition and learned to play the harpsichord, and whatever he attempted musically, he acquired without difficulty.

In 1656, Lully composed music for a scene in a ballet, *Psyche*, and from that time on, his compositions became the most popular of any at court. Although he was born an Italian, his music was French, and he even shared the French dislike of the Italian opera. In spite of his love of acting in the ballets, of dancing, and of courting social favor with the King and nobles, Lully was a thorough musician. When he went into music he found that few of the singers could read notes, but they learned their parts by ear. He soon changed this, and by the time he died, all singers and players of orchestral instruments could read well. In this reform, he did a great service to the growth of music.

His first stage works were called comedy-ballets. One of his early works was ballet music written for a performance of Cavalli's opera, *Xerxes*, which was performed upon

Mazarin's invitation at Versailles (1660). He next was given the position of "Superintendent of Music," became a naturalized French citizen, and was married. Lully wrote 19 ballets, 12 comedy-ballets, and 18 operas, besides about 23 motets for special occasions. His ballets included recitatives, airs, dialogues and symphonies, which was the name given to music written for orchestra. From 1672 until the time of his death in 1687, he wrote an opera a year, and sometimes two!

The splendor and extravagance of the costuming and stage settings of these ballets and operas of Lully are almost unbelievable! At times, even the orchestra wore costumes of the period represented on the stage. Lully conducted the orchestra for one opera in a magnificent Egyptian dress. Louis XIV loved these elaborate performances, and took part in some of them.

After the downfall of Perrin and Cambert, which many said was caused by Lully, he became absolute ruler in all musical matters. He used his power to close a rival opera house, and no opera could be given anywhere in France without his permission, for which he received a sum of money. He was such a tyrant that he had many enemies, some of whom tried to poison his snuff, in order to get rid of the King's favorite.

"Le Roi Soleil" (The Sun King), as Louis XIV was called, had to be entertained, and Lully understood so well how to keep him amused, that the King could not get along without his composer whose performances dazzled all beholders!

You must read French history of that period in order to understand just how gorgeous and how extravagant life at the palace of Versailles was and how eventually it led to the revolt of the people and the French Revolution. Or perhaps you have seen the elaborate gardens, fountains and palace,—a playground built at fearful cost where the Kings of France might forget their cares! The King went so far as to give Lully a post of royal secretary, usually held by nobles. It is said that his only claim to the position was that he made people laugh!

In 1681, his ballet *Triomphe de l'Amour* (Triumph of Love) was given, in which, for the first time, women instead of men danced. Indeed, ladies of the nobility took part in the ballet!

The French Overture introduced by Lully, was in two parts or movements,—the first slow and serious, the second by way of contrast fast, and bringing in the contrapuntal-style of the church composers; sometimes a third part resembling the first was added. These overtures were very much liked in Lully's time and during the 18th century, and was the form used by the German composers in their orchestral suites and by Handel. Lully was very successful in composing military music, and his military marches were used not only by the French army, but by the armies marching *against* France. All of his music is simple and clear in outline, it is easy to remember, its rhythm is vigorous and definite, and the people, as well as musicians of his day, loved and understood it. One writer said that one of his songs from *Amadis*, an opera (1684), "was sung by every cook in France and Lully would stop his carriage on the Pont Neuf (the New Bridge across the Seine) to set some poor fiddler right who was playing one of his airs." His works reached Italy, Germany, England, Holland and Flanders, and influenced many of the composers like Purcell, Humphrey and Handel to say nothing of the French composers who followed him.

Lully built up the orchestra, and used the different groups of instruments in entirely new ways.

Lully died in 1687 as the result of having dropped the stick with which he directed his orchestra on his foot. This does not sound possible, but the baton used in his time was very large and heavy, and the accident caused blood poisoning. He was very much missed, for there was no one with his talent for conducting and disciplining the singers and dancers to replace him.

RAMEAU

In 1683, was born another French composer who carried on the work that Lully had begun, a work so much loved by the French public, that Jean Philippe Rameau found as strong a rival in the dead Lully as his contemporaries had in the living. Rameau's father was organist of a church at Dijon, and although the family was very poor, the father was determined to give his three children a musical education, and began to teach them before they could read. As a result of this early training little Jean Philippe, when he was only seven years old, could play at sight on the harpsichord any music put before him, and when he was sent to school, he was very unruly and sang out loud in class or scribbled music all over his papers instead of doing his lessons.

When he was eighteen, he went to Italy, but as he did not like the music, he left. He was always headstrong and self-willed, and this was one of the hasty decisions for which he was afterwards sorry. He traveled from place to place on this journey, playing his way as he went, on the organ in churches and the violin in a band of traveling musicians. In the south of France, old Provence, the home of the troubadours, he became organist at Clermont, and lived quietly for six years. Here he wrote his first pieces for clavecin (spinet) and three cantatas. (The cantata was a new form which came from Italy, and was a small opera to be sung in a drawing-room.) When Rameau grew tired of his work as organist at Clermont, he showed his discontent by playing as badly as he possibly could, by using untuneful organ-stops and by playing fearful discords. An attempt was made to shut him off but he paid no attention until a choir boy was sent to him with a message, whereupon he left the organ and walked out of the church. He finally succeeded in making the directors give him his release, but before many years he returned to his old post, and was taken back in spite of his disagreeable temper, and so proud was Clermont of its organist, that his chair is still kept and exhibited.

From Clermont he went to Paris where he studied with the organist Marchand, and read the old books of musical theory such as Zarlino's, for Rameau during his career wrote five important books on musical theory and harmony. He was the first to establish definitely the classic principles of harmony, and to put them into a form that for many years was used by all students. You must remember that up to the 17th century, counterpoint was the chief study, but when Italian opera succeeded in breaking down the polyphonic habit, a new science had to be made to explain the new system of *chords* that had been gradually built up by the Italians and also by Luther and his chorals. This was the *science of harmony*, and Rameau's *Treatise of Music, containing the Principles of Composition* (1722), was one of the first books of its kind.

Until Rameau was fifty, he was known as an organist, a teacher of composition and a writer of many charming works for harpsichord and clavecin. He married a young singer when he was 43, and the year after, he made the acquaintance of a wealthy patron of the arts, at whose house he met artists, literary men, princes and embassadors. Rameau taught his patron's wife, and had the use of his organ and private orchestra. Here he first found himself among friends who understood and appreciated his talents; here he met the great French writer, Voltaire, and the Abbé Pellegrin, both of whom wrote librettos for his operas. There is a tale that the Abbé made the composer sign an

agreement about payment for the use of his book but after
hearing the first rehearsal he tore it up—so pleased was he
with Rameau's first opera, *Hippolyte et Aricie* (1733).
Now Rameau met the jealousy of Lully's followers, who
tried to prevent the success of the work. They hissed it
and wrote slighting verse about it:

> If difficulties beauty show,
> Then what a great man is Rameau.
> If beauty, though, by chance should be
> But nature's own simplicity,
> Then what a small man is Rameau!—

(Frederick H. Martens' translation of *A History of Music*
by Paul Landormy.)

It is curious how often a new style in music has been
greeted with just such criticism and prejudice as the
"Lullyists" showed for Rameau's opera! They claimed
that the work was not French, that he used strange chords,
that his music was too difficult to be understood! In fact
they said exactly the same things that are said today
about new works which are different from what the public
is used to hearing. Voltaire said that it takes a whole
generation for the human ear to grow familiar with a new
musical style!

His third opera, *Castor and Pollux*, in 1737, was his first
real success. With this work, he became famous, and was
regarded as France's greatest composer. An English
noble in Paris at the time stated "that although everyone
was abusing Rameau's 'horrible' work, yet it was impossible to get a seat at the opera."

Although Rameau brought nothing new to opera, he
was the step between the Lully traditions and the innovators who came with Gluck. The French composers today
turn to him in their search for the direct road along which
French music has traveled.

In spite of Rameau's unfriendly reserved nature, he won fame by force of his genius. He was as unlike Lully as two men could possibly have been. Rameau accepted favors from no one, and was generous in his attitude towards his fellow composers. He talked very little and was not popular. However, he was at the height of his career, when a company of Italian singers arrived in Paris (1752), and played *La Serva Padrona* by Pergolesi. The fresh sparkling little opera took Paris by storm, and this was the beginning of a sharp fight known as the war of the buffoons (page 330), which divided Paris into two factions,—those who stood by Lully and Rameau, and those who wanted to see French opera replaced by the new Italian comic opera.

"The charm of these light operas," says Mary Hargrave in her little book, *The Earlier French Musicians*, "lay in the simplicity of their subjects, taken from scenes and persons in ordinary life, humorously treated. They came as a delightful relief after the stilted classical heroes and heroines, the threadbare episodes of gods and goddesses, the Greek and Roman warriors in tunics, with ribbons and helmets on powdered wigs, in short, all the artificial conventions of which people had at last grown unutterably weary."

Even the court was divided: Louis XV was on the side of French music, but the Queen was for the Italian, and crowds gathered nightly at the opera near the royal boxes, which were known as the "King's corner," and the "Queen's corner." Word bombshells were thrown from one camp into the other, and sometimes these became real insults! Poor Rameau! First he was the butt of the Lullyists because he was too modern, and now storms of abuse were heaped on his head because he was too old-fashioned! Nevertheless, to the end of his life his operas were received with great enthusiasm, and on one occasion when the old man of eighty was seen hiding in the corner of a box during one of his operas, he was called out with storms of applause. He was always very shy about appearing in public, applause embarrassed him, and no doubt much of his disagreeableness was due to his being bashful.

Rameau looked upon his scientific studies as more important than his composing, and Bach, Handel and many other composers studied his theory work even when they were not great admirers of his compositions. We never hear his operas, but his lovely pieces for the harpsichord, many of which are out of his operas are played in piano recitals and are unsurpassed as examples of the French dance suite. Following the fashion of his time, he gave his pieces amusing titles such as *The Call of the Birds*, *The Hen*, *The Whirlwinds*, *The Egyptian*.

A list of his works show that he wrote 26 operas, 2 cantatas, 5 books on theory, and 4 volumes of harpsichord music.

His death occurred in 1764, and all France mourned their "greatest composer" and for years held memorial services in his honor.

Piron, a French writer, said of him: "All his mind and all his soul were in his harpsichord and when he had closed that, the house was empty, there was no one at home."

French Composers for Clavecin and Harpsichord

In every collection of French instrumental music of the 17th and 18th centuries, besides the names of Lully and Rameau, we find Jacques Champion de Chambonnières (1602–1672), Jean Baptiste Loeilly, or Loeillet (?–1728?), François Couperin (1668–1733), Jean François Dandrieu (1684–1740), Jean Louis Marchand (1669–1733), Louis Claude Daquin (1694–1772) and Schobert (1720–1768).

These writers for clavecin and harpsichord of the French school were the first to write music for instruments to which they gave names describing the nature of the compositions. So, now, in addition to the names of dances which formed the suites, we find *The Coucou, Butterflies, Tambourine, The Windmill, The Turtle-Doves,* and so on. This was an important step for it led directly to the kind of titles given to piano pieces in the 19th century by the German romantic school.

The most important of this group was François Couperin, called "the great," as he was the most gifted member of a family, who supplied France with musicians for two centuries. From 1665 to 1826, there were eight Couperins who were organists of St. Gervais' Church in Paris.

We can compare the Couperin family to the Bachs who flourished at the same time in Germany. François (1668–1733), was only a year old when his father died, but a friend, who was an organist, taught him and in time he, too, became organist at St. Gervais. He was harpsichord player to the King, and was a favorite in court circles. No fashionable affair was complete without Couperin at the harpsichord, and every Sunday evening he played chamber music for Louis XIV, the royal patron of Lully. One of the books of pieces for the clavecin was published under the title of *Royal Concerts,* and in the preface, Couperin told that they were written for "*les petits concerts du roi*" (the little concerts of the king), and he also said that he hoped the public would like the pieces as much as the King did. For twenty years Couperin played in the King's household, and taught several princes and princesses.

You know the old proverb, "All roads lead to Rome." We would change it, and say that all roads lead to Bach! And Couperin is one of the main highways, for without knowing that he was doing so, he prepared the way for Bach, Haydn, Mozart and Beethoven. Everything he wrote, and most of his pieces were in the dance form of the suite, was exquisite in refinement and taste. The French musicians of today look upon him as one of their composers, most truly French, and they try to follow in the way he led, so as to be able to write music that will express the French people, in heart and character. Later in the story of music, the German classic school and then the romantic school had a very strong influence on the music of every country in the world, and in France there was the desire to brush aside the outside influences, and to find the road that the early French composers of the 17th and 18th centuries had traveled. Paul Landormy, a French writer on musical history has summed up Couperin as "one of the miracles of the French spirit in music, and across the gulf of time he clasps hands on one side with Jannequin and Costeley, (p. 154), on the other with Fauré and Debussy" (p. 519).

All the important music outside of opera written in France at this time was for the clavecin and harpsichord, and if the flute or the viol was invited to take part in a concert, it was only to double the melody played by the harpsichord, and did not have a part especially created for it.

Wouldn't you be surprised today if you should see an announcement of a concert to be given by the President's chauffeurs? But in the time of Couperin and Lully wind instruments were used in all the court festivals, balls and ballets, and were played by men attached to the great hunting stables of the king. The band was called *la musique de la grande écurie du Roi* (music of the King's stables). There were twelve trumpets, eight fifes and drums, the cromornes (krumhorn—a curved reed instrument), four to six Poitou oboes and bag-pipes, and twelve large oboes under which title were included oboes, (or violins), sack-buts and cornets. The wind instrument players accompanied the royal hunting parties and made the beautiful forests of France ring with their merry music. Each family had its own hunting call, by which it was recognized from afar. We heard a phonograph record in

Paris of these ancient calls, and with each one, the name of the family to whom it belonged was announced.

By the way, do you know the difference between a band and an orchestra? (This is not a conundrum!) A band was originally a group of musicians who played while standing or marching, while the orchestra was always seated. This word comes from the Greek word meaning dance, and was first given to a group of players who accompanied the dancers in the dramas, and were seated in that section of the theatre which is still called the orchestra.

CHAPTER XVII

Germany Enters—Organs, Organists and Organ Works

IT is rather hard to believe that the largest of all instruments, the pipe organ, is a descendant of Pan's Pipes, played by the shepherds on the hillsides of ancient Greece, is it not? The pipes of the church organ of today are of different lengths and are built on the same principle as were the pipes of Pan, our goat-footed friend, who broke off the reeds by the bank of a stream way back when the world was young, to pour out his grief in music for his lost love, Syrinx.

The next step was to supply the organ pipes with wind so they could be made to produce tones without blowing on each one separately. A wooden box was invented, and each pipe inserted into a hole in the top of the box, which is still called the wind-chest. At first this was supplied with air by two attendants who blew into tubes attached to the wind-chest. Soon the tubes were replaced by bellows, and were worked with the arms, and as the instrument grew larger, with the feet like in a treadmill. An organ is spoken of in the Talmud as having stood in the Temple of Jerusalem, and the hydraulic (water) organ in which air was supplied to the pipes by means of water power was built in Alexandria, Egypt, about the year 250 B.C. The small organ with keys that could be carried from place to place was called a portative (from the Latin *porto* —to carry); the larger organ sometimes stationary and sometimes moved on wheels was called a positive. The levers needed to produce the sound were soon exchanged for keyboards which at first had only a few keys, and you may remember our telling how the keys were pounded with the fists and elbows, in the Winchester organ.

A Greek writer of the 4th century A.D. gives us a vivid description of an organ: "I see a strange sort of reeds—they must methinks have sprung from no earthly, but a brazen soil. Wild are they, nor does the breath of man stir them, but a blast, leaping forth from a cavern of oxhide, passes within, beneath the roots of the polished reeds."

It is not known just when the organ was first used in the churches, but there are records of its having been known in Spanish churches as early as the 5th century A.D. Pope Vitalian introduced it in Rome in 666, and in the 8th century in England, organ building became a very popular profession. Cecil Forsyth says: "In those days a monk or bishop who wished to stand well with society could not take up essay-writing or social-welfare: what he could do was to lay hands on all the available timber, metal, and leather, and start organ-building."

Pepin, the father of Charlemagne, imported an organ into Compiègne, France, from Byzantium in the 8th century. Charlemagne had it copied at Aix-la-Chapelle. The Arabians must have been organ-builders, too, for one of their most famous rulers, Haroun-al-Raschid, sent Charlemagne a pneumatic organ noted for its soft tone. The instruments made in Germany and France up to the 10th century were small and unpretending, but were objects of astonishment and curiosity.

In Magdeburg, in the 11th century, we find the first keyboard with keys 3 inches broad. In 1120, we hear of an organ in the Netherlands that had 2 manuals (keyboards) and pedals. Organ-building was growing up! In the 14th century the manuals of many organs had 31 keys.

The organ was not always accepted in the church, for in the 13th century its use was regarded as scandalous just as the English Puritans in the 17th century called it a "squeaking abomination," and it is not even now admitted in the Greek Catholic Church!

Until the 14th century, the organ had been used only in a most primitive way to guide the singers of plain-song. It became a solo instrument when it was possible to grade its tone from soft to loud, which was done by the invention and use of three manuals: the upper one played *"full organ"* (very loud); the middle, the *discant*, (softest), played a counterpoint to the subject; the subject was played on the lowest keyboard.

So we see how one invention led to another until the organ became an instrument of almost unlimited possibilities, and how keyed instruments had shown the composers how to develop music along new lines. By the end of the 16th century, organ compositions and organ-playing had made rapid progress all over Europe, and you will recall the great organists in all the churches and cathedrals in the Netherlands, in England, Italy, France, Spain, and even in Germany which up to this time had not been on the "musical map." (Chapter XI).

Are you wondering why we have gone back into "ancient history" at this point, or have you already discovered that these grand old organists are leading us directly Bach-ward?

FRESCOBALDI

Just a century before Bach's time, the greatest of all Italian organists, Girolamo Frescobaldi (1583–1644), was born at Ferrara, Italy. So popular was he, that he filled the vast Cathedral of St. Peter's, whenever he played. His compositions were the most important produced for organ in the early 17th century, and his fugues were the first to be treated in modern fashion, in form, fancy, and feeling for tone color, and were a foundation on which Bach's were built. His compositions include *canzone, toccatas, ricercari,* and numerous pieces in the popular dance forms. Most of these are found in two collections published for *cembalo e organo* (spinet and organ). He was not interested in opera, but went his own musical way expressing himself in an original and individual language far ahead of his period. With Frescobaldi, Italy ceased to be the world's center for organists.

GERMAN ORGANISTS

At this point, Germany came into the musical field, and soon became the artistic center of organ-playing. Up to this time, the country had produced less music than any of its neighbors: Italy had written the greatest Church music, and invented opera; France had followed closely in Italy's footsteps; the Low Countries had helped in music's growth by their early work in polyphony and had taught all Europe including Germany; England had led the world in her compositions for virginals and harpsichord, the forerunners of piano music. Although Germany did not at first rank musically with these countries, the religious fervor and devotion to the cause of Protestantism bore fruit in the grand chorales of Luther. In these we find the birth of German music destined to rule the world for two centuries, the 18th and the 19th, just as the Italian had in the 16th and the 17th. The religious inspiration, the direct simplicity and sincerity of the chorales are the qualities found in the works of the first great German composer, Johann Sebastian Bach!

The religious wars of the first half of the 17th century crushed almost all the music out of Germany. In the second half, the organists became the leaders, and their music for organ inspired by the chorale was the first real contribution that Germany made to the growth of music.

One of the earliest of these German organists was Johann Jacob Froberger (1605–1667), of Saxony, who was a pupil of Frescobaldi, and court organist at Vienna. He went to London (1662), and as he was robbed on the way, he arrived penniless. He found work as organ-blower at Westminster Abbey. On the occasion of Charles II's marriage, he overblew the bellows and interrupted the playing, which so enraged the organist Christopher Gibbons, son of Orlando, that he struck him. Poor Froberger! But he had a chance to redeem himself, for he sat down to the organ a few moments later, and started to improvise in a manner for which he was famous in Vienna. A former pupil of his, recognizing his style, was overjoyed to find him, and presented him to the King. He was invited to play on the harpsichord which he did to the astonishment of every one.

A Dutch organist, Johann Adam Reinken (1623–1722) and a Dane, Dietrich Buxtehude (1637–1707) belong to this school, as they lived in Germany most of their lives and worked along the lines the Germans were developing. Reinken was a pupil of Frescobaldi; he had a direct influence on Bach who often walked from Lüneburg to Hamburg to hear the far-famed organist. When Reinken was 99 years old he heard Bach improvise on his Chorale "By the Waters of Babylon," which drew from him the praise, "I thought that this art was dead, but I see that it still lives in you."

ABSOLUTE MUSIC

It is very probable that had Buxtehude not lived, Bach would have written his organ works in a different style, so deeply did the younger composer study the older man's compositions. Buxtehude was organist in Lüneburg and there he started a series of concerts which became so popular that they were continued into the 19th century. Bach walked fifty miles to hear Buxtehude play; and he probably made himself known to the great man; it was no doubt to hear the concerts which had the poetic name of *Abendmusik* (Evening Music), that he went. Buxtehude was one of the first to try to make instrumental music stand as music (a language in itself), without a danceform, a plain-song or chorale or poetic idea behind it, to act as a Biblical text does in a sermon. This music for music's sake is called "Absolute Music" and Bach was one of its strongest disciples. Absolute music, which was so beautifully handled by Buxtehude, became the basis of the Classic School of the 18th and early 19th centuries.

The organ chorale prelude which was so important a musical form during this period had a very interesting history. Today the organist in our churches plays the hymn through before it is sung; he plays it quite simply just as it is written in the Hymnal, but in the day of these old German organists, the artistic feeling was deeper, and the organist was allowed to weave the chorale or hymn into a beautiful and complete composition. But in his love of composing and of showing how many different ways he could decorate the chorale, he often exceeded his time limit, and the chorale-prelude was left behind. In its place the organ fantasia and the sonata appeared.

. Johann Pachelbel (1653–1706), of Nüremberg, was a pupil of another celebrated director and organist, Johann Kaspar Kerl (1628–1693), who was said to be one of the best teachers of composition of his day. There were also three German organists born late in the 16th century, all of whom were followers of the famous Dutch composer Jan Sweelinck. They were known as the "three S's"—Heinrich Schütz was the greatest of them. He wrote organ music, but also worked out a scheme for combining the chorale with the ideas of Peri and Caccini for use with Bible texts in the Lutheran Church. This was called Passion music and was originally written for Good Friday. On this foundation Bach built some of his grandest oratorios. The Italian influence came into Schütz's work while he was a pupil of Gabrieli in Venice. Johann Heinrich Schein was a Cantor at St. Thomas' School before Bach, and wrote many chorales. The third of the "three S's" was Samuel Scheidt who was called the German Frescobaldi. "What plain-song was to Palestrina and his school, the chorale was to Schütz and his followers." (Quoted from Charles Villiers Stanford.)

THE INVENTOR OF THE SONATA AND OF "PROGRAM MUSIC"

Johann Kuhnau (1660–1722), wrote many compositions which today we find very amusing! For his day, however, he must have been looked upon as ultra-modern! The composition which first brought him into public notice was a motet, written for the election of the town council. Could you imagine anyone writing a serious composition for an election today, or anyone willing to listen to it at the polls? He was organist of St. Thomas', in Leipsic, a graduated lawyer, master of several languages, writer of satirical poems, musical director of the University, and finally Cantor in two Churches. He was admired and honored after his death as one of the greatest musicians of his day and one of the most learned men. He invented a style of music for the clavier which he called Sonata. It was in several movements and was not based on dance tunes as were the suites. While it was not in the form that later was known as sonata-form, it was a sign-post pointing the way. Seven of these sonatas he named *Fresh Clavier Fruit!* And it was fresh in style as well as in name.

He was the first German composer to write "program music," that is the kind which tries to tell a story, or to imitate the actual sounds of natural objects, such as the crash of thunder, the motion of a windmill, the rocking of a cradle, and the cackling of a hen. You can see how long a list one might make and how easy it would be for anyone with a vivid imagination to make up all sorts of pictures in music. This is just the opposite from music for music's sake which we described to you as "Absolute Music," and most of it which follows this period when music comes of age can be put into one of the two camps, —the Program Music Camp, or the Absolute Music Camp.

Kuhnau's program music took a queer turn! He was living at a time when religion was uppermost in every one's thoughts, when the Bible stories were bedtime stories and when the leading compositions were the sonatas written for organ. So in 1700 he published six Biblical-history Sonatas. In *David and Goliath*, he attempts to put into music the rude defiance and bravado of the giant; the fear of the Hebrews; David's courage and fearlessness, and the battle and fall of the giant; the flight of the Philistines (can't you imagine how the composer would represent this with all kinds of runs and scales?); the joy of the Hebrews; the celebration of the women who probably came out to meet David "with timbrels and harps"; and general jubilation.

At the end of the 17th century, Germany was strongly under the influence of France and Italy, especially in opera. In Dresden, Berlin, Munich and Vienna, one heard only opera in Italian sung by Italian singers, but Hamburg tried to develop a national music by giving German opera sung by German singers, and attracted many serious musicians. Johann Mattheson (1681–1764) a singer, conductor and composer, is remembered chiefly for a book called *A*

German Roll of Honor, in which he gathered up all the information he could find about German composers up to his time. He asked all the living composers to write accounts of themselves for his book, so we take it for granted that it must be truthful!

Music had changed more in the 17th century than in any that had gone before. If we tried to sum it all up in one word we should say that it was a century of *transition* or the passage from one condition to another. It began with the old Ecclesiastical, or Church, modes, and ended with the major and minor scales which we still use today; the reign of counterpoint was over, and now had to share the throne on equal terms with harmony.

Sonata-Form

The dominating musical form after Bach's time was to be the Sonata, a name we have often used. The sonata which found its champions in Haydn, Mozart and Beethoven, was the child of the sonata written by D. Scarlatti, Kuhnau, and Bach and his sons. It is built on the principle of contrast as were the suites. A sonata is a collection of three or four related pieces called movements: one, fast—one, slow—then fast. If in four movements, the first is moderately fast; the second, very slow; the third, fast (scherzo); the fourth fast (usually rondo form).

Sonata-form is the name given to the first movement of a sonata, a string quartet, trio, quintet, etc., concerto or a symphony. It has two main themes which are announced, then developed and then re-announced, forming three contrasting sections or panels: *Statement* or *Exposition*, *Development*, and *Restatement*. From now on, when we speak of *sonata-form*, this picture should come to you.

The stage is now all set for Bach and those who came after him.

Music Has Grown Up

CHAPTER XVIII

Bach—The Giant

BACH and Handel rescued the Germans from the reputation of being musical barbarians, for Germany had not had a Lully or a Palestrina. But just in time, Bach and Handel entered and Bach carried composition to maturity and religious musical art to its highest point, while Handel was one of the foremost opera and oratorio composers of his day.

And indeed not until Mozart's day did the Italians think that Germany was anything but barbarous, not in fact until they were outranked in Italian Opera by a German.

Of all the unassuming men of genius Johann Sebastian Bach (1685–1750) is the most lovable. Never did he seem to realize that he was doing anything, but the will of God, never did he seem to care what people thought of his work, but went on composing, supporting a large family, often with so little money that he tutored and played at funerals to eke out a living. In his life there was little glitter. Bach was a saint, if there was ever a saint. Although some few admired Bach during his lifetime, it was not until one hundred years after his death that his works were known and that he received the fame he deserved.

The Bach family for six generations were musicians,

beginning with his grandfather "to the 5th power," Veit Bach, a Thuringian baker in the 16th century whose pleasure "was to use a small zither, which he took with him to play, while the mill was moving." All his descendants became musicians down to and beyond Johann Sebastian.

The Bachs were great family lovers and every year they held reunions, at which all of the different members living in various parts of Germany, met together and enjoyed a jolly time singing and playing.

Sebastian was born in 1685 in Eisenach, the town where Martin Luther wrote his stirring chorales. His father Ambrosius began very early to teach him music, the family profession, and Sebastian started with the violin.

But the poor little boy lost both father and mother when only ten years of age, and he was left to be brought up by his elder brother, Johann Christopher. Sebastian was passionately fond of music and although Christopher taught him to play the clavier, nevertheless this sad little tale is told:

Sebastian had seen Christopher with a book of music including pieces by Froberger, Pachelbel, Buxtehude, and others. Sebastian was very anxious to get it and play bits from it. Christopher forbade him to touch it and put it away in a cupboard, which fortunately had a lattice door, for Sebastian, every night during the full moon, (because he did not dare to use a candle), copied the book note for note. When Christopher discovered this, the little lad was soundly scolded and the work of many months was taken from him.

It did not seem to daunt him, for from this time on, he copied great works whenever he could.

It became necessary for Sebastian to earn money to save Christopher's purse, and in 1700 he became a choir boy at St. Michael's in Lüneburg, where he received lessons without paying for them. He was happy here, with a library where he could copy music to his heart's content, and every vacation he went on foot to Hamburg to learn of the great organist, Reinken. He visited too the court of Celle where he heard Couperin's music, which no doubt helped to develop his style.

Soon he left Lüneburg and went to Saxe-Weimar where he entered the orchestra of Prince Johann Ernst. But his interest was in the church and when he was eighteen he tried for the post of organist in the Church at Arnstadt. He played so delightfully, despite his youth, that he was accepted at the first hearing!

He composed many works here and learned much about the organ, that was to be valuable to him and to us. He was well liked, too, and his playing was enjoyed. Nevertheless, his interest in others was so great, that he decided to go to see Buxtehude in Lübeck, and he was so interested in the master's art that he forgot about his church in Arnstadt and stayed four months instead of one! When he returned he was severely reprimanded. Later, he received a second reprimand which is of tremendous interest for he was accused of "interspersing the chorale with many strange variations and tones, to the confusion of the congregation." He was charged with the crime of being original!

Due to this lack of sympathy, he accepted a post as organist at Mühlhausen in 1707 and later in the year married his cousin, Maria Barbara, with great rejoicings. They had seven children, two of whom were the famous Wilhelm Friedemann and Karl Philipp Emanuel.

The next year he became Concertmaster (first violinist), to the Duke of Weimar and remained there until 1718. This was a very fruitful composing period, for he had no money worries. He studied the Italian masters, especially Vivaldi, and wrote some excellent cantatas. However, he went soon to the Prince of Anhalt-Cöthen, as Court Choir Master.

He made concert trips from here to Dresden and Leipsic, and it was in Dresden that he challenged the proud Marchand, the French organist to a public improvisation contest on a theme, new to both of them. But the contest never took place, because, unknown to Bach, Marchand heard him play and when the time for the contest came, Marchand had left town hurriedly in an early post-chaise. And strange as it may seem, Emperor Frederick I gave Marchand one hundred ducats and Bach got nothing!

Bach's new patron was a fine man and a Protestant and gave Bach every chance. At Weimar, he had become well known for his religious works and beautiful playing. But, as he had no organ, he wrote music for harpsichord, violin, chamber music, and for the orchestra which was far from "grown up." Here, too, he wrote the Brandenburg Concertos and the first part of his epoch-making work *The Well-tempered Clavichord* (48 Preludes and Fugues, 1722) which he finished in 1744. It is still the greatest work of its kind. In it he reaches the highest point of contrapuntal writing.

In 1720, while Bach was traveling with the Prince, his wife died. Four of their seven children survived her. After a year and a half he married a charming singer, Anna Magdalena Wulkens, with whom he lived happily. They had thirteen children, only six of whom outlived Bach. The lovely little tunes that he wrote for Anna Magdalena and his children, many of us have played in the first years of our music study. The great Bach, who wrote some of the masterpieces of the world, could also write simple little Minuets and Preludes that any child can play.

But with all Bach's comfort he missed an organ. Deep in his soul, he craved the making of religious music—it was part of his thinking. His religous ideas tied up with his music, were his life. So this saint left comparative comfort at Cöthen for an ill-paid post in Leipsic, where he succeeded Johann Kuhnau (1723) as Cantor at the school of St. Thomas. There he stayed the rest of his life and wrote many of his greatest works.

Bach wrote to a friend that he thought a long while before leaving his "gracious, music-loving and discriminating Prince. . . . but it happened that my master married a . . . princess who . . . weaned my master from the loving interest he had . . . toward our glorious art. And so God arranged that the post of Cantor at St. Thomas' should fall vacant. . . . I took three months to consider the future and was induced to accept, as my sons were studious and I was desirous . . . of gratifying their bent by entering them in the school . . . and thus, in the name of the Most High, I ventured and came to Leipsic."

Note, dear reader, the nobility, spirituality and sweetness here, thinking of his children and not of his career!

He struggled against the unsympathetic town council, the school, and lack of money. He wrote to his friend Erdman, "My present income averages $700. When funerals are numerous I make more, but if the 'air is healthy' then my income falls. During the past year I have earned $100 less, owing to the small number of deaths."

In 1732 he wrote one of his few attempts at comedy. —the *Coffee Cantata* set to music on a text by Picander. Leipsic had become a slave to the new luxury, coffee, and in this Picander found material for a satire.

Besides his regular work, he had to teach dull, undisciplined pupils, attend to services in four churches, and be satisfied with the few singers and players he found for the performances he directed.

Yet, fed with the spirit of love that was within him, he was happy and his home was a center of joy. He never became too sad until he lost his sight three years before his death. Even then he dictated his compositions and conquered discouragement!

Bach's life was made happier when his son, Karl Philipp Emanuel, became Court musician and clavier player to Frederick the Great, and he talked so much of his father that Bach was invited to Potsdam.

When Frederick the Great, who was playing the flute in his orchestra, heard that Bach was in Potsdam, he put down his flute and interrupted the concert saying, "Gentlemen, old Bach has arrived." Bach appeared in his traveling clothes and was invited to improvise a fugue in six parts, which he did to the great admiration of all.

Yet many felt that his writings were lacking in charm! This was no doubt because people were getting accustomed to the Italian melodies which had become popular in Germany. Furthermore, when he wrote "The Art of Fugue" his son could sell but thirty copies and finally sold the plates for the mere cost of the metal! Students are grateful that copies of this work were saved, for it is still the greatest authority on fugue writing.

In 1749, Bach underwent an operation on his eyes but lost his sight and in 1750 died of apoplexy. So little was he appreciated that his grave was destroyed in the renovation of the Johanneskirche grounds. His supposed remains were discovered in 1894 and re-interred one hundred and forty-four years after his death. But—what remains of Bach, no known or unknown grave can bury.

A quarter of a century after Bach's death, Mozart said, on hearing a Bach Cantata, "At last I have heard something new and have learned something." Then later Mendelssohn re-discovered him, and Schumann, too, helped to bring him to the world's notice. And not until 1850, a century after his death, was the Bach Society formed to honor Bach, the corner-stone of modern music.

Bach was a stalwart man with fine deep eyes, broad forehead and a grave face, lit with kindly humor. He had dignity and calm, was always courteous, and criticised only his pupils whom he wanted to help. When asked one time, how he played so well, he remarked, "I always have had to work hard." He could stand no one who was pretentious and conceited. He wanted his rights but never boasted. One year besides fulfilling his other duties he wrote a cantata every Sunday! He wrote them as a preacher writes sermons. They had to be done and he never neglected his duty.

Bach was a devoted father and husband and his home was one of the happiest of any great genius. Many of his children were musical and he said that he had an orchestra in his own home!

Even his little half-witted son had genius and during the last years of Bach's life when he had become blind, the little boy sat at the clavier, Bach's favorite instrument, and improvised to the joy of his father.

Bach's Works

It is impossible to describe in words just what Bach accomplished, so surpassing in beauty are his best works.

He brought the art of polyphonic writing to its highest and most sublime point. His value to the student cannot be exaggerated, for he is the musical Bible to all who would be musicians.

The organ was the core of his musical thinking and it is in the things which center about the organ that his art is loftiest.

Although he was most ingenious in writing counterpoint, he was never dry and tricky as were other writers. His subjects were always original and his melodic line always of rare beauty.

His works are most varied: fugues, motets, cantatas, passions, oratorios, concertos, sonatas and suites. He was a radical in his day, for he threw over conventional notions of harmony as to proper keys and insisted upon a new system of tuning the clavier, so as to use the whole range of tones. The "Well-tempered Clavichord," two groups of 24 Preludes and Fugues in 24 keys, was the outcome of this. It was so called because it was written to show the possibilities of a clavier (or clavichord) tuned according to an idea of his, enabling one to play in all keys. This was one of the greatest discoveries in the whole story of music, for it made possible all the music which has followed. The keyboard was divided into equal half-steps. This made twelve half-steps within each octave and thus all the intervals became fixed, and modulation from key to key was possible. Heretofore, if one went from one key to another, the instrument sounded out of tune, but now instruments were tuned, as we glibly say, "to scale."

He invented a new fingering in which the thumb and little finger were used for the first time. We wonder why the thumb had been snubbed!

The pianoforte was just coming into prominence in Bach's day but he preferred the clavier, on which he felt he could play with more expression.

He developed the fugue to its highest point. A fugue is an enlarged canon in which the fragments of theme or melody are taken up and answered by two, or more, voices. One voice declares the subject and the answer is repeated usually in the dominant key a fifth above, while the first voice gives the counter-subject. There are various kinds of fugues, depending on their construction. After every voice has entered, separated from each other by little passages called "episodes," a section in which the subject is freely developed comes, and then frequently there is a stretto, in which the parts overlap each other, building up to a climax; then follows the last cadence or ending.

To write a noble or lofty fugue, neither dry nor pedantic, takes art to the *nth* power! Bach had the art that touched Heaven's borders! In truth you can safely divide fugues into two classes—Bach's and all others!

None of Bach's works were published until he was forty years old, many not until long after his death, and some of his manuscripts were lost and never published at all.

The list of his works is stupendous; the Bach Gesellschaft (Bach Society, 1850) published them in sixty volumes! Among them were the 48 Preludes and Fugues (The Well-tempered Clavichord Collection); 12 Suites; many Inventions in 2 and 3 parts; partitas; 12 concertos for 1, 2, 3 and 4 claviers with orchestra; many sonatas and concertos for violin, flute, viola da gamba, clavier, and orchestra; several overtures for orchestras; vocal works; 200 motets and cantatas; 5 *Passions*, of which the greatest are the St. Matthew and the St. John; 5 masses of which his *B Minor Mass* is a world masterpiece; oratorios; magnificats; many organ works, and old German chorales harmonized for voices.

Try to hear Bach compositions on the harpsichord. It reveals the beauty of the saintly Bach. The art of harpsichord playing has been revived by Wanda Landowska and others.

Also try to hear the Bach Festival, in Bethlehem, Pennsylvania, in the Moravian Church, where it has been held annually for many years.

In a list of great men, Bach would be classed with Euripides, Sophocles, Shakespeare, Milton, da Vinci, Michelangelo and Goethe.

Bach did not write for people, he wrote for his own soul. He never seemed able to write theatric music, for his was the drama of the spirit. Always, his music was the result of his musings, the confessions of his ideals. So he attained a loftiness, grandeur and sublimity far removed from even some of the most dramatic writers.

BACH'S SONS

Bach's sons reached great eminence. The eldest was Wilhelm Friedemann (1710–1784) an unusually talented man on whom the father built great hopes. But while Friedemann inherited his father's musical talent he did not have his character, and was looked upon as a disgrace to the family on account of his dissolute ways. He was the greatest organist of his time and most of his compositions which were considered very fine, have been lost to the world, for he did not take the trouble even to write them down, but played them from memory.

The third son, Karl Philipp Emanuel (1714–1788), although trained to be a lawyer, could not resist the urge of music, and after going through two universities decided to become a musician to Frederick the Great. He was "general manager" of all the music at court until the Seven Years' War put an end to his position after almost thirty years' service. He then spent the rest of his life in Hamburg. As composer, conductor, teacher and critic his influence was great. He was loved and respected by the whole city. In his day he was regarded as being as important as his father, but we know that he was not in the same class, although he was the greatest of his contemporaries. He did not imitate his father's style but developed the sonata into the form that Haydn, Mozart and Beethoven perfected. He was an innovator, not only in form, but in the treatment of melody and harmony. His best sonatas were written at the court of Frederick the Great.

In the growth of music he is the link between his immortal father and Haydn. Haydn was more gifted than he and made the seeds planted by Philipp Emanuel blossom luxuriantly.

Johann Christoph (1732–1795) was an upright, modest, amiable man, and a splendid musician keeping up the family traditions.

Johann Christian (1735–1782) the youngest of those who outlived the father, is known as the Italian or English Bach, because he went to Italy in 1754, became organist of the Milan Cathedral, and wrote vocal music in the Neapolitan style. He left his position as organist, married an Italian prima donna, wrote many operas and spent the last twenty years of his life in London, as director of concerts, and music-master to the Queen. He exerted a strong influence on the development of music in England, and was a friend of Mozart.

Curious as it may seem, the great and gifted Bach family died out in 1845, with a grandson of Johann Sebastian. Out of twenty children there seems not to have been one to carry the line to the present day.

CHAPTER XIX

Handel and Gluck—Pathmakers

George Frederick Handel—Master of Oratorio

(1685–1759)

IN the last chapter we saw Bach rescue music from the danger of emptiness and frivolity, by perfecting polyphonic music and dignifying church music as it had not been since Palestrina.

Bach and Handel were alike in that they were both born in Germany when music, especially opera, had become mechanical and full of set rules. They were both Lutherans and Thuringians. They worked about the same time, and tried to encourage the hearts and minds of their country, torn by the Thirty Years' War; both were polyphonic masters; both organists. Bach attached himself to Frederick the Great, the protector of the faith, and Handel went to England, where there was liberty of thought; and both became blind and died of apoplexy.

The differences, with so many similarities, are most interesting. Bach, modest, retiring, was always a German subject; Handel became an English subject. Bach was a homebody with many children; Handel was a traveler and never married. Bach wanted only to satisfy himself; Handel, to satisfy the public. Bach was humble, Handel arrogant. Bach seldom fought for his rights, while Handel would dismiss even his masters. Bach cared

little for applause, but Handel could not live without it.
Bach was devoted to the lyric, Handel to the epic. Handel
is usually (not always) heroic, Bach is usually religious (not
always, of course). Handel is popular, easy to understand;
Bach is deep, coming from the soul, and it takes more
thought than the crowd is always willing to give to appreciate this giant.

Handel achieved great worldly success, and treated
nobles as equals. Poor Bach worked contentedly in an
humble position and struggled for money and profited by
"bad air." (See page 248.)

Bach demanded faith and love of art, Handel demanded
ready ears. Bach's first intention was not to make music,
but to express his devotion in the best medium he had;
Handel wanted fame and riches and the approval of the
crowd. Handel died rich and Bach died poor.

George Frederick Handel (1685–1759) composer of the immortal oratorio *Messiah*, and one of the greatest opera composers of his time, was born in Halle, Saxony. His father
was a barber-surgeon, and managed to get the title "Cham-
berlain to the Prince of Saxe-Magdeburg."

Handel's father wished him to study law, but George
Frederick did not like the idea and besides he showed
great musical gifts. One day when he was a little boy, he
found hidden in the attic, a clavichord upon which he
secretly played every chance he had.

Not long after this "find," something most important
happened. His father was going to Weissenfels to the
Duke's castle and had no intention of taking George
Frederick with him. So, Father Handel seated himself in
the coach, taking things comfortably, when he spied little
George Frederick dashing along by the great wheels. He
paid no attention to him, but after going a mile and realizing that the little boy was still following, he called out
"What do you want?" "I want to go with you," answered

Handel, and although his father was quite annoyed, George Frederick's will, as always, prevailed and he went with his father! At the court the Duke saw, very quickly, how gifted the little Handel was. His father relented and on his return to Halle, George Frederick was given instruction on the organ, harpsichord and in composition with Zachau, and taught himself the oboe and violin, greedily mastering all the music he could find.

Although he studied music he seems to have respected his father's wishes and studied law and even after his father died in 1697, he continued, but later gave it up for music. At seventeen he entered the University, and studied, besides music, the literary classics which were of great use to him later.

On leaving the University he went to Hamburg, the musical center of Germany, where he heard Keiser's works and received good advice from Johann Mattheson, the composer, tenor and conductor, who later engaged George Frederick in a duel.

The quarrel came about in this way: Handel was to lead Mattheson's opera, *Cleopatra*, in order to relieve Mattheson, who sang the part of Antonio. After Antonio was "killed," Mattheson being free to lead, entered the orchestra pit to take Handel's place as leader. Handel was infuriated. They met later and fought a duel in which Handel was saved by a large metal button which snapped Mattheson's rapier! What a little thing a button is and what it did for music!

Handel's first four operas were written here for the Hamburg stage. But *Almira* (1705) is the only one ever heard now.

HANDEL IN ITALY

Next he visited Florence, Rome and Venice during which time he had the happiest three years of his life. He composed a cantata, an oratorio and other works; he learned much of melody and sweet flowing music, which softened his dry, stiff use of German counterpoint, and he gathered material for his later London work.

An amusing story is told of him in Venice. There was a carnival going on and Handel went to it. At one of the costume balls, he sat down to a harpsichord uninvited and began improvising, thinking that no one would know him. A gorgeously garbed figure dashed through the crowd to his side, and almost overcome by the music, gasped, "This; is either the Devil or the Saxon." (Handel was called "The dear Saxon"—"*Il cáro Sarsone*" in Italy.) It was Domenico Scarlatti's first meeting with Handel, and forever after they remained warm friends.

In Vienna he met Steffani (Chapel Master) who persuaded him to go to Hanover and after a short time, the Elector, who became George I of England, appointed him Chapel Master and gave him permission to go to England for a visit before taking up his new work.

This visit was the turning point in Handel's career, for later he became an English subject and he—but we must not get ahead of our story!

HANDEL IN ENGLAND

Handel went to England about fifteen years after the death of Purcell, "The Orpheus of England." Handel was quick to see Purcell's good points and modelled his first English work to celebrate the Peace of Utrecht, on Purcell's *Te Deum*.

After arriving in London he wrote *Rinaldo* with an Italian libretto in fourteen days! He was the speed maniac of the 17th and 18th centuries. His librettist said of him, "Mr. Handel barely allowed me time to compose my verses." Later he arranged *Rinaldo* for harpsichord and all England played it, especially the lovely aria *Lascia ch'io Piango* (Let Me Weep).

Yet Handel doesn't seem to have made money out of *Rinaldo*, which brought the publisher, Walsh, $10,000, about which Handel said, "My dear fellow, the next time you shall compose the opera and I will publish it." (*History of Music*, by Paul Landormy.)

Later, he became the guest of the Duke of Chandos, at whose house he wrote at least sixteen compositions.

King George had been very angry with Handel for leaving Hanover and remaining in England, but forgave him later, and Handel was made Director of the Royal Academy of Music which the King founded in 1719. Among Handel's duties was procuring the artists for the operas. This meant much to him and allowed him to travel all over Europe. He composed operas almost as people wrote their letters, for in eight years he produced eleven successful operas! Think of that for work!

HANDEL AND HIS RIVALS

But—he had a rival, Battista Bononcini, protégé of the mighty Duke of Marlborough, and a musical war raged in London. John Byrom, a humorist of the day wrote:

> Some say, as compared to Buononcini
> That Mynheer Handel's but a ninny
> Others aver that he to Handel
> Is scarcely fit to hold a candle.
> Strange all this difference should be
> 'Twixt tweedledum and tweedledee.

Handel won, however, and Bononcini left England. In 1729, another opera venture was started, an Italian opera society, of which Handel was made the Director. Off he went to Dresden and brought back Senesino, a tenor, and other famous singers. But Handel did not get along well with his singers and subordinates. He was too high-handed and because of his quarrels the opera was given up! On one occasion he dragged the singer, Cuzzoni, to the window and threatened to throw her out if she did not sing the way he wished. Various other reasons were given too,— one, the dispute between Cuzzoni, who was called the "Golden Lyre" and another soprano, Faustina, the wife of Hasse, a rival conductor. Colley Cibber, a critic of the time said: "These costly canary birds contaminate the whole music loving public with their virulent bickerings. Cæsar and Pompey did not excite the Romans to more violent partisanship than these contentious women."

And now we see Handel bankrupt and superseded in another theatre by his two rivals, Porpora and then Hasse (1699–1783) of Hamburg. However, they too were unsuccessful.

On went Handel, writing operas and oratorios and conducting at special functions. His health snapped, but his will was so powerful that this forceful man recovered, and presented two more operas, which were not successful. In spite of all his failures and lack of tact, he had faithful friends who arranged a successful benefit concert in 1738 for him. At about the same time a statue was erected in Vauxhall Gardens, an honor never before paid to a living composer!

He composed, while writing for the stage all these years, twelve sonatas for violin or flute with figured bass, thirteen sonatas for two violins, oboes or flutes and bass, twelve *concerti grossi*, twenty organ concertos, twelve concertos for strings, many suites, fantasies and fugues for harpsichord and organ. It is difficult to understand how one brain could do all this!

HANDEL FORSAKES OPERA

After his ill success with the Italian Opera House, he gave up writing operas and devoted himself to oratorios. In thirteen years (1739–1752) he wrote nineteen. Among these are *Saul* in which is the famous "Dead March," *Joseph*, and many other important ones, but towering over all *The Messiah*, and *Heracles*, which Romain Rolland says is "one of the artistic summits of the 18th century."

They are not all oratorios, for *Heracles* and several others are not religious in subject, but are dramatic epics.

Handel's sight failed him, but even this did not stop his torrential activity to his death in 1759.

He had become an English subject, so was buried with pomp at Westminster Abbey.

He was loved even though he was fiery of temper, and had a will that no one could conquer.

His music is full of his gusts of feeling but always correct and his art perfect. In his work he always held himself under great control and it mirrors his power and balance. He loved wind instruments and people often considered his music noisy!

He wrote forty-two operas, two passions, ninety-four cantatas, ten pasticcios, serenatas, songs and the instrumental works mentioned above. The famous Handel *Largo* comes from one of his operas, *Xerxes*, and was an aria *Ombra mai fu* (Never was there a Shadow).

Handel used counterpoint, but always knew when to unbend and use delightful flowing melody, which made his music popular.

Other men, Hasse, Telemann and Graun, contemporaries of Handel, followed the popular Italian models but without Handel's genius for melody and sublimity, and their music was rarely heard after their own generation had passed away.

Handel's *Messiah*, which he wrote in twenty-four days, was first given in Dublin. It took the people by storm and when the king heard it, thrilled by the "Hallelujah Chorus," he rose to his feet, and since then it is the custom to stand during that number. It has become the Christmas Oratorio and is sung in churches and societies all over the world. It has lost none of its first popularity among the people and is loved as few works have ever been. It thrills because it is sincere, big, and arouses religious feeling. Oratorio was his special gift to the world and one never hears the name of Handel without thinking of *The Messiah*.

Handel seemed to reunite the forms: oratorio and opera, under his massive will. At first some of his oratorios were given in costume, showing the influence of opera.

Handel had many enemies in England, but he also had friends. Although imperious, he had a sweet side, and made friends with humble folk who loved music, even though he hobnobbed with royalty. Thomas Britton, a coal heaver, his friend, is sketched by an artist of the day in a picture where Handel is playing *The Harmonious Black-smith* to Alexander Pope, the Duchess of Queensbury, Colley Cibber and other famous folk. Yet he stormed at everyone and even royalty "quaked in their boots" and were forced to behave themselves at rehearsals and concerts which Handel directed.

Accused of using someone's melody, he answered, "That pig couldn't use such a melody as well as I could!" He helped himself to so many that he was called the "Great Plagiarist."

His latter life was spent quietly, with a few intimate friends, drinking his beer and smoking his beloved pipe. He was always generous and as he grew older seemed to become kindlier and softer. He contributed largely to the Foundling Asylum and even played the organ there.

He wanted to die on Good Friday, "in hopes," he said,

of meeting his good God, his sweet Lord and Saviour on the day of his resurrection," and on Good Friday, April 6th, 1759, he died.

CHRISTOPH WILLIBALD GLUCK—FATHER OF MODERN
OPERA

1714–1787

Now we come to the next genius, Christoph Gluck (1714–1787) born when George Frederick Handel was twenty-nine years old. He also attacked the frivolous drift of his time, but in another field from Handel and Bach, and he gave the fashionable, aimless Italian opera its death blow for all time.

Gluck's life is different from Handel, Bach, Haydn, Mozart and Beethoven as you will see later when you have read about all of these. For, until he was almost forty years old, Gluck did nothing to make him great, whereas these other men showed from their earliest years that they were unusual.

Gluck belongs to two periods for his life bridges Bach's and Haydn's. You will see how he first belonged to the frivolous fashion-loving composers like Hasse, Jomelli and Piccinni, and how later he blossomed into the great renewer and constructor of opera and escapes into a class of his own! His is the most remarkable instance of a man who starts with an ordinary talent, and later in life grasps a vision that never came to him in his early youth and which was not caught by others in his day.

Furthermore he was able to carry his point and not merely see the vision and let it go by. But first let us see how his life unfolded, for a man's life helps us to understand his works.

Christoph Willibald Gluck, born July 2nd, 1714, at Weidenwang, near Nüremburg, was the son of a gamekeeper, who moved from estate to estate in the service of princes and nobles, and at the time of Christoph's birth, was ranger to Eugene, Prince of Savoy. So, this little boy destined to become the great Chevalier von Gluck, was a child of the people even as was Haydn and others.

Gluck Starts Traveling

At the age of three he was taken to Bohemia, (Czecho-Slovakia), for his father entered the service of Prince Lobkowitz, a member of a family of music-lovers, of which you will hear again. His parents were quite poor, yet it is remarkable that they gave Christoph a good education and at twelve he went to a Jesuit school near Eisenberg, the home of Prince Lobkowitz.

Here he learned to sing and to play the organ, the violin, the 'cello and the clavier. He was diligent and became most proficient and was loved and admired by the school fathers. But little did they dream that some day he was to write classic operas, based not on Christian stories but the pagan dramas of the Greeks!

When nearly nineteen, he left the seminary and said good-bye to the Church of St. Ignatius and went to Prague. To support himself and to carry on his scientific and musical studies he gave lessons, played for rustic festivals and earned money the best way he could, until Prince Lobkowitz, became interested in him and introduced him to the musical circle at court. Here he met Count Melzi who took him to Milan, where he was taught by Giovanni Battista Sammartini, a celebrated organist and teacher of counterpoint. After four years of study he completed his musical education.

In Milan, he wrote his first opera, *Artaserse* which was

performed in 1741. Metastasio, the popular librettist, wrote the words to *Artaserse*, as he did for many of Gluck's works written in the loose style of Italian opera. Gluck was now twenty-eight and in the five years spent here, he composed eight operas, through which he gained great popularity. But not yet had it come to him to revolutionize opera; he simply used the old pattern which was really nothing but groups of songs, recitatives and choruses having very little connection except to give the performers the chance to do musical feats to amaze the audience with their skill. The story of these operas, meagre as it was, stopped short, for some long and elaborate cadenza, and then it went on again with no thought of the meaning of the drama but rather to tickle the taste of the audience and the performer. The orchestra, too, was a step-child, for no one cared where it came in as long as it was politely subdued, keeping the singers on the key, and doing its best to be heard only when bidden. So, Gluck followed these ideas in the beginning and perhaps it was better that he did, otherwise he might never have realized how far opera had strayed from the ideals of Monteverde.

Having eight operas to his credit, he began to get commissions from other cities and countries, and next accepted an invitation, in 1745, to go to London as composer of opera at the Haymarket Theatre. In 1746 he wrote *La Caduta de Giganti* (The Fall of the Giants), with no doubt a libretto of Metastasio's, then he gave his *Artamene* and was assisted in their production by Handel, who is supposed to have treated the works with contempt. He is said to have exclaimed, "Even my shoe-black can write better counterpoint than Gluck." But we must remember that Gluck had not yet become the *great* Gluck. His visit to England was fruitful, for Gluck heard and digested the great oratorios of Handel, and realized that the voice and orchestra might be handled the same way in opera. No doubt his mission was beginning to dawn on him; it came, not as a great revelation, but gradually.

He Makes Success of Failure

Another thing that gave him a push forward and shows how great people can make a success of failure: he was asked to write a *pasticcio* (Italian word meaning a meat-pie), or a string of melodies, very fashionable in his day. He strung together his best airs from his Italian operas, and called it *Pyramus and Thisbe*, but it was a dismal failure. "Ah, ha!" he must have thought, "why shouldn't this musical drivel fail, for it is naught but trash, and with nothing that is needed to make a good literary drama." So this was one of the experiences that led him to reform opera, making the words fit the music and not stopping a performance, so that a popular soloist could sing a meaningless trill and then start again with the other part of the word,—the way that opera was being written at that time.

After his London ups and downs he went to Paris and heard the operas of Rameau. He realized now the value of musical declamation and recitative to the meaning and action of opera if used with thought, and he was not slow in taking suggestions.

Gluck was probably the most all round man of his day, for he knew literature and science as did few musicians. He knew all the influential people in the arts, sciences, and music in London, Hamburg, Dresden and Vienna, and his home was a center of learned and delightful people. When in Vienna but a short time, he was commissioned to write an opera and he produced, with success, *La Semiramide*, after which he went to Copenhagen. His next opera, *Telemacco*, in which he began to work out his new ideas, was well received in Rome and Naples.

In 1750 after many disappointments, he was married to a lady he had long adored. They lived happily together, for Marianne Pergin not only brought him money which was a great joy, but was always his devoted and understanding help-mate. She was an accomplished woman, and a companion that many might envy. But, sad to say, they had no children, so they adopted a niece of Christoph's, a lovely little girl with great musical talent. The three lived lovingly together until the poor little child sickened and died, making the Glucks most unhappy, for they adored her, as is often the case, even more than if she had been their own child.

In 1751 Gluck journeyed to Naples. Didn't he travel a lot in the days of the stage coach and brigands! In the same year he became conductor to Prince Frederick at Vienna and in 1754 was officially attached to the opera, and Maria Theresa made him court chapel master.

Soon after, the Pope pleased with what he had done in Rome, made him Chevalier of the Golden Spur and from that time he always styled himself Ritter (Chevalier) von Gluck.

In *Il re pastore* (The Shepherd King), we see the dawning of Gluck's best period of writing (1756). The overture is better music than he had written before, and from this time on, Gluck became the genius in the opera world for which he is known. From 1756 to 1760 he lived apart from the world studying and after this he began to broadcast his ideas in writing and composing.

When the Archduke Joseph of Austria, afterwards the Emperor, married Isabella of Bourbon, Gluck wrote *Tetide* which was performed with great pomp. After this he wrote the ballet *Don Giovanni*, or *The Libertine*, particularly interesting, for it certainly gave Mozart an idea for his own great work *Don Giovanni*.

Again our "wandering minstrel" moved, this time to

Bologna where he conducted a new opera which, strange
to say, showed not a sign of his new ideas!

"Orpheus and Euridice" is Born

Soon he met Calzabigi, another librettist, with whom he
wrote his first epoch-making opera *Orpheus and Euridice.*
Although in some parts it is written like the older operas,
he used many of his new ideas. The public at first were
bewildered but they liked it. The next opera written with
his new librettist was *Alceste,* so different was it, and so
full of his best thought that the public did not like it.
The pleasure-loving people went to be amused and heard
music almost as serious as oratorio. It was austere, and
its climax was not satisfactory. Yet it and *Orpheus and
Euridice* mark the birth of music-drama which Mozart
and Wagner developed further.

In *Orpheus and Euridice* the chorus was an important
part of the drama as it had been in the old Greek drama
from which Gluck took many of his stories; and was not
something dragged in to fill up space. Instead, too, of the
over-embroidered arias they were simple and expressive,
and the characters were real living beings, instead of figures on which to drape showy melodies. Naturally, the
composers were jealous of him and went so far as to
say that the principal singer had written *Orpheus and
Euridice.*

Gluck said of his *Alceste:* "I seek to put music to its
true purpose; that is, to support the poem, and thus to
strengthen the expression of the feelings and the interest
of the situation without interrupting the action. . . .
In short, I have striven to abolish all those bad habits
which sound reasoning and true taste have been struggling
against now for so long in vain." He abolished the unnecessary cadenza, a showy flourish composed by the soloist

himself to display his technical agility. You will see in a later chapter how Beethoven dealt with it.

Happily Gluck and Calzabigi still continued working together and in 1770 he wrote *Paride and Elena* (Paris and Helen) which proved Gluck to be a writer of beautiful romantic song.

By now Vienna and Paris were enthusiatic about him, yet he was severely criticized because he dared to write and compose differently from everyone else. The adventurer into new paths must always expect trouble from those who have not caught up with him.

TROUBLE BREWS FOR GLUCK

Now our traveler goes to Paris where he presents *Iphigenia in Aulis*. The story was taken from a play of the French dramatist Racine. Although this was the fourth work in Gluck's new style it was not as good as the others. His enemies did their utmost to hurt him as they resented his coming into Paris to reform French opera. And as the musicians and singers were not good artists, it was almost impossible to give it well, and probably it would never have reached the stage had it not been for Marie Antoinette the French Queen who was later guillotined. She had been a real friend and pupil of Gluck, when a young princess in Vienna. Nevertheless the opera pleased its audiences, and it paid well, and Gluck was given a new court office in Vienna.

In 1776 the trouble that had been brewing with Gluck's opponents came to a climax. Piccinni was his great Italian rival and the city of Paris was torn as to who was the better composer. All the literary men and the court were divided into factions, one for and one against Gluck. Some great men, including Jean Jacques Rousseau were Gluckists, while others of importance were Piccinnists.

Never had there been so great a contention for musical glory or struggle against new ideas. It was a most extraordinary thing, but it does show that there was great musical interest or people would never have wasted so much time in argument and in writing for or against these men. Finally it came to a head, and it was decided to give them both the same libretto of *Iphigenia in Tauris* to see who could write the better opera. Gluck completed his within the year and after nearly three years, Piccinni finished his. They were both performed and needless to say Gluck won the award and even Piccinni said himself that Gluck's was the better. It is nice to know that after Gluck's death, Piccinni tried to collect funds to raise a memorial as a tribute to him! So artistic rivalry need not dim admiration.

In *Iphigenia in Tauris* again the master rises to great heights. His overture was splendid, his orchestral color was superb. He pictured the different characteristics of the various groups of people and of the individuals themselves in word and music as it never had been done before.

He wrote *Armide* in 1777. It did not succeed although it was very lovely and dreamy and in it, he suggested the sounds of babbling brooks and the song of the nightingales.

Gluck wrote thirty operas, seven of which are in his new style: *Don Giovanni, Orpheus and Euridice, Paris and Helen, Alceste, Iphigenia in Tauris, Iphigenia in Aulis* and *Armide.*

NEW PATHS

And thus this great path-breaker advanced *opera seria* (grand opera).

The old *sinfonia* in three movements which opened the opera, disappeared, and instead came the introduction or overture, suggesting the opera itself. He taught and wrote that composers could do anything to assist the action of the opera; he elevated the story to an important place; the characters in the plot were thought of as people and not as puppets, and they were studied individually and not as machinery only. The situations in the story governed the kind of music he used and he tried hard to make the orchestra a main part of the opera. It seems odd that nobody had thought of this before. Yet you have seen how much time had been given to the voice throughout the ages, and how long it had taken instruments to arrive at their full importance. So we see Gluck improving as he worked with a better librettist. From now the opera writer had to use thought in composition, as he would in writing a play.

A Very Cross Conductor!

But Gluck had trouble with the singers on account of his innovations. He was the crossest conductor of his time, would allow no one to dictate to him, and scolded the singers as they had never been scolded before.

He must have looked droll conducting, for he used to take off his wig during rehearsals, and wrap a cloth about his head to keep the draughts from fanning him! He would rage if the singers tried to do what they had been permitted to do in other operas! Some singers demanded extra pay when Gluck conducted. Sometimes he would repeat a passage twenty or thirty times and no *pianissimo* was soft enough and no *fortissimo* loud enough! Someone said of him while he was conducting, "He lives and dies with his heroines, he rages with Achilles, weeps with Iphigenia and in the dying scene of *Alceste* throws himself back in his chair and becomes as a corpse."

Otherwise he was always the kind soul who attracted everybody from Marie Antoinette down. She used to receive him in her boudoir so that they could enjoy conversation without court formalities.

One day two prima donnas refused to obey him when rehearsing *Iphigenia*, and he said: "Mesdemoiselles, I have been summoned here to Paris especially to produce *Iphigenia*. If you sing, well and good, but if not, that is your business; only I shall then seek an audience with the Queen, and inform her that the opera cannot be performed, and I shall put myself into my carriage and straightway leave for Vienna." You may know that the ladies did their best!

In closing let us tell you what Berlioz, a master of orchestration, said of Gluck's orchestration in *Alceste:* "Of its kind I know nothing more dramatic, nothing more terror-inspiring." And this was said of a man who had only the simplest orchestra with which to work. After much fighting, he was the first to introduce into the orchestra the kettle-drums and cymbals, which moderns have used with grandeur.

Gluck lived to see his own success, but the Piccinni strife and the jealousies may have weakened his constitution, for he died rather suddenly in 1787, a few weeks after the first performance of Mozart's *Don Giovanni*.

There are many memorials in Europe to Gluck, not the least being his bust which stands beside Lully and Rameau in the Grand Opera of Paris.

PUBLIC CONCERTS

It is very hard to realize that time was when there were no public concerts. Music was confined for so many centuries to the churches, to the public squares, to the King's Chamber, or to the ball rooms of wealthy nobles, that it had not become the democratic art that it is now. Of course the first opera houses in Italy had been steps in the

direction of bringing music to the people.   The concerts
begun by the Danish organist, Buxtehude, in Lübeck about
1673, and the *Tonkünstler-societät* in Vienna of the same
period were the first public concerts.   In England, John
Banister started concerts at about the same time, which
were the first to admit an audience by payment of a fee.
Handel's friend, Thomas Britton, the coal-heaver, gave
concerts at his home for 10 shillings the series!

The 18th century saw a great development in giving public concerts.   In France, the *Concerts Spirituels* were begun in 1725.   The object of these were to give music to the
people on the days of religious festivals when the opera
house was closed.   There were about 24 concerts a year;
the political events of 1791 put an end to the society but it
had already given the people a taste for concerts, and many
new societies grew out of it.   The festivals of Three Choirs
in West England (see page 190) were founded in 1724, and
the Academy of Ancient Music in 1710.   The *Musikverein*
in Leipsic was founded in 1743 and was later turned into
the famous *Gewandhaus* concerts in 1781.

This movement for public concerts went hand in hand
with the development of instruments and the perfecting of
performers.   In fact the word concert came from "*consort*
—the union or *symphony* of various instruments playing in
concert to one tune."

THE MANNHEIM SCHOOL

The symphony came to life in Germany.   Paul Landormy in his *History of Music* tells us that it was the time of
the "poor scholars" who were educated free from expense
in the schools with the understanding that they were to
learn the "musician's trade" and take part in the concerts
organized by the cities and the courts.   Thus symphony
orchestras grew up all over Germany,—Munich, Stuttgart,

Dresden, Darmstadt, Hamburg where Telemann conducted, in Leipsic, Berlin and Mannheim.

In Mannheim appeared the most important group of composers, known as the *Mannheim School*, and many wrote the early symphonies which led from the works of Bach to those of Haydn and Mozart. The best known of these composers are: Johann Stamitz (1717–1757), Franz Xavier Richter (1709–1789), Anton Filtz, Christian Cannabich, Ignaz Holzbauer, Ernst Eichner and Giovanni Battista Toeschi. Under the direct influence of the Mannheim School were: François Joseph Gossec (1734–1829), a Belgian living in Paris who wrote many symphonies; Luigi Boccherini (1743–1805) known as one of the first writers of chamber music in the form used by the classic writers; Giovanni Battista Sammartini (1701–1775) of Milan; the sons of Bach, Karl Ditters von Dittersdorf, and Joseph and Michael Haydn.

CHAPTER XX

"Papa" Haydn and Mozart—the Genius

FRANZ JOSEPH HAYDN

1732–1809

ABOUT the time in history when Franz Joseph Haydn was born, the world was very much upset. No one knew what to think or how. It was a time of battle and struggle as he was born in the midst of the Seven Years' War and lived during the French Revolution. Everyone except for a few great persons felt bitter and discontented and doubt was everywhere. This seems to be the way wars and conflicts effect all peoples and it is why wars are so damaging.

Yet out of this mixture of feeling and thinking, the great classic period of music was created by such men as Bach and Haydn and Mozart and the finishing touches were put on it by Beethoven, the colossus.

Franz Joseph Haydn was born in Rohrau (1732), a little town in Austria near Vienna. His father was a wheelwright and his mother was a very good cook. Beethoven's mother, too, was a professional cook.

These simple parents, his brothers and sisters, measuring not a baker's, but a wheelwright's dozen, had an hour or two of music every evening after the hard day's work, and Mathias, the father, played the harp and sang. It was during these evenings that little Joseph's father noticed that at the age of six he was passionately fond of music.

One time at a festival the drummer failed to appear and there was no one who could play for the choristers who were to march through the town. His teacher, Frankh, called Joseph and showed him how to make the drum stroke and told him to practice it. When he was left by himself he found a meal tub, over which he stretched a cloth, put it on a stool and drummed with such vigor that the whole thing toppled over and he and his drum were covered with meal! But he learned to drum! And the people laughed when in this solemn church festival, the little six year old Joseph was seen drumming the big drum carried by a hunchback in front of him. The drums on which he played are still at Hainburg. But, we forget, we have not brought him from Rohrau!

Not long before J. M. Frankh, a relative, came to visit the Haydns, and it was decided that he should take Joseph to Hainburg to teach him. The excitement, of course, was great and little Joseph felt very important with all the hustle and bustle preparing for his departure. Little did Saperle (his nickname) realize what a hard master he was getting in Frankh, who only cared for the pay he received from Joseph's father. Nevertheless he learned much and showed great talent while at Hainburg and one day a great thing happened. Reutter, the organist of St. Stephen's in Vienna, visited Frankh and as they talked of music the conversation turned to the choir school which Reutter directed. Frankh sent for Joseph, a slight, dark haired, dark eyed little boy, and Reutter asked him to read a piece of music at sight. Joseph looked at it and said: "How can I, when my teacher couldn't?" Yet, Joseph did sing it sweetly and he entered the choir school. Here his life was a misery, for Reutter was harsh and unsympathetic, but soon Joseph's hard life in the choir school was over, for one very cold winter night, he felt a little frisky, as many a healthy lad does, and pulled off the wig of a man in the choir. Reutter, who had wanted an excuse to rid himself of Joseph, because his voice had begun to break, threw him out into the cold. Poor Saperle had no other place to go and wandered about all night, until he met his acquaintance Spangler, a tenor who was very poor and so had sympathy with Haydn. He took him home to live with him and his wife and child in his attic,—one small room with no comfort and no privacy. All this time young Haydn was forced to earn his daily bread by teaching as much as he could, playing for weddings, baptisms, funerals, festivals, dances and street serenadings. This street serenading was a charming, pretty custom of the time.

One night Haydn and some other youths serenaded Kurz, a prominent comedian. Kurz, pleased by the music below his window, called to the lads: "Whose music is that?" "Joseph Haydn's," called back Haydn. "Who is he and where?" asked Kurz. "Down here, I am Haydn," said Joseph. Kurz invited him upstairs and Haydn, at the age of seventeen, received a commission for a comic opera, which had two special performances.

All this time he mixed with the poor and laboring people, and their songs became his songs, and his heart was full of their frolics and their pains. He was of the people and was so filled with their humor that later he was called the father of humor in music.

Soon, in order to be alone, and to work in peace, he took a room in another attic, and bade good-bye to his very good friends. His room was cold in winter and let in the rains and snows, but it did have a spinet on which Haydn was allowed to play, and fortunately Metastasio the librettist lived in this house. Here Haydn studied the works of Karl Philipp Emanuel Bach, Fuchs' *Gradus ad*

Parnassum (Steps to Parnassus, Parnassus meaning the mountain upon which the Greek Muses lived and so comes to mean the home of learning). He practised too, during this time, on any instrument he could find and learned so much that he became the founder of the modern orchestra.

When Metastasio discovered that there was a hard working musician in his house he met him and then introduced him to Porpora the greatest Italian singing teacher in Vienna. Not long after meeting him, Porpora entrusted to his care Marianne Van Martines, his ten year old pupil, the future musical celebrity. At seventeen Marianne wrote a mass which was used at St. Michael's Church and she became the favorite singer and player of Empress Maria Theresa. You see women even in those days composed and performed!

So began Haydn's successes. Porpora engaged him as accompanist, and treated him half way between a valet and a musician, but Haydn's sweet nature carried him through all unpleasantnesses and he was so anxious to learn and to earn his six ducats that he did not care if he did have to eat with the servants.

In 1751–2, he wrote his first mass, his first string quartet, and his first comic opera for Kurz, *The Crooked Devil*, the music of which has been lost. Soon after he met Gluck at the concerts of the Prince of Hildburghausen, where Haydn acted as accompanist; at the prince's house too, he met Ditter von Dittersdorf, violinist and composer. The nobles of these days did much for music for it was usually at their homes and under their guidance that the composers received opportunities to work.

Nevertheless, we see Haydn during these days slaving to make his daily bread, but with the money he made he bought books on music theory and held himself sternly down to hard work, morning, noon, and night.

In 1755 Baron von Fürnburg, a music amateur, who gave

concerts at his home, asked him to compose for him, and
he wrote eighteen quartets, six *scherzandi* for wind instruments (the ancestors of his own symphonies), four string
quartets, to be played by the village priest, himself, the
steward, and the 'cellist Albrechtsberger.

All these pieces show how much happier he was since
becoming part of the Baron's staff, for they are merry and
jolly, and filled with that humor which Haydn was the
first to put into music.

Here, too, he met the cultivated Countess Thun, who was
so interested in his struggle for success, and in the youth himself that she became his pupil. From this time on he began
to earn more and to live more comfortably.

Everything seemed to be clearing up for him now. The
Countess introduced him to Count Morzin, a Bohemian
nobleman of great wealth, and in 1759 he became his musical director. His orchestra had eighteen members and
here he wrote his first Symphony (the first of one hundred
and twenty-five!)

All this time he kept up his teaching and very soon married the daughter of a wig-maker, who did not understand
him and with whom he was very unhappy, but he lived
with her like the good man he was until within a few years
of his death.

Haydn and the Esterhazys

Soon after Haydn's marriage, Count Morzin had to cut
down expenses and dismissed his musical staff, but Prince
Paul Anton Esterhazy engaged him and he lived with him
thirty years under salary with all his expenses paid,—thus
ended his struggles to make a living. He composed in
comfort and had a few able musicians to play whatever
he wrote. He had quiet, solitude and appreciation,—the
need of all art workers.

From 1761 to 1790 in the Esterhazy home he wrote most of his immortal works,—six of his best symphonies; the oratorio *The Seven Words from the Cross* (1785) which he himself thought was a masterpiece; six string quartets.

His orchestra here had six violins and violas, one violoncello, one double bass, one flute, two oboes, two bassoons and four horns,—seventeen in all; later he had twenty-two to twenty-four including trumpets, kettle drums and from 1776–1778 the newest arrival, the clarinet.

His duties were to rehearse the orchestra daily, give music lessons, compose for the orchestra and instruct the singers engaged by the prince. Oh, yes! he had to tune his own harpsichord, on which he played when he led the orchestra.

Haydn led a beautiful life with the Esterhazy family. In the summer he hunted and fished, and in the winter, went off to Vienna to hear the orchestra and meet great personages attracted by the art, music and court life. But he had to keep on composing for the Esterhazys, who were constantly entertaining and there were many special occasions to be celebrated with Haydn's lovely music.

It seems hard for us to realize that one family could play the compositions of one man continually, but we have rarely had so great a man to listen to!

Haydn in England

In 1790 Haydn's fame had spread abroad, especially to England. Salomon, a violinist and concert manager begged him to come to conduct concerts with a new composition for each concert, for which he wrote twelve of his best symphonies. He gave his first concert February 25th, 1791. He was now about sixty years old and his popularity was so great that the Prince of Wales engaged him for twenty-six court concerts. He forgot to pay him, but later Parliament sent him one hundred guineas (about $525). Money at that time bought four or five times what it buys now, so Haydn went back to Austria, rich and famous and with a degree from Oxford. The English asked him many times to return and finally in 1794 he went again and was greeted with even more enthusiasm. Few composers in all the world have lived to see such triumphs as did the jovial, charming "Papa Haydn," as his warm friend and pupil Mozart called him. But withal, Haydn was modest and unassuming and never hesitated to give his services in concerts for the poor or to give money to the sick.

Besides his London fees, he had a generous pension from the Esterhazys. So now, with leisure, he could do his greatest works. At this period he wrote two oratorios, *The Creation* and *The Seasons*. The first was on a text from Milton's *Paradise Lost;* the second was based on Thomson's poem. Emil Naumann says this of *The Seasons:* "It is not until we come to Haydn that we witness the joys and sorrows of men and women of our own time and dwellers in our own land, the tiller of the soil, the wine-presser and shepherd, or homely figures like Simon the farmer, his daughter Anna and the peasant Lucas, in *The Seasons*." Then he says of *The Creation:* "We move with him through the German spinning room, where the girls relate stories to the accompaniment of the musical hum of the spinning wheel, or we rove through woods to follow the chase. His whole heart is in nature. He loves to depict her in her many varying aspects, and at all seasons, and all is touched with a light, tender hand. His types are of home. . . . His delineation of nature is ever the same, fresh and loving, whether we look at *The Seasons* or at *The Creation*."

Haydn said of his English experience, "It is England which has made me famous in Germany."

In 1797 he wrote *God Preserve the Emperor* which became the Austrian National Hymn; and later put it in his quartet called the Kaiser Quartet. From this time on, nearly every nation honored him,—Russia, France, Sweden, England, Austria, Germany. And as Haydn was leaving for England, when Mozart said to him, "Papa, you are scarcely fitted for such an undertaking, mixing with the big world without the gift of language," he replied, "Aye, but *my* language is understood by the whole world."

And this is the keynote of Haydn's greatness, his music is and was understood by the whole world, so true and simple and melodious is it.

A Gala Performance

One year before his death when he was seventy-six years of age, he was so feeble that he had to be carried to the concert hall where a great performance of *The Creation* was given in his honor under the direction of Salieri, who later taught Beethoven. Princes and nobles and grand ladies did him homage and the ladies threw their beautiful cloaks over his couch to keep him warm, for it was a cold night in March, 1808. When that part of the oratorio came where they sing, "And there was light," it is said that Haydn exclaimed, "Not I, but a power from above created that."

He died on May 30th, 1809, from shock, it is said, caused by the booming of cannon near his house when the French besieged Vienna.

So passed this conscientious musician, whose belief is summed up in these sentences: "I know that God appointed me a task. I acknowledge it with thanks, and hope and believe I have done my duty and have been useful to the world. May others do likewise."

HAYDN'S GIFT TO MUSIC

1. He made over the orchestra, he discovered that muted strings made a beautiful winning effect.

2. He and Mozart at about the same time, added the clarinet to the orchestra.

3. He was the first composer who brought humor, that difficult thing which is neither wit nor comicalness, to music, although others had brought fun and boisterousness.

4. He was the first to use the individual tone color of each instrument, so, rightly he has been called the father of the modern orchestra.

5. He developed sonata-form in the sonata itself, the quartet, concerto and symphony. He was one of the first to establish two themes instead of one in the movements of sonata-form. This was a great innovation and made the sonata a far more living thing and gave the composers who followed him a richer field to carry out musical design and human feeling.

6. He wrote about 1,407 works! There are 104 authenticated symphonies, 83 string quartets, 66 piano sonatas, 5 oratorios, 42 German and English songs, 336 Scotch songs, 40 canons, 13 part songs for three and four voices, 5 German marionette operas written for the Esterhazy theatre, 14 Italian operas, 163 pieces for the baryton (viola da bordona) a favorite instrument of one of the Esterhazy princes, 47 divertimenti and trios, 15 concertos for different instruments, 15 masses, 5 other sacred works, 400 single minuets and waltzes. (Emil Naumann.)

7. Among his larger vocal works with orchestra are: *Alcide* (1762), *Philemon and Baucis, entre acte* music for *King Lear* and many others. His symphonies are so numerous and so many in the same key that in order to tell them apart some have been given such names as *Surprise*

Symphony, The Farewell Symphony, the *Military Symphony, Queen of France, The Oxford*, the fascinating *Kinder Symphonie* (children's symphony) and on and on!

MOZART AND HAYDN

Mozart was years younger than Haydn and died while still very young, but they were the closest friends. Haydn was his teacher, but lived to think of Mozart as his superior and didn't hesitate to say so. This again shows the great spirit of Haydn.

Although Haydn was an innovator and a master of form his rules were never cast into molds he could not break through inspiration. A critic once asked him about the introduction to the Mozart Quartet in C major which had been much discussed on account of its complex harmonies, —a work which today we look upon as one of the greatest examples of his genius. Haydn replied in a decided tone, "If Mozart has written it, be sure he had good reason for so doing." Albrechtsberger, a strict technician, questioned him about the use of consecutive fourths which was breaking a good old-fashioned law of harmony. Haydn replied, "Art is free and must not be fettered by handicraft rule. The cultivated ear must decide, and I believe myself as capable as any one of making laws in this respect." Thus spoke the great musician and not just the teacher and follower.

He loved his art so well that he welcomed the young Mozart to Vienna generously, because of his genius. Haydn, when asked by a manager to have one of his operas follow the night after one of Mozart's refused, saying: "It would be too much to venture, for next to the great Mozart it would be difficult for anyone to stand. Could I force home to every lover of music the grandeur and inimitableness of Mozart's operas, . . . and display of genius, and were I able to impress all others with the same feelings which excite me, the nations would contend for the possession of so rare a gem. Let Prague strive to hold fast the priceless man. But reward him adequately, for without this the history of great men is truly sad and offers to posterity little inducement to exertion, as indeed many a hopeful mind lies fallow for want of encouragement. It angers me *only* that Mozart has not yet been engaged at some Imperial court. Pardon this digression but I love the man dearly." When he left Mozart he wrote to his friend Frau von Gennzinger, "I am inconsolable at parting," and then he tells with the simplicity of a child "a happy dream" he had, listening to a performance of Mozart's *Marriage of Figaro*. (Adapted from Naumann.)

And thus we see this cheerful-hearted man according honor and love even to his rivals, his broad realistic humor showing itself, as well as charm, dignity and beauty, in all his works whether in music or in life.

Papa Haydn was a good and truly religious man. He leaves us an example of kindliness and thoughtfulness, for even the people who loaned him money, which he repaid, were remembered in his will. A touching story is told of him; that when he returned to his parent's home, he kissed the floor upon which his mother and father used to walk, so well had he remembered them, yet so simple had he remained, he who played among and played with and played for the greatest people who lived in his time.

WOLFGANG AMADEUS MOZART

1756–1791

Now we come to the greatest musical genius of all time. For, whereas Bach, Handel, Haydn, Gluck, and Beethoven excelled in many things, Mozart excelled in everything;

living but thirty-five years, about half the time of most of these, he outstripped them all in natural genius.

Wolfgang Amadeus, born in Salzburg on the 27th of January, 1756, was the son of Leopold Mozart, under chapel master to the hated Archbishop of Salzburg. His mother was the daughter of a minor official in Hildenstein, and was not a cook as were the mothers of Haydn and of Beethoven. However, Madam Mozart's not having been of that profession did not lessen her son's genius!

One day when little Wolfgang was four years old, his father found the boy busily writing. He warned his father not to disturb him, as he was writing a concerto for the harpsichord. And, sure enough, when the father looked over the boy's shoulder he saw that he was not scribbling as most children of four years do, but was actually composing a work for harpsichord and orchestra, which he afterwards played to show how it should go. In spite of the blots of ink, it could easily be read.

Mozart's father was a wise and kindly man. He soon appreciated that the boy was destined for a great career, and decided that he must be properly trained.

Wolfgang was a sweet and loving child, very kind and easy to control, although he and his sister "Nannerl" were "regular" children and loved to play as other children. The father decided to take them both on a concert tour through Europe, in order to meet the great musicians and to earn money for their education.

In May, 1765, Wolfgang and his pretty little sister gave their first concert in London "for the benefit" so the sign read, "of Miss Mozart aged thirteen and Master Mozart eight years of age, prodigies of nature . . . a concert of music, with all the overtures of this little boy's composition."

The people, tired of all the pomp and ceremony of fashion, were eager for something different and were ready to listen to youthful prodigies, so the hall was crowded, and everyone was amazed.

They were beautifully brought up, charming, merry and unspoiled by the gifts showered upon them. Father Mozart gave the presents to them by degrees, teaching them the value of all things, from jewels to flattery.

Because of this training, Mozart always remained modest, did everything with gratitude to God and greatest love for his parents. He was especially loving to Nannerl to whom he brought every new idea. In fact Mozart radiated friendship and love.

The Children Tour Europe

On this concert tour (1765) in Paris, London, Holland and Switzerland, Mozart was received with great enthusiasm everywhere. When they came back, Mozart had no time to become conceited for he began a strict course of study and at twelve he composed his first mass and his first opera *Bastien et Bastienne*, which is still played and is charming. At fourteen he was assistant concertmaster to the Archbishop of Salzburg, and then began a series of woes, for the Archbishop was a mean character and treated him most unjustly.

However, in 1777, we see him in Paris with his mother, where to his great advantage he heard Gluck's operas and met Gluck. Shortly after that his mother died, and it made a very deep scar in his heart. Soon he was absorbed in composing and finishing *Idomeneo* and in this year (1781) took up his residence in Vienna. In the next, he married Constance Weber and wrote *Il Seraglio* in which his heroine is called Constance. They say he was teased for this, but he did not mind very much. In 1786 he wrote the unexcelled *Marriage of Figaro*, which at first was not appreciated, but soon came into its own.

Prague began to love Mozart and gave him ovations. To show his appreciation he composed *Don Giovanni* (1787) and so great was the people's delight in this masterpiece that Emperor Joseph made him court composer at the salary of $400 a year! Too bad it was not more, for poor Mozart was never free from the heart-breaking struggle to make enough money to live. You will recall the letter of Haydn in the last section where he wished some nation would adopt Mozart and free him from care, so great was Haydn's appreciation and love for Mozart, which Mozart returned. When listening to a piece of Haydn's, a critic once said: "I wouldn't have written it like that, would you?" "No," replied Mozart, "and do you know why? Because neither of us would have had the idea!" Isn't it refreshing to see men so great in wisdom and works that they become greater because of their loyalties.

Yet this man, a genius almost divine, was so hated by petty musicians, so badgered by unjust criticism, that when he was dying he believed that someone had poisoned him!

In spite of his enemies, he was known for his gaiety and bubbling fun, which ever overflowed into his music. No one seems to know why his country did not free him of money worry.

Appreciation Comes Late

As it so often happens with great men, after his death public subscriptions were collected and statues erected as a tribute to his memory. At Salzburg you can see a statue of him, and yearly festivals of his works are held in his honor; and in Vienna, the opera house is decorated with frescoes of scenes from the *Magic Flute!*

After his visit to Prague he was never well, and when he had finished the inimitable *Magic Flute* he started work on his last composition, the great Requiem (a mass played for the dead) which influenced Catholic Church music for years. He became very despondent, in great contrast to his usual high spirits, and poor Constance did everything to cheer him. One day, while writing the Requiem, Mozart began to weep and declared he was writing it for himself, "I feel I am not going to last much longer, some one has certainly given me poison, I cannot get rid of this idea."

In November, being an ardent member of the Masonic brotherhood, as were also Beethoven and Haydn, believing as they did in the freedom and brotherhood of man, he wrote a cantata and led it himself at his lodge. Ill and despondent, he continued work on the Requiem, not quite finished when he died. During this time he longed to hear his *Magic Flute* which was constantly given at the opera house, and like a child, he would say: "I guess they have just reached this or that point," and he would hum the music as he thought it must be progressing at the opera. The day before he died, Roser, his friend, played some of the opera on the harpsichord to cheer him.

The afternoon before his death, after working on the Requiem, he and some of his friends sang it. At the *Lacrymosa*, Mozart wept. He said to Sussmayer, his friend, "Did I not say I was writing the Requiem for myself?" Later he asked his wife to tell Albrechtsberger of his approaching end, so that he would be ready to take his post at St. Stephen's. During his last hours he was informed that he had been made director of all the music at St. Stephen's with a salary that for the first time in his life would have enabled him to live in comfort, but it was too late! At midnight, on December 5th, 1791, he lost consciousness and fell into a slumber from which he did not awake. His wife was so overcome with grief that she was too ill to attend his funeral. A few faithful friends followed the coffin, but had to turn back as a furious tempest was raging and they could not force their way through the driving rain and sleet. Thus passed one of the rarest spirits that has ever brought Music to earth, and he lies in a grave unknown and unmarked. In 1859, the city of Vienna erected a monument to his memory near the spot where he was probably buried.

Sad, sad end for so great a man! He and Raphael, Keats and Shelley and Jesus, Himself, all died early in their careers and yet had time to leave the world a finer and more lovely place for us.

MOZART PRINCE OF MUSICIANS

Why do we celebrate Mozart in what seems to be exaggerated terms?

Where Handel was a great epic composer, Bach a great religious composer, Gluck, a dramatic writer, Haydn more versatile than many of the others yet not dramatic, Beethoven lyric, free and hating all tyrannies, in Mozart we have great opera, great masses, great epics, symphonies and chamber-music quartets and quintets.

The list of his works is gigantic! How he was able in the short span of his life, to write down so much, to say nothing of composing them, is a problem that cannot be solved!

With his usual tendency not to finish work until the last minute, he wrote the overture to *Don Giovanni* the night before the first performance. He composed and scored it for orchestra in less time than it took the copyists to copy the parts, and the audience was forced to wait almost an hour until Mozart appeared at the conductor's stand to direct the unrehearsed overture. When the curtain rose on the first act Mozart said, "The overture went off very well on the whole, although a good many notes certainly fell under the desks!"

Mozart promised a group of country dances to a count,

but failed to keep his word. The count invited him, putting dinner time an hour ahead. When Mozart arrived he was shown into a room, was given music paper, quills and ink and was asked to compose, then and there, four country dances to be performed the next evening. In a half hour's time he wrote the entire orchestra score and earned his dinner!

Mozart could be not only humorous, but tragic in the same work, making his humor seem greater by contrast. *Don Giovanni* and the *Magic Flute* could be called tragic-comedies they are so rich in both moods.

In the *Marriage of Figaro* he originated what Emil Naumann calls conversational opera. Although Rossini's *Barber of Seville*, and Donizetti's *Daughter of the Regiment* follow it in style they do not reach it in real fun, melody and quality. When we say some of his operas were humorous we do not mean that they were comic operas.

In *Don Giovanni* he originated romantic opera, and although Weber in *Oberon* and other operas have their fine moments, none approach the awe-inspiring, continuous beauty of Mozart's.

He was the first to write a great fairy opera, *The Magic Flute*, composed when he was writing the Requiem! Although the librettist wrote it for money, Mozart wanted it idealistic and true to his beliefs.

Cosi Fan Tutti (They're All Alike) was really and truly comic opera, and *Titus* shows his mastery of the formal and severe style. So in all these he left models for those who followed him. Had he done but this one thing he would have been great indeed.

Coming into the world when he did, he was the connecting link between the old Italian opera and Gluck, who idealized what the old Florentines did, on the one hand, and the romantic and romantic-comic opera of the later masters of Germany and France, on the other.

In instrumental music he is the link between Haydn and Beethoven. Let us see how! He furthered the work of Haydn in the quartets and quintets by making them more human and more expressive of sorrow, pain, passionate grief and the deeper things than Haydn. In his six quartets dedicated to Haydn he says, "I labored over these." This does not agree with the usual statement, says Naumann, "that he shook his music out of his sleeve."

Out of his forty-nine symphonies nine rank, some think, with Beethoven's nine! In the finale of the Jupiter symphony he does so great a musical feat that as yet no one has surpassed it. For in it he writes a fugue along with the sonata form of the symphony, so spontaneous and so lovely that even Bach himself could not have reached the freshness of it.

Mozart treated the fugue with the same limpid mirthfulness that he used in less strict forms of music. This Beethoven never achieved for his fugues were always a bit labored, but Mozart was perfectly at home in contrapuntal writing.

Mozart also was one of the first to write art songs. In the art song the music changes from verse to verse to make the meaning of the poem or words more expressive. Thus he paved the way for Schubert, Schumann, Brahms and other great song writers, as he did for the symphonist Beethoven and those born later.

He opened the gate, not to a national art, but to an international art.

So, we leave Mozart, the Genius, for Beethoven, the Colossus, who deepened and glorified music and gave it a broader path along which to travel.

CHAPTER XXI

Beethoven the Colossus

1770–1827

L ET us see what was happening in the world into which
Beethoven was born.

The French Revolution had closed the 1700s with blood
and terror, and the American Colonies were uneasy under
British rule, and before Beethoven was six, the American
Revolution was in full blast.

It was another time like the Renaissance, when people
began to think for themselves. In other words, the individual was commencing to count more than the nation.

Slowly we see the idea die out that only the nobles and
the wealthy had the right to life, liberty and happiness,
and we see the ideas of freedom and equality taking the
place of serfdom and slavish obedience to over-lords.
All this may seem strange to appear in a book on music
but art always mirrors the life and feelings of the people
of its time.

Then came Napoleon, who dragged the French army
through the continent of Europe, until he was defeated at
Waterloo by the English.

Then, too, came the War of 1812 between England and
America, and unrest seemed to be over the face of the
world.

But through it all came the insistent demand of the

people for more democratic governments, and these new demands grudgingly granted by monarchs caused revolts and uprisings everywhere.

This was the time when men like Goethe, Schiller, Kant, Fichte and other famous poets and philosophers did their thinking and writing.

And into this world, the great democrat, Beethoven, came to add his contribution to life, liberty, and beauty, as have few others of our race.

And so the road is made easy for the people who followed Beethoven,—Weber, Schubert, Mendelssohn, Schumann and Chopin, and later Wagner, who helped make the 19th century, a great musical era.

ROMANTICISM

Instead, now, of people writing around a well known song, as they did in the cantus-firmus days, originality was the keynote; instead of conventional forms, composers began to find new forms and to compose from the heart; instead of writing dainty and graceful music, they wrote music of power; instead of holding back what they wanted to say, they poured out in rich melody their very deepest, loveliest and most exalted feelings,—caring more for what they felt themselves than for the effect on their audiences. Instead, too, of mathematical rules, they wrote themselves, their hopes and their fears into their compositions, and this freedom is labeled the Romantic Movement in Music.

Now appeared the great vocal and instrumental soloists (virtuosi). They developed because of the advance in the making of instruments. Beethoven could write more richly with the piano he had, than if he had lived in Bach's time. For the advance in instruments helps the composer and the composer, the instruments.

Since music became of age, we have seen many things happen to it: the advance in instruments, of the orchestra, and opera, and the development of the sonata and symphony.

Ludwig van Beethoven was the bridge between the classic writers and those to follow him: Schubert, Schumann, Mendelssohn, Chopin, and Liszt, members of the "Romantic School."

Before explaining what Beethoven did to advance music, you must hear about his life, for he was so interesting that knowing him will help you to understand his work.

Although born in Bonn, Germany, his ancestors on his father's side were of Dutch-Flemish stock like our old friends, Okeghem and Willaert. You will notice that the syllable before his last name is "van." If his name had been German, it would have been "von." He was proud of his Dutch origin and corrected anyone who misspelled it. This frankness, you will see, was a part of his character.

An Unhappy Boyhood

He was born December 16th, 1770, and his mother was the chief cook in the Castle of Ehrenbreitstein. His father, a tenor, and his grandfather were musicians in the band of the Elector of Cologne at Bonn. His mother was sweet and loving, but his father was unkind and intemperate. According to some accounts, his boyhood was spent in poverty and his father tried to drive him to earn money for the family. It was very hard on Beethoven that his mother should have died early in his life.

At four years of age Ludwig's father insisted upon his learning to play the piano, and as he did not want to practise, he was whipped often. Later he started to work in earnest and in spite of hating it, played in public when he was eight and at eleven he had mastered Bach's forty-eight Preludes and Fugues, a difficult task even for a grown up. Besides, he had written three piano sonatas published in 1781. We think he wasted little time after his first whippings!

When thirteen, he went on the opera staff where he played accompaniments for rehearsals, without pay. Not a bad job for a lad!

One of his first teachers was Pfeiffer, who belonged to the opera troupe and boarded with the Beethovens. Beethoven now was growing most enthusiastic about music and took up the study of the organ. Not only this, but he wrote a funeral cantata for organ, which excited the whole town.

He played the piano very beautifully, as did Mozart, and when he went to Holland with his mother, at eleven, he played at many private houses, and gained confidence in himself.

Think of it! When Beethoven was twelve, Neefe, his teacher and organist at Bonn, left town and Beethoven took his place. This proves his great ability, because playing for services was complicated. He was so successful that Neefe prophesied he would become a second Mozart!

In 1787, Beethoven, despite his poverty, went to Vienna, where Mozart said that he would "make a noise in the world," and gave the young pianist a few lessons. Not long afterwards, Beethoven was recalled to Bonn where his life was much saddened by the deaths of his mother and his little sister.

At this time he made the acquaintance of the von Breuning family,—mother, three boys and a girl, whose friendship was one of the inspiring events of his boyhood. He gave lessons to Eleanore and to a brother, and was a close friend to them all. Here he was introduced to the marvels

of literature, which proved to be a life-long love and a sol-
ace for the sad hours after he became deaf. He also accompanied the von Breunings on holidays in the country, and
through them met Count Waldstein, a young noble and
amateur musician, who was most enthusiastic over Beethoven's budding talent. Through Count Waldstein he
was brought to the attention of the Elector of Bonn, who
gave the young musician a place as viola player in the
orchestra of his national theatre. Here he made several life-
long friends,—Franz Ries, who probably taught him to
play the violin and viola, the two Rombergs, Simrock and
Stumpff. His old teacher Neefe, was pianist and stage
manager in the theatre.

Now his home became most unhappy because of his
father's drunkenness and bad habits. The Court, however, in 1799, looked after Beethoven and saw that part
of his father's salary was paid to him to help him care for
the family. In addition to this the money he earned by
playing and by giving lessons enabled him to support his
brothers and sister.

He Meets Papa Haydn

When Papa Haydn passed through Bonn on his way
to London, Beethoven went to visit him, and brought with
him, instead of candy or flowers, a cantata which he had
written for the occasion. Haydn was delighted with
him and offered to teach him if he would go to Vienna.
So, in 1792, on the advice of Count Waldstein, we see him
again in Vienna, studying counterpoint with Haydn. At
first he frankly imitated his master, and although he
leaned more toward Mozart's colorfulness of style than
Haydn's, from the older composer he learned how to
treat and develop themes, and how to write for the
orchestra.

When Haydn left Vienna for his second visit to England, Beethoven studied with Albrechtsberger, also with Schenck, Salieri and Förster. Although he was an amazing student his teachers were afraid of and for him, for his ideas were ahead of his day. They failed to see in him the great pathfinder, and naturally thought he was a dangerous radical or "red" as we would say.

Beethoven's Friendships

The story of Beethoven's life is a story of a few faithful friendships. He was not befriended for his personal beauty, but for his inner beauty. His head was too big for his body, he did not care what sort of clothes he wore, nor did he have any regard for conventions, fashions or great personages. He was a real democrat and cared nothing for titles and the things smaller men respect. Once Beethoven's brother called on him and left his card upon which was written, next his name, "Man of Property." Beethoven in return sent his card on which he wrote, "Man of Brains."

Thinking that Napoleon was going to free mankind, he dedicated the *Eroica*, the third symphony, to him. But when he heard that Napoleon had set himself up as Emperor, in a violent rage, he trampled on the dedication page.

One day he and Goethe were walking along the street when the King passed by. Goethe stood aside with uncovered head but Beethoven refused to alter his path for royalty and kept on his hat, for he felt on an equality with every man and probably a little superior. But he lost his friendship with Goethe because of his many failures to conform to customs.

At twenty-seven Beethoven began to grow deaf. It made him very morose and unhappy. In 1800 he wrote to his

friend Wegeler, the husband of Eleanore von Breuning,
"My hearing during the last three years has become gradually worse. I can say with truth that my life is very
wretched. For nearly two years past I have avoided all
society because I find it impossible to say to people 'I am
deaf.' In any other profession this might be tolerable
but in mine, such a condition is truly frightful."

Beethoven was forceful and noble in spirit, quick tempered, absent-minded, gruff, and cared little for manners
and customs except to be honest and good. But although
he was absent-minded he never neglected his work or
his obligations to any man, and his compositions show
the greatest care and thought. He worked a piece over
and over before it was finished and not, like Mozart, did it
bubble from him whole and perfect.

He was too high-strung and impatient to teach much and
Ferdinand Ries, the son of Franz, and Czerny seem to be
his only well-known pupils. But he taught many amateurs
among the nobility, which probably accounts for many of
his romances. In later years, he withdrew unto himself
and became irritable and suspicious of everybody, both
because of his deafness and the misery his family caused
him. This great man, tortured with suspicions and doubt,
and storming often against his handicap, was innately honest
and desperately sincere in spite of his fear of poverty which
made him drive hard bargains on occasions. In fact he
was very moral by nature and he lived and composed according to the dictates of his soul, rarely ever writing to
order or to win favor.

He made valuable friends among music lovers and patrons such as Prince and Princess Lichnowsky, Prince
Lobkowitz, Count Rasoumowsky, Empress Maria Theresa
and others, to whom he dedicated many of his great works.
This he did only as a mark of his friendship rather than
for gain.

He was clumsy and awkward and had bad manners and a quick temper, and he had a heavy shock of black hair, that was always in disorder, but the soul of the man shone out from his eyes and his smile lit up his face.   Although he is said to have been unkempt, he was exceedingly clean, for when he was composing he would often interrupt his work to wash.

When the *Leonore* overture was being rehearsed, one of the three bassoon players was missing.   Prince Lobkowitz, a friend of Beethoven, jokingly tried to relieve his mind by saying, "It doesn't make any difference, the first and second bassoon are here, don't mind the third."   Beethoven nearly pranced with rage, and reaching the street later, where the Prince lived, he crossed the square to the gates of the Palace and stopped to shout at the entrance, "Donkey of a Lobkowitz!" and then passed on, raving to himself.   But there was a warm, sweet streak in his nature for his friends loved him dearly, and he was very good to his nephew Carl, who lied to him and deceived him. Carl added to Beethoven's unhappiness, for when he was lonely and in need of him, Carl never would come to him unless for money.

Beethoven had a high regard for women and loved Countess Guicciardi, who refused to marry him.   He dedicated *The Moonlight Sonata* and some songs to her.   He fell in love many times but never married.

We see his great heart broken by his nephew, we see his sad letters begging him to come and take pity on his loneliness, we see him struggle to make money for him; and all Carl did was to accept all and give nothing.   Finally this ungrateful boy was expelled from college because he failed in his examinations.   This was such a disgrace that he attempted to commit suicide.   As this was also looked upon as a crime he was given twenty-four hours to leave Vienna and so enlisted in the army.   Nevertheless

Beethoven made Carl his sole heir. This was one of many ways in which he showed himself a great person.

BEETHOVEN THE PIANIST

While at Vienna he met the great pianists and played far better than any of them. No one played with such expression, with such power or seemed worthy even to compete with him. Mozart and others had been charming players and composers, but Beethoven was powerful and deep, even most humorous when he wanted to be.

He worked well during these years, and with his usual extreme care changed and rechanged the themes he found in his little sketch books into which, from boyhood he had put down his musical ideas. Those marvelous sketch books! What an example they are! They show infinite patience and "an infinite capacity for taking pains" which has been given by George Eliot as a definition of genius.

THE THREE PERIODS

At his first appearance as a pianist in Vienna he played his own C major Concerto in 1795. From 1795 to 1803 he wrote all the works from opus 1 to 50. In these were included symphonies 1 and 2, the first three piano concertos, and many sonatas for piano, trios and quartets, a septet and other less important works.

This is the first period of Beethoven's life. His second period in which his deafness grew worse and caused him real physical illness, extended to 1815—in this the trouble with his nephew and the deceit of his two brothers preyed on his mind to such an extent, that he became irascible and unapproachable. His lodgings were the scene of distressing upheavals and Beethoven was like a storm-beaten mountain!

For consolation, he turned to his music, and in the storm and stress he wrote the noble opera *Fidelio*, and the third symphony, *Eroica*, concertos, sonatas and many other things.

Someone once asked him, "Why don't you write opera?" He replied, "Give me a libretto noble enough for my music." Evidently this is the reason why he wrote only one opera. We find another example of his patience and self-criticism, as he wrote four overtures for *Fidelio*. Three of them are called *Leonore* overtures and one *Fidelio*. The third *Leonore* seems to be the favorite, and is often played.

By 1822, the beginning of the third period, the great music maker was stone deaf! Yet he wrote the magnificent Mass in D and his last symphony, the Ninth, with the "Hymn of Joy," two of the great masterpieces of the world, although he was unable to hear one note of what he had composed as he could not hear his beloved violin even when he held it close to his ears.

Imagine Beethoven—stone deaf, attending a performance of the Ninth Symphony in a great hall—not knowing that it had had a triumphal success until one of the soloists turned him around to see the enthusiastic faces and the hands clapping and arms waving, for he could hear not a sound! He who had built such beautiful things for us to hear, knew them only in his mind!

Beethoven was a great lover of nature. He used to stroll with his head down and his hands behind his back, clasping his note book in which he jotted down the new ideas as they came to him. He wrote to a friend, "I wander about here with music paper among the hills and dales and valleys and scribble a bit; no man on earth could love the country as I do."

Beethoven Makes Music Grow

If you have ever seen a sculptor modeling in clay you know that his great problem is to keep it from drying, because only in the moist state can it be moulded into shape. In the same way, we have seen in following the growth of music, that no matter how beautiful a style of composition is, as soon as it becomes set in form, or in other words as soon as it hardens, it changes. Let us look back to the period of the madrigal. You remember that the early madrigals were of rare beauty but later the composers became complicated and mechanical in their work and the beauty and freshness of their compositions were lost. The people who felt this, reached out for new forms of expression and we see the opera with its arias and recitatives as a result. The great innovator Monteverde, broke this spell of the old polyphonic form, which, like the sculptor's clay, had stiffened and dried.

The same thing happened after Bach brought the suite and fugue to their highest. The people again needed something new, and another form grew out of the suite, the sonata of Philipp Emanuel Bach, Haydn and Mozart. The works of these men formed the Classic Period which reached its greatest height with the colossus, Beethoven. As we told you, he used the form inherited from Haydn and Mozart, but added much of a peculiar power which expressed *himself*. But again the clay hardened! Times and people changed; poetry, science and philosophy led the way to more personal and shorter forms of expression. Up to Bach's time, music, outside of the folk-song, had not been used to express personal feeling; the art was too young and had grown up in the Church which taught the denial of self-expression.

In the same way, the paintings up to the time of the 16th century did not express personal feelings and happenings, but were only allowed to be of religious subjects, for the decorating of churches and cathedrals.

Beethoven, besides being the peak of the classic writers. pointed the way for the music of personal expression, not mere graceful expression as was the fashion, which was called the "Romantic School" because he was big enough to combine the sonata form of classic mould with the delicacy, humor, pathos, nobility and singing beauty for which the people of his day yearned.

This led again to the crashing of the large and dried forms made perfect by Beethoven and we see him as the bridge which leads to Mendelssohn, Chopin, Schubert and Schumann and we see them expressing in shorter form every possible human mood.

Beethoven was great enough to bring music to maturity so that it expressed not only forms of life, but life itself.

How and what did he do? First, he became master of the piano and could from childhood sit down and make marvelous improvisations. He studied all forms of music, counterpoint, harmony, and orchestration. At first he followed the old forms, as we see in the first two symphonies. In the third symphony, the *Eroica*, he changed from the minuet (a relic of the old dance suite) to the scherzo, an enlarged form of the minuet with more chance for musical expression,—the minuet grown up. In sonatas like *The Pathetique*, he used an introduction and often enlarged the coda or ending, to such an extent that it seems like an added movement, so rich was he in power in working over a theme into beautiful musical speech.

Later we see him abandoning set forms and writing the *Waldstein* Sonata in free and beautiful ways. Even the earlier sonatas like *"The Moonlight"* and its sister, Opus 27, No. 2, are written so freely that they are called Fantasy Sonatas, so full of free, flowing melody has the sonata become under his hand.

His work becomes so lofty and so grand, whether in humorous or in serious vein, that when we compare his compositions to those of other men, he seems like one of the loftiest mountain peaks in the world, reaching into the heavens, yet with its base firmly standing in the midst of men.

A Composer of Instrumental Music

Beethoven was distinctly a composer of instrumental music, although he wrote the opera *Fidelio*, also the Ninth Symphony in which he made great innovations in symphonic form and introduced the Choral.

Up to this time, composers in the Classic School had paid more attention to the voice and to the soloists in the concertos than to the orchestra. Thus we see men like Mozart leaving a space toward the end of the movement in a concerto for the soloist to make up his own closing salute to his audience before the orchestra ended the piece. These cadenzas became acrobatic feats in which the players wrote the most difficult "show-off" music. Beethoven, with his love for the orchestra and his feeling that the soloist and the orchestra should make one complete unit, wrote the cadenza *himself* and thereby made the composition one beautiful whole rather than a sandwich of the composer, soloist and composer again.

Fancy all this from a man who, when he multiplied 14 x 26 had to add fourteen twenty-sixes in a column! We saw this column of figures written on a manuscript of Beethoven's in an interesting collection, and the story goes that Beethoven tried to verify a bill that was brought to him in the midst of a morning of hard work at his composing.

Besides his symphonies, concertos and sonatas in which are light moods, dark moods, gay and sad moods, spiritual heights and depths, filling hearers with all beauty of emotion,—he wrote gay little witty things, like the German Dances, The Fury over the Loss of a Penny (which is really funny), four overtures, many English, Scotch, Irish, Welsh and Italian folk-song settings. He also wrote one oratorio called *The Mount of Olives*, two masses, one of which is the magnificent *Missa Solemnis*, one concerto for the violin that is the masterpiece of its kind, and the one grand opera *Fidelio*.

Thus we have told you about the bridge to the "Romantic Movement" which will follow in the next chapter.

Beethoven could have said with Robert Browning's "Abt Vogler"

> Ye know why the forms are fair, ye hear how the tale is told;
> It is all triumphant art, but art in obedience to laws. . . .

> And I know not if, save in this, such gift be allowed to man,
> That out of three sounds he frame, not a fourth sound, but a star.

CHAPTER XXII

The Pianoforte Grows Up—The Ancestry of the Pianoforte

THE ANCESTRY OF THE PIANOFORTE

WE feel so familiar with the Pianoforte that we call it piano for short and almost forget that it is dignified by the longer name. We forget too, that Scarlatti, Rameau and Bach played not on the piano but on its ancestors; and that Byrd, Bull and Gibbon did not write their lovely dance suites for the instrument on which we play them today.

The Pianoforte's family tree has three distinct branches, —strings, sounding board and hammers. First we know the piano is a stringed instrument, although it hides its chief characteristic, not under a bushel, but behind a casing of wood.

WHERE STRINGED INSTRUMENTS CAME FROM

We have seen the stringed instrument developed from the bow when primitive man winged his arrow in the hunt, and heard its twang. Later desiring fuller tone, the sounding board grew, when early peoples sank bow-like instruments and reeds into a gourd which increased and reflected the sound as the metal reflector behind a light intensifies it.

Strings to produce sound, must be rubbed, like the bow drawn across violin strings, plucked as the mandolin or the harp is plucked, or struck with a hammer as was the dulcimer.

In the ancient times there were two instruments much alike, the *psaltery* and the *dulcimer*, both with a triangular or rectangular sounding box across which are stretched strings of wire or gut fastened to tuning pins. The difference between these two "relatives" is that the *psaltery* is plucked with fingers or a plectrum, and the *dulcimer* is struck with hammers. So the *psaltery* is the grandfather of the virginal, spinet, clavecin, and harpsichord, while the *dulcimer* is the remote ancestor of the pianoforte.

The first record we find of a *dulcimer* is a stone picture near Nineveh, of an Assyrian king in 667 B.C., celebrating a triumphal procession. This *dulcimer*, suspended from the neck of the player, is being struck with a stick in his right hand, while his left palm on the string checks the tone. Here we have the first stringed instrument which was hammered and muffled, two important elements in the piano.

In Persia the *dulcimer* was called the *santir* and is still used under different names in the Orient and other places. In Greece and other countries it was called the *psalterion*, and in Italy, the *dolcimelo*. Later, the Germans had a sort of *dulcimer* called the *Hackbrett*, probably because it was "hacked" as the butcher hacks meat! We see the *dulcimer* in many shapes according to the fancy of the people who use it. The word comes from *dulce*—the Latin for "sweet" and *melos*—the Greek for "melody."

As people grew wiser and more musical, they padded their hammers or mallets; this gave the idea for the padded hammer of the piano for checking the tone as our Ninevehan did with his left palm.

Should you ever listen to a gypsy band, you will hear the *dulcimer* or *cembalo*.

THE KEYBOARD

The third element in the making of the piano is the keyboard.

It is evident that the piano keyboard and the organ keyboard are practically the same. The water organs of the Greeks and Romans had keyboards, but as the Christian Church forbade the use of organs as sacrilegious, keyboards were lost for almost a thousand years.

The keyboard seems to have developed from the Greek *monochord* used in the Middle Ages to give the pitch in convent singing. It was tuned with a movable bridge or fret pushed back and forth under the strings and fingers. First it was stretched with weights hung at one end. It was a simple matter to add strings to produce more tones, later tuning pins were added and finally a keyboard. This was the whole principle of the *clavichord*. (We might say that the *monochord* and *dulcimer* are the Adam and Eve of the pianoforte family.)

THE CLAVICHORD

In the clavichord, each key drove a metal tangent against a string and was held there as was the bridge of the monochord. The tone was dependent on the place where the tangent struck. The string vibrated on one side of the tangent, but the other part of the string was deadened by a strip of cloth. The strings were about the same length and often two or three keys operated the same string so that it was possible to make a very small instrument. In the 16th century, it usually had twenty keys; in the 18th century, four octaves or fifty keys, but of course there were less than fifty strings! Later, every key had its own string and these were called *bundfrei* or unfretted clavichords, while the others were called *gebunden* or fretted. The clavichord was usually small enough to carry under the arm, although sometimes it was made with legs. Should you be in New York you must see the collection of beautifully ornamented clavichords and harpsichords at the Metropolitan Museum of Art in the Crosby Brown Collection.

Bach liked the clavichord better than the harpsichord and the early pianos that blossomed in his day. Because of the pressure of the tangent, it was possible to get a delicately graded tone when the key was pressed, a wavy, rocking, pulsating effect, which made each player's performance very individual, but to us, now, it sounds thin and metallic. The word "clavichord" comes from *clavis*—a key, and *chord*—a string. Clavichords and also virginals were often played in pairs, no doubt for richer effect and for volume.

Large instruments developed slowly because before the 11th century, wire-drawing (making) was not known, so all keyed string instruments were strung with gut.

Harpsichord

128TH SONNET

SHAKESPEARE AND THE HARPSICHORD

How oft when thou, my music, music play'st
Upon that blessed wood, whose motion sounds
With thy sweet fingers when thou gently sway'st
The wiry concord that my ear confounds,
Do I envy those *jacks* that nimble leap
To kiss the tender inward of thy hand:
Whilst my poor lips, which should that harvest reap,
At the wood's boldness, by thee blushing stand!
To be so tickled they would change their state
And situation with those dancing chips,
O'er whom thy fingers walk with gentle gate,
Making dead wood more blessed than living lips.
Since saucy *jacks* so happy are in this
Give them thy fingers, me thy lips to kiss.

The harpsichord, we like to call the "Jack and Quill" instrument—for it is played by keys, jacks and quills which pluck its strings, instead of pressing or hammering. This is like a keyboarded zither, and is shaped something like our grand piano.

Each key has a string. Pressing the key pushes a jack, from whose side projects a small quill or spine which twangs the string. When the key is released, the quill slips back into the first position and a damper falls upon the string. The strings vary in length according to the pitch for the harpsichord has no tangent to divide off the string as had the clavichord and monochord. Thus the harpsichord on account of its long and short strings is not square like the clavichord but is shaped more like the harp and the grand piano.

Some one said that the harpsichord tone was "a scratch with a note at the end of it." And yet, when we hear Wanda Landowska play the harpsichord today, it sounds very beautiful indeed. Smaller varieties are called virginals and spinets. Perhaps the spinet is named for its inventor Spinetti, or perhaps the word comes from "spinet" meaning spine, a thorn or point. The virginal comes from the word *virgo*—meaning maiden and was the popular instrument for the "ladies" of the day. There were larger harpsichords, too, with two and three keyboards and very many varieties, both small and large. The clavichord and the harpsichord were known from the 15th century and were associated with the organ until the 17th century, when the Ruckers family developed harpsichord making into a fine art. The first mention of the harpsichord, is in the "Rules of the Minnesingers" (1404).

The First Pianofortes

Early in the 18th century, music ceased to be just pretty sounds, and musicians wanted instruments on which they could express deeper feelings and began to look around for some way to make the harpsichord meet this need.

It came about in this way. Pantaleone Hebenstreit, a fiddler at the Saxon court played a dulcimer which he enlarged by adding to it a second system of strings. He tuned it in equal temperament, as Bach had the clavichord, and used hammers on it which produced very beautiful and loud tones. Louis XIV saw this, and liking it, called it the Pantaleone. But, shortly after this, Gottlieb Schroeter heard it and said, "only through hammers can the harpsichord become expressive."

So in 1721 Schroeter submitted to the King of Saxony his idea of a harpsichord which could play soft and loud or in Italian *piano* and *forte* (the *fortepiano* or *loud-soft* instrument). But as he had none made he did not get credit for the invention until after much argument, based on accounts in his diary. As always, when a thing is needed someone will invent it.

The man who actually made the first pianoforte was an Italian, Bartolommeo Cristofori (1653–1731) of Padua; and the Frenchman Marius, and the German, Christoph Gottlieb Schroeter, followed suit. In 1709, Cristofori exhibited harpsichords (*gravicembali*) with hammer action capable of producing *piano* and *forte* effects. He advertised it in the paper as a *gravicembali col piano e forte*. By 1711, the fame of his invention had spread into Germany. In February, 1716, Marius in France tried to improve the harpsichord with hammers which he called the *clavecin à mallets*, and made two types.

Schroeter about this time made the two kinds also. The piano had little standing, however, until Gottfried Silbermann took advantage of Bach's criticism of his pianos and made a *grand* type.

The next experimenters in pianos were, Frederici of Gera (died in 1779), who made the *square*. Spaeth, who made *grands* and George Andreas Stein in Augsburg, who was trained by Silbermann, invented the Viennese action on which a light touch was possible and for this reason Mozart used it.

Burkhardt Tschudi, a piano maker in London, had a Scotch assistant, James Broadwood, who became his partner (1770). Later the firm became John Broadwood and Sons, which it has remained. It was the first to use the damper and the soft pedals. For some time they used Zumpe's style of square piano but later made their own. This house used the Cristofori action which made a more solid and heavier tone than the Viennese action, and was known as the English action, excellent for large rooms and concerts. These actions suited the different methods of piano playing.

Stein's daughter Nanette Streicher, an excellent pianist and a cultivated woman, upon inheriting her father's piano business moved to Vienna and for forty years was considered an expert in the piano world. Thayer, in his life of Beethoven says: "In May, Beethoven, on the advice of medical men, went to Baden, whither he was followed by his friend Mrs. Streicher . . . who took charge of his lodgings and his clothes, which appear to have been in a deplorable state." Thayer says that Beethoven always preferred the piano of Stein to any others. Beethoven wrote to Nanette: "Perhaps you do not know, though I have not always had one of your pianos, that since 1809 I have invariably preferred yours."

So, you see a woman could keep house and be a manufacturer as well, even in the early 19th century!

Then came Sebastien Erard (1752–1831) who made the first French piano in 1777. Erard invented many new things for the piano and formed a company in England. This firm was advertised on the hand bill announcing Liszt's concert in Paris when he was twelve years old.

Added to these names is Ignaz Josef Pleyel (1757–1831), who also made a piano with a very sympathetic tone which Chopin made famous from 1831. The Pleyel and the Erard are still the leading pianos of France.

For some years the pianoforte went through many changes. As you are not learning to make a piano, you will have to take it for granted that there were many many steps taken from this time on to make the modern piano. However, the thing that held it back was the all-wood frame which could not stand the strain of the tightly drawn strings and it was a long time before the makers gave up the beautiful wood for the sturdier metal. About the time of Beethoven, playing the piano became a more complicated thing than it had been, and a grown up instrument was needed, so musical instrument makers had to "step lively" to keep pace with the music. At every concert, and often in the middle of a piece, the player would have to stop to retune the instrument on which he was playing. Therefore, all energy was bent to making the frame of the piano rigid, the strings more elastic and the pins firmer, and the metal frame was used.

All these special things were accomplished in later years. Some of the inventors were John Isaac Hawkins, an Englishman, who patented the upright pianoforte in 1800 in the United States, William Allen, a Scotchman, who introduced metal braces in 1820 and Alpheus Babcock, who patented the iron frame in a *single cast*, in Boston, in 1825. It was an American, Jonas Chickering, of Boston, who invented the complete iron frame for the concert grand, and at present, after many years, the instrument which seventy-five years ago bent under the pull of the strings, can now stand the strain of thirty tons! Chickering made pianos as early as 1823.

After this there was much experimentation in pianos,

culminating here, in the pianos made by Steinway and Sons the ancestor of which was the firm of Heinrich Englehard Steinweg, of Brunswick, Germany, starting as organ makers. In 1848 Heinrich's sons went to New York City and changed their name to Steinway, where Theodore, the eldest, continued the firm as Steinway and Sons.

Of course, the methods of stringing and tuning a piano have taken years to develop—all of which we cannot go into in this book. Now, instead of twenty strings, as we saw them in the clavichord, we have 243 strings to produce 88 tones.

So now we have the harpsichord with hammers "grown up" into the pianoforte, with its myriad parts, no longer made by hand, but carefully manufactured by machinery and the finest of them are American.

PIANO BUYING CREATED A HOLIDAY IN THE 18TH CENTURY

"When the pianoforte was completed and ready to be delivered at the house of the impatient purchaser (in Germany) a festival took place; the maker, was the hero of the hour, and accompanied the piano followed by his craftsman and apprentices, if he had any. (In those days the pianos took months and months to make, for they were made by hand and the makers received cash in part payment and the rest was made up in corn, wheat, potatoes, poultry and firewood!)

"The wagon which conveyed the precious burden was gaily decorated with wreaths and flowers, the horses magnificently decked out, a band of music headed the procession, and after the wagon followed the proud maker, borne on the shoulders of his assistants; musicians, organists, schoolmasters and dignitaries marching in the rear. At the place of destination the procession was received with greetings of welcome and shouts of joy. The pastor of the place said a prayer and blessed the new instrument and its maker. Then the mayor or the burgomaster of the place delivered an address,—dwelling at great length upon the importance of the event to the whole community, and stating, perhaps, that the coming of such a new musical instrument would raise their place in the eyes of the surrounding country. Then followed speeches by the schoolmaster, doctor, druggist, and other dignitaries, and songs by the *Männerchor* (men's chorus) of the place. Amidst the strains of the band, the pianoforte was moved to its new home. A banquet and a dance closed the happy occasion." (From *Reminiscences of Morris Steinert* by Jane Marlin.)

"The Piano and Pneumatics"

It is very difficult to know just when this important instrument first was invented. It seems to have started with a mechanical organ and many were the experimenters among whom was John McTammany, a soldier in the Civil War who while disabled turned his mind to mechanics and became one of the great pneumatic (air power) experts. And so, just as we arrive at the beautiful instrument, the piano, comes another instrument far more complicated, whose possibilities are still in its infancy. At present the automatic piano is operated by bellows and pneumatic tubes (which look together like a bunch of gray spaghetti) and through which the air is exhausted and acts in such a way that the piano hammers fall against the piano strings. Into these instruments are placed perforated music rolls which travel over a tracker bar full of holes, each one having its rubber spaghetti tube. When the bellows work and the perforation of the roll passes over a perforation of the tracker bar, the air is released and its exhaustion causes the hammer to fall on the strings. This sounds simple,—but it is not!

There are three kinds of automatic players,—one, the *piano player*, which is now practically extinct in this country, a cabinet which moves up to the piano, and with a series of keys corresponding to the keys on the piano which, when in action presses down the piano keys and the tune starts.

Then we have the *player piano*. In this, whether it be an upright or a grand piano, the machinery is inside the piano itself (instead of being in the outside cabinet), so that one can hardly tell at first glance whether it is an automatic instrument or not. The perforated roll is put on inside the piano.

All these piano player bellows work either by electricity or by the feet. So in the latter, one cannot help playing with "sole"!

The *reproducing piano* is the third type of player. This is magical, for it reproduces the player's performance as he plays it himself. Therefore we can entice Paderewski, Bauer, Rachmaninoff and all the other great players into our own drawing rooms and hear them with their superb skill. These are usually operated by electricity, yet the Aeolian Company and some others, have had a *reproducing piano* which is propelled by the pedals as were the old ones before the invention of the electric player. Furthermore, some of the reproducing pianos have a mechanism with which you yourself can interpret any piece you desire. This gives the music lover who has been denied the study of music a chance to enjoy interpreting great music. It is an impossibility to overestimate the value of the player piano to the young student, to increase his auditory repertory. And yet this valuable aid in music appreciation has been almost completely superseded by the phonograph and the radio.

Their Contribution to Art

For a long time, the mechanical player has been looked on as a step-child, to be made fun of and scorned. Today, the great critics and best musicians recognize its value which is not as a substitute for a piano but as an instrument in itself. Sir Henry J. Wood of England says: "I realize the value . . . of the pianola . . . for a good many of the people in our audiences . . . are acquiring by its means a closer acquaintance with the great musical masterpieces."

He says in another place, "It's a foolish and a short-sighted policy to despise any means by which we may add to the sum total of musical appreciation."

And Edwin Evans, English critic and writer, says: "The player piano relieves the musician of the technical difficulties of the keyboard. . . . It does not relieve him from the duty of thinking musicianly, on the contrary, . . . it makes it a point of honor with him to give . . . fuller employment to his brain and sensibility. . . . There are dozens of scores nowadays which it is an impossibility to read at the piano and very trying to read on paper. Here the player piano is a boon and a blessing for it unravels every mystery and solves every problem."

Besides this, it can be played so skilfully by some that even musicians can be fooled as to whether human or mechanical fingers are playing. Gustave Kobbé said, in his *Pianolist*, something like this: "There are only about five professionals who can play the piano better than an accomplished pianolist."

To prove its artistic worth further, Percy Grainger, Alfredo Casella and Igor Stravinsky and other great moderns wrote some music especially for the player piano because they could use all the eighty-eight notes with full orchestral effects, without stopping to think of the meagre ten fingers of man! So we see the possibility of mechanical instruments becoming creative instruments.

OTHER "CANNED" MUSIC

Then we have the phonographs and radio. These cannot be considered instruments in the same way as the player piano and reproducing piano, but are invaluable means of musical education and are doing, with the player piano, a marvelous work in introducing people to the great music of the world. Of course, it depends upon the way all these music carriers are used, for if you have poor music on them, it will mean nothing to you, but if you hear the "wear evers" on them, you will have a touch of heaven in your life, forever.

PIANISTS COME TO VIEW

As an outcome of the work of Bach, Beethoven, and Mozart, the piano appeared because of the need of a more powerful instrument than the harpsichord and clavichord. At this time there were two particular schools of piano playing,—the Viennese, light and delicate in tone, and the English school, producing a more solid and more brilliant tone.

The principal pianists of the Viennese school were Johann Hummel, who, as a boy of seven, was a pupil of Mozart, Franz Duschek, Mozart and Pleyel. Later Beethoven himself appeared, the profound pianist in this group, but also an advocate of Clementi's methods.

The Clementi School is named from Muzio Clementi (1752–1832), the "Father of the Pianoforte." He was a composer of piano pieces, especially of sonatas which are still of musical value. Who of us has not studied Clementi's sonatinas? Besides being a great player, a teacher and a composer, Clementi published a work called *Gradus ad Parnassum*, piano studies, a form which sprang up because of the need to develop a technic for the new instruments when the piano was young.

Clementi, at fourteen, went to England, where he lived all his life and became interested in the making of pianos. He was associated with the firm of Clementi and Company, later Collard and Collard, and it is said that he gave the Broadwoods much advice in the making of their "grand" piano. So we see Clementi as a founder of piano technic, and an instrument maker. He lived eighty years, during the last years of Handel and Scarlatti, and he survived Beethoven, Schubert and Weber. It is said that Mozart took a theme from a Clementi sonata for one of his operas. His pupils were quite famous: John B. Cramer, the composer of many important piano studies still in use; Johann L. Dussek, one of the first to invent and write down finger exercises, and there were many others.

There were two schools with Clementi at the head of one, and Mozart, of the other. With Hummel, a pupil of Mozart, the Classic School closed, and then Clementi's ideas came to the fore in the new Romantic School.

THE NEW ROMANTIC SCHOOL

One of the earliest of these new Romanticists was John Field, who was born in Ireland, visited London, had quite a career in Russia and foreshadowed Chopin. (See page 343.) Then there was Ferdinand Ries, son of Beethoven's early friend and teacher, Franz Ries; but the most famous of this period were Ignaz Moscheles and Frederick Kalkbrenner, a fluent composer and writer of studies. He was the first pianist to teach Clementi's *Gradus ad Parnassum*.

Ignaz Moscheles (1794–1870) was a Bohemian and

from about 1815, the most brilliant pianist in Germany, France, Holland and England. He was Mendelssohn's teacher. Chopin wrote three études (studies) on an order from Moscheles. He is a *very* important figure in the growing up of piano music.

Carl Czerny (1791–1857) was another *very* important pianist and one of the few pupils of Beethoven. He was a follower of Hummel and Clementi and won great fame as a teacher in Vienna, where he lived. He wrote a great many pieces, about a thousand in all, making many arrangements of orchestral works and many piano studies, which we still use today. Beethoven encouraged him to make a piano version of his *Fidelio*. Czerny was the teacher of many able musicians.

Frederick Chopin, you will find out later (Chapter 24) changed piano music from the bravura to a poetic and deeper style. His touch and tone were so enchanting that he created a completely new fashion in piano playing which has not been lost. (See page 322.)

Clara Schumann (1819–1896), the wife of Robert Schumann, was the leading woman pianist of the day, in fact, of many days.

In the times of Mozart and of Liszt, improvising was very popular and a part of a musical education; around 1795, after the Paris Conservatory was founded, it seemed to die out. However, organists today often have occasion to improvise. Dupré, one of the famous French organists, who has played in the United States, improvises whole sonatas on given themes. And Alec Templeton, the blind English pianist, is a genius at improvisation.

After Chopin, Schumann and Schubert there was a great love of the short piano piece and as the piano was being developed more and more, it was natural that pianists should become numerous. So piano playing was heard in the concert hall and in the parlor where it was, to be sure, often light and frivolous and yet quite often,—serious and delightful. The light and decorated pieces were usually called *salon music* and today many are written which are classed as *salon pieces*. Cécile Chaminade, as delightful and clever as her pieces are, is a typical *salon* composer, Rubinstein, also, with such pieces as *Melody in F*, is a writer of salon pieces, and there are countless others.

Among the people who were prominent as pianists and composers in that day, especially in Poland, where Chopin was born, were Alois Tausig, a pupil of Thalberg and Josef Wieniewski, who was the teacher of the "Lion of Pianists," Ignace Jan Paderewski.

Around Paris gathered many pianists among whom were Ignace Leybach an organist and composer at Toulouse, Henry Charles Litolff the famous publisher, Louis Moreau Gottschalk, American pianist and the author of *The Last Hope*, and Eugene Ketterer. The following, with many others, centered around Vienna: Joseph Löw, Theodore Kullak, Louis Köhler, Gustav Lange and Louis Brassin.

BRAVURA PLAYING

A little later, due to the improvements of the piano, another school grew up called by some, the Bravura Pianists, because the pieces for these pianists were written to show off brilliant technic. Most of the people were flashy pianists, yet there were some very marvelous performers, for among them, Liszt himself figures and Thalberg, a Swiss, who was Liszt's rival for piano honors.

Another set of pianists and composers was Henry Herz, Alexander Dreyschock, Emil Prudent and Adolph Henselt, a Bavarian, who was an amazingly poetic and beautiful player.

Practically all these pianists were prominent composers in their day.

About this time we see women coming into great prominence as professional pianists. The first one to interest us is Marie Felicité Denise (Moke) Pleyel, who was Miss Moke, the beloved of Berlioz and the lady whom he intended to kill but changed his mind! She was an inspiring teacher, a pupil of Herz, Moscheles and Kalkbrenner and was admired by Mendelssohn and Liszt.

THE GROWTH OF VIOLIN MUSIC

The same things seem to have happened to violin playing and violin music at this time as happened to the piano. There was always the competition between writing fine, deep music and showy, spectacular music, which, when played, would please an audience. But the violin was the same then as it had been for years,—the only advance it had made was the perfecting of the bow by François Tourte, assisted by Giovanni Battista Viotti, Pugnani's greatest pupil. We use his bow today. It has about one hundred white horsehairs, the tension of which is controlled by a screw at the nut in the finger grip. But the thing that did affect violinists and violin playing was the fact of the rise in the 19th century of the orchestra and chamber music. From the time that madrigals were first accompanied by instruments, we have heard about *Chamber Music*, but the string quartet in sonata form as we know it today, had as its father, Haydn, and Luigi Boccherini (1743–1805) as a godfather. The link between the Corelli School of violinists and this school was Viotti who was one of the first men to write a violin concerto in sonata form.

The violinists of this period were also given to bravura playing as were the pianists. This was a safe thing for great violinists like Paganini to do, but for the less gifted

it often developed into, not music at all, but musical cal-
isthenics. Here is the group which appeared in the early
19th century: Rudolph Kreutzer, to whom Beethoven dedicated his famous *Kreutzer Sonata;* Andreas Romberg (1767–
1821) who knew Haydn and Beethoven at Vienna and took
Spohr's place as concert master at Gotha. He wrote music
somewhat in the style of Mozart. Then comes the "Wizard of the Bow," Nicolo Paganini, standing alone and belonging to no school.

He was born in Genoa and began to play in public in
1795, when he was thirteen years old. A very pretty story
is told of Paganini and the spider:

When Nicolo was a very poor and lonely student, he had
a pet spider that used to listen to him practise. Every
time Nicolo would touch the bow to the strings, out came
Mr. Spider to listen attentively. Now there was a little
girl, the daughter of a shop-keeper near by; she adored
the great, tall, slender youth who spent most of the day
and most of the night playing on his violin. She fell ill
and died, and by a curious coincidence, the spider was
killed. Paganini was so overcome by the loss of his admir-
ing comrades that he left home at once and wandered
from place to place, playing the guitar when he could not
get work with his violin.

Later he played all over Europe and had the crowd with
him for his matchless brilliancy in rapid work, his deep
pathos and exceptional beauty of tone. He has probably
never been surpassed in double stopping, chromatics and
his *pizzicati* (plucking the strings). Isn't it too bad the
greatest violinist in the world lived before the gramophone was invented, so we have no records of his playing
as we have of Mischa Elman, Fritz Kreisler, Jascha Heifetz,
Albert Spalding and Maud Powell!

In this period, Ludwig Spohr was of great importance.
He was a friend of Mendelssohn and, curious enough, **was**

an admirer (one of the early ones) of Wagner. He had been an intimate of Weber and played with Paganini at Rome and knew Rossini. His rank as a violinist was acknowledged. He did not encourage "fire works" but demanded fine music. He was always a classical musician, for his early love was Mozart. You will meet him again in the next chapter. He traveled all over Europe and met many great men and his autobiography is a rich store of anecdotes and interesting facts.

At this time too, there were many great violinists in France, Austria, Germany and Italy. We would like to write a whole volume on the brilliant pianists of the late 19th and 20th centuries such as Paderewski, De Pachman, Godowsky, Busoni, Rosenthal, Harold Bauer, Gabrilowitsch, Hofmann, Rachmaninov, Teresa Carreno, Myra Hess, Guiomar Novaes, Katherine Bacon, John Powell, Percy Grainger, Levitzki and innumerable others!

MORE ABOUT RADIO

1927 witnessed the broadcasting of concerts by the Boston Symphony under Serge Koussevitzky, The New York Philharmonic Orchestra (Willem Mengelberg), The New York Symphony (Walter Damrosch), Children's Concerts (Ernest Schelling), and other organizations. The broadcasting companies have their own orchestras, such as the fabulous National Broadcasting Company's Symphony Orchestra under Arturo Toscanini. A valuable radio musical field for pleasure and education has developed. Dr. Damrosch's musical lectures on the Ring elicited nearly one million letters! 1929 saw the capitulation of Leopold Stokowski and the Philadelphia Orchestra in a series of broadcasts. Since 1931, opera has been broadcast from the stage of the Metropolitan Opera House in New York. On many programs are heard the world's greatest artists.

CHAPTER XXIII

Opera Makers of France, Germany and Italy—
1741 to Wagner

AS with all things that are over-popular and over-used, the opera in the 18th century became trifling and empty, except for the work of some few geniuses.

The music of the ancient Egyptians and Chinese advanced very little, on account of fast and firm laws, and opera remained the same for a long time, because of the strict rules. For there were laws governing the kind of arias, the number of men's parts and women's parts, when and where ballets and choruses should come in, the number of acts and many another clogging rule. But, worst of all, the people in the audiences knew the rules so well that they made a fuss when any composer dared to depart from them. Such was the case when Gluck came on the scene, and when he left it, with all the changes he made, other rules became just as binding!

You saw the effort of Gluck to reform opera in order to arrive at truth and sincerity; you saw how Mozart dignified the forms that were being used by enriching them, by his sparkling humor, by his new musical devices and limitless outpourings of melody. Beethoven, too, made his one masterpiece, *Fidelio*, stand for sincerity rather than triviality, and now von Weber we see adding to opera the story of peasant life in Germany, combined with mystery and beauty. Yet, with all these forerunners of a newer opera, many composers had to work very hard and much time had to pass by until we reach the great change under Wagner's genius.

Von Weber Writes Fairy Tale Opera

Because Carl Maria von Weber (1786–1826) had so great an influence on opera writers, we will start with him.

Weber was the founder of romantic German opera,— the opera that dealt with people and their feelings and the folk song of the German nation. He was the first to combine the story of everyday life with the charm of imagination. Being of a long line of barons and also a great pianist, he raised the position of musicians to a high level in society, so that after him, pianists and violinists were looked upon as artists and not as artisans.

He seemed to understand the life of his time, and suited his work to his surroundings so beautifully, that it immediately led away from the trivialities into which Italian opera had drifted, into something more worth while. He was a true romantic, as he put into his operas warmth of feeling, elegance and delightful melody. He had a lovely sense of what was dramatic or theatric, and he knew the orchestral instruments as well as he knew the piano, for which he wrote skilfully.

He was born at Eutin, near Lübeck, where Bach had lived, and showed great musical gifts when he was a little boy. And although he was delicate, his father dearly wanted him to be a second Mozart. Michael Haydn, brother of Papa Haydn taught him and Weber showed great ability at the piano and could sit down and improvise and read music at sight.

He was taught by Abbé Vogler in Vienna, who first introduced him to folk music, which he used with such pleasing skill later. (By the way, Abbé Vogler, a famous organist and teacher, was the Abt Vogler of Robert Browning's poem.)   Weber became conductor of the orchestra at Breslau at 18.   But, being a delicate boy, he could not stand many of the things he did and he broke down in health.

Later he was unfortunate enough to become secretary to Duke Ludwig of Württemberg at Stuttgart who was not a fit companion for a young man.   Weber mixed in the gay life of the Duke and his friends, fell into bad habits, and drifted into money difficulties.   Strange to say, during this time he read much and even wrote some music encouraged by Danzi, his friend.

However, he got into a scrape trying to help his father out of a financial difficulty, angered the King and was banished in 1810; and though cleared of his guilt, he remained in exile for some time.   Then deciding to turn over a new leaf, with a mind teeming with ideas, he settled down to work.

He soon became known for his compositions and was made Musical Director at the Prague Theatre, where he won popular favor by writing national songs.   He undertook to organize a Dresden troupe, after having done a similar work in Prague, but he was annoyed by bad health and the jealousies of his rivals.   Nevertheless, here he produced *Der Freischütz, Enchanted Huntsman*, which Berlin received in 1821 with wild enthusiasm, while *Euryanthe*, given almost at the same time, was not, in Vienna, very successful.

Weber's operas, as the beginning of German romantic opera, are on the direct road to Wagner's.   Wagner inherited from Gluck and Weber, and Gluck inherited directly from the German *Singspiel* (sing-play) of the 18th century, which was a play composed of dances and songs not unlike the English masque and the French ballet and vaudeville.

It came before opera in Germany, yet made the basis for a German school, for it used German song and German subjects. Mozart, too, was one of Weber's musical fathers, especially in his *Magic Flute*.

We see Weber, now, as we saw Mozart, combining the supernatural with national or German melody, and using both imagination and realistic effects. His *Oberon* is full of fairy atmosphere and *Der Freischütz* is often uncanny and awesome. He keeps the spoken dialogue of the old *Singspiel* and in *Der Freischütz* deals for the first time with peasant life. His orchestration is lovely and his skill with it was so great that he is still looked upon as one of the important men in the development of the orchestra. He paints the individual characters beautifully by giving each one suitable music to sing.

He reached dramatic heights by his contrasts between mellow quietness and brilliant effects. He made use of all the resources on his instruments, their defects as well as their good points. No one had ever before written more weird music than in the scene of the Wolf's Glen, in *Der Freischütz*.

His piano music, including many fine sonatas, was rich with new and brilliant effects and his *Concertstück* (Concertpiece) was the father of the symphonic poems which were later written by Franz Liszt, Hector Berlioz, Tchaikowsky, and Richard Strauss. Thus did Weber give much to music's growth.

Louis Spohr (1784–1854) who was later a kind friend to Wagner, wrote ten operas which belong, too, in the Romantic School of Weber. He, however, was best known for his violin concertos, written in the classic style of Haydn and Mozart. He wrote these because he lived in the time of the great piano and violin virtuosi (brilliant performers) in Vienna. His work is tiresome to us because of his many mannerisms.

Grétry and Opéra Comique

Now we will go back a little and take up the French School with Grétry. Although a Belgian, he was the first man of importance in France after Rameau, and was the founder of the comedy opera (*opéra comique*).

André Ernest Modeste Grétry (1741–1813), was born in Liége. He excelled in the *opera buffa* imported from Italy, which, due to the great sense of humor of the French, immediately became popular. In spite of their vulgarity there was much in these comedy operas that was delightful and they were on subjects which interested the people. Grétry was very skilful and successful in this kind of opera of which he wrote fifty in addition to much church music, six symphonies and many instrumental pieces.

Later, *opéra comique*, a more refined form of this *opera buffa*, had a long vogue in France. It became more serious, too, getting very close to grand opera, except that it had spoken words. *Opéra comique* always kept its naturalness, was simple, straightforward in story and informal in action. Another important difference from grand opera was that it could be easily given in small theatres, for it needed no spectacular scenes. This of course made *opéra comique* popular, for composers liked to write it, as they had a better chance to have their works performed than if they had written grand opera with costly scenes. This form has been the inspiration of many of the French composers of the 19th and 20th centuries.

Opéra comique is first found in Paris at the time of the War of the Buffoons in 1752 the year that Pergolesi's little opera *La Serva Padrona*, took Paris by storm.

Now, Paris had become the great meeting place for composers, and we find Italians and Germans going there to give operas, combining the ideas of Rameau, Lully and Gluck, with their own national styles. They often dis-

After a painting by Giacometti.

Georges Bizet.

Vincent d'Indy.   *Camille Saint-Saëns.*

Jules Massenet.   *Gustave Charpentier.*

French Composers of the 19th Century.

Hector Berlioz.

(Father of the Tone Poem.)

Franz Liszt.

Sympathetic Teacher, Composer, Pianist and Friend to Young Musicians.

placed the French musicians and Paris was a center of jealousies and heart aches in the midst of its brilliancy.

CHERUBINI—MUSICAL CZAR OF PARIS

The first of these foreigners to invade France was Luigi Cherubini (1760–1842), a Florentine, who became the musical czar of Paris. He was educated in Italy and in the beginning wrote Italian opera in the popular style. He went to London on invitation and was made composer to the King. In 1788 we see him in Paris giving his opera *Demophon*. In this, instead of being trivial in the waning Italian style, he became "grand" and pompous! Nearly every one that followed, copied him. Beethoven thought him to be the greatest living composer, because of his *Lodoiska* (1791) and *The Water Carrier* (1800).

Cherubini started as a composer of church music and wrote most of his operas from 1780 to 1800. He returned to church music later in life and wrote his great Credo for eight voices. He composed in all forms required of the Roman Catholic service and one of the noblest, sacred writings is his Requiem in C.

But his opera writing influenced his church music and made him and many who followed him, compose such spectacular church music that the solemn polyphony of the 17th century was well-nigh lost. About a generation ago, the Pope decided that this style of writing was not suitable for the church and so ordained it, that only Gregorian Chant should be sung in the Roman Catholic Church. History repeats itself and Church music, as in the time of St. Gregory and of Palestrina, had to have another "house-cleaning."

Cherubini's orchestration was broad and fine and his overtures were classic models. He seemed to have followed Mozart's style rather than Gluck's and joined the classic style with the modern. He had vigor, and was free from mannerisms, and was looked upon as a great man. As the head of the Paris Conservatory he was able to befriend many a struggling composer. He died after a long useful life, at 82.

His *Medée* and *The Water Carrier* (*Les deux journées*) mark the greatest accomplishment in his life—both are tragic yet are *opéra comique* because they contain spoken dialogue. Remember this instance of tragic *opéra comique* and it will explain how it differs from what we call comic opera.

FOLLOWERS OF GLUCK

Following the time of Gluck in Paris there was a group of composers who were so much influenced by him that they are looked upon as his disciples. One of these was his own pupil, Antonio Salieri (1750–1825), who in turn taught Beethoven, Schubert and others.

One of the links between the 18th and 19th centuries was Etienne Nicholas Méhul (1763–1817), a Frenchman, who worked with Gluck. He dared to take his themes from life and wrote *opéra comique* with a serious aim. Even though he lived in the turbulence of the French Revolution, he wrote thirty operas, among which the greatest is *Joseph*. He was made inspector at the new Conservatory and also an Academician, and was one of the most loved composers of his day. He was often noble in musical expression and handled his chorus and orchestra with skill. He wrote little of anything but opera, but pointed the way for others, especially in the use of local color and national feeling.

The next follower of Gluck, Gasparo Spontini (1774–1851), born in Italy, of peasant stock, was one of the first to write historic opera, which was further developed by

Meyerbeer and others. Technically, this is known as French Grand Opera, which was being developed at the same time as *opéra comique*. It appealed to hearts and imagination, for the people loved the great scenes and patriotism portrayed.

Spontini first went to Paris in 1803 and the people did not like his work. But he persisted, studied Gluck and Mozart as hard as he could, and produced *Milton*, which showed the public that his work had some beauty. After this he wrote *La Vestale*, a noble work which swept him into favor, and he won a prize offered by Napoleon and judged by Méhul, Gossec (a composer), and Grétry.

Weber, however, while Spontini was absent came to Paris with *Der Freischütz*, and took his place in the hearts of the people. Cast down by losing his popularity, Spontini returned to Italy. His musical ability was not equal to his great plots, yet, as the first writer of historic opera he deserves a place in the growing-up of musical drama.

Grétry made French *opéra comique* out of *opéra bouffe*. Among the well known writers of *opéra comique* in France were François Adrienne Boieldieu, Daniel François Esprit Auber, Louis Joseph Ferdinand Hérold, Jacques François Halévy.

Boieldieu (1775–1834) was born in Rouen and became, in 1800, professor of piano at the Paris Conservatory. He wrote piano pieces and operas, and is best known for his *La Dame Blanche* (*The White Lady*) which is still heard in Paris. His operas combine sweet melody, amusing rhythm with not a little dramatic style. He shows in his works a real understanding of how characters and action should be handled.

Auber (1782–1871) called "The Prince of Opéra Comique," was born in Paris, and later he became the Director of the Conservatory and Imperial Chapel Master to Napoleon III. His best known operas are *Fra Diavolo*, *The Black*

Domino, Masaniello, or *La Muette de Portici (The Dumb Girl of Portici).* He had great popularity during his day.

Hérold (1791–1833) was not as accomplished as either Auber or Boieldieu. He was the son of a piano teacher and studied at the Conservatory under Méhul. In 1812 he won the *Prix de Rome* (the prize given by the Conservatory for composition, which permitted the student to go to Rome to perfect himself in his art, and to increase his culture, at the expense of the Government.) His best operas are *Zampa* and *Le Pré aux Clercs.* He was particularly good in orchestration, and his works are still heard.

The last one in this group is Jacques François Halévy (1799–1862), who is chiefly famous for *La Juive (The Jewess),* a type of historic opera, even though he wrote many in the style of *opéra comique.* It is still given today, and it was while singing in this opera, at the Metropolitan Opera House that Caruso was stricken with his fatal illness and Martinelli, a few years later was taken ill, and so it is looked upon with superstition by some of the singers.

MEYERBEER COMPOSES VERY GRAND "GRAND OPERA"

Next, comes Giacomo Meyerbeer (1791–1864), and he followed the historic style that Spontini had begun. He, though a German, captured the French audiences and is famous chiefly for writing grand scenes, rather than for noble music in grand opera. His name was Jacob Liebmann Beer, but he changed it to Meyerbeer. He was the son of a Jewish banker and had no struggle for money as did so many of the composers. He began as a pianist and was also a pupil of Abbé Vogler. He was unsuccessful in Germany, so went to Italy. After an invitation to hear his opera *Il Crociato (The Crusader)* performed in Paris, he took up his residence there.

His style was a queer mixture of German counterpoint,

Italian melody and French rhythm, and after blotting up all the popular fashions of the day, he gave his *Robert le Diable* (*Robert the Devil*), *The Huguenots* and *Le Prophète* (*The Prophet*) with different degrees of success in Paris. Eugèn Scribe was chief librettist in this period.   Later Meyerbeer's operas were given in Berlin, with Jenny Lind in the title rôles and he became very famous. *Dinorah* and *L'Africaine* (*The African Maid*) were very popular and are still in the repertory of opera companies. But his style seems insincere and showy according to those who expect more of opera than grand effects, glitter and elaborate scenery. *The Huguenots* was probably his finest piece of work.

Among other composers in Germany whose names you may come upon in other places are: Heinrich Marschner (1795–1861), Conradin Kreutzer, Lortzing (1801–1851), von Flotow (1812–1883), composer of *Stradella* and *Martha*, and Otto Nicolai (1810–1849) who wrote the delightful bit of fluff, *The Merry Wives of Windsor*.

Later we see the old *Singspiel* take the form of Comic Opera (not *opéra comique*) with such Germans as Carl Millocker and von Suppé and Victor Nessler in his *Trumpeter of Sakkingen* and *The Pied Piper of Hamelin*, and Johann Strauss, the great Viennese Waltz King, whose *Blue Danube* and other waltzes are so familiar. (Vienna was as famous for the waltz as America is for jazz.)

OFFENBACH'S TALES OF HOFFMANN

Another German who went to Paris was Jacques Offen‑ bach (1819–1880) from Cologne, who became more of a Parisian than the Parisians. He was quite a fop and Wag‑ ner once called him "the musical Clown" for he was often seen wearing a yellow waist-coat and trousers, sky blue coat, grey gloves, a green hat and he carried a red sun shade.

How like an electric sign he must have looked! But withal, he was so popular in Vienna that when Wagner approached the Opera House about his *Meistersinger* he was told that they were too busy producing Offenbach's operas to consider his. He was the best box-office attraction of his time, and the managers could not get enough of his works. Offenbach was important because he founded a new kind of light opera, or the operetta, which is light in story, charming and winsome. His chief operas are *The Grand Duchess of Gerolstein, La Belle Hélène* and his masterpiece *The Tales of Hoffmann* of which you probably know the often-played Barcarolle. He felt that it was his finest work and was very eager to be present at its first performance at the Opéra Comique in Paris, but before he had finished orchestrating it, he died. When it was given, the following year, it was praised as the work of a genius.

His followers were Planquette, with *Chimes of Normandy*, Lecocq and his *La Fille de Mme. Angot*, and *Giroflé-Girofla*, and Franz von Suppé with *Fatinitza, Boccaccio* and the *Poet and Peasant* overture, played at all movie-houses!

In Vienna Johann Strauss with his waltzes, and the most perfect comic opera of its kind, *Die Fledermaus (The Bat)* still sparkling and delightful, *Zigeuner-Baron (Gypsy-Baron)*, all owe their start in life to Offenbach's genius. We too, in America, have had the gifted Victor Herbert with his *Mlle. Modiste, The Serenade, The Red Mill* and many other lovely operettas and Reginald De Koven with *Robin Hood*. The inimitable pair in England, Sir Arthur Sullivan and his librettist W. S. Gilbert, wrote comic operas that have become classics. (See page 341.)

So, the foppish Offenbach sowed fruitful seed, and the crop that followed him have given high pleasure and delightful times to many, and probably will, for years to come.

An Italian Trio—Rossini, Bellini, Donizetti

We have dipped into Germany and France so now we must see what was going on in Italy.

Few Italians realized that great musical advances were being made in other countries and kept on doing the same old things. But one or two became famous because they left Italy to mingle with the other composers and audiences of Europe.

Among the best known of these was Gioacchino Rossini (1792–1868), who became director of the *Theatre Italien* in Paris, after visits to Vienna and London. His grand opera, *William Tell*, was based on the Schiller poem dealing with the hero of Swiss history. His masterpiece, the *Barber of Seville*, a most delightful *opera buffa*, was modelled after the *Marriage of Figaro* by Mozart. Both texts were from Beaumarchais' comedies and deal with the same characters.

Rossini had genius for writing well for the voice. His church music, such as the *Stabat Mater* and the *Solemn Mass*, is full of beautiful living melody, and is often heard. He was a brilliant composer, an innovator, and helped to rid opera of the ornate cadenza. He improved orchestration and changed the "dry" recitative into a more dramatic accompanied type. His work shows special skill in concerted pieces,—choruses and the finales of the acts.

One of the best known followers of Rossini in Italy was Gaetano Donizetti (1797–1848) with his *Daughter of the Regiment*, *Lucrezia Borgia* and *Lucia di Lammermoor* from Sir Walter Scott's story, *The Bride of Lammermoor*. He wrote showy brilliant things like the sextet and the mad scene from *Lucia* and by his very skill in these musical fireworks, kept back opera founded on truth and sincerity.

Vincenzo Bellini (1801–1835), unlike Donizetti, wrote only in the grand style and not in the *comique*. His best known works are *Norma*, *I Puritani* (*The Puritans*) and *La*

Sonnambula (*The Sleep Walker*). Though he was a better writer than Donizetti, Bellini is heard far less often today. In our time, Rosa Ponselle was a noted singer of the role of Norma at the Metropolitan.

Opera Singers of the Period

As there cannot be successful opera without opera singers, here are the names of a few who have gone down to history: Angelica Catalani, Giuditta Pasta, Henriette Sontag, Wilhelmine Schroeder Devrient, Maria Garcia Malibran, Pauline Viardot Garcia, Henriette Nissen, Giulia Grisi, Jenny Lind, Caroline Carvalho, Euphrosyne Parepa-Rosa, Zelia Trebelli, Pauline Lucca, and Adelina Patti, and Manuel Garcia, John Braham, Domenico Ronconi, Nicholas Levasseur, Joseph Tichatschek, Giuseppe Mario, Enrico Tamberlick, Theodor Wachtel, Charles Santley and John Sims Reeves.

English Opera Ballad

18th Century

Fifteen years after the period in which Purcell glorified English music, Handel went to England and gathered about him composers who wrote along the lines which he popularized. In addition to this, ballad-operas, part-songs, "catches" (separate songs or ballads) were very popular. In London, there were comic plays made of strings of songs such as Gay's *Beggar's Opera* which were sisters to *opera buffa* in Italy, *opéra bouffe* in France, and the *Singspiel* in Germany.

Forty-five of these ballad-operas were produced in 15 years. The arrangers of these amusing song-plays included the names of Dr. Pepusch, a German who lived in

London; Henry Carey (1692–1743), famous as the composer of *Sally in our Alley, God Save the King* (our *America*); and Thomas Arne (1710–1778) who wrote many masques, numerous ballad operas, and set many of the Shakespeare lyrics and wrote many glees and ballads. Some of these part songs were very beautiful and somewhat like the madrigals of earlier days.

Many of the church composers in their lighter moods wrote some of these ballad-operas, among them: Samuel Arnold, with his *Maid of the Mill*, a *pasticcio*, "Notable," says Waldo Selden Pratt, "as the first native music drama, since Purcell"; William Jackson; Thomas Atwood and Charles Dibden who was so successful with his *Shepherd's Artifice* that he wrote seventy others, and thirty musical monologues, among which were *Sea Songs*. Some other well known men were Michael Arne, son of Dr. Thomas Arne with his *Fairy Tale, Almena* and *Cymon* from Garrick's play of the same name; James Hook with some two thousand songs and twenty-five plays; William Shield, the viola player and song writer; Stephen Storace, clever violinist and the author of *The Haunted Tower* and *Pirates*, and his sister Ann Storace, a singer. At this time there were two clubs, one called the "Catch Club" and another the "Glee Club," and one also called "Madrigal Society," and before 1800 we have a list of glee writers including the two Samuel Webbs, Sr. and Jr., Benjamin Cook and his son Robert, John Wall Callcott, a pupil of Haydn, who won many medals from the "Catch Club."

From now on, England was influenced by foreign composers, especially Mendelssohn, Weber and Gounod, and made ballad operas and operettas freely adapted from continental works, besides glees and songs and music for the Church of England services. The interest in music was great and some of the church music and glees at the time were excellent. In this period, the Birmingham Festivals were started, Horsley founded the *Concentores Sodales* (1748–1847), a group formed along the lines of the earlier Catch and Glee Clubs. The Philharmonic Society also was formed (1813) and among its great leaders were Cherubini in 1815, Spohr 1820 and 1843 and Weber 1826 and Mendelssohn many times after 1829. Through the effort of the Earl of Westmoreland, the Royal Academy of Music was organized in 1822. Among the composers of this period were Samuel Wesley (1776–1837), a Bach enthusiast who wrote much church music and other classic forms; William Crotch (1775–1847); George Stark, an intimate of Weber and Mendelssohn, who edited *Gibbon's Madrigals*; William Horsley, who edited *Callcott's Glees* and wrote glees himself, symphonies and songs and handbooks. There were many others in this period but too numerous to mention here.

In the next period England's composers free themselves from the Mendelssohn School and begin to branch out. Do not think that Mendelssohn was not good for them. He gave much that England needed, and also brought English composers in contact with European music. But they liked church music and the ballad opera and the charming part songs, rather than the heavier operas of Europe. Among writers of cathedral music are Sir George A. McFarren, John Bacchus Dykes, whose name appears in our hymn books, Joseph Barnby, Samuel Wesley mentioned above, and Henry Smart. In 1816, Sir William Sterndale Bennett was born, he was a choir boy and entered the Royal Academy of Music in 1835. The House of Broadwood (English piano makers) sent him to Leipsic to study and he came under the influence of Mendelssohn and Schumann. He was the director of the Royal Academy of Music, a fine pianist and wrote many compositions, among which his Cantata *A Woman of Samaria* is not as dry as the usual sacred works of this period. He died in 1875.

Another great writer of this time was Sir John Stainer (1840–1901). Some of his things are given today in our churches and are very beautiful and impressive. He is the author of valuable text-books.

LIGHT OPERA

At this time, some writers of a sort of belated ballad opera appeared in the persons of:

Michael William Balfe who wrote thirty operas among which is *The Bohemian Girl*, still played and greatly admired; William Vincent Wallace, like Balfe an Irishman, who is famous for his *Maritana;* and then of course, Sir Arthur Seymour Sullivan (1842–1900), who probably needs very little introduction to any American or any Englishman for he wrote *The Mikado, Pirates of Penzance, Iolanthe*, the only fairy opera without a mortal in it, *Pinafore, Patience, Princess Ida, Trial by Jury, Ruddigore* and many others, in which he and W. S. Gilbert, as librettist, worked together. W. S. Gilbert was the author of the inimitable and amusing *Bab Ballads*. If you haven't read them you have a treat in store for you! They wrote together in a fresh, mock-heroic, humorous vein, and it seems as if they were made for each other, so delightfully did they play into each other's hands. Sullivan's first light opera was *Cox and Box* on a book by Burnand.

Sullivan was the son of a clarinet player and teacher. He also began, as did so many British Islanders, as a choir boy and entered the Royal Academy of Music on a Mendelssohn Scholarship. Later he went to the Leipsic Conservatory and wrote some music to Shakespeare's *Tempest*, which established his fame in England. Besides his operas he wrote much incidental music, some anthems and cantatas, among these *The Golden Legend* and *The Prodigal Son* are the best. He wanted very much to write grand opera, but he never seemed to work well in this vein and his *Ivanhoe* did him little good.

And so, we leave opera until the wand of the Wizard Wagner changes the whole path of music.

CHAPTER XXIV

The Poet Music Writers—Romantic School

SCHUBERT—MENDELSSOHN—SCHUMANN—CHOPIN

YOU have seen how Romantic Music began, and why Beethoven is often the first name mentioned when Romanticism is talked about, for he was the colossal guide-post pointing the way.

He was as far from the classical forms of Bach, as from later writers who have "jumped over the musical traces" altogether. All were, and still are, trying to free themselves from conventions, and to express their feelings satisfactorily.

It is natural to begin the Romantic school with Schubert, the first figure of great importance. But there was one John Field (1782–1837) from totally different surroundings who is still remembered for his fine piano nocturnes.

Impressed with the quiet and solemnity of the night, he knew how to put it into beautiful melody. He was born in a little out-of-the-way street in Dublin, not far from St. Patrick's Cathedral, and near the birthplace of that romantic poet, Tom Moore. His father and his grandfather, both musicians, forced the infant prodigy, and at ten, he played, publicly, a concerto composed by his father.

At twelve, the boy was apprenticed, or "hired out," as pupil and salesman to Clementi, the composer and piano manufacturer in London. He showed off the pianos so well to the customers, that Clementi soon realized he had made a good bargain. The boy played in London as the "ten-year-old pupil of Clementi," on whom he no doubt tried out his *Gradus ad Parnassum*. (Page 320.)

Five years later he played his own "Concerto for the grand *forte-piano*, composed for the occasion." Clementi was shrewd, and started a branch of his piano business in St. Petersburg, taking Field with him.

One of the ear-marks of Romantic music is the title of the piano piece or song. Until the romantic period music was designated usually by the number of the work or by its form such as *gavotte, minuet, rondo, sonata*, etc., but the Romantics wrote what they felt, and with the exception of Chopin, gave descriptive names to their pieces. In 1817 John Field wrote a concerto named *L'incendie par l'orage* (*The Fire from the Storm*), a musical picture.

His influence was more important than his music. We see his hand in the playing and composing of the poet-pianist, Frederick Chopin.

Although Weber appeared in a different musical field he, too, had a strong influence. He was four years younger than Field but had greater opportunities and was one of the first of the Romantic School.

Charles Mayer (1799–1862) was a direct follower and pupil of Field. His *études* (studies) ranked with those of Henselt, who wrote the delightful *If I Were a Bird*, and he had an influence upon Chopin, too.

SCHUBERT—MAKER OF SONGS

And now we come to Franz Peter Schubert (1797–1828), born in Vienna of a schoolmaster father, and a mother, who, like Beethoven's, was a cook.

The musical comedy, *Blossom Time*, was built upon some

of Schubert's most beautiful melodies and episodes from his life. We must never trust too far stories told this way, which often contain unreliable details, however this charming operetta gives an interesting glimpse of Schubert's devotion to composition. It is true that he wrote wherever he was, covering his cuffs as well as the menus and programs in the taverns with the endless flow of themes which eventually became world-famous songs. Schubert was not a mere writer of songs; he established the form known as the art song or *Lied* and through all his works, torrents of melody seemed to spring from him eternally.

He was the twelfth of nineteen children, five of whom were of a second marriage, and there was no wealth or luxury for Franz, so his father worked hard to pay for his music lessons.

His teacher said that no matter what he tried to teach him in violin, piano, singing, the organ or thorough-bass, Franz knew it already, for he learned everything almost at a glance.

He was first soprano in the church choir of Lichtenthal and the beauty of his voice attracted much attention. He also played the violin in the services, and stole little stray minutes to write songs or pieces for strings and piano.

When he was sent to the school for Imperial choristers the boys laughed at his coarse, grey clothing, the big "Harold Lloyd spectacles," and his retiring, bashful manners. They soon changed when they discovered the astonishing things he could do. His home-spun clothes were exchanged for the uniform trimmed with gold lace worn by the Imperial choristers, who formed an orchestra to practise daily, music by Haydn, Mozart, Cherubini and Beethoven. Among them was Spaun and when he won his confidence, Franz told him that he had written many pieces and he would write more, but could not afford to buy the music paper.

His new friend made it possible for Schubert to have the paper and other necessities, by which Spaun did something to benefit the world.

The ease with which Schubert absorbed all learning perhaps made him neglect the study of counterpoint. Before he was twenty, he could not give all his time to music as he taught in his father's school. His heart was not in his work, for while hearing the pupils recite he wrote themes on every scrap of paper he could find. He had an endless struggle with poverty, even when he gave music lessons in the Esterhazy family. Perhaps he fell secretly in love with one of the young daughters, or perhaps he missed his comrades, but he was unhappy away from Vienna.

He was of the people and wrote from the heart and to the heart. While the early songs met with favor among his companions, they did not immediately reach the wider public. Yet he was encouraged to write in larger forms. He hoped for success with his symphonies and chamber music, and his disappointment was keen when the critics did not rate them as highly as they did the songs.

The steady flow of melody and the torrent of themes in his chamber music, which is regarded as comparable to that of Beethoven and Brahms, is like a song with lovely play of instruments. Who can forget the haunting beauty of the *Unfinished Symphony?* Left unfinished not by Schubert's death, as many suppose, but because the composer felt that he had arrived at a summit of beauty in the second movement, and dared not add a third, lest he could not again reach the heights. Of his last symphony in C major, which takes an hour to perform, Robert Schumann wrote that it was of "Heavenly length."

Schubert lived when the romantic poets gave him wonderful verse for his texts. He loved the literature of Goethe and Heinrich Heine, both of whom knew the hearts of the simple people.

The world will never forget the wonderful heritage of vast quantities of great works left by this genius, who died at thirty-two. Besides creating new forms in song he also gave the pianists pieces that were new and important. He left no concertos, nor did he write for solo violin, but his piano sonatas and chamber music are of value. *Der Erl-Koenig* (*The Erl King*), *Der Doppelganger* (*The Shadow*), and *Death and the Maiden*, all sounded the last note in tragedy, and he also wrote many lovely songs in lighter mood.

THE WELL FAVORED MENDELSSOHN

Most masters who have left the world richer for having lived, were born in poverty and knew the sorrows of privation, not so with Felix Mendelssohn-Bartholdy (1809–1847), loved by the many who have played his *Songs Without Words*, or who have heard Elman's fingers fly over his violin in the concerto, said to be the best writing ever done for that instrument.

Popular as are many works from the polished and fluent pen of Mendelssohn, the oratorios *Elijah* and *Saint Paul* are noble, for these contain some of the most dramatic and inspired writing. In that work which is typical of Mendelssohn and his personality, he showed more characteristics of the older classical school than of the romantic. If he had lived during the classical period he would have been a greater composer, for he was romantic by influence and classic in taste.

Has not the *Spring Song* the shimmer of spring and the *Spinning Song* the whir of the wheels? One can easily imagine the kindly touch of a loving hand in *Consolation*, while the *Hunting Song* is alive and going. This is the romantic music that became the model for thousands of small pieces.

It is said frequently that if Mendelssohn had been less conventional, his work would have been more forceful, because he had much that was truly fine.

Mendelssohn lived among the most brilliant literary lights of his day. His refinement was reflected in his music. He was petted by an adoring father, mother and sisters, who gave him every opportunity to study and compose, and he was much sought after socially. He devoted much time to the study of languages, sketching in water colors and traveling in Italy and Switzerland. His sister Fanny, whose musical education was of the utmost assistance to her brother whom she idolized, would have been famous but for her father's prejudice against women in professional life. She was a gifted composer and it is claimed that she wrote many of her brother's songs and some of the *Songs Without Words*.

Her death was a mortal blow from which Mendelssohn never recovered. Extremely sensitive, his affection for his family was most intense and filled his life.

His grandfather was the eminent philosopher Moses Mendelssohn, who being a Hebrew, was open to the sorrows caused by prejudice. He was such a great man, however, that he succeeded in breaking down barriers not only for himself, but for his race.

Abraham Mendelssohn was pleased to call himself, "First the son of the famous Moses Mendelssohn, then the father of the eminent Felix Mendelssohn." His banking house in Berlin continued into this century.

The most noted musicians and artists were entertained in the Mendelssohn home, and heard the compositions of the gifted young man. In 1821 the boy was taken to Goethe's home where he played and improvised for the poet. He was delighted with him for his musical talent, and because he had inherited the gift of conversation and letters from his grandfather, of whom Goethe was very fond. Young Mendelssohn never shocked the great old poet as did Beethoven, for his manner was always correct.

In 1825 Mendelssohn went to Paris to Cherubini who was asked whether his talent justified cultivation beyond the average stage. The master was very enthusiastic, but his father would not leave him in Paris, even in charge of the noted teacher. Returning to Berlin he wrote the incidental music to *Midsummer Night's Dream* for an amateur performance in the Mendelssohn home. It reflects the humor of Shakespeare, while the orchestration shows great delicacy and perfection. Mendelssohn was only seventeen when he wrote it, with all its finish and its flawless musical treatment. Much that he did at that period shows his natural flow of genius. Music seemed to gush from his soul like pure, fresh water from a spring, making one think of cool fountains, sparkling with melody and clarity. These qualities are also in the *Fingal's Cave* or *Hebrides* overture, and he takes you on his delightful trips in *Calm Sea and Prosperous Voyage*. The way these numbers reflect his impressions and the way he transmitted them to others is typical of the Romantic School. The purity of his musical form related him to the classical and gave inklings of the Symphonic Tone Poem.

In his symphonies Mendelssohn also told tales of his travels, as in the *Italian Symphony*, and in his *Scotch Symphony* in which he made use of Scotch folk tunes. He also wrote much chamber music. He left some piano concertos which still attract the professionals of today, and are the joy of many piano students who play them arranged for two pianos.

Mendelssohn tried operas but like many others failed to find a good libretto. This was the trouble with one he produced in Berlin. Added to this there were many intrigues and jealousies at the opera house which turned him bitterly against that city.

However, he accomplished one of the greatest things ever done for music. The works of Bach and Handel had been so neglected that they were almost forgotten. He knew them well, and wanting others to love them as he did, he assembled a great chorus and gave Bach's *Passion according to Saint Matthew*. This was the first performance since Bach's death, and it brought these works back to us. Imagine Mendelssohn's popularity and talent as a conductor to have been able to do this at the age of twenty! Then he traveled again, and after roaming through Italy, Switzerland and France, he went to London where he created a stir as pianist, composer and conductor. Besides his splendid education he had a winsome and attractive personality, and his success was very great. He made, in all, nine visits to England.

Having been brought up in the Christian faith, he married the daughter of a French Protestant minister and had five children. They went to live in Germany, and becoming conductor of the Leipsic Gewandhaus orchestra, he made the city the musical center of Germany. He founded the Leipsic Conservatory of Music (1843), where he gave his old teacher Moscheles an important post. This conservatory is well known here, for many American musicians of former generations were educated there.

Mendelssohn conducted many festivals and he always aroused new interest in Bach, whom he presented at every opportunity.

His *Saint Paul* had success in Duesseldorf (1837), and during his last visit to England (1846), he gave at the Birmingham festival, *Elijah*, second today in popularity only to Handel's *Messiah*.

When Mendelssohn returned to Leipsic, he showed traces of overwork and the death of his sister coming at the same time, made him unable to resist the strain. He died November 4, 1847, when only 38. His happy life shines through his music so full of beauty and sunshine.

Schumann—The Supreme Poet

Robert Schumann (1810–1856), a tower of beauty, strength, imagination and dramatic fervor even judged by 20th century standards, still thrills us as we recognize his genius. What a price he paid for his life filled with joys and griefs!

We are grateful for the solidity of his building, his breadth of vision, the wonders of his imagination, the beauty of his poetic fancy, and above all, the vastness of his musical knowledge. A peak among the composers of the Romantic School, he has scaled the heights of dramatic fervor as he has touched the sun-flecked valleys. To him we owe the naming of pieces, and the feeling of emotion which the composer felt when he named them,—*The Happy Farmer, The Prophet Bird, The Rocking-Horse, End of the Song, The Child Falls Asleep,* etc.

All who have been milestones in music have been well educated, yet how unjustly people say musicians know nothing but music. Many have not had only culture from their studies, but also have come from refined homes. So Schumann, born at Zwickau, Saxony, had an educated father, a book-seller. His mother wanted Robert to be a lawyer, and did not wish his musical talent to interfere. He began to compose and study music at seven, but he studied law, literature and philosophy, later, at the University of Leipsic.

After a year he went to the famous University of Heidelberg (1829), which has always been proud that the great composer was one of its students.

Schumann returned to Leipsic on account of the musical life. With his return began the romance of his life, one

of the most beautiful love stories in musical history. He
studied with Frederick Wieck, whose little daughter Clara
was a prodigy pianist. He became a member of the household and was charmed by the talent of the child. Mean-
while he was studying as pianist, and being ingenious,
he invented an instrument to develop his weak fourth
finger, but it ruined his hand and unfitted him for his
career.

Now he gave more attention to composition and to
musical criticism. He founded a music journal which gave
him the chance to help some of the brilliant musicians of
the day. He brought Chopin to the notice of Germany,
and proclaimed the genius of young Johannes Brahms. He
also formed a deep friendship for Mendelssohn.

Valuable as are all writings which reveal his thoughts,
his richest gift to the world was his music, in which he
preached the gospel of beauty.

As Schumann grew into manhood he began to know the
depths of sorrow, some of his finest works having been an
outburst of his tortured soul. Clara Wieck was now a
young woman and a great pianist. It was natural that
an affection should spring up between them. But Clara's
father had greater hopes. He could not see a struggling
young musician and critic as the husband of his talented
child. During this long and painful courtship when Schumann dared not speak his love to Clara he wrote compositions with which to tell his story, and she understood. One
of these expressions was the lovely *Warum* asking the
question, "Why?" so longingly.

In those days a case could be brought into court and the
reason demanded why a parent should refuse to allow a
marriage. Schumann went to law, and the court decided
that Wieck's objections were without cause. But the year
of strain told upon his health and nerves and he began
his married life under a cloud of illness. The young pair

were ideally happy, he wrote glorious music, and she took pride in playing his piano works on all her programs.

With all her accomplishments—and she was a great artist—she was first a devoted wife who cared for her husband as though he had been her child. Schumann's very finest work was done during these years. His inspiration drove him chiefly to songs, full of lyric beauty like Schubert's; indeed, when speaking of *Lieder* the names of Schubert and Schumann are always linked.

Mendelssohn urged Schumann to teach in the Leipsic Conservatory, but he left there soon to make a tour of Russia with his wife. That year they settled in Dresden, a quieter city, because his nerves were beginning to forecast the shadow of his future.

Mendelssohn loved Schumann and admired him as composer, writer and critic. He conducted the first performance of Schumann's B flat symphony at a Gewandhaus concert of Clara Schumann, and the happiness of the three was tremendous. Schumann did not think of himself alone, but was always trying to help his colleagues. Schubert wrote his C major symphony in March of the year he died and never heard it, but Schumann had the score sent to Mendelssohn in Leipsic for its first performance after a wait of eleven years.

Notwithstanding his nerves, Schumann was now in his full power and the amount he wrote is incredible. Most of his chamber music was written in 1842, three of the string quartets being dedicated to Mendelssohn. The work that gave him fame all over Europe was the quintet for piano and strings, opus 44; with Clara at the piano, Berlioz heard its first performance and spread the news of his genius through Paris. About this time the *Variations for Two Pianos* were written and played by Robert and Clara Schumann. He wrote in all, four symphonies.

Another interesting and popular number is *Carnaval*, a

collection of named sketches in three-four time each one portraying some person or thing. *Eusebius* and *Florestan* have caused much curiosity—the secret is that Schumann was a student of himself and these were meant to show his conflicting moods. Chopin is represented, also Mendelssohn, while *Chiarina* is Clara.

A strange thing happened to Schumann in Vienna. He was visiting the graves of Beethoven and Schubert which are not far apart, and he found a steel pen on Beethoven's tomb. He took this for an omen, but used it only for his most precious works. He wrote the B flat symphony with it and the magic seemed to work!

Schubert is universally praised for the beauty of his themes, but who could surpass the loveliness of Schumann's melodies? The contrasts between the exquisite little tone-pictures of *Kinderscenen* and the grandeur of the sonatas and the *Fantasia* mark the breadth of his genius, while the amount he accomplished in his short span of life was marvelous.

He was but twenty-five when he first showed mental trouble, and at forty-four his case was hopeless. He tried to end his life by jumping into the Rhine and was taken to an asylum near Beethoven's birthplace, Bonn, where he died two years later, survived by his wife and five children.

What a price he paid for his life filled with joys and griefs!

Chopin—"Proudest Poet-Soul"

Robert Schumann wrote that Chopin was "the boldest, proudest poet-soul of his time." Such a tribute from him meant more than all the praise we can give him now; it shows that he had admiration and respect from his rivals as he had idolatry from the literary, artistic and refined circles of Paris.

Frederic Chopin (1810–1849) was born in Poland of a French father and a Polish mother. The difference one finds in the date of his birth, February 22 or March 1, is owing to the difference between the Russian and Polish calendars, and those of other countries.

Like Mozart he showed talent very early and at nine played his first public concert. His mother, unable to be present, asked him what the audience liked best. "My collar, Mamma!" he answered, proud of the little lace collar on the black velvet jacket! He was elegant then, and always kept his air of distinction, and a love for beauty.

Shortly after beginning music-study, Chopin tried to compose, and felt such authority that he undertook to change certain things written by his teacher. His earliest work was a march dedicated to the Grand Duke Constantin, which was arranged for brass-band and printed without the composer's name.

From his two teachers in Poland, both ardent patriots, Chopin must have absorbed much of the national feeling so strongly marked in his works. As it was a day of flashy *salon* (Page 322) playing, his teacher, Joseph Elsner, felt that Chopin was the founder of a new school in which poetic feeling was leading music out of the prevailing empty acrobatic finger feats!

The world owes much to that wise teacher who instilled a love of Bach into his young pupil. He answered some one who blamed him for allowing Chopin too much freedom: "Leave him alone! he treads an extraordinary path because he has extraordinary gifts and follows no method, but creates one. I have never seen such a gift for composition." Later he marked his examination papers: "Chopin, Frederic (pupil for three years), astounding capacity, musical genius."

At fifteen Chopin was adored by his companions and

always held the affection of those who knew him. He seems to have been the original "matinee idol" of Paris, whenever he played, for he was the most poetic and finest pianist ever heard.

Though Chopin was seemingly French in manner, habits and tastes, he was extraordinarily patriotic and his music is perhaps the finest expression of Poland the world has ever seen.

No one has surpassed, or even equalled Chopin in writing for the piano. He understood its possibilities, limitations, tonal qualities and power to express emotion.

He did not leave a great quantity of compositions, but a well-ordered collection of music, so individual that even today, with all his imitators, when we hear Chopin—(and there is seldom a piano recital without at least one number) —we instantly recognize it as his.

Strongly marked rhythms are among his most fascinating characteristics. He glorified and elaborated the dances of Poland, as had others in the past, who made art pieces of the gavotte, minuet, bourrée, gigue, etc.

What lovelier numbers on a program than Chopin's mazurkas, polonaises, waltzes? There is also irresistible rhythm in the *Ballades*, *Impromptus*, the *Berceuse*, *Barcarolle*, and what could rival in fantasy the *Nocturnes* or *Preludes?* The *Etudes* cover a variety of moods, while his *Scherzos* stand alone in piano literature.

Chopin left no symphonies, no chamber music, except two piano sonatas and one for 'cello and piano, and what he did for voice could be told in a few words. He also wrote two piano concertos in which the piano work is beautiful but the orchestration is not as fine.

These concertos and his piano sonatas were the largest forms in which he wrote, proving that he could have succeeded here had he not chosen to perfect music in the smaller forms.

Chopin never had a fair start in life in the way of health, and while his delicate appearance made him the more interesting, especially to the ladies, he was a real sufferer. It would be unfair to believe that his work would have been greater had he enjoyed complete health, for his unhappiness and his sufferings gave him a sense of the mysterious and the beyond. He lived in a world far from material things and seemed able to translate all he felt into music.

He had the devotion of many idolizing friends, tireless in their efforts to make him happy and keep him working so that he should not brood over his illness (tuberculosis). Foremost among these was the famous French novelist George Sand, whose love and companionship were the source of rare inspiration and comfort. She was a woman of vast mental and physical power and seemed to impart her strength to him. But Chopin was a favorite not only with women but among the men, as we learn through the letters he left. We find many from Schumann, Mendelssohn, Liszt, Delacroix, the French painter, and from his Polish compatriots in exile.

Concertizing began to fatigue him beyond endurance. Returning to Paris from a tour during a hard winter in England, he grew so ill that he rarely left his bed, although he did not die until the following October, 1849.

Chopin had asked that the Mozart Requiem be given at his funeral, which occurred October 30, from the Madeleine Church in Paris. The singer Lablache who had sung the Mozart number at Beethoven's funeral also performed this tribute for Chopin.

In addition to the Requiem, Lefebure-Wely, one of the fine organists of Paris, played Chopin's preludes in B and E minor, and the familiar funeral march from the first sonata was arranged for orchestra and played for the first time.

HELLER—THE CHILDREN'S CHOPIN

We may not find the name of Stephen Heller (1813-1888) on many of the "grown-up" programs, but no pupils' recitals are complete without several of his lovely melodies.

He was the friend of children and devoted himself more to teaching and writing for the young minds and small hands than did any of his companions. Heller was intended for a lawyer, but his talent as shown at nine was great enough for him to study with Carl Czerny in Vienna. He became a fine concert pianist and toured Europe. Taken ill during one of these tours, he was adopted by a wealthy family who allowed him all the time he wanted for composing. Most of his study was done in Paris where he was a friend of Berlioz, Chopin, Liszt and other prominent artists of the day.

He left several hundred piano pieces, nearly all masterpieces in a field where he stands practically alone. He wrote in the style developed by Mendelssohn and Schumann, and what Chopin is to the music world of the "grown-ups," Heller is to the young student.

CHAPTER XXV

Wagner—the Wizard

<small>WILHELM RICHARD WAGNER</small>

1813–1883

RICHARD WAGNER, the Wizard, called out of the past a vast company of gods and goddesses, giants, knights and heroes, kings and queens. He made them live for us with all their joys and sorrows, loves and hates, in his great music dramas, for which he has been recognized as one of the rare geniuses of the world.

Evoked by his music-magic they pass before us,—the gods and heroes of Walhalla,—Wotan, Brünnhilde, valiant Siegfried, Fafner the giant who is turned into a dragon, Mime the dwarf, the Rhine-Maidens and the Valkyries; Parsifal the guileless youth who became the Knight of the Holy Grail, and Lohengrin his son, the beautiful knight who marries Elsa, a lady of rank of the Middle Ages.

We see the minnesingers, Tannhäuser and Wolfram von Eschenbach, in one of their famous Minstrel Tournaments with the hand of the lovely Elizabeth as a prize; we also meet the lovable shoemaker-mastersinger Hans Sachs in Nüremberg, of the 16th century, and David his merry apprentice, lovely Eva Pogner and the charming knight Walter von Stolzing, and Beckmesser the clownish mastersinger; then there are the imperious Irish Queen, Isolda, and Tristan, her lover, with Kurvenal his faithful servant, and Brangaene, her attendant. Wagner makes not only the mythological persons relive but he brings back realistic pictures of the everyday life and customs of the German people of the Middle Ages.

Wagner had his idea of what opera should be and nothing short of his ideal interested him. He kept to his purpose and accomplished miraculous things whether he suffered or starved or was banished from his country.

Richard was born at a time, favorable for hearing and knowing the Viennese composers of the 18th and early 19th centuries, who had increased the importance of the orchestra. He could hear too the music of Schumann and Schubert, with all the new beauty and warm feeling they radiated. This new depth appeared not only in the orchestra but also in piano and vocal music. In Wagner's time, people felt deeply about everything,—science, philosophy, literature, and especially politics; and many were the quarrels and discontents among nations. Even our own country was torn by a cruel war.

Wagner listened to the works of Mozart and of Beethoven, whom he admired immensely. He approved of Beethoven's use of the chorus in the *Ninth Symphony*, which had no little effect on his work and ideals.

Among the people who most influenced Wagner was Gluck, who first fought for sincerity and truth in opera drama. Gluck did not have the advantage of the grown-up orchestra and freer forms, yet Gluck did so much to free opera that Wagner was fortunate indeed to have come after him. Another great influence was Weber, who mixed everyday story in a delightful play of fancy and picturesqueness. Wagner, after hearing Weber's *Der Freischütz*, was very much impressed.

Meyerbeer, a contemporary, although rather artificial

and always working for effects, nevertheless showed Wagner the value of gorgeous scenic productions. Wagner was fond of the stage, and Meyerbeer's big scenes sank into the mind of the young composer-poet, who liked to be called a poet rather than a musician!

Musically, Franz Liszt was probably the greatest influence in Wagner's life and we often hear in Wagner's works bits of melody which remind us of Liszt.

It is not fair to say that he was great just because he followed Gluck, Weber, and Mozart, for he brought music out of its old ruts and was copied by hundreds of composers.

The hero of this chapter was born in Leipsic in 1813 and was the youngest of nine children. His father died shortly after his birth and his mother married an actor playwright named Geyer and they all went to live in Dresden. His stepfather felt that Richard had musical gifts and he proved a very kind and wise parent. He died when the boy was only eight.

Richard must have been a most interesting little chap, for he always did everything with what we would call "pep" and persistence. He loved poetry and was devoted to the theatre. His stepfather had always allowed him to go "back stage" at the playhouse, so the youth became familiar with stage craft, which he used later in producing his music dramas.

He read the Greek and German poets and dramatists at a very early age. He was the first of the musical geniuses to be trained in the arts before he started music. So we can picture a little chap, "stage-struck," studying when he should, seeing plays when he could, and listening to the works of Weber and Beethoven which enchanted him, and storing up ideas, but as yet showing no great leaning toward music as a profession.

The family moved back to Leipsic in 1827 where he

went to school until he entered the university in 1831. He heard much orchestral music and became so deeply charmed with Beethoven, that he copied the *Ninth Symphony* from a score, to become familiar with it. The *Ninth Symphony* with chorale takes about two hours to perform, imagine how long it took to copy it! An instance of the wizard's energy and "stick-to-it-iveness"!

A KILLING PLAY

He began to study music with C. G. Müller, for Beethoven's works made him decide that he wanted to know more. He also was taught by Theodore Weinlig, the cantor or singer of St. Thomas' school. At sixteen, he wrote a play which had so tragic a plot that he killed off forty-two of the characters, and afterwards said, he had to bring some back as ghosts to wind up the drama, for there were no characters left alive! His drama reading made him exaggerate tragedy in his own play! After this he wrote a sonata, a polonaise, and a symphony, in classic style, performed in 1833.

In 1830 there had been a political revolution in Germany and it greatly impressed the young man for he was an independent thinker in politics as well as in music.

He visited Vienna in 1832 but he found it so appreciative of Hérold's opera *Zampa* and Strauss' waltzes that he could not bear it and left almost immediately. He was much like Beethoven in disposition for he was quick to anger and kind in great gusts, and could be most agreeable to his friends.

HIS EARLY OPERAS

He had gone to Vienna with his symphony but showed it to no one; it is said that Mendelssohn saw it but forgot

Johannes Brahms at Home.

After the painting by Rongier.

César Franck.

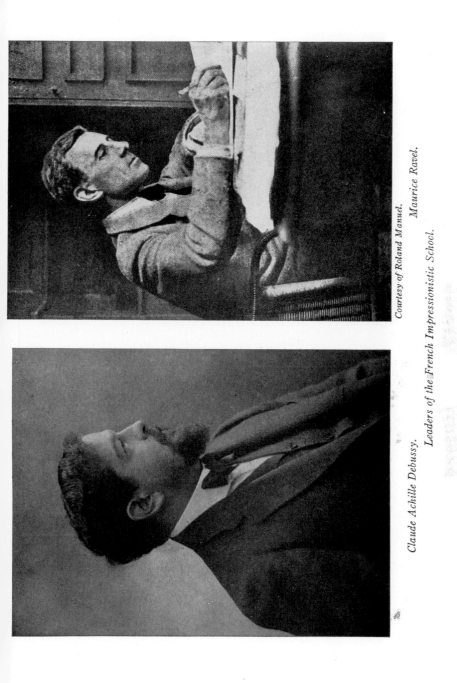

Courtesy of Roland Manuel.

Claude Achille Debussy.   *Maurice Ravel.*

Leaders of the French Impressionistic School.

Courtesy of "Musical America."

Arnold Schoenberg (Austrian).

Igor Stravinsky (Russian).

about it. Here he wrote the poem and some poor music for an opera *Die Hochzeit* (*The Wedding*) which he tore up the next year.

Then off to Prague went he (1832), and wrote his first libretto, for you must remember he did not go to people like Metastastio or Molière for opera texts but wrote his own. Had he not been a composer he certainly would have been a literary man. In fact, he was, for he wrote more pamphlets and books than many a writer! Yet, he showed his real genius as a composer.

But he was so poor now that he was glad to get a job as a chorus master at the mean salary of 10 florins ($5) a month! It was here he wrote the opera *Die Feen* (*The Fairies*) a wildly romantic work, after which he returned again to Leipsic. For the first time he heard Wilhelmine Schroeder-Devrient sing, whose marvelous talent influenced him all his life. In 1834 as a conductor of a troupe with headquarters in Magdeburg, he tried to produce his second opera, the tragic *Das Liebesverbot* (*Forbidden Love*), modeled after Shakespeare's *Measure for Measure;* but it was so badly given that it was a dismal failure. The opera was like Bellini and Auber, whose works he admired, and it was too early in his life (twenty-one) to show new ways of composing.

Soon he went to Königsberg, where (1836) he married Wilhelmina Planer, a young actress whom he met in the theatre, and he spent the year trying to get his Magdeburg troupe out of difficulties. Later he was given a post in Riga.

While at Riga his duty was to lead orchestral concerts, at many of which Ole Bull, the Norwegian violinist, played. Here, too, he read *Rienzi* of Bulwer-Lytton, the English author, and wrote a libretto and opera in the showy style of Meyerbeer. He said himself that it "out-Meyerbeered Meyerbeer." Leaving hastily, debts and all, with *Rienzi* in his hand, he went to Paris (the goal of all composers) in a sailing vessel, with his new wife and a dog named Robber, stopping over in England. The trip took four long perilous weeks. From the sailors he learned the story of the Flying Dutchman, which he afterwards used in his opera of that name.

We wish we could tell you the whole story of this gale-tossed, unhappy mariner, the Flying Dutchman, and how at last he found happiness and relief from storms and troubles of life by finding his mate in the maiden Senta. You will love the music and the story which is woven about Senta in the beautiful ballad bearing her name.

In this opera, Wagner first used the *leit-motif* or leading theme (particularly in the overture) which he used as we use a name or description of a person, idea or thing, except that he used them in music instead of in words. For example, when Senta comes in to the story, either as someone's thought or as a person, or when she is spoken of, her theme is heard, woven into the music. So it is when Siegfried appears in the operas of the *Ring of the Nibelungen*, you hear the Siegfried theme; when the Gold is mentioned, you hear the Gold theme; or if the Giants appear, their theme is heard,—so it is with the Dragon and everything connected with the story. You hear in some form, their name plates, as it were, and so by listening, you can follow just what is going on through the music. This is one of the things that Wagner developed, though Gluck and others had attempted to use it.

During his stay in Paris, he had a struggle for existence and did everything possible to gain a livelihood, while striving to get a hearing for his compositions. He wrote, in his misery, the *Faust Overture*, the first work to win recognition.

He went to see Meyerbeer on his way to Paris, for Meyerbeer was very popular and his approval could have aided

poor Richard. Some say Meyerbeer helped him and others
say he did not. Wagner gained little from him. Even
when he first went to see Liszt, who later became his best
friend, it is said that Liszt snubbed him. Wagner never
stopped writing his theories for the papers, and a hot-headed
young scribbler he was! Yet withal he submitted the
story of *The Flying Dutchman* to the director of the Paris
Opera House who rejected it as an opera, but gave the story
to Dietsch, the conductor, to write the music. This did
not daunt Wagner, who, after a defeat, worked harder on
his next task. So he wrote another *Flying Dutchman*, story
and music and orchestration, in seven weeks!

However, luck began to favor him, and *Rienzi* (1842) was
accepted by the Dresden Opera and was so successful that
he became conductor in Dresden, which saved him for a
while from money worries, and *The Flying Dutchman*,
which had gone begging so long, was loudly demanded.
Strange to say, this wonderful legend did not succeed, for
the people missed the little tricks of Meyerbeer and they
could not understand the flowing music in new form.
Wagner was very disappointed for the story was one of the
old German (Teuton) legends and he thought the German people would love it.

Later, however, Spohr gave it with great success at
Cassel, and won Wagner's gratitude for his understanding
and kindness.

Now comes *Tannhäuser*, an entrancing legend which
inspired him to study more deeply into the Teutonic legends. This he produced in Dresden, and other German
cities played it later. Everything became topsy-turvy in
the musical and political world. Wagner was writing fiery
things about freedom in music and politics, nothing to
amount to much, but enough to rouse his enemies, who
became hateful and hissed *Tannhäuser*,—calling it nerve-
killing, distressing music without melody. How could

anyone fail to find melody in *Oh Thou Sublime Sweet Evening Star*, the *Pilgrim's Chorus*, the *Venusburg* music and the colorful overture with themes of the whole opera? Yet music affects people this way when it is new in structure. "There is no melody" is said today when the so-called modern music is played. This should make us stop and listen carefully and look back on what happened to the writers of the past when they dared differ from the crowd. Perhaps calling your attention to this will make you listen with open ears and open minds to the new, which so soon becomes the familiar.

So Wagner, while conducting other operas in Dresden, began on *Lohengrin* and finished it in 1847. But he was impetuous and his written articles irritated the people. His ideas were fiery and his musical speech so odd, that even Schumann, who was very sympathetic, only partially understood him or his music. However he did say that Wagner would have a great influence on German opera, but Mendelssohn, after hearing *Tannhäuser*, only liked the second finale. Even his friend Madame Devrient, though she loved and admired him, said: "You are a man of genius but you write such eccentric stuff, it is hardly possible to sing it."

Never did Wagner feel that he was at fault, so great was his faith in his ideas of doing away with arias, of not having stopping places in an opera, just to begin some other song, and of making the words equally important to the music.

The Nibelungen Ring

While working at *Lohengrin* he had started his studies of the Icelandic and Germanic Saga, the *Nibelungenlied*. These tales changed under his pen into the story of Siegfried, which he wove into the trilogy known as *The Nibel-*

ungen *Ring* or *Trilogy with a Prologue,* as he called it, and as we call it now—*The Tetralogy* (in four parts).

The four dramas of the *Ring of the Nibelung* are:

(1) *The Rhinegold* (*Das Rheingold*)
(2) *The Valkyries* (*Die Walküre*)
(3) *Siegfried*
(4) *The Twilight of the Gods* (*Die Götterdämmerung*)

Many things happen in these tales but it takes the four to tell the one big story:

Alberich the wicked Nibelung, a gnome, in his greed steals the gold from the Rhine Maidens who were guarding it, hidden in the Rhine. They tell him that the one who fashions a ring out of the gold will rule the world, but must forego love. Alberich makes the ring but Wotan the god of the gods wrests it from him. During the drama various people secure the Ring but it had been cursed by Alberich and brings disaster to all who get it. Finally the very gods themselves are doomed to destruction, and Brünnhilde, the oldest of the Valkyries, the daughters of Wotan, returns the stolen treasure to the waters of the Rhine.

The Wizard has painted in magnificent music the great Rhine River, flowing across the stage; the fire surrounding Brünnhilde until she is rescued by the valiant Siegfried, who knows no fear; Valhalla the home of the gods; the hunt in which Siegfried drinks from the magic horn of memory; and his funeral pyre into which Brünnhilde casts herself and her horse, carrying the ring which she has taken from Siegfried's finger, back to the Rhine Maidens from whence it came.

The scenes are gigantic and so is the music. Wagner, with his ideals for freedom and the betterment of humanity, used these legends as a cloak to cover his personal opinions which would have been looked upon as anarchism if he had not used such clever and artistic symbols. In Alberich's greed for the gold, is hidden Wagner's ideas of the Government's greed for power against which he had fought so strenuously. Another lesson is that anyone possessing the gold is denied love, showing that greed kills human feelings.

Because the Opera at Dresden did not use the things he liked, he rebelled openly against the popular political and musical ideas; he was banished and went to Zürich, Switzerland. Here he wrote more fiery literature and made more enemies and a few friends, and the enmity he stirred up against himself delayed his success. He hoped for a better state of political life in order to write freer and more beautiful music.

While he was in Zürich, Liszt, in Weimar, produced *Lohengrin* with success. It was given to celebrate Goethe's birthday (1850), before a brilliant audience, and now Wagner's fame seemed sure, though his "pockets were empty." *Lohengrin's* success was slow in Germany, as it took about nine years to reach Berlin and Dresden. It was thought to be without melody! Can you hear Lohengrin's song to the Swan, the Wedding March or the Prelude? Listen to it in your mind's ear or auralize it! Wagner's themes were so marvelously interwoven and he did such amazing things with his orchestra, that it was difficult for people to unravel the torrential new music. They were not prepared for endless music flowing on like speech, suiting the music to the word and not stopping the action to show off the singer's skill. What Gluck *tried* to do, Wagner did. His operas were music dramas because the action or drama was his first thought.

For fifteen years in exile, he gave himself to literary work and composition. He had ample time now to write of his musical theories and his feelings about life.

Soon, London called him to lead the Philharmonic Society, which he did during the time he was completing *The Valkyries* and sketching *Siegfried*. He tried to interest the

English in Beethoven and others whom he loved, but of little avail. The people preferred the delightful delicacy of Mendelssohn to the solidity of Beethoven. So here again he made more enemies than friends, and his bitter pen did not help to smooth things over. By the time he left London, he had finished *The Valkyries*.

In this great music drama, he tells the story of Siegmund and Sieglinde, Brünnhilde and the Valkyries who carried the dead warriors from the battle-fields on their saddles to Valhalla. You hear in the galloping music of the *Ride of the Valkyries*, and the *Fire Music*, and *Love Song* of the first act, such music as never was written by anyone but Wagner! Oh, it is a wonderful legend, explaining itself in Wagner's own poems, and with the short music name tags (leit-motifs) which are enlarged and turned around and intermingled with other name tags, and which stand out beautifully when you know how to listen.

Tristan and Isolda and Meistersinger

While in Zürich, Wagner met the merchant Otto Wesendonck, whose beautiful and poetic wife Wagner loved dearly. She was a great influence in his life and they were friends for many years. It was during this friendship that he started the love drama of *Tristan and Isolda*.

In 1859 he finished the love drama which tells of Tristan and the lovely Queen of Ireland and how they drank the love potion and how they loved and were separated. A noble story with some of the most grippingly beautiful music ever written!

But with this masterpiece of masterpieces completed, he could get nobody to produce it. Everyone said it was impossible to sing it, and we know even today that it takes very special musical gifts and few can do it well. For it is quite true that Wagner, with all his theories about composition; thought little of the singer's throat muscles and more of what he wanted to say.

Poor Wagner was disconsolate! He could not get his works performed and he was still prevented from returning to Germany, the country he loved. So off he went to Paris and there *Tannhäuser* failed utterly after three terrible, turbulent, horrible performances, which almost ended in riots, obviously planned ahead by his enemies.

But to offset this disaster, he was allowed to return home and everyone rejoiced in his arrival. No doubt his treatment in Paris softened the German heart.

Not long after this Wagner and his wife separated and some years later in 1871, he married Cosima Liszt, who had been the wife of Hans von Bülow.

After Wagner conducted opera on a tour through Russia, Hungary, Bohemia (Czecho-Slovakia) and many German cities, Ludwig II, King of Bavaria, sent for Wagner and offered him an income, and from this time on Wagner composed without financial worries. He was commissioned in 1865 to complete *The Ring*, and *Tristan and Isolda* was performed by Hans von Bülow.

Again political intrigues and his enemies drove him to Switzerland, and after *Tristan and Isolda* was given and while he was in Switzerland, he completed *The Ring* and *Die Meistersinger*, the most beautiful comic opera in the world, which was also produced by von Bülow in Munich, June 21st, 1868. And now we fulfill our promise to you, which we made in Chapter VIII about the Meistersinger:

Walther von Stolzing, a young knight, falls in love at first sight with Eva the beautiful daughter of Pogner, the goldsmith of Nüremberg, who has promised her to the winning singer in the coming Festival of the Mastersingers. Beckmesser, the old town clerk, counts on winning as he also loves Eva. As Walther does not belong to the music guild, he has to pass the examination. Beckmesser gives him so many bad marks for not keeping the committee's rules that he is not admitted.

But Hans Sachs, the greatest Mastersinger of all, the town cobbler, thought Walther a beautiful singer even though he broke musical laws, and the very freedom and the new loveliness in his music charmed him.

In the evening just as Walther and Eva try to run away, Beckmesser comes to serenade Eva. Hans Sachs, cobbling shoes in his doorway interrupts Beckmesser's ludicrous serenade with a jolly song, in which he marks all Beckmesser's mistakes with his hammer, just as Beckmesser had marked Walther's. The neighborhood is aroused, confusion follows, Beckmesser gets a beating and Hans Sachs slips Eva and Walther into his own house.

Next day Walther sings a song to Hans which he has dreamed and Hans writes it down. Beckmesser comes in and finding the words, steals them, sure he could win if he sang a song of Hans Sachs.

Beckmesser fails miserably and Sachs calls on Walther to sing it. Here Walther sings the famous *Prize Song*, which wins the approval of the Mastersingers, and the prize—lovely Eva.

Here we get a splendid idea of what Wagner felt about new music, for in *The Mastersingers* he tried to picture the jealousies of composers, who condemned the beauty of his inspiration and new ideas and methods.

Never was there an opera more delightful for young people, who love the melodies and charming pictures of medieval Nüremberg.

BAYREUTH

About this time *The Valkyries* and *Rhinegold* had been given at the Court Theatre in Munich (1869–1870). The King gave up his plan to build a new theatre for these stupendous works, which needed special machinery because of the elaborate stage effects. Wagner insisted that scenery was as important as the words and music. So he started to build, by general subscription over all Europe, a theatre at Bayreuth. He succeeded so well that not only did Europe contribute, but America, also, and groups of people banded together to collect money for it. Wagner was now the fashion and finally the new opera house opened August 13th, 1876, with *The Ring*, for he had finished *Die Götterdämmerung* the year before.

Artistically it was successful but not financially. If his pen had been dipped in honey and not in bitters, he would have won his public more easily, but he seemed unable to be diplomatic. So off he went to London and other places to conduct concerts to make money to pay the debts of his new theatre. Later he wrote the Festival March, for the Philadelphia Centennial (1876), which helped financially.

The people were divided into two camps,—those for Wagner, and those against him. So strong was the feeling, that during the 1880's, in Germany, signs in cafés read: "It is forbidden to discuss religion or Wagner"! The proprietors wished to save their chairs and china which the fists of their patrons would destroy.

Parsifal

During this time he was at work on *Parsifal*, a drama in music as serious as oratorio yet with the most thrilling stage effects and richness of music. *Parsifal, Tristan and Isolda, The Ring* and *Die Meistersinger* are to every other opera what a plum pudding is, compared to a graham cracker. In fact, all Wagner's late music dramas are like plum puddings, so rich and compact are they.

Parsifal was produced in 1882 in Bayreuth and was

not given again for six years. Later it was the occasion for
yearly pilgrimages to Bayreuth, as if to a shrine. It is so
long that it takes the better part of an afternoon and evening to perform it, yet you sit enraptured before its gripping
spell of beauty and holiness.

In 1903 the musical world was startled by the first performance in America of *Parsifal*, as Wagner, in his will,
had forbidden a stage performance outside of Bayreuth.
It was covered by copyright until 1913, which was supposed to have protected it from performance. Heinrich
Conried, director of the Metropolitan Opera Company in
New York City, in his eagerness for novelties, disregarded
the master's wish, and mounted an elaborate production
under the direction of Alfred Hertz. This so offended
the Wagner family that they refused to allow anyone who
had taken part in that performance to appear in Bayreuth.

Bayreuth became a Mecca, to which pilgrims went every
other year, to attend the festivals. After the World War,
Wagner's family turned to America for help to continue
these festivals, interrupted by the war, as the Wizard
himself had done, when building his theatre. In 1924 his
son, Siegfried, visited America, conducted some symphony
concerts and secured funds to carry on the festivals.

Parsifal is a combination of three legends—of which
one is the *Parsifal* of our old friend the Minnesinger Wolfram von Eschenbach (1204). (Chapter VIII.)

It is the story of the Redemption of Mankind, told in
symbols with great beauty of poetry, music and scenery.
It is certain to fill you with religious fervor, for it reaches
the depths of your soul and raises you above the things of
the earth. Amfortas, the guardian of the Holy Grail, whose
wound represents the suffering of mankind, hears the mystic
voice of his father, Titurel, who tells him that not until a
sinless one comes with pity in his heart will the wound be
healed. Parsifal, "the guileless fool," is his redeemer.

The year following the first production of *Parsifal* Wagner's health began to fail and he went to Venice where he died suddenly in 1883. He was buried with fitting honors at Bayreuth which always honors the memory of the Great Master of German Opera.

Here is a picture of Wagner in the words of his brother-in-law: "the double aspect of this powerful personality was shown in his face; the upper part beautiful with a vast ideality, and lighted with eyes which were deep and severe, gentle or malicious, according to the circumstances; the lower part wry and sarcastic. A mouth cold and calculating and pursed up, was cut slantingly into a face beneath an imperious nose, and above a chin which projected like the menace of a conquering will."

How the Wizard Changed Opera

When Wagner reached his full power, he composed drama rather than opera in the old sense.

His music explained the words and action and expressed the state of mind of the character.

The melodies are used very much like the theme in a sonata. These leit-motifs (leading motives) are usually carried, as we told you, in the weavings of his wonderful orchestral webs. This theme or leit-motif or name tag, is tossed from instrument to instrument in numberless entrancing ways. Sometimes he uses a flickering theme for flames as in the fire music of *The Valkyries* or glorious chimes or trumpetings as in *Parsifal* to cast a holy spell; but, whatever he uses, he charms and holds you spellbound.

He combines the counterpoint of the 16th century masters, with a most modern feeling for harmony, inherited from the classic Germans. He used harmony in a new way with a freedom it never before had reached, and pointed the way for modern composers of today.

As the Wizard, Wagner throws a glamor over the most
mystic happening, as when Siegmund, in *The Valkyries*, with-
draws the Sword from the tree; or in the most common-
place fact as when Eva tells Hans Sachs that she has a
nail in her shoe. In *The Mastersingers*, you can always tell
that he is making fun of Beckmesser, because his name tag
shows him to be petty and ridiculous.

Although Wagner's music is rich, very clear to us and
beautiful, in his day it seemed complicated and discordant,
because of its great volume and sonority, the result of the
perfect part writing.

For the first time, he makes the brasses of equal importance to the string and wind instruments. It is thrilling
to hear the trombones and his effective use of trumpets.
He used many of Berlioz's ideas in muffling horns, and
added new instruments, too, among them, the bass clarinet and the English horn (*cor anglais*), which is an alto
oboe and not a horn at all!

Wagner had a beautiful way of dividing up the parts for
violins and other instruments into smaller choirs which
answered each other and with which he could get special
effects. For example, the Prelude of *Lohengrin* is probably the nearest thing in shimmering music to what the
angels must play, so heavenly is it. Here he divides the
violins into many parts and it is far more beautiful than
if they all played the same thing. Thus, he gave more
value to the instruments and greatly improved the orchestra.

His preludes in which you hear the leading motives or
name tags, are a table of contents for what follows.

Wagner did not use tricks of decoration like Meyerbeer
nor did he give show-off pieces for his singers' benefit.
His idea was to use sincere musical speech to tell the story
and not one bit did he care how hard the singer worked to
carry out his idea.

Wagner, above all, was a dramatist, choosing lofty and noble themes of heroic and ideal subjects in which his imagination could play. He loved the sublime and the great spectacle.

The chief interest of Wagner's opera is in the orchestra which carries the theme webs. He used neither the folk song in its simple beauty nor accepted classic arias which could be taken out and sung. His song is often declaimed and appears not to sing with the orchestra, for the voices are used as instruments and not to show off vocal skill. Yet, Liszt was quick to take out from the operas and transscribe for piano the Fire Music, the Ride of the Valkyrie and many others which we now sing and whistle.

Finally, Wagner by his example has given courage to the man of ideas, if he will believe in himself and work without ceasing.

CHAPTER XXVI

More Opera Makers—Verdi and Meyerbeer to Our Day

AFTER reading about the feats of the Wizard it is not surprising that he had many followers,—those who openly claimed to take him for an example, and others who did not realize how much they received from him and would not like to have been called his followers!

VERDI—THE GRAND OLD MAN OF ITALY

After following the Italian methods of writing opera and having become a very famous composer, Verdi received inspiration from Wagner in the last three or four years of his very long life. He was much loved and it is difficult to tell whether it was his operas or his beautiful character which prompted the affection. He was called "the Grand Old Man of Italy." A national hero was he, and the Italians' idol. Praise and flattery did not make him proud but spurred him to work through trouble and good fortune, and so he became one of the greatest opera writers. He was born a few months after Wagner, in the village of Roncole near Parma, and his life was interesting, for he lived at the time when opera was popular and was going through the Wagner upheaval which spread all over Europe. He had a unique chance to make opera more important in Italy, and succeeded in giving it a new impetus, even though in the beginning his popular things followed popular patterns.

VERDI AND THE ORGAN-GRINDER

Giuseppe Verdi (1813–1901) was the son of an innkeeper and, as a little boy, showed marked musical talent. He was a good obedient little fellow, but always rather melancholy in character and never joined the village boys in their noisy amusements. "One thing only could rouse him from his habitual indifference, and that was the occasional passing through the village of an organ grinder. To the child, who in after years was to afford an inexhaustible repertory to those instruments for half a century all over the world, this was an irresistible attraction. He could not be kept indoors, and would follow the strolling player as far as his little legs could carry him." (Grove's Dictionary.)

Who has not heard the *Miserere* from *Il Trovatore* played, all out of tune, by an Italian organ grinder who sends a little monkey around with a cup to gather in the pennies? We remember an organ grinder in San Francisco who ground out the *Miserere*. Each year or two that we returned there were more of the notes missing. Ten years later, the performance was quite "toothless" and sounded very funny.

All his life, Verdi kept a little spinet that his father bought for him in 1820. We see him then, at seven, deep in musical study and at ten he was the organist of Roncole, going to school in Busseto, a nearby town. One night when he was walking the three miles to go back to Busseto after church, the poor little fellow was so weary that he missed the road and fell into a canal, narrowly escaping death! Is it not splendid that his village appreciated his talent and gave him a scholarship which made it possible for him to go to Milan to continue his musical studies!

HIS OPERAS

He did not compose an opera until 1839 when his *Oberto* in the style of Bellini was produced in Milan with such success that he received orders to write three more from which he gained much good-will and fame.

It must have been a thrilling time for opera writers, because Wagner was composing, too, and you know the great excitement he caused. Amidst this interesting whirl of opinion, Verdi wrote one of the operas ordered by the Milan director, and during this time he was sorely stricken by the deaths of his wife and two lovely children. Besides this, his opera failed and in his discouragement the poor young man made up his mind to give up composition. However, a rare good friend coaxed him back to his work after a little rest, and he produced his successful *Nebucco* (*Nebuchadnezzar*) (1842), *I Lombardi* the next year and his well known *Hernani* (1844). In this, his first period, he used as models, Bellini and men of his type, not writing anything startlingly new.

In his second period he wrote operas nearly as fast as we write school compositions, and among the famous things are *Rigoletto* (1851), *Il Trovatore*, *La Traviata* (story from Dumas' *Camille* or *Dame aux Camelias*), (1853), and *The Masked Ball* (1859). *Hernani* and *Rigoletto* are founded on stories by Victor Hugo. The first performance of *La Traviata* in Venice was a failure due more to the performers, than to the opera itself which still crowds opera houses of the world.

The best known work of his third period is *Aida* (1871), one of Verdi's masterpieces. An opera on an Egyptian subject was ordered by the Khedive of Egypt for the opening of the Italian Opera House in Cairo, for which Verdi received $20,000. Mariette Bey a famous Egyptologist made the first sketch in order to give the right local atmosphere to the libretto. Curiosity ran so high that every seat was sold before the first night and it was a great success. Think how electrified the audience must have been by the tenor solo, *Celeste Aida*, one of Caruso's greatest successes; by the realistic Nile scene; the voice of the priestess in the mammoth Egyptian temple, and the famous march with trumpets made specially for it!

Dear old lovable Verdi was a wise man as well as an accomplished composer. He used more modern methods in *Aida* to hold audiences who were hearing about Wagner and his startling innovations.

Other operas of this third period were *La Forza del Destino*, in which Rosa Ponselle made her Metropolitan debut (1918) with Caruso, and *Don Carlos*, which was given at the Paris Grand Opera. Until this time he showed great technical skill and a sense of color and melody. Singers have revelled in the operas of his second period. In our era, Marcella Sembrich, Nellie Melba, Frieda Hempel, Luisa Tetrazzini, Amelita Galli-Curci, Lily Pons, and others have sung the coloratura,—florid, soaring, elaborate style. One of Lucrezia Bori's most popular roles was that of Violetta in *La Traviata*. However, in *Aida*, Verdi departed much from the usual, and people said that he was copying Wagner because they didn't know the difference between the influences which change a person's ways, and imitation.

So he deserted the old models, Auber, Meyerbeer and Halévy, for something more substantial, his deeper and gigantically conceived *Aida*. After this, Verdi's splendid mass, the *Requiem*, was written for the death of the Italian poet Manzoni. In it he approaches the German school in depth and seriousness, veering away from the superficial Italian style.

In his last efforts he seems definitely influenced by Wagner; for, with his *Otello* and *Falstaff* we find a new Verdi, surpassing in form and sincere melody anything that he had done. Arrigo Boito, his friend, wrote librettos based on Shakespeare's *Othello* and *Merry Wives of Windsor*. When *Falstaff* was given in New York (1925) a young American baritone, Lawrence Tibbett, in the role of Ford, flashed into fame. In the season of 1938–39, the same singer appeared in the title role in the revival of this great work. The year before, Giovanni Martinelli, the famous Italian tenor, sang the title role in a successful revival of *Otello* at the Metropolitan. *Simon Boccanegra* was revived for Tibbett (1932). Besides Tibbett, some great baritones who have sung *Rigoletto* in New York were Antonio Scotti, Titta Ruffo, and Maurice Renaud.

Verdi was a man of the people, loving Italy and being loved in return, a master of voice, ready to take good suggestions to improve his work, always kind, high-minded, and generous. He knew the orchestra and wrote for it in a way that gave, in his last masterpieces, a new flavor to Italian opera, and led the way for future composers.

BOITO AND HIS "MEFISTOFELE"

Arrigo Boito (1842–1918), journalist, poet, and composer sprang into prominence with his *Mefistofele*, in which the Russian singer, Chaliapin, attracted huge audiences at the Metropolitan. When it was first given in Italy, the audiences missed the coloratura arias, and the critics were very hard on the young composer. So he went back to journalism for many years. His next opera *Nero* has a gory plot, but is real and not embroidered as were most of the Italian operas. Boito had studied in Germany and had absorbed much of the realism and truthfulness that Gluck and Wagner taught. *Nero* had an elaborate first performance (1924) by the celebrated Arturo Toscanini, one of the greatest living conductors, at *La Scala* in Milan. It is a tremendous stage spectacle, surpassing in scenic effect many of the older melodramas.

"Cavalleria Rusticana" and "I Pagliacci"

In 1890 the first truly realistic opera was written in Italy. A prize was offered by the publisher Sonzogno and an unknown man, Pietro Mascagni, won it with *Cavalleria Rusticana* (*Rustic Chivalry*). He was born in 1863, the son of a baker. He was a musical boy, but his father wished him to be a lawyer, so he had to work at the piano in secret. One day when he had been locked up by his father who did not want him to practise, he was discovered by his uncle, who sympathized with him and took him to Count Florestan, who helped the young musician to study in Milan.

Mascagni's work in *Cavalleria Rusticana* was vivid and he used both the old and the new style of writing. It is full of the most entrancing melody (the Intermezzo, the Brindisi, or drinking song, and Santuzza's aria, *Voi lo sapete*). He also wrote *Iris* and *Amico Fritz*, which never equalled *Cavalleria* in popularity.

With Ruggiero Leoncavallo (1858–1919) it was only after writing a number of operas that he produced a success in the world-famous *I Pagliacci*. He wrote the tragic story of these strolling players as well as the music, which is not as popular in style as *Cavalleria*, but it is superbly put together and very dramatic. As these operas are both short, they are often performed together. The rôle of Canio (*I Pagliacci*) was one of Caruso's masterpieces. How wonderful to think that his voice has been preserved for the future generations through his records of

which *Ridi Pagliacci* (*Laugh Clown*) is one of the finest.
It is generally admitted that Caruso's voice was the most
glorious of our age, and certainly there was no artist more
idolized than he. In this same opera Antonio Scotti's
performance of the famous Prologue was equally beautiful.

GIORDANO

Umberto Giordano (1867) goes into peculiar realms for
subjects for his operas. He uses local political intrigues
and literature for his themes, and is known especially for
his *André Chenier* and *Fedora* which are given in many
opera houses of the world. In *Siberia* he uses folk songs of
Russia. He has recently set *The Jest* by Sem Benelli librettist of *L'Amore dei Tre Re* (*The Love of Three Kings*) by
Italo Montemezzi.

PUCCINI THE POPULAR IDOL

Now we come to a delightful opera maker, Giacomo
Puccini (1858–1924). He is the greatest modern Italian
with the exception of Verdi. He has a distinctive touch
that gives him individuality. He keeps a nice balance
between voice, orchestra and melody. His music is always
full of color and feeling. His themes, for the most part,
touch the heart and have gained wide popularity.

His first opera was *Manon Lescaut*, the same story which
Massenet used in his delightful opera *Manon; La Bohème* is
his next and is often said to be his best. It is a tale of artist
life in the Latin Quarter of Paris and is full of romance,
color, gaiety and sadness. His story is taken from Murger's
Vie de Bohème, which was a fortunate choice. *Madame
Butterfly* is another of his glittering successes. It has a
decided Japanese flavor in its musical phrases. It is based
on a story by John Luther Long, which was made into a

play by David Belasco. Butterfly was one of Geraldine Farrar's loveliest rôles.

Tosca, in which Farrar, Caruso and Scotti made a famous trio, is a blood curdling drama of murder, cruelty and love, full of music which mirrors the story. The libretto was taken from Victorien Sardou's *La Tosca*, a celebrated drama in which the "divine Sarah" (Bernhardt) made one of her most brilliant successes.

He uses interesting little musical devices which make it easy to recognize a Puccini piece, and his music has charm. It is built on Italian tradition but is distinctly late 19th century. He enjoyed the greatest popularity of his day, and there have been few, excepting perhaps Verdi and Wagner, whose operas have been so well known. His beautiful melody, piquant airs, fine rhythms, clever orchestration and humanness of plot, make Puccini very often touch the edge of *opéra comique*. Although he uses a musical phrase over and over again, it is not like the Wagner *leit-motif*. There are no concerted finales or clearly defined stopping-places as there used to be in earlier operas. So you see, Puccini profited by Wagner and Verdi.

His *Girl of the Golden West*, a California story of the days of '49, had its world première (first production) at the Metropolitan Opera House (1910). For some time Puccini had been looking for a libretto for a new opera. While in New York, to be present at the Metropolitan production of *Madame Butterfly*, he was also searching for material in the hope of finding an American story. Again David Belasco came to his aid. His own *Girl of the Golden West*, a picturesque play, was being given and he invited Puccini to see it. He was interested and turned it into an opera. The rehearsals at the Metropolitan were most interesting with Puccini and Belasco working together. Emmy Destinn and Caruso sang the leading rôles.

It is realistic, dramatic, beautiful in parts, and not written for coloratura exhibitions! But when it was produced it proved too Italian for Americans and too American for the Italians, so Puccini was disappointed in its lack of success.

Puccini's operas, as well as Verdi's and others, have a new popularity, that of the mechanical player audience, the gramophone and player-piano, as well as the radio.

Wolf-Ferrari and "The Jewels of the Madonna"

One of the most delightfully witty opera writers is Ermanno Wolf-Ferrari (1876), son of a German father and Italian mother, and writer of *The Secret of Suzanne* (her secret was that she smoked!) a very droll and amusing story. He is musical grandchild to Mozart, so delicately does he sketch and so charming is his melody. If you hear his operas, including the tragic and exciting but beautiful *The Jewels of the Madonna*, you will certainly say that he can make more out of a little, than almost anyone. With a small orchestra he seems to work miracles, and his melodies are gracious and his rhythms captivating.

Montemezzi Visits America

Whether it was Lucrezia Bori (Spanish soprano) or its composer who made *L'Amore dei Tre Re* (*The Love of Three Kings*) so entrancing, is hard to say. Here is lovely music flowing on endlessly! The voice is handled delightfully, and the rich orchestration is masterly and beautiful throughout. *The Love of Three Kings* by Italo Montemezzi (1875) is a music drama on a medieval subject and few other operas have so fine a libretto as this by Sem Benelli.

Montemezzi, with his American wife, visited America in 1925. He was fittingly received at the Metropolitan Opera

House where Edward Johnson and Lucrezia Bori sang the lovely opera. They were here again in 1939.

Some other 19th century names in Italy are Giovanni Sgambati (instrumental pieces); Giuseppi Martucci (instrumental pieces); Marco Enrico Bossi, a famous Italian organist whose visit to this country in 1925 ended tragically, as he died on the boat on his way home, and Buongiorno, Eugenio di Parani and Franchetti, and Amilcare Ponchielli (1834-1886), composer of *La Giaconda*.

Now let us turn to what France has done in opera in the second half of the 19th century.

FRENCH OPERA

When Meyerbeer was musical czar of Paris, we see not only Wagner in France, but six other important composers. Hector Berlioz (1803-1869) was a tone poet; Charles Ambroise Thomas (1811-1896), Charles François Gounod (1818-1893), and Georges Bizet (1838-1875) were opera writers; Charles Camille Saint-Saëns (1835-1921) was a composer of concertos, piano and chamber music, and of operas, one of which is famous; and César Franck the Belgian (1822-1890) who lived in Paris, although not an opera writer, influenced the composers of opera who lived after him.

Mignon came from the heart of one of these, Ambroise Thomas, winner of the *Prix de Rome*, and in 1871 the director of the Paris Conservatory. He wrote several works, among them a successful opera *Hamlet*, yet none have added as much to his reputation as *Mignon*.

Félicien David (1810-1876) is known for his symphonic poem *Le Desert* and his *Lalla Rookh*, an opera which was given at the *Opéra Comique*.

Another well known name is Benjamin Godard (1849-1895). Do you remember the *Berceuse* from his opera

Jocelyn? He wrote *Le Dante* and *La Vivandière*, besides many salon pieces for young students of the piano.

GOUNOD'S "FAUST"

Faust, in connection with music, makes us think of Gounod. Gounod was born in Paris and showed musical ability when a boy. He was graduated from the Conservatory and won the *Prix de Rome* (1837).

His interest always seemed to be in religious music for he went to Italy to study Palestrina and Bach. His study resembled a church for it had stained-glass windows and an organ, and furnishings which gave it a religious atmosphere. After he returned from Rome he studied for the priesthood but soon gave it up.

Gounod's musical training was very broad for at first he was influenced by Rossini, Weber and Mozart, and later by Bach and Palestrina.

His *Messe Solennelle* (*Solemn Mass*) was given in 1861 and his *Faust* in 1859. This is considered to be one of the most tuneful operas written in the 19th century, and packs opera houses all over the world. His *Romeo and Juliette*, though not as popular, is still given, and his *Médecin Malgré Lui* (*Doctor in Spite of Himself*) (from Molière's play) "is a gem of refined setting," says Clarence Hamilton.

Among his other operas are *Philemon and Baucis*, *La Reine de Saba* (*The Queen of Sheba*) both inferior to *Faust*.

During the Franco-Prussian war he lived in London where he produced his oratorios, *The Redemption* and *Mors et Vita* (*Death and Life*), with his Gounod Choir, and held in England a somewhat similar place to Handel and Mendelssohn, for he, too, had many disciples.

He was a master of beautiful melody and instrumentation.

There is a new school in Paris whose slogan is, "Back to Gounod" in order to recapture his way of writing melody.

Everybody Loves "Carmen"

In Georges Bizet we see a man of genius who produced but one great work. To be sure he lived only thirty-seven years, two years longer than Mozart with his hundreds of pieces, yet Bizet is of great importance in French opera and is looked upon by musicians as a man of rare power, and he is loved by everyone for his marvelous *Carmen*. Louis Gruenberg, the American composer, said, "I have looked in vain for a flaw in *Carmen* but it is perfection throughout. It is the one opera in the world that wins both musicians and the masses alike, and it disarms criticism."

Emma Calvé will always be remembered as Carmen, for she not only sang the part with its intense melody and Spanish color, but she lived it on the stage.

Bizet is an amazing orchestral tone painter, and has a unique place among opera writers.

The story of *Carmen* is taken from a novel of Prosper Mérimée and is full of the sun, the shadows, the fascinating dances, the bull fight and the romance which belong particularly to Spain. *Carmen* is an *opéra comique*, for, in spite of its tragic ending, in the original version as played in Paris it has spoken dialogue.

His other things are *Jeux d'enfants* (*Children's Games*), four-hand pieces, and the *Arlesienne Suite* (dances) so pictureful and emotional. It is used as ballet sometimes for *Carmen*.

Bizet was not appreciated and at first *Carmen* was a failure, but many geniuses ahead of their time have shared the same fate.

It seems quite reasonable that after all the experiences France has been through in the early and middle 19th

century she should now blossom out, not with remodelled
Italian opera, but with her own opera and her own ways of
writing music.

The two influences were without doubt from César Franck
and Bizet whose sincerity not only influenced musicians
but rather quickly gained the public. The third influence
was of course, Wagner, who, though he infuriated many,
gained followers everywhere that his music was listened to
seriously. In France, Reyer and Chabrier were both Wagner
enthusiasts and did much to bring him finally into the Paris
Opera House a little before the 20th century (adapted
from *The Art of Music*). Out of these influences came a
fine group of gifted composers,—d'Indy, Dukas, Charpentier
and others.

Ernest Reyer (1823–1909), who was an ardent follower of
Wagner, had a hard time because of the new harmonies he
used. His last opera *Salammbo* is better known than the
others, although several of his works are still played in Paris
at the Grand Opera.

Emmanuel Chabrier (1841–1894), famous as composer of
the tone poem, *España*, must come in here, for at the time
of his death, he was writing a most interesting opera, *Briseis*,
which was finished by his pupils. Illness and impending
death seem not to matter to men and women who have
genius. The day before he died, Robert Louis Stevenson
stopped in the middle of a sentence, in his novel *The Weir
of Hermiston*, one of his best. The first woman to receive
the *Prix de Rome* in France, Lili Boulanger (1892–1918) did
much of her composing in bed during her last illness; her
devoted sister Nadia, a prominent musician in Paris, who
had received the second *Prix de Rome*, finished the deathbed
works. And did we not see Mozart finishing his *Requiem*
on the last day of his life?

This French group, striking out for something new, was
influenced by Wagner's theories, Franck's return to the

old classic style, the Russian school, the re-action against
Wagner and the renewed interest in orchestral concerts
in Paris (adapted from C. G. Hamilton).

SAINT-SAËNS—THE CHILD PRODIGY AND OCTOGENARIAN

Camille Saint-Saëns (1835–1921) wrote in all styles from
classic to the newest of program music. He is another
who gave concerts before he was twelve years old; he
studied at the Conservatory, lived in Paris as a composer,
organist and pianist, was a learned man and a very good
musical critic. Later in life he lived in Algiers, which
accounts for the oriental touch in his music. He journeyed
over much of the world and we heard him in Carnegie Hall,
on his last trip to this country in 1915, on his way to the
San Francisco exposition where he played the organ and
conducted his opera *Samson and Delilah*. He played some
of his most technically difficult pieces when he was in his
eighties. He wrote some symphonies, some descriptive
symphonic poems, *Le Rouet D'Omphale*, *Phæton*, *Dance
Macabre* (very weird and rhythmic) and others. Out of
five, his G minor is the most brilliant piano concerto.

He is best known for his opera *Samson and Delilah* which
is carried into fame by the two arias, *My Heart at Thy
Sweet Voice* and *Love Come to My Aid*. This last is of
the finest lyric writing in French opera and the first is surpassingly emotional. The choral parts (often sounding
like early Hebrew music) show a real master at work, and
the effect of the whole is very dramatic, whether sung as
oratorio or opera.

It is not as an opera writer, however, that Saint-Saëns
wished to go down to history for he threw his whole strength
into trying to make the French public know and love the
classics. Paul Landormy says: "From the historic point
of view, Saint-Saëns is a notable figure. Saint-Saëns is

the French Mendelssohn. . . . He undertook the musical education of France at the exact moment when Berlioz despaired of succeeding with the task, and he prepared the public for the great French School of symphonists which arose toward the end of the 19th century."

In 1871 Saint-Saëns was made president of the newly formed National Society of Music of which you will read later.

The ballet was used to advantage by Clement Philibert Léo Délibes (1836–1891) a master of this form of music and dance. He built up a certain atmosphere that is particularly French. His ballets, *Coppelia* and *Sylvia*, and his opera *Lakmé* are conventional and very popular. *Lakmé* is *opéra comique* because of the spoken words and of its romantic character. Délibes always has a certain delicacy of color, and charm which captivates.

Another composer who writes in an exotic vein (or an out-of-the-nation-to-which-he-belongs way, with all the color of the other nation in costumes and scenes) is Edouard Victor Antoine Lalo (1823–1892). Lalo was trained to sincerity by his models, Beethoven, Schubert and Schumann. This does not mean copying, for his music is not anything like the music of these men. He skilfully drew a variety of effects from his orchestration, and his music has individuality. His best known work in opera is *Le Roi d'Ys*. He also wrote a work for violin and orchestra *Symphonie Espagnole* which is a pet of all the violinists because of its brilliancy and beauty.

MASSENET

Jules Massenet (1842–1912) was something like a modern French Meyerbeer and an Offenbach combined, yet his work is far more worth while. Before he died he was at the height of his popularity in Europe and America, and the repertory of the Hammerstein Opera in New York included many of Massenet's works. He composed operas so rapidly that his public could not forget him!

He built on Gounod and Ambroise Thomas and gained much from Wagner. He used continuous melody and some of the principles of the leit-motif. Wagner's music compared to Massenet's was thick for Massenet's is thin!

Whether Massenet will always remain popular is a question. His operas are engaging and clever, and he knew how to write theatre music to please the public. The most important of his operas (about fifteen), are *Manon* and *Le Jongleur de Notre Dame*. The title parts of both were sung by the brilliant Mary Garden, in this country. (See Chapter VIII.) *Manon* ranks second to the *Jongleur*. You know, too, the *Meditation* from *Thäis*, another of his popular successes. It was written for Sybil Sanderson, an American singer, in Paris. Massenet's operas did not show his tremendous knowledge of counterpoint, of which he was professor at the Conservatory. His position was later filled by André Gédalge who has taught most of the composers of today. Gédalge is also the composer of some very fine symphonies, sonatas and an extraordinary *Treatise on the Fugue*.

Other writers of this period are Xavier Leroux (1863–1919), Gabriel Pierné (1863–1937), composer of a delightful oratorio, *Children's Crusade*. He was conductor of the Colonne Orchestra in Paris. André Messager (1853–1929) was the composer of some very charming light operas of which *Veronique* is the best known. There are also the great organists Charles Marie Widor (1845–1937) with ten organ symphonies and many other works, and Alexandre Guilmant (1837–1911), who came to America while one of the writers of this book (Ethel Peyser) was a student at Vassar College, where he inaugurated the new organ.

Followers of César Franck

Although César Franck was not a successful opera writer, he influenced composers by showing how to combine modern harmony successfully with the classic form.

Among the many César Franck's revival of the classic style influenced are Gabriel Pierné, Henri Duparc (1848–1933), and Ernest Chausson (1855–1899), Franck's pupils. Chausson was first known through *Helen*, a three-act opera, and *Le Roi Arthus*, which show what he might have accomplished had not an accident caused his death.   Besides the operas he wrote beautiful chamber music, a fine symphony and songs.   His *Poem* for violin is full of gentle, yet deep feeling.   All his work has veiled mystery and is very lovely.

The most important pupil of César Franck is Vincent d'Indy (1851–1931), one of the leading figures in France. He founded, with Charles Bordes and Guilmant, the organist, the *Schola Cantorum*, and revived interest in sacred music.   He conducted in this country and is admired for his symphonic works, his operas *Fervaal* and *L'Étranger* (*The Stranger*), piano pieces and chamber music.   One of his symphonic poems, *Istar*, was made into a ballet for Mme. Ida Rubenstein and was performed for the first time at the Grand Opera in Paris, in 1924.

Alfred Bruneau (1857–1934) links Wagner's period with Debussy's.   His operas are rarely given outside of Paris. His manner was new and caused much discussion.   He based many of his plots on Émile Zola's writings, and was conductor of the *Opéra Comique*.   *The Attack on the Mill* was given in America.

Charpentier's "Louise"

Gustave Charpentier (1860) comes next.   He made his name with the delightful opera about the dressmaker apprentice *Louise*, a musical story on the life in Montmartre, one of the artist quarters of Paris. Charpentier wrote the book, which was the story of his own life. He also wrote its sequel *Julien*. No one who has ever been in Paris fails to be deeply stirred by this picture of the simple home life of the *midinette* or sewing girl. Mary Garden created the part of Louise in America and it was the first rôle of her operatic career. In one scene, you hear the almost forgotten street cries of Paris. He has also written a charming work for orchestra, *Impressions of Italy*, which is the result of his having won the *Prix de Rome* in his youth.

This brings us up to the 20th century to which we shall devote an entire chapter. But in order to finish our story of French opera, we will merely introduce you to Claude Achille Debussy, the ultra-modern harmonist and weaver of mystery and beauty, who ushered in the 20th century with his lovely and enchanting opera, *Pelleas and Melisande*, written on the play by Maurice Maeterlinck. For ten years the composer worked over this masterpiece, and it was produced for the first time at the *Opéra Comique*, in Paris in 1902. Here we find something that never had been before,—opera completely separated from all the old ideas of what opera should be. But in tearing down the old, Debussy gave something very rare, beautiful, sensitive, touching a very high artistic peak, in its place. This was pure impressionism in music, just what romanticism was to the early 19th century. This carries the French School to its highest degree of mystic beauty.

After Debussy's opera came Maurice Ravel's *L'Heure Espagnole* (*The Spanish Hour*), Henri Rabaud's *Marouf*, Paul Dukas' *Ariane et Barbe Bleue* (*Ariadne and Blue Beard*), a Maeterlinck libretto second only to *Pelleas and Melisande* in atmospheric charm, Albert Roussel's *Padmavati*, an Oriental opera. that has been produced very recently at the Grand Opera in Paris, and Florent Schmitt's *Le Petit Elfe Ferme l' Oeil* (*The little elf winks its eye*) presented at the *Opéra Comique* in 1924.

HUMPERDINCK—THE FAIRY-TALE MAN—GERMANY

Outside of the operas of Richard Strauss, of which we have written elsewhere, there have been few outstanding opera-writers in Germany since Wagner. Among those are Ludwig Thuille (1861–1907), whose *Lobetanz* was given at the Metropolitan Opera House in 1911; Eugène d'Albert (1864–1932), who lived in Germany most of his life, although he was born in Scotland, and wrote the lovely *Tiefland* which was performed in America; Max Schillings (1868–1933), whose *Mona Lisa* was performed at the Metropolitan; Hans Pfitzner (1869), who wrote an operatic legend based on Palestrina; Siegfried Wagner (1869–1930), son of Richard; and Leo Blech (1871).

One exception was Engelbert Humperdinck (1854–1921), born in Bonn, Beethoven's birthplace. He is perhaps closer to the hearts of children than any other composer, and when you hear that it was he who wrote music for that beautiful little fairy story *Hansel and Gretel*, we are sure you will agree. The Metropolitan Opera gives special performances of it and it is frequently presented elsewhere in English. Would it not be nice if more operas were given in English? You would then find out for yourselves that this is the story of *Babes in the Woods*.

How fine it would have been had you been able to hear in your own language *Koenigskinder* (*Children of the King*), another opera written by Humperdinck! This gave one of the loveliest roles to the well-loved American prima donna, Geraldine Farrar, and brought a large flock of real geese on the Metropolitan stage to take part in the performance. The other name of the opera is *The Goose-Girl*, which explains the presence of the geese. Geraldine Farrar always brought one or two with her when she acknowledged the applause and there was always an awful squawk! In this opera too, there is a horrid old Witch. Humperdinck found joy and inspiration in the folk music of Germany, much of which deals with fairies, elves, witches and inhabitants of the world of imagination.

Humperdinck was a great musician and he had the honor of being asked to prepare the score of *Parsifal* for the publishers.

Because of the beauties of his melodies, the lovely subjects he selected and his sympathy with the finer and higher things of life, it is a pity that Humperdinck left so few works.

He was attracted to the theatre and wrote much music as theatre music for plays. This is called incidental music, that is, it is incidental and the play's the thing! Just before he died Humperdinck wrote the incidental music for the *Miracle* which is a great spectacle in pantomime. This means that there is no speaking, only tableaux and acting. He did not live to finish it, but it was completed by his son, for the production made by Max Reinhardt.

CHAPTER XXVII

Some Tone Poets

PROBABLY you think that any music on a program is program music! Of course it is, but not in the special use of the word, for when it is program music, it has a story of its own and has to be described in more or less detail so that the audience can understand what it is about. Therefore, we find two classes of music—*absolute music*, which needs no story to explain it, and—*program music*, which does. Beethoven's best works are known by their opus number while most of Schumann's have descriptive titles. Early composers sometimes wrote music describing or imitating something, like Daquin's *Cuckoo*, Jannequin's *Battle of Marignan*, *The Carman's Whistle*, etc. These pieces were program music in a way, but the modern tone poets went further by writing music with rather extended stories and with music not as simple as it used to be, but nevertheless an outgrowth of ballad form, sonata and the symphony.

Suppose you wanted to write a tone poem! First you must have a subject and then you must write music to explain it. Let us say you were going to write a Subway Tone Poem, your program notes might read something like this: The hero rushes away from his office, into the hurrying, scurrying street, down the slippery, crowded subway steps, and when he reaches the noisy turnstile, slips in his fare and meets his young lady. He leads her through the crowd, protecting her from the jostling mob. Then they enter the train and above the noise and bustle they cast sweet glances at each other and converse. The train stops occasionally and finally they get off at their station. They walk to her home, along an empty side street where it is quiet and charming. He doffs his cap and we leave them, both thinking lovely things about each other.

Don't you think you're ready now to write a tone poem?

BERLIOZ, INNOVATOR

Up to Hector Berlioz' time (1803–1869), there was no definite attempt to write a tone poem with an elaborate story. This man, one of the most complicated in musical history, did much to help music and future musicians, for he started to tell stories in music without scenery or dialogues.

He was born near Lyons, France, the son of a doctor who wanted him to study medicine, but as he almost fainted several times in the dissecting room, he gave it up. This was his first rebellion and all his life he struggled against nearly everything that existed. His was a noble discontent in many ways, for he believed deeply in his own ideas and suffered much putting them into practice. He lived shortly after the French Revolution when everything was topsy-turvy. Many of the old things that people had looked upon with reverence had vanished and he tried, as other young men of his day, to forge new ideas according to his sense of right.

One day he saw some musical score paper and realized in a moment, what wonderful things might be done with it and exclaimed: "What an orchestral work one might write on that!" and quite suddenly, he decided to write music! He could only play the guitar, the flute and the flageolet and knew practically nothing of harmony. He certainly paid well for his decision, for he had a hard struggle with himself and circumstances.

He took one of his compositions to Professor Lesueur at the Paris Conservatory, and was admitted.

BERLIOZ VERSUS CHERUBINI

Cherubini, Director of the Conservatory, made a rule that men and women should use separate doors leading into the library. Not knowing this rule, Berlioz entered by the door reserved for the women and sat down to read a score of his beloved Gluck. Cherubini, thin, pale-faced, with tousled hair and fiercely shining eyes, came up to Hector and reprimanded him for breaking the rule. They had a noisy fight, chasing in and out among the desks and when Berlioz reached the door, he looked back at Cherubini and called out: "I am soon coming back to study Gluck again." Being a determined boy, he did come back, but Cherubini, on whom his future depended, was his staunch enemy for life.

His parents were infuriated with Hector for his conduct. His mother, a pious woman, practically disowned him and his father gave him a small allowance, stipulating that unless he could soon prove his ability in music, he should have to go back to medicine. So he tried desperately to earn money, by singing in choruses, playing the flute and teaching. He hoped to win the *Prix de Rome*, which would give him a few years in Rome and three thousand francs. In spite of terrific opposition from Cherubini, and held back, too, by his own lack of diplomacy, either by submitting works that were written too poorly or too well, finally, after four attempts, he won the coveted award with his cantata *Sardanapalus*. He left out the parts then looked upon as modern and difficult, which would have lost him the prize, but the first time it was played in public, he put them all in, and the piece was successful. 1830 was an eventful year for Berlioz. He won the *prix de Rome*, and he gave the first performance of his revolutionary score, *The Fantastic Symphony*.

After a hectic courtship, he married the Irish actress, Harriet Smithson. They were unhappy and unfortunate. He even had to put aside composing to earn a living by writing, and he proved an exceptionally gifted writer and critic. Later he married a singer, Marie Recio.

His autobiography, too, is most interesting for he sees himself as a romantic hero and tells the tale with great dramatic energy and exaggeration.

With Intent to Murder!

Once he was engaged to another woman who married some one else and he wrote: "Two tears of rage started from my eyes and my mind was made up on the spot to kill without mercy." But being impetuous and quick-tempered, he never reached the scene of murder, for, when about to sail to where she was, he either fell or jumped into the water, which very much dampened his ardor for killing.

One night, Chopin and Schumann followed him because he had threatened to kill himself. But, at the crucial moment Berlioz changed his mind!

Life for Berlioz was a drama in which he was the leading man, and he watched his own performance, as if he were a part of the audience. He craved novelty at every turn. He was sensitive, high-strung and vain, and yet withal, he had the dignity of being loyal to his beliefs in himself, and did not want to deceive anybody. He wrote with humor, brilliancy and understanding, he had faith in his work, and was sufficiently heroic to stick to his course whatever the cost. He was a martyr, for he suffered in order to do what he wished in music, and was never appreciated.

Although he went to England, Germany, Austria and Russia, and was very successful, Paris, only, interested him. In 1863, his opera *The Trojans in Carthage* failed and in 1868, he died, a broken-hearted man.

BERLIOZ'S CONTRIBUTION TO MUSIC

It seems strange, but Berlioz disliked Bach and Palestrina and worshiped Beethoven, Gluck and Weber. He was jealous of Wagner and did everything he could to make *Tannhäuser* a failure in Paris.

Berlioz invented new ways, as have our own Jazz Bands, to make the instruments produce different sounds. He put bags over the horns, hung up the cymbals and had them struck with sticks instead of clapping them together, dressed up the drumsticks in sponges, and was much pleased at the effect made when a trombone played a duet with a piccolo. He made propaganda for new instruments especially for the horn, invented by Adolphe Saxe, which was called Sax Horn, and from which descended the Saxophone, so behold Berlioz, the founder of the Jazz Band!

Where other composers would use four trombones or one, he used sixteen! In his *Requiem* for example, he used sixteen trombones, twelve ophicleides (cornets with extra levers or keys), eight pairs of kettle drums, two bass drums, a gong and of course, all the regular string and reed instruments. He boasted after the first performance, that a man had a fit from the excessive noise!

THE INTIMATE FRIEND OF INSTRUMENTS

He wrote the sort of melody that showed off each particular instrument to its best advantage. He studied them as if they were human beings, and he understood their characters and temperaments, what they could do and at what they would balk. He showed the possibilities of the choirs of woodwind instruments, a rich heritage for us today. The orchestra playing a piece of his, directed by him, was matchless in its effect. *Effect* was the keynote of his writings. As the first great master of tonal effect, he is unsurpassed, and his book on orchestration is still one of the most practical text books on the subject.

Berlioz used the *idée fixe* (fixed idea) or *leit-motif*, not as Wagner used it later, but quite definitely, twisting a theme in many ways to bring out different phases of the same subject. Thus, Berlioz founded the dramatic in orchestral music, without scenery and without words, which is the Symphonic Tone Poem.

The majority of the people did not understand him any more than they understand Stravinsky today. His greatest work was his *Symphony Fantastic* written in 1830, in which he used the *idée fixe* to tell about the life of the artist, in true program music style for which he fought and almost bled. In *Harold in Italy*, he makes a departure by giving to the viola, the rôle of the "leading lady" which had not been done up to his day. He often used voices with the orchestra as he did in his tone poem *Romeo and Juliet*, and "concert opera," *The Damnation of Faust*.

The noisy *Requiem* is one of the finest things he did, and his overtures, such as *The Roman Carnival* and the opening to his opera, *Benvenuto Cellini*, are fine works. The oratorio, *The Infancy of Christ*, written in classic style, was well received, but his operas never succeeded.

He paved the way for new orchestral effects and prepared the ground for Franz Liszt, Richard Wagner, Richard Strauss, and many other orchestral composers. He was a musical Byron, for he was more interesting than beautiful, more vivid than noble, a sincere *poseur*, faithful to his ideas and always searching for romance.

He was well versed in literature, always carried Virgil in his pocket, and loved and admired Shakespeare, Goethe, Byron, Walter Scott and other great writers on whose works he based many compositions. In his fascinating autobiography, he said, "The dominant qualities of my music are passionate expression, internal fire, rhythmic animation and unexpected change," and he was right.

And so we leave this romantic man, craving sensation in his life and in his music, exaggerated in word and tone, and thank him for what Daniel Gregory Mason calls, "His contribution to the unresting progress of art."

He was not appreciated in Paris until after his death, and some one said that the stones hurled at him in contempt were soon piled up for him in the pedestals of his monuments.

Franz Liszt

Another Mozart seems about to appear, for Franz Liszt (1811–1886), too, was an infant prodigy!

He was born in Raiding, Hungary, and his father, Adam Liszt, who was steward to Prince Esterhazy, gave Franz piano lessons and managed his first concert tours.

At nine Liszt played in public, then went to Vienna and took lessons from Carl Czerny and Salieri. When twelve years old he played in Paris and "set the world on fire" with his brilliancy. Some one said that after his first concert he had a triumphal progress to fame over the laps of great ladies, for he was petted and "bon-bonned" and kissed by all.

Liszt wanted to go to the Conservatory in Paris, but as he was a foreigner, Cherubini, though a foreigner himself, would not admit him.

ADVERTISING LISZT

Here is a handbill used for advertising the little boy Liszt:

"AN AIR"

With grand Variations by Herz, will be performed on Erard's New Patent-Grand Pianoforte, by:

MASTER LISZT

Who will likewise perform an Extempore Fantasia and respectfully requests two written Themes from any of the Audience upon which he will play his Variations

This shows two interesting things: the mention of the *grand pianoforte*, which had not been in use long and the fashion of improvising in public, a "stunt" almost like solving a cross-word puzzle without a dictionary!

For a long time, he was advertised as two years younger than he was, and his father carried him to the piano; but he soon rebelled at this pretense and it was discontinued.

LISZT SHOWS HIS UNSELFISHNESS

After Liszt's father died in 1827, he gave up concert tours for a while, and settled down in Paris with his mother for eight restful years to study and teach the piano. He gave her all he had made in his concert tours because, he said, she had made so many sacrifices for him. He grew spiritually deeper and well fitted for the glories to come. Like Berlioz, Liszt was born a short time after the French Revolution, when new ideas were coming into literature, religion and art, through which this gifted youth tried to guide himself in a wise way that shaped his future life. Later he traveled in Switzerland and Italy with Countess Marie d'Agoult who became the mother of his three children. The second, Cosima, became Wagner's second wife.

Liszt again made concert tours through Europe (1839), and astounded everyone with his playing and the charm of his personality. Musicians and audiences were at his feet! He made a great deal of money, too, and grew so popular that artists painted him, ladies knelt before him in adoration, tableaux were given in his honor, monuments erected to him and societies named after him.

His kindness to the poor and needy was unfailing. When Pesth was inundated by a flood, he sent a generous gift to the sufferers; he established a fund for the poor in Raiding and completed the necessary sum for the Beethoven monument at Bonn. He never accepted money for teaching after he was "grown up" for he wanted to be a help to his some three hundred pupils. It is said that after 1847 he never gave a concert for his own benefit! An extraordinary character!

In 1843, he went to Weimar, as a visiting artist. Soon he met Princess Von Sayn Wittgenstein of Russia who realized his great gifts and influenced him to become more than a pianist. Later in the year we see him as conductor living at Weimar and attracting the greatest people of the musical world to him. Here Liszt was able to help young musicians who came from all over the world. Wagner would never have been so successful, had not Liszt aided him during his exile. He stood by him with patience and loving kindness and helped him to produce his operas. He was of untold assistance to Schumann and Berlioz, Rubinstein, Cornelius and countless others by performing their works when nobody else dared to. Liszt was in high favor with society, and having a love for the new in music, he used his popularity to help music grow. Wagner himself said: "At the end of my last stay in Paris, when ill, broken down and despairing, I sat brooding over my fate, my eye fell on the score of my *Lohengrin*, totally forgotten by me. Suddenly I felt something like compassion that this music should never sound from off the death-pale paper. I wrote two lines to Liszt; his answer was the news that preparations for the performance were being made on the largest scale the limited means of Weimar would permit." Liszt's motto was, "First Place to the Living."

Liszt's Professional Life

Liszt's services were demanded for concerts and festivals in many towns from 1852–1859. The people, however, could not understand how their idol could believe in Wagner and Berlioz, and there were many rabid discussions. Very soon Liszt brought out his own symphonic poems, among them, *Tasso, Prometheus, Mazeppa, Les Preludes*, and his two piano concertos (1855–1857), utilizing his romantic ideas and inventing new forms.

After leaving Weimar, which some biographers claim was because of the adverse criticism of Cornelius' opera, *The Barber of Bagdad*, Liszt went to Rome. Here his deep mystical nature and his need for rest and time for contemplation, led him to enter one of the Holy Orders of the Church, and the Pope gave him the honorary title of Abbé. Pope Pius IX adored him and called him his Palestrina. The church music which he composed there included his oratorios *St. Elizabeth, The Christus*, his unfinished *Stanislaus*, the *Hungarian Coronation Mass* and the *Requiem*.

Liszt returned to Weimar every spring and summer and conducted many festivals and concerts, including the centenary of Beethoven's birth. He was also much interested in the National Academy at Pesth, so now he divided his time between Rome, Pesth, and Weimar.

He wrote many brilliant piano pieces, among them his nineteen remarkable Hungarian Rhapsodies based on the melodies he heard from the gypsies. Besides composing music, teaching and helping other musicians and giving to the needy, he wrote essays and criticisms.

In appearance Liszt was tall and thin with deep-set eyes and bushy eyebrows and a mouth which turned up at the corners when he smiled. His charm of manner won all who came in contact with him.

A story is told of him that he as a youth was sitting to the artist Scheffer for his portrait, and fell into a theatrical pose, probably with his head thrown back and one hand thrust into the breast of his buttoned coat, which was characteristic. As this did not impress the painter, Liszt, realizing it, cried with much embarrassment, "Forgive, dear master, but you do not know how it spoils one to have been an infant prodigy."

In spite of Liszt's outward affectation and posing, he had a noble character. He was simple and whole-souled, free from jealousy and the love of money. He died highly honored in 1886 at the age of seventy-five in Bayreuth, while attending a Wagner festival. In fact it was difficult to tell who received more honor at Bayreuth, Liszt in the audience or Wagner at the conductor's desk.

Liszt's Accomplishments

As a pianist, no one has surpassed Liszt who revealed the piano's possibilities. Besides his many compositions, he made transcriptions of symphonies, chorals, operas, songs and every other form, which brought them closer to the people. His brilliant arrangements, although often over-decorated and cheap in effect, show that the piano can almost reproduce the orchestra.

Liszt was not as great a composer as he was a pianist

and stimulator of other musicians, yet he made music grow
by introducing many new ideas and forms. His fine critical
judgment and interest in music for the future led him to be
sympathetic with young composers, for many of whom he
opened the way. The people who gathered about him disliked old forms and were looking for new music in which
he encouraged them. Among the musicians who were
friends and pupils at Weimar, were: Joseph Joachim Raff,
Peter Cornelius, Eduard Lassen, who took Liszt's place
when he left Weimar, Leopold Damrosch, the father of
Walter and Frank Damrosch of New York, Alexander
Ritter, the pianist and inspirer of so many great people,
and hundreds of others.

Liszt wrote many symphonic and choral pieces which
showed marked originality. Although not as profound as
Wagner, he helped Wagner so much that their names
would be forever linked, even if his daughter Cosima had
not been Wagner's wife.

RUBINSTEIN AND VON BÜLOW

Among other friends of Liszt of value to musical history were Anton Rubinstein (1829–1894) (page 443), the
Russian, and Hans von Bülow (1830–1894), a German.
Both these men were great pianists and wrote noteworthy
compositions. Liszt was a great stimulus to them and
they had many points in common. Rubinstein was romantic and von Bülow, classic. Rubinstein did much to
link Germany and Russia musically, which was a help to
both nations. Von Bülow was an illustrious pianist,
friend of Wagner, famous conductor, and editor of many
musical scores, among them an edition of Beethoven's
Sonatas, still in constant use. Both these men did much
for pianists all over Europe.

Other great pianists and composers of their day were:

Nikolai Rubinstein (Anton's brother) (1835-1881); Theodor Leschetizky (1830-1915), trained by Carl Czerny, and he in turn trained hundreds of pianists; Karl Tausig and many others.

Of course, the effect of these pianists was to make music and the piano more popular, thus adding greatly to the musical culture of the world.

TCHAIKOVSKY

You probably know of Piotr (Peter) Ilyitch Tchaikovsky (1840-1893) as a great symphony writer, but he was also a successful writer of tone poems such as *The Tempest*, *Francesca da Rimini*, *Manfred*, based on Byron's *Manfred*, and called a symphony, *Hamlet*, *The Storm*, *Romeo and Juliet*, and two incomplete poems, *Destiny* (*Fatum*) and *Voyevoda*.

Tchaikovsky was born in Russia, he went to the school of Jurisprudence and later entered the Ministry of Justice but soon began to compose music and studied at the St. Petersburg Conservatory. Among his most popular works is *The Nut Cracker* Suite for orchestra, adapted from the score of a Ballet. It includes a Russian dance, an Arab dance, a Chinese dance, flower waltz, and other fascinating, whirling, delightful dances.

Many of Tchaikovsky's works not called tone poems have very definite programs, such as *The Snow Maiden* (*Snegourotchka*) a favorite legend and music to a fairy tale—the parts are named *Chorus of Blind Gusslee Players*, *Monologue of the Frosts*, *Appearance of the Wood Demons* and so on, and he wrote it as incidental music to a play.

SERGEI RACHMANINOV

Boecklin's painting *Isle of Death*, inspired Sergei Rachmaninov (1873) to write a most beautiful musical poem about its sombre trees and the sea. As a distinguished pianist he has glorified the art in all countries, especially in America. He was a student of Siloti and of Zvierev, a friend of Tchaikovsky. His masters in harmony and theory were Taneiev and Arensky. He has held musical posts of honor and has written remarkable piano concertos, chamber music works, choruses and one opera, *Aleko*. You probably know his popular C sharp minor Prelude which has been a sort of visiting card of Rachmaninov to the public, although this is only one of many of his fine compositions for pianoforte.

RICHARD STRAUSS, THE PROTEUS OF MUSIC

Among tone poets, Richard Strauss (1864), or Richard II one might call him, is one of the most important. It is strange that he should have the same name as Wagner, for his father Franz Strauss, a skilled horn player, disliked Wagner and his compositions intensely. Richard's mother was the daughter of a brewer and they all lived in Munich, where the son was born.

When he was a little boy, he wrote musical notes before he could write the alphabet, and at six, composed little pieces. By the time he was twenty he had written compositions which put him with Schubert, Mendelssohn and Mozart, in the ranks of musical prodigies.

Until his sixteenth work *Aus Italien* (*From Italy*) (1886), his first tone poem, he did not depart from the classic forms, although there were a few signs of change in style in a violin sonata which he wrote just before the tone poem. In fact, he was so much against Wagner and his innovations, that no one could have guessed that later he himself would be considered an innovator and would be accused of imitating Wagner.

During his youth, after hearing *Siegfried*, he wrote to a friend about the music of Mime: "It would have killed a cat and the horror of musical dissonances would melt rocks into omelettes."

When he met von Bülow, the old master thought little of his talents, but the young man gave him a surprise. For, when Richard went to Meiningen he had never led an orchestra in his life and without one rehearsal, conducted his *Serenade for Strings*, opus 7. Von Bülow realized his great ability, made him assistant conductor, and a year later when he left Meiningen, Strauss took his place.

It was about now that Richard met Alexander Ritter the violinist and radical thinker who, he said, changed his life by introducing to him new ideas. He became converted to Wagner. When he heard *Tristan and Isolda* he was thrilled by it. So, like Proteus, the god who changed his form to suit his adventure, Strauss, the musical Proteus, changed his ideas to suit his opinions.

Wearied by hard work after writing many classical pieces including a sonata, an overture, the *Festmarsch*, a violin concerto, songs, a horn concerto and other things, he became very ill. He said to a friend that he was ready to die, and then added, "No, before I do, I should love to conduct *Tristan*." This shows that the young man could change his opinion and become devoted to what he loathed years before, a fine quality which continually brought down upon his head criticism from smaller folk. Yet this Proteus-like quality, was a sign of his power for growth.

Because he did not gain strength quickly from his illness, he went to Italy and then wrote his first symphonic poem *Aus Italien* (*From Italy*) in a new and modern vein.

When he returned, he led the orchestra in the Court Theatre of Munich and then went to Weimar for two years, and this former young classicist was now hailed as the leader of modern composers! He produced, here, three tone poems: *Macbeth, Don Juan* and *Tod und Verklärung* (*Death and Transfiguration*) (1888–1890).

Then, on account of illness (1892) he went to Greece, Egypt and Sicily. During this tour, he wrote an opera, *Guntram*, which he produced on his return to Weimar.

He became interested in the Bayreuth festivals and in 1894 he conducted a production of *Tannhäuser*, after which he married Pauline de Ahna who played Elizabeth. Before this, he had made her the heroine of his first opera, *Guntram* (1893).

Not long after this he gave up the Weimar post and went to Munich with his bride. He became the conductor there and at the same time, led the Berlin Philharmonic concerts until the double work and commuting became too much for him. He gave up Berlin and Arthur Nikisch succeeded him,—the same Arthur Nikisch who later took the baton of the Boston Symphony Orchestra in America.

In 1899 he became the leader of the Royal Opera in Berlin in which city he decided to live and from there made trips all over the world including the United States, first in 1904 and later, after the World War. During his last tour, we heard him play the piano for his songs which are unsurpassed in beauty, and conduct some of his own orchestral works with skill and enthusiasm.

He is tall and slender, with kindly blue eyes, rather informal in manner. He has the air of a happy man even if he has received some of the harshest criticism from friends and foes that any composer has had from earliest times. His wife used to sing his songs in public. He is fond of games, especially the card game "skat" and like the true grandson of a brewer enjoys his glass of beer.

STRAUSS'S CONTRIBUTION TO MUSIC

Among Strauss' greatest works are his operas *Electra*, *Salome* and *Der Rosenkavalier* and his nine tone poems. Despite all the harsh things critics have said of him, Strauss has always maintained that, although he did not write in accepted forms, he felt that the form should always be suitable to the subject, for "as moods and ideas change so must forms." This, Ernest Newman said in defence of Strauss, and it may be applied to all arts.

So Strauss is not formless but like Proteus, has many forms. Cecil Gray said, "he seems to have an irresistible itch to provoke the amazement and the horror of the multitude." This is quite true, especially in *Salome*, *Electra* and *Der Rosenkavalier* in which opera he went back to Mozart form as a model. It seems incredible that a man who could write the noble songs that he has written should have chosen such unpleasant plots for his operas!

In *Death and Transfiguration* he was distinctly a follower of Liszt. His friend Alexander Ritter is said to have written the poem after the music had been composed.

At the time that it was first played, it caused so much comment that Strauss, like Browning, laughed at people for trying to "read" more into it than he wrote. Browning was asked whether he meant a certain thing in one of his poems, and his reply was something like this: "Madam, I never thought of it, but if you think it is there, I am more than glad to know it."

His *Don Juan* is delightful, too, but his *Till Eulenspiegel* (1895) which tells of the mischievous pranks of Till, is one of the finest examples of *humor* in music and probably will outlive many works of this modern period, his own as well as others. He wrote it in the form of a classical Rondo, because he could picture Till's ever recurring deviltry and exploits in this form. Poor Strauss was reviled for this daringly written music, too, yet this tone poem is an amazing piece of work and was given gloriously as a ballet in New York City a few years ago by Diaghilev's Russian Ballet.

In *Also Sprach Zarathustra* (*Thus Spake Zarathustra*),

Strauss uses the *idée fixe* or *leit-motif*. This is based on a prose poem of Nietzsche.

In *Don Quixote* he uses variation form, an ingenious way of showing the varying sides of the character of Don Quixote. Here he shows events and not ideas, a most definite story in tones. You can almost see the attack on the wind-mills and you can actually hear the sheep bleating, the church music of passing pilgrims, and the love tale of Dulcinea. In this piece, program music reaches its height.

In *Ein Heldenleben* (*A Hero's Life*) (1898) Strauss frankly quotes from his musical works. He does not have to prove that he is the hero, for he admits it! When Strauss was asked what the poem meant, he said, "There is no need of a program, it is enough to know that there is a hero fighting his enemies." In it, you can really hear the carping critics, his retorts, the triumphs and the defeats. It is very interesting and amazingly well written.

The *Domestic Symphony* (*Sinfonia Domestica*) is the story of a family for one day. There is the father motif, the mother motif and the baby motif! The alarm clock wakens the family, baby is bathed, played with, spanked, and visited by relatives, and the routine of the day is described in music. Program music indeed!

His early works include an opera, *Feuersnoth*, and his songs are among the greatest of the German *Lieder*, ranking him with Schubert, Schumann, Brahms and Hugo Wolf. He has also written the *Alpine Symphony;* two ballets and eight operas, including *Ariadne auf Naxos, The Woman Without Shadows, The Egyptian Helen, Arabella, Daphne,* etc.

Strauss shows in all his work great pictorial power. He paints in tones if ever a man does. His humor in music is amazing. He tries to make vivid in music a thing as simple as a fork and as complex as a philosophic idea. Some one said of him, comparing him to Wagner, that he started out to write symphonic poems and really wrote music dramas, while Wagner started out to write music dramas and ended by writing *Tristan and Isolda*, a super-symphonic poem with voices added.

Richard Strauss is the last of the great German classic and romantic composers who have ruled the musical world for the past two centuries. Still living in Germany he has opened the way to many of the younger composers, who have learned much from his methods of orchestration and handling music in the large forms. While he out-Wagnered Wagner in strange and new harmony, he now seems old fashioned in comparison to Schoenberg, Stravinsky and Honegger. Although Strauss seemed to us very complex and exaggerated a few years ago, it was very interesting to notice that when his works were revived in America after the War, the audiences had grown up musically to the point where they seemed no longer unintelligible or ultramodern.

We remember when we were leaving the opera house after the first performance of *Salome* in this country, hearing one ill bred, untutored woman say, "Gee! Goit, but that was one big noise!" By this time she has probably reached the point where she listens to a swing version of the Salome dance with real pleasure and understanding!

Strauss did unusual things with instruments, added many new ones, and as someone said, he loves to have the "trombone play like a piccolo!"

No one can say where Strauss will stand as a composer, for time alone can place him. However, we make bold to state that he will stand high in the company of the world's composers.

CHABRIER (1841–1894)

As imitation is the sincerest form of flattery, there is no proof of the success of the tone poem more telling than the fact that practically every composer in the musical world has written symphonic tone poems. In fact today, one hundred tone poems are written to one symphony! Berlioz had his followers in France, and in the group around César Franck were several who wrote tone poems. One of the most charming of these poets was Alexis Emanuel Chabrier (1841–1894) who took up music first as an amateur while studying law in Paris, and while he was Minister of the Interior. Later he became so devoted to music that he gave all his time to it.

Among his works are operas and many other forms of music, the loveliest of which is the Rhapsody on Spanish tunes called *España*. It is a model of its kind and in it he uses the collected material with rare skill. It shows him very clever in reproducing foreign atmosphere and feeling. He was born in Ambert, France, and died in Paris.

DEBUSSY

Claude Achille Debussy (1862–1918) although talked of in another chapter, must be mentioned as a composer of tone poems in this. Among his most famous works are *L'Après-midi d'un Faune (The Afternoon of a Faun)*, *La Mer (The Sea)*, *Les Nuages (Clouds)*, *Fêtes (Festivities)*, and *Sirènes (Sirens)*, which are all surpassingly lovely, written in Debussy's special harmonies with which he wove a mystical, far-away atmosphere, so compelling and yet so magical that you think you are in a mysterious cloudland. He often uses a scale of whole tones. In *Pelleas and Melisande*, his greatest work (opera), you seem to look into a distant land which never did and never will exist, except in the glorious reaches of his or our imaginations. So to those of us who love fairy realms, cloudland and beauty of idea and serene expression, Debussy will be a rare treat and never vanish from our mind's ear.

RAVEL

Maurice Ravel (1875–1937), who lived in Paris, seemed to love Spanish themes as did Chabrier and Bizet. One of the loveliest tone poems is his *Rhapsodie Espagnole* in four movements. His *Mother Goose* suite and *La Valse* are also charming, modern, short orchestral works.

He wrote with rare distinction and beauty. In the chapter on 20th century music, Ravel will make another appearance.

PAUL DUKAS (1865–1935)

Among the most humorous and delightful tone poems is *L'Apprenti-Sorcier* (*The Sorcerer's Apprentice*) by Paul Dukas, who, also, will appear in another chapter.

CHAPTER XXVIII

Late 19th Century Composers Write New Music on Old Models

BRAHMS IN GERMANY—FRANCK IN FRANCE

AFTER calling Beethoven a Colossus, there does not seem to be room for any one else, and yet Brahms (1833–1897) is no less of a genius. You will often hear people speak of "the three Bs,"—Bach, Beethoven and Brahms; and of these, Brahms being closer to our own day has had the advantage and influence of the past. But perhaps he also had the disadvantage of having had some one else say what he would like to have been the first to say! That Brahms continued along the lines that Beethoven began, may be seen from the fact that many call Brahms' first symphony *The Tenth*, meaning that Brahms had begun his symphonies where Beethoven left off.

It is not easy to write of Brahms without seeming to exaggerate, because if we speak of his songs we must say that no one ever created more beautiful song form; if we speak of his chamber music we must acknowledge that he understood writing for instruments as no one before or since has surpassed. His piano pieces, too, are pure delight! Where will one find finer work than his one concerto for violin and the two for piano? His four symphonies have so far been unsurpassed and his choral works, too. If he **had** never written anything but the *German Requiem* this would have marked him as one of the world's masters. Has he not justified Schumann's exclamation upon meeting him in 1853, when Brahms was twenty years old: "Graces and Heroes have watched the cradle of this young genius who sprang 'like Minerva, fully armed from the head of Jove?' " But Brahms was very modest and was always embarrassed in the presence of praise. While he was compared to Beethoven he waited until very late in life to write symphonies. "How can I write a symphony," he is reported to have said, "when I feel the shadow of the great Beethoven treading constantly behind me?"

He was born in Hamburg. His father, who was a musician, rejoiced greatly when little Johannes at an early age gave proof that he was gifted. The Brahms family was very poor, and instead of becoming a great artist according to his desire, Johannes' father from the time he was old enough to earn his living, was a double-bass player. Even though he was the best in Hamburg, he and his wife, who was fond of music, had to struggle and save to give their little son the best teachers in piano and composition.

In order to make more than the small amount gained by playing in the orchestras the father organized what we call "the little German band" which played in the open air. Father Brahms and five other musicians attracted the people wherever they went. The boy who had begun to earn a few pennies by arranging dances and marches for the little bands of the cafés, wrote music for his father's band, and early in the morning even while he brushed shoes before others were awake, the thoughts which became his loveliest songs came to his mind.

Brahms meets Remenyi

When Johannes was fifteen he gave his first public piano recital and made a deep impression. It started him on the road to fame, for he played so well that he was engaged to accompany the Gypsy violinist, Remenyi, who played all over the world and became very famous. Brahms went into many countries with him but never came to America, where Remenyi was a great idol. Gypsy-like, he was happy in his wanderings and when he was old went into vaudeville, drawing thousands wherever he played. He was about to face one of these immense audiences in San Francisco but drew only a few tones from his beloved violin when his magic fingers were stilled in death!

Remenyi was a great influence in Brahms' life, for it was through him that Brahms became fascinated with the Gypsy Dances which the composer gave the world as *Hungarian Dances.* He wrote them for piano solos, duets and bits of them may be found all through Brahms' orchestral writings. This is folk music, even though it was not the folk music of the country in which Brahms was born.

Another important thing that came into his life through Remenyi was his meeting with Joachim, one of the greatest violinists and teachers of the world. At a concert given by Remenyi when playing the *Kreutzer* sonata of Beethoven the piano was tuned so low that Brahms was compelled to transpose the entire piano part a semitone (half-step) higher while playing it. Joachim who was in the audience came behind the stage to congratulate the players. He gave Brahms letters of introduction to Liszt, then at Weimar, and Schumann at Düsseldorf. This visit led to Schumann's article about him, mentioned at the opening of this chapter.

BRAHMS AND THE SCHUMANNS

Brahms became a favorite visitor at the home of Schumann and his brilliant wife Clara Schumann. He was hailed by all the celebrities who assembled at the frequent soirées and musicales, as a musician of great promise. His compositions show a strong influence of this early friendship. But Brahms repaid this kindness, for when the ill-fated Schumann died, he became like a son to the bereaved Clara Schumann, who loved him as one.

As this splendid pianist had played her husband's piano works all over Europe, so she made known the first piano concerto of her young friend. She made a success in spite of the fact that it was not particularly well received at its first performance at the Leipsic Gewandhaus, probably because Brahms was not as great a pianist as he was a composer. His feeling seems to have made him want to turn the piano into an orchestra. He felt everything in a massive way and was very exact.

At the age of twenty-one Brahms became Director of the Court Concerts and of the Choral Society of the Prince of Lippe-Detmold. Being very conscientious he learned much from this experience, which helped him to become a great writer of choral works as his *German Requiem* and *The Song of Fate* prove.

Outside of his music Brahms led an uneventful life. He never married, and devoted such affection as he might have given to a family to music. It is told that someone who knocked at his door, receiving no answer, entered to find him sobbing violently under the emotion caused by some music that he was composing.

When Brahms was about forty he visited Vienna and was so delighted with the musical life he found there that he remained for the rest of his days. As we note the delightful rhythm of his *Waltzes*, it is easy to believe that he felt the Viennese moods, which found their way into his compositions.

There is little to say of his general habits except that he was devotedly fond of out-door life and he interrupted his work only to take long jaunts in the open, usually in company with sympathetic friends, for he was friendly, and needed companionship. He did not give up all his time to composing, for he was director of the great *Singverein* (Choral Society) and he gave some excellent performances of the choral works of Bach, Beethoven, and of other oratorios and masses.

Brahms died (1897) at sixty-four from an illness which was aggravated by a cold he caught while attending the funeral of his friend Clara Schumann. His ashes lie in the same cemetery where Beethoven and Schubert are buried.

His Contribution to Music

Although Brahms did not create any new forms, there are so many different sides to his compositions, that it is hard to describe any one in particular. He came into the world at the time when music was turning toward the dramatic, because of Wagner's influence. It seemed that Brahms, himself, was afraid to hear Wagner, whose work he admired. Brahms never wrote an opera and he never wrote pictorial works such as tone poems. His writings were "absolute music" that is, music in its purest form, neither imitating nor representing anything but music. Here was Brahms between the tone poems of Liszt and the operas of Wagner, and he remained true to pure music! It is said that Hans von Bülow invited him to attend the first performance of *Parsifal* but he refused saying that he had a dread of Wagnerians, (but not of Wagner)! Although Brahms wrote when the romantic school was at its height, he brought back classicism with a force that influenced the entire musical world. In addition to the classic and romantic forms, many works are called *classic* to distinguish them from *popular* music.

Brahms was of the peasant type, and honesty was one of his strongest qualities. This honesty, sincerity and simplicity may be found in every line of his music, which shows throughout that he loved Bach. He left a large number of very great works, including four symphonies; two piano concertos, one for violin, and one for violin and violoncello; three string quartets and many trios, quintets and sextets; sonatas for piano, violin, violoncello, and clarinet; many piano pieces, songs, and choral numbers.

He was the center of a group of composers to whom he must have been an inspiration and an example. His lyrical gift and form, which mean that his melodies almost sing themselves, was so great that it is hard to understand why his symphonies and sonatas, to many people, sounded complex, thick and confused.

The song writers of this period were numerous as they have been in every country. Many write one or two songs that are lucky enough to become popular, but this does not make a great composer, for the great either bring something new into the world, or create music which by its quality moves other people to write good and beautiful music.

Song Writers

Brahms towered among song writers after the time of Schubert and Schumann. He carried forward the form which gave Germany fame for her *Lieder* (songs). Great beauty with simplicity of vocal melody against an accompaniment that had the character of a full-fledged piano piece distinguished Brahms' songs from those by composers of an earlier period in which the piano part was intended to give just a little support to the singer. The old songs, however, were often appealing by their very simplicity for they had almost a folk song manner.

Franz Abt (1819–1885) was one of these writers. He must have made a fortune out of *When the Swallows Home-*

ward Fly—only, as the composer can not control these things, he probably never knew that this song was to be found on nearly every piano in America for almost fifty years!

Robert Franz (1815–1892) made the world want to sing German *Lieder* for the haunting beauty of his songs. *The Rose Complained* and *In Autumn* are fair examples of a collection said to include 350 published songs.

In Chapter XXIV you have seen the place in song occupied by Schubert and Schumann. From them to Brahms does not seem such a great stretch, but only the musician knows how wide it is. The form in which Brahms wrote *Lieder* brought a new feeling to the composers, not by way of imitation, but because vocal music developed naturally into the paths along which he led the way.

Richard Strauss, known for his great tone poems, also for his operas *Salome*, *Elektra* and *The Rose Cavalier*, shortly after Brahms, wrote some of the most beautiful songs in the world.

We also find many by his colleagues, Felix Weingartner (1863), Hans Pfitzner (1869), Mahler and others, whose songs, though beautiful, showed their skill less than their operas, symphonies, and choral works.

Hugo Wolf—Song Genius

Hugo Wolf (1860–1903) has come to be regarded as one of the great composers of the 19th century. This, in spite of the fact that he composed 260 songs, almost nothing for orchestra, and in chamber music, he wrote only the *Italian Serenade*, a fascinating work for string orchestra which he arranged also for quartet. It was played in America over thirty years ago by the Flonzaley Quartet. Such a master would, no doubt, have been one of the musical beaconlights of the world, had his life not been so tragic.

His story, indeed, exceeds in unhappiness that of Schubert, Schumann, or Beethoven. Early in his life his mind began to give way, and during periods of sanity he wrote with unbelievable fluency only to be suddenly cut off. He was fully aware of his fate, and his letters describing his agony are too sad to write about.

Hugo Wolf, born at Windischgratz in Styria, was the fourth son of a musical leather-currier. The home was the scene of much chamber music in which Hugo played the second violin. Wolf frequently expressed the belief that he had some Latin blood in his veins. This seemed to show in his music for he wrote songs in Italian and Spanish style, and his opera *Der Corregidor* was from a Spanish novel. Could greater songs have been written than his *Spanish Song Book* (*Spanisches Liederbuch*)? It includes not only some brilliant folk melodies, but also noble religious songs. Romain Rolland, the French writer on musical subjects, wrote: "It has been said that the *Spanisches Liederbuch* is to Wolf's work what *Tristan* is to Wagner's."

Indeed many have compared his vivid power of expression and inspiration to Wagner's. The poems by Goethe, Moerike, Michelangelo, Heyse, Geibel, Eichendorff, etc., which he selected, proved what a high literary taste he had. For a time he was a music critic and made bitter enemies because of the abuse he hurled at Brahms. His greatest tragedy was his inability to conform to his fellowmen as pupil, teacher, critic, or human being.

Although he went to the Vienna Conservatory, he got most of his education from libraries and from reading the great masters' scores. Having no piano he could be found daily sitting on a bench in the park studying the Beethoven sonatas. But he loved Wagner best of all, and held his meeting with that master his life's greatest joy. Wolf had composed little until after he was twenty-eight; then his writing was feverish, interrrupted only by his mental lapses.

In one of these spells, he died of pneumonia, at 43. All his work was done in four or five years, for of the last nine years during five of them (1890–95) he was prostrated and often unable to speak.

BRUCKNER

Among the composers around this time and later, there are but few who have left more than a ripple on the musical ocean. Some created a stir in their own day and even now there is hot discussion about them among the critics, while some people like them and others do not.

In those days, as now, every composer had his friends and followers who thought it their duty not only to stand up for their friend, but to ridicule "the other fellow." So it was with Brahms, for in the same way that he was abused by those who measured him against Wagner, his friends refused to recognize in Anton Bruckner (1824–1896) a rival of their idol (Brahms).

Brahms was living in Vienna but he was not born there, so the feeling was strong against him when he began to threaten the position of the Viennese, Anton Bruckner, who though nine years older than Brahms, was not recognized so early. There was much in favor of Bruckner. He was a very fine musician. Themes, melodies, bubbled forth constantly like an oil-gusher, but he did not know how or when to stop them. If he had only had a keener sense of self criticism, he might have been as great a figure as Brahms and the story of his life been different.

It is wonderful, however, what he made of himself, for he was a poor schoolmaster and organist who had only his natural gifts to start with, and had little education. But he wrote nine symphonies and they were so long that at first they fairly terrified conductors to whom he brought them. He won his point, however, and lived to gain much recognition. He died in Vienna in 1896. Several of his symphonies were played in America in 1924, the centenary of his birth in Ansfelden, Upper Austria. More recently a Bruckner Society was formed.

Anton Bruckner wrote during the time of the height of Richard Wagner's glory and the dawn of Richard Strauss's fame, and was eleven years younger than Wagner, whom he idolized, and whose methods he tried to use in symphonic form.

MAHLER IN AMERICA

It would be difficult to make a definite statement about Gustav Mahler (1860–1911), for whatever be said for or against him, is sure to draw argument. He had been a storm-center for years before his death, and even afterward those against him waged war as bitterly, while those for him fought more valiantly than ever.

America was in the thick of this fight and many friendships of long standing were broken on account of it. Mahler, living in New York as recently as 1908–1911, makes us realize the more fully what men of genius have had to suffer.

Mahler was a musical genius, with astounding ability to work and amazing skill in handling his massive scores. He died at the age of fifty-one leaving so many symphonies, choral and festival works that it was a wonder how one man could have accomplished that much even had he lived to be a hundred.

We marvel at his genius, but do we want to hear often works that last for hours? Some can follow his themes, his amazing treatment of them and his ingenious writing for instruments. Others are fatigued by the length of time he dwells upon one subject and by the length of the work itself, and they sometimes object to his strong contrasts in light and shade. We are, however, thankful that America enjoyed the benefits Mahler brought, for he was one of the world's greatest conductors.

He made his American debut at the Metropolitan Opera House, January 1, 1908, and in 1909 he became conductor of the New York Philharmonic Orchestra. The labor was so hard, more in trying to adjust himself to the ideas of his Board of Directors than in the work itself, that it broke his health and he returned to his home to die.

He came here with a tremendous career behind him. Having all his life led operas and produced them in lavish fashion yet he did not write one! Like for Bruckner, whose disciple he was, a Mahler Society was founded to encourage performances of his works. He wrote nine symphonies in several of which he used large choruses. One of his most important works is *Das Lied von der Erde* (*The Song of the Earth*) for tenor, contralto and orchestra.

Gustav Mahler was born in Kalischt, Bohemia, and died in Vienna. He studied philosophy at the Vienna University and among his teachers of music were Julius Epstein and Anton Bruckner.

When Anton Seidl left the opera house of Prague, 1885–86, Gustav Mahler jointly with Angelo Neumann succeeded him. He made a great success of the Court Opera of Vienna where he was director of the house and conductor for ten years, but he demanded nothing short of perfection. His insistent ardor for the best in music and in its performance caused him the greatest unhappiness and really cost him his life.

Max Reger

Max Reger (1873–1916) caused a stir during the latter part of the 19th century and the beginning of the 20th. His father, a schoolmaster and good organist, wanted

Max to be a schoolteacher, but at an early age young Max began to write for piano and organ. After hearing *Die Meistersinger* and *Parsifal* in Bayreuth (1888) he was so stirred that he began to write big works. Reger was perhaps most influenced by Bach, and notwithstanding his very modern ideas he never lost sight of the old classic form which may have made his work seem stiff and formal at times. Some of his songs are very fine and his orchestral numbers are frequently played in America.

Max Bruch 1838–1920 was born in Berlin and besides being a composer of chamber music, three symphonies and familiar violin concertos, he wrote many choral works.

FATHER FRANCK

From this period, but not from this same country, arose one of the most important and most beautiful influences of the 19th century. We have learned enough about the world's great men to know that we can never judge by appearances, unless we are keen enough to recognize a beautiful soul when it looks through kindly eyes.

Such was the countenance of César Franck (born in Liége, Belgium, 1822—died in Paris, 1890), often called the "French Brahms"—but he was neither French, nor was he enough like Brahms to have been so called. While César Franck was not French, we may say that the entire French school of the second half of the 19th century was of his making. This, because instead of devoting himself to playing in public and making long concert tours, he preferred to have a quiet home-life so that he could compose. This seriously disappointed his father who had sent him from Liége to the Paris Conservatory.

He was but five years of age when Beethoven died, but his work throughout his entire life strongly showed the influence of the Master of Bonn, perhaps because his first teacher in Paris was Anton Reicha, a friend and admirer of Beethoven.

While all of Beethoven's nine symphonies are known and played all over the world, César Franck is known by one which is played very often and by all orchestras. Where Beethoven wrote many sonatas both for piano alone and for piano and violin, when we hear the name of César Franck, we immediately think of the one famous sonata for violin and piano which was so popular that it was also arranged for violoncello. This was written in very free and practically new form.

César Franck has written a number of fine works for piano and for orchestra, and for stringed instruments, but when it comes to organ works, it would take a large volume to carry them. Most pianists play the *Prelude*, *Aria* and *Finale*, also the *Prelude*, *Chorale* and *Fugue*, just as nearly all the violinists play the sonata, which are masterpieces. Being deep in church music, and also a very religious man, it was perhaps natural that among his best known works should be *Les Béatitudes* for orchestra, chorus and soloists, and *Redemption*, a work sung frequently by the Oratorio Societies of America and Europe. It was d'Indy who said: "In France, symphonic music originated with the school of César Franck." Although there was only one symphony, he composed a number of symphonic poems. The best known among these are *Les Éolides* (*The Æolides*), *Les Djinns* on Victor Hugo's impressive poem of that name and *Le Chasseur Maudit* (*The Accursed Hunter*). Also very well known are the piano quintet, the string quartet, and we hear sometimes the Symphonic Variations for piano and orchestra.

FRANCK AT THE PARIS CONSERVATORY

César Franck was different from most composers, for *his* father, like Father Mozart, was very determined that he

should be a pianist and took the boy on a concert tour
when he was only ten years of age! He gave concerts
throughout Belgium, and at fourteen his father took him
with his brother Joseph to the Paris Conservatory, where
later he became a distinguished professor.

There are many examples in life where a talent runs away
with its possessor. So it was with young César, who, after
only a year's schooling, entered the *concours* or competition. He covered himself with glory in the piano piece
he had to play, but when he was tested for reading at sight,
it flashed through his head how funny it would be to transpose the piece three notes lower! And so he did, without a
mistake! But the judges were so horrified that he should
dare do anything different from what was expected that
they decided not to give him the prize because he had
broken the rules! But, Cherubini, our old acquaintance
there was great enough to know what the boy had done,
and through his influence a special prize was created for
César Franck called the Grand Prix d'Honneur which has
never since then been conferred upon anyone!

César Franck was very mild and sweet in nature but
when it came to his music he was almost rebellious in his
independence. To understand the degree of his daring you
must know what a *concours* means.

The graduating classes of the Paris Conservatory are
drawn up to play their pieces and to receive the criticism
of the judges and the prizes. They all play the same thing
so the judges can tell exactly how each compares with the
other. Five of the most famous musicians of the world
are selected and they sit in judgment. Imagine this ter-
rifying ordeal! A couple of years after the first occurrence,
César Franck had to enter an organ competition, and
again his genius got away from his judgment. He was
expected to improvise a sonata on one subject given him
by the judges and a fugue on another subject. Franck

passed in very orderly fashion through the first part, but when it came to the fugue he thought how amusing it would be to work the sonata subject into the fugue subject, a feat which startled these wise judges by its colossal daring and the stupendous manner in which he accomplished it. But did they give him the first prize? Not they! Talk about "Red Tape"—he had not followed the rules and all he received out of the brilliant feat was a second prize! But the world got César Franck.

Composer, Teacher, Organist

We little realize how a tiny deed may influence the world! We may almost reckon that a kind-hearted priest was responsible for what César Franck became as a composer. After he had had the wonderful musical training at the Conservatory he refused to travel as a concert artist, but wanted to remain at home and marry. This separated him completely from his father. Besides wanting his son to play, he objected to his marrying an actress when he was twenty-six. Here is where the priest first befriended him, for he performed the ceremony that made them man and wife.

But the days of revolution in Paris (1848) were upon them and pupils did not come in great numbers. Poverty such as Franck had never known faced him and his bride. But his good friend the priest was called to a church and he immediately appointed César Franck as organist. The instrument was very fine and his happiness was complete for he loved church services above everything. This brought him directly under the musical influence of Bach, which after all, was the greatest in his life. Later he became organist of Saint Clothilde where the organ was even finer and his composing hours were fairly absorbed by writing for the organ.

The programs given by concert-organists are usually divided between Bach and César Franck, with a few numbers by Alexandre Guilmant, the great French organist, Charles Marie Widor, Theodore Dubois and a few other Frenchmen.

With all the composition that this grand old man of musical France left behind him, he left a still greater thing in the young men who were his pupils, some of whom were among the most important figures in the late 19th century.

It is a singular fact that César Franck died almost exactly as did two of his most famous pupils, Ernest Chausson and Emmanuel Chabrier. The former was killed in the Bois de Boulogne while riding a bicycle and Chabrier was killed by a fall from a horse. Their beloved professor was knocked down by an omnibus, and although he seemed to recover and continue with his lessons and composing, he became ill from the effects and died a few months later, in his 68th year.

During this last illness he wanted to get out of bed to try three new *chorales* for organ, which he read through day after day as the end approached. This was the last music from his pen for the manuscripts were lying beside him when the priest gave him the last rites of the Catholic Church.

If one could sum up the outstanding features of César Franck's music, they would be nobility and lofty spirit, true reflections of his unfaltering religious faith.

Franck's Pupils

César Franck did more than just devote teaching hours to his pupils. He had them come to his home, and surrounded by youth and enthusiasm, his own power grew greater. They played their new works for each other and for the Master, and out of this was born the *Societé Na-*

tionale (National Society). It swung both the public taste and the composers out of the light, frivolous opera of the day into a love for, and a support of French symphonic and chamber music. The Society was founded in 1871, just following the Franco-Prussian war and was a protest against the German musical domination in France, in fact it was a direct aim against Wagner. In spite of the fact that Franck was influenced by Bach, Beethoven and Wagner, he worked sincerely to develop the classic French school outside of opera form.

Another great national institution which grew out of the influence of César Franck was the famous Schola Cantorum founded by Vincent d'Indy and Charles Bordes, his pupils, and Alexandre Guilmant.

Among the Franck pupils in addition to d'Indy and Bordes may be mentioned, as a few of the foremost, Alexis de Castillon (1838–1873), Emmanuel Chabrier (1842–1894), Henri Duparc (1848–1933), famous for a group of beautiful songs, Ernest Chausson (1855–1899), Guillaume Lekeu (1870–1894), a native of Belgium and composer of *Hamlet*, a tone poem and other pieces, Pierre de Bréville (1861), Guy Ropartz (1864), Gabriel Pierné (1863–1937), Paul Vidal (1863–1931), and Georges Marty (1860–1908).

But Franck's influence touched many others including such close friends as Alexandre Guilmant and Eugène Ysaye, the renowned violinist, as well known in America as in Europe. He was a countryman of César Franck and played for its first performance anywhere, Franck's violin sonata dedicated to him.

Alberic Magnard (1865–1914) was related musically to Franck through d'Indy, his chief teacher. Magnard met death by the enemy in his own home during the World War.

We could fill many pages concerning these interesting men, but we must continue our musical journey. From among them, however, we must learn a little more about Vincent d'Indy, not only because he was famous as composer and teacher, but he also taught many Americans.

VINCENT D'INDY

Vincent d'Indy (1851–1931) a musician of rare qualities and countless achievements, was a cultured and educated gentleman. He was brought up by his grandmother, a woman of education and refinement, for his mother died when he was very young. He therefore learned to love culture and elegance early in his life, but this did not prevent him from doing the sort of work which make men a benefit to art and to mankind. In addition to being a musician, he was a skilled critic and writer, also a great teacher and organizer, proof of which may be found in what he did for France, indeed, for the world, in founding the *Schola Cantorum.* He wrote many books as well as magazine and newspaper articles and an immense number of musical compositions. He was born in Paris and was a member of the Garde-Mobile during the Franco-Prussian war.

Until the time that he left home for military service he studied the piano with Louis Dièmer, a noted pianist and teacher of Paris, and harmony with Marmontel and Lavignac, both equally famous. Upon his return from war service, his days with César Franck began, and these were precious hours for the pupil as well as for the teacher who recognized the young man's power.

He made several trips to Germany, the first in 1873 when he carried to Brahms the César Franck score of *Redemption* sent with the composer's compliments. At this time he also met Liszt and Wagner, and later he attended the Bayreuth performances including the world première (first performance) of *Parsifal.* His musical activities led him from the organ loft to becoming tympani (kettledrums) player in the Colonne Orchestra, where he went, no doubt, to learn the instruments of the orchestra and how to handle them. He found out, because he was most skilled in writing for orchestra.

He had many prominent pupils, and it was his pride and his ambition to continue along the lines laid down by César Franck. He had more than ordinary success as a conductor, going to many countries to conduct his own compositions. He came twice to America as guest conductor of the Boston Symphony appearing with that organization in its home and also in New York.

Vincent d'Indy, following the ideal of Franck, was largely responsible for the return of music in his country to symphony, from which it had strayed far. In this period there was a general feeling to bring music back to classical form. This young school was doing it in France as Brahms had done it in Germany and the result was that many composers wrote symphonies. If we look through musical history since then, we will find that the revival of a feeling for the classics helped to make the latter part of the 19th century very rich.

Although d'Indy wrote several operas, there has been no attempt to give them in this country, which is strange because it is very difficult to get operas that are worth producing at the Metropolitan Opera House or in Chicago, the only other city in America that supports its own opera on a large scale.

Until his death, d'Indy lived in Paris, where the life around him bristled with study, achievement and ambition. He was as much of an inspiration to his pupils as was his own teacher, but this is the 20th century, in which conditions, and men, are different from those of the past! He did not stand still but went steadily ahead, although his influence upon the very modern writers must have been healthy and restraining, notwithstanding the fact that only a few years ago he was regarded as a modern.

GABRIEL FAURÉ

In the musical history of France, the name of Gabriel Fauré (1845–1924) looms high. He was born in Pamiers and was taught by the Dean of French musical folk, Camille Saint-Saëns. Like all the musicians of France, no matter whether or not they planned to use it as a profession, they devoted as much time to the organ as to the piano, and most of them became famous organists even though they had not so intended. For this reason France had more fine organists and organ compositions to offer than any other country in the 19th century.

Gabriel Fauré became the organist of Rennes and later went to Saint Sulpice and Saint Honoré, and finally he became organist of the Madeleine in 1896. These churches are among the greatest in France, and to be organist in any one of them means that he was a great musician.

Fauré had honors showered upon him for he gave his country some of the most brilliant works contributed by any of her sons. In France the compositions of Gabriel Fauré are highly valued, but with the exception of a few songs, are not known in America, the more the pity. Fauré is better known here as the head of the Conservatory in which his life was spent until his recent death. He went there to share the classes in composition, counterpoint and fugue with André Gédalge, succeeding Jules Massenet, and in 1905 Fauré succeeded Théodore Dubois as Director of the Conservatory. Still more honors heaped upon him made him a member of the *Académie*, for which no one can be named until there is a vacancy. He was therefore the successor to Ernest Reyer.

In 1910 the musical world was stirred when Gabriel Fauré was made Commander of the Legion of Honor, a distinction given only when a man has done something great.

In addition to these tributes to his standing in the community and his achievements as an artist, he took numerous prizes for his compositions of which there were three operas, much incidental music, symphonies, a well known violin and piano sonata, some fine chamber music and much music for the organ and for choruses. But beyond the appreciation always shown Fauré for his larger works, he will always be loved in France because he was regarded as the French Schubert, so lovely were his melodies and so lavishly did he write.

He kept pure and true the ideals and characteristics of French music, more so, indeed, than did many who may be better known to the concert-goers of this country.

English Composers in Classical Forms

While the Germans, French and Austrians were writing, England had composers, who although not so famous, nevertheless kept music alive in England. Among them were:

Sir William Sterndale Bennett (1816–1875) with his many orchestral and choral works of which his cantata, *The Woman of Samaria*, is best known; Sir George A. Macfarren (1813–1887) with operas and oratorios, especially his cantata, *Rebekah;* his brother, Walter Cecil Macfarren (1826–1905), conductor, and composer of orchestral music; Sir John Stainer (1840–1901), organist, composer of famous anthems, and much church music, and Professor of Music at Oxford; Sir Frederick Bridge (1844–1924), organist of Westminster Abbey, writer of text-books on music, of anthems, part songs and oratorios; Sir Arthur C. Mackenzie (1847–1935), composer of many works including two Scotch symphonies and a cantata, *The Cottar's Saturday Night;* Sir Charles Hubert Hastings Parry (1848–1918), Professor of Music at Oxford after Stainer, and writer of many important books on music and of compositions in many forms; Arthur Goring Thomas (1851–1892), who wrote operas, cantatas, and many songs; Sir Frederick Hyman Cowen (1852–1935), with operas, cantatas, symphonies, chamber music; Sir Charles Villiers Stanford (1853–1924), born in Dublin, Ireland, Professor of Music at Cambridge since 1887, student of Irish folk music, and writer of chamber music and short pieces, also of valuable books on musical history and other musical subjects; Edward German (1862–1936), famous for his *Henry VIII* Dances, incidental theatre music, and an operetta, *The Moon Fairies*, in which he used the last libretto written by Sullivan's inimitable partner, Sir W. S. Gilbert; and Samuel Coleridge Taylor (1875–1912), an Englishman of African descent, whose music for chorus and for orchestra is based on American Indian legend, and on Negro folk songs.

Until his death, Sir Edward Elgar (1857–1934) was regarded as the dean of English composers. He is famous for many pieces, among which are the oratorios *The Dream of Gerontius*, *The Apostles*, other choral works, *The Enigma Variations*, symphonies, and his march, *Pomp and Circumstance*. In 1924, he was made "Master of the King's Musick."

Women Writers in England

Among the women in England, Dame Ethel Smyth (*Dame* is an honorary title in England) (1858) is known for her opera *The Wreckers*, and her comic opera *The Boatswain's Mate*. Some of her operas have been performed at the Metropolitan Opera House in New York and at Covent Garden, London. Besides she has written songs for the Suffrage Movement, incidental music, and music in large forms.

Liza Lehman (1862–1918), wrote *In a Persian Garden*, *Nonsense Songs*, and *The Daisy Chain*, which made her famous.

"Poldowski," Lady Dean Paul (d. 1932), daughter of Wieniawski, the Polish composer and violinist, wrote piano pieces and lovely songs in Debussy style. She had considerable influence in getting the work of the younger British composers and her countryman, Szymanowski, heard in London.

Rebecca Clarke, a talented Englishwoman, has written several chamber music works which place her in the foremost rank of women composers. On two occasions she received "honorable mention" in the Berkshire chamber music prize competition offered by Mrs. F. S. Coolidge, at Pittsfield, Massachusetts.

CHAPTER XXIX

Music Appears in National Costumes

WE cannot tell you very much about the early history of music in Russia, for until the 19th century, the Russians had little but their folk songs and church music. For many centuries the Christian priests disliked to have them sing their legends and folk songs because they were not of Christian origin and so music had a very difficult road to go.

Another thing which kept music as an art from growing, was the edict in the Church against the use of instruments. But as there is always a silver lining to every cloud the unaccompanied singing became very lovely.

For ages, then, there was the most strikingly beautiful natural music in the folk tunes of this gigantic country, three times as large as the United States. Its cold bleak steppes or plains and its nearness to the East gave them fascinating and fantastic legends, and a music sad, wild and colorful, with strange harmonies—their inheritance from the Slavs and Tartars. All these date back to days before the Christian era, so you can understand even though they are of surpassing beauty, the Church was afraid of the wild, tragic, pagan melodies and rhythms.

In the early 18th century, at the time of and after Peter the Great, there were many Europeans who came to Russia and brought along their music or their own national ideas of music, so that Russia had foreign opera and foreign teachers. When Catharine the Great was Queen she appreciated the wonderful store of folk legends and was very good to composers both Italian and Russian, of whom there were very few.

Very soon, a Venetian, Catterino Cavos, went to Russia and wrote Italian opera based on Russian folk songs and legends. This gave suggestions to Russians as to what could be done with their folk songs. Next came the terrible defeat of Napoleon, in 1812, by the Russians and the burning of Moscow. When important political things happen and when a favorite city is nearly destroyed, people's imaginations are stirred and it makes them think about the things of their own land. After the way was prepared by Vertowsky, Dargomyzhsky, and Seroff, Michael Glinka (1804–1857) wrote his opera, *A Life for the Tsar*, for the time was ripe for serious Russian national music. He was tired of the music of the Italians, introduced into Russia in 1737, and the French music introduced by Boieldieu and others a little after 1800. He made a close study of Russian folk song and of composition, and became the father of the new Russian music. He studied in Leningrad (St. Petersburg) with Charles Mayer and John Field, the Irish composer of nocturnes who found his way into Russia with Clementi. Glinka's travels for his health brought him to Paris where he was much interested in the works of Berlioz. When he wrote his first opera, he said he wanted the Russians "to feel at home," so he used in it the magic background of Russia with the flavor and interest of the Orient. His opera, *Ruslan and Ludmilla*, also pictures their national life. Besides this, Glinka, in some Spanish caprices, brought Spanish folk songs before the eyes of the musical art world.

Rubinstein and Tchaikovsky

An important group followed in the footsteps of Glinka, called "The Five." The members wanted national music and sincere opera in any form they desired. The Russian Ballet, which tells a story and is not a mere exhibition of fancy steps, was an outcome of this freedom.

There were two schools constantly at odds with each other. The "Russian Five" was one, and the leaders of the other were Anton and Nikolai Rubinstein and Peter Ilytch Tchaikovsky (1840–1893) whose fame is probably greater than any other Russian. Tchaikovsky was interested in the European composers and studied composition with Anton Rubinstein. He was made professor of harmony at the Moscow Conservatory in 1866. While there he wrote many operas and articles for Moscow papers. He married unhappily and had a nervous breakdown in 1877, and lived quietly, a sensitive nervous man all his life. He was aided financially by a wealthy patroness, Mme. von Meck, whom he never met. He visited New York City in 1891 and conducted his *Marche Solennelle* at the opening of Carnegie Hall. He died in Russia of cholera. Besides his symphonic poems (see page 409), he wrote several overtures, six symphonies, of which the Fourth, Fifth, and Sixth (the *Pathetic*), are famous, four suites, three ballets, eleven operas, two of which, *La Pique Dame* and *Eugèn Onegin*, have been given outside of Russia.

His works, usually very emotional and tragic, have captivating melodies, often based on folk songs, and have rich orchestral color. But withal, they were based more on the German tendencies and forms of music than those of the younger Russians, therefore, Tchaikovsky and Rubinstein were pitched in musical battle for some years against this other school.

"THE FIVE"

Alexander Borodin (1834–1887), a scientist and physician and a friend of Liszt, wrote crashing and flashy music with

what they called "Modern harmonies." It seemed full of
discords for the people of his time but to us is fascinating
and piquant! His *Prince Igor*, a story of adventure and
war not unlike *Le Chanson de Roland*, is a beautiful opera
with striking melody and dances, and Oriental color.

Modeste Moussorgsky (1839–1881) probably had more
natural genius than any of the rest of "The Five," even
though his work had to be edited by Nikolai Rimsky-
Korsakov. Moussorgsky's music had the real spirit of
Russia, sad, colorful, full of exciting dances based, as is
most of this Russian music, on the folk songs of his native
land. Besides this, it is very human and touches the soul
of people as they listen. His songs are real treasures. His
music is truly a portrait of the Russian people.

He wrote a very beautiful opera, called *Boris Godounov*,
richly laden with the Oriental color, and pathos and tragedy
of Russia's past. A very interesting thing to know is that
Rimsky, because of his wider knowledge of harmony and
orchestration, corrected Moussorgsky's works and very often
changed things that seemed to him quite wrong. Recently
we have examined a score of Moussorgsky and compared it
with the changed version of Rimsky and we now find that
Moussorgsky's score was even more vivid and modern to
our ears than Rimsky's. Several composers have arranged
for orchestra Moussorgsky's piano pieces, *Pictures from an
Exposition*, and have brought out beauties in color, humor
and scenic painting in the music.

The next man, Mily Balakirev (1837–1910), a country
boy steeped in folk songs, became the founder and leader of
this Group of Five. After founding a free music school in
St. Petersburg, he became the conductor of the Royal
Musical Society, of the Imperial Musical Society, and Imperial Chapel. His works are chiefly in orchestral form, brilliantly and effectively orchestrated. Some of his piano pieces,
such as *Islamey*, and songs are very beautiful, but his great-

est gift to music was his careful study of Russian national
story and song, and he furthered the revival of the Oriental
in Russian musical art.

César Cui (1835–1918), born at Vilna, Poland, was the
son of a French officer, and became a great authority on
military science. He wrote eight operas which were more
lyric than dramatic and, as Balakirev's friend and first disciple among "The Five," he helped this younger Russian
School principally with his writings for the press about its
members.

Last but not the least of this "Five" is Nikolai Rimsky-
Korsakov (1844–1908), who was born in Novgorod, and
while a student at the Petrograd Naval College, became an
advocate of the theories of Balakirev to keep Russian music,
Russian. While on a three-year cruise, as a young naval
officer, he wrote his first symphony, and touched the shores
of America.

Very soon he left the navy and became a teacher and
conductor in St. Petersburg. He is well known for his
orchestral suite, *Shéhérazade*, which gives a glamorous picture of some of the stories from *The Arabian Nights* as told
by the Persian Queen, Shéhérazade. Another famous work
is his second symphony, *Antar*. Probably no other person
among the Russians could give you the effect and colorfulness of the Orient as Rimsky. He takes most of his stories
from Russian legends and his operas are entrancing. The
best of these are *The Snow Maiden*, *Sadko*, and the humorous, fantastic and tuneful *Coq d'Or* (*The Golden Cockerel*).
He has written works for the piano, and some of the songs
out of his operas, such as *The Song of India* and *Shepherd
Lehl* are probably familiar to you.

Rimsky's works have been popular in this country. Concert and radio orchestras play his symphonies, tone poems,
and excerpts from his operas. *Sadko* and *Le Coq d'Or* have
been produced successfully at the Metropolitan.

These five men and the group including Anton and Nikolai Rubinstein, Sergei Tanieiev (1856–1915) and Tchaikovsky, were very antagonistic, as we said before, until finally some of the Five went on the staff of the various conservatories in Russia and the breech seemed to be healed; since then others have appeared, out-distancing even the Five in modern harmony, Alexander Scriabin (1872–1919) and Igor Stravinsky (1882).

Coming after the older Russians were Anton Arensky (1861–1906), Alexander Glazounov (1865–1936), writers of symphonies, piano pieces and chamber music, Anatole Liadov (1855–1914), Serge Liapunov (1859–1924), Nikolai Medtner (1879), Catoire, Reinhold Glière (1875), Ippolitov-Ivanov (1859–1935), Alexander Gretchaninov (1864), Serge Vassilenko (1872), Theodor Akimenko and Sergei Rachmaninov (1873) who has spent many years in America where he is known as a brilliant composer and gifted pianist. (Page 409.)

BOHEMIA—CZECHO-SLOVAKIA

Another country rich in national characteristics, donning national costume in art music as well as in folk music, is Bohemia—or Czecho-Slovakia. It is the land of harp players, street musicians and the gypsy, where nearly everybody seems to be musical. The Esterhazy family, nobles who were patrons of Haydn and other composers, were Bohemians.

In Prague, their principal city, Gluck, Mozart, Weber and many other foreigners were appreciated when their own countries turned deaf ears to them, but it is not until the middle of the 19th century, that Bohemia gave the world its own composers. Among these were Frederick Smetana (1824–1884), a pupil of Liszt and a fine pianist. He became the opera conductor at Prague and like

Beethoven, became afflicted with deafness, but it unbalanced his mind and he died in an insane asylum at sixty. He wrote a number of pieces for chamber combinations, symphonic poems, symphonies and operas of which the best known is the *Bartered Bride*, a picture of Bohemian life.

The greatest Bohemian and one of the ablest musicians of the 19th century, is Antonin Dvorak (pronounced Dvorjak) (1843–1904), a peasant and son of an innkeeper and butcher at Mühlhausen. Coming from the people, he was familiar with the folk songs, and although his father wanted him to be an innkeeper and butcher, Antonin used to follow the strolling players and showed a decided talent for music. He learned to sing, to play the violin and the organ, and studied harmony. Later he went to Prague to continue his work. He was very poor but Smetana befriended him, and five years after he entered school, he wrote his first string quartet. Thirteen years afterwards, he became organist at $60.00 a year at St. Adalbert's Church. He is another man whom Liszt helped by performing his works and finding publishers for them. He became famous through his fascinating *Slavonic Dances* and was soon invited to London after his *Stabat Mater* had been performed there. He wrote *The Spectre's Bride* for the Birmingham Festival of 1885, and his oratorio for the Leeds Festival, *St. Ludmilla*, in the following year. The University of Cambridge made him Doctor of Music and before that, he had been Professor of Music at the Prague Conservatory. Soon he came to New York and received a salary of $15,000 a year as director of the New York Conservatory of Music. Homesickness overcame him and he went back to Bohemia where his opera, *Armide*, was given before he died.

Dvorak was a sound musician. He had studied Mozart, Beethoven and Schubert but was devoted to his own folk lore and the harmonies which appealed to his nation. He

was particularly interested in national types of music and
when in America, the Negro music appealed to him tremen-
dously. While here, he knew H. C. Burleigh, the Negro
composer and singer, with whom he had an interesting and
fruitful friendship. When he went back to Bohemia, he
wrote the *New World Symphony*, built on Negro folk ideas,
and a string quartet in which he has used Negro themes.
Isn't it curious that it often takes an outsider to show us the
beauties at our own doorstep?

He wrote many songs, symphonic poems, five symphonies
and other forms of music. Although strict in the use of
form, his work was free, full of melody and imagination.
It is distinguished by warm color, beautiful rhythms and
flowing melody, daring modulations and naturalness. He
was a master of orchestration. Probably you know his famous *Humoresque* and his incomparable *Songs My Mother
Taught Me*.

Roumania

Georges Enesco (1881), a most gifted violinist, conductor
and composer, born in Moldavia, is the principal represen-
tative of Roumania. He was trained at the Paris Conservatory. His first work is *Poème Roumain*, in which, as well as
in his *Rumanian Rhapsodies*, symphonies, suites, etc., he
shows national characteristics. He wrote other orchestral
works, chamber music and songs. Since 1936 he has appeared as guest conductor of the New York Philharmonic-
Symphony Orchestra.

The Land of the Polonaise

Poland sprang into prominence in music with Frédéric
Chopin, but it has produced many other pianists and pianist-
composers,—among them, Carl Tausig.

If you like brilliant salon and much decorated pieces, you will enjoy the works of Moritz Moszkowski (1854–1924), who was born of Polish descent in Breslau. He was a fine pianist and had a long list of pupils including the brilliant American, Fannie Bloomfield-Zeisler.

Poland has given us Ignace Jan Paderewski (1860), whose *Minuet* you probably know, and whose amazing piano skill is familiar to you. While he has written many piano pieces, a fairly successful gypsy opera, *Manru*, an interesting piano concerto and a symphony, it is as pianist that he will be remembered. He has been the idol of every nation in which he has played.

His pupil, Sigismond Stojowski (1870), has lived in America since 1906 and has written orchestral works, a piano concerto and many piano pieces.

THE LAND OF THE FIORDS AND SKALDS—NORWAY AND SWEDEN

Here is another country with a rich folk-lore, half pagan and half Christian.

Ole Bull, the violinist, also did much for Norwegian music in the 19th century. One of the first composers was Halfdan Kjerulf (1815–1868) who was born in Christiania (Oslo) and studied in Leipsic. He gave up his life to composition. Henrietta Sontag as well as Jenny Lind introduced his songs to the public; like his piano pieces they are national in flavor. If you have the chance, hear his *Lullaby* and *Last Night*.

Norway! The land of the Vikings, of Odin and Thor, of the eddas and sagas, of skalds and harpists, of sprites and trolls, fiords, mountain kings and the mischievous Peer Gynt—all brought to life by the magic wand of Edvard Hagerup Grieg (1843–1907).

Surely one of the greatest poet-composers of recent

times, he brought out the beauties of the Norwegian folk song and dance, and dressed up serious music in national costume. Ole Bull assisted Grieg by recognizing his ability when he was a very young man. Grieg was sent to the Leipsic Conservatory but he overworked and became ill, and went to Copenhagen, where he met Niels Gade, under whose guidance some of his earlier works were written. He returned to Norway and was again stimulated by Ole Bull; he met a young composer, Rikard Nordraak, and together they did a good deal of work toward establishing a national school. Again Liszt acts as an international aid society to young musicians, for he now befriends Grieg in Rome. The government of Norway granted a life pension to Grieg so that he might give all his time to composition, after which he wrote incidental music to the celebrated *Peer Gynt* of Ibsen. He lived in the country and in 1885 built his villa "Troldhaugen" near Bergen. His wife, Nina, who sang many of his songs, died in 1935.

His short pieces are like portraits of Norway and he is able to catch with marvelous ease and simplicity, the peculiar harmonies, mingling minor and major keys together in a most charming way. Although a lyric writer, he has written a piano sonata, three sonatas for violin and piano, and a most effective piano concerto, all of which show brilliancy and keen dramatic sense. His *Holberg Suite* for piano and the *Elegiac* melodies and the Norwegian theme for strings are full of rich, romantic feeling. As a song writer, too, Grieg ranks very high.

Some of the other Norwegians are: Johan Severan Svendsen (1840–1911), Wagnerian in feeling yet writing his compositions with strong Norwegian color. Christian Sinding (1856), whose *Rustling of Spring* you will remember, puts on the national costume of his native Norway in his writings, although educated in Germany. Among others are Johan Selmer, Gerhard Schjelderup and Madam Agathe Backer-Gröndahl, pianist-composer of decided charm.

Jenny Lind, the "Swedish Nightingale" (1820–1887) and Christine Nilsson (1843–1921), did much to bring Norse folk songs to the attention of the world. These melodies were very much admired because they reflected the coolness and the sadness of the land of the fiords.

DENMARK

We now go to the land of Buxtehude, the celebrated organist of Lübeck. Although J. Hartmann, director of the Conservatory of Copenhagen, has been called "The Father of Danish Music," the first great composer was Niels Wilhelm Gade (1817–1890). He started as a maker of instruments, became a member of the Royal Orchestra at Copenhagen and won a prize with his first work, an orchestral overture, *Echoes from Ossian*. Mendelssohn played this in Leipsic and from this time on they were great friends. Gade succeeded him as conductor of the Gewandhaus Concerts in Leipsig; in 1848, he returned to Copenhagen and held many positions, among which was court chapel master. Gade's works were a mixture of the Romantic and the Classic Schools to which he added Danish qualities. He wrote well in symphonic style and in choruses, songs and piano pieces.

Among others were Asger Hamerik (1843–1923), a pupil of Von Bülow and Berlioz, Otto Malling (1848–1915), Ludwig Theodor Schytte (1850–1909), a student of Gade and Liszt, who lived for a long time in Germany, where he died. His short piano pieces are classics for all young piano students. Edward Lassen, Victor Emandel Bendix and August Enna are other well known Danes.

SWEDEN

The first of the romantic writers in Sweden is Anders Hallen (1846–1925). His music was somber and Wagnerian in effect, showing the influence of his native province Bohuslän. He had a great sense of melody and his marches and dances in his native style are delightful. Emil Sjögren (1853–1918) was called "The Schumann of the North," for he wrote mostly piano pieces, a beautiful violin sonata and vocal solos, showing much charm and warmth of feeling. We might add Wilhelm Stenhammar (1871–1927), who wrote operas, symphonies, chamber music and choral works, and Hugo Alfven (1872), composer of symphonies and music director at Upsala University.

MUSIC IN THE COUNTRY OF LAKES—FINLAND

Finland, "the land of a thousand lakes," and of virgin forests and meadows, has always been a country of great beauty and sadness. Jan Sibelius is the greatest (1865) of her composers. He was educated as a lawyer but being a violinist, he decided to pursue a musical career. He is remarkable as a writer of symphonic poems, and sings with compelling beauty the legends of his country taken from *The Kalevala*, the epic poem which ranks with the greatest legendary poems of all times. Besides *The Kalevala* are the short lyrics or Kanteletar, sung to the lute of steel strings, which is called *The Kantele*. These legends and songs were first arranged by Elias Lönnrot in the early part of the 19th century. The symphonic poems of Sibelius are *Karelia*, *The Swan of Tuonela* and *Lemminkäinen* from *The Kalevala*. He wrote other compositions, of course, including cantatas and ballads and string quartets and choruses. His *Finlandia* is a true picture of the Finnish people and country, and the

Fourth of his seven symphonies is one of the 20th century's monumental works. One notes in his Finnish songs a peculiar five-four rhythm which is haunting and fascinating. He was recognized as a great musician, for he is the only one of this time who drew a government pension. In 1914, Sibelius was in America for the Norfolk Festival for which he had written a special work, a symphonic poem, *Aalottaret* (Daughter of the Ocean). At the same time Yale University conferred a degree upon him. He lives far north in Finland away from cities, surrounded for many months of the year by great snow fields.

Selim Palmgren (1878) is a writer of charming piano pieces, operas and orchestral pieces. From 1923 to 1926, he was teacher at the Eastman Conservatory in Rochester, New York.

Other composers in Finland were Bernard Crusell (1775-1838), and Frederick Pacius (who was born in Hamburg in 1809 and died in Helsingfors in 1891), the Father of Finnish Music and the author of the National Hymn *Wartland* and *Suomis Song* (Suomi means Finland). He was a violinist, a follower of Spohr and composed a great many musical works.

Among others is Armas Järnefelt (1869), an orchestral conductor and composer living in Stockholm.

SPAIN—THE LAND OF THE FANDANGO

One of the most adventurous and likeable men that we have met in the history of music is Isaac Albeniz (1860-1909). He was born in Spain and started his travels when he was a few days old. He ran away from home when he was nine years old and toured about, making money by playing the piano. He loved travel and his life as a young man is a series of runnings-away-and-being-brought-back. He became a very great pianist and Alphonso XII was so pleased with his playing and so delighted with his personality, that at fifteen he was granted a pension and being free from money worry, he realized the dream of his life and went to see Franz Liszt.

He became a player approaching Von Bülow and Rubinstein in skill.

He kept composing attractive and popular Spanish tunes using the rich, rhythmic Spanish folk songs in rather new and modern harmony. He finally decided to give up his life as a popular composer and brilliant pianist, and settled down to serious composition. The next thirty pieces took him longer to write than his four hundred popular songs!

In 1893 he went to Paris in a most wonderful period, and met Debussy, Fauré, Duparc and d'Indy.

His most important composition is *Iberia*, a collection of twelve Spanish piano pieces. Among his other things are *Serenade*, *Orientale* and *Aragonaise*, all in Spanish dress.

He was a very rare personality with a rich nature, exuberant, happy and merry, even until his death.

He was the real center of Spanish music and influenced all who came after him. He was to Spain what Grieg was to Norway, Chopin to Poland, Moussorgsky to Russia, and Dvorak to Bohemia or Czecho-Slovakia.

ENRIQUE GRANADOS

Following Albeniz, was another great Spaniard, Enrique Granados (1867–1916), who was born in Lérida, Spain, and met a tragic death on a transport in the English Channel during the World War. Unlike Albeniz, he did not write in a modern vein, but rather in the accustomed harmonies. He was more Spanish for this reason than Albeniz, less original and without the great charm of the other master.

The only opera in Spanish that has ever been sung at the Metropolitan Opera House was his *Goyescas* in 1916. The principal rôle was sung by Anna Fitziu. First he wrote this as an opera in 1899. Later he made a piano version of it, very much like a suite, which was played with great success by Ernest Schelling. He also wrote symphonic poems among which was *Dante* with a vocal part, sung by Sophie Braslau, in 1915, with the Chicago Symphony Orchestra.

He is one of Spain's great sons and the rich and sincere national spirit which he put into his music makes him beloved of his compatriots.

CHAPTER XXX

America Enters

NOT long ago we visited the medieval castle of Amboise in Touraine, France, for the 400th celebration of the birth of the French poet, Ronsard. (Chapter XI.) A program of madrigals by Jannequin, Costeley, Lassus and others who had used Ronsard's poems as texts, was given in the room where the poet himself had entertained his friends. We were impressed by the beauty of the old castle and the aged towers and ramparts. It was here that we realized the meaning of TRADITION!

The peasant children passing under the watch tower in the village below the castle are reminded daily of a past replete with history and romance! They know without having been taught that here their poet, Pierre de Ronsard, and the Italian painter, Leonardo da Vinci, lived, worked and died. This watch tower was old when Columbus discovered America!

The lack of tradition, this unconscious knowing of the past, that Europe has in abundance is often held up to us in America as a serious loss in our art life. The question came to us: Is there nothing in our country to make up for the absence of this historical and romantic background?

As in a motion picture, there passed before our minds the Grand Canyon of Arizona, the Rocky Mountains, the snow-capped peaks of the Pacific slope, the Columbia River, the Mississippi and the Hudson, Golden Gate of California,

Niagara Falls, and the Plains, lonesome stretches of sand and sage-brush vast as the sea! Surely such wondrous beauty should inspire artists to create great works.

But this is a day of cities, aeroplanes, automobiles, speed and unrest, when the mind rules instead of the heart! And we must "watch our step" or we will become the slaves of this Age of Invention instead of being the masters. All this is reflected in our art life and we must guard our creative talent if we would rank with European nations in the making of music.

We already rank with them in performing it, and in organizations, such as our orchestras, opera houses, chamber music organizations, music schools, music settlements, music club activities, community singing, glee clubs, oratorio societies, and amateur orchestras. America needs music and loves it as never before. Perhaps out of all this music study and concert-giving in addition to what is being done with the radio and mechanical instruments, which are now making records of the world's finest compositions, there will come a race of real music lovers and creators. They will study our national traits and will unite them with the earnest work of American composers of today and yesterday; they will open their minds to the natural beauties of nature; they will try to raise the standard of the general public, and they will make music in America grow. May every American reader take this to heart!

In our chapter on "National Portraits in Folk Music" we told you that we have no definite traits in our music that could be called national because this country was settled by people of many different nationalities and races. All these peoples brought to the "Promised Land" their customs and traditions, their song and story world. We can still see traces in the present generation of the early settlers: New England and the South are Anglo-Saxon; Louisiana and the northern border, French; California,

Spanish; New York, Dutch; Minnesota, Scandinavian; Pennsylvania, Missouri and Wisconsin, German. Besides, the Italians, Irish, Russians and Germans have settled in all parts of this huge "melting pot"!

There is however an *Americanism* that is hard to define, but is the result of the intermingling of all nationalities. It is the spirit of the pioneer that sent our forefathers, foreigners many, across the plains in the "covered wagon"; the spirit of youth and enthusiasm of a country still new; the spirit that works out gigantic commercial problems and miraculous inventions with the same fervor with which an artist creates; it is the spirit of an inspired sculptor before the unfinished block of marble. All of which must combine in our music before we can create a national idiom.

But we must go back and travel with you the rocky road, —"Music in America."

PILGRIMS AND PURITANS

The Pilgrims and Puritans who reached our "stern and rock-bound coast" early in the 17th century did not approve of music, except for the singing of five hymn tunes! The first book printed in America was the *Bay Psalm Book* (1640) at Cambridge, Massachusetts. Its heading was:

"The Psalmes in Metre: Faithfully translated for the Use, Edification, and comfort of the Saints in publick and private, especially in New England."

"Spiritual Songs" were not at first included, but later about fifty English hymn-tunes, sung in unison were used. It went into many editions, found its way to England and Scotland, and was preferred by many to all others.

Music was forbidden as a trade in New England and a dancing master was fined for trying to start a class. The early settlers thought "to sing man's melody is only a vain show of art" and objected to tunes because "they are inspired"! So the Puritans were forbidden to invent new tunes. You can understand that an art could not easily flourish in such stony ground.

Mr. Oscar G. Sonneck, an authority on the history of American music, says in his book, *Early Concert-life in America:* "The Puritans, the Pilgrims, the Irish, the Dutch, the Germans, the Swedes, the Cavaliers of Maryland and Virginia and the Huguenots of the South may have been zealots, adventurers, beggars, spendthrifts, fugitives from justice, convicts, but barbarians they certainly were not. . . . Possibly, or even probably, music was at an extremely low ebb, but this would neither prove that the early settlers were hopelessly unmusical nor that they lacked interest in the art of 'sweet conchord.' . . . What inducements had a handful of people, spread over so vast an area, struggling for an existence, surrounded by virgin-forests, fighting the Red-man, and quarreling amongst themselves, to offer to musicians? We may rest assured that even Geoffrey Stafford, 'lute and fiddle maker' by trade and ruffian by instinct, would have preferred more lucrative climes and gracefully declined the patronage of musical Governor Fletcher had he not been deported in 1691 to Massachusetts by order of his Majesty King William, along with a batch of two hundred other Anglo-Saxon convicts.

"There were no musicians by trade, . . . and as the early settlers were not unlike other human beings in having voices, we may take it for granted that they used them not only in church, but at home, in the fields, in the taverns, exactly as they would have done in Europe and for the same kind of music as far as their memory or their supply of books carried them. That the latter, generally speaking, cannot have been very large, goes without saying. . . . Instruments were to be found in the homes of

the wealthy merchants of the North and in the homes of
the still more pleasure seeking planters of the South.
Indeed, there can be little doubt that the nearest approach
to a musical atmosphere . . . was to be found in the
South rather than in the North. Still, we might call the
period until about 1720 the primitive period in our musical
history.

"After 1720 we notice a steadily growing number of
musicians who sought their fortunes in the Colonies, an
increasing desire for organs, flutes, guitars, violins, harpsichords, the establishment of 'singing-schools,' an im-
provement in church music, the signs of a budding music
trade from ruled music paper to sonatas and concertos, the
advent of music engravers, publishers and manufacturers
of instruments, the tentative efforts to give English opera
a home in America, the introduction of public concerts, in
short the beginnings of what may properly be termed the
formative period in our musical history, running from 1720
until about 1800."

The first organ in America came from London in 1713 for
the Episcopal Church of Boston, but it remained unpacked
for seven months, as many objected to an organ at divine
services. The fate of music hung in the balance with the
Puritans but fortunately it won out.

Rev. James Lyon, a graduate of Princeton University,
"Patriot, preacher and psalmodist," published in 1792 a
collection of psalms, anthems and hymns, called *Urania*,
to which he added a few of his own compositions and a
dozen or so pages of instructions for his singing-school
in Philadelphia. Other collections followed.

WILLIAM BILLINGS (1746–1800)

William Billings, born in Boston, in 1746, was one of
our first composers. He took his music seriously, was self-

taught, and wrote his first music on leather with chalk, in the tannery where he worked. He was queer and was laughed at, but he was so sincere in his love of music that he won friends who encouraged him to publish (in 1770) a new psalm-book, *The New England Psalm Singer, or American Chorister.* As singing-schools had been formed to learn how to read and to sing the church music, the time was ripe for more difficult music than had been allowed by the Pilgrim Fathers. Billings, although he knew nothing about it, tried some experiments in counterpoint, and introduced some "fugue-tunes," which really were not fugues at all, into his hymns. That he enjoyed the result may be seen from this quotation: "It has more than twenty times the power of the old slow tunes, each part straining for mastery and victory, the audience entertained and delighted, . . . sometimes declaring for one part, and sometimes for another. Now the solemn bass demands their attention, next the manly tenor; now the lofty counter, now the volatile treble. Now there; now here again, O ecstatic! Rush on, you sons of harmony!"

In the preface to his book we find the first American musical declaration of independence, for he states that Nature and not Knowledge must inspire thought, and that "it is best for every composer to be his own carver." But later he showed a bigness of spirit, for he writes humbly: "Kind Reader, no doubt you remember that about ten years ago I published a book . . . and truly a most masterly performance I then thought it to be. How lavish was I of encomiums (praise) on this my infant production! . . . I have discovered that many of the pieces were not worth my printing or your inspection."

This second book was called *Billings' Best* because it became very popular. Many of his tunes were sung around the camp-fires of the Revolutionary Army, and even the

Continental fifers played one of his airs. He was a fiery patriot, and when Boston was occupied by the British, he paraphrased the 137th Psalm, and wrote:

> By the rivers of Watertown, we sat down;
> Yea, we wept as we remembered Boston!

This was the time when the young Mozart was astonishing the courts of Europe, and the Colossus Beethoven was born!

For a long time there was prejudice against instrumental music in New England, so the first concerts gave selections from Handel's *Messiah* and Haydn's *Creation*, which after all were oratorios.

Later William Billings' singing class in Stoughton, Massachusetts, founded in 1774 to study and perform psalm tunes and oratorios became the Stoughton Musical Society in 1786 and was looked upon as the earliest musical organization in America. It is still in existence. But Mr. Sonneck discovered that in Charleston, South Carolina, the St. Cecilia Society was founded twenty-four years earlier.

The next important society founded was the Boston Handel and Haydn. It is still alive and has had great influence on musical life not only in its native city but throughout America. After the war of 1812, a musical jubilee was held in Boston. It was so successful, that a society was formed from the fifty members of the Park Street Church choir and others interested in "cultivating and improving a correct taste in the performance of sacred music." This was the Handel and Haydn, which has lived up to its intention. The young society showed American spirit and asked Beethoven to write a work for it! The Colossus was pleased with this recognition from over the seas, and in one of his note books had written "The oratorio for Boston."

Music in Benjamin Franklin's Philadelphia

Although New England was the cradle of music, Philadelphia was the art-center in the second half of the 18th century, and went ahead of Boston in culture, because it was not held down by Puritan laws. In 1741 Benjamin Franklin published Dr. Watt's hymns, and later invented an instrument called the harmonica,—not the little mouthorgan. Franklin's instrument was a set of thirty-five circular glasses arranged on a central rod, tuned to play three octaves and enclosed in a case that looked like a spinet. There is one in New York City at the Metropolitan Museum of Art. Try rubbing the edge of your tumbler with a moist finger and you will hear the sound this instrument made.

In Goldsmith's *Vicar of Wakefield*, we read that fashionable ladies "would talk of nothing but . . . pictures, taste, Shakespeare and the *musical glasses.*" These had been invented by no less a person than Gluck! He played a concerto on twenty-six drinking glasses, accompanied with "the whole band," and claimed he could play anything that could be performed on a violin or harpsichord! It was after hearing them in London, that Franklin improved upon them and made his harmonica.

Francis Hopkinson, "First American Poet-Composer"

The title of first American composer falls on Francis Hopkinson (1737–1791), who was born nine years before William Billings. In 1759, Hopkinson wrote a secular song, *My Days Have Been so Wondrous Free*, eleven years before Billings' *New England Psalm Singer* saw the light of day. Billings was the product of New England Psalmody, was an uncouth self-taught son of the people. Hopkinson was born in Philadelphia, was a college bred man, lawyer, poet, essayist, patriot, composer, harpischord player, organist, and inventor.

He was an intimate friend of Franklin, Washington, Jefferson and Joseph Bonaparte; a member of the Continental Congress, and one of the signers of the Declaration of Independence.

He wrote in the style of Carey and Dr. Arne in England, and we have eight songs dedicated to "His Excellency George Washington, Esquire," and in the dedication Hopkinson says: "With respect to this work . . . I can only say that it is such as a lover, not a master, of the arts can furnish."

The Beggar's Opera was presented in New York in 1750 and in Philadelphia in 1759. In 1787, Washington went to a puppet opera in Philadelphia. In 1801 selections from Handel's *Messiah* were given in the hall of the University of Pennsylvania. We hear of Francis Hopkinson's playing on the first organ in Christ Church, Philadelphia, and as early as 1749, John Beals, a "musick-master from London" comes to the Quaker city to teach "violin, hautboy (oboe), flute and dulcimer," and advertises as ready to play for balls and entertainments. So we see Philadelphia growing up rapidly, with opera, oratorio, instrumental music and music teachers!

Franklin and Washington often commented on the unusually fine music that they heard in the town of Bethlehem (Pennsylvania). The early appreciation of music is continued in the yearly Bach Festival held in the Moravian Church for many years directed by Frederick Wolle (1863–1933). Musicians from everywhere attend these remarkable performances at Bethlehem.

Trinity Church in New York had an organ in 1741, although there were concerts at least ten years earlier. An English schoolmaster, William Tuckey, was the first to train choir boys for the services about 1756.

Early Opera

We should hardly expect to find French and Italian operas in America before the 1800s, but way down south in New Orleans in 1791, a troupe was giving performances of parts of operas and *vaudeville*, and perhaps an occasional opera of Grétry or Boieldieu. From 1810, the company performed opera regularly, and until recently, there was French opera in New Orleans.

Every time an opera company came to New York, *The Beggar's Opera* was played, along with other *Ballad-Operas*. In 1796, there were two operas by Americans, Benjamin Carr and Pellisier, but all details have been lost.

Louis Elson says, "At the beginning of the 19th century Charleston and Baltimore entered the operatic field, and travelling troupes came into existence, making short circuits from New York through the three large cities, but avoiding Boston, which was wholly given over to Handel, Haydn, and psalms." (*History of American Music*.)

The first time that New York heard *Home, Sweet Home* was on November 12, 1823, in a melodrama by John Howard Payne, *Clari, the Maid of Milan*. Payne, an American, wrote the words, and Henry Carey, the English composer, the music.

The first grand opera that New York heard was Weber's *Der Freischütz*. It was probably a very crude performance as they made many changes to suit public taste, but it was a great success, especially the melodramatic scenes.

In 1825, Manuel Garcia, a Spanish tenor, came to New York with his family of singers, including his daughter, who afterwards became the famous Mme. Malibran. He gave *The Barber of Seville* and ten other Italian operas which were a revelation to the new world. They called Garcia the "Musical Columbus."

After this, New York was never without some opera venture. One company followed another, and although the
people seemed to enjoy the novelty for a while, they never
gave it whole-souled patronage.

The first opera written (1845) by an American was
Leonora by William H. Fry (1813–1864). It was performed
in Philadelphia, and thirteen years later in New York. It
was in the Balfe and Donizetti style. Fry composed symphonies, and wrote for the New York *Tribune* on musical
subjects, and did much to make people realize the benefit
to be derived from cultivating music.

In 1855 George Bristow composed the second American
opera, *Rip Van Winkle*. He and Fry started a crusade
against the German musicians who had come over to
America after the revolution of 1848, fearing that they
would extinguish the feeble American flame of composing.

Orchestras

The father of American orchestras was a German oboe
player, Gottlieb Graupner. When Haydn went to London
to direct the largest orchestra formed up to that time,
Graupner played with him. Graupner went to Boston
(1799), and at once formed the first American orchestra.
About the same time in New York, a society called the "Eu-
terpian" was founded; it gave one concert a year for thirty
years! From 1820 to 1857 there was in Philadelphia, a
"Musical Fund Society"; its object was to improve musical
taste and to help needy musicians. It gave the first performance in America of Beethoven's First Symphony, as
well as choral works.

In Boston the last concert of the Philharmonic Orchestra
as Graupner's band was called, took place in 1824, and
another more important orchestra was formed sixteen
years later. Before the Boston Symphony came, an or-

chestra was given to the city by the Harvard Musical Association. It was controlled by a group brought up on Handel, Haydn and Beethoven, who would not permit their idols to be replaced by such anarchists as Berlioz and Wagner! Many of the young foreign orchestral players wanted the new works so they seceded from the Harvard Musical Association and called themselves the Philharmonic Society. As there were not enough people of musical taste to support two orchestras they were soon replaced by the Boston Symphony Orchestra, which was put on a permanent basis by Colonel Henry L. Higginson, who founded it and supported it during his lifetime. Georg Henschel conducted the first concert in 1881, and the Boston Symphony Orchestra has always been one of the greatest musical institutions in America. The conductors have been Wilhelm Gericke, Arthur Nikisch, Max Fiedler, Karl Muck, Henri Rabaud, Pierre Monteux, and Serge Koussevitsky.

The New York Philharmonic Society was founded (1842) through the efforts of a violinist, Ureli Hill, its first conductor. Among its conductors have been: Theodore Thomas, Leopold Damrosch, Anton Seidl, Walter Damrosch, Emil Paur, Wassili Safonoff, Henry Hadley, Gustav Mahler, Theodore Spiering, Josef Stransky, Artur Bodansky, Willem Mengelberg, Willem van Hoogstraten, Wilhelm Furtwängler, Arturo Toscanini, Bruno Walter, John Barbirolli, Georges Enesco, and many distinguished guest conductors.

Theodore Thomas (1835–1905), who was born in Germany but arrived here at the age of ten, was the first great musician to live in America and to advance musical conditions and standards. He gave this country its first taste for the aristocrat of music, chamber music, and with William Mason, the pianist, presented Schumann and Brahms to America. They were young radicals, and wanted to make everybody love the music they loved. Thomas introduced Wagner, too. Imagine the discussions his music raised when even Europe was torn in its opinions of the master innovator! Franz Liszt sent Thomas parts of Wagner scores which the young conductor tried out before they had been played abroad. In 1864, his own orchestra ran a close race with the New York Philharmonic Society. He toured with his men, thus giving other cities the chance to hear orchestral music. Theodore Thomas was a musical missionary! He was conductor of the New York Philharmonic (1877–79), and in 1890 the Chicago Orchestra was formed, which he conducted until his death in 1905. Frederick Stock followed Thomas, and the Chicago Orchestra has helped to cultivate music in the Middle West.

The Damrosch Family

In 1871, a German conductor, destined to develop music, came to New York and after a few months, sent for his family. This was Dr. Leopold Damrosch, who founded the Oratorio Society (1873) and the New York Symphony Society (1877), which was merged with the Philharmonic in 1928. The Oratorio Society, for many years directed by Walter Damrosch, is today conducted by a gifted American, Albert Stoessel.

In the early years, feeling ran high between the followers of Theodore Thomas and of Dr. Damrosch. Many stories are told of the rivalry in playing new European scores. One of Damrosch's greatest early triumphs was the performance of Berlioz's *Damnation of Faust*. He also gave the first performance of Brahms' First Symphony, scheduled for performance by the rival orchestra.

Dr. Damrosch's young son, Walter, played second violin in the orchestra, learning through experience, his father's profession. From 1903 to 1928 he was head of the New York Symphony Orchestra. A pioneer in directing radio orchestras, he is today the conductor of the National Broadcasting Company's Music Appreciation Hour for school children, and a commanding figure in America.

Dr. Damrosch was also a pioneer in introducing Wagner to us. Two years after the Metropolitan Opera House was built (1882), he was made director and conductor of German opera. He imported some of the great Wagnerian singers, Madame Materna, Marianne Brandt, Mme. Seidl-Kraus, Anton Schott, and others. Wagner opera had come to stay. After a short illness, Dr. Damrosch died (1885) and Walter, then twenty-three years of age, fell heir to the position of conductor at the Metropolitan and of the Oratorio Society. Through his efforts, Lilli Lehmann, foremost Wagnerian singer, was engaged, also Emil Fischer, basso, Max Alvary, tenor, Anton Seidl, conductor, and Mme. Lillian Nordica (Lillian Norton), one of the first Americans at the Metropolitan.

Walter Damrosch composed *Danny Deever* on the poem by Rudyard Kipling. One never can think of this stirring song, without remembering David Bispham, who sang it into fame. Bispham was another native, who was for years a member of the Metropolitan Opera Company, and an oratorio singer. Damrosch is the composer of three grand operas, *The Scarlet Letter* on a text from Nathaniel Hawthorne's novel, *Cyrano de Bergerac*, of Edmond Rostand's, made into a libretto by W. J. Henderson, and *The Man Without a Country* on E. E. Hale's story. He also wrote incidental music to three Greek Tragedies *Iphigenia in Aulis*, *Medea* and *Electra*, first performed in the open air theatre of the University of California, by Margaret Anglin and her company. *Cyrano* was completely revised in 1939.

Damrosch married the daughter of James G. Blaine in 1890, and soon after, he started an opera venture which for several years visited the large cities and brought Wagner into many places where his music had been merely a hearsay.　Damrosch was a pioneer in championing the cause of new composers, and many well known European works had their first American performances at his New York Symphony concerts.

Dr. Frank Damrosch (1859–1937), an older brother, was an important educator, the head of the Institute of Musical Art, and was once conductor of the Oratorio Society and of the "Musical Art Society." Dr. Frank Damrosch also founded the People's Choral Union in which working men and women were taught singing and became members of a chorus of twelve hundred voices which performed the classic oratorios. He also founded the Young People's Concerts, which have brought to young people of New York the finest music the world has produced. For several years, Walter Damrosch had these in charge, and his talks explaining the works performed were quite as enjoyable as the music. Since 1924, Ernest Schelling has continued the children's concerts with what is now the Philharmonic-Symphony.

THE MASON FAMILY

Another famous family in American music is the Mason family, dating back to Lowell Mason (1792–1872) who was born at Medfield, Massachusetts. His principal work was a collection of hymn tunes which he harmonized, and won him the title of "Father of American Church Music." He was president and conductor of the Handel and Haydn Society, and was a born teacher. He travelled from one society to another in distant cities, training choruses, giving encouragement and advice. He moved to New York in 1851.

Lowell Mason's third son, Dr. William Mason (1829–1908), was also a pioneer. In his long life he saw music grow in America from crude beginnings to a height that seems almost unbelievable, in one short century. He not only heard, but he played piano concertos with orchestras as fine as those he found in Europe when he went to study with Moscheles, Hauptmann, Richter, and Franz Liszt. Mason was one of the young artists permitted to be a friend as well as a pupil of the kindly Music Master. Dr. Mason and Theodore Thomas were the first to give chamber music concerts, and thus introduced many masterpieces of Brahms and Schumann, for as "modernists" they loved to bring new compositions to the public. Dr. Mason, in his whole-hearted love of his art, his sincerity and geniality, is worthy of our deepest respect and admiration. He composed about fifty piano pieces, and with W. S. B. Mathews, arranged a piano method that was very popular and successful. We feel sure that if you search in that old box of music that mother used to study, you will find a copy. No doubt she played his *Silver Spring*, *Rêverie Poetique* and *Danse Rustique*.

Daniel Gregory Mason (1873), one of the foremost composers, lecturers and writers on music, is a nephew of Dr. William Mason and grandson of Lowell Mason. He was graduated from Harvard University in 1895. His compositions include sonatas, a string quartet on Negro themes, a piano quartet, three symphonies, a fugue for piano and orchestra, a Russian Song Cycle, piano pieces, etc. Dr. Mason has written many valuable books on musical subjects and on Music Appreciation, and is at present MacDowell Professor of Music at Columbia University.

GOTTSCHALK—THE PICTURESQUE

We have been telling you about the composers in the northern part of the United States, and those who had come from Germany like the Damrosch family, but here is one composer and gifted pianist who brought a new color into American music. Louis Moreau Gottschalk (1829–1869), born in New Orleans, was the child of an English father and Creole mother, thus mixing Spanish, French and English blood. He was an infant prodigy; he played the piano at four, the organ at six, and at thirteen he went to Paris to study. He was praised by Chopin, and appeared in concerts with Hector Berlioz. He charmed everyone who heard him, and was the first American pianist to receive European honors. The Infanta of Spain made a cake for him and a celebrated bull-fighter gave him a sword! He toured Cuba and North and South America, giving more than a thousand concerts. But the life was too hard on him and he died at the age of forty in Rio Janeiro, Brazil.

The Last Hope, Ojos Creollos (*Creole Eyes*), *Banjo, Souvenirs of Andalusia* are among the most popular of his ninety compositions for piano, which showed the strong influence of life in Louisiana, his love of sunshiny Spain, and his study in France. Here we find rhythms closely related to rag-time and jazz, as well as the slow fascinating Spanish dance. Today his works are forgotten, but for many years they were played throughout the land.

Stephen Collins Foster

Stephen Collins Foster (1826–1864), for whom we have claimed the right to be called a composer of folk songs, was born in Lawrenceville (Pittsburgh), Pennsylvania, on the fiftieth anniversary of our Declaration of Independence. The understanding he had of the Negro came to him because his parents were Southerners. He showed talent for music when he was very young, and learned by himself to play the flageolet when he was seven years old. He was very self-willed and did not like discipline, so he taught himself practically all he knew of music. His first composition, *Tioga Waltz* for four flutes, was written when he was a school boy. It was first played in school, with Stephen in the lead. His first song, *Open thy Lattice, Love*, was published in 1842. For several years, five boys met at the Foster home, and Stephen taught them to sing part songs. He composed many pieces for them, among them *Oh, Susannah, Old Uncle Ned* and *Old Black Joe.*

About 1830, an actor, Thomas Rice, had the idea of dressing up like an old negro porter in Pittsburgh, from whom he borrowed the clothes, and singing a song he had heard from a negro stage driver:

> Turn about and wheel about, and do jist so,
> And ebery time I turn about, I jump Jim Crow.

The song, accompanied by a dance, took the audience by storm, especially when the porter appeared on the stage, half dressed, and demanded his clothes, because the whistle of the steamboat had just blown and the old fellow had to "get back on the job." So "Daddy" Rice became the father of "Negro Minstrels," and travelled all over America and even England, singing and dancing negro songs. A few years later Stephen Foster sent his *Oh, Susannah* to a travelling minstrel troupe, and the song took "like wild fire." He decided to write songs as a profession, in spite of his family who thought he had wasted time "fooling around" with music, and insisted on his going to work.

While *Oh, Susannah* is a "rollicking jingle," *Old Uncle Ned* is the "first of the pathetic negro songs that set Foster apart from his contemporaries and gave him a place in musical history," says Harold Vincent Milligan. "In this type of song, universal in the appeal of its naïve pathos he has never had an equal."

Another claim he has as a folk song composer, is that

he never studied as most people do who want to be composers. He knew very little about harmony and less of counterpoint, and his is "music that has come into existence
without the influence of conscious art, as a spontaneous
utterance, filled with characteristic expression of the feelings of a people." (H. E. Krehbiel.) Perhaps he was right
when he said that he was afraid that study would rob
him of the gift of spontaneous melody that was his to such
a marked degree, because he was not naturally a student
and might never have carried his studies far enough. At
any rate we have every reason to be grateful for the simple
direct songs which are dear to us and as near to our hearts
as any folk song of any age or country whose author has
been forgotten!

He was sweet-natured, irresponsible, refined and sensitive, but easily influenced. His publishers made $10,000
out of his songs, but he made little and spent much. He
married in 1850, but the union was not happy.

During his last years spent in New York, he was poverty-
stricken and miserable, and sold his songs, as soon as they
were written, for a few dollars in order to live. It seems too
bad to have to say that much of his money and his life
were squandered thoughtlessly.

Curiously enough, his favorite poet was Edgar Allan
Poe, whose life resembled his own in many sad details.
He loved to go up and down in the Broadway stages, often
thinking out his melodies as he rode. This reminds us of
Walt Whitman, who rode up and down Fifth Avenue along-
side his friend Pete Dooley, the driver of the stage coach!

Stephen Foster died in New York in 1864 as the result
of an accident in which he had severed an artery. He was
saved from burial in Potter's Field, by the arrival of his
brothers and his wife, and he was buried in Pittsburgh
beside his parents whom he had immortalized in *The Old
Folks at Home.*

CHAPTER XXXI

America Comes of Age

FOR many years Boston was a center of musical life. At the close of the Civil War a school was well under way in New England, which we might call the classical period of American music.

B. J. LANG

Although Benjamin J. Lang (1837–1909) never published his compositions and never allowed them to be heard, he had much influence on Boston's musical life, having been conductor of the Handel and Haydn and of the St. Cecilia societies, and the piano teacher of such musicians as Arthur Foote, William Apthorp, Ethelbert Nevin and Margaret Ruthven Lang, his daughter.

JOHN KNOWLES PAINE

John Knowles Paine (1839–1906), was the first professor of music at Harvard. In 1862, he gave his services without pay for a course of lectures on music, but they were not appreciated. When President Eliot became head of the University, music was made part of the college curriculum. In 1875 Paine became head of the department. In 1903, Walter R. Spalding was made assistant, and after Paine's death was head until 1928.

Professor Paine was the first American who wrote an oratorio. *St. Peter* was performed in 1873 in Portland, Maine, his birthplace. Next, he wrote two symphonies, one of which was often played by Theodore Thomas. Paine's *Centennial Hymn* opened the Philadelphia Exhibition, with more success than the Wagner March, it is said.

Professor Paine was a pioneer in many fields of American composition and taught American composers to follow in the lines of sincerity and honesty which he carved out for himself.

DUDLEY BUCK

Dudley Buck (1839–1909), was a noted organist, composer and teacher. He did not remain in New England (Hartford, Connecticut) where he was born, but held church positions in Chicago, Cincinnati, Brooklyn, and New York, and was active in the musical life of these different cities. His principal works were anthems and hymns, still in use, music for the organ and valuable text-books, also many popular cantatas.

GEORGE CHADWICK

George Chadwick, one of our most important composers, was born in Lowell, Massachusetts, in 1854. He studied in Germany with Reinecke, Jadassohn and Rheinberger, three celebrated teachers who had more to do with forming the taste of the 19th century American composers than any American teacher.

Chadwick came of a musical family. His musical life began as alto singer in a Lawrence church choir, where later he blew the bellows of the organ, but soon was promoted from blowing to playing it. He began composing while in High School. He was a student at the New England Conservatory, founded in 1867, but was not allowed to study with the idea of becoming a professional. When he saw that he would receive no further help from his father toward music-training, the young musician of twenty-two went to Michigan for a year. He taught music, conducted a chorus, gave organ recitals, saving enough to study in Leipsic. Jadassohn told Louis Elson that Chadwick was the most brilliant student in his class.

In 1880, Chadwick returned to Boston where he lived until his death. From 1880 he was first, teacher, then musical director of the New England Conservatory. Some of his pupils became leaders in American music,—Horatio Parker, Arthur Whiting, J. Wallace Goodrich (organist), Henry K. Hadley and others.

Chadwick composed more orchestral works than any other American of his time. His list includes three symphonies, a sinfonietta, six overtures, three symphonic sketches for orchestra, a lyric sacred opera, *Judith*, music to the morality play, *Everywoman*, much chamber music, many choral works and about fifty songs, best known of which is *Allah*. He died in 1931.

ARTHUR FOOTE

Arthur Foote (1853–1937) is one prominent composer whose training bears the label "made in America," for he never studied abroad. He was born in Salem, Massachusetts, and worked with Stephen Emery, a prominent theory teacher. Foote was graduated from Harvard in 1874, where he studied music in Professor Paine's department. After organ study with B. J. Lang, Foote became organist of the First Unitarian Church founded in 1630, which post he filled from 1878 to 1910. This is doubtless the longest record of an organist in one church in America. Foote was one of America's finest teachers, and influenced many, not only by his teaching, but by his broad-minded criticism. His harmony text-book, written with Walter R. Spalding, is one of the most valuable and reliable in the musical world.

Foote wrote scholarly and beautiful chamber and orchestral music which placed him in the foremost ranks of American composers, but he won the hearts of the entire English-speaking world by two little songs, *Irish Folk Song* and *I'm Wearing Awa'*.

HORATIO PARKER

Horatio Parker (1863–1919) inherited his talent from his mother who played the organ in Newton, Massachusetts, but she had a hard time interesting her son in music, for he disliked it very much. But at fourteen he had a change of heart going to the other extreme of having literally to be dragged away from the instrument. He studied with Emery and Chadwick, and then went to Germany to work with Rheinberger. He was organist in several churches and in 1894 was made professor of music at Yale University where he remained until his death.

In 1894, his best known work was performed in Trinity Church, New York. It is an oratorio, *Hora Novissima* (*The Last Hour*), on the old Latin poem by Bernard de Morlaix, with English translation by Parker's mother also the author of the librettos for two other of his oratorios. *Hora Novissima*, one of America's most important works, has been performed often, not only in this country, but it was the first American work given at the English Worcester Festival. It was so successful that Dr. Parker received the commission to write for another English festival at Hereford, and he composed *A Wanderer's Psalm*. This was followed by *The Legend of St. Christopher* which contains some of Parker's most scholarly contrapuntal writing for chorus. As another result of England's recognition of his music, Cambridge University conferred upon the American composer the honorary degree of Doctor of Music.

Parker won the prize of $10,000 offered by the Metropolitan Opera Association (1911) for the best opera by an American. This was *Mona*, a story of the Druids in Britain, for which Brian Hooker, the American poet, wrote the libretto. In spite of having been a prize winner, it had no public success and did not outlive its first season.

In 1915, Parker and Hooker won another $10,000 prize offered by the National Federation of Music Clubs, with an opera called *Fairyland*. It has not seen the light of day since its performances in Los Angeles.

FREDERICK CONVERSE

Frederick Converse (1871) of Boston, was graduated from Harvard (1893) when his opus 1, a violin sonata, was publicly performed. After study with Chadwick, he went to Germany to Rheinberger, returning in 1898 with his first symphony under his arm. He has since written three others, and many orchestral and chamber music works. He has often set Keats, the English poet, or used his writings as inspiration for his music,—*Festival of Pan* and *Endymion's Narrative*, two symphonic poems, and *La Belle Dame sans Merci*, a ballad for baritone voice and orchestra. He also wrote a fantasy on Walt Whitman's *Mystic Trumpeter*, and his humor is revealed in *Flivver Ten Million*. Converse was the first American to have an opera, *The Pipe of Desire*, produced by the Metropolitan Opera Association (1910).

TWO COLLEGE PROFESSORS

David Stanley Smith, a native of Toledo, Ohio (1877), belongs to this New England group, for he was graduated from Yale University. He taught in the music department and became its dean in 1919. He has composed four symphonies and excellent chamber music. Several of his early string quartets were played by the famous Kneisel Quartet (1886–1917) which organization had a generous share in improving American musical taste.

Edward Burlingame Hill (1872), grandson of a former president of Harvard, was made head of its music department in 1928. He has composed three symphonies, symphonic poems, ballets, chamber music, songs, and piano pieces. He has written articles on music and a book, *Modern French Music.*

Mrs. H. H. A. Beach Prepares the Path for American Women

One of the most important composers of the New England group, is Mrs. H. H. A. Beach (1867). She was Amy Marcy Cheney, an astonishing little child who, before her second year, sang forty tunes. Louis Elson tells that at the age of two she was taken to a photographer, and just as he was about to take the picture, she sang at the top of her voice, *See, the Conquering Hero Comes!* She could improvise like the old classic masters, and could transpose Bach fugues from one key to another, at fourteen. When sixteen, she made her début as a pianist, and at seventeen she played piano concertos with the Boston Symphony Orchestra, also with Theodore Thomas' orchestra.

Mrs. Beach received her training in America. Her first work in large form was a mass sung in 1892 by the Handel and Haydn Society. She next composed a *scena* and *aria* for contralto and orchestra, sung with the New York Symphony Society. It was the first work by a woman and an American to be given at these concerts, which Walter Damrosch conducted.

In 1893, Mrs. Beach's *Festival Jubilate* opened the woman's building at the Chicago Columbian World's Exposition. She has composed two piano concertos, a symphony (*The Gaelic*), a violin sonata, a quintet for flute and strings, a piano trio, many piano pieces and splendid songs, among which must be mentioned *The Year's at the Spring*, *June*, and *Ah, Love, but a Day*. She has recently written many fine sacred choral numbers.

Mrs. Beach prepared the way for other American women, not only by showing that women could write seriously in big forms, but also by her sympathetic encouragement of talent and sincerity wherever she finds it.

Margaret Ruthven Lang (1867), daughter of B. J. Lang, is also a Boston composer. *Irish Mother's Lullaby* is the best known of her many art songs, in addition to which she has written an orchestral *Dramatic Overture* which Arthur Nikisch played, when he was conductor of the Boston Symphony Orchestra.

Among our best song writers are many women:—Harriet Ware, Gena Branscombe, Alice Barnett, Fay Foster, Eleanor Freer, Mana Zucca (who has written also a piano concerto, and piano pieces), Rhea Silberta, Ethel Glenn Hier (piano pieces and songs), Fannie Dillon (piano pieces and violin compositions), Mabel Wood Hill (songs, chamber music and Bach arrangements for string orchestra), Marianne Genet (songs and fine choral works), Lily Strickland, Mabel Daniels (orchestral and important choral works), Katherine Ruth Heyman (songs, and a book, *Relation of Ultramodern Music to the Archaic*), Rosalie Housman (songs, piano pieces and a Hebrew Temple Service), Gertrude Ross, Mary Turner Salter, Florence Parr Gere, Clara Edwards and Pearl Curran, writers of several popular successes. And although she is not a composer of art songs, we must not forget Carrie Jacobs Bond, whose *End of a Perfect Day* has sold in the millions, and her songs for little children have brought joy to many.

One of Our Most Scholarly Musicians

Another Boston musician and composer, teacher of piano and composition was Arthur Whiting (1861–1936), nephew of the organist and composer George Whiting. He made a specialty of harpsichord music, and added to musical culture by his recitals on the old instrument. After 1895, he lived in New York City until his death.

Charles Martin Loeffler—First Impressionist in America

Charles Martin Loeffler was a composer belonging to a different class from any of the Boston group just mentioned. He was French by birth, as he was born in Alsace in 1861, French in his musical training and in his musical sympathies. For fifty-three years he lived in Boston, twenty of them at the second desk (next to the concert-master) of the Boston Symphony Orchestra. He was the first composer to write in this country, the kind of music that existed at the end of the 19th century in France,—like that of Fauré, Dukas, Chausson and Debussy. The seed he planted did not fall on fertile soil, for all his fellow musicians as well as the orchestral conductors, from whose hands the public received its music, were Germans and German trained. They knew their "three B's," their Wagner and even the French Berlioz, but Loeffler brought something different, something disturbing, something not easy to place. His music belonged neither to the classical nor to the romantic school.

Not only in America did this new French music have a fight, but on its own ground in France was it misunderstood! But you have seen from Monteverde to Wagner that the path of true innovation never ran smooth!

Loeffler's work was original, the work of a musician completely master of the modern orchestra and of modern harmony with its colorful and expressive effects. Besides this there was a spirit that never before had come into art. This was given the name of *Impressionism*, the getting of effects from objects, painted, or described in literature, without elaborate details. In music, composers who try to suggest to the hearer an image existing in their own minds are called Impressionists. This image may be a thought, an emotion, a definite object, a poem, a picture, a beautiful tree, the grandeur of Niagara, any one of a thousand things that await the hand of the Alchemist-Musician to be transmuted into tone.

All Loeffler's compositions reflect this impressionism, and he was the first, but not the last of these poetic tone impressionists in America. He was foremost a composer of symphonic poems: *La Mort de Tintagiles* (*The Death of Tintagiles*) after the play by Maurice Maeterlinck, *A Pagan Poem* after Virgil, *La Bonne Chanson* (*The Good Song*) after Verlaine, *La Villanelle du Diable* (*The Villanelle of the Devil*), *The Mystic Hour* with male chorus, *Psalm 137* with female chorus. He also wrote an eight part mixed chorus, *For One who Fell in Battle*. Other orchestral works include a suite in four movements for violin and orchestra, *Les Veillées de l'Ukraine* (*Evening Tales of the Ukraine*), concerto for 'cello and orchestra, first played by Alwyn Schroeder with the Boston Symphony Orchestra, *Divertissement* for violin and orchestra, and *Spanish Divertissement* for saxophone and orchestra. Important works for chamber music include: two rhapsodies for clarinet, viola and piano, an octet for strings and two clarinets, a quintet, *Music for Four Stringed Instruments*, and a quartet built on Gregorian modes; and he wrote songs for medium voice and viola obligato with French texts by Verlaine and Baudelaire. He died in 1935 near Boston.

The Red Man Attracts Composers

The next composer, Henry F. Gilbert, born in Somer-
ville, Massachusetts (1868), brings us into an interesting
field, the study of Negro and Indian folk music. After
working with Edward MacDowell, Gilbert turned his
attention to a thorough investigation of Negro music,
resulting in orchestral works based on Negro themes
such as, *American Humoresque, Comedy Overture on Negro
Themes, American Dances, Negro Rhapsody,* and *The Dance
in Place Congo,* a symphonic poem which was mounted as
a ballet at the Metropolitan Opera House (1918).

Gilbert tells that the *Comedy Overture* was rescued from
a wreck that was to have been a Negro Opera, based on
Joel Chandler Harris' *Uncle Remus.* What a pity he did
not complete it!

The *American Humoresque* is based on old Negro minstrel
tunes like *Zip Coon, Dixie,* and *Old Folks at Home.*

Gilbert was one of the founders of the Wa-Wan Press,
established at Newton Center, Massachusetts, by Arthur
Farwell. It was organized (1901) by composers in the
interest of American compositions, and to study and encourage the use of Indian music. Gilbert died in 1928.

Arthur Farwell was born in St. Paul, Minnesota (1872).
He attended college in Boston and studied music with
Homer Norris (1860–1920), a Boston organist and composer,
whose cantata *Flight of the Eagle* was based on a Walt
Whitman poem. Farwell was also a pupil of Humperdinck
in Berlin and Guilmant in Paris. The Indian music research, in which he is a pioneer, led him into the West to
live among the Redskins and to make phonograph records of hundreds of tunes. He is also interested in community singing and music for the people. Practically a
new field is his music for Percy MacKaye's pageants *Cali-
ban* and *The Evergreen Tree.*

Carlos Troyer, a very old Californian who died recently, spent his life collecting Zuni and Mojave-Apache songs, having realized their artistic value long before any one else. In his youth he was an intimate friend of Liszt. He travelled, later, through South American jungles, with his violin and music-paper, writing down the tunes he heard, and several times he would have been burned by the savages, but saved himself by playing for them.

Harvey Worthington Loomis (1865–1930) contributed a piano version of Omaha Indian melodies to the Wa-Wan Press (1904) called *Lyrics of the Redman*. In the preface Loomis shows that Indian themes should be used impressionistically, for he says: "If we would picture the music of the wigwam and the war path we must aim by means of the imagination to create an art work that will project, not by *imitation* but by *suggestion*, the impression we have ourselves received in listening to this weird savage symphony in its pastoral *entourage* (surroundings) which, above all, makes the Indian's music sweet to him."

Natalie Curtis' valuable service to Indian and Negro music was cut off by her tragic death in Paris (1921), from an automobile accident. Fortunately she left several works in which she gave not only information on the music of these primitive Americans and also the *Songs and Tales of the Dark Continent of Africa*, but in them she set down quite unconsciously the beauty of her character and the sincerity of her purpose. There are four volumes of Negro Folk Songs, and *The Indians' Book*, besides the African book. Recently we heard two Spanish-Indian melodies, a *Crucifixion Hymn* and *Blood of Christ*, that Miss Curtis found in use in religious festivals near Santa Fé, New Mexico. They are Spanish in character, and are almost unaltered examples of the songs of the Middle Ages brought down to us by the Indian. These were arranged by Percy Grainger according to directions left by Miss Curtis.

Several American operas have been written on Indian legends and it would be difficult to find more picturesque subjects.

Our Light Opera Genius

Victor Herbert's *Natoma*, given by the Chicago Opera Company in 1911, is an Indian story and one of his two grand operas. Born in Dublin, Ireland (1854), Herbert was the grandson of the novelist Samuel Lover. He was educated in Germany, and was a fine 'cellist. He came to the Metropolitan Opera orchestra as first 'cellist in 1886, and since then until his death in 1924, he delighted every one with his incomparable melodies in light operas.

After Patrick Gilmore's death, Herbert in 1893, became bandmaster of the 22nd Regiment band which had become famous in 1869 and 1872 for two monster Peace Jubilees held in Boston. We think the 20th century, the age of gigantic enterprises, but——! for the first Jubilee, Gilmore had a chorus of 10,000 voices, and a band of 1,000! Not satisfied with this volume, in the second Jubilee he doubled the number! He also had cannons fired to increase the drum battery!

From Gilmore's Band, Herbert became conductor of the Pittsburgh Symphony, also guest conductor of the New York Philharmonic Orchestra, but he had made such a success as composer of light operas, that he finally devoted all his time to the theater. Among Herbert's most popular successes are: *The Serenade*, *The Idol's Eye*, *Babes in Toyland*, *Mlle. Modiste*, *Naughty Marietta*, *The Madcap Duchess*, etc.

Julian Edwards (1855–1910), like Victor Herbert was born a British subject, in Manchester, England, and was a successful composer of light opera. He also wrote many sacred cantatas.

Sousa, the March King

Our most famous bandmaster was the "March King," John Philip Sousa (1856–1932), once leader of the United States Marine Band. Who was not marched to *Stars and Stripes Forever*, *Washington Post*, or *Liberty Bell?* Who does not love them, be he "high" or "low brow"? With Sousa leading, the band played around the world, and no American composer was better known abroad. In fact, Sousa's music was considered as "typically American" a generation ago as is swing today.

Cadman's Indian Opera

Charles Wakefield Cadman's Indian opera *Shanewis* was given at the Metropolitan in 1918. He is known for many songs which had popularity, among them *At Dawning* and *The Land of the Sky-blue Water* on a lovely Indian theme. Born in Johnstown, Pa. (1881), Cadman studied music in Pittsburgh. He lectured for years on Indian music. He has written other operas, including *A Witch of Salem*, orchestral and choral works, and chamber music. He makes California his home.

Arthur Nevin (1871), brother of Ethelbert Nevin, lived among the Blackfoot Indians, studying their music and gathering themes for his opera *Poia*, which was produced in Berlin (1910). For several years he was head of the choral and extension work at the University of Kansas.

A professor at the same college is the New Englander, Charles Sanford Skilton (1868), writer of cantatas, Indian operas, and orchestral works based on Indian themes.

Thurlow Lieurance (1878), also an authority on Indian music lore, is well known for the song *By the Waters of Minnetonka*, a genuine Indian melody. He has written other songs and a drama based on Indian themes, among which is a Navajo blanket song.

The blankets woven by the Navajo women are not only remarkable examples of primitive art, but tell the stories of the tribe. No two blankets are the same, and like the music we write, are expressions of the weaver's hopes, fears, joys and sorrows.

Homer Grunn (1880) who taught piano in Phoenix, Arizona, profited by the opportunity to gather Indian tunes, which he has put into songs, a music-drama and orchestral works. In 1910 he settled in Los Angeles.

ETHELBERT NEVIN—POET-COMPOSER

Ethelbert Nevin (1862–1901) told his father that he would not mind being poor all his life if he could just be a musician! And the father, a music lover himself, allowed his sensitive, dream-loving, poetic son to study in America and in Europe. Perhaps "Bert's" mother had something to do with the decision, for she, too, was sensitive and fine, and so much of a musician that her grand piano was the first to cross the Allegheny mountains into Edgeworth, the town near Pittsburgh where the Nevins were born.

Ethelbert Nevin was a romanticist who found the medium of his expression in short songs and piano pieces. He had a gift of melody surpassed by few and he reached the heart as perhaps no other American except Stephen Foster had done. *Narcissus* for piano and *The Rosary* have swept through this country selling in the millions. *Mighty Lak' a Rose*, published after his early death, was a close third. Several others of his songs may be ranked among the best that America has produced. Nevin was what Walt Whitman would have called a "Sweet Singer."

ROBIN HOOD AND HIS MERRIE CREW COME TO LIFE IN THE 19TH CENTURY

Reginald de Koven (1859–1920) will ever be remembered for his delightful light opera *Robin Hood* on which we were brought up. His song, *Oh, Promise Me*, will probably be sung when he will have been forgotten. De Koven's last two works were operas, of which *Canterbury Tales* after Chaucer was performed at the Metropolitan Opera House and *Rip Van Winkle* from Washington Irving and Percy Mackaye, by the Chicago Opera Company. One of his best songs is a setting of Kipling's *Recessional*.

"Pilgrim's Progress"—An American Oratorio

One of the most respected American composers is Edgar Stillman Kelley, born in Sparta, Wisconsin, in 1857, whose American forefathers date back to 1650. After study in Stuttgart, Kelley went to California, where he was composer, teacher, critic, lecturer, writer and light opera conductor. Later he was professor at Yale, dean of composition at the Cincinnati Conservatory, and since 1910, a fellowship at the Western College at Oxford, Ohio, gives him the leisure and economic freedom to compose. His orchestral works include incidental music to *Ben Hur*, *Aladdin*, Chinese suite, a comic opera, *Puritania*, *Alice in Wonderland*, two symphonies, *Gulliver* and *New England*, incidental music to *Prometheus Bound*, and an oratorio based on Bunyan's *Pilgrim's Progress*. If you do not know Kelley's delightful song, *The Lady Picking Mulberries*, allow us to introduce the little Chinawoman to you. You will meet at the same time an old acquaintance,— Mr. Pentatonic Scale.

Several of the older school of composers in America, faithful pioneers whose works are rarely heard now were Silas G. Pratt (1846–1916); Frederic Grant Gleason (1848–1903), who lived and worked in Chicago from 1877 to the time of his death; William Wallace Gilchrist (1846–1916), a writer of cantatas and psalms, Episcopal church music, two symphonies, chamber music and songs. who spent most of his life in Philadelphia; Homer N. Bartlett (1846-1920), composer of piano pieces; William Neidlinger (1863-1924), writer of many charming children's songs.

Frank van der Stucken, who was born in Texas, in 1858, lived in Europe from 1866 until 1884. He was the first conductor to give an entire program of American orchestral works in America and also at the Paris Exposition of 1889. For years he was conductor of the Cincinnati Symphony Orchestra and he composed many large orchestral works. He died abroad in 1929.

Rossetter Gleason Cole (1866), composer of songs, piano pieces, organ pieces, cantatas and works for orchestra and 'cello, takes his themes from American and general sources. He is organist in Chicago and has charge of the music courses of the summer session of Columbia University. He has held many important posts and taken numerous prizes. His cantata *The Rock of Liberty* was sung at the Tercentenary Celebration, 1920, of the settlement of Plymouth.

Arne Oldberg, born in Youngstown, Ohio (1874) is director of the piano department of Northwestern University (Michigan) and has many orchestral works, symphonies, concertos and overtures, which have had frequent hearings. He has also composed much chamber music.

There are also Harry Rowe Shelley (1858) writer of much important church music; James H. Rogers, critic and composer of piano teaching pieces and many fine songs, including a cycle *In Memoriam*, which is a heartfelt expression of sorrow in beautiful music; Wilson G. Smith (d. 1929), composer of piano teaching pieces and musical writer; Louis Coerne (d. 1922), writer of opera and of works for orchestra; Ernest Kroeger (d. 1934) of St. Louis who also used Indian and Negro themes in works for orchestra and piano; Carl Busch of Kansas City, composer of orchestral works, cantatas, music for violin and many songs, in some of which we see the Indian. In California were Wm. J. McCoy (d. 1926) and Humphrey J. Stewart (d. 1932) who composed church music and wrote often for the yearly outdoor "High Jinks" of the San Francisco Bohemian Club, in which many important composers have been invited to assist; Domenico Brescia (d. 1939), a South American composer, who lived in San Francisco, and wrote interesting chamber music played at the Berkshire Chamber Music Festivals; and Albert Elkus, a composer of serious works for orchestra and piano.

But this grows into a musical directory! Although neglecting many who have helped to make music grow in America, we must proceed to important mile-stones ahead.

For many years New York has been the American center of music. Few of the people in musical life are native New Yorkers, but have come from all parts of the States and Europe to this musical Mecca.

MacDowell Greatest American Poet-Composer

The greatest romanticist and poet-composer of America up to the present is Edward MacDowell (1861–1908). Some of the romanticism of the early 19th century has become mere imitation of the style which arose as a protest against the insincere forms of the 18th century. But the true spirit of romance never dies and never becomes artificial,—such romance had MacDowell. He was sincere, always a poet, always himself, and in spite of his Irish-Scotch inheritance, German training and love of Norse legends, he expressed MacDowell in every note. He lived before the time when we question "How shall we express America in Music"? In fact he was much against tagging composers as American, German, French, and so on.

Edward MacDowell, born in New York City, began piano lessons when he was eight. One of his teachers was the brilliant South American Teresa Carreño, who later played her pupil's concerto with many world orchestras. At 15, he entered the Paris Conservatory where he was fellow student with Debussy.

While there, MacDowell studied French, and during a lesson amused himself by drawing a picture of his teacher. When caught, the teacher, instead of rebuking him, took the sketch to a friend, a master at the *École des Beaux Arts*, the famous old art school of Paris. The artist found the sketch so good that he offered to train him without charge but Edward had made up his mind to be a musician and did not accept the offer.

In 1879, MacDowell studied composition at Frankfort with Joachim Raff, one of the composers of the Romantic period. Raff introduced him to Liszt, who invited Mac-Dowell to play his first piano suite at Zürich (1882). The composer's modesty is reflected in these words which Lawrence Gilman quotes: "I would not have changed a note in one of them for untold gold, and *inside* I had the greatest love for them; but the idea that any one else might take them seriously had never occurred to me." This suite was his first published composition.

In 1884, he married Miss Marian Nevins of New York, and theirs was one of the most beautiful marriages in musical history, although their meeting was amusing! The young girl had crossed the ocean to continue her music studies at a time when it was not a common occurrence, and when she went to Raff for lessons, he sent her to a young countryman of hers, "an extraordinary piano teacher." She was indignant to be sent to a young inexperienced American in that fashion, but she went! The young inexperienced American did not want to teach an American girl, because he felt she would not be serious enough to do the kind of work he demanded, but he accepted her! Later she accepted him!

In 1888, he established himself in Boston as pianist and teacher. His first concert was with the Kneisel Quartet, and in 1889 he successfully played his concerto with the Boston Symphony Orchestra. He made tours through the States giving recitals and appearing with the orchestras. Winning immediate recognition, his position as an exceptional composer grew. In 1896 the Boston Symphony Orchestra presented his first piano concerto and his orchestral *Indian Suite* on the same program in New York. Such an honor had never before been shown an American!

In 1896, he became professor of the new Chair of Music at Columbia University in New York City. After resigning his post in 1904, his health broke as the result of an accident, and for several years he was an invalid. All the care of physicians, devoted friends, his parents, and his courageous wife, could not restore his memory, and in 1908, he died in New York and was buried in Peterboro, N. H. A natural boulder from where he often watched the sunset, marks the spot—fitting for one who loved Nature as he did.

Shortly before his passing, a group of friends formed a society, the MacDowell Club of New York, which has for its object the promoting of "a sympathetic understanding of the correlation of all the arts, and of contributing to the broadening of their influence, thus carrying forward the life-purpose of Edward MacDowell." He wished musicians to know the value of associating with artists outside of the field of music. Eugene Heffley (1862–1925), an intimate friend of MacDowell and first president of the MacDowell Club, did much to make the MacDowell music known and loved, just as he did for Charles Griffes, Debussy, Ravel, Scriabin and others who have come with new messages.

Some people have statues erected, others have towns and

streets named for them, but besides the numerous Mac-Dowell Clubs throughout the States, the most beautiful memorial is the MacDowell Association at Peterboro. Early in his career, MacDowell found it impossible to work well in the city, and by happy chance he and his wife discovered a deserted farm which they bought for the proverbial "song." Here the composer spent his summers in the beautiful New Hampshire woods, in the heart of which he built the little log cabin, which in his words, is

> A house of dreams untold
> It looks out over the whispering tree-tops
> And faces the setting sun.

And in this "house" he told many of his dreams in lovely melody! While ill, he often expressed the desire to share the inspiration-giving peace and beauty of his woods with friends, workers in music and the sister arts. Out of this wish has grown the colony for creative workers, which has been a haven to hundreds of composers, poets, painters, sculptors, dramatists, and novelists. The "Log Cabin" is the seed out of which twenty-four studios have sprung. The small deserted farm has spread over 500 acres, and Mrs. MacDowell with the aid of faithful friends has made a dream come true!

MacDowell was a composer for the pianoforte, although he wrote some lovely songs; a few orchestral works, best known of which is *The Indian Suite*, in which he employs Indian themes; and several male choruses written when he conducted the New York Mendelssohn Glee Club. We love and remember him for his *Woodland Sketches*, *Sea Pieces*, *Fireside Tales*, *New England Idyls* (opus 62 and his last work), virtuoso-studies, and the four sonatas—the *Tragica*, *Eroica*, *Norse* and *Keltic*.

W. H. Humiston (1869–1924), composer, lecturer, musical critic, organist, assistant conductor of the New York

Philharmonic Orchestra and a pupil of MacDowell, had the
most complete collection of Bach and Wagner in this country and was a great authority on their writings. This collection now belongs to the MacDowell Association, and is
in the Savidge Memorial Library at Peterboro.

HENRY HOLDEN HUSS

Henry Holden Huss (1862), born in Newark, New Jersey,
has lived in New York since returning from study with
Rheinberger in Munich. Before that, he was a pupil of
his father, George J. Huss, a Bavarian who came to America
during the 1848 revolution, and was a fine musical educator.
Huss also studied with O. B. Boise (1845–1912), an American
theorist and teacher. As concert pianist, Huss has played
his piano concerto with all the important orchestras. Raoul
Pugno, the much loved French pianist, and Adele aus der
Ohe also played it abroad and in America. Huss is an
idealist as teacher, composer and pianist. A classicist at
heart, his works are written on classic models,—a beautiful
violin sonata with poetic slow movement, two string quartets, a viola sonata, a concerto for violin and orchestra,
besides *The Seven Ages of Man* for baritone and orchestra,
sung by the late David Bispham, *Cleopatra's Death* for soprano and orchestra, a female chorus, *Ave Maria*, and many
fine art songs and piano pieces, including *To the Night*, a
lovely impressionistic composition ranking with the best that
America has produced.

Ernest Hutcheson (1871), an Australian, and Howard
Brockway (1870), a Brooklynite, both pupils of O. B. Boise,
have done much to make music grow in America. Hutcheson,
who was a prodigy pianist, studied with Max Vogrich in
Australia and Reinecke in Leipsic. He has had a great career

in Europe and in his adopted country as pianist and teacher, but he also has a symphony, a double piano concerto and several other large works in manuscript. Hutcheson is president of the Juilliard School of Music. Since 1911 he has been head of the piano department of the Chautauqua Institution.

Brockway, who harmonized *Lonesome Tunes*, folk songs from the Kentucky Mountains collected by Loraine Wyman, composed a symphony played in Boston (1907) by the Orchestra, a suite, ballad-scherzo for orchestra, many piano works and songs. Hutcheson, Brockway, and Boise were teachers in the Baltimore Peabody Institute, one of the important music schools, under direction of Harold Randolph, a fine musician and pianist.

George F. Boyle (1886) of New South Wales taught at the Peabody Institute, and at the Juilliard School since 1928. He has composed piano pieces, songs and orchestral works.

RUBIN GOLDMARK

Rubin Goldmark (1872–1936) was known as the best toast-master in the music world! Born in New York, he was one of Dvorak's most talented pupils and inherited his gifts from his noted uncle Carl Goldmark (1830–1915), a Hungarian composer of *Sakuntala, The Queen of Sheba*, the symphony *The Rustic Wedding*, etc. Rubin Goldmark wrote several important tone poems,—*Samson, Gettysburg Requiem, Negro Rhapsody*, based on Negro themes, and other fine things for orchestra, chamber music, piano and violin numbers, and as a teacher he laid the foundations for several American composers, among whom are Frederick Jacobi, Aaron Copland and George Gershwin. His last years were spent as teacher of composition in the Juilliard Graduate School.

HENRY HADLEY

Henry K. Hadley (1871–1937) by birth and training was a New Englander, but he spent most of his life in Germany where he got his orchestral experience, and in Seattle, San Francisco and New York, where he conducted orchestras. He was one of the few Americans who directed the New York Philharmonic Orchestra. He took many prizes for opera, symphony, cantata and an orchestral rhapsody. Among his best known works are his operas, *Cleopatra's Night* (Metropolitan, 1920), *Bianca, Azora;* orchestral works, *Lucifer, In Bohemia, Culprit Fay,* four symphonies; choral works, *Ode to Music, Mirtil in Arcadia, Belshazzar;* chamber music, and about 150 songs.

ALBERT MILDENBERG'S "MICHAEL ANGELO"

It seems regrettable that an opera ready for production should lie idle because of the death of its composer. Perhaps no composition has had a more tragic story than *Michael Angelo* by Albert Mildenberg (1878–1918). In 1908, Mildenberg signed a contract in Vienna for the production of the opera. The following year on the way to Europe, the ship, *Slavonia,* was wrecked, and although the composer escaped, his entire orchestral score and parts went to the bottom of the sea. Courageously he rewrote the work, and sent it to the Metropolitan Opera House in competition for the $10,000 prize, won by Horatio Parker. Before it had reached the judges, in some way, still unexplained, the major part of the score disappeared! Again, Mildenberg set to work with the sketches he had, and made a third score, but it cost him his life. The opera was completed before his death, but he was too ill to carry it further.

Mildenberg, a pupil of Rafael Joseffy, also wrote many piano pieces; *The Violet, I Love Thee,* and *Astarte,* songs that had a popular vogue and are still sung; the romantic comic operas, *The Wood Witch* and *Love's Locksmith*, besides a cantata and many choruses.

John Alden Carpenter—Modernist

John Alden Carpenter (1876), one of America's foremost composers, was born in Park Ridge, Illinois, and educated at Harvard where he took the music course, studying afterwards in Rome with Edward Elgar, the English composer, and later with Bernard Ziehn in Chicago. A business man, Carpenter still has time to devote to composing music. In his early work, his tendencies were impressionistic, and none understands better than he the charms of rich and unusual harmonies, the use of modern melodic and orchestral effects, and the value of humor in music. All these we find in his *Adventures in a Perambulator* for orchestra, and his ballet *Krazy Kat*, where jazz rhythms are used to great advantage. One of the most beautiful works of its kind is the ballet after Oscar Wilde's *The Birthday of the Infanta*, performed by the Chicago Opera Company; his first ballet, presented by the Metropolitan Opera Association, is called *Skyscrapers*,—certainly American! In this he made use of jazz idioms and popular melodies. Carpenter's settings of Tagore's *Gitanjali* are among America's finest songs; he has many others, a concertino for piano and orchestra, a violin sonata, a string quartet, and a piano quintet. Carpenter received the Cross of the French Legion of Honor (1921) and an honorary degree from Harvard (1922).

An All-American Symphony

Eric Delamarter (1880), born in Lansing, Michigan, wrote a *Symphony After Walt Whitman* in which he used twenty-year old street songs from the "Barbary Coast" (San Francisco), *Lonesome Tunes* of Kentucky, and a fox-trot rhythm with newer street songs. These, Delamarter has woven into a symphony, the material of which is all-American although neither Negro nor Indian.

Delamarter is a well known organist, composer of many other works for orchestra, organ, and oratorios, incidental music for drama, cantatas and songs. He served for many years as assistant conductor of the Chicago Symphony Orchestra.

Noble Kreider and Edward Royce, son of Professor Josiah Royce of Harvard University, have both written well for the piano. Harold Bauer has played variations and short pieces by Edward Royce.

Ernest Schelling—Pianist-Composer-Conductor

Ernest Schelling (1876), born in New Jersey, appeared as pianist at the Academy of Music in Philadelphia at the age of four! His pianistic training included lessons with Paderewski. He has toured Europe and America as pianist, and for many seasons has conducted the children's concerts of the New York Philharmonic-Symphony Society. He is "Uncle Ernest" to thousands of young concert-goers. His important orchestral works include a Symphony; Symphonic Legends; *Morocco, Suite Phantastique* and *Impressions From An Artist's Life* for piano and orchestra, and *The Victory Ball*, which has enjoyed wide popularity. He has also written piano pieces and chamber music.

John Powell—Virginian

The charm and refinement of the Southern gentleman are reflected in John Powell's personality, along with deep sincerity and conviction. He was born in Richmond, Virginia (1882), is a graduate of the University of Virginia, and a

pupil of Theodor Leschetizky and Navratil in Vienna. He
has an international reputation as brilliant pianist and gifted
composer. Powell's works show classical training in form
combined with rich romantic feeling and love for folk music.
He believes that music should draw on the folk element
for its strength, and has proved his theory by his intensive
study of Anglo Saxon tunes of the Southern mountains, and
by his free use of the music of the Negro. *In the South*,
At the Fair, piano pieces, show this early influence and his
fund of humor, and in his *Negro Rhapsody* for piano and
orchestra, Powell has painted a picture of the Negro in
many moods—smoldering and aroused, religious, primitive
bordering on barbaric, as well as humorous, and carefree.
Sonata Teutonica first brought him before the public. He
has written other sonatas for piano and for violin, songs,
chamber music and orchestral works, including *Natchez on
the Hill*, three Virginia country dances.

Negro Spirituals Versus Jazz

This brings us to a much discussed question: the influence
of Negro music and jazz on serious composition. The pure
Negro music is the Spiritual and *not* jazz, which seems to
be the typically American idiom many have been waiting
for.

It is not Negro but is developed from the Negro dance
rhythm, a real folk music; it is the result of Negro music
played upon by American life and influences; through it
some have learned to free themselves musically, and have
showed the American spirit of adventure and daring which
until recently had been absent from our native compositions.
The path has been travelled from the songs of Stephen
Foster, Negro Minstrels, "coon songs" and "cake walks,"
to jazz with its elaborate orchestration unlike any other
existing music, and its complicated rhythms. Jazz rhythm

is contrapuntal rhythm. The people of Europe say that it is our one original and important contribution to music! This is a strong statement, but as "imitation is the sincerest form of flattery," serious 20th century European composers have flattered us by writing jazz, and we have *Piano Rag* by Stravinsky, a *Syncopated Sonata* by Jean Wiéner, jazz by Darius Milhaud, Casella, Honegger, and even Debussy was tempted into writing *Golliwogg's Cake Walk.* Some of our American composers have tried their hands at jazz in art music.

More recently, with the commercial exploitation of jazz, a new term, "Swing," has come into use. The musicians in a swing band have to be virtuoso instrumentalists as they improvise brilliant melodic and rhythmic variations.

HARRY THACKER BURLEIGH—NOTED NEGRO COMPOSER

His arrangement of the Spiritual, *Deep River*, has made Harry Burleigh's name known on two continents. Burleigh (1866) came under Dvorak's influence at the National Conservatory. For many years he has been leading baritone in St. George's Church and was also at Temple Emanu-El in New York. His name is found on practically every program where Spirituals are sung. He has written other works too.

Of Burleigh's race is R. Nathaniel Dett (1882), conductor of the Hampton Singers, also director of the music department of Hampton College. Percy Grainger introduced his characteristic Negro *Juba Dance* in Europe and America. Dett's numerous arrangements of Spirituals and choruses in Negro style are among the finest of their kind; his oratorio, *The Ordering of Moses*, is a recent success. Grainger wrote of him: "There is in his treatment of blended human voices that innate sonority and vocal naturalness that seem to result only from accumulated long experience of untrained im-

provised polyphonic singing, such as that of Southern Negroes, South Sea Polynesians and Russian peasants. . . ."
David Guion (1895) of Texas has made an intensive
study of American folk tunes. His piano settings of *Turkey
in the Straw, Home on the Range, Arkansas Traveler*, etc.,
are famous.

Louis Gruenberg Finds New Paths

Louis Gruenberg (1884) came to New York from Russia
at the age of two. At nineteen he studied with Ferruccio
Busoni, the Italian pianist-composer, in Berlin and Vienna.
Gruenberg first followed conventional lines of composition, receiving prizes in Berlin and New York (in 1922 he
was awarded the Flagler prize for a symphonic poem *Hill
of Dreams*). These early works comprise symphonic poems,
a string quartet, a piano concerto, a symphony, a suite for
violin, also a sonata, two operas, songs and piano pieces.
He then asked himself what was the spirit of Americanism
that had not yet found its way into music, and his answer
was the white man's jazz expressing the "spirit of the times."
As a result he changed his way of writing. The compositions of this period are a violin sonata, a set of piano pieces
called *Polychromatics*, a *Poem* for 'cello, four pieces for string
quartet, a viola sonata, *Vagabondia*, Jazz Suite for orchestra,
short piano pieces with the amusing name of *Jazzberries*,
three violin pieces in the same style, a group of songs *Animals and Insects*, texts by Vachel Lindsay, and that poet's
Daniel which Gruenberg set as *Daniel Jazz* for tenor and
chamber orchestra, and *Creation*, a Negro sermon by James
Weldon Johnson, a Negro poet. This period culminated in
Gruenberg's greatest success, his opera on Eugene O'Neill's
Emperor Jones (Metropolitan, 1933). Gruenberg also col-
laborated with John Erskine in an impressionistic fairy
opera, *Jack and the Beanstalk;* he wrote a radio opera, *Green*

Mansions, commissioned by the Columbia Broadcasting System (1937), and won the RCA-Victor Co. prize in 1930, the Lake Placid Club prize with a piano quintet, and wrote a quartet on commission from Mrs. E. S. Coolidge (1938). He is at present in California.

Two Jazz Geniuses

Irving Berlin (1888), a genius in writing typical American jazz, was born in Russia and had no musical training. He picks out his irresistible melodies by ear and his aide writes them down to the delight of the millions in all corners of the earth, where the phonograph has carried them. The sheiks no longer sing in ancient pentatonic melody to their lady loves, but turn on the phonograph which ably plays some of his hundred numerous American songs: *My Wife Goes to the Country*, *Snooky Ookums*, *Along Came Ruth*, *If You Don't Want Me Why Do You Hang Around*, *Mandy*, *Say It With Music*, *What'll I Do*, *All Alone*, and many from the musical revues (Music Box Revue, especially). His earlier *Alexander's Rag Time Band* goes back to cake-walk days and has become a classic of its kind. He rose from poverty to riches through giving delight to the public.

George Gershwin (1898–1937) flashed into the limelight when he played his jazz piano concerto *Rhapsody in Blue* with Paul Whiteman's Orchestra. Here is a merging of classic form with the "voice of the people." He was a Brooklyn boy brought up as a "song-plugger," using his extraordinary talents to play popular songs in vaudeville and in cafés. He was the writer of successful musical comedies such as *Lady Be Good*, *Strike Up the Band*, *Of Thee I Sing*. His brother Ira was his librettist. At the time of his premature death in Hollywood, he was writing for the sound films. He studied with Rubin Goldmark to equip himself to write such scores as his *Piano Concerto*, commissioned by Walter Damrosch for the New York Symphony, *An America in Paris*, and his opera *Porgy and Bess* to the play by Dubose and Dorothy Heyward.

CHARLES TOMLINSON GRIFFES

Charles Tomlinson Griffes (1884–1920) was a poet composer whose early death was a serious loss to America, for every thing he wrote was an addition to our music. He was impressionistic in style, and we are grateful for the lovely art songs, *Five Poems of Ancient China and Japan*, three songs with orchestral accompaniment to poems of Fiona MacLeod, ten piano pieces and the Sonata which have never been surpassed in beauty and workmanship by any American, the *Poem* for flute and orchestra, the string quartet on Indian themes, and his orchestral tone-poem, *The Pleasure Dome of Kubla Khan*. For the stage, Griffes composed a Japanese mime-play, *Schojo*, a dance drama, *The Kairn of Korwidwen* and Walt Whitman's *Salut au Monde*, a dramatic ballet. The last two were interesting experiments presented at the Neighborhood Playhouse by the Misses Alice and Irene Lewisohn.

Griffes was a native of Elmira, New York, and his first studies were made with Miss Mary S. Broughton, who recognized her young pupil's unusual talent and took him to Germany for study. His composition work was done with Humperdinck, and Rüfer, and from 1907 until his death he taught music at Hackley, a boys' school in Tarrytown, New York.

Lawrence Gilman, American critic, said: "He was a poet with a sense of comedy. . . . Griffes had never learned how to pose. . . . It was only a short while before his death that the Boston Symphony Orchestra played for the first time his *Pleasure Dome of Kubla Khan* . . . and the general concert-going public turned aside . . . to bestow an approving hand upon this producer of a sensitive and imaginative tone-poetry who was by some mysterious accident, an American! . . . He was a fastidious craftsman, a scrupulous artist. He was neither smug nor pretentious nor accommodating. He went his own way,—modestly, quietly, unswervingly . . . having the vision of the few. . . ."

WHITHORNE'S AMERICAN IMPRESSIONS

Emerson Whithorne (1884) was born in Cleveland, Ohio, and studied there and in Europe. After writing in Oriental and European fashion, he composed *New York Days and Nights*, piano pieces in which are cleverly pictured Times Square, Hudson River ferry boats, Trinity Church Chimes, etc. *Saturday's Child* for tenor, soprano, and chamber orchestra is also an American expression. His ballet, *Sooner and Later*, written with Irene Lewisohn, and the incidental music for *Marco's Millions*, show talent for the theatre. He has composed many orchestral and chamber music works.

ALBERT SPALDING—AMERICA'S VIOLINIST-COMPOSER

When Walter Damrosch took the New York Symphony Orchestra on tour in Europe, Albert Spalding (1888, Chicago) went along as joint soloist with John Powell, playing his violin concerto. Spalding has also written many small pieces for violin, other orchestral and piano works, and a string quartet played (1924) by the Flonzaley Quartet. Spalding ranks with the great violinists of the world.

Three other violinists showing talent as composers are Edwin Grasse (1884), who in spite of the handicap of blindness, has composed some charming violin pieces, violin sonatas and string quartets; Samuel Gardner, who has written orchestral works, chamber music and short violin pieces; and Cecil Burleigh, short poetic pieces for violin and for piano, and a violin concerto.

AMERICAN MUSIC GUILD

To encourage the composing and appreciation of American composition, ten composers formed the *American Music Guild* (1921). The members were Marion Bauer, Chalmers Clifton, Louis Gruenberg, Sandor Harmati, Charles Haubiel, Frederick Jacobi, A. Walter Kramer, Harold Morris, Albert Stoessel, and Deems Taylor.

Albert Stoessel (1894, St. Louis) is director of the Opera School and the Orchestral Department of the Juilliard Graduate School; of the music at Chautauqua, N. Y.; conductor of the New York Oratorio Society and of the Worcester, Mass., Festival, and composer of chamber music, orchestral works, and of the opera *Garrick*.

Deems Taylor (1885, New York), music critic, writer, and composer of songs and orchestral works (*Through the Looking Glass* Suite), has written much choral and incidental music for plays and motion pictures. A graceful work is the ballet in *The Beggar on Horseback*. His operas, *The King's Henchman* (1927) and *Peter Ibbetson* (1931), were given at the Metropolitan. He was narrator for the Metropolitan Opera broadcasts, and is the commentator for the New York Philharmonic broadcasts.

A. Walter Kramer (1890, New York) is a critic and writer on musical subjects, composer of many songs that have made his name familiar, orchestral works, a *Rhapsody* for violin and orchestra, pieces for violin, organ and piano, and a symphonic tone poem on Masefield's *Tragedy of Nan*.

Harold Morris (1889, Texas) has studied only in America and writes chiefly in large forms for orchestra: *Poem* after Tagore, two symphonies, a piano concerto, Variations on a Negro Spiritual, a violin concerto, and much chamber music. He has won several important performance and publication prizes, and his works have been played by the leading orchestras.

Frederick Jacobi (1891, San Francisco) has a special gift of poetic expression which shows itself in his orchestral works, *Two Assyrian Prayers* for voice and orchestra, a symphony, *Indian Dances*, concertos for cello, for piano, and for violin; his choral works, *The Poet in the Desert* and the Synagogue Service; his chamber music, two string quartets, *Scherzo* for wind instruments, and piano quintet, the *Hagiographa*; songs, and piano pieces. Since 1936 he has taught composition at the Juilliard Graduate School.

Chalmers Clifton (1889, Jackson, Miss.), after graduating from Harvard, studied in France. He turned from writing chamber music and music for a pageant to conducting. He directed the American Orchestral Society, a training orchestra for young artists, and later was associated with the Federal Music Project in New York as conductor and regional director, from which position he resigned in 1939.

Sandor Harmati (1894-1936), a Hungarian by birth, founded the Lenox String Quartet and composed several string quartets and orchestral works. He took numerous prizes for his compositions and was for several years conductor of the Omaha Symphony Orchestra.

Charles Haubiel (1894, Ohio) has won many prizes beginning with the International Schubert Centennial Contest (1929) with *Karma*, a symphonic work; another prize was that of the Philharmonic-Symphony Society (1938) for his *Passacaglia*. He is Assistant Professor in the music department of New York University. He has written for the theatre, orchestra, also choral works, and chamber music.

Marion Bauer (1887) was born in Walla Walla, Washington. She has written songs, piano pieces, two violin sonatas, a string quartet, a viola sonata, a chamber music ballet, choruses, and a work for orchestra. She is the author of *Twentieth Century Music*. She writes and lectures on music, and is Associate Professor at New York University.

American Academy in Rome

In 1905, MacDowell was one of the founders of an Academy in Rome for American students on the principle of the Roman prize of the Paris Conservatory. Several composers have visited the ancient city of learning as guests of the Academy. Unfortunately, the music fellowship does not admit women!

One of the prize winners was Leo Sowerby (1895, Grand Rapids, Michigan), who has written three piano concertos and a double piano concerto, other orchestral works, *Vision of Sir Launfal* for chorus, also chamber music and a piano work, *Synconata*, which has been played by Paul Whiteman. Sowerby lives in Chicago.

Another Roman Fellow was Howard Hanson (1896, Wahoo, Nebraska), who has stimulated interest in American composers by annual festivals at Rochester, N. Y., where he is director of the Eastman School of Music. He wrote the opera *Merrymount* (Metropolitan, 1932), three symphonies, many symphonic poems, choruses with orchestra, chamber music, piano pieces, and songs. He is important in educational circles also, and has received commissions for special works.

Other Roman Fellows are: G. H. Elwell, Vittorio Giannini, Walter Helfer, Herbert Inch, Werner Janssen, Hunter Johnson, Normand Lockwood, Robert L. Sanders, Roger Sessions, Alexander Steinert, Randall Thompson, Samuel Barber, Kent W. Kennan, Frederick Woltmann, and Charles Naginski.

Experimentalists

When Leo Ornstein (Russia, 1895) was very young he stated: "I am not concerned with form or with standards of any nature." And in his early compositions he lived up to this declaration of independence. In one of his piano works,

Wild Men's Dance, he went back to primitive man for his inspiration and wild rhythms. He was one of the most daring and original of any of the American innovators. His *Poems of 1917* for piano reflect his restless and fearless spirit. He came to America as a child after having survived a pogrom. He was unusually gifted,—a pianist prodigy, who was trained by Bertha Tapper and Percy Goetschius. He wrote the incidental music to *Lysistrata*, also a piano concerto, a symphony, two Nocturnes, and *Nocturne and Dance of the Fates* for orchestra, commissioned by the League of Composers, besides much chamber music. He teaches in Philadelphia.

Henry Eichheim (1870), a student of Oriental music, turned his Chinese and Japanese impressions into colorful orchestral scores.

Carl Ruggles (1876), an independent thinker, experimented with harmonic and instrumental combinations in orchestral works: *Men and Angels*, *Men and Mountains*, *Portals*, and *Sun Treader*.

Charles Ives (1874) experimented with acoustics and dissonances and tried to reflect the New England life in his orchestral and chamber music, and in his songs. His piano sonata, *Concord, Mass.* (*1840–60*), is daring in form and content.

SONG WRITERS

There are many composers famous as song-writers, only a few of whom can be listed: Alexander Russell, R. Huntington Woodman, Carl Deis, William Arms Fisher, Charles Fonteyn Manney, Clayton Johns, Sidney Homer, Charles Gilbert Spross, Oley Speaks, Louis Campbell-Tipton, Wintter Watts, William C. Hammond, G. Bainbridge Crist, Marshall Kernochan, Eastwood Lane, Richard Hammond, Harry Osgood, Charles B. Hawley, Adolph Martin Foerster, Richard Hageman, Edward Ballantine, Clough Leighter, Victor Harris, Isidore Luckstone, Percy Lee Atherton, John Beach, Paolo Gallico, Arthur Bergh, Morris Class, Walter Morse Rummel, Blair Fairchild, Eugen Haile (German-American), Frank LaForge, Harold Vincent Milligan, Timothy Spelman, Edward Horsman, Tom Dobson, Oscar G. Sonneck. Mr. Sonneck (1873–1928) was less known as a composer than as a musicologist whose vast knowledge made him invaluable as the first librarian of the music division of the Library of Congress in Washington (1902–1915). His books are an important addition to musical *Americana*. He was editor of the *Musical Quarterly*, and secretary of the Beethoven Association.

Foreigners Writing in America

Many musicians who are making music grow in America were born in Europe. They may not be *American* composers, but are composers in America and most of them have become American citizens.

Ernest Bloch, born in Geneva, Switzerland (1880), came here in 1916, at which time the Flonzaley Quartet played his *String Quartet*. His work shows his Jewish descent rather than Swiss nationalism. Among his important orchestral works are *Three Jewish Poems*, *Israel* symphony, *Schelomo*, Rhapsody for 'cello and orchestra, a prize symphonic rhapsody, *America*, and a *Concerto Grosso* for strings. He took the Coolidge Prize with his *Viola Suite*, and has also a violin sonata and a piano quintet. He has written an opera, *Macbeth*, and a great choral work, the *Sabbath Service*. He taught in New York, Cleveland, and San Francisco, and among his pupils were many who have become well known composers.

Rudolph Ganz, born in Zürich, Switzerland (1877), has composed a symphony and *Animal Pictures* for orchestra, as well as numerous piano pieces and songs. He is at present head of the Chicago Musical College, and an important pianist and conductor. He was for many years conductor of the St. Louis Symphony Orchestra.

Percy Aldridge Grainger, born in Melbourne, Australia (1882), appeared as a pianist at the age of ten and since then has never stopped! His mother was his first teacher and later he was a pupil of Busoni and intimate friend of Grieg, whose concerto he played upon his first American appearance (1915). During the World War he became naturalized and served in the American army. As composer he is unique, being self-taught, and although knowing the compositions of all the great masters, he goes to folk music for his themes and ideas, and has become an authority on British and Scandinavian folk music, and is collecting music of the American Indian and the Negro.

Among Grainger's best known pieces are: *Molly on the Shore, Colonial Song, Shepherd's Hey, Irish Tune from County Derry*, and *Country Gardens*, all folk melodies around which he has woven most fascinating modern harmonies. In 1925 he gave two concerts which he called, with true Grainger originality, "Room Music" instead of chamber music. He has recently spent much time in his native country. He is an original thinker and an interesting personality.

Carl Engel, born in Paris (1883) and educated in France, is an American citizen. He was director of the Music Division of the Library of Congress in Washington, D. C., and is now president of G. Schirmer's and editor of the *Musical Quarterly*. Engel has written in addition to essays in delightful style, a *Triptych* (a violin sonata in three movements) and songs, which mark him as a lover of modern harmony.

Two Frenchmen in New York, Carlos Salzedo (1885), one of the world's leading harpists, and Edgar Varese (1885) were foremost innovators a few years ago, bringing to the public, through the now defunct *International Composers' Guild*, the latest styles in music. They presented the new works of the most extreme composers, including their own, before the ink was dry on the manuscript. Salzedo wrote a harp concerto with seven wind instruments, *Préambule et Jeux*, Sonata for piano and harp, and many solos for harp. Varese is known for his orchestral work *Amériques*, and chamber music, *Offrandes*, *Integrales*, and a work for percussion, *Ionisation*. Through the efforts of these men, of the *League of Composers*, and of the *Pro Musica* Society (E. Robert Schmitz, founder and president), many contemporary compositions have been heard in America.

Lazare Saminsky, a Russian, choirmaster at Temple Emanu-El, New York, has written several symphonies, a chamber opera, *Gagliarda of a Merry Plague*, an opera ballet, *Jephtha's Daughter*, and many choral works. He is a student of Hebrew music and has written an authoritative book, *Music of the Ghetto and the Bible*, and also *Music of Our Day*.

Kurt Schindler (Berlin, 1882–1935), first conductor of the chorus, New York Schola Cantorum, was an authority on Russian, Spanish and Finnish folk music, of which he made many collections. He also wrote art songs and choruses.

Leopold Godowsky (1879–1938), of Polish birth, was one of the great pianists and teachers. He wrote much for piano and made many musicianly transcriptions.

Among the world famous violinists living in America, Mischa Elman (1892), Jascha Heifetz (1901), and Efrem Zimbalist (1889), have added to violin literature, arrangements of piano pieces and songs, and original compositions. Fritz Kreisler (Austria, 1875) now a French citizen, wrote the music with Victor Jacobi, for the light opera *Apple Blossoms*. He is a frequent visitor to America.

SOME PATRONS OF MUSIC IN AMERICA

America has had its patrons who like the Esterhazys and Lobkowitzes of old have advanced music by founding and maintaining orchestras, music schools, chamber music, festivals and prize competitions. Among these are Henry Lee Higginson, Boston Symphony; Harry Harkness Flagler, New York Symphony; W. A. Clark, Los Angeles Philharmonic; George Eastman, Rochester Symphony and Eastman School of Music; Augustus Juilliard, Juilliard Musical Foundation; Mrs. Edward Bok, Curtis Institute of Music; Edward J. de Coppet, the Flonzaley Quartet; Carl Stoeckel, festivals at Norfolk, Connecticut; Adolph Lewisohn, Stadium Concerts; Louis Eckstein, Ravinia Opera; Mr. and Mrs. Daniel Guggenheim and Mr. and Mrs. Murry Guggenheim, summer concerts by Edwin Franko Goldman's Concert Band; Mrs. Elizabeth Sprague Coolidge, Berkshire Chamber Music Festivals and the Coolidge Foundation of the Library of Congress, Washington, D. C., under the auspices of which concerts are presented, prize competitions held, and composers are commissioned for the development of chamber music. Also the Society for the Publication of American Music, the Juilliard School of Music Publication Award, the Eastman School publications, the Guggenheim Fellowships, the Walter Naumberg prize, the National Federation of Music Clubs, the League of Composers, the National Bureau for the Advancement of Music, and many music schools and settlements have helped to make music grow.

We include here Arthur P. Schmidt (1846–1921) of Boston as a patron of music, who, by his devotion to American composers and the faith with which he published their works as early as 1876, has made music grow. Under this heading must also be included Gustav Schirmer (1829–1893) and Oliver Ditson (1811–1888).

Symphony Orchestras

Besides Boston, New York, and Chicago, other cities have helped the advancement of music in America by maintaining symphony orchestras. Among these are: Philadelphia,

Detroit, San Francisco, Los Angeles, Cincinnati, St. Louis, Cleveland, Rochester, Pittsburgh, Syracuse, Omaha, Portland, Ore., Seattle, Minneapolis, St. Paul, Miami, etc. Among the conductors who have headed these organizations have been Leopold Stokowski, Eugene Ormandy, Ossip Gabrilowitsch (1878–1936), Alfred Hertz, Walter H. Rothwell (1872–1927), Fritz Reiner, Artur Rodzinski, Nikolai Sokoloff, Eugene Goossens, Vladimir Shavitch, Sandor Harmati (d. 1936), Willem van Hoogstraten, Emil Oberhoffer, Henri Verbrugghen, Arnold Volpe, Dmitri Metropoulos, etc.

Organizations which helped to build love of music in this country were the New York Symphony Orchestra (Walter Damrosch) the Russian Symphony Orchestra (Modest Altschuler), the Volpe Symphony Orchestra (Arnold Volpe), and the People's Symphony Concerts (F. X. Arens), all of which are out of existence.

There are civic orchestras in many smaller cities, besides those which were organized under the Federal Music Project of the Works Progress Administration in various centers. The growth of high school orchestras, bands, and choral groups has been almost unbelievable. In some motion picture houses excellent music is presented by local orchestras, although most of the music is now supplied by sound films.

Another notable development has been the broadcasting of concerts by several major orchestras throughout this country, and the formation of radio orchestras such as the National Broadcasting Company's Orchestra under the direction of Arturo Toscanini, one of the greatest musicians of the age. NBC also broadcasts the Saturday matinee opera performances from the Metropolitan stage. The Columbia Broadcasting System not only broadcasts the New York Philharmonic-Symphony Sunday programs but has its own orchestra under Howard Barlow, and station WOR has an orchestra under Alfred Wallenstein.

An American Conductor and Prize-Winning Composer

For seven years the Bamberger Little Symphony Orchestra of Station WOR was directed by the American conductor and composer, Philip James (1890), whose musical education was 100% American. In 1932 he received the NBC prize for his satirical suite *WGZBX*, and in 1937, honorable mention in the Philharmonic-Symphony contest for his *Bret Harte* overture, and the Juilliard Publication Award. He is chairman of the music department of New York University. He has written a ballet with narrator, *Judith*, incidental music for several plays, a suite for string orchestra, many symphonic works, many choral works, a string quartet, a woodwind quintet, an organ sonata, piano pieces and songs.

Outdoor Music

Within the last years, the desire for music in the summer has led to open air concerts and operas. Of these, the concerts of the Philharmonic-Symphony in the Lewisohn Stadium (New York); those in the Hollywood Bowl (California); Robin Hood Dell (Philadelphia, Pa.); the Berkshire Music Festivals with the Boston Symphony Orchestra under Dr. Serge Koussevitsky; Goldman Concert Band (Edwin Franko Goldman, conductor) playing in Central Park (New York) and Prospect Park (Brooklyn); and the Ravinia Festivals (near Chicago) are the most widely known.

For twenty years (1911–1931), Ravinia Park provided magnificent opera performances which made a delightful summer night playground for Chicago music lovers. Since the death of Louis Eckstein (1935), the generous patron of Ravinia opera, there have been summer concerts in the Park. Cincinnati has had several seasons of successful opera at the "Zoo," and St. Louis also has its summer opera.

The musical activities of Chautauqua Institution (Lake

Chautauqua, N. Y.) under the direction of Albert Stoessel,
have led to calling that place the "Salzburg of America."
For a few weeks each summer, a fine orchestra with soloists
gives five or more concerts a week in the outdoor Amphi-
theatre, and there is a series of five operas (two performances
of each) presented by young American artists drawn largely,
though not exclusively, from the Juilliard Opera School.
There are also frequent chamber orchestra, string quartet,
and choral concerts during the short season.

OPERA IN AMERICA

Opera has not kept pace with the symphony orchestras
in this country. The Metropolitan Opera Association with
the famous tenor, Edward Johnson, as general manager
(New York), the Chicago Civic Opera Association (Jason
F. Whitney, manager), the San Francisco and Los Angeles
Grand Opera Company (G. Merola, director), the San Carlo
Opera Company (a traveling organization managed by For-
tune Gallo), are in operation.

FESTIVALS

Important in American musical life are the music festivals
held usually in the spring, although one of the oldest, the
Worcester (Mass.) Festival, under the direction of Albert
Stoessel, takes place in October. Many of these organiza-
tions combine choral and orchestral societies; some of them
also present opera. Among the most famous are the Cin-
cinnati; the Ann Arbor (Mich.) May Festivals; the Chicago-
North Shore, since 1937 revived as the Evanston Festivals;
Maine festivals at Portland and Bangor; at Springfield,
Mass.; Mrs. E. S. Coolidge's Chamber Music Festivals at
Pittsfield and Washington, D. C.; Westchester County Fes-
tivals at White Plains, N. Y.; American Music Festivals at
Rochester and at Yaddo, Saratoga Springs, N. Y.; Bach

Festivals at Bethlehem, Pa.; and more recently the Berkshire Festivals of the Boston Symphony Orchestra under Dr. Serge Koussevitzky; Westminster Choir Festivals featuring native choral and instrumental compositions at Princeton, N. J., under the direction of Dr. John Finley Williamson, and the Ridgefield (Conn.) Mozart opera Festivals on the estate of William M. Sullivan.

The biennial meetings of the National Federation of Music Clubs deserve to be included here, as more and more their activities take on the nature of festivals of American music.

In educational, cultural, and amusement circles, there is every reason to be proud of the recent growth of music in America. New York City is, today, the music center of the world.

CHAPTER XXXII

Twentieth Century Music

THERE was once an old man who said: "I have lived to see the post-chaise give way to the locomotive but I *cannot* and *will not* accept the automobile!" What would he have said to the aeroplane? But this old man was not different from the people today, who seem unable to accept the new music and take it as a personal affront when they must listen to it. Like the automobile and the aeroplane, however, it is here, and is a part of the 20th century!

Nothing that lives stands still; there must be constant change and growth, or decay sets in. This is as true of music as it is of ourselves and the things around us. We have watched this process of change in music from pre-historic man to the 20th century; we have seen certain periods bursting with new ideas, works and forms; we have seen individuals tower above their fellows, marking epochs to which their names have become attached, like the Palestrinian era, the Bach era, and the Wagner period; and we are living in a moment of new ideas, works and forms, on which we cannot pass final judgment. Time alone must be the judge!

There is no point at which a period ends and a new one begins, for they overlap. We saw harmony grow out of polyphony; we saw the romantic Beethoven rise out of

the classic Beethoven; in the romantic Chopin, we found
the germs of impressionism (for definition, see page 483),
and in Debussy's impressionism, we see the breaking away
from traditions into a new world of sound.

Polyform Music

When we begin our music lessons, we are taught the musical alphabet,—the major scale, and then, the minor and
the chromatic. So accustomed are we to these scales
that we forget there was a time when they did not exist,
and that new ones may be added, for they are not fixed
for all time. There have been, as you know, the no-scale
time, the pentatonic scale, the Greek modes, the Ecclesiastical or Church modes, the diatonic (major and minor)
scale, the chromatic scale and the so-called whole-tone
scale of Debussy. Beethoven and all the writers of the
classic period used the diatonic scales which gave their
works a definite tonality, that is, a home tone to which
all the tones try to return. If, for example, you sing *Yankee
Doodle* and stop before the last note, you feel very uncom-
fortable, because you have not sounded the home tone
towards which all the tones are reaching. To the diatonic
modes, Chopin and Wagner added a frequent use of the
chromatic scale, which enriched music. In addition to diatonic and chromatic harmony, along came Debussy with
his melodies in whole steps, and he also went back to the
old Greek modes, using them in new and unexpected ways.
Today we have all the past to draw upon and the composers are quick to take advantage of their rich inheritance
and to add innovations.

In the 20th century the influences have come from Paris
and Vienna,—Debussy and Schoenberg,—and later Stravinsky, the Russian. From the French has come a style of
writing called *polytonality*, and from Vienna has come

atonality. Don't be afraid of these names for they are easily explained!

Having said that *tonality* is a system in which all tones gravitate to a central tone (they all come home to roost!) it is not difficult to understand through the formation of the word *poly*—many, *tonal*—tones, that it means the use of several keys or tonalities at the same time, a counterpoint of key against key, or scale against scale, instead of note against note as it was in the Golden Age of Polyphony. Think of a *cantus firmus* in C major, and a counter melody in F♯ minor! (Between ourselves if *skilfully handled*, it has possibilities!) Ravel, Milhaud and Honegger know how to do it. Of course in the old system we change from key to key by means of a musical bridge called *modulation*, but in polytonality, the bridge is discarded, and the unrelated keys are heard piled on top of each other in layers.

Atonality, the system which Schoenberg and his followers use, is based on the chromatic scale of twelve half steps, creating new melodic and harmonic combinations, and new methods of chord building. This gives a more varied tonal paint-box than the old diatonic modes and the chromatic scale of former days, for it has now become an independent scale, and is not a part of the diatonic family.

MULTI- AND POLY-RHYTHMS

Rhythm also reflects this age of unrest, and there have been decided changes which seem to return to the Middle Ages to the period of bar-less music writing. Instead of finding a piece written throughout in $\frac{3}{4}$ metre or $\frac{4}{4}$, it will be *multi-rhythmic* or *poly-rhythmic*. *Multi-rhythmic* means many shiftings from one rhythm to another; *poly-rhythmic* means a counterpoint of different rhythms all played at the same time. The English composer, Cyril Scott, uses multi-rhythms (where almost every measure changes its metre), and the French Florent Schmitt uses poly-rhythms.

(for example, triplets against eighth notes in common time in the right hand, and ⅜ metre in the left).

In the 15th and 16th centuries every one wrote motets, masses and madrigals; in the 17th century every one wrote suites and from this time on, opera; in the 18th, sonata form; in the 19th, sonatas and short romantic pieces. In the 20th century, no one form is used more than another, but all forms are undergoing changes as the composers reach out for freedom. This is the day of the large orchestra and of the small chamber music groups; symphonies have been replaced by the shorter symphonic poem, the tendency being for short forms. The four-hour music drama has given way to the one-act operas, and the dance drama or ballet as the Russian Diaghilev introduced it, is a 20th century development. The orchestral writing has changed greatly from the methods of Berlioz, Wagner and Strauss, for while they were masters of large mass effects, the composers of today are treating each instrument individually, in other words, they are using orchestration, *poly-instrumentally!* In chamber music, we have the string quartet, but in addition, many experiments are being made in combining solo instruments of unrelated families, like strings, wind, brass and percussion, as we find in Stravinsky's chamber music.

It is often said that modern music has no melody, but it would be more correct to say that it has *new* melody, resulting from the attempt to push aside old forms, old harmonies, old rhythms; now we have arrived at a new era of polyphony, abounding in dissonance, that often is cacophonous rather than harmonious. We call this period the POLYFORMIC era.

ANOTHER RENAISSANCE

The men who ushered in this POLYFORMIC era were Claude Debussy in Paris, Arnold Schoenberg in Vienna, and Alexander Scriabin in Russia. Richard Strauss, then at his height, is a good example of the overlapping of two periods, for he represents the romantic German school of the 19th century, and has also pointed the way to the future. Igor Stravinsky, although younger, is one of the strongest factors in this new Renaissance which in scope and power reminds us of the rebirth of learning in the Middle Ages.

Another cause for the breaking away from old forms and conditions was the World War, which cut off the composers from the usual sources of musical supply, and forced them to develop their own ideas. This led to new groups arising in all parts of the world, who, rebelling against restraint, put wild experiments in the place of time honored customs.

Claude Achille Debussy

Although Claude Achille Debussy (1862–1918) was almost forty when the 20th century came in, only in this century has his work been known and imitated. He was the direct outcome of a movement in France, after the Franco-Prussian War to develop French music along the lines started by Rameau and Couperin. This meant breaking away from the classic models of Beethoven and the dramatic music of Wagner. He exchanged the romantic style of Schumann and Chopin for a new impressionistic style.

Claude Debussy was born in St. Germain-en-Laye, near Paris. He attended the Paris Conservatory when he was eleven and studied with Marmontel, Lavignac and Guiraud. In 1884, with a cantata, *L'Enfant Prodigue*, he won the *Prix de Rome* which has started the career of so many French composers! During this, his first period, he wrote many lovely songs to poems by Verlaine and Baudelaire, the same impressionistic poets who inspired Charles Martin Loeffler in America; *Suite Bergamasque*, which includes the lovely *Clair de Lune* (*Moonlight*); the work which first brought him fame, *L'Après-midi d'un Faune* (*Afternoon of a Faun*); the beautiful string quartet; *Chansons de Bilitis; Three Nocturnes for Orchestra*, and the unique opera *Pelleas and Melisande*, which took him ten years to write! It was first given in the Paris *Opéra Comique* (1902).

In this opera, Debussy showed himself an innovator; it was a new kind of harmony and melody and never before had an opera like it been written. He gave an exact impression in music of Maeterlinck's imaginative, mystic play. This is not a case where music drowns the meaning of the story but each word is colored and interpreted by the music. Debussy accomplished what the Camerata, Gluck and Wagner tried to do. By the time he wrote *Pelleas and Melisande*, his style was established and the proof of his high attainment is seen in his many imitators.

He worked very slowly and carefully and often destroyed what had taken him hours to write. Although an innovator, he was a deep student well grounded in the traditions of the past, a lover of Mozart and of the 18th century French writers, and when he seemingly broke all rules he gave something new in their place, not in the spirit of experiment but of sincere conviction.

He was surrounded by painters who like Claude Monet, Pissarro and Sisley did not paint *actual things*, but rather ideals of things; and by poets who like Verlaine, Gustave Kahn, Henri de Régnier, Pierre Louys and Stéphane Mallarmé did not write about *things* but rather the *impression* and *images* things gave them. He was absorbed and delighted by this non-photographic kind of art and translated into his music the veiled, mystic, idealistic, silver glimmering impressions that others put into paint and into words. This is *Impressionism* in art.

Musically, Debussy was influenced by Wagner, although he fought against him, and by some of the French composers in whose day he began to write, like Chabrier and Chausson. From Moussorgsky and other Russians he learned much about old modes, color effects and free expression; and with Erik Satie he talked over many musical problems, no doubt gaining much from this curious musical caricaturist and humorist. No matter how extreme and absurd Debussy's music might have sounded forty years ago to the people, they must have felt the mystic beauty and rare poetic charm of his work.

Someone, as a joke, put a Butterick pattern on a player-piano roll as a music record, and it sounded so ridiculous that a composer hearing it, said: "Ah, that must be a Debussy piece!" But, you see this was forty years ago!

No matter how revolutionary his piano pieces may have sounded, today they have become almost classics! The combination of poetic imagination, romanticism and impressionism are seen in the titles: *Reflets dans l'eau* (*Reflections in the Water*), *L'Isle joyeuse* (*Happy Island*), *La Cathédrale engloutie* (*The Engulfed Cathedral*), *Jardins sous la pluie* (*Gardens in the Rain*).

For his daughter Claude, who died the year after her father, Debussy wrote six little piano pieces called the *Children's Corner*. At the time he was writing them, little Claude used to drag the manuscripts around like a ragdoll, telling anyone she met, "These are *my* pieces, my father is writing them for me." They were: *Dr. Gradus ad Parnassum*, *Jimbo's Lullaby*, *The Doll's Serenade*, *The Snow Falls*, *The Little Shepherd* and *Golliwogg's Cakewalk*.

Among his later works are: Three symphonic sketches, *La Mer* (*The Sea*); the mystery play on a book by d'Annunzio, *Le Martyre de St. Sebastien* (*The Martyrdom of St. Sebastian*); a work for two pianos, *Noir et Blanc* (*Black and White)*; a *Sonata for Violoncello and Piano* and twelve *Studies for Piano.*

In *Minstrels, Children's Corner* and *General Lavine—eccentrique* we find *humor*, a characteristic of 20th century music.

His music was vague and dreamy, and many composers were weakened rather than strengthened by trying to imitate him, for they had neither his genius nor his poetry. What he gave us was genuine, what others tried to copy was affected. His use of the whole-tone scale and the pastel shades of music were so much a part of him that to employ them today shows a lack of originality. But to those coming after him, who did not imitate him but worked out their own ways, he was a path-breaker of great value.

MAURICE RAVEL

Maurice Ravel (1875–1937) lived in or near Paris most of his life, although he was born in Ciboure, Basses-Pyrénées. He was a student at the Conservatory under Gabriel Fauré and André Gédalge. He did not receive the *Prix de Rome,* perhaps because in his early works he already showed tendencies, which must have seemed revolutionary to musicians who had not yet grown accustomed to the innovations of Debussy. Ravel developed his ideas at the same time and under the same influences as Debussy. You will often hear that Ravel imitated Debussy, but it is less an imitation than a development along the same lines. Ravel, too, was an impressionist, a poet, a lover of veiled mystic effects, *suggesting* images rather than *reproducing* them. He had a keen rhythmic sense, perhaps a heritage of his birthplace, so close to the Spanish border.

No 20th century composer understands the orchestra better than Ravel did, as may be seen in his ballet *Daphnis and Chloe, Rhapsodie Espagnole,* his delightful *Mother Goose, La Valse,* and *Bolero.* His short opera, *L'Heure espagnole* is full of charming music and splendid workmanship; his quartet written in 1902–03 is one of the finest examples of 20th century chamber music. For piano he added a rich contribution in the *Sonatina, Pavane for a Dead Infanta, Valses nobles et sentimentales, Les Miroirs (Mirrors), Gaspard de la Nuit (Gaspard of the Night), Le Tombeau de Couperin (The Tomb of Couperin)*, and his songs are very beautiful. They include *Histoires Naturelles (Nature Stories)* and the Greek and Hebrew folk songs.

Ravel's *L'Enfant et les Sortilèges (The Child's Sorceries)* is a revelation of his abilities. It is a ballet in early form with modern music, a fantasy tale about a little boy who will not do his lessons and in his fury, injures a squirrel. The chairs, grandfather's clock, frogs, fairies, sprites, squirrels, arithmetic dwarfs from the book he has destroyed, and tea-pots, rebel and talk "at him," until he binds up the wound of the squirrel. Into this Ravel put humor and even sentiment; he made some of the chairs dance a minuet, other characters a fox trot, and he included many old and new dances. He showed his magic handling of the orchestra. With extreme cleverness he even had the chair and the shepherdess sing a song in canon form! At the end all join in singing a fugue of "heavenly beauty."

A follower of Ravel is Maurice Delage (1879), who has written some very interesting songs and an orchestral work in which he has imitated the sounds of an iron foundry! He also studied Indian music and has written Hindu songs.

An enthusiastic follower and friend of Ravel is Roland Manuel, critic, writer and composer. He has never written what is called *ultra* (very) modern music, but everything he does,—songs, chamber music, operetta, or ballet is marked with good taste, refinement and fine musicianship.

Other Frenchmen who added to the 20th century style in music are Paul Dukas (1865–1935), whose opera based on Maeterlinck's *Ariane et Barbe Bleue (Ariadne and Blue Beard)* is second only to Debussy's *Pelleas et Melisande;* Vincent d'Indy (1851–1931); Déodat de Séverac (1873–1921), a writer of charming piano music whose impressionism reflects his love of Nature; Albert Roussel (1869–1937), a pupil of the Schola Cantorum, whose four Symphonies, chamber music, songs, and opera *Padmavati* show unique talent; Florent Schmitt (1870), whose orchestral works and piano quintet are important; André Caplet (1880–1925), Charles Koechlin (1867), who has written important books on musical theory, and Erik Satie (1869–1925).

Erik Satie—Cartoonist

Erik Satie is a riddle! Many are the heated discussions he has caused. His influence has been exerted through what he has said, not what he has done. He was a caricaturist and gave amusing titles to frivolous little pieces in which one never knows whether he was laughing *at* or *with* the world. He loved short disconnected pieces and did much to make the young composer break away from long symphonic forms. He was a friend of Debussy, godfather to the *Group of Six*, and later to four younger men who call themselves the "School of Arcueil" where Satie lived. His name should have been Satyr for, with his pointed ears, eye-brows, and beard, he looked the part! Among his compositions are the ballets, *Parades* and *Relâche*, and a dramatic aria with orchestra, *Socrates*.

The School of Arcueil includes Henri Sauguet, Maxime Jacob, Roger Desormière, and Henri Clicquet-Pleyel, who take pleasure in American jazz effects, with which they have tried amusing experiments.

The Group of Six

The World War reacted both directly and indirectly upon a group of composers in France. Daring and brutality are the keynote of almost all the works of the years from 1914 to the present day. Debussy and Ravel with their poetic imagery did not express the feelings of the younger men, so they were pitilessly brushed aside by *Les Jeunes* (*The Young*) who also overthrew the accepted forms for their own experiments. One of these experiments was the development of the classic spirit of the 18th century clothed, however, in 20th century dissonance. It was called *neo-classicism*, and was a reaction from the 19th century romanticism.

These composers did not band together like the "Russian Five." A French critic called them simply "The Six," and the name stuck. They were not united by unity of purpose or ideal, they just happened to be friends whose music was often presented on the same programs, and Erik Satie "who had been throughout thirty-five years the instigator of all audacity, the manager of all impudence," was their confidential adviser. The six are Germaine Tailleferre (1892) who played her piano concerto in America (1925) and has written two charming ballets; Louis Durey (1888); Georges Auric (1899) and François Poulenc (1899), both of whom have written ballets; Darius Milhaud (1892), and Arthur Honegger (1892).

Of these, Milhaud and Honegger are the most important. Milhaud has written operas, ballets, chamber music and orchestral works with great fluency, often showing fine gifts and flashes of beauty. His opera, *Christophe Colomb*, was produced in Berlin (1930), and his piano pieces, *Saudades do Brazil* (*Souvenirs of Brazil*) are popular examples of polytonality. His ballet *La Creation du Monde* is a characteristic blend of jazz and an imitation of Bach!

Honegger was amazingly successful with a work in oratorio form, *Le Roi David* (*King David*), and with a tone poem, *Pacific 231*, which is a type of locomotive. He broke from the Group, and has gone his own independent way, writing beautiful songs, orchestral and chamber music, and operas, including *Judith*, *Antigone*, and *L'Aiglon*. He recently wrote music for Paul Claudel's mystery play *Jeanne d'Arc at the Stake*.

Of the young French composers showing the varied tendencies of the day, some are writing in classic form, some in romantic, but all are very independent. One of these is Jean Françaix (1912), a pupil of Nadia Boulanger. He has written ballets, a sinfonietta, a piano concerto, piano pieces, chamber music, etc., in neoclassic style.

ALEXANDER SCRIABIN

Alexander Nicolai Scriabin (1872–1915) was born in Moscow, Russia, and was trained in a military school; instead of becoming an army officer, he turned to music, and was a pupil of Safonov, for several years conductor of the New York Philharmonic Orchestra, and of Taneiev. His early works show the influence of Chopin and Arensky, but he soon developed a style of his own, which made him one of the important composers of the beginning of the 20th century. An English writer, Eaglefield Hull, thinks that "the sonatas of Scriabin are destined in the future to occupy a niche of their own, together with the forty-eight Preludes of Bach, the thirty-two Sonatas of Beethoven, and the piano works of Chopin." To explain briefly the innovations of Scriabin would be impossible, but he broke away from fixed scales and tonality, and opened new musical roads. He used neither polytonality nor atonality, although his methods border on the latter. He built new chords, not major and minor as we know them, but in intervals of fourths. Here is a typical Scriabin chord which he used as we use a major triad (c–e–g) as the center around which to build a composition:

This chord contains the upper harmonics or overtones evolved primarily from the theory of Pythagoras (see page 41). Scriabin called this combination the "mystic chord" for he was a student of Theosophy and tried to use music as a means to express occult ideas. So he wrote a tone-poem, *Prometheus*, which, according to his directions, Modest Altschuler conducted in New York (1915) with a color-organ throwing colors on a screen while the orchestra played the music. Two other of his symphonic works *Le Divin Poème* (*Divine Poem*) and *Le Poème de l'Extase* (*Poem of Ecstasy*) show his extraordinary harmonic originality.

Besides the ten sonatas in very free form, he wrote hundreds of shorter piano pieces, disclosing his deep, poetic, mystic nature. Composers have imitated him, but his music is so tagged with Scriabin's individuality that, like the whole-tone scale of Debussy, imitation is easily detected.

L'Enfant Terrible of Modern Music—Stravinsky

Igor Stravinsky (1882) has influenced more young musicians than any other living composer! He intended to become a lawyer, but instead took up composition, and studied orchestration with Rimsky-Korsakov, and his early works reflect his teacher. We never know how meeting someone may change our course in life, and Stravinsky's meeting with Serge Diaghilev changed his!

Diaghilev, director of the *Russian Ballet*, recognized a gift in the young Stravinsky, who was busy writing an opera from a fairy tale of Hans Christian Andersen, *The Nightingale*. He commissioned him to write a ballet on a fairy tale, *L'Oiseau de Feu* (*The Fire Bird*) which was produced in Paris (1910) and brought Stravinsky instant fame. The next year this was followed by the delightful *Petrouchka*. His most famous score *Le Sacre du Printemps* (*Rites of Spring*) was produced in Paris in 1913, causing a near-riot, as it was received with hissing and catcalls by a public unprepared for its brutality, its savage rhythm, and raucous dissonance.

In this work Stravinsky went back to primitive times when Russia was pagan, and he explains, "Thus we see Russian peasants dancing in the springtime, accompanying the rhythms by their gestures and their feet." An English critic, Edwin Evans, sees behind the pagan rite, "The marvelous power . . . in all Nature to grow, to develop, and to assume new forms." (We have watched this happen in music.)

After *Le Sacre du Printemps*, Stravinsky wrote *Les Noces*, a ballet founded on pagan Russian marriage customs. Here he has used a chorus of voices, four pianos and percussion instruments in place of an orchestra. He finished the opera *The Nightingale* and in 1917 wrote an orchestral poem based on the themes from the opera.

In the short ballet, *L'Histoire du Soldat* (*Story of the Soldier*), Stravinsky has used popular music of the fair, circus, music-hall, not folk music, and we find our jazz and tango in it, as also in his *Piano Rag Music* and *Ragtime* for orchestra. His songs composed for the most part to nonsense verses, are among the cleverest things he has done.

Stravinsky wrote a group of string quartet pieces in which he made the violins sound like bells. This was not because he tried to imitate bells but on the strings he uses the harmonics or overtones that are heard in bells. This is one of the secrets of his unusual harmonies.

OVERTONES

We hear so much about overtones and harmonics that perhaps we can trace for you the growth of music along the path of Pythagoras' theory, showing how we arrived at this era of dissonance.

HARMONIC SERIES

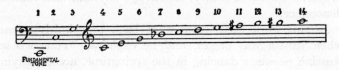

First men and women singing in unison produced music in octaves, 1 and 2 of the harmonic series. Next came the centuries of *organum* when the parts were sung in fifths and fourths, 2, 3, and 4 of the harmonic series. Then followed the centuries of the major triad (c–e–g), 4, 5, and 6 of the harmonic series. When the 7th overtone in the harmonic series appeared, we had the very important dominant 7th chord (c–e–g–b♭), looked upon as outrageous heresy and dissonance! It was years, even centuries, before it was admitted as a respectable member of the family! The 9th harmonic forming the dominant 9th chord (c–e–g–b♭–d) had the same hard row to hoe, and is one of our modern chords. César Franck shocked the musicians by opening his famous violin sonata with this chord! We can trace the whole-tone scale of Debussy to the 7th, 8th, 9th, 10th, and 11th overtones of the series, (b♭–c–d–e–f♯). Scriabin's "mystic chord" is formed from the 8th, 11th, 7th, 10th, 14th, and 9th overtones (c–f♯–b♭–e–a–d). It is a short step now to *polytonality* and *atonality*, to Stravinsky, Schoenberg, Milhaud, and Honegger.

You have seen the white ray of sunlight enter your window, which upon a second glimpse divides into all the colors of the rainbow. In other words, the white light is the *fundamental tone*, which is the *sum* of *all the other colors*, much as any *single tone* is the *sum* of *its overtones*, and it is with these overtones that our modern composers are experimenting. Here we see that modern music is the result of *evolution* (slow growth) and not *revolution*!

HEART MUSIC DISAPPEARS

Stravinsky, *l'enfant terrible* in music, the most daring composer of a most daring period, seemed to throw over all restraint! His music had little heart quality, and so strongly did he influence the younger men, that "heart music" went out of style. A brusque, unemotional music took its place because the composers feared that to show sentiment would be thought to be weakness! However, the best workers tried to express humor, action and vigor, and because of this our jazz appealed to Europeans. The World War made Stravinsky the "man of the hour" in music. He was the direct opposite of the refined, beauty worshipping Debussy and Scriabin, the mystic. The composers, upset by the devastating war, needed strong food; so they hungrily pounced upon the suggestions flung out by Stravinsky, the ring leader.

But withal, "the worm will turn!" Already those with ears to hear, realized a change in the air, which became a new classic period (neo-classic) in which the younger composers tried to revive the 18th century spirit in 20th century dress. Stravinsky himself changed, and wrote in this *neoclassic* style. After he had written several ballets for Diaghilev, his countryman, he turned his attention to chamber music and wrote works for small groups of wind instruments and a string quartet, *Concertino*, and a concerto for piano and wind instruments in which he tried to imitate Bach in modern harmonies with jazz rhythms. He believes in *absolute music*, and has written works without *program*, relying on the music to express what he has to say.

Stravinsky's neoclassicism found expression in an opera-oratorio, *Oedipus Rex*, after Sophocles (1927), a classic ballet, *Apollon Musagètes*, commissioned by Mrs. E. S. Coolidge for the opening of the Library of Congress Chamber Music Festival (1928), the *Symphony of Psalms* (1930) commissioned for the fiftieth anniversary of the Boston Symphony

Orchestra, and *Persephone*, a melodrama for chorus, orchestra and narrator. He has also written a violin concerto, a concerto for two pianos without orchestra, a concerto for sixteen instruments called *Dumburton Oaks*, and a ballet, *Card Party* "in three deals" which had its first performance under the composer's direction in New York (1937). Stravinsky is supreme master of orchestration and is largely responsible for treating each instrument as though it were playing a solo, which we described as poly-instrumentation. We should not have enjoyed Stravinsky as a neighbor, for he begged, borrowed or bought every kind of instrument, which he played himself in order to learn all their tricks! In 1935 he wrote an autobiography, *Chronicle of My Life*. The year before, he had become a French citizen.

Prokofieff and Other Russians

Serge Prokofieff (1891), a Russian second in fame only to Stravinsky, was a child prodigy as composer and pianist. By the time he was graduated from the Petrograd Conservatory in 1914, he had composed an opera, two of his five piano concertos, four sonatas, piano pieces and songs. A characteristic rhythmic driving force, humorous grotesqueries, individual style, and boldness in his use of dissonance were in evidence in these early works. He wrote the famous *Classical* Symphony and a powerful choral number, *Sept, ils sont sept* (*Seven, they are seven*) in 1917. He left Russia in 1918, gained an international reputation as pianist and composer, made his home for several years in Paris, but returned to Moscow in 1934. He wrote *The Love for Three Oranges* for the Chicago Civic Opera; some ballets, *Chout* (*The Buffoon*), *Le Pas d'Acier* (*The Age of Steel*), and *L'Enfant Prodigue* (*The Prodigal Child*) for Diaghilev. His later works include a second violin concerto, incidental music for the films, a cello concerto, symphonic scores, and a clever novelty for children, *Peter and the Wolf* for orchestra and narrator, in which every character is represented by a different instrument.

When Nicholas Miaskovsky (1881) wrote his first symphony it won him a scholarship at the Petrograd Conservatory where he was a fellow student with Prokofieff. He has composed eighteen symphonies, which began in the pre-war romantic style. His later works show the composer's acceptance of the Soviet ideas and are based on Russian modes. He has also written chamber music, piano sonatas, and songs. He is the teacher of many Soviet composers in Moscow.

Soviet Composers

Russian music in the 19th century struggled to express the national spirit inherent in its folk songs and church music. At the time of the revolution, it was far removed from the masses. Then a new world was opened for the creative artists, a new foundation was laid for Russia's music. Not all the hopes to reach the mass audience were realized but the first two decades have brought forward new names and new talents. Eugen Braudo wrote in an article for *Modern Music* (1933) "All through the years immediately following the revolution the old masters suffered a kind of paralysis of creative effort; the problems of reconstruction awaited solution by a younger generation. These new men were at first completely inexperienced. . . . Soon, however, a vigorous struggle to better serve the new audience began. The older composers gradually succeeded in re-orientating themselves. . . . Recently a successful effort has been made to enlist the complete cooperation of the older masters . . . that they may aid in the artistic reconstruction of the country. . . ."

The Union of Soviet Composers is helping to organize Russian music. The members include old and young, and all are pledged to support with their art the socialist program of construction.

Alexander Krein (1883) has written symphonies of revolution and an opera, *Zagmuk*, on a Babylonian character, although his earlier tendencies were impressionistic. His brother Gregory (1880) has written chamber music and a symphonic cycle depicting the life of Lenin.

Samuel Feinberg (1890) shows the influence of Scriabin in almost all his compositions, especially in his piano sonatas. Michael Gniessen (1883) is both composer and teacher. Alexander Mossoloff (1900) is known outside Russia for his noisy orchestral work imitating a *Steel Foundry*. Leonid Polovinkin (1898) wrote several symphonies and musical pieces for the Moscow Children's Theatre.

Many of the younger men are writing operas on themes dealing with the social struggle, but as yet no new revolutionary forms of music drama have been evolved. Among these composers are Vasilenko, Pashchenko, Knipper, Deshevov, and Shostakovitch. Other composers are Maximilian Steinberg (1883), Nikolai Roslavetz (1881), known as the "Russian Schoenberg," Victor Bielyi (1904), Boris Schechter, writer of mass choruses, Alexander Davidenko, Maryan Koval (1908), and Nikolai Chemberdji.

Two Russian composers who live in Paris and are not of the Soviet group are Nicolas Tcherepnin (1873) and his son, Alexander (1899). The father has written operas, ballets, symphonic works, and completed Moussorgsky's unfinished opera *The Fair at Sorochintzy*. The son is a pianist as well as composer and has studied the music of China and Japan at first hand. He writes in the 20th century style.

Igor Markevitch (1912), although born in Russia lives in Paris, where he became a pupil of Nadia Boulanger in 1926. He has written orchestral works in neoclassic style, *Rebus* for orchestra, a choral *Psalm*, symphonies, and piano concertos.

DMITRI SHOSTAKOVITCH

The most widely known of the Soviet composers is Dmitri Shostakovitch (1906), a pupil of Steinberg at the Petrograd Conservatory. His first symphony, written when he was nineteen, is frequently played and is well known through its phonograph recording. It has unusual melodic quality and rhythmic verve. He has written five symphonies and some operas, including *The Nose* and *Lady Macbeth of Mzensk*. The latter was condemned as vulgar, a "leftist monstrosity" and a menace to true art. Soviet critics accused him of having fallen in the path of decadent composition of Western Europe. It seemed as though the most gifted composer of 20th century Russia was a fallen star! His ballet, *The Limpid Stream*, was also attacked as frivolous and over-simplified. However, with the success of his Fifth Symphony in Leningrad and in Moscow, Shostakovitch was reinstated. He has written piano music including 24 Preludes, *Three Fantastic Dances*, a sonata; chamber music; and incidental music for sound films.

POLAND

In modern Poland, Karol Szymanowski (1883–1937) wrote symphonies, chamber music, songs, piano sonatas and many other piano pieces which reflect Polish national color and French impressionism. One of his most beautiful works is his *Stabat Mater*. His last work was a ballet, *Harnasie*, which was given at the New York World's Fair (1939). He did much to encourage the younger Polish composers.

Lady Dean Paul, who wrote under the name of Poldowski, was a Pole, although she lived and died in London (1932). (Page 439)

Tadeusz Jarecki, of New York City, received a prize in Poland for writing the best composition by a native composer. This same quartet took the first Berkshire Chamber Music Prize (1918) and was published in New York by the Society for the Publication of American Music.

Alexandre Tansman (1892), a talented Pole, has met with success in Paris, where he writes works for orchestra, chamber music, and ballet.

Arnold Schoenberg, Musical Anarchist

Arnold Schoenberg, born in Vienna (1874), taught himself until he was twenty. He then studied with Alexander von Zemlinsky, who became his brother-in-law. Zemlinsky once said of him, "He is in his early twenties and I have taught him all I know; he brought me a work recently for which he had to paste two pieces of score paper together to hold his score, so large an orchestra had he employed!" (His tone poem, *Pelleas and Melisande*, 1904.) To this early period belong some songs, a song cycle with orchestra on texts by Jens Peter Jacobsen, *Gurrelieder*, and the sextet, *Verklärte Nacht* (*Illumined Night*).

Both Richard Strauss and Gustav Mahler were Schoenberg's friends. Through Mahler's efforts many of his compositions were performed. His first string quartet was played in America by the Flonzaley Quartet. His chamber symphony and his second string quartet, with solo voice, performed (1924) at the Berkshire Chamber Music Festival, belong to this same period. He has since written two other string quartets.

Schoenberg's early works were based more or less on models of the past, but being naturally an anarchist in music he tried to escape from doing what others had done. Instead of writing works that took fifty minutes to play like his first string quartet (in one movement), he wrote five orchestral pieces and piano pieces (Op. 19) that were mere samples of compositions, so short were they. He cut out long development of themes, all feeling for tonality, writing in the twelve-tone scale, which we explained as *atonality*. He built his chords in intervals of fourths instead of thirds, and changed many rules. He distorted intervals, using a seventh or ninth instead of the octave, and making the fourths and fifths a half step larger or smaller than was customary. His melodies are marked by large skips and queer intervals, but when one once knows his language, it is easily recognized as Schoenberg's. Although he has broken away from the slavery of old traditions, he may have "jumped out of the frying-pan into the fire!" His piano pieces, Op. 11 and Op. 23, and his song cycle *Das Buch der hängenden Gärten* (*The Book of the Hanging Gardens*) are characteristic of his newer style.

In *Pierrot Lunaire*, a cycle of twenty-one songs with chamber music accompaniment, he uses a curious effect for the voice "which must be neither sung nor spoken." This effect he uses also in chorus in his music drama, *Die Glücklische Hand* (*The Hand of Fate*) on his own libretto. Although this and another music drama, *Erwartung* (*The Awaiting*), were begun in 1909, they were both performed for the first time in 1924 in Vienna. This delay was due to the prejudice against the work of this innovator, who either has been laughed at, scorned, and reviled, or worshipped by a small group of disciples and imitators whose works sound very much like his. Schoenberg has become an American citizen and makes his home in Southern California.

Among these pupils are Egon Wellesz (1885) who has gone his own way in writing music for the stage and combining the old ideas of ballet and orchestral music with Greek drama in a modern dance-drama. He has also written chamber and orchestral music. Dr. Wellesz is an authority on musical history. He has written many books and articles, especially on early opera and Byzantine and Oriental music. He has written a book on Schoenberg (1921).

Alban Berg (1885–1935), also a Schoenberg pupil, wrote unusually fine chamber music and an opera, *Wozzeck*, fragments of which were played at a festival in Prague (Czecho-Slovakia) in May, 1925, by the International Society for Contemporary Music, which has been valuable in encouraging and developing modern music. This society holds yearly meetings in various European centers, at which are heard the works of contemporary composers of the world. Each country has a branch, which sends its share of new works to be used in the festival's programs. *Wozzeck* has been produced as an opera both in Europe and America and was an artistic success. At the time of his death, Berg was completing another opera, *Lulu*.

Others of the Schoenberg group are Anton von Webern (1883), Karl Horvitz (1884–1925), Paul Pisk (1893), Ernst Toch (1887), and Ernst Krenek (1900). These last three are in America.

Von Webern has worked in Vienna, Prague and provincial cities as conductor. His compositions are in the twelve-tone system and are extremely short. He has written orchestral and chamber music and many songs. Krenek, another Austrian composer, studied with Franz Schreker, but has been much interested in Schoenberg's methods. He attracted attention in this country by his jazz opera, *Jonny spielt auf* (*Johnny Strikes Up the Band*), which was given at the Metropolitan. One of his recent operas, *Karl V*, is written in the twelve-tone system. He has recently written a book, *About New Music*. He has composed many orchestral scores, chamber music, and songs. Ernst Toch held many important teaching posts in his native Austria and in Germany. He has written much for theatre: opera, incidental music, and music for radio productions in Germany, England, and the United States. He also writes orchestral, chamber, choral, and piano music, as well as songs. He went to Hollywood to live in 1937.

ERICH KORNGOLD

Erich Wolfgang Korngold (1898) startled the musical world just before the War, with astonishing compositions he wrote as a little boy. Among these were orchestral works and a piano sonata of extraordinary promise. He was born in Vienna and is the son of a musician and musical critic. Korngold was first known in America as the composer of *Die Tote Stadt* (*The Dead City*) an opera in which the soprano, Maria Jeritza, made her first appearance at the Metropolitan Opera House. In many ways the opera goes back to the old pre-Wagner form and is full of melody, unusual in a young 20th century composer! He has written other operas bordering on the lighter Viennese operetta and has kept away from the Schoenberg influence. He has written music for the sound films in Hollywood, and is living in Los Angeles.

BUSONI THE GREAT

Ferruccio Busoni (1866–1924) although an Italian, had a strong influence in two fields of German music, those of piano playing and composing. He lived in Berlin and was one of the brilliant thinkers and musicians of the period. He left behind him chamber music and orchestral works, also several operas, one of which, *The Harlequin*, he finished just before his untimely death. This combines traditional form with radical ideas. His monumental work, *Doktor Faustus*, was completed by Philipp Jarnach. His sonatinas for piano and a set of studies on American *Indian Themes* are important. He made a deep study of all methods of composition,—old and new, and gave his pupils the advantage of his experience.

Although the younger Germans did not copy the huge symphonic form of Bruckner and Mahler, these two have

gained greatly in popularity and are serving as models.
Hans Pfitzner (1869), opera composer, is one of the most
typical Germans of the living composers of the pre-war
period; Franz Schreker (1878-1934), an Austrian who lived
in Berlin, taught many of the younger composers. He wrote
operas and songs.

MODERN GERMAN MUSIC

HINDEMITH

Richard Strauss was the last of the pre-eminent classic
school of German composers, which for two hundred years
had led the world in music. One of the most talented of
the young Germans is Paul Hindemith (1895). Lawrence
Gilman wrote: "He seems to be able to write polytonally or
atonally if he chooses, and also to write as the Academies
might observe, like a gentleman. Richard Strauss is reported
to have said to him: 'Why do you write atonally when you
have talent?' " Although he was violist in the Amar Quartet, he had played in cafés, in the "movies," dance halls,
operetta theatres, and jazz bands, as well as having been
concertmaster of the Frankfort Opera orchestra. He was
active in festivals of modern music held at Donaueschingen
(1921-26) and many of his works have been heard at the
annual festivals of the International Society for Contemporary Music. He wrote a number of works for small orchestra under the general title of *Kammermusik* or Chamber
Music, a long list of chamber music including string quartets,
sonatas for piano, for violin and viola; much piano music,
and the beautiful song cycles, *Das Marienleben* (*The Life of
Mary*) and *Die Junge Magd* (*The Young Maiden*) for voice
and chamber music accompaniment; several operas, among
them *Cardillac*, *Neues vom Tage* (*News of the Day*), *Sancta
Susanna* (*Holy Susanna*), *Hin und Zurück* (*There and Return*), *Mathis der Maler* (*Mathis, the Painter*), and a ballet

on St. Francis of Assisi, *Nobilissima Visione;* also orchestral scores.

Hindemith was also interested in a movement called *Gebrauchsmusik* which might be translated as useful or usable music. He felt that music had grown too far away from the layman or non-musician and had become too exclusively the property of the highly specialized musician. With this in mind he started, about 1926, to write simplified music, technically easy, for the amateur. This included *Music to Sing or Play,* a children's cantata *Let Us Build a Town, Songs for Singing Groups,* educational work for violin ensembles, etc.

Because of the unusual character of his work, it was banned in 1934 by the nationalistic movement in power. Hindemith, the man, was welcome to remain in Germany where he taught at the Berlin *Hochschule* (High School of Music) from 1927 to 1937, but his music was no longer welcome. He has paid annual visits to the United States and has been teaching music to children in Turkey, where his original ideas are not tabu!

Another German is Heinz Tiessen (1887), who, besides piano music in *atonality,* wrote incidental music to a drama by Hauptmann, and songs. He became interested in *Gebrauchsmusik* and founded and directed a chorus of workingmen's children.

Philipp Jarnach (1892), of Spanish parentage, French birth and education, a pupil of Busoni, lived in Berlin and wrote much orchestral, chamber, and piano music in 20th century style.

Heinrich Kaminski (1886) was accepted in Germany as the composer who was trying to build a bridge from Bach to modern times. His *Concerto Grosso* for double orchestra commands respect. He also wrote an opera, *Jurg Jenasch,* and much chamber music.

Kurt Weill (1900), another pupil of Busoni, has attempted

to create a new type of musical play. He is known by his *Dreigroschenoper* (*Three Penny Opera*), a modern version of Gay's *Beggar's Opera*; *Der Jasager* (*The One Who Says Yes*), a children's opera in *Gebrauchsmusik* style; *Mahagonny*, a *singspiel* in the jazz manner. He also wrote the incidental music for *The Eternal Road* and *Johnny Johnson* (New York, 1936), as well as for *Railroads on Parade*, the show at the Railroad Building at the New York World's Fair (1939).

Karol Rathaus (1895), an Austrian pupil of Schreker, has written a ballet, two symphonies, other orchestral and choral works, and chamber music. He lives in America.

Music Under the Third Reich

Perhaps some of the readers of this book will in the next generation tell their grandchildren and children of the nightmare the world lived through in the 1930's. It is hard to believe that so sharp and definitive a detour could be made as that which has taken place in the country which produced Bach, Beethoven, Schumann, and Brahms, to say nothing of Haydn, Mozart, Schubert, Wagner, etc.

"During these six years I have seen many a casual music tourist leave Germany convinced that business goes on as usual," writes "Fugitivus," in *Modern Music* (May-June, 1939). "And why not? Concert halls and opera houses are filled with apparently enthusiastic young audiences. Festivals are lavishly presented, even though the international public is absent. New works are continuously commissioned and premières are mounted with pomp and circumstance."

But "Fugitivus" shows the reverse of the picture, too. Although the tradition of centuries cannot be destroyed easily, the country is subject to a *Kulturpolitik*, of which the *Musikkammer* (Music Chamber) headed by Dr. Joseph Goebbels, Minister of Propaganda and Enlightenment, is a part. "Fugitivus" says that the head of the *Musikkammer* is not musically enlightened. "Non-Aryan" composers and those who have contracted non-Aryan marriages have been weeded out. Every town has an official, a Local Commissar of Music, whose duty is to pass on the merits of all artists and all works to be presented in that town. Many of the best composers have left the country, while many less gifted remain. Although all these are "pure Aryan," other disqualifications, political, cultural, and personal, may lead to their downfall at any moment.

"Fugitivus" says that the press has neither freedom of expression nor opinion. The critics are mere "observers" and the practice of criticism is nil. Many works by foreign composers, as well as Germans, are "undesirable." The repertory is reactionary and the houses are filled by members of a social organization, who are compelled to buy cheap tickets for opera and concert series. In the meantime, many wait the day when release from such standardization may become possible.

HUNGARY—BARTÓK AND KODÁLY

Béla Bartók (1881) and his friend Zoltan Kodály (1882) have done much to bring Hungarian folk music into the modern world, for they are steeped in folk tunes, which they use with skill and imagination. Bartók has written a short opera, ballets, orchestral works, string quartets, violin sonata, and many piano compositions. His children's pieces are delightful, based as they are on Hungarian folk tunes. Kodály's best known works are the comic opera *Hary Janos* and his choral work *Psalmus Hungaricus*.

We have spoken at length of the gypsy music of the Hungarians brought to us by Brahms, Liszt and Sarasate (violinist and composer). We also told you that the Hungarians were Magyars. Adjoran Otvos, in the *League of*

Composers Review says: "Bartók and Kodály have accomplished a pioneer work of quite a different nature, an exploration into the folk music of Hungary which has yielded a collection of historic significance, the most important and only authentic one made in that country.

"Bartók, poor and supported only by a scholarship, started in 1905, an investigation of the music of his race. Spending a week with a friend in the country, he heard a servant, while at work, singing a tune quite different from the hybrid (mixed breed) gypsy airs which pass for Magyar music, in Hungary and elsewhere. He contrived to conceal himself and day after day, while the servant worked, recorded a number of songs whose primitive character, he at once recognized. With this impetus, he embarked on a tour which lasted over two years, as long as his money held out. On his journeys among the peasants he met Kodály, out on a similar mission of research. Without previous inkling of each other's aims, they proceeded together, recording the ancient songs of the Magyars in the compilation which is famous today."

Ernst von Dohnányi

Ernst von Dohnányi (1877) a noted pianist and composer of Hungary has spent most of his life in Berlin and has toured Europe and America in piano recitals. He has written many works for orchestra, chamber music, piano and opera, all of which show more influence of Brahms than of men of his own land. He was conductor of the State Symphony Orchestra of New York for the season 1925–26.

A pupil of Béla Bartók, Georg Kosa, shows decided gifts in his first orchestral work, *Six Pieces for Orchestra*.

Czech School

The Czech school founded by Smetana and Dvorak and Zdenko Fibich (1850–1900) and continued by Vitezslav

Novak (1870), Josef Suk (1874), and Vaclar Stepan (1889), had a rebirth in the 20th century. Leos Janacek (1854–1928), composer of many operas, one of which, *Jenufa*, was presented at the Metropolitan was the leading spirit; Rudolf Karel (1881), pupil of Dvorak, Bohuslav Martinu (1890), follower of Stravinsky, Ernst Krenek (1902), before he left Europe, and Alois Haba (1893), pupil of Novak and Schreker are the working forces.

The Quarter-Tone Man

Alois Haba first wrote chamber music, then he tried some interesting experiments for which he is known as the "quarter-tone man." We have heard of quarter-tones among the Hindus and Arabs (Chapter VI) and as the human ear has become more educated, the possibility of dividing the scale into quarter-tones is much discussed, and seems to be the next step in developing music along the line of overtones (see above). Did you ever realize that as with eyes that are far-sighted or near-sighted, ears may vary too, in the amount they hear? Most people think that every one hears alike, but this is not so. Stravinsky was one day sitting with a friend on the shore of a Swiss Lake near which he lived. The friend said the water was calm and still, but Stravinsky heard a definite musical sound! Many of these musical sounds unheard by our ears he has shown us in his music. In the same way it is said that Haba has an extraordinarily keen ear and in trying to express what he hears, he has written two string quartets in the quarter-tone system. Stringed instruments are not in *tempered* scales and lend themselves to any division of the interval, into third-tones, as Busoni tried, and quarter-tones as Haba has written. Hans Barth, an American pianist and composer, has gone further and has made a piano on which quarter-tones may be played. This may prove to be the basis of music of the future, or it may be merely one of the numerous experiments without lasting value. Mr. Barth wrote a concerto for his quarter-tone piano which he played with Stokowski and the Philadelphia Orchestra.

ITALY AND THE NEW ORDER

For many centuries Italy has been known as the opera-producing country of the world. With the coming of the 20th century, however, a group of composers were working in Italy to get away from only opera writing and to develop along the line of orchestral and chamber music.

Alfredo Casella (1883) is perhaps responsible for this movement as he lived in Paris for many years and came in contact with Debussy's music and the modern movement there. Casella is an excellent pianist. One of his earliest works to attract attention in America was *War Films*, a series of orchestral pictures that were very realistic. He has written piano pieces, chamber music, orchestral works, and a ballet, *La Giara* (*The Jar*), which was given at the Metropolitan. Casella's style has changed from impressionism to polytonality and neoclassicism, and in the ballet he used a folk song basis. More recently he wrote an opera inspired by the conquest of Ethiopia and dedicated it to Mussolini.

G. Francesco Malipiero (1882) with Casella, Pizzetti, and Respighi, wrote music which gave Italy an important place in 20th century music. His harmonic idiom was modern, dissonant, and original. He wrote many symphonic works including *Pause del Silenzio* (*The Pauses of Silence*) which first attracted to him the attention of European audiences. One of his string quartets, of which there are four, received a Coolidge prize in the Berkshire Chamber Music Festival contests. He has written ballets, piano music, much chamber music, and more recently he has turned to opera and has composed nine. Another recent score which created a profound impression was his oratorio *La Passione* in which he deliberately returns to the style of the 15th and 17th centuries. Malipiero has devoted his time and attention to bringing out an edition of Monteverde's works, and has published a book about this great 17th century composer.

Ildebrando Pizzetti (1880) has written twelve operas, three of which have been on texts by Gabriele d'Annunzio. *Fra Ghirardo* was performed at the Metropolitan (1929) with Edward Johnson in the title role. He has also made an important contribution to Italian choral music in a Requiem Mass for solo voices and *De Profundis* for seven mixed voices unaccompanied, and to Italian song. He has written orchestral, piano, and chamber music.

Ottorino Respighi (1879–1936) wrote operas in traditional vein, but deserted them for chamber music and orchestral works. *Pines of Rome* and *Fountains of Rome*, we hear often. His *Violin Concerto in Gregorian Mode* was played by Albert Spalding. One of his operas, *La Campana Sommersa* (*The Sunken Bell*) was given at the Metropolitan in 1928. His "mystery" play, *Maria Egiziaca* (*Mary of Egypt*) had its première in New York (1932).

And now *Noah's Ark* has been made into a ballet by an Italian, Vittorio Rieti (born in Egypt, 1898), a pupil of Respighi. He wrote two ballets for Diaghilev, and an opera as well. He has written a piano concerto which is said to have stemmed from "the invention of Liszt," a symphony, concerto for clavichord and orchestra, *Madrigal* for twelve instruments and other works in neoclassic style. Another of the younger Italians, Virgilio Mortari (1902), a pupil of Pizzetti, shows special ability in handling voices although he has written works for chamber orchestra, also in neoclassic style. Luigi Dallapiccola (1904) was for a time interested in Schoenberg's twelve-tone system, but recently changed to a Palestrinian idiom with modern yet diatonic effect in his three choruses from Dante. He has written several works for voices with orchestra.

MANUEL DE FALLA

In Spain, one man who has continued along the lines of Albeniz and Granados is Manuel de Falla (1876). He studied first with Felipe Pedrell, the father of the modern Spanish school. In 1907 he went to Paris where he met Debussy and Dukas. He wrote a ballet, *El Amor Brujo* (*Love, the Magician*). He combines a picturesque Spanish folk style with a modern way of writing music. One of his most attractive works is a scenic arrangement as Spanish as a Spanish fandango from a chapter in *Don Quixote*, Cervantes' masterpiece. It is a marionette ballet called *El Retablo de Maese Pedro* (*Master Pedro's Puppet Show*). His writings have a simplicity and freshness which can come only from deep study and so perfect a mastery of art that there is no self-consciousness. He is a true nationalist delighting in Spanish color. His music has nobility and humanness and captivating charm. He wrote a harpsichord *Concerto* for Wanda Landowska in modern dissonant neoclassic style (1923–26). His Seven Spanish Popular Songs, based on folk music, are very beautiful. Falla was made President of the Institute of Spain in 1938.

Ernesto Halffter (1905), a pupil of Falla, is a composer of the younger generation. He writes in neoclassic, polytonal idiom, for orchestra, chamber music, piano, and songs. He has composed one opera, *The Death of Carmen*, and he wrote *Sonatina* for the lovely dancer, La Argentina (1890–1936).

Another eminent Spanish composer, Joaquin Turina (1882), studied with Vincent d'Indy and was friendly with many of the French Impressionists whose style he combined with the Spanish. He has written four operas, works for orchestra, also chamber music, songs, and piano pieces.

THE NETHERLANDS

Clarence G. Hamilton says in his *Outlines of Music History* that Netherland composers are patriotically laboring for a distinctive school. Few names are known outside of Holland, with the exception of Alphonse Diepenbroek (1862–1921), Dirk Schaefer (1873–1931), Sem Dresden (1881), James Zwart (1892), Julius Roentgen (1855–1932), who collected many of the Dutch folk songs, and Cornelius Dopper (1870), conductor and composer for orchestra. Among the younger men are Willem Pijper (1894) and Johan Franco (1908). Bernard van Dieren (1884–1936), who spent most of his life in London, wrote much music in a very modern and original style.

In Belgium, Jan Blockx (1851–1912) wrote successful operas and chamber music; Paul Gilson (1865) has written orchestral and chamber music works which have won him a high place among modern Flemish composers; both César Franck and Guillaume Lekeu were Flemish (Belgian); Joseph Jongen (1873), while not writing in very modern style, is well known for his symphonic poems, chamber music, a ballet, *S'Arka* (produced at the Théâtre de la Monnaie, Brussels), songs, piano pieces, and organ works.

SWITZERLAND

Jacques-Dalcroze (1865) is better known as the inventor of Eurythmics, a system of music study from the standpoint of rhythm, than as composer, but he has written many charming songs in folk style. Gustave Doret (1866), has written several operas, cantatas, oratorios which have been performed in his native land and in Paris. Hans Huber (1852–1921) has a long list of compositions in all forms. Ernest Bloch, though born in Switzerland is living in America and is by far the greatest innovator of these Swiss writers. Emile Blanchet (1877) is a writer of piano music, rather more poetic than of the very modern style. Arthur Honegger (1892) a leading composer of France, though born in Havre, is often claimed as a Swiss composer, because his parents are Swiss. Rudolph Ganz, pianist, composer and conductor in America was born in Switzerland.

With Frederick Delius (1863–1934) we first meet a new feeling in English music. He wrote orchestral pieces (*Brigg Fair*, concertos, *On Hearing the First Cuckoo in Spring*), choral works (*Appalachia*, *The Song of the High Hills*, *Mass of Life*, etc.), chamber music and songs. He was the first Englishman to write in the impressionistic way. His opera *The Village Romeo and Juliet* is modern in form. The music interprets the story and is not based on Italian models.

Delius, of Dutch-French-German stock, was born in England, but much of his life was passed in France. He lived for a short time in Florida. He never tried for music posts or prizes but remained apart to compose. Though his work occasionally sounds like the 18th century virginal music, it was often romantic in style with rich harmonic color.

He has, in his choral compositions, done some of the best work since Beethoven, says one biographer, and in them are strength, power and beauty, quite different indeed from the sensuous and sweet smaller works. He was a careful worker, a great idealist, and a truly great musician.

There are many well-trained musicians like Holbrooke and Hurlstone who have done much for music in England but this chapter belongs to those who are carrying on 20th century ideas.

Among them is Ralph Vaughan Williams (1872) to whom folk music is as bread to others. He uses it whenever he can. In his *London Symphony*, his most famous work, he has caught the spirit of the city and it is a milestone of the early 20th century. Isn't it curious that the most important music written on the poetry of our American Walt Whitman is by an Englishman! This is the *Sea Symphony* for orchestra and chorus, an impressive work by Vaughan Williams. His operas include *Hugh the Drover*, *St. John in Love*, *The Poisoned Kiss*, a comedy; and *Job*, a masque for dancing.

He has also written *Five Mystical Songs*, *Willow Wood* (cantata), *On Wenlock Edge* (six songs), three *Norfolk Rhapsodies*, *In the Fen Country*, and *Pastoral* Symphony.

Sir Granville Bantock (1868) is a musical liberator for he was the first to free English composers from the old style of Mendelssohn and the new kind of classicism of Brahms, and release them to write as they felt. He wrote music on the *Rubaiyat of Omar Khayyam* (Persian), *Sappho*, *Pierrot of the Minute*, *Fifine at the Fair*, *Hebredean* (Scotch) *Symphony*, which shows his love of Scotch music, and many other works, including songs, choral numbers and piano pieces. He succeeded Elgar at Birmingham University and has made valuable studies and collections of folk music.

A lover of chamber music, the fantasy and fancy, is Frank Bridge (1879). He is a thorough musician and has written *The Sea*, the *Dance Rhapsodies* for orchestra, symphonic poem *Isabella* on Keats' poem of the same name. *Three Idylls for Strings*, much chamber music, and other works.

Gustave Holst (1874–1934) whose original name was von Holst although he was not of German descent, was a pupil of Sir Charles V. Stanford and was an inspiring teacher and conductor. He had many posts and wrote many important works: an opera, *The Perfect Fool*, the *Hymn to Jesus*, one of the finest choral works of the century, *The Planets*, a fine orchestral work, *St. Paul's Suite* for strings, military band music, songs and part songs, some of which are written with violin accompaniment,—a charming idea!

John Ireland (1879), has written a fine piano sonata and a violin sonata, *Decorations* (a collection of small pieces), *Chelsea Reach*, *Ragamuffin* and *Soho Forenoons*, chamber music and orchestral pieces.

Cyril Scott (1879) was trained in Germany. He is a mixture of French impressionistic influence and Oriental mysticism, as you can see from the titles of his pieces: *Lotus Land* (Lotus is an Egyptian flower), *The Garden of Soul*

Sympathy, and *Riki Tiki Tavi*, a setting of Kipling's little chap of the Jungle Book, which is very delightful. He is one of the first English Impressionists who paved the way for the younger English School. He has made many inter, esting experiments in modern harmony and rhythm.

Arnold Bax (1883), of Irish parentage, is a gifted and poetic composer who has written many things in small and large forms, six symphonies, chamber music and piano sonatas, *The Garden of Fand* for orchestra, *Fatherland*, a chorus with orchestra, and other things, all of which show him to have a creative imagination and rich musical personality.

Lord Berners (1883) (Gerald Hugh Tyrwhitt-Wilson), a lover of the works of Stravinsky and Casella of the modern Russian and Italian Schools, was trained in an old-fashioned way, and then Stravinsky and Casella, seeing in his music possibilities for freer writing, encouraged him to break away from old ways, and he became one of the most modern of the young English composers. He writes interestingly in caricature and sarcasm, in fact he is a musical cartoonist in such pieces as the *Funeral March of a Pet Canary*, *Funeral March of a Rich Aunt*, full of originality and of fun in choosing subjects. He wrote, too, three pieces, *Hatred*, *Laughter* and *A Sigh* which are amazing musical studies. His work is interesting because of its daring in his very correct surroundings.

Eugene Goossens (1893), of Flemish ancestry, understands dissonance and modern combinations, which he uses with fascinating charm. His violin sonata and *Nature Pieces* for piano show his depth of feeling, his *Kaleidescopes* (12 children's pieces) show his humor and love of the grotesque, and *Four Conceits*, his power to be musically sarcastic. His *Five Impressions of a Holiday* and *Two Sketches for String Quartet* are so delightful that modern music would have lost much without them. He wrote *Judith*, a one act opera, and *Don Juan de Mañara*, and much chamber music in neoclassic style. He is a gifted conductor and has directed concerts in London and Rochester (New York), was engaged as guest conductor of the New York Symphony in 1925–26, and is the present conductor of the Cincinnati Orchestra.

Arthur Bliss (1891), like Stravinsky, whom he admires, was the *enfant terrible* of English music and was not held down by any rule or fixed standards except those of good taste. He used instruments in daring ways and showed a natural knowledge of them. One of his pieces is for an unaccompanied *Cor Anglais* (*English horn*). Among his works are *The Committee, In the Tube* (*Subway*) *at Oxford Circus, At the Ball.* He wrote a *Color Symphony,* so-called because when composing it, he experienced a play of color sensation, although he did not write it to be used with the color organ, as does Scriabin in *Prometheus.* Among his chamber music is a well known Quintet for oboe and strings. In *Rout,* a gay piece for voice and chamber orchestra, he used meaningless syllables in place of words. He spent several years in Los Angeles, but has returned to England. He has since become more conservative, as was shown in his Concerto for piano and orchestra, written for the British concert of the New York World's Fair (1939).

ENGLISH SONG WRITERS

The 20th century has produced many beautiful songs in England, written by Rutland Boughton, composer of an opera *The Immortal Hour;* Cecil Armstrong Gibbs; Peter Warlock (1894–1930), which was the assumed name under which the critic and writer, Philip Heseltine, wrote music; Herbert Howells; John Ireland, who has composed in other forms than songs; Norman O'Neill, who wrote the incidental music for several plays; Norman Peterkin; Roger Quilter; Martin Shaw, and Gerrard Williams.

WALTON AND LAMBERT

Of English composers born in this century, William Walton (1902) and Constant Lambert (1905) easily take first rank. Walton, whose father was a music teacher, was brought to the notice of the musical world by Edward J. Dent, professor of music at Cambridge, prominent writer, and president for many years of the International Society for Contemporary Music. Prof. Dent introduced Walton's string quartet to the Society, and it was performed in 1923 at the Salzburg Festival of the I. S. C. M. His next important works were the orchestral overture, *Portsmouth Point*, and the satirical ballet, *Façade*, written to accompany Edith Sitwell's poems. A work of importance was the viola concerto played at the Liége Festival of the I. S. C. M. in 1930. His choral work, *Belshazzar's Feast*, shows skilful handling of chorus, solo baritone voice, and orchestra. He has written his first symphony and also was the composer of the march *Crown Imperial* written for the coronation of George VI.

Constant Lambert comes from a family of painters and sculptors. Diaghilev commissioned a ballet, *Romeo and Juliet*, when the composer was hardly out of his 'teens. He is best known for his work for chorus, piano, and orchestra, *Rio Grande*, on a poem by Sacheverell Sitwell, employing jazz rhythms skilfully. A second ballet, *Pomona*, was performed at the London Festival of the International Society for Contemporary Music in 1931. He has recently written a third ballet, *Horoscope*, and a masque for chorus and orchestra, *Summer's Last Will and Testament*. Mr. Lambert is a conductor and critic, and is the author of a book, *Music, Ho!*

PRESENT DAY AMERICAN COMPOSERS

In this country we hear the works of all the composers of whom we have spoken in this chapter. We also have musicians, native born and foreign, many of whom have recently left their homes in middle Europe, who practise contemporary methods of composing. New York City to-day is the music center of the world, and in no country are there more young talents than in America. We have reason to be encouraged by the progress that has been made by our musicians in the 20th century.

A generation of composers has arisen, forming a new American school. Different tendencies, styles, educational backgrounds and influences are represented by men (and women) most of whom were born since 1900. Among these are George Antheil (1900), whose *Ballet Mechanique* shocked music lovers in 1925; Samuel Barber (1910), whose scores were played by Toscanini and the National Broadcasting Company's Orchestra, and by Stokowski and the Philadelphia Orchestra; Robert Russell Bennett (1894), who has won a reputation as a brilliant orchestrator, and composer of the *Abraham Lincoln* Symphony, the opera *Maria Malibran*, produced by the Juilliard Opera School, and of the *Water Music* for the New York World's Fair (1939); Nicolai Berezowsky (1900, Russia), composer of three symphonies, a violin concerto and much chamber music, whose scores have been played by Koussevitzky and the Boston Symphony Orchestra; Marc Blitzstein (1905), whose opera, *The Cradle Will Rock*, created a sensation; Elliott Carter (1908), whose ballet, *Pocahontas*, has been performed; Abram Chasins (1903), composer of two piano concertos, which he has played with major orchestras, and of popular piano pieces, including *Rush Hour in HongKong;* Israel Citkowitz (1909), whose song cycles and chamber music have won praise; Henry Cowell (1897), whose experiments in "tone clusters," rhythmical and acoustical problems have won him a unique place in American music; Ruth Crawford (1901), the first woman composer to hold a Guggenheim Fellowship; Chester MacKee (1894) writing fine songs with orchestra;

Paul Creston (1906); Robert Delaney (1903); David Diamond (1915), who received the Juilliard Publication Award for his *Psalm for Orchestra;* A. Lehman Engel (1910), conductor and composer of many choral works, incidental music to *Murder in the Cathedral, Within the Gates, A Hero is Born,* etc.; Vittorio Giannini (1903), who has written three operas and was commissioned by the Columbia Broadcasting System to write a special opera for radio performance (1938); Frederic Hart (1898), composer of a successful one-act opera *The Romance of Robot* produced by the Federal Music Project in New York; Robert McBride (1911), who has an original and humorous style of his own in chamber music, especially for woodwind instruments; Colin McPhee (1901, Canada), who has made a study of Balinese music; Charles Naginski (1909, Egypt), who won the American Prix de Rome (1938); Paul Nordoff (1909), composer of two piano concertos and chamber music; Gardner Read (1913), who won the first prize, with his first symphony, offered by the Philharmonic-Symphony Society (1937); Wallingford Riegger (1885), who has been writing for chamber orchestra, film and ballet; Elie Siegmeister (1909), who has written many choral numbers of popular appeal; William Grant Still (1895), an important Negro composer of contemporary tendencies; Gerald Strang (1908, Canada), an assistant to Schoenberg in California; Virgil Thomson (1896), composer of a sensational success, *Four Saints in Three Acts,* an opera to a text by Gertrude Stein; David Van Vactor (1906), whose first symphony won a Philharmonic-Symphony prize; Adolph Weiss (1891), a disciple of Schoenberg and an American atonalist. This list could be more than doubled if space permitted.

COMPOSERS AND PROFESSORS

Several composers born in the last decade of the 19th century are influencing American music not only by their own excellent works, but because they teach composition and theory in some of the leading universities and music schools.

Douglas Moore (1893), Associate Professor of Music at Columbia University, wrote an opera on Stephen Vincent Benet's text, *The Devil and Daniel Webster* (produced by American Lyric Theatre, 1939). His *Pageant of P. T. Barnum* and *Moby Dick* are popular orchestral numbers in which Mr. Moore has developed a direct and characteristic American idiom. He has written a string quartet published by the Society for the Publication of American Music, and choral works by the American poets, Benet, Lindsay and MacLeish.

Walter Piston (1894) is Chairman of the Music Division at Harvard. As a student he won fellowships, including the Guggenheim, and he has had several important commissions. He has written a Concerto and a Prelude and Fugue for orchestra, a concertino for piano and chamber orchestra, and chamber music.

Quincy Porter (1897) has written six string quartets, two violin sonatas, a symphony and incidental music for plays. He was professor of music at Vassar and in 1938 became Dean of the Faculty of the New England Conservatory. He, like Mr. Piston, has had important commissions from the League of Composers and the Columbia Broadcasting System.

Richard Donovan (1891) is a member of the faculty of Yale University School of Music, and organist and director of the choir of Christ Church, New Haven. He is particularly interested in plain song and early polyphonic music and writes choral works and chamber music in modern, dissonant style.

Bernard Rogers (1893), whose training was entirely American, received Pulitzer and Guggenheim fellowships. He teaches composition at the Eastman School of Music,

Rochester, N. Y. His orchestral scores have been performed by leading orchestras, and include three symphonies; he has also written works for chamber orchestra, choral works, a string quartet and an opera, *The Marriage of Aude*.

Randall Thompson (1899), a Fellow of the American Academy in Rome, has taught in Wellesley, Harvard, University of California, and in 1939 was made head of the Curtis Institute of Music in Philadelphia. He has composed two symphonies which have been played internationally. He has won a reputation also as a choral writer (*Americana*, a delightfully humorous chorus for mixed voices and *The Peaceable Kingdom*, commissioned by the League of Composers), and many of his works have been heard over the radio.

Roger Sessions (1896), who has been president of the United States Section of the International Society for Contemporary Music since 1934, is Assistant Professor of Music at Princeton University. His Symphony No. 1, and his Piano Sonata have been played at I. S. C. M. Festivals. His String Quartet No. 1 was presented at a Festival of the Library of Congress. He has held the Guggenheim, the American Academy at Rome, and the Carnegie Fellowships. His suite from *The Black Maskers* first brought his name before the musical public. He has composed three symphonies, one of which was commissioned by the League of Composers in the American Composers series. In 1928 with Aaron Copland he organized the Copland-Sessions concerts.

Bernard Wagenaar (1894, Holland) came to this country in 1921, since which time he has held an important position because of his orchestral works, which include three symphonies and a *Divertimento*, and a Triple Concerto for Harp, Flute, 'Cello and Orchestra, and his chamber music, *Three Songs from the Chinese*, sonatas for violin and for piano, and two string quartets. His works have been heard in America and Europe. He has received publication awards from the Eastman School, the Juilliard Foundation and the Society for the Publication of American Music. Since 1927 he has been a member of the faculty of the Juilliard Graduate School.

In the Music Department of New York University Philip James, Charles Haubiel and Marion Bauer are well known composers.

AN ITALIAN-AMERICAN OPERA WRITER

One of the youngest composers in this country to win acclaim is Gian-Carlo Menotti (1911), who was born in Italy and educated musically at the Curtis Institute. He has thus far devoted himself to operas in a 20th century version of the Italian *opera buffa*. So successful was he, that his first venture, *Amelia Goes to the Ball*, was given at the Metropolitan. He was commissioned to write a radio opera, which was presented by the National Broadcasting Company (1939). *The Old Maid and the Thief* proved to be a delightful farce, skilfully handled.

Another naturalized American composer is Anis Fuleihan (1900), who was born on the Island of Cyprus and came to the United States as a boy. He began his composing career with ballets written for the dance group of the Neighborhood Playhouse, for Adolf Bolm, the Denishawns and others. His orchestral suite, *Mediterranean*, and his symphony have been performed by major orchestras. He has composed two piano concertos with string orchestra, a viola concerto, chamber music, piano preludes and sonatas, choral works and songs.

A recent arrival in New York is Stefan Wolpe, whose Russian father settled in Berlin, Stefan's birthplace. He spent five years in Palestine, where he studied Arab and Jewish music. He has an unusual command of technical resources, which he uses in songs on Biblical texts, orchestral works and chamber music.

AARON COPLAND

One of our most important 20th century composers is
Aaron Copland (1900), who studied first with Rubin Goldmark and later in Paris with Nadia Boulanger, two teachers
who have trained many of the younger American group.
In 1925, he received a Guggenheim Fellowship. Mr. Copland has written many large scale works which have been
played by major orchestras: his early symphony for organ
and orchestra; two other symphonies and a *Dance Symphony;*
Symphonic Ode a commission for the celebration of the fiftieth anniversary of the Boston Symphony Orchestra; *Concerto* for piano and orchestra; *Outdoor Overture*, written for
and played by the orchestra of the High School of Music
and Art, New York; *Second Hurricane*, a "play-opera" for
high school performance; his ballets, *Hear Ye; Hear Ye!*
and *Billy the Kid*; *Music for the Theatre*, commissioned by
the League of Composers, for chamber orchestra; choral
works and chamber music, including his piano trio, *Vitebsk*,
on a Jewish melody; and his piano *Variations*. He has
turned from compositions of extreme dissonace to a type
which might be described as neoromantic. He also experimented with jazz rhythms in large forms—such as his concerto, and *El Salon Mexico*. In this brilliantly orchestrated
score, Mr. Copland has translated into music the Mexico
of the tourists as he found it reflected in a popular dance
hall in Mexico City. He has made use of Mexican folk
songs combined with rhythmic vitality, which produced an
exciting and effective piece.

Mr. Copland has been tireless in his interest in and encouragement of contemporary American music. He has
found time to examine scores of both younger and older
colleagues, to criticize, advise, and in many cases he used
his influence to get the works performed. Besides his share
in the Copland-Sessions Concerts (1928–1931), he was first

director of the American Festivals of Contemporary Music at Yaddo, Saratoga Springs, N. Y. and is active in work on the executive board of the League of Composers. In 1937 he helped to found the American Composers Alliance of which he is president. The object of the organization is to improve the economic position of native composers throughout the country.

Mr. Copland is the author of *What to Listen for in Music,* in the preface of which he states his musical creed: "The composer has something vital at stake. In helping others to hear music intelligently, he is working toward the spread of a musical culture which in the end will effect the understanding of his own creations."

Roy Harris

A most interesting career is that of Roy Harris (1898), who was born in Oklahoma and was brought up in California. He did not take up the study of composition until he was grown, and after he had decided to become a farmer and had served in tbe army during the World War. His first symphony was written before young Harris had had much training, but it showed unusual natural talent. He had studied in California and later he went to Paris where he became a pupil of Nadia Boulanger. At this time he received the Guggenheim Fellowship award for two years. In spite of his training, Mr. Harris is largely self taught, and his compositions have an individuality, a forceful, primitive quality, unlike the work of his teachers and colleagues. He has tried to apply the principles of Plain song to modern melody writing as shown in his third symphony.

His works have been performed by the important orchestras and chamber music organizations, as well as the radio companies which have often commissioned him to write special scores. His orchestral works include three symphonies, besides the Andante from the early symphony; a Symphony for High School Orchestras; *Johnny Comes Marching Home*, elaboration of the popular song; *Farewell to Pioneers*; a Chorale and a Prelude and Fugue for string orchestra; and concertos for violin and for piano. Among his choral compositions is a setting of Walt Whitman's *Song of Occupations*, which was commissioned by the League of Composers and sung on the Russian tour of the Westminster Choir. Mr. Harris has written many other choral works, such as his Symphony for Voices, and much chamber music. He was for a few years head of the Composition Department of the Westminster Choir School at Princeton, N. J., and director of the Princeton Festival of American Music.

WILLIAM SCHUMAN

Attention has been attracted to William Schuman (1910), one of the younger American composers by performances of his second symphony, an orchestral *Overture*, and his *Prologue* for chorus and orchestra, performed by the New York High School of Music and Art. Mr. Schuman is teacher of composition at the Sarah Lawrence College, Bronxville, N. Y., holder of the 1939 Guggenheim Fellowship and a recently elected member of the Executive Board of the League of Composers.

LEAGUE OF COMPOSERS

Several organizations have worked for the cause of modern music by presenting concerts devoted to works by contemporary Europeans and Americans. The *Pro Musica* Society has been responsible for the visits to this country of Maurice Ravel, Béla Bartók, Darius Milhaud, Alexandre Tansman, Arthur Honegger, and others.

The *League of Composers* (founded 1923) has had many notable "first performances" of compositions by Schoenberg, Bloch, Bartók, Stravinsky, Gruenberg, Malipiero, Hinde-

mith, Copland, de Falla, Whithorne, Carrillo, Sessions, and
many of the younger Americans. The League has enlarged
the scope of its activities to include commissions to American
composers, stage productions, radio programs, regional
broadcasts, and is planning (1939) to establish exchange programs with European countries. It publishes the quarterly
magazine, *Modern Music*, and has recently reorganized to
include, besides its executive board, a composers' committee,
an auxiliary board, and a committee for stage performances.

Its executive board with Mrs. Arthur M. Reis as chairman
includes: Marion Bauer, Nicolai Berezowsky, Aaron Cop-
land, Frederick Jacobi, Minna Lederman, editor of *Modern
Music*, Douglas Moore, Lee Pattison, Lazare Saminsky,
William Schuman, Roger Sessions, Randall Thompson, and
Dr. Thaddeus Hoyt Ames.

The *National Association for American Composers and
Conductors*, which also performs American works at its concerts, was founded by Henry Hadley to promote the interests of American composers and conductors. Sigmund
Spaeth is its president; Gena Branscombe, Horace Johnson
and Howard Murphy, its vice presidents; and it has a board
which arranges its programs with Harold Morris as its
chairman.

The *American Composers' Alliance*, with Aaron Copland
as president, is a new organization with a nation-wide membership. (See page 563.)

Our Good-bye

This book has been longer than it should have been, yet
our sins have been of omission rather than commission.
But if we have only made you realize that the world cannot
stand still, that music is always growing whether we understand it or not, and the good is handed on to the next generation even though much "falls by the wayside," we will
not have written in vain.

SOME OF THE BOOKS WE CONSULTED

Afro-American Folk Music, H. E. Krehbiel. (Schirmer, 1914.)

The History of American Music, Louis C. Elson. (Macmillan Co.)

Music in America, Dr. Frederick Louis Ritter. (Charles Scribner's Sons, 1890.)

My Musical Life, Walter Damrosch. (Charles Scribner's Sons, 1923.)

Stephen Collins Foster, Harold Vincent Milligan. (G. Schirmer, 1920.)

Francis Hopkinson and James Lyon, Two Studies in Early American Music, O. G. Sonneck. (Printed by the Author in Washington, D. C., 1905.)

Early Concert Life in America (1731–1800), O. G. Sonneck. (Leipzig, Breitkopf & Haertel, 1907.)

Musicians of Today, Romain Rolland. (Henry Holt, 1917.)

La Musique Française d'aujourd'hui, Jean Aubry. (Perrin & Cie.)

The History of Pianoforte Music, Herbert Westerby. (E. P. Dutton & Co.)

Gustav Mahler, Paul Stefan. (G. Schirmer.)

The Symphony Since Beethoven, Felix Weingartner. (Oliver Ditson Co., 1904.)

Voyage Musical au Pays du Passé, Romain Rolland. (Librairie Hachette & Sons, Ltd., 1909.)

Modern Composers of Europe, Arthur Elson. (Sir Isaac Pitman Sons, Ltd., 1907.)

The Player-Piano Up-to-Date, William Braid White. (Edward Lyman Bill.)

Outlines of Music History, Clarence G. Hamilton. (Oliver Ditson Co.)

The Romantic Composers, Daniel Gregory Mason. (Macmillan Co.)

Contemporary Russian Composers, M. Montagu-Nathan. (Frederick A. Stokes Co.)

The Story of Music, W. J. Henderson. (Longmans, Green & Co., 1889.)

Histoire Generale de la Musique, François Joseph Fetis.

Primitive Music, R. Wallaschek.

Grove's Dictionary of Music and Musicians. (Macmillan & Co.)

Music of the Most Ancient Nations, Carl Engel. (South Kensington Museum Art Handbooks.)

American Primitive Music, Frederick R. Burton.

The Art of Music: A Narrative History of Music. (D. G. Mason, Editor-in-Chief.)

Music: Its Laws and Evolution, Jules Combarieu. (Paul, Trench, Trübner & Co., 1903.)

Histoire de la Musique, Felix Clement.

History of Music, Emil Naumann.

Marcotone, Edward Maryon.

Mythology: Age of Fable, Bulfinch.

History of Music, W. J. Baltzell. (Theo. Presser.)

History of Rome, Dionysius Cassius.

Metropolitan Museum of Art Handbook No. 13.

Catalogue of Musical Instruments of All Nations.

Familiar Talks on the History of Music, A. J. Gantvoort. (G. Schirmer.)

Analysis of the Evolution of Musical Form, Margaret H. Glyn. (Longmans & Co.)

La Musique Gregorienne, Dom Augustin Gatard.

The Music of the Bible, Sir John Stainer. (Novello & Co. H. W. Gray.)

Critical and Historical Essays, Edward MacDowell. (A. P. Schmidt.)

Histoire de la Musique, H. Lavoix fils. (Concienne Maison Quantin.)

Early History of Singing, W. J. Henderson.

The History of British Music, Frederick J. Crowest.

Story of the Art of Music, F. J. Crowest. (Appleton's.)

La Musique des Troubadours, Jean Beck. (Laurens.)

Story of Minstrelsy, Edmondstoune Duncan. (Scribner's.)

Trouvères et Troubadours, Pierre Aubry. (Alcan.)

Lecture on Trouvères et Troubadours, Raymond Petit. (MS.)

Cours de Composition Musicale, Vincent d'Indy. (Durand et Cie.)

Encyclopédie de la Musique et Dictionaire du Conservatoire, Albert Lavignac (fondateur). V Vols.

The Threshold of Music, William Wallace. (Macmillan Co.)

Palestrina, Michel Brenet. (Alcan.)

Monteverdi, Henry Prunières. (Alcan.)

Twelve Good Musicians, Frederick Bridge. (Kegan Paul, Trench, Trübner & Co.)

Les Clavecinistes, André Pirro. (Laurens.)

Lully, Henry Prunières. (Laurens.)

The Earlier French Musicians (1632–1834), Mary Hargrave. (Kegan Paul, Trench.)

A History of Music, Paul Landormy. (Translated, F. H. Martens.) (Scribner's).

Chippewa Music, Frances Densmore. (Smithsonian Institution Bureau of American Ethnology.) (Bulletin 45.)

Teton Sioux Music, Frances Densmore. (Bureau of American Ethnology.) (Bulletin 61.)

Alla Breve, Carl Engel. (G. Schirmer.)

Complete Book of the Great Musicians, Percy A. Scholes. (Oxford University Press.)

Baker's Biographical Dictionary of Musicians. (3rd. revised Edition.) (G. Schirmer, 1919.)

Pianoforte and its Music, H. E. Krehbiel.

The Story of Music and Musicians, Lucy C. Lillie. (Harpers.)

Johann Sebastian Bach, Johann Nikolaus Forkel.

Irish Folk Music, Capt. Francis O'Neill. (1910, Regan Printing House. Lyon & Healy, Chicago.)

Histoire et Theorie de la Musique de L'Antiquité, par Fr. Aug. Gevaert, 1881.

Grand Opera Singers of Today, Henry C. Lahee. (The Page Co., Boston.)

Richard Strauss (Living Masters of Music), Ernest Newman. (John Lane, The Bodley Head.)

Great Singers—Series 1, 2, George T. Ferris. (T. Appleton Co., N. Y., 1893.)

Richard Strauss the Man and His Works, Henry T. Finck. (Little Brown & Co.)

The History of the Art of Music, W. S. B. Mathews. (The Music Magazine Pub. Co., Chicago, 1891.)

Haydn (The Great Musicians), Pauline D. Townsend. (Samson, Marston & Rivington, 1884.)

Mozart (The Great Musicians), Dr. F. Gehring. (Scribners, 1883.)

The World of Music, Anna Comtesse de Bremont. (Brentano's, 1892.)

Contemporary Musicians. Cecil Gray. (Oxford University Press, 1924.)

Music and Its Story, R. T. White. (Cambridge University Press, 1924.)

Evolution of the Art of Music, C. Hubert H. Parry. (Appleton, 1896.)

Modern Composers of Europe, Arthur Elson. (Sir Isaac Pitman & Son Ltd., London, 1909.)

One Hundred Folk Songs of All Nations, Granville Banstock. (G. Schirmer.)

Sixty Patriotic Songs of All Nations, Granville Banstock. (G. Schirmer.)

The Life of Ludwig van Beethoven, Alexander Wheelock Thayer. Translated by H. E. Krehbiel. (Beethoven Association, 1921.)

Complete Opera Book, Gustave Kobbé. (G. P. Putnam's Sons, 1924.)

In the Garret, Carl Van Vechten. (Alfred Knopf, 1920.)

The Music and Musical Instruments of the Arab, Francisco Salvador Daniel.

Songs of the Russian People, Kurt Schindler.

Appreciation of Music, Thomas Whitney Surette and Daniel Gregory Mason.

My Favorite Folk Songs, Marcella Sembrich. (Oliver Ditson Co.)

One Hundred Folk Songs, Cecil Sharp. (Oliver Ditson Co.)

Sixty Russian Folk Songs, Kurt Schindler and Deems Taylor. (G. Schirmer Co.)

Russian Folk Songs, M. Balakirev. (M. P. Belaieff, Leipzig.)

Old Irish Folk Music and Song, P. W. Joyce. (Longmans, Green Co.)

Ancient Irish Music, P. W. Joyce. (Longmans, Green Co.)

English Melodies, Vincent Jackson. (J. M. Dent & Son L't'd, 1910.)

Songs Every Child Should Know, Dolores M. Bacon. (Doubleday Page, 1906.)

The Orchestra and Its Instruments, Esther Singleton. (The Symphony Society of New York, 1917.)

Reminiscences of Morris Steinert, Jane Marlin. (G. P. Putnam's Sons, 1900.)

Edward MacDowell, Lawrence Gilman. (John Lane, 1906.)

The Study of Folk-Songs, Countess Martinengo-Cesaresco. (E. P. Dutton & Co.)

A History of Music, Sir Charles Villiers Stanford–Cecil Forsyth. (The Macmillan Co., 1924.)

The History of Music, Waldo Selden Pratt. (G. Schirmer, 1907.)

The New Encyclopedia of Music and Musicians, Waldo Selden Pratt, Editor. (The Macmillan Co., 1924.)

Ancient Art and Ritual, Jane Harrison. (Henry Holt & Co., 1913.)

Der Auftakt (*Czecho-Slovakian Magazine*). (Festival No., May, 1925).

Musical Quarterly, O. G. Sonneck, Editor. (G. Schirmer, April 1924.)

German Music of the Last Decade, by Hugo Leichtentritt. League of Composer Review. (New York.)

Franco-American Musical Society Bulletin. Ely Jade, Editor, (N. Y.)

Book of American Negro Spirituals. James Weldon Johnson. (Viking Press, N. Y.)

Miniature Essays. (J. &. W. Chester, Ltd.)

Program Notes of the Philharmonic Society of New York. Lawrence Gilman.

La Revue Musicale. Henry Prunières, Editor. (Paris.)

The Sackbut, Ursula Greville, Editor. (London.)

Musical America. (New York.)

Musical Courier. (New York.)

Musical Leader.

A History of Musical Thought, D. N. Ferguson (F. S. Crofts & Co., 1935)
Music Through the Ages, Marion Bauer and Ethel Peyser (G. P. Putnam's Sons, 1932)
Twentieth Century Music: How It Developed, How to Listen to It, Marion Bauer (G. P. Putnam's Sons, 1933)
How to Enjoy Music, Ethel Peyser (G. P. Putnam's Sons, 1933)
An Introduction to Music, Martin Bernstein (Prentice-Hall, Inc., 1937)
National Music, R. Vaughan Williams (Oxford University Press, 1934)
Discovering Music, H. D. McKinney and W. R. Anderson (American Book Co., 1934)
The Story of Music, Paul Bekker (W. W. Norton & Co., Inc., 1927)
Beethoven, The Man Who Freed Music, Robert Haven Schauffler (Doubleday, Doran & Co., Inc., 1929)
The Unknown Brahms, R. H. Schauffler (Dodd, Mead & Co., 1933)
Music of Our Day, Lazare Saminsky (Thomas Y. Crowell Co., 1932)
Brahms: His Life and Works, Karl Geiringer (Houghton Mifflin Co., 1936)
The Chamber Music of Brahms, D. G. Mason (The Macmillan Co., 1933)
International Cyclopedia of Music and Musicians, Edited by Oscar Thompson (Dodd, Mead & Co., 1939)
A History of Music, Theodore M. Finney (Harcourt, Brace & Co., 1935)
Music Since 1900: An Encyclopedic Survey, Nicolas Slonimsky (W. W. Norton & Co., Inc., 1937)
The Oxford Companion to Music, Percy A. Scholes (Oxford University Press, 1938)
Science and Music, Sir James Jeans (The Macmillan Co., 1937)
Composers in America, Biographical Sketches of Living Composers With a Record of Their Works, Claire Reis (The Macmillan Co., 1938)
Our American Music, John Tasker Howard (Thomas Y. Crowell, 1933)
Collected Essays, W. H. Hadow (Oxford University Press, 1927)
Listening to Music, Douglas S. Moore (W. W. Norton & Co., Inc., 1932)
What to Listen For in Music, Aaron Copland (Whittlesey House, McGraw-Hill Book Co., Inc., 1939)
World History of the Dance, Dr. Curt Sachs (W. W. Norton & Co., Inc., 1937)
Mozart, Marcia Davenport (Chas. Scribner's Sons, 1932)
Art-Song in America, William Treat Upton (Oliver Ditson Co., 1930)
The Changing Opera, Paul Bekker (W. W. Norton & Co., Inc., 1935)
The Progress of Music, George Dyson (Oxford University Press, 1932)
Essays in Musical Analysis, Donald Francis Tovey (Vols. I & II, *Symphonies;* Vol. III, *Concertos;* Vol. IV, *Polyphony and Illustrative Music;* Vol. V, *Vocal Music.* (Oxford University Press, 1935)
Modern Music, Minna Lederman, Ed. (League of Composers Quarterly)

Some Music Writers According to Forms of Composition

SOME MUSIC WRITERS ACCORDING TO FORMS OF COMPOSITION

Troubadours and Trouvères

TROUBADOURS
(*12th Century*)

Guillaume d'Acquitaine (1070–1127)
Bernart de Ventadorn (d. 1195)
Bertran de Born (d. c. 1215)
Richard the Lion Hearted (1169–99)
Peire Vidal (d. 1215)
Le Moine de Montaudon (The Monk of)
Guiraut de Borneil (Maestre dels trobadors) (d. c. 1220)
Gaucelm Faidit (Jongleur)

(*12th and 13th Centuries*)

Peire Cardinal

(*13th Century*)

Pierre Mauclerc (Duke of Bretagne)
Uc de Saint-Circ
Thibaut de Champagne (King of Navarre) (1201–1253)
Jean Bretel
Adam de la Hale (c. 1220–1287)
Guillaume de Machaut (c. 1300–1377)

TROUVÈRES
(*12th Century*)

Blondel de Nesle (d. c. 1200)
Chrétien de Troyes
Chatelain de Coucy (d. 1203)
Gace Brulé (d. c. 1210)

(*13th Century*)
Colin Muset (d. c. 1250)

Minnesingers
(*12th Century*)

Kürenberger
von Aist
Spervogel

(*13th Century*)

Wolfram von Eschenbach
Walther von der Vogelweide (c. 1164–c. 1227)
Prince Witzlav
Tannhäuser
Nitthart
Bitterolf
Prince Konrad

Meistersingers

Heinrich von Meissen ("Frauenlob") (12?–1318)
Till Eulenspiegel
Hans Sachs (1494–1576)

Motets and Madrigals

FRANCO-BELGIAN PERIOD

Guillaume Dufay (1400–1474)
Jakob Obrecht (1430–c. 1506)
Jan de Okeghem (1430–1495)
Josquin Des Près (c. 1445–1521)
Heinrich Isaak (1450–1517)
Jean Mouton (c. 1475–1522)
Heinrich Finck (German) (1444–1527)

573

Jakob Clemens non Papa (1475–1567)
Claude Goudimel (1505?–1572)
Johannes de Tinctoris (1446–1511)

FLEMISH PERIOD

Clement Jannequin (14?–15?)
Jakob Arcadelt (1514–c. 1570)
Adrian Willaert (1480–1562)
Nicolas Gombert (c. 1495–c. 1570)
Cyprian de Rore (1516–1565)
Philippe de Monte (1521–1603)
Orlandus Lassus (1530–1594)
Philippe Verdelot (16th cent.)

ITALIAN PERIOD

Alfonso della Viola (15?–c. 1567)
Constanza Festa (14?–1545)
Giovanni Animuccia (c. 1500–1571)
Andrea Gabrieli (1510–1586)
Giovanni Pierluigi da Palestrina (c. 1525–1594)
Orazio Vecchi (1550?–1605)
Matteo Asola (15?–1609)
Luca Marenzio (1550?–1599)
Giovanni Gabrieli (1557–1613)
Giovanni Gastoldi (c. 1550–?)
Carlo Gesualdo (c. 1560–1613)
Felice Anerio (1560–1614)
Andriano Banchieri (1567–1634)
Claudio Monteverde (1567–1643)

FRENCH PERIOD

Nicolas de la Grotte (16th cent.)
Claudin de Sermizy (1490–1562)
Claudin le Jeune (c. 1530–c. 1600)
Guillaume Costeley (1531–1606)
Jacques Mauduit (1557–1627)

GERMAN PERIOD

Heinrich Isaak (c. 1450–1517)
Ludwig Senfl (c. 1490–1500)
Hans Leo Hassler (1564–1612)

ENGLISH PERIOD

John Taverner (c. 1495–1545)
Richard Edwards (c. 1523–1566)
William Byrd (1543–1623)
Thomas Morley (1557–1604?)
Thomas Weelkes (?–1638?)

George Kirbye (?–1634)
John Dowland (1563–1626)
John Wilbye (1574–1638)
Michael Este (c. 1550–1625)
Thomas Ford (c. 1580–1648)
Orlando Gibbons (1583–1625)
Thomas Ravenscroft (c. 1590–c. 1633)

SPANISH PERIOD

Pedro Guerrero (15?–?)
Cristóbal Morales (1500–1553)
Francisco Guerrero (1527–1599)
Tomas Luis de Vittoria (c. 1535–1611)

Fugues

ITALIAN

Andrea Gabrieli (1510–1586)
Giovanni Gabrieli (1557–1613)
Adriano Banchieri (1567–1634)
Girolamo Frescobaldi (1583–1643)

ENGLISH

Thomas Tallis (c. 1510–1585)
William Byrd (1543–1623)
John Bull (1562?–1628)

DUTCH

Jan Pieters Sweelinck (1562–1621)

DANISH

Dietrich Buxtehude (1637–1707)

GERMAN

Samuel Scheidt (1587–1654)
Johann Jacob Froberger (1605–1667)
Johann Reinken (1623–1722)
Georg Muffat (c. 1645–1704)
Johann Pachelbel (1653–1706)
Johann Krieger (1652?–1735)
Johann Joseph Fux (1660–1741)
Johann Sebastian Bach (1685–1750)
George Frederic Handel (1685–1759) (English citizen)
Friedrich Marpurg (1718–1795)
Johann Georg Albrechtsberger (1736–1809)

FRENCH

François Couperin (1631–1698)
Jean Louis Marchand (1669–1732)
Louis Nicolas Clérembault (1676–1749)

Modern Fugues

GERMAN

August Klengel (1783–1852)
Wolfgang Amadeus Mozart (1756–1791)
Felix Mendelssohn - Bartholdy (1809–1847)
Robert Schumann (1810–1856)
Johannes Brahms (1833–1897)
Salomon Jadassohn (1831–1902)
Max Reger (1873–1916)

FRENCH

César Franck (Belg.) (1822–1890)
André Gédalge (1857–1926)
Camille Saint-Saëns (1835–1921)

AMERICAN

Mrs. H. H. A. Beach (1867)
Daniel Gregory Mason (1873)
Charles Haubiel (1892)
Roy Harris (1898)

SWEDISH

Emil Sjögren (1853–1918)

CZECHO-SLOVAKIAN

Felix Petyrek (1892)

Suites

(*Sonate da Camera, Sonate da Chiesa, Sonatas, Ordres, Suites, Exercises, Partitas*)

ITALIAN

Girolamo Frescobaldi (1583–1644)
Michel Angelo Rossi (159?–16?)
Giovanni Legrenzi (1625–1690)
Bernardo Pasquini (1637–1710)
Giovanni Bononcini (1640–1678)
Giovanni Battista Vitali (1644–1692)
Giuseppe Torelli (1645–1708)
Arcangelo Corelli (1653–1713)

Domenico Zipoli (c. 1675–c. 1726)
Evarista Felice d'all'Abaco (16?–17?)
Domenico Scarlatti (1685–1757)

FRENCH

Jacques Champion de Chambonnières (1610–1671)
François Couperin (1668–1733)
Jean Philippe Rameau (1683–1764)
Jean François Dandrieu (1684–1740)
Jean Marie Leclair (1687–1764)

ENGLISH

Henry Purcell (c. 1659–1695)

GERMAN

Johann Schein (1586–1630)
Samuel Scheidt (1587–1654)
Johann Philipp Krieger (1652?–1735)
Johann Kuhnau (1660–1722)
Georg Böhm (1661–1733)
Johann Mattheson (1681–1764)
Georg Philipp Telemann (1681–1767)
Johann Sebastian Bach (1685–1750)
George Frederic Handel (1685–1759)

Modern Suites

GERMAN

Joseph Joachim Raff (Swiss) (1822–1882)
Karl Reinecke (1824–1910)
Ignaz Brüll (1846–1907)
Ferdinand Hummel (1855–1928)
Max Reger (1873–1916)
Ernst Toch (1887)
Arnold Schoenberg (1874) (Austrian)

FRENCH

Georges Bizet (1838–1875)
Charles Marie Widor (1845–1937)
Benjamin Godard (1849–1895)
Claude Debussy (1862–1918)
Jean Roger-Ducasse (1873)

Maurice Ravel (1875–1937)
Darius Milhaud (1892)

RUSSIAN

Peter Ilich Tchaikowsky (1840–1893)
Michael Ippolitoff-Ivanoff (1859–1935)
Serge Rachmaninoff (1873) (American)
Igor Stravinsky (1882) (French)

HUNGARIAN

Emanuel Moor (1863–1931)
Ernst von Dohnanyi (1877)

ENGLISH

Edward German (1862–1936)
Eugen d'Albert (1864–1932)
Granville Bantock (1868)
Ralph Vaughan Williams (1872)
Gustav Holst (1874–1934)
York Bowen (1884)

NORWEGIAN

Edvard Grieg (1843–1907)
Christian Sinding (1856)
Johan Halvorsen (1864–1935)

AMERICAN

Edgar Stillman-Kelley (1857)
Edward MacDowell (1861–1908)
Arthur Whiting (1861–1936)
Louis Victor Saar (1868–1937)
Leopold Godowsky (1870–1939)
John Alden Carpenter (1876)
Louis Gruenberg (1884)
Harold Morris (1889)
Charles Haubiel (1892)
Albert Stoessel (1894)

POLISH

Alexandre Tansman (1897)

FINNISH

Jan Sibelius (1865)

ITALIAN

Ferruccio Busoni (1866–1924)
Lorenzo Perosi (1872)
Ottorino Respighi (1879–1936)

Sonatas

(Before Beethoven)

GERMAN AND AUSTRIAN

Johann Kuhnau (1660–1722)
Johann Mattheson (1681–1764)
Georg Philipp Telemann (1681–1767)
Johann Sebastian Bach (1685–1750)
George Frederic Handel (1685–1759)
Franz Richter (1709–1789)
Karl Philipp Emanuel Bach (1714-1788)
Johann Stamitz (1717–1757)
Leopold Mozart (1719–1788)
Joseph Haydn (1732–1809)
Karl von Dittersdorf (1739–1799)
Karl Stamitz (1746–1801)
Wolfgang Amadeus Mozart (1756–1791)
Ludwig van Beethoven (1770–1827)

ITALIAN

Giovanni Vitali (c. 1644–1692)
Arcangelo Corelli (1653–1713)
Giovanni Bassani (c. 1657–1716)
Tommaso Vitali (c. 1665–?)
Antonio Vivaldi (1675–1743)
Francesco Maria Veracini (1685–1750)
Domenico Scarlatti (1685–1757)
Giuseppe Tartini (1692–1770)
Pietro Locatelli (1693–1764)
Giovanni Sammartini (1701–1775)
Baldassare Galuppi (1706–1784)
Pietro Domenico Paradies (1710–1792)
Pietro Nardini (1722–1793)
Gaetano Pugnani (1731–1798)
Luigi Boccherini (1743–1805)
Giovanni Battista Viotti (1753–1824)

(Contemporaries of Beethoven)

GERMAN AND AUSTRIAN

Johann Dussek (Bohemian) (1761–1812)
Johann Cramer (1771–1858)
Johann Woelfl (1772–1812)

Johann Hummel (1778–1837)
Ferdinand Ries (1784–1838)
Karl Maria von Weber (1786–1826)
Friedrich W. M. Kalkbrenner (1788–1849)
Ignaz Moscheles (Bohemian) (1794–1870)
Franz Schubert (1797–1828)

ITALIAN

Muzio Clementi (1752–1832)
Luigi Cherubini (1760–1842)

ENGLISH

Samuel Wesley (1766–1837)
John Field (1782–1837)

(After Beethoven)

GERMAN AND AUSTRIAN

Franz Schubert (1797–1828)
Heinrich Marschner (1795–1861)
Felix Mendelssohn - Bartholdy (1809–1847)
Robert Schumann (1810–1856)
Franz Liszt (1811–1886)
Joseph Raff (Swiss) (1822–1882)
Karl Reinecke (1824–1910)
Johannes Brahms (1833–1897)
Ludwig Thuille (1861–1907)
Richard Strauss (1864)
Georg Schumann (1866)
Alexander Zemlinsky (1872)
Max Reger (1873–1916)
Heinz Tiessen (1887)
Hermann Scherchen (1891)
Egon Kornauth (1891)
Philipp Jarnach (1892) (French-Spanish)
Paul Pisk (1893) (living in America)
Paul Hindemith (1895)
Erich Wolfgang Korngold (1897) (American)
Ernst Krenek (1900) (living in America)

CZECHO-SLOVAKIAN

Rudolph Karel (1881)
Emil Axman (1887)

HUNGARIAN

Franz Liszt (1811–1886)
Emanuel Moor (1863–1931)
Ernst von Dohnanyi (1877)
Béla Bártok (1881)
Zoltan Kodály (1882)

FRENCH

César Franck (Belgian) (1822–1890)
Camille Saint-Saëns (1835–1921)
Felix Alexandre Guilmant (1837–1911)
Gabriel Fauré (1845–1924)
Charles Marie Widor (1845–1937)
Benjamin Godard (1849–1895)
Paul Vincent d'Indy (1851–1931)
Claude Achille Debussy (1862–1918)
Gabriel Pierné (1863–1937)
Guy Ropartz (1864)
Paul Dukas (1865–1935)
Charles Koechlin (1867)
Guillaume Lekeu (Belgian) (1870–1894)
Florent Schmitt (1870)
Maurice Ravel (1875–1937)
Rhené-Baton (1879)
Gabriel Grovlez (1879)
Arthur Honegger (1892)
Darius Milhaud (1892)
Germaine Tailleferre (1892)
Raymond Petit (1893)

DUTCH

Samuel de Lange (1840–1911)
Dirk Schaefer (1873–1931)
James Zwart (1892)
Willem Pijper (1894)
Johan Franco (1908)

RUSSIAN

Anton Rubinstein (1829–1894)
Georg Catoire (1861–1926)
Joseph Wihtol (1863)
Alexander Glazounov (1865–1936)
Alexander Scriabin (1872–1915)
Paul Juon (1872)
Serge Rachmaninoff (1873) (American)

Fedor Akimenko (1876)
Nicholas Medtner (1880)
Nicolai Miaskovsky (1881)
Igor Stravinsky (1882)
Samuel Feinberg (1890)
Alexander Tcherepnin (1899)

POLISH

Frédéric Chopin (1810–1849)
Xaver Scharwenka (1850–1924)
Ignace Jan Paderewski (1860)
Miecyslaw Karlowicz (1876–1909)
Karol Szymanowski (1883–1937)

SCANDINAVIAN

Johan P. E. Hartmann (Danish)
(1805–1900)
Niels Wilhelm Gade (Danish)
(1817–1890)
Edvard Hagerup Grieg (Norwegian) (1835–1919)
Emil Sjögren (Swedish) (1853–1918)
Bror Beckman (Swedish) (1866)
Wilhelm Stenhammar (Swedish)
(1871–1927)

ITALIAN

Enrico Bossi (1861–1925)
Ferruccio Busoni (1866–1924)
Ildebrando Pizzetti (1880)
Alfredo Casella (1883)

SPANISH

Isaac Albeniz (1860–1909)

ENGLISH

William Sterndale Bennett (1816–1875)
C. Hubert H. Parry (1848–1918)
Charles Stanford Villiers (1852–1924)
Marie Wurm (1860–1938)
John B. McEwen (1868)
Wm. Y. Hurlstone (1876–1906)
John Ireland (1879)
Cyril Scott (1879)
Arnold Bax (1882)
York Bowen (1884)

AMERICAN

John Knowles Paine (1839–1906)
Arthur Foote (1853–1937)
Edward MacDowell (1861–1908)
Ernest Kroeger (1862–1934)
Henry Holden Huss (1862)
Mrs. H. H. A. Beach (1867)
Frederick Converse (1871)
Edward B. Hill (1872)
Daniel Gregory Mason (1873)
John Alden Carpenter (1876)
David Stanley Smith (1876)
Louis Campbell-Tipton (1877–1921)
Alexander MacFayden (1879)
Ernest Bloch (Swiss) (1880)
Arthur Shepherd (1880)
Fanny Charles Dillon (1881)
John Powell (1882)
Charles Griffes (1884–1920)
Emerson Whithorne (1884)
Louis Gruenberg (1884)
George Boyle (Australian) (1886)
James Friskin (Scottish) (1886)
Marion Bauer (1887)
Chalmers Clifton (1889)
Harold Morris (1889)
Donald Tweedy (1890)
Elliot Griffis (1892)
Albert Stoessel (1894)
Bernard Wagenaar (1894)
Leo Ornstein (Russian) (1895)
Aurelio Giorni (It.) (1895-1938)
Roger Sessions (1896)
Quincy Porter (1897)
Roy Harris (1898)
George Antheil (1900)
Ulric Cole (1905)
Ross Lee Finney (1906)

Classic Concertos

GERMAN

(*Before Mozart*)

Johann Sebastian Bach (1685–1750)
George Frederic Handel (1685–1759)
Johann Gottlieb Graun (1701–1759)
Franz Benda (Bohemian) (1709–1786)

Wilhelm Friedemann Bach (1710–1784)
Karl Philipp Emanuel Bach (1714–1788)
Franz Joseph Haydn (1732–1809)

FRENCH

Jean Marie Leclair (1697–1764)
Jean Philippe Rameau (1683–1764)

ITALIAN

Giuseppe Torelli (1650–1708)
Arcangelo Corelli (1653–1713)
Antonio Vivaldi (1675–1743)
Francesco Maria Veracini (1685–1750)
Giuseppe Tartini (1692–1770)

Concertos

GERMAN AND AUSTRIAN

Wolfgang Amadeus Mozart (1756–1791)
Johann Dussek (1761–1812)
Ludwig van Beethoven (1770–1827)
Joseph Woelfl (1772–1812)
Johann Hummel (1778–1837)
Ferdinand Ries (1784–1838)
Ludwig Spohr (1784–1859)
Karl Maria von Weber (1786–1826)
Friedrich Kalkbrenner (1788–1849)
Ignaz Moscheles (Bohemian) (1794–1870)
Wilhelm Molique (1802–1869)
Felix Mendelssohn - Bartholdy (1809–1847)
Robert Schumann (1810–1856)
Georg E. Goltermann (1824–1898)
Karl Reinecke (1824–1910)
Johannes Brahms (1833–1897)
Max Bruch (1838–1917)
Josef Rheinberger (1839–1901)
Heinrich Hofmann (1842–1902)
Ignaz Brüll (1846–1907)
Richard Strauss (1864)
Hans Pfitzner (1869)
Max Reger (1873–1916)
Arnold Schönberg (1874) (American)

Alban Berg (1885–1935)
Heinrich Kaminski (1886)
Ernst Toch (1887)
Paul Hindemith (1895)
Ernst Krenek (1900)

CZECHO-SLOVAKIAN

Antonin Dvorák (1841–1904)
Vaclav Talich (1883)
Erwin Schulhoff (1894)

HUNGARIAN

Franz Liszt (1811–1886)
Joseph Joachim (1831–1907)
Jeno Hubay (1858–1937)
Julius Major (1859–1925)
Emanuel Moor (1863–1931)
Ottokar Novacek (1866–1900)
Ernst von Dohnanyi (1877)
Béla Bártok (1881)

FRENCH

François Baillot (1771–1842)
Jacques Rode (1774–1830)
Henri Vieuxtemps (1820–1881)
César Franck (Belgian) (1822–1890)
Edouard Lalo (1823–1892)
Camille Saint-Saëns (1835–1921)
Charles Marie Widor (1845–1937)
Gabriel Fauré (1845–1924)
Benjamin Godard (1849–1895)
Ernest Chausson (1855–1899)
Gabriel Pierné (1863–1937)
Maurice Ravel (1875–1937)
Darius Milhaud (1892)
Germaine Tailleferre (1892)
Jean Francaix (1912)

BELGIAN

Eugen Ysaye (1858–1931)
Théophile Ysaye (1865–1918)
Joseph Jongen (1873)

DUTCH

Julius Roentgen (1855–1932)
Dirk Schaefer (1873–1931)
James Zwart (1892)

SWISS

Hans Huber (1852–1921)

RUSSIAN

Anton Rubinstein (1830–1894)
Peter Ilich Tchaikowsky (1840–1893)
Nikolai Rimsky-Korsakov (1844–1908)
Serge Liapounov (1859–1924)
Anton Arensky (1861–1906)
Georg Catoire (1861–1926)
Alexander Glazounov (1865–1936)
Alexander Scriabin (1872–1915)
Serge Rachmaninoff (1873)
Fedor Akimenko (1876)
Nicolai Miaskovsky (1881)
Igor Stravinsky (1882)
Serge Prokofieff (1891)
Alexander Tcherepnin (1899)

POLISH

Frédéric Chopin (1809–1849)
Joseph Wieniawski (1837–1912)
Philipp Scharwenka (1847–1917)
Franz Xaver Scharwenka (1850–1924)
Ignace Jan Paderewski (1860)
Emil Mlynarski (1870–1935)
Sigismond Stojowski (1870) (living in America)
Karol Szymanowski (1883–1937)
Alexandre Tansman (1897)

FINNISH

Jan Sibelius (1865)
Selim Palmgren (1878)

SCANDINAVIAN

Eduard Lassen (Danish) (1830–1904)
August Winding (Danish) (1835–1899)
Emil Hartmann (Danish) (1836–1898)
Johan Svendsen (Norwegian) (1840–1911)
Edvard Grieg (Norwegian) (1843–1907)
Christian Sinding (Norwegian) (1856)
Johan Halvorsen (Norwegian) (1864)
Tor Aulin (Swedish) (1866–1914)

Wilhelm Stenhammar (Swedish) (1871)
Hugo Alfven (Swedish) (1872)
Halfdan Cleve (Norwegian) (1879)
Kurt Atterberg (Swedish) (1887)

ITALIAN

Nicolo Paganini (1780–1840)
Giuseppe Martucci (1856–1909)
Alberto Franchetti (1860)
Enrico Bossi (1861–1925)
Ferruccio Busoni (1866–1924)
Leone Sinigaglia (1868)
Ottorino Respighi (1879–1936)
G. Francesco Malipiero (1882)
Alfredo Casella (1883)
Vittorio Rieti (1898)

SPANISH

Isaac Albeniz (1860–1909)
Manuel de Falla (1876)
Juan de Manen (1883)

ENGLISH

John Field (1782–1837)
George MacFarren (1813–1887)
William Sterndale Bennett (1816–1875)
Frederick Hymen Cowen (1852–1935)
Tobias Matthay (1858)
Frederick Delius (1863–1934)
Eugen d'Albert (Scotch) (1864–1932)
Arthur Hinton (1869)
Samuel Coleridge-Taylor (1875–1912)
Wm. Y. Hurlstone (1876–1906)
Cyril Scott (1879)
York Bowen (1884)
Arthur Bliss (1891)
Dorothy Howell (20th Century)
William Walton (1902)

AMERICAN

Leopold Damrosch (German) (1832–1885)
Frederick Grant Gleason (1848–1903)
Max Vogrich (Transylvanian) (1852–1916)
Helen Hopekirk (Scotch) (1856)

Harry Rowe Shelley (1858)
Victor Herbert (1859–1924)
Edward MacDowell (1861–1908)
Edmund Severn (1862)
Henry Holden Huss (1862)
Mrs. H. H. A. Beach (1867)
Gustav Strube (German) (1867)
Ernest Hutcheson (Australian)
    (1871)
Felix Borowski (1872)
Arne Oldberg (1874)
Ernest Schelling (1876)
Josef Hofmann (Polish) (1876)
John Alden Carpenter (1876)
Blair Fairchild (1877–1933)
Ernest Bloch (Swiss) (1880)
John Powell (1882)
Louis Gruenberg (1884)
Cecil Burleigh (1885)
George F. Boyle (Australian)
    (1886)
Albert Spalding (1888)
Harold Morris (1889)
A. Walter Kramer (1890)
Frederick Jacobi (1891)
Mana Zucca (1893)
Leo Ornstein (Russian) (1895)
Leo Sowerby (1895)
Roger Sessions (1896)
Aaron Copland (1900)
Nicolai Berezowsky (1900)
Anis Fuleihan (Syrian) (1900)
Abram Chasins (1903)
Paul Nordoff (1909)

Symphonies

German and Austrian

Franz Xaver Richter (1709–1789)
Karl Philipp Emanuel Bach (1714–1788)
Johann Stamitz (1717–1757)
Karl Friedrich Abel (1725–1787)
Franz Joseph Haydn (1732–1809)
Michael Haydn (1737–1806)
Johann Christian Bach (1738–1782)
K. D. von Dittersdorf (1739–1799)
Karl Stamitz (1746–1801)
Wolfgang Amadeus Mozart (1756–1791)
Ludwig von Beethoven (1770–1827)

Ludwig Spohr (1784–1859)
Carl Maria von Weber (1786–1826)
Franz Schubert (1797–1828)
Franz Lachner (1803–1890)
Felix Mendelssohn - Bartholdy
    (1809–1847)
Otto Nicolai (1810–1849)
Robert Schumann (1810–1856)
Robert Volkmann (1815–1883)
Joseph Joachim Raff (Swiss)
    (1822–1882)
Anton Bruckner (1824–1896)
Johannes Brahms (1833–1897)
Max Bruch (1838–1920)
Herman Goetz (1840–1876)
August Klughart (1847–1902)
Felix Weingartner (1863)
Richard Strauss (1864)
Georg Schumann (1866)
Siegmund von Hausegger (1872)
Alexander von Zemlinsky (1872)
Karl Bleyle (1880)
Heinz Tiessen (1887)
Ernst Toch (1887) (in America)
Karol Rathaus (1895) (in America)
Eduard Erdmann (1896)

(Dance Symphony)

Egon Wellesz (1885)
Ernst Krenek (1900)

Czecho·slovakian

Frederic Smetana (1824–1884)
J. J. Abert (1832–1915)
Antonin Dvořák (1841–1904)
Gustav Mahler (1860–1911)
Josef Suk (1874–1935)
Otakar Ostrcil (1879–1937)
Emil Axman (1887)
Erwin Schulhoff (1894)

Hungarian

Franz Liszt (1811–1886)
Karl Goldmark (1830–1915)
Julius Major (1859–1925)
Emanuel Moor (1863–1931)
Ernst von Dohnanyi (1877)

French

François Joseph Gossec (Belgian)
    (1734–1829)

Henri Méhul (1763-1817)
Hector Berlioz (1803-1869)
Napoleon - Henri Reber (1807-1880)
Charles François Gounod (1818-1893)
César Franck (Belgian) (1822-1890)
Edouard Lalo (1823-1892)
Camille Saint-Saëns (1835-1921)
Charles Widor (1845-1937)
Gabriel Fauré (1845-1924)
Augusta Holmès (1847-1903) (Irish)
Vincent d'Indy (1851-1931)
Ernest Chausson (1855-1899)
André Gédalge (1857-1926)
Guy Ropartz (1864)
Paul Dukas (1865-1935)
Alberic Magnard (1865-1914)
Albert Roussel (1869-1937)
Henri Rabaud (1873)
Darius Milhaud (1892)

BELGIAN
Théophile Ysaye (1865-1918)

DUTCH
Richard Hol (1825-1904)
Bernard Zweers (1854-1924)
Julius Roentgen (1855-1932)
Cornelius Dopper (1870)
Bernard Dieren (1884-1936)
Willem Pijper (1894)

SWISS
Hans Huber (1852-1921)

ROUMANIAN
Georges Enesco (1881)

RUSSIAN
Anton Rubinstein (1829-1894)
Alexander Borodin (1833-1887)
Mily Balakirev (1837-1910)
Peter Ilich Tchaikowsky (1840-1893)
Nikolai Rimsky-Korsakov (1844-1908)
Sergius Taneiev (1856-1915)
Joseph Wihtol (1863)
Alexander Gretchaninov (1864)

Alexander Glazounov (1865-1936)
Vassili Kilinnikov (1866-1900)
Paul Juon (1872)
Alexander Scriabin (1872-1915)
Serge Vassilenko (1872)
Serge Rachmaninoff (1873) (in America)
Reinhold Glière (1875)
Nicholas Miaskovsky (1881)
Igor Stravinsky (1882)
Maximilian Steinberg (1883)
Alexander Krein (1883)
Youri Shaporin (1889)
Serge Prokofieff (1891)
Lev Knipper (1898)
Leonid Polovinkin (1898)
Vissarion Shebalin (1902)
Dmitri Shostakovitch (1906)
Igor Markievitch (1912) (in Paris)
Julian Krein (1913)

POLISH
Philipp Scharwenka (1847-1917)
Franz Xaver Scharwenka (1850-1924)
Ignace Jan Paderewski (1860)
Emil Mlynarski (1870-1935)
Sigismund Stojowski (1870) (in America)
Miecyslaw Karlowicz (1876-1909)
Felix Nowowiejski (German) (1877)
Karol Szymanowski (1883-1937)
Alexandre Tansman (1897)

FINNISH
Jan Sibelius (1865)
Leevi Madetoja (1887)

SCANDINAVIAN
Johan P. E. Hartmann (Danish) (1805-1900)
Niels Gade (Danish) (1817-1890)
Eduard Lassen (Danish) (1830-1904)
Emil Hartmann (Danish) (1836-1898)
Johan Svendsen (Norwegian) (1840-1911)
Peter Lange-Müller (Danish) (1850-1926)

Jacob Adolph Hagg (Swedish) (1850)
Victor Bendix (Danish) (1851–1926)
Christian Sinding (Norwegian) (1856)
A. Carl Nielson (Danish) (1865–1931)
Wilhelm Stenhammar (Swedish) (1871–1927)
Sigurd Lie (Norwegian) (1871–1904)
Natanael Berg (Swedish) (1879)
Kurt Atterberg (Swedish) (1887)

ITALIAN

Giovanni Battista Sammartini (1704–1774)
Carlo Toeschi (1724–1788)
Luigi Boccherini (1743–1805)
Giovanni Toeschi (1745–1800)
Antonio Salieri (1750–1825)
Muzio Clementi (1752–1832)
Giovanni Sgambati (1843–1914)
Giuseppe Martucci (1856–1909)
Franco Alfano (1876)
Ildebrando Pizzetti (1880)
G. Francesco Malipiero (1882)
Alfredo Casella (1883)
Victor da Sabata (1892)
Vittorio Rieti (1898)

MEXICAN

Carlos Chavez (1899)

ENGLISH

Sir G. A. Macfarren (1813–1887)
Sir Arthur Sullivan (1842–1901)
Sir Charles Hubert H. Parry (1848–1918)
Sir Frederick H. Cowen (1852–1935)
Sir Charles V. Stanford (1852–1924)
Sir Edward Elgar (1857–1934)
Dame Ethel M. Smyth (1858)
Algernon Ashton (1859–1937)
Granville Bantock (1868)
Arthur Hinton (1869)
Walford Davies (1869)
Percy Pitt (1870-1932)
Ralph Vaughan Williams (1872)

Gustav Holst (1874–1934)
Hamilton Harty (1879)
Arnold Bax (1883)
York Bowen (1884)
Benjamin Dale (1885)
Arthur Bliss (1891)

AMERICAN

Leopold Damrosch (1832–1885)
John Knowles Paine (1839–1906)
Silas G. Pratt (1846–1916)
Max Vogrich (Transylvanian) (1852–1916)
George Chadwick (1854–1931)
George Templeton Strong (1856)
Arthur Bird (1856-1924)
Edgar Stillman Kelley (1857)
Henry Schoenefeld (1857–1936)
Charles Martin Loeffler (1861–1935) (French)
Ernest Kroeger (1862–1934)
Horatio Parker (1863–1919)
Gustav Strube (1867)
Mrs. H. H. A. Beach (1867)
Howard Brockway (1870)
Henry K. Hadley (1871–1937)
Frederick Converse (1871)
Frederick Stock (1872)
Edward B. Hill (1872)
Daniel Gregory Mason (1873)
Arne Oldberg (1874)
Ernest Schelling (1876)
Mortimer Wilson (1876–1932)
David Stanley Smith (1877)
Ernest Bloch (Swiss) (1880)
Eric Delamarter (1880)
Lazare Saminsky (1882) (Russian)
Edwin Grasse (1884)
Louis Gruenberg (1884)
Emerson Whithorne (1884)
John J. Becker (1886)
Harold Morris (1889)
Edwin Stringham (1890)
Frederick Jacobi (1891)
Bernard Rogers (1893)
Bernard Wagenaar (1894) (Dutch)
Robert Russell Bennett (1894)
William Grant Still (1895)
Roger Sessions (1896)
Howard Hanson (1896)
Quincy Porter (1897)
Roy Harris (1898)
William Dawson (1899)

Werner Janssen (1899)
Harl McDonald (1899)
Randall Thompson (1899)
Anis Fuleihan (Syrian) (1900)
Aaron Copland (1900)
Nicolai Berezowsky (1900) (Russ'n)
Charles Naginski (b. Egypt) (1909)
Samuel Barber (1910)
William Schuman (1910)
Gardner Read (1913)
David Diamond (1915)

Orchestral Music

(Symphonic Tone Poems, Overtures, Suites, etc.)

GERMAN AND AUSTRIAN

Ludwig van Beethoven (1770–1827)
Carl Maria von Weber (1786–1826)
Felix Mendelssohn - Bartholdy (1809–1847)
Robert Schumann (1810–1856)
Richard Wagner (1813–1883)
Johann Strauss (1825–1899)
Johannes Brahms (1833–1897)
Alexander Ritter (1833–1896)
Heinrich Hofmann (1842–1902)
Engelbert Humperdinck (1854–1921)
Felix Weingartner (1863)
Richard Strauss (1864)
Georg Schumann (1866)
Max von Schillings (1868–1933)
Siegmund von Hausegger (1872)
Paul Juon (Russian) (1872)
Max Reger (1873–1916)
Arnold Schoenberg (1874) (American)
Paul Amadeus Pisk (1893) (in America)
Paul Hindemith (1895)
Erich Korngold (1898) (in America)
Karol Rathaus (1895) (in America)

CZECHO-SLOVAKIAN

Frederick Smetana (1824–1884)
Antonin Dvořák (1843–1904)
Zdenko Fibich (1850–1900)

Vitezslav Novak (1870)
Josef Suk (1874–1935)
Otakar Ostrcil (1879–1937)
Rudolf Karel (1880)
Karl Horwitz (1884–1925)
Bohuslav Martinu (1890)
Fidelio Finke (1891)

HUNGARIAN

Franz Liszt (1811–1886)
Karl Goldmark (1830–1915)
Emanuel Moor (1863–1931)
Ernst von Dohnanyi (1877)
Béla Bártok (1881)
Zoltan Kodaly (1882)
George Kosa (1897)

FRENCH

Hector Berlioz (1803–1869)
Félicien David (1810–1876)
César Franck (Belgian) (1822–1890)
Camille Saint-Saëns (1835–1921)
Théodore Dubois (1837–1924)
Georges Bizet (1838–1875)
Alexis Emanuel Chabrier (1841–1894)
Jules Massenet (1842–1912)
Gabriel Fauré (1845–1924)
Vincent d'Indy (1851–1931)
Ernest Chausson (1855–1899)
Georges Huë (1858)
Gustave Charpentier (1860)
Claude Achille Debussy (1862–1918)
Gabriel Pierné (1863–1937)
Guy Ropartz (1864)
Paul Dukas (1865–1935)
Erik Satie (1866–1925)
Charles Koechlin (1867)
Albert Roussel (1869–1937)
Florent Schmitt (1870)
Déodat de Sévérac (1873–1921)
Henri Rabaud (1873)
Roger-Ducasse (1873)
Max d'Ollone (1875)
Maurice Ravel (1875–1937)
Louis Aubert (1877)
André Caplet (1878–1925)
Gabriel Grovlez (1879)
Maurice Delage (1879)
Jacques Ibert (1890)
Roland Manuel (1891)

Darius Milhaud (1892)
Arthur Honegger (1892)
Lili Boulanger (1893–1918)
Jean Francaix (1912)

BELGIAN

Théophile Ysaye (1865–1918)
Paul Gilson (1865)
Guillaume Lekeu (1870–1894)
Joseph Jongen (1873)
M. Brusselmans (1886)

DUTCH

Richard Hol (1825–1904)
Julius Roentgen (1855–1932)
Alfons Diepenbrock (1862–1921)
Johan Wagenaar (1862)
Bernard van Dieren (1884–1936)
Johan Franco (1908)

ROUMANIAN

Georges Enesco (1881)

RUSSIAN

Anton Rubinstein (1829–1894)
Alexander Borodin (1833–1887)
César Cui (1835–1918)
Mily Balakirev (1837–1910)
Peter I. Tchaikowsky (1840–1893)
N. Rimsky-Korsakov (1844–1908)
Anatole Liadov (1855–1914)
Ippolitov-Ivanov (1859–1935)
Antonin Arensky (1861–1906)
Alexander Glazounov (1865–1936)
Vassili Kilinnikov (1866–1900)
Alexander Scriabin (1872–1915)
Paul Juon (1872)
Serge Rachmaninoff (1873)
Reinhold Glière (1875)
Nicholas Miaskovsky (1881)
Igor Stravinsky (1882)
Michael Gniessen (1883)
Serge Prokofieff (1891)
Alexander Mossoloff (1900)

POLISH

Jean Louis Nicodé (1853–1919)
Ignace Jan Paderewski (1860)
Sigismund Stojowski (1870) (in America)

Miecyslaw Karlowicz (1876–1909)
Karol Szymanowski (1883–1937)
Ludomir Rozycki (1883)
Alexandre Tansman (1897)

FINNISH

Robert Kajanus (1856–1933)
Jan Sibelius (1865)
Armas Järnefelt (1869)
Leevi Madetoja (1887)

SCANDINAVIAN

Edvard Hagerup Grieg (1843–1907)
Anders Hallen (1846–1925)
Otto Malling (1848–1915)
Peter Lange-Müller (1850–1926)
Ludwig T. Schytte (1850–1926)
Gerhard Schjelderup (1859–1933)
Hugo Alfven (1872)
Natanael Berg (1879)
Kurt Atterberg (1887)

ITALIAN

M. Enrico Bossi (1861–1925)
Ferruccio Busoni (1866–1924)
Leone Sinigaglia (1868)
Ottorino Respighi (1879–1936)
Ildebrando Pizzetti (1880)
Vincenzo Tommasini (1880)
Riccardo Pick-Mangiagalli (1882)
G. Francesco Malipiero (1882)
Alfredo Casella (1883)
Guido Guerrini (1890)

SPANISH

Felipe Pedrell (1841–1922)
Isaac Albeniz (1860–1909)
Enrique Granados (1867–1916)
Pablo Casals (1876)
Manuel de Falla (1876)
Joaquin Turina (1882)
Ernesto Halffter (1905)

BRAZILIAN

Hector Villa-Lobos (1884)
Burle Marx (20th Century)

ENGLISH

Arthur Sullivan (1842–1900)
Alexander Campbell Mackenzie (1847–1935)

Charles Hubert Hastings Parry (1848–1918)
Charles Villiers Stanford (1852–1924)
Edward Elgar (1857–1934)
William Wallace (1860)
Edward German (1862–1936)
Frederick Delius (1863–1934)
Granville Bantock (1868)
Arthur Hinton (1869)
Cecil Forsyth (1870)
Ralph Vaughan Williams (1872)
William H. Bell (1873)
Gustav Holst (1874–1934)
Samuel Coleridge-Taylor (1875–1912)
Norman O'Neill (1875–1934)
H. Balfour Gardiner (1877)
Josef Holbrooke (1878)
John Ireland (1879)
Cyril Scott (1879)
Frank Bridge (1879)
Arnold Bax (1883)
Lord Berners (1883)
York Bowen (1884)
Armstrong Gibbs (1889)
Arthur Bliss (1891)
Eugene Goossens (1893) (in America)
William Walton (1902)
Constant Lambert (1905)

AMERICAN

John Knowles Paine (1839–1906)
Silas G. Pratt (1846–1916)
Frederick Grant Gleason (1848–1903)
Arthur Foote (1853–1937)
George Chadwick (1854–1931)
George Templeton Strong (1856)
Frank Van der Stucken (1858–1929)
Victor Herbert (1859–1924)
Edward MacDowell (1861–1908)
Charles Martin Loeffler (1861–1935)
Ernest Kroeger (1862–1934)
Carl Busch (Danish) (1862)
Horatio W. Parker (1863–1919)
Henry K. F. Gilbert (1868–1928)
William H. Humiston (1869–1924)
Henry Eichheim (1870)

Frederick Converse (1871)
Henry K. Hadley (1871–1937)
Frederick Stock (German) (1872)
Frank E. Ward (1872)
Rubin Goldmark (1872–1936)
Edward Burlingame Hill (1872)
Felix Borowski (Polish-English) (1872)
Camille Zeckwer (1875–1924)
Mortimer Wilson (1876–1932)
John Alden Carpenter (1876)
Carl Ruggles (1876)
Ernest Schelling (1876)
Rudolph Ganz (Swiss) (1877)
Blair Fairchild (1877–1933)
David Stanley Smith (1877)
Franz C. Bornschein (1879)
Ernest Bloch (Swiss) (1880)
Arthur Shepherd (1880)
John Powell (1882)
Reginald Sweet (?)
Percy Grainger (Australian) (1882)
Charles Griffes (1884–1920)
Louis Gruenberg (1884)
Emerson Whithorne (1884)
Albert Elkus (1884)
Edgar Varese (1885)
Deems Taylor (1885)
Joseph Achron (1886) (Russian)
Edward Ballantine (1886)
Wintter Watts (1886)
Victor Kolar (Hungarian) (1889)
Harold Morris (1889)
Philip James (1890)
Edwin Stringham (1890)
Adolph Weiss (1891)
Frederick Jacobi (1891)
Timothy Spelman (1891)
Sandor Harmati (Hungarian) (1892–1936)
Albert Stoessel (1894)
Robert Russell Bennett (1894)
Walter Piston (1894)
Leo Sowerby (1895)
Howard Hanson (1896)
Henry Cowell (1897)
George Gershwin (1898–1937)
Roy Harris (1898)
Ernst Bacon (1898)
George Antheil (1900)
Robert Mills Delaney (1903)
David van Vactor (1906)

Chamber Music

(String Quartets, Trios, Quintets, etc., various combinations of instruments.)

(Before Haydn)

ENGLISH
William Byrd (1543–1623)
Thomas Morley (1557–1604)
Orlando Gibbons (1583–1625)
John Jenkins (1592–1678)
Matthew Locke (1632–1677)
Henry Purcell (1658–1695)

ITALIAN
Salomon Rossi (1598–1623)
Tarquinio Merula (born before 1600)
Giovanni Battista Fontana (born before 1600–d. 1630)
Carlo Farino (17th Century)
Biagio Marini (1600–1660)
Giovanni Legrenzi (1625–1690)
Giovanni Battista Vitali (1644–1692)
Arcangelo Corelli (1653–1713)
Alessandro Scarlatti (1659–1725)
Antonio Vivaldi (1675–1743)
Francesco Geminiani (1680–1762)
Giuseppe Tartini (1692–1770)
Antonio Veracini (late 17th Cent.)
Pietro Locatelli (1693–1764)
Giovanni Battista Pergolesi (1710–1736)
Felice de Giardini (1716–1796)
Pietro Nardini (1722–1793)
Giovanni Battista Sammartini (1730–1770)
Gaetano Pugnani (1731–1798)
Luigi Boccherini (1743–1805)

GERMAN
J. Hermann Schein (1586–1630)
Jan Adam Reinken (1623–1722)
Nikolaus Hasse (1630–1706)
Johann P. Krieger (1649–1725)
Johann Pezel (16?–1686)
Johann Sebastian Bach (1685–1750)
Johann Schenck (17th Century)
Johann J. Quantz (1697–1773)
Johann Graun (1698–1771)

Johann Adolph Hasse (1697–1783)
Ignaz Holzbauer (1711–1783)
Frederick the Great (1712–1786)
Karl Philipp Emanuel Bach (1714–1783)
Johann W. A. Stamitz (1717–1757)
Johann Schobert (1720?–1767)
Carlo Giuseppe Toeschi (Italian) (1724–1788)
Johann T. Goldberg (1730–1760?)

FRENCH
Henri Desmarets (1662–1741)
François Couperin (1668–1733)
Jean Marie Leclair (1697–1764)

(Haydn and Later)

GERMAN AND AUSTRIAN
Joseph Haydn (1732–1809)
Johann G. Albrechtsberger (1736–1809)
Michael Haydn (1737–1806)
Karl Ditters von Dittersdorf (1739–1799)
Wenzel Pichel (1741–1805)
Johann Wenzelstich (1746–1803)
Abt Vogler (1749–1814)
Wolfgang Amadeus Mozart (1756–1791)
Paul Wranitsky (1756–1808)
Ignaz J. Pleyel (1757–1831)
Daniel Steibelt (1765–1823)
Rudolph Kreutzer (1766–1831)
Anton Reicha (1770–1836)
Ludwig van Beethoven (1770–1827)
Johann Hummel (1778–1837)
Ferdinand Ries (1784–1838)
Ludwig Spohr (1784–1859)
Friedrich Kuhlau (1786–1832)
Carl Maria von Weber (1786–1826)
Heinrich Marschner (1795–1861)
Franz Schubert (1797–1828)
Franz Lachner (1803–1890)
Felix Mendelssohn - Bartholdy (1809–1847)
Robert Schumann (1810–1856)
Otto Nicolai (1810–1849)
Ferdinand Hiller (1811–1885)
Robert Volkmann (1815–1883)
Fritz Spindler (1817–1905)
Cornelius Gurlitt (1820–1901)

Friedrich Kiel (1821–1885)
J. Joachim Raff (Swiss) (1822–1882)
Theodore Kirchner (1823–1903)
Anton Bruckner (1824–1896)
Carl Reinecke (1824–1910)
Waldemar Bargiel (1828–1897)
S. Jadassohn (1831–1902)
Johannes Brahms (1833–1897)
Karl Navratil (1836–1914)
Max Bruch (1838–1920)
Joseph Rheinberger (1839–1901)
Hermann Goetz (1840–1876)
August Klughardt (1847–1902)
Robert Fuchs (1847–1927)
Hugo Wolf (1860–1903)
Ludwig Thuille (1861–1907)
Richard Strauss (1864)
Robert Kahn (1865)
Paul Ertel (1865–1933)
Georg Schumann (1866)
Alexander Zemlinsky (1872)
Max Reger (1873–1916)
Arnold Schoenberg (1874) in America
Anton von Webern (1883)
Karl Horovitz (1884–1925)
Egon Wellesz (1885)
Alban Berg (1885–1935)
Heinrich Kaminski (1886)
Heinz Tiessen (1887)
Ernst Toch (1887) in America
Hermann Scherchen (1891)
Egon Kornauth (1891)
Paul Pisk (1893) in America
Alois Haba (1893)
Paul Hindemith (1895)
Ernst Krenek (1900) in America
Otto Siegl (1896)

CZECHO-SLOVAKIAN

Johann Ladislaus Dussek (1761–1812)
Bedrich Smetana (1824–1884)
Franz Bendel (1832–1874)
Antonin Dvorák (1841–1904)
Zdenko Fibich (1850–1900)
Leos Janacek (1854–1928)
Josef Bohuslav Foerster (1859)
Vitezslav Novak (1870)
Josef Suk (1874–1935)
Ottakar Ostrcil (1879–1937)
Rudolf Karel (1880)

Emil Axman (1887)
Vaclar Stepan (1889)
Fidelio Finke (1891)
Erwin Schulhoff (1894)
Hans Krasa (1899)

HUNGARIAN

Karl Goldmark (1830–1915)
Julius Major (1859–1925)
Emanuel Moor (1863–1931)
Ottokar Novacek (1866–1900)
Ernst von Dohnanyi (1877)
Béla Bártok (1881)
Zoltan Kodaly (1882)
Leo Weiner (1885)
Imre Weishaus (20th Century)

FRENCH

François Joseph Gossec (1734–1829)
André Ernest Modeste Grétry (1741–1813)
Marie Alexandre Guenin (1744–1814)
Hyacinthe Jadin (1769–1800)
Jacques F. Mazas (1782–1849)
Chrétien Urhan (1790–1845)
Napoleon - Henri Reber (1807–1880)
Félicien David (1810–1873)
Ambroise Thomas (1811–1896)
César Franck (1822–1890)
Edouard Lalo (1823–1892)
Camille Saint-Saëns (1835–1921)
Théodore Dubois (1835–1924)
Alexis de Castillon (1838–1873)
Gabriel Fauré (1845–1924)
Charles Marie Widor (1845–1937)
Vincent d'Indy (1851–1931)
Ernest Chausson (1855–1899)
André Gédalge (1856–1926)
Sylvio Lazzari (Tyrolese) (1858)
Auguste Chapuis (1858–1933)
Claude Achille Debussy (1862–1918)
Guy Ropartz (1864)
Alberic Magnard (1865–1914)
Charles Koechlin (1867)
Albert Roussel (1869–1937)
Florent Schmitt (1870)
Henri Rabaud (1873)
Maurice Ravel (1875–1937)
Jean Roger Ducasse (1873)

André Caplet (1878–1925)
Paul le Flem (1881)
Louis Durey (1888)
Jacques Ibert (1890)
Roland Manuel (1891)
Georges Migot (1891)
Arthur Honegger (1892)
Darius Milhaud (1892)
Germaine Tailleferre (1892)
Lili Boulanger (1893–1918)
Marcelle Soulage (1894)
Georges Auric (1899)
Francis Poulenc (1899)
Raymond Petit (1893)

BELGIAN

Chas. de Bériot (1802–1870)
Guillaume Lekeu (1870–1894)
Joseph Jongen (1873)
Victor Vreuls (1876)
Arthur Hoerée (20th Century)

DUTCH

Richard Hol (1825–1904)
Julius Roentgen (1855–1932)
Johan Wagenaar (1862)
Dirk Schaefer (1873–1931)
Bernard van Dieren (1884–1936)
lived in England
James Zwart (1892)

SWISS

Jean Xavier Lefèvre (1763–1829)
Hans Huber (1852–1921)

ROUMANIAN

Georges Enesco (1881)

RUSSIAN

Michail Ivanovitch Glinka (1804–1857)
Anton Rubinstein (1829–1894)
Alexander Borodin (1833–1887)
César Cui (1835–1918)
Piotr (Peter) Ilich Tchaikowsky (1840–1893)
Nikolai Rimsky-Korsakov (1844–1908)
Serge I. Taneiev (1856–1915)
Anton Arensky (1861–1906)
Georg Catoire (1861–1926)
Alexander Gretchaninoff (1864)
Alexander Glazounov (1865–1936)

Paul Juon (1872)
Serge Rachmaninoff (1873)
Reinhold Glière (1875)
Gregory Krein (1880)
Nicolai Miaskovsky (1881)
Leonid Sabaneyef (1881)
Nicholas Roslavets (1881)
Igor Stravinsky (1882)
Maximilian Steinberg (1883)
Serge Prokofieff (1891)
Alexander Tcherepnin (1899)
Dmitri Shostakovitch (1906)

POLISH

Ignaz Felix Dobrzysnki (1807–1867)
Ladislas Selenski (1837–1921)
Philipp Scharwenka (1847–1917)
Franz Xaver Scharwenka (1850–1924)
Emil Mlynarsky (1870–1935)
Ludomir Rozycki (1883)
Karol Szymanowski (1883–1937)
Tadeusz Jarecki (1889)
Alexandre Tansman (1897)
Jerzy Fitelberg (1903)

FINNISH

Jan Sibelius (1865)
Armas E. Launis (1884)
Aare Merikanto (1893)

SCANDINAVIAN

Johan P. E. Hartmann (Danish) (1805–1900)
Niels W. Gade (Danish) (1817–1890)
August Winding (Danish) (1835–1899)
Emil Hartmann (Danish) (1836–1898)
Johan Svendsen (Norwegian) (1840–1911)
Edvard Hagerup Grieg (Norwegian) (1843–1907)
Ole Olsen (Norwegian) (1850–1927)
Peter Lange - Müller (Danish) (1850–1926)
Gerhard Schjelderup (Norwegian) (1859–1933)
A. Carl Nielson (Danish) (1865–1931)

Christian Sinding (Norwegian) (1856)
Wilhelm Stenhammar (Norwegian) (1871–1927)
Sigurd Lie (Norwegian) (1871–1904)
Kurt Atterberg (Swedish) (1887)

ITALIAN

Giuseppe Verdi (1813–1901)
Antonio Bazzini (1818–1897)
Giovanni Sgambati (1843–1914)
Giuseppe Martucci (1856–1909)
M. Enrico Bossi (1861–1925)
Ferruccio Busoni (1866–1924)
Leone Sinigaglia (1868)
Mario Tarenghi (1870)
Alfredo d'Ambrosio (1871–1915)
Lorenzo Perosi (1872)
Ermanno Wolf-Ferrari (1876)
Ottorino Respighi (1879–1936)
Vincenzo Tommasini (1880)
Ildebrando Pizzetti (1880)
G. Francesco Malipiero (1882)
Riccardo Pick-Mangiagalli (1882)
Alfredo Casella (1883)
Vincenzo Davico (1889)
Guido Guerrini (1890)
Mario Castelnuovo-Tedesco (1895)
Mario Labroca (1896)
Vittorio Rieti (1898)

SPANISH

Enrique Granados (1867–1916)
Manuel de Falla (1876)
Joaquin Turina (1882)
Oscar Esplà (1886)
Adolfo Salazar (1890)
Ernesto Halffter (1905)

ENGLISH

George Onslow (1784–1852)
Michael Balfe (1808–1870)
George Alexander MacFarren (1813–1887)
William Sterndale Bennett (1816–1875)
Ebenezer Prout (1835–1909)
Alexander Campbell Mackenzie (1847–1935)
Charles Hubert H. Parry (1848–1918)

Charles Villiers Stanford (1852–1924)
Frederick H. Cowen (1852–1935)
Edward Elgar (1857–1934)
Ethel M. Smyth (1858)
Algernon Ashton (1859–1937)
William Henry Hadow (1859–1937)
Marie Wurm (1860–1938) (lived in Germany)
William Wallace (1860)
Frederick Delius (1862–1934)
Eugene d'Albert (1864–1932)
John Blackwood McEwen (1868)
Frederick Lamond (1868)
Granville Bantock (1868)
Walford Davies (1869)
Cecil Forsyth (1870)
Ralph Vaughan Williams (1872)
Gustav Holst (1874–1934)
H. Waldo Warner (1874)
Samuel Coleridge-Taylor (1875–1912)
Donald Francis Tovey (1875)
Norman O'Neill (1875–1934)
William Yates Hurlstone (1876–1906)
Thomas Dunhill (1877)
H. Balfour Gardiner (1877)
Josef Holbrooke (1878)
John Ireland (1879)
Frank Bridge (1879)
Cyril Scott (1879)
Arnold Bax (1883)
York Bowen (1884)
Benjamin Dale (1885)
Rebecca Clarke (1886)
Gerrard Williams (1888)
Armstrong Gibbs (1889)
Arthur Bliss (1891)
Herbert Howells (Australian) (1892)
Eugene Goossens (1893)
William Walton (1902)

BRAZILIAN

Hector Villa-Lobos (1884)

AMERICAN

John K. Paine (1839–1906)
Frederick Grant Gleason (1848–1903)
Arthur Foote (1853–1937)

Adolph M. Foerster (1854–1927)
George W. Chadwick (1854–1931)
George Templeton Strong (1856)
Edgar Stillman Kelley (1857)
Henry Schoenefeld (1857–1936)
Abraham W. Lillienthal (1859)
Arthur Whiting (1861–1936)
Charles Martin Loeffler (1861–1935)
Samuel Baldwin (1862)
Carl Busch (Danish) (1862)
Edmund Severn (1862)
Ernest R. Kroeger (1862–1934)
Henry Holden Huss (1862)
Horatio Parker (1863–1919)
William H. Berwald (1864)
Mrs. H. H. A. Beach (1867)
Louis Adolphe Coerne (1870–1922)
Frederick Stock (German) (1871)
Henry K. Hadley (1871–1937)
Arthur Nevin (1871)
Frederick Converse (1871)
Felix Borowski (1872)
Rubin Goldmark (1872–1936)
Frank E. Ward (1872)
Daniel Gregory Mason (1873)
Arne Oldberg (1874)
Camille Zeckwer (1875–1924)
Frederick Ayres (1876–1926)
David Stanley Smith (1877)
Blair Fairchild (1877–1933)
John Beach (1877)
Franz C. Bornschein (1879)
Heniot Levy (Polish) (1879)
Ernest Bloch (Swiss) (1880)
Eric Delamarter (1880)
John Powell (1882)
Percy Grainger (Australian) (1882)
Mary Howe (1882)
Ethel Leginska (English) (1883)
Eastwood Lane (1884)
Louis Gruenberg (1884)
Charles Griffes (1884–1920)
James P. Dunn (1884–1936)
Emerson Whithorne (1884)
Wallingford Riegger (1885)
Deems Taylor (1885)
Carlos Salzedo (French) (1885)
George F. Boyle (Australian) (1886)
Marion Bauer (1887)

Burnet C. Tuthill (1888)
Albert Spalding (1888)
Leslie Loth (1888)
Chalmers Clifton (1889)
Harold Morris (1889)
Alois Reiser (Czech) (1889)
Edwin Stringham (1890)
Richard Donovan (1891)
Frederick Jacobi (1891)
Charles Haubiel (1892)
Sandor Harmati (Hungarian) (1892–1936)
Douglas Moore (1893)
Bernard Wagenaar (1894) (Dutch)
Mitya Stillman (Russian) (1894–1936)
Albert Stoessel (1894)
Walter Piston (1894)
Mark Wessel (1894)
Wm. Grant Still (1895)
Leo Sowerby (1895)
Howard Hanson (1896)
Roger Sessions (1896)
Richard Hammond (1896)
Quincy Porter (1897)
Lamar Stringfield (1897)
Roy Harris (1898)
Werner Janssen (1899)
William Dawson (1899)
Aaron Copland (1900)
Nicolai Berezowsky (1900)
Ruth Crawford (1901)
Paul Nordoff (1909)
Elie Seigmeister (1909)
Israel Citkowitz (1909)
Robert McBride (1911)

Pianoforte Music

(*Lyrical Pieces, Songs without Words, Nocturnes, Impromptus, Ballads, Intermezzi, Preludes, and Program Music, etc.*)

German and Austrian

Johann N. Hummel (1778–1837)
Carl Maria von Weber (1786–1826)
Friedrich Kuhlau (1786–1832)
Franz Schubert (1797–1828)
Charles Mayer (1799–1862)
Joseph Kessler (1800–1872)
Felix Mendelssohn - Bartholdy (1809–1847)

Robert Schumann (1810–1856)
Ferdinand von Hiller (1811–1885)
Adolf von Henselt (1814–1889)
Robert Volkmann (1815–1883)
Fritz Spindler (1817–1905)
Theodor Kullak (1818–1882)
Albert Loeschorn (1819–1905)
Friedrich Kiel (1821–1885)
Joseph Joachim Raff (Swiss) (1822–1882)
Theodor Kirchner (1823–1903)
Carl Reinecke (1824–1910)
Ernst Pauer (1826–1905)
Gustav Merkel (1827–1885)
Waldemar Bargiel (1828–1897)
Gustav Lange (1830–1889)
Hans von Bülow (1830–1894)
Salomon Jadassohn (1831–1902)
Franz Bendel (1833–1874)
Johannes Brahms (1833–1897)
Adolf Jensen (1837–1879)
Joseph Rheinberger (1839–1901)
Heinrich Hofmann (1842–1902)
Hugo Reinhold (1854–1935)
Alexander von Fielitz (1860–1930)
Hugo Kaun (1863–1932)
Adele aus der Ohe (1864–1937)
Georg Schumann (1866)
Alexander Zemlinsky (1872)
Max Reger (1873–1916)
Arnold Schoenberg (1874) (in America)
Siegfried Karg-Elert (1877–1933)
Walter Braunfels (1882)
Arthur Schnabel (1882)
Karl Horwitz (1884–1925)
Heinz Tiessen (1887)
Ernst Toch (1887) (in America)
Egon Kornauth (1891)
Hermann Scherchen (1891)
Philipp Jarnach (1892)
Otto Siegl (1896)
Erich Wolfgang Korngold (1897) (in America)
Ernst Krenek (1900) (in America)

Czecho-Slovakia

Johann Ladislaus Dussek (1761–1812)
Ignaz Moscheles (1794–1870)
Alexander Dreyschock (1818–1869)

Antonin Dvořák (1841–1904)
Josef Rebicek (1844–1904)
Zdenko Fibich (1850–1900)
J. B. Foerster (1859)
Vitezslav Novak (1870)
Josef Suk (1874–1935)
Rudolf Karel (1880)

Hungarian

Franz Liszt (1811–1886)
Stephen Heller (1813–1888)
Karl Goldmark (1830–1915)
Emanuel Moor (1863–1931)
Arpad Szendy (1863–1922)
Eduard Poldini (1869)
Ernst von Dohnanyi (1877)
Béla Bártok (1881)
Zoltan Kodály (1882)

French

Napoleon-Henri Reber (1807–1880)
Charles Alkan (1813–1888)
Ignace Leybach (1817–1891)
Jean Henri Ravina (1818–1906)
César Franck (1822–1890)
Auguste Durand (1830–1909)
Eugène Ketterer (1831–1870)
Camille Saint-Saëns (1835–1921)
Théodore Dubois (1837–1924)
Louis Brassin (1840–1884)
Alexis Emmanuel Chabrier (1841–1894)
Gabriel Fauré (1845–1924)
Théodore Lack (1846–1921)
Benjamin Godard (1849–1895)
François Thomé (1850–1909)
Vincent d'Indy (1851–1931)
Raoul Pugno (1852–1914)
Sylvio Lazzari (Tyrolese) (1857)
Auguste Chapuis (1858–1933)
Mme. Cécile Chaminade (1861)
Xavier Leroux (1863–1919)
Gabriel Pierné (1863–1937)
Isidor Philipp (1863)
Erik Satie (1866–1925)
Charles Koechlin (1867)
Claude Achille Debussy (1867–1918)
Florent Schmitt (1870)
Louis Vierne (1870–1937)
Louis Vuillemin (1873–1929)
Henri Rabaud (1873)

Déodat de Sévérac (1873–1921)
Jean Roger-Ducasse (1873)
Maurice Ravel (1875–1937)
Louis Aubert (1877)
Gustave Samazeuilh (1877)
André Caplet (1878–1925)
Rhené-Baton (1879)
Gabriel Grovlez (1879)
Paul Le Flem (1881)
Jacques Ibert (1890)
Georges Migot (1891)
Arthur Honegger (1892)
Darius Milhaud (1892)
Francis Poulenc (1899)
Jean Françaix (1912)

BELGIUM
Théophile Ysaye (1865–1918)

DUTCH
Richard Hol (1825–1904)
Johan Wagenaar (1862)
Dirk Schaefer (1873–1931)

SWISS
Sigismund Thalberg (1812–1871)
Hans Huber (1852–1921)
Emile Blanchet (1877)

RUSSIAN
Michail Ivanovitch Glinka (1804–1857)
Anton Rubinstein (1830–1894)
Alexander Borodin (1833–1887)
Nicolai von Wilm (1834–1911)
César Cui (1835–1918)
Nicolai Rubinstein (1835–1881)
Mily Balakirev (1837–1910)
Modest Moussorgsky (1839–1881)
Peter Ilich Tchaikowsky (1840–1893)
Nikolai Rimsky-Korsakoff (1844–1908)
Nicolas Stcherbatchev (1853)
Alexander Kopylov (1854–1911)
Anatole Liadov (1855–1914)
Eduard Schütt (1856–1933)
Genari Karganov (1858–1890)
Alexander Ilyinsky (1859–1919)
Serge M. Liapounov (1859–1924)
Anton Arensky (1861–1906)
Joseph Wihtol (1863)
Alexander Glazounov (1865–1936)

Vladimir Rebikov (1866–1920)
Arseni Korestchenko (1870–1918)
Paul Juon (1872)
Alexander Scriabin (1872–1915)
Serge Rachmaninoff (1873)
Reinhold M. Glière (1875)
Ossip Gabrilowitsch (1878–1936) (American)
Nicholas Medtner (1880)
Gregory Krein (1880)
Leonid Sabaneyef (1881)
Alexander Krein (1883)
Samuel Feinberg (1890)
Serge Prokofieff (1891)
Alexander Tcherepnin (1899)
Dmitri Shostakovitch (1906)
Igor Markievitch (1912) (in Paris)

POLISH
Frédéric Chopin (1810–1849)
Theodore Leschetizky (1830–1915)
Alexander Zarzycki (1834–1895)
Philipp Scharwenka (1847–1917)
F. Xaver Scharwenka (1850–1924)
J. L. Nicodé (1853–1919)
Moritz Moszkowski (1854–1925)
Ignace Jan Paderewski (1860)
Emil Mlynarski (1870–1935)
Sigismund Stojowski (1870) (in America)
Poldowski (Lady Dean Paul) (187?–1932) (London)
Karol Szymanowski (1883–1937)
Alexandre Tansman (1897) (Paris)

FINNISH
Robert Kajanus (1856–1933)
Jan Sibelius (1865)
Oskar Merikanto (1868–1924)
Armas Järnefelt (1869)
Selim Palmgren (1878)
Armas E. Launis (1884)

SCANDINAVIAN
Halfdan Kjerulf (Norwegian) (1815–1868)
Niels Gade (Danish) (1817–1890)
August Winding (Danish) (1835–1899)
Edmund Neupert (Norwegian) (1842–1888)
Edvard Hagerup Grieg (Norwegian) (1843–1907)

Agathe Backer-Gröndahl (Norwegian) (1847–1907)
Ludwig T. Schytte (Danish) (1850–1909)
Emil Sjögren (Swedish) (1853–1918)
Cornelius Rybner (Danish) (1855–1929) (American)
Christian Sinding (Norwegian) (1856)
August Enna (Danish) (1860–1923)
Johan Halvorsen (Norwegian) (1864–1935)
A. Carl Nielson (Danish) (1865–1931)
Olof Peterson-Berger (Swedish) (1867)
Sigurd Lie (Norwegian) (1871–1904)

ITALIAN

Giovanni Sgambati (1843–1914)
M. Enrico Bossi (1861–1925)
Ferruccio Busoni (1866–1924)
Mario Tarenghi (1870)
Franco Alfano (1876)
Ermanno Wolf-Ferrari (1876)
G. Francesco Malipiero (1882)
Alfredo Casella (1883)
Victor da Sabata (1892)
Mario Castelnuovo-Tedesco (1895)

SPANISH

Pedro Albeniz (1795–1855)
Isaac Albeniz (1861–1909)
Enrique Granados (1867–1916)
Alberto Jonás (1868) (American)
José Vianna di Motta (Portuguese) (1868)
Manuel de Falla (1876)
Joaquin Turina (1882)
Federico Mompou (1893)

BRAZIL

Hector Villa-Lobos (1884)

ENGLISH

John Field (1782–1837)
William Sterndale Bennett (1816–1875)
Walter C. MacFarren (1826–1905)

Charles Hubert H. Parry (1848–1918)
Tobias Matthay (1858)
Algernon Ashton (1859–1937)
Herbert F. Sharpe (1861–1925)
Eugen d'Albert (1864–1932)
Granville Bantock (1868)
Arthur Hinton (1869)
Percy Pitt (1870–1932)
Ernest Austin (1874)
Norman O'Neill (1875–1934)
Samuel Coleridge-Taylor (1875–1912)
William Y. Hurlstone (1876–1906)
H. Balfour Gardiner (1877)
Roger Quilter (1877)
Josef Holbrooke (1878)
John Ireland (1879)
Frank Bridge (1879)
Cyril Scott (1879)
Arnold Bax (1883)
Lord Berners (1883)
York Bowen (1884)
John R. Heath (1887)
Norman Peterkin (1888)
Gerrard Williams (1888)
Alec Rowley (1892)
Eugene Goossens (1893) (in America)

AMERICAN

Hermann Adolf Wollenhaupt (German) (1827–1863)
L. M. Gottschalk (1829–1869)
William Mason (1829–1908)
Sebastian Bach Mills (1838–1898)
Homer N. Bartlett (1846–1920)
Emil Liebling (1851–1914)
Max Vogrich (Transylvanian) (1852–1916)
Constantin Sternberg (1852–1924)
Rafael Joseffy (Hungarian) (1852–1915)
Percy Goetschius (1853)
Arthur Foote (1853–1937)
William H. Sherwood (1854–1911)
Adolph M. Foerster (1854–1927)
George W. Chadwick (1854–1931)
Wilson G. Smith (1855–1929)
Arthur Bird (1856–1923)
George Templeton Strong (1856)
Carl V. Lachmund (1857–1928) (German)

Harry Rowe Shelley (1858)
Bruno Oscar Klein (German) (1858–1911)
Edward MacDowell (1861–1908)
Arthur Whiting (1861–1936)
Ethelbert Nevin (1862–1901)
Henry Holden Huss (1862)
William H. Berwald (German) (1864)
Rosseter Cole (1866)
Mrs. H. H. A. Beach (1867)
Margaret Ruthven Lang (1867)
Florence N. Barbour (1867)
Louis Victor Saar (1868–1937)
Henry F. Gilbert (1868–1928)
Paolo Gallico (Italo-Austrian) (1868)
Louis Adolph Coerne (1870–1922)
Leopold Godowsky (Polish) (1870–1939)
Howard Brockway (1870)
Samuel Bollinger (1871)
Arthur Nevin (1871)
Rubin Goldmark (1872–1936)
Felix Borowski (1872)
Arthur Farwell (1872)
Edward Burlingame Hill (1872)
Daniel Gregory Mason (1873)
Ernest Schelling (1876)
Mortimer Wilson (1876–1932)
Josef Hofmann (Polish) (1876)
John Alden Carpenter (1876)
John Beach (1877)
Louis Campbell-Tipton (1877–1921)
Rudolph Ganz (Swiss) (1877)
Blair Fairchild (1877–1933)
Albert Mildenberg (1878–1918)
Benjamin Lambord (1879–1915)
Heniot Lévy (Polish) (1879)
Arthur Shepherd (1880)
Fanny Charles Dillon (1881)
Noble Kreider (1880?)
F. Morris Class (1881–1926)
Gena Branscombe (1881)
R. Nathaniel Dett (1882)
John Powell (1882)
Percy Grainger (Australian) (1882)
Eastwood Lane (1884)
Charles Tomlinson Griffes (1884–1920)
Emerson Whithorne (1884)
Louis Gruenberg (1884)

Cecil Burleigh (1885)
George F. Boyle (Australian) (1886)
Edward Royce (1886)
Walter Morse Rummel (1887)
Marion Bauer (1887)
Leslie Loth (1888)
A. Walter Kramer (1890)
Frederick Jacobi (1891)
Rosalie Housman (1892)
Charles Haubiel (1892)
Elliot Griffis (1893)
Mana Zucca (1893)
Albert Stoessel (1894)
David W. Guion (1895)
Leo Ornstein (1895)
Richard Hammond (1896)
Henry Cowell (1897)
George Antheil (1900)
Aaron Copland (1900)
Otto Luening (1900)
Abram Chasins (1903)

Some Writers of Song

GERMAN AND AUSTRIAN

Christoph Willibald Gluck (1714–1787)
Johann Adam Hiller (1728–1804)
Wolfgang Amadeus Mozart (1756–1791)
Karl Zelter (1758–1832)
Johann Zumsteeg (1760–1802)
Ludwig van Beethoven (1770–1827)
Carl Maria von Weber (1786–1826)
Luise Reichardt (1788–1826)
Heinrich Marschner (1795–1861)
Johann Carl Gottfried Loewe (1796–1869)
Franz Schubert (1797–1828)
Heinrich Dorn (1804–1892)
Felix Mendelssohn - Bartholdy (1809–1847)
Heinrich Proch (1809–1878)
Otto Nicolai (1810–1849)
Robert Schumann (1810–1856)
Richard Wagner (1813–1883)
Robert Franz (1815–1892)
Franz Abt (1819–1885)
Joseph Joachim Raff (Swiss) (1822–1882)

Peter Cornelius (1824–1874)
Alexander Ritter (1833–1896)
Johannes Brahms (1833–1897)
Adolf Jensen (1837–1879)
Max Bruch (1838–1920)
Joseph Rheinberger (1839–1901)
Engelbert Humperdinck (1854–1921)
Felix Mottl (1856–1911)
Hugo Wolf (1860–1903)
Ludwig Thuille (1861–1907)
Felix Weingartner (1863)
Hugo Kaun (1863–1932)
Richard Strauss (1864)
Robert Kahn (1865)
Hans Pfitzner (1869)
Hans Hermann (1870–1931)
Siegmund von Hausegger (1872)
Max Reger (1873–1916)
Arnold Schoenberg (1874)
Erich Wolff (1874–1913)
Franz Schreker (1878–1934)
Karl Bleyle (1880)
Joseph Marx (1882)
Walter Braunfels (1882)
Anton von Webern (1883)
Egon Wellesz (1885)
Heinz Tiessen (1887)
Hermann Scherchen (1891)
Eduard Erdmann (1896)
Erich Korngold (1897)
Kurt Weill (1900)

CZECHO-SLOVAKIAN

Bedrich Smetana (1824–1884)
Eduard Napravnik (1839–1916)
Antonin Dvorák (1841–1904)
Zdenko Fibich (1850–1900)
Gustav Mahler (1860–1911)
Karl Navratil (1867–1936)
Vitezslav Novak (1870)
Fidelio Finke (1891)
Hans Krasa (1899)

HUNGARIAN

Franz Liszt (1811–1886)
Karl Goldmark (1830–1915)
Francis Korbay (1846–1913)
Emanuel Moor (1863–1931)
Ottokar Novacek (1866–1900)
Ernst von Dohnanyi (1877)
Béla Bártok (1881)
Zoltan Kodály (1882)

Deszo Zsives (1885)
Tibor Harsanyi (1898)

FRENCH

Luigi Cherubini (Italian) (1760–1842)
Hector Berlioz (1803–1869)
Napoleon-Henri Reber (1807–1880)
Félicien David (1810–1876)
Charles Gounod (1818–1893)
César Franck (Belgian) (1822–1890)
Edouard Lalo (1823–1892)
Camille Saint-Saëns (1835–1921)
Leo Délibes (1836–1891)
Théodore Dubois (1837–1924)
Georges Bizet (1838–1875)
Jules Massenet (1842–1912)
Emile Paladilhe (1844–1926)
Charles Marie Widor (1845–1937)
Gabriel Fauré (1845–1924)
René Lenormand (1846–1932)
Henri Duparc (1848–1933)
Benjamin Godard (1849–1895)
Augusta Holmès (Irish) (1849–1903)
Alexandre Georges (1850–1938)
Vincent d'Indy (1851–1931)
Raoul Pugno (1852–1914)
Ernest Chausson (1855–1899)
Alfred Bruneau (1857–1934)
Sylvio Lazzari (Tyrolese) (1857)
Georges Huë (1858)
August Chapuis (1858–1933)
Gustave Charpentier (1860)
Pierre de Breville (1861)
Cecile Chaminade (1861)
Henri Bemberg (1861)
Claude Achille Debussy (1862–1918)
Gabriel Pierné (1863–1937)
Paul Vidal (1863–1931)
Charles Koechlin (1867)
Albert Roussel (1869–1937)
Florent Schmitt (1870)
Louis Vierne (1870–1937)
Deodat de Sévérac (1873–1921)
Henri Rabaud (1873)
Reynaldo Hahn (Venezuelan) (1875)
Max d'Ollone (1875)
Maurice Ravel (1875–1937)

Camille Decreus (1876–1939)
Raoul Laparra (1876)
Louis Aubert (1877)
André Caplet (1878–1925)
Gabriel Grovlez (1879)
Rhené-Baton (1879)
Jean Cras (1879–1932)
Jeanne Herscher-Clément (1880)
Félix Fourdrain (1880–1924)
Paul Le Flem (1881)
Louis Durey (1888)
Jacques Ibert (1890)
Georges Migot (1891)
Roland Manuel (1891)
Darius Milhaud (1892)
Arthur Honegger (1892)
Raymond Petit (1893)
Marcelle Soulage (1894)
Georges Auric (1899)
Francis Poulenc (1899)

BELGIAN

Gustav Huberti (1843–1910)
Jan Blockx (1851–1912)
Edgar Tinel (1854–1912)
Sylvain Dupuis (1856–1931)
Paul Gilson (1865)
Louis Mortelmans (1868)
Guillaume Lekeu (1870–1894)
Victor Vreuls (1876)

DUTCH

Richard Hol (1825–1904)
Bernard Zweers (1854–1924)
Julius Roentgen (1855–1932)
Alfons Diepenbrock (1862–1921)
Jan Brandt-Buys (1868–1933)
Cornelius Dopper (1870)
Dirk Schaefer (1873–1931)
Bernard van Dieren (1884–1936)
Dirk Foch (1886)
Willem Pijper (1894)

SWISS

Hans Huber (1852–1921)
Rudolph Ganz (1877) (American)
Emile Blanchet (1877)
Ernest Bloch (1880) (American)

RUSSIAN

Michael Glinka (1804–1857)
Anton Rubinstein (1830–1894)

Alexander Borodin (1833–1887)
César Cui (1835–1918)
Mily Balakirev (1837–1910)
Modest Moussorgsky (1839–1881)
Peter Ilich Tchaikowsky (1840–1893)
Nicolai Rimsky-Korsakov (1844–1908)
Alexander Kopylov (1854–1911)
Alexander Ilyinsky (1859–1919)
Anton Arensky (1861–1906)
Georg Catoire (1861–1926)
Erik Mayer-Helmund (1861)
Joseph Wihtol (1863)
Alexander Gretchaninov (1864)
Alexander Glazounov (1865–1936)
Vladimir Rebikov (1866–1920)
Arseni Korestchenko (1870–1918)
Serge Vassilenko (1872)
Serge Rachmaninov (1873)
Reinhold Glière (1875)
Miecyslaw Karlowicz (1876–1909)
Nikolaus Medtner (1880)
Gregory Krein (1880)
Igor Stravinsky (1882)
Alexander Krein (1883)
Michael Gniessin (1883)
Alexander Davidenko (1899)
Victor Bielyi (1904)

POLISH

Frédéric Chopin (1810–1849)
Felix Nowowiejski (German) (1877)
Poldowski (Lady Dean Paul) (187?–1932) (English)
Karol Szymanowski (1883–1937)
Alexandre Tansman (1897)

FINNISH

Jan Sibelius (1865)
Oskar Merikanto (1868–1924)
Armas Järnefelt (1869)
Selim Palmgren (1878)
Armas E. Launis (1884)

SCANDINAVIAN

Adolf Lindblad (Swedish) (1801–1878)
Johan P. E. Hartmann (Danish) (1805–1900)
Halfdan Kjerulf (Norwegian) (1815–1868)

Niels Gade (Danish) (1817–1890)
Eduard Lassen (Danish) (1830–1894)
Jorgen Malling (Danish) (1836–1905)
Rikard Nordraak (Norwegian) (1842–1866)
Julius Bechgaard (Danish) (1843–1917)
Edvard Grieg (Norwegian) (1843–1907)
Mme. Agathe Backer-Gröndahl (Norwegian) (1847–1907)
Otto Malling (Danish) (1848–1915)
Ludwig Schytte (Danish) (1850–1909)
Ole Olsen (Norwegian) (1850–1927)
Peter Lange - Müller (Danish) (1850–1926)
Emil Sjögren (Swedish) (1853–1918)
Cornelius Rybner (1855–1929)
Christian Sinding (Norwegian) (1856)
August Enna (Danish) (1860–1923)
Johan Halvorsen (Norwegian) (1864–1935)
A. Carl Nielsen (Danish) (1865–1931)
Bror Beckman (Swedish) (1866)
Olof Peterson-Berger (Swedish) (1867)
Wilhelm Stenhammar (Swedish) (1871–1927)
Sigurd Lie (Norwegian) (1871–1904)
Hugo Alfven (Swedish) (1872)
Halfdan Cleve (Norwegian) (1879)
Natanael Berg (Norwegian) (1879)
Ture Rangström (Swedish) (1884)

ITALIAN

Giuseppe Verdi (1813–1901)
Luigi Arditi (1822–1903)
Ciro Pinsuti (1829–1888)
F. Paolo Tosti (1846–1916)
P. Mario Costa (1858)
Ruggiero Leoncavallo (1858–1919)
Enrico Bossi (1861–1925)

Franco Leoni (1864)
Leone Sinigaglia (1868)
Carlo Perinello (1877)
Stefano Donaudy (1879–1925)
Ottorino Respighi (1879–1936)
Gabrieli Sibella (?–1925)
Ildebrando Pizzetti (1880)
Vincenzo Tommasini (1880)
Francesco Malipiero (1882)
Francesco Santoliquido (1883)
Alfredo Casella (1883)
Riccardo Zandonai (1883)
Ferdinando Liuzzi (1884)
Pietro Cimara (1887) (in America)
Adriano Lualdi (1887)
Vincenzo Davico (1889)
Guido Guerrini (1890)
Mario Castelnuovo - Tedesco (1895)

SPANISH

Pedro Albeniz (1795–1855)
Felipe Pedrell (1841–1922)
Joaquin Valverde (1846–1910)
Enrique Granados (1867–1916)
Joaquin Valverde, Jr. (1875–1918)
Manuel de Falla (1876)
Carlos Pedrell (Uruguayan) (1878)
Joaquin Turina (1882)
Joaquin Nin (1883)
Julian Huarte (?)

ENGLISH

John Barnett (1802–1890)
William Sterndale Bennett (1816–1875)
Arthur Seymour Sullivan (1842–1900)
Alexander C. Mackenzie (1847–1935)
Charles Hubert H. Parry (1848–1918)
Arthur Goring Thomas (1851–1892)
Frederick H. Cowen (1852–1935)
Charles Villiers Stanford (1852–1924)
Maud Valerie White (1855–1937)
Edward Elgar (1857–1934)
Ethel M. Smyth (1858)
"Anton Strelezki" Sir Francis Bernand (1859–1907)

Algernon Ashton (1859–1937)
Edward German (1862–1936)
Liza Lehmann (1862–1918)
Frederick Delius (1863–1934)
Arthur Somervell (1863–1937)
Eugene d'Albert (1864–1932)
Herbert Bedford (1867)
Granville Bantock (1868)
Walford Davies (1869)
Percy Pitt (1870–1932)
Cecil Forsyth (1870)
Ralph Vaughan Williams (1872)
Landon Ronald (1873–1938)
Gustav Holst (1874–1934)
Ernest Austin (1874)
Norman O'Neill (1875–1934)
Samuel Coleridge-Taylor (1875–1912)
Martin Shaw (1876)
H. Balfour Gardiner (1877)
Roger Quilter (1877)
Graham Peel (1877)
Josef Holbrooke (1878)
Rutland Boughton (1878)
Frank Bridge (1879)
John Ireland (1879)
Cyril Scott (1879)
Bryceson Treharne (1879)
Arnold Bax (1883)
Lord Berners (1883)
Hubert Bath (1883)
Felix White (1884)
Benjamin Dale (1885)
John Heath (1887)
Gerrard Williams (1888)
Leigh Henry (1889)
Armstrong Gibbs (1889)
Arthur Bliss (1891)
Alec Rowley (1892)
Eugene Goossens (1893)
Peter Warlock (1894–1930)
Eric Fogg (1903)

AMERICAN

Francis Hopkinson (1737–1791)
Stephen Collins Foster (1826–1864)
Harrison Millard (1830–1895)
Oscar Weil (1839–1921)
Dudley Buck (1839–1909)
George L. Osgood (1844–1923)
William Wallace Gilchrist (1846–1916)

Homer N. Bartlett (1846–1920)
Jules Jordan (1850–1927)
Arthur Foote (1853–1937)
George W. Chadwick (1854–1931)
Adolph M. Foerster (1854–1927)
Wilson G. Smith (1855–1929)
John Hyatt Brewer (1856–1931)
Helen Hopekirk (Scotch) (1856)
Mary Turner Salter (1856–1938)
Clayton Johns (1857–1932)
James H. Rogers (1857)
Edgar Stillman Kelley (1857)
Frank Lynes (1858–1913)
Harry Rowe Shelley (1858)
Charles B. Hawley (1858–1915)
Gerrit Smith (1859–1912)
Reginald de Koven (1859–1920)
Charles Whitney Coombs (1859)
Victor Herbert (1859–1924)
Alfred G. Robyn (1860–1935)
William C. Hammond (1860)
Pietro Floridia (Italian) (1860–1932)
Homer A. Norris (1860–1920)
Edward MacDowell (1861–1908)
Charles Martin Loeffler (1861–1935) (French)
Isidore Luckstone (1861)
R. Huntington Woodman (1861)
William Arms Fisher (1861)
Ethelbert Nevin (1862–1901)
Walter Damrosch (1862)
Henry Holden Huss (1862)
Ernest R. Kroeger (1862–1934)
Carl Busch (1862)
Carrie Jacobs Bond (1862)
Horatio Parker (1863–1919)
William H. Neidlinger (1863–1924)
Frederick Field Bullard (1864–1904)
Sidney Homer (1864)
Emilie Frances Bauer (Francisco di Nogero) (1865–1926)
Harvey Worthington Loomis (1865–1930)
Louis Koemmenich (German) (1866–1922)
Daniel Protheroe (Welsh) (1866–1934)
Frank Seymour Hastings (?)
Clarence Lucas (1866)
Harry T. Burleigh (1866)

Rossetter Gleason Cole (1866)
Mrs. H. H. A. Beach (1867)
Margaret Ruthven Lang (1867)
Florence N. Barbour (1867)
Louis Victor Saar (Dutch) (1868–1937)
Henry F. Gilbert (1868–1928)
Paolo Gallico (Austrian) (1868)
Victor Harris (1869)
William Henry Humiston (1869–1924)
Louis Adolph Coerne (1870–1922)
Howard Brockway (1870)
Bruno Huhn (1871)
Samuel Bollinger (1871)
Frederick Converse (1871)
Arthur Nevin (1871)
Henry K. Hadley (1871–1937)
Percy Lee Atherton (1871)
Theodore Spiering (1871–1925)
Walter Henry Rothwell (English-Austrian) (1872–1927)
Rubin Goldmark (1872–1936)
Arthur Farwell (1872)
Rupert Hughes (1872)
Charles Fonteyn Manney (1872)
Edward Burlingame Hill (1872)
George A. Grant-Schaeffer (1872)
Daniel Gregory Mason (1873)
John Adam Hugo (1873)
Eugen Haile (German) (1873)
Edward Horsman (1873–1918)
Oscar G. Sonneck (1873–1928)
Charles Gilbert Spross (1874)
Henry Clough-Leighter (1874)
Hallett Gilberté (1875)
Frederick Ayres (1876–1926)
Oley Speaks (1876)
Ernest Schelling (1876)
Mortimer Wilson (1876–1932)
John Alden Carpenter (1876)
John Beach (1877)
Louis Campbell-Tipton (1877–1921)
Blair Fairchild (1877–1933)
David Stanley Smith (1877)
Harriet Ware (1877)
Albert Mildenberg (1878–1918)
Thurlow Lieurance (1878)
Franz C. Bornschein (1879)
Benjamin Lombard (1879–1915)
Mary Helen Brown (1864–1937)
Frank LaForge (1879)

Heniot Lévy (Polish) (1879)
Harry Osgood (1879–1927)
Mabel Daniels (1879)
Marianne Genet (?)
Alexander Macfayden (1879)
Alexander Russell (1880)
Homer Grunn (1880)
Marshall Kernochan (1880)
Ernest Bloch (Swiss) (1880)
Arthur Shepherd (1880)
F. Morris Class (1881–1926)
Gena Branscombe (1881)
Charles Wakefield Cadman (1881)
Fanny Charles Dillon (1881)
Amy Ashmore Clark (1882)
R. Nathaniel Dett (1882)
Arthur Bergh (1882)
John Powell (1882)
Ward Stephens (?)
Percy Grainger (Australian) (1882)
Pearl Curran (?)
Richard Hageman (Dutch) (1882)
Bainbridge Crist (1883)
Carl Deis (1883)
Carl Engel (1883)
Charles Griffes (1884–1920)
Emerson Whithorne (1884)
Louis Gruenberg (1884)
Eastwood Lane (1884)
Deems Taylor (1885)
Cecil Burleigh (1885)
Fay Foster (1885)
Katherine Ruth Heyman (?)
Florence Turner Maley (?)
Wintter Watts (1886)
Louis Edgar Johns (1886)
George F. Boyle (1886)
Edward Ballantine (1886)
Edward Royce (1886)
Walter Golde (1887)
Lily Strickland (1887)
Walter Morse Rummel (1887)
Dwight Fiske (?)
Marion Bauer (1887)
Leslie Loth (1888)
Albert Spalding (1888)
Harold Vincent Milligan (1888)
Chalmers Clifton (1889)
Philip James (1890)
A. Walter Kramer (1890)
Mabel Wood Hill (1891)
Rhea Silberta (?)
Frederick Jacobi (1891)

Rosalie Housman (1892)
Clara Edwards (?)
Mana Zucca (1893)
Albert Stoessel (1894)
Bernard Wagenaar (1894)
Chester MacKee (1894)
Charles Earnest (?)
Richard Hammond (1896)
Aaron Copland (1900)
Alexander Steinert, Jr. (1900)
Alice Barnett (?)
Tom Dobson (?–1921)
Kathleen Lockhart Manning (?)
Ruth Crawford (1901)

Oratorios

ITALIAN

Emilio del Cavalieri (1550?–1602)
Domenico Mazzocchi (1590–1650)
Luigi Rossi (1598–1653)
Giacomo Carissimi (1605–1674)
Giovanni Paolo Colonna (1627–1695)
Carola Pallavicini (1630–1688)
Alessandro Stradella (1645–1681)
Alessandro Scarlatti (1659–1725)
Francesco Pistocchi (1659–1726)
Jocopo Perti (1661–1756)
Antonio Caldara (1678–1763)
Niccolo Porpora (1686–1767)
Leonardo Leo (1694–1746)
Nicola Jommelli (1714–1774)
Felice de Giardini (1716–1796)
Pietro Guglielmi (1727–1804)
Antonio Sacchini (1734–1786)
Giovanni Paisiello (1741–1816)
Domenico Cimarosa (1749–1801)
Antonio Salieri (1750–1825)
Nicola Zingarelli (1752–1837)
Gioacchino Rossini (1792–1868)
Gaetano Donizetti (1797–1848)
Giuseppe Verdi (1813–1901)
M. Enrico Bossi (1861–1925)
Giovanni Gianetti (1869–1934)
Alfredo d'Ambrogio (1871–1915)
Lorenzo Perosi (1872)
Ermanno Wolf-Ferrari (1876)
Franco Alfano (1876)
Ottorino Respighi (1879–1936)

GERMAN

Heinrich Schütz (1585–1672)
Johann Sebastiani (1622–1683)

Johann J. Fux (1660–1741)
Reinhard Keiser (1674–1739)
Johann Mattheson (1681–1764)
Georg Philipp Telemann (1681–1767)
Johann Sebastian Bach (1685–1750)
George Frederick Handel (1685–1759) (English)
Johann Adolph Hasse (1699–1783)
Karl Heinrich Graun (1701–1759)
Karl Philipp Emanuel Bach (1714–1788)
Johann Heinrich Rolle (1718–1785)
Franz Joseph Haydn (1732–1809)
Johann Gottlieb Naumann (1741–1801)
Wolfgang Amadeus Mozart (1756–1791)
Ludwig van Beethoven (1770–1827)
Sigismund Neukomm (1778–1858)
Ludwig (Louis) Spohr (1784–1859)
Friedrich Schneider (1786–1853)
J. K. G. Loewe (1796–1869)
Felix Mendelssohn-Bartholdy (1809–1847)
Robert Schumann (1810–1856)
Ferdinand Hiller (1811–1885)
Johannes Brahms (1833–1897)
Max Bruch (1838–1920)
Joseph Rheinberger (1839–1901)
August Klughardt (1847–1902)
Otto Taubmann (1859–1929)
Pater Hartmann (1863–1914)
Paul Hindemith (1895)

HUNGARIAN

Franz Liszt (1811–1886)
Mauritius Vavrineoz (1858–1913)
Zoltan Kodály (1882)

CZECHO-SLOVAKIAN

Antonin Dvorák (1841–1904)
Leos Janacek (1854–1928)

RUSSIAN

Anton Rubinstein (1829–1894)
Igor Stravinsky (1882)

POLISH

Felix Nowowiejski (1877)
Karol Szymanowski (1883–1937)

ENGLISH

Maurice Greene (1696–1755)
Thomas A. Arne (1710–1778)
John Stanley (1713–1786)
Samuel Arnold (1740–1802)
William Crotch (1775–1847)
John Barnett (1802–1890)
Michael Costa (1808–1884)
George Alexander MacFarren (1813–1887)
William Sterndale Bennett (1816–1875)
Frederick Ouseley (1825–1889)
Joseph Barnby (1838–1896)
John Stainer (1840–1901)
Arthur Seymour Sullivan (1842–1900)
Frederick J. Bridge (1844–1924)
Alexander Campbell Mackenzie (1847–1935)
Charles Hubert Hastings Parry (1848–1918)
Charles Villiers Stanford (1852–1924)
Frederick Hymen Cowen (1852–#1935)
Henry John Edwards (1854)
Harvey Löhr (1856)
Edward Elgar (1857–1934)
Frederick Delius (1862)
Alfred Herbert Brewer (1865–1928)
John Blackwood McEwen (1868)
Granville Bantock (1868)
H. Walford Davies (1869)
Gustav Holst (1874–1934)
Samuel Coleridge-Taylor (1875–1912)
William Walton (1902)

FRENCH

François Lesueur (1760–1837)
Félicien David (1810–1876)
Charles Gounod (1818–1893)
César Franck (Belgian) (1822–1890)
Camille Saint-Saëns (1835–1921)
Théodore Dubois (1837–1924)
Vincent d'Indy (1851–1931)
Claude Achille Debussy (1862–1918)
Gabriel Pierné (1863–1937)

Charles Silver (1868)
Henri Rabaud (1873)
Reynaldo Hahn (Venezuelan) (1875)
André Caplet (1878–1925)
Arthur Honegger (1892)

BELGIAN

Pierre Benoit (1834–1901)
Edgar Tinel (1854–1912)

SPANISH

Felipe Pedrell (1841–1922)
Isaac Albeniz (1861–1909)

AMERICAN

Dudley Buck (1839–1909)
John Knowles Paine (1839–1906)
Julian Edwards (English) (1855–1910)
Humphrey J. Stewart (1856–1932)
Edgar Stillman Kelley (1857)
Horatio W. Parker (1863–1919)
Clarence Lucas (1866)
Rossetter Gleason Cole (1866)
Paolo Gallico (Austrian) (1868)
Henry K. Hadley (1871–1937)
Frederick S. Converse (1871)
Ernest Bloch (1880)
R. Nathaniel Dett (1882)
Frederick Jacobi (1891)
Nicolas Nabokov (1903) (Russian)

Some Opera Writers

ITALIAN

Claudio Merulo (1533–1604) (Madrigal Play)
Vincenzo Galilei (1533–1591)
Giulio Caccini (1546–1618)
Emilio del Cavalieri (1550–1602)
Jacopo Peri (1561–1633)
Claudio Monteverde (1567–1643)
Francesco Manelli (1595–1670)
Benedetto Ferrari (1597–1681)
Francesco Cavalli (1602–1676)
Giacomo Carissimi (1604–1674)
Marc Antonio Cesti (1620–1669)
Giovanni Legrenzi (1625–1690)
Domenico Gabrieli (1640–1690)
Alessandro Stradella (1645–1681)
Alessandro Scarlatti (1659–1725)

Jacopo Antonio Perti (1661–1756)
Attilio Ariosti (1666–1740)
Antonio Lotti (1667–1740)
Antonio Caldara (1670–1736)
Giuseppe Porsile (1672–1750)
Marc Antonio Bononcini (1675–1726)
Niccolo Antonio Porpora (1686–1766)
Leonardo Vinci (1690–1730)
Leonardo Leo (1694–1744)
Giovanni Battista Pergolesi (1710–1736)
Nicola Jommelli (1714–1774)
Niccola Piccinni (1728–1800)
Giuseppe Sarti (1729–1802)
Antonio Sacchini (1734–1786)
Giovanni Paisiello (1741–1816)
Domenico Cimarosa (1749–1801)
Antonio Salieri (1750–1825)
Niccolo Vaccai (1790–1848)
Gioacchino Antonio Rossini (1792–1868)
G. Saverio Mercadante (1795–1870)
Giovanni Pacini (1796–1867)
Gaetano Donizetti (1797–1848)
Vincenzo Bellini (1801–1835)
Errico Petrella (1813–1877)
Giuseppe Verdi (1813–1901)
Carlo Perdrotti (1817–1893)
Alberto Randegger (1833–1911)
Amilcare Ponchielli (1834–1886)
Filippo Marchetti (1835–1902)
Arrigo Boito (1842–1918)
Luigi Mancinelli (1848–1921)
Niccolo Ravera (1851)
Alfredo Catalani (1854–1893)
Sylvio Lazzari (1857) (living in Paris)
Giacomo Puccini (1858–1924)
Ruggiero Leoncavallo (1858–1919)
Alberto Franchetti (1860)
Pietro Mascagni (1863)
Franco Leoni (1864)
Crescenzo Buongiorno (1864–1903)
Giacomo Orefice (1865–1923)
Ferruccio Busoni (1866–1924)
Francesco Cilèa (1866)
Umberto Giordano (1867)
Giovanni Gianetti (1869–1934)
Antonio Luzzi (1873)

Italo Montemezzi (1875)
Domenico Monleone (1875)
Ermanno Wolf-Ferrari (1876)
Franco Alfano (1876)
Stefano Donaudy (1879–1925)
Ottorino Respighi (1879–1936)
Alberto Iginio Randegger (1880–1918)
Ildebrando Pizzetti (1880)
G. Francesco Malipiero (1882)
Giuseppe Gino Marinuzzi (1882)
Riccardo Zandonai (1883)
Francesco Santoliquido (1883)
Adriano Lualdi (1887)
Vincenzo Davico (1889)
Ettore Lucatello (?)
Victor de Sabata (1892)

SPANISH

Salvador Giner (1832–1911)
Felipe Pedrell (1841–1922)
Tomas Breton y Hernandez (1850)
Costa Nogueras (?)
Isaac Albeniz (1861–1909)
Enrique Granados (1867–1916)
Amedeo Vives (1871–1932)
Manuel de Falla (1876)
Joan Manen (1883)
Maria Rodrigo (1888)

SOUTH AMERICA

Carlos Gomez (Brazilian) (1839–1896)
José Valle - Riestra (Peruvian) (1859)
Antonio Berutti (Argentine) (1862–1938)

FRENCH

Robert Cambert (1628–1679) (Wrote with Perrin)
Jean Batiste Lully (Italian) (1632–1687)
Pascal Colasse (1649–1709)
Marin Marais (1656–1728)
André Campra (1660–1744)
André Destouches (1672–1749)
Jean Phillippe Rameau (1683–1764)
Egidio Romualdo Duni (Italian) (1709–1775)
Jean Jacques Rousseau (1712–1778)

François André Danican Philidor (1726–1795)
Pierre Berton (1727–1780)
Pierre Alexandre Monsigny (1729–1817)
André Ernest Modeste Grétry (1741–1813)
François Joseph Gossec (1743–1829)
Luigi Cherubini (Italian) (1760–1842)
Jean François Lesueur (1760–1837)
Etienne Henri Méhul (1763–1822)
Gasparo Luigi Pacifico Spontini (Italian) (1774–1851)
François Adrien Boieldieu (1775–1834)
Nicolo Isouard (1775–1818)
Daniel François Esprit Auber (1782–1871)
Louis Joseph Ferdinand Hérold (1791–1833)
Jacques F. F. E. Halévy (1799–1862)
Adolphe Adam (1803–1856)
Hector Berlioz (1803–1869)
Napoleon-Henri Reber (1807–1880)
Félicien C. David (1810–1876)
Ambroise Thomas (1811–1896)
Louis Lacombe (1818–1884)
Charles François Gounod (1818–1893)
Jacques Offenbach (German) (1819–1880)
Victor Massé (1822–1884)
Edouard Lalo (1823–1892)
Louis Ernest Reyer (1823–1909)
Florimond Ronger Hervé (1825–1892)
Alexandre Charles Lecocq (1832–1918)
Camille Saint-Saëns (1835–1921)
Ernest Guiraud (American) (1837–1892) (born in New Orleans)
Théodore Dubois (1837–1924)
Georges Bizet (1838–1875)
Clément P. Léo Délibes (1839–1891)
Félix Victorin de Joncières (1839–1903)
Emmanuel Chabrier (1841–1894)

Jules Massenet (1842–1912)
Émile Paladilhe (1844–1926)
Joseph Arthur Coquard (1846–1910)
Robert Planquette (1848–1903)
Benjamin Godard (1849–1895)
Augusta Holmès (Irish) (1849–1903)
François Thomé (1850–1909)
Alexandre Georges (1850–1938)
Vincent d'Indy (1851–1931)
Hillemacher Frères (Brothers) Paul (1852–1933) Lucien (1860–1909)
Raoul Pugno (1852–1914)
André Messager (1853–1929)
Samuel A. Rousseau (1853–1904)
Ernest Chausson (1855–1899)
Alfred Bruneau (1857–1934)
Silvio Lazzari (It.) (1857)
Georges Huë (1858)
Gustave Charpentier (1860)
Gabriella Ferrari (1860–1921)
Pierre de Bréville (1861)
Claude Achille Debussy (1862–1918)
Xavier Leroux (1863–1919)
Camille Erlanger (1863–1919)
Gabriel Pierné (1863–1937)
Paul Vidal (1863–1931)
Alfred Bachelet (1864)
Alberic Magnard (1865–1914)
Paul Dukas (1865–1935)
Albert Roussel (1869–1937)
Florent Schmitt (1870)
Henri Büsser (1872)
Déodat de Sévérac (1873–1921)
Henri Rabaud (1873)
Reynaldo Hahn (Venezuelan) (1875)
Max d'Ollone (1875)
Antoine Mariotte (1875)
Maurice Ravel (1875–1937)
Jean Nougués (1875–1932)
Henri Février (1875)
Raoul Laparra (1876)
Louis Aubert (1877)
Gabriel Dupont (1878–1914)
Félix Fourdrain (1880–1924)
Albert Wolff (1882)
Roland Manuel (1891)
Arthur Honegger (1892)
Darius Milhaud (1892)

BELGIAN

André Ernest Modeste Grétry (1741–1813) (lived in Paris)
François Auguste Gevaert (1828–1908)
Pierre Benoit (1834–1901)
Jan Blockx (1851–1912)
Edgar Tinel (1854–1912)
Valentin Neuville (1863)
Paul Gilson (1865)
Alfred Kaiser (1872)
Charles Radoux (1877)
Albert Dupuis (1877)
Joseph van der Meulen (?)

DUTCH

Anton Berlijn (1817–1870)
Johan Wagenaar (1862)
Jan Brandt-Buys (1868–1933)
Cornelis Dopper (1870)
Charles Grelinger (?)

SWISS

Emile Jacques-Dalcroze (1865)
Gustave Doret (1866)
Othmar Schoeck (1886)

GERMAN

Heinrich Schütz (1585–1672)
Johann Fux (1600–1741)
Johann Thiele (1646–?)
Johann Christoph Pepusch (1667–1752) (lived in London)
Johann Conradi (1670?–?)
Reinhard Keiser (1674–1739)
Johann Mattheson (1681–1764)
George Frederick Handel (1685–1759) (English)
Johann Adolph Hasse (1699–1783)
Karl Heinrich Graun (1701–1759)
Christoph Willibald Gluck (1714–1787)
Johann Adam Hiller (1728–1804)
Karl Ditters von Dittersdorf (1739–1799)
Abt (Georg Joseph) Vogler (1749–1814)
Johann Friedrich Reichardt (1752–1814)
Peter von Winter (1754–1825)
Wolfgang Amadeus Mozart (1756–1791) (Austrian)

Joseph Weigl (1766–1846)
Ludwig van Beethoven (1770–1827)
Christoph Ernst Friedrich Weyse (Danish) (1774–1842)
Konradin Kreutzer (1780–1849)
Ludwig (Louis) Spohr (1784–1859)
Carl Maria von Weber (1786–1826)
Peter Joseph von Lindpainter (1791–1856)
Giacomo Meyerbeer (1791–1864) (lived in Paris)
Heinrich Marschner (1795–1861)
Karl Gottlieb Reissiger (1798–1859)
Gustav Albert Lortzing (1801–1851)
Otto Nicolai (1810–1849)
Friedrich von Flotow (1812–1883)
Richard Wagner (1813–1883)
Franz von Suppé (Austrian) (1819–1895)
Peter Cornelius (1824–1874)
Felix Draeseke (1835–1913)
Max Zenger (1837–1911)
Hermann Goetz (1840–1876)
Victor Nessler (Alsatian) (1841–1890)
Heinrich Hofmann (1842–1902)
Ignaz Brüll (Austrian) (1846–1907)
August Bungert (1846–1915)
August Klughardt (1847–1902)
Cyril Kistler (1848–1907)
Ivan Knorr (1853–1916)
Engelbert Humperdinck (1854–1921)
Heinrich Zöllner (1854)
Paul Geisler (1856–1919)
Wilhelm Kienzl (1857)
Alexander von Fielitz (1860–1930)
Joseph Maria Erb (Alsatian) (1860)
Emil Nikolaus Reznicek (Czecho-Slovakian) (1861)
Ludwig Thuille (1861–1907)
Hugo Kaun (1863–1932)
Felix Weingartner (1863)
Richard Strauss (1864)
Waldemar von Baussnern (1866–1931)
Max Schillings (1868–1933)

Hans Pfitzner (1869)
Siegfried Wagner (1869–1930)
Alexander von Zemlinsky (Austrian) (1872)
Leo Fall (Austrian) (1873–1925)
Paul Gräner (1873)
Waldemar Wendland (1873)
Julius Bittner (1874)
Arnold Schoenberg (1874)
Joseph Gustav Mrazek (Austrian) (1878)
Franz Schreker (Austrian) (1878–1934)
Edgar Istel (1880)
Walter Braunfels (1882)
Ignatz Waghalter (1882)
Egon Wellesz (Austrian) (1885)
Alban Berg (Austrian) (1885–1935)
Paul Hindemith (1895)
Erich Korngold (American) (1897)
Karl Krafft-Lortzing (18?–1923)
Ernst Krenek (Austrian) (1900)
Kurt Weill (1900) (in America)

CZECHO-SLOVAKIAN

Bedrich (Friedrich) Smetana (1824–1884)
Eduard Napravnik (1839–1916)
Antonin Dvorák (1841–1904)
Zdenko Fibich (1850–1900)
Leos Janacek (1855–1928)
Hans Trnecek (1858–1914)
Josef Bohuslav Foerster (1859)
Emil Nikolaus Reznicek (1861)
Karl Kovarovic (1862–1920)
Karel Weis (1862)
Stanislaus Suda (1865)
Karl Navratil (1867–1936)
Vitezslav Novak (1870)
Adolf Piskacek (1873–1919)
Camillo Hildebrand (1876)
Ottokar Ostrcil (1879–1937)
Ottokar Zich (1879–1934)
Rudolf Karel (1880)
Bohuslav Martinu (1890)
Jaromir Weinberger (1896)

HUNGARIAN

Karl Goldmark (1830–1915)
Alphons Czibulka (1842–1894)
Jeno Hubay (1858–1937)

Julius J. Major (1859–1925)
Emanuel Moor (1863–1931)
Georg Jarno (1868–1920)
Béla Bártok (1881)
Emil Abrányi (1882)

SCANDINAVIAN

Johan P. E. Hartmann (Danish) (1805–1900)
Ivar Hallström (Swedish) (1826–1901)
Eduard Lassen (Danish) (1830–1904)
Emil Hartmann (Danish) (1836–1898)
Anders Hallén (1846–1925)
Peter Lange - Müller (Danish) (1850–1926)
Christian Sinding (Norwegian) (1856)
Gerhard Schjelderup (Norwegian) (1859–1933)
August Enna (Danish) (1860–1923)
Wilhelm Stenhammar (Swedish) (1871–1927)
Hakon Boerresen (Danish) (1876)
Paul August von Klenau (Danish) (1883)
Ture Rangström (Swedish) (1884)

FINNISH

Jan Sibelius (1865)
Franz Oskari Merikanto (1868–1924)
Selim Palmgren (1878)
Armas E. Launis (1884)

RUSSIAN

Michail I. Glinka (1804–1857)
Alexander S. Dargomyzsky (1813–1869)
Alexander Serov (1820–1871)
Anton Rubinstein (1830–1894)
Alexander P. Borodin (1833–1887)
César Cui (1835–1918)
Modest Moussorgsky (1839–1881)
Peter I. Tchaikovsky (1840–1893)
Nikolai Rimsky-Korsakov (1844–1908)
Michail Ippolitov-Ivanov (1859–1935)

Anton Arensky (1861–1906)
Alexander Gretchaninov (1864)
Alexander Glazounov (1865–1936)
Vladimir Rebikov (1866–1920)
Arseni Korestchenko (1870–1918)
Serge Rachmaninov (1873)
Igor Stravinsky (1882)
Serge Prokofieff (1891)
Dmitri Shostakovitch (1906)
Ivan Dzerjinsky (1909)

POLISH

Ladislas Zelenski (1837–1921)
Sigismund Noskowski (1846–1909)
Ignace Jan Paderewski (1860)
Karol Szymanowski (1883–1937)
Ludomir von Rozycki (1883)
Raoul Koczalski (1885)

ROUMANIAN

Theodor Flondor (?–1908)

ENGLISH

Thomas Campion (1575–1620)
John Coperario (Cooper) (1570–1627)
William Lawes (1582–1645)
Henry Lawes (1596–1662)
John Banister (1630–1679)
Matthew Locke (1632–1677)
Henry Purcell (1658–1695)
Thomas Arne (1710–1778)
William Shield (1748–1829)
Stephen Storace (1763–1796)
Henry R. Bishop (1786–1855)
John Barnett (1802–1890)
Julius Benedict (1804–1885)
Michael William Balfe (1808–1888)
George A. MacFarren (1813–1887)
William Vincent Wallace (1814–1865)
Frederic Clay (French) (1838–1889)
Arthur Sullivan (1842–1900)
Alfred Cellier (1844–1891)
Alexander Campbell Mackenzie (1847–1935)
A. Goring Thomas (1851–1892)
Charles Villiers Stanford (1852–1924)
Frederick Corder (1852–1932)

Frederic Hymen Cowen (1852–1935)
Ethel Mary Smyth (1858)
Isidore De Lara (1858–1935)
Marie Wurm (1860–1938) (lived in Germany)
Liza Lehmann (1862–1918)
Edward German (1862–1936)
Frederick Delius (1863–1934)
Eugene d'Albert (1864–1932)
Edward Woodall Naylor (1867–1934)
Gustav Holst (1874–1934)
Josef Holbrooke (1878)
Albert Coates (1882)
Hubert Bath (1883)
Lord Berners (1883)

AMERICAN

William H. Fry (1813–1864)
George Bristow (1825–1898)
John Knowles Paine (1839–1906)
Frederic Grant Gleason (1848–1903)
William J. McCoy (1848–1926)
Max Vogrich (Transylvanian) (1852–1916)
George W. Chadwick (1854–1931)
Julian Edwards (English) (1855–1910)
Humphrey John Stewart (English) (1856–1932)
Reginald DeKoven (1859–1920)
Victor Herbert (Irish) (1859–1924)
Pietro Floridia (Italian) (1860–1932)
Walter Damrosch (1862)
Horatio W. Parker (1863–1919)
Ernest Carter (1866)
N. Clifford Page (1866)
Paolo Gallico (Austrian) (1868)
Wallace A. Sabin (English) (1869–1937)
Louis Adolphe Coerne (1870–1922)
Joseph C. Breil (1870–1926)
Henry K. Hadley (1871–1937)
Frederick Converse (1871)
Arthur Nevin (1871)
Frank Patterson (1871)
Mary Carr Moore (1873)
Theodore Stearns (?–?)
John Adam Hugo (1873)

H. Lawrence Freeman (1875?)
Albert Mildenberg (1878–1918)
Ernest Bloch (Swiss) (1880)
Charles Wakefield Cadman (1881)
Simon   Buchhalter   (Russian)
    (1881)
Lazare Saminsky (Russian) (1882)
Louis Gruenberg (1884)
Deems Taylor (1885)
W. Frank Harling (1887)
Isaac Van Grove (?)
Eugene Bonner (1889)
Timothy Spelman (1891)
Albert Stoessel (1894)
Robert Russell Bennett (1894)
Howard Hanson (1896)
Virgil Thomson (1896)
John Laurance Seymour (189?)
Frederic Hart (1898)
Beryl Rubinstein (1898)
George Antheil (1900)
Marc Blitzstein (1905)
Gian-Carlo Menotti (1911) (It.)

Modern Ballets

RUSSIAN

Peter I. Tchaikovsky (1840–1893)
Nikolai Rimsky-Korsakov (1844–
    1908)
Alexander Glazounov (1865–1936)
Arseni Korestchenko (1870–1918)
Nikolai Tcherepnin (1873)
Igor Stravinsky (1882)
Maximilian Steinberg (1883)
Serge Prokofieff (1891)

POLISH

Karol Szymanowski (1883–1937)
Alexandre Tansman (1897)

FRENCH

Léo Délibes (1836–1891)
Emanuel Chabrier (1841–1894)
Jules Massenet (1842–1912)
Vincent d'Indy (1851–1931)
André Messager (1853–1929)
Alfred Bruneau (1857–1934)
Claude Debussy (1862–1918)
Gabriel Pierné (1863–1937)
Erik Satie (1866–1925)
Charles Silver (1868)

Albert Roussel (1869–1937)
Florent Schmitt (1870)
Jean Roger-Ducasse (1873)
Maurice Ravel (1875–1937)
Louis Aubert (1877)
Louis Durey (1888)
Roland Manuel (1891)
Darius Milhaud (1892)
Arthur Honegger (1892)
Germaine Tailleferre (1892)
François Poulenc (1898)
Georges Auric (1899)
Henri Sauguet (1901)

ITALIAN

Franco Alfano (1876)
Ottorino Respighi (1879–1936)
Ildebrando Pizzetti (1880)
G. Francesco Malipiero (1882)
Alfredo Casella (1883)
Vittorio Rieti (1898)

SPANISH

Manuel de Falla (1876)

HUNGARIAN

Béla Bártok (1881)

SCANDINAVIAN

Kurt Atterberg (Swedish) (1887)

AUSTRIAN

Egon Wellesz (1885)

GERMAN

Paul Hindemith (1895)

CZECHO-SLOVAKIAN

Karl Kovarovic (1862–1920)
Georg Kosa (1897)
Bohuslav Martinu (1890)

ENGLISH

Arthur Seymour Sullivan (1842–
    1900)
Ralph Vaughan Williams (1872)
Gustav Holst (1874–1934)
Constant Lambert (1905)

AMERICAN

Henry F. Gilbert (1868–1928)
Arnold Schoenberg (1874) (Aus-
    trian)
John Alden Carpenter (1876)

Charles Griffes (1884–1920)
Louis Horst (20th Century)
Emerson Whithorne (1884)
Wallingford Riegger (1885)
Deems Taylor (1885)
Leo Sowerby (1895)
Virgil Thomson (1896)
Cole Porter (1897)

Henry Cowell (1897)
Aaron Copland (1900)
George Antheil (1900)
A. Lehman Engel (1910)
Robert McBride (1911)

MEXICAN

Carlos Chavez (1899)

INDEX